BALDERDASH

BALDERDASH

A TREATISE ON ETHICS

Antti P. Balk

THELEMA PUBLICATIONS
Helsinki • Washington D.C. • London

Thelema Publications, LLC

UK: BCM Agape, London WC1N 3XX

US: PO Box 10102, Washington, DC 20018-0102

First published 2012

British Library Cataloguing in Publication Data

Balk, Antti P.
Balderdash : a treatise on ethics.
1. Ethics. 2. Nihilism (Philosophy)
I. Title
170-dc23

Library of Congress Control Number: 2012934838

ISBN-13: 978 952 5700 40 4
ISBN-10: 952 5700 40 2

To the Goddess Nina,
Queen of Heaven

Acknowledgements

The author would like to acknowledge the aid and influence
of the following individuals and institutions:

Bill Heidrick, Calle Abrahamsson, Rodney Orpheus, Lon DuQuette,
Jim Wasserman, Richard Kaczynski, Mordechai Shapiro, Mike Marduk,
Kjetil Fjell, M. Dionysius Rogers, Bjarne Salling Pedersen,
Jukka Nieminen, Kane Kanera, Timo Lehtinen,
Erwin Hessle and Ryan Adam Murray.

Peter Schiff, Jim Rogers, Marc Faber, Rick Santelli, Walter E. Williams,
Karl Denninger, Kalle Isokallio, Jeffrey Tucker, Lew Rockwell,
Judge Andrew Napolitano and Dr. Ron Paul.

David E. Kelley, Chuck Lorre, Trey Parker, Matt Stone, Penn Jillette,
Paul McKenna, Henry Rollins, Jack Hunter, John Stossel, Tuomas Enbuske,
Martti Backman, Jukka Relander, Tuomas Nevanlinna, Jaakko Hämeen-Anttila,
Simo Parpola, Antti Heikkilä, Antti Tuuri, Arto Paasilinna,
Mark Morford and Chuck Palahniuk.

My late Grandpa and Grandma,
everyone at Thelema Publications,
Kathie and Ken Jarva,
and
the Arts Council of Finland.

Author's Note

The idea for this work came to me circa 1998, about the same time as I started writing my first book, *Saints & Sinners*, then just known as *An Account of Western Civilization*. The draft manuscript of the latter was not finished until the spring of 2004, so most of the research for the present work was carried out between then and 2006—except for the research on economics, much of which was prompted by the global financial crisis in 2008. All references to works or statistics published after 2010 were added at either the editing or the proofreading stage.

Table of Contents

"Ethics is balderdash."

— Edward Alexander Crowley (1875–1947)
poet, mountaineer, adventurer

"Morality is temporary, wisdom is permanent."
— Hunter S. Thompson

"I am treated as evil by people who claim
that they are being oppressed because
they are not allowed to force me
to practice what they do."
— D. Dale Gulledge

"The difference is, I know I am
playing for the devil
and they don't."
— Jerry Lee Lewis

1

Primus in Orbe Deos Facit Timor

Atheism is admittedly a thoroughly Christian phenomenon. I do not imply the common assertion by the believers that the atheist is inversely tied to the divinity he or she denies; "Atheism is no more a religion than abstinence is a form of drinking," as Marilyn Burge pointed out. What I refer to is the fact that atheism is practically unknown in any but Christian cultures. Other cultures do undergo "secularization"—the reduction in the influence of religion in everyday life. But have you ever met a person from an Islamic culture that would profess atheism as his or her actual world view?

I have been led to conclude that there are no atheists, just "secularized Christians": practically every Christian-turned-atheist continues to live by an artificial code of ethics that would not exist had Christianity not created it. Why, you ask? Well, to quote Carl Sagan: "One of the saddest lessons of history is this: If we've been bamboozled long enough, we tend to reject any evidence of the bamboozle. We're no longer interested in finding out the truth. The bamboozle has captured us. It is simply too painful to acknowledge—even to ourselves—that we've been so credulous. (So the old bamboozles tend to persist as the new bamboozles rise.)"[1]

One of the oddities of Christian culture is that should a person announce he is taking part in a Bible class, his fellow-men are very shocked and concerned. "What?

1. 1995, 241.

Has he lost his mind?" Imagine a Muslim country where it would be considered provocative to study the Koran. Most Westerners no longer know what it is to be truly religious, nor have they for a while. Over the last two centuries, people in the West have challenged their faiths to the point of these losing all their significant content and power. Our Churches now ask little of anyone, nor play a vital part in our politics. In fact, we are astonished and terrified by the truly religious, who follow the logic of submission of the individual to political and moral ideas, and to the arbitrary will of God. To us, "belief" is a dangerous notion and we would like to think that there is little of it among us.

"Morality is of the highest importance," said Albert Einstein in 1927, "but for us, not for God."[2] Man is a social animal, and morality is a human invention. God commands man not to kill, for it is evil, but if God commanded us to kill would killing suddenly be good? Of course not, God's opinion and will are irrelevant—murder of a fellow human being is wrong to us in our own view. Buddhists have no God, yet only the Pope could call them immoral with a straight face. The daily acts of road rage, gangland shootings, school yard bullying, spousal abuse, and televised sports violence are not caused by a lack of belief in a higher being, but a lack of belief in the rights of man.

The influences that have raised humans to a high moral level are education and freedom, the humanizing tendency of a better-equipped and more stimulating life. It is science and liberalism, two fundamentally skeptical forces continuously at work in all human progress, that have accomplished the exact things for which the Judaeo-Christian religion claims the credit. The concepts of Sin and Virtue have very little to do with ethics—no Christian minister preaches salvation by good behaviour. It would be extremely bad business for Roman Catholicism to advertise the salvation of only the upright, temperate, intelligent, and ethical. Yet how common is the scientist who believes she is an atheist, but still sends her son to a Catholic school for "proper moral education"?

The "harmless" myth of Santa Claus has to be one of the most potent means ever devised for intimidating children, twisting their behaviour, distorting their values, eroding their self-esteem, and impairing their development of critical thinking skills. The credit for disseminating and consolidating Christmas as a permanent secular holiday lay largely with the primary school system with its seasonal pageants. The Church may have ceased to interfere with advanced education, but she still wields power over our children, meaning that they have to learn about Adam and Eve, Noah and the Deluge, instead of about evolution. What is worse, they are taught that accepting statements without any evidence is a virtue, not only making them an easy prey to all kinds of quacks in later life, but also leaving them ill-disposed to accept the methods of thought required by modern science.

Would it not make more sense for a scientist to subscribe to the ethics of a non-theistic religion such as Buddhism? No, if you consider the fact that a scientific atheist is predisposed to treat all religious philosophies as opposed to science and thus steer clear of them. And why is this harmful? Were religion merely theoretical it might be

---

2. 1979, 66.

dismissed as inconsequential, but it is virtually impossible to separate theory and practice. Regardless of the innumerable inconsistencies between the two, organized religion has always had a tendency to enforce its theories in practical life. Churches have never implied dogmatism only in abstract thinking, but intolerance in legal and social action as well.

Agnostics, on the other hand, are mere cowards. One cannot logically prove a negative, so agnosticism is just admitting to a fact, not voicing an opinion. And anyone can have the facts, having opinions is an art. The point Thomas Henry Huxley tried to make when he coined the term "agnosticism" was that: "Irrationally held truths may be more harmful than reasoned errors."[3] Still, if you do not understand Einstein's Theory of Relativity it does not make it incorrect. Our democratic society assumes that everyone's opinion is equally valuable and needs to be voiced as loudly as possible. But facts are facts, and it is not a valid argument to deny them because of the insufficiency of one's personal knowledge. As Det. Harry Callahan so prosaically put it: "Opinions are like assholes, everybody's got one."[4]

People brought up as atheists are rare indeed, and whether they remain one depends on which type of atheist they have been raised as. There are four general types, from the largest to the smallest: nihilistic, mad-at-god, philosophical, and scientific. The nihilistic type is what most people think of as being an atheist. Quite a few nominal "believers" identify with this group, making it so large that it has to be divided into three smaller sub-groups: the people who "don't believe in anything" because they simply do not think; the people who simply "could not care less"; and finally those who are simply "concerned about other things."

The atheist of the first sub-type has never even bothered to think about God or anything else. His "beliefs" are but a potpourri of nonsense—old saying, urban legends, latest fads, uninformed opinion, and pious homilies all rolled into one. Should you ask him to explain his reasons for his beliefs, he will give you no more than a blank stare and try to avoid you in the future. Many of the atheists who subsequently converted to Christianity are of this type, from St. Paul to C. S. Lewis. They only became Christians because they had never thought about their beliefs before, and the moment someone presented them with a decent religious song and dance, they simply could not think of a reason to remain an atheist. The thing is, it does not matter whether Jesus existed or not: had he done what he is told to have done, he would only have been re-enacting myths, and had he said what he is told to have said, he would have only been repeating old sayings; in fact, if Jesus did exist, so much the worse for Christianity.

The second sub-type of nihilistic atheist does not even care whether there is a God or not. These are the people who "claim to be interested in art, which means they really aren't interested in anything at all."[5] And even if you do get this type to care about anything, he will likely choose religion over atheism, just because there are

---

3. 1893, 128.

4. *The Dead Pool.* Dir. Buddy Van Horn. Warner Bros. Pictures, 1988.

5. J. Bronowski, as quoted in Lucie K. B. Hall, "Atheist Taxonomy: The Five Varieties of Atheists," *San Diego Humanist,* March–April 1999.

more believers than atheists, and thus more chance of finding others like him. The third and last sub-type is formed by those with a different agenda. Those whose lives are consumed by other pursuits they engage in with quasi-religious fervour, such as money, sports, politics, sex, et cetera. They are prime examples of the type of atheist that the Rev. William T. Cummings failed to find in the foxholes during WWII.

The second general type of atheism, namely the mad-at-god variety, is nearly as large as the first group. It constitutes the types of persons who, on account of a personal tragedy or an unrealized dream, have declared God dead or incompetent. However, the answer to the question that, if God is good why does He let bad things happen to me and mine is, and has always been, "free will." Besides which, it is impossible to be angry at something in which you do not believe. The early French existentialist are also among this group, mad at God for daring not to exist. To paraphrase Dr. Ludwig von Shtickfitz, they know two and two are four, but cannot stand it.

The philosophical atheists form a much smaller group, but one that can still be divided into two dissimilar sub-types, logical and emotional. The emotional type may have witnessed untold horrors, such as mass murders or ethnic cleansings, and on observing God's apparent indifference, become doubtful of not only His benevolence, but His very existence. While bearing a superficial resemblance to the mad-at-god atheist, his conviction is much deeper and more compelling. Moral disagreement with the revealed word of God or its adherents will more than often lead to this type of atheism. After all, most of humanity is considerably more moral than the best gods it has created, though frequently the moral disagreement is with a religion that has marginalized them as a social group in the name of God, as with homosexuals. However, it is not an effective argument that "the Bible is one of the most genocidal books in history"; nor does criticism of the founder or followers of a religion, by itself, constitute a negation of any part of the religion.

The logical type of philosophical atheist is a deep-thinking individual who, after weighing the logical absurdity of the simultaneous attributes of omniscience, omnipotence, and omnibenevolence, finally summons up the courage to ask Thomas Aquinas: "If God had to exist in order for the universe to be created, then who created God?" The trouble is, "Making fun of born-again Christians is like hunting dairy cows with a high powered rifle and scope."[6] Logic itself is nothing more than a careful series of steps that only preserves the truth-value of the starting assumption. Should your starting assumption prove false, the whole chain of logic derived therefrom becomes equally wrong. Since, again, one cannot prove a negative, the logical atheist needs to take a stand one way or the other.

Scientific atheists constitute the smallest and the most modern group, although they were not unknown in ancient Greece. These people usually start out as philosophical atheists, and through their scientific training, come to the realization that the actions of a deity have no place in a controlled experiment. That is to say, you cannot practise science with the assumption that on weekdays, God interferes with your experiments to demonstrate his greater glory, but on weekends, He leaves them

---

6. O'Rourke 1988, 95.

to proceed "naturally," with the same end in mind. This so-called "naturalistic hypothesis" forms the basis of scientific atheism, and is probably the main reason why so many scientists are atheists. Every time a scientist performs an experiment, he is testing the validity of the naturalistic assumption, any support for which is a mark against the theist hypothesis.

Thus, atheism is not a world view in itself; atheism is defined by the view it does not support, that is, theism. Atheists are frequently charged with blasphemy, which is the one crime they cannot commit. When an atheist denounces or mocks the deities, he is dealing with ideas, not with beings. If he does not admit the existence of God, how could he be capable of insulting Him? Atheism attacks not God but the belief in God, not a being but an idea, not a fact but a fancy. The atheist does not deny God, for he is without the idea of God; he cannot deny that of which he has no conception, the conception of which by its affirmer is so imperfect that he is unable to define it to him.

When Prof. Arthur O. Lovejoy was asked at a government investigation if he believed in God, he recited thirty-three different definitions of god from memory, and inquired which one the questioner had in mind. Of course, it did not really matter to the questioner—to avow a belief in the existence of a higher being simply assures one's participation in our socio-cultural system, where everyone knows that God exists, even though we are too ignorant to accurately comprehend or define Him. A nation can assume that adding the words "under God" to its pledge of allegiance will give evidence that her citizens believe in God, when all it really proves is that they believe in believing in God.

Yet it is not the atheist who should be apologizing for his beliefs, or lack of them; the theist is the one who is actually undermining morality. The question is not whether a personal divinity exists or not (or whether it would be reasonable to suppose that one does), but whether it would be a good or a bad thing if one did—and this is where even most of the scientific atheists get it wrong. The problem with a personal divinity: ***Deus est demon inversus.*** How is worshipping or taking orders from God any better than worshipping or taking orders from the Devil? "Power corrupts, and absolute power corrupts absolutely."

If a God who keeps tinkering with the universe is absurd, a God who interferes with human freedom and creativity is a tyrant. In fact, should someone walk up to me and convince me that God was real, that would be the most frightening proposition I could ever imagine. God says you have free will, but make the wrong choice and you will be tortured for eternity in Hell. That is no different from a man telling his girlfriend she can do what she likes, but if she chooses to leave him, he will hunt her down and kill her. Yet when a man says this, we will lock him up, when God says it, we call him "merciful" and build churches for his greater glory. An omnipotent and omniscient tyrant is still a tyrant, no better than the earthly dictators who turn everybody into mere cogs in the machinery they control—an atheism that rejects such a deity is abundantly justified. In the immortal words of Mark Twain: "If there is a God, he is a malign thug."

A theist thinks all deities but his are false, an atheist make no exception for the last one. When the former understands why he dismisses all other possible divinities, he will understand why the latter dismisses his. Of course, there are no truly polytheistic religions—the Easterners are not stupid. All the so-called "polytheistic" religions got formed courtesy of social integration and are in actual fact either atheistic (non-theistic) or gravitating towards atheism. Indeed, from the monotheists' point of view, "The equal toleration of all religions . . . is the same as atheism."[7] However, rigid monotheism also leads inevitably to atheism: the idea of an only but *jealous* god, to be *worshipped*, is preposterous. Lastly, in order to "rebel" one has to first acknowledge an authority; atheists do not acknowledge the divine variety.

Verily, the fear of God is not "the beginning of wisdom," but the root of all evil. "God has done nothing for men and women except to scare them out of their wits," wrote Lemuel K. Washburn[8] and I tend to agree. According to a report published in the *Journal of the American Medical Association*, people with strong religious beliefs appear to want doctors to do everything they can to keep them alive as death approaches; those who prayed on regular basis were more than three times more likely to ask for intensive life-prolonging care than those who relied least on God.[9] Epictetus said it in the first century of the Christian era: "Why, do you not know, then, that the origin of all human evils, and of all baseness, and of cowardice, is not death, but rather the fear of death?"[10] The human ego is a defence-mechanism. There are many others, but they all occur as a response to an immediate danger. When the ego contemplates its future annihilation, the thought of death renders it immediate, and to protect itself, the ego denies death. It cannot deny that the body will die and rot, the evidence is too strong, but it can pretend to be not a transient creation of its environment, but an immortal soul.

"Your soul will be dead even before your body: fear nothing further," Nietzsche instructed us.[11] More importantly, it is not even desirable that the ego should live forever; it is the cause of all our troubles. Eastern "soul" or spirit is impersonal—just like the Eastern god(s). For the ego, eternity in Heaven would be just as pointless and tedious as eternity in Hell. However, time itself is a human, egocentric concept. "It's better to burn out than to fade away," or, to put it another way, "if there is a sin against life, it consists perhaps not so much in despairing of life as in hoping for another life and in eluding the implacable grandeur of this life."[12] Christianity, then, is a cult of death.

On the other hand, "If death is the end of everything, then living is everything."[13] Life neither would nor could have any meaning if we lived forever, nor would our actions have any consequences. Without death, there would be no change, no evolution. As Garrison Keillor once observed: "A sense of mortality should make us

---

7. The Encyclical "Imortale Dei," Given by His Holiness Pope Leo XIII, November 1, 1885.

8. 1911, 209.

9. Andrea C. Phelps, et al. "Religious Coping and Use of Intensive Life-Prolonging Care Near Death in Patients With Advanced Cancer," *JAMA* 301(11), March 18, 2009, 1140–1147.

10. *Discourses*, III, xxvi, § 2.

11. *Thus Spoke Zarathustra*. 1954, 132.

12. *Summer in Algiers*. Camus 1991, 153.

13. Richardson 1995, 375.

smarter." It is our mortality that leads to our morality, as surely as the greedy desire for immortality leads to immorality. *Memento mori;* know, not fear, that you are going to die. Death, after all, is the first condition of immortality; or conversely, "that which is the most awful of evils, death, is nothing to us, since when we exist there is no death, and when there is death we do not exist."[14]

There is something sad and contemptible about a man who is unable to face the perils of life without the aid of comforting myths. Undoubtedly some part of him knows full well that they are just myths, and that he believes in them only because they are comforting. But he dare not face the truth, and being aware that his beliefs are not true, he becomes furious whenever they are challenged. "I took my life and the Church seriously," wrote Dr. Alfred F. Loisy in *My Duel with the Vatican*, "and the consequence is that I have wasted one and disturbed the other."[15]

The fear of being laughed at is one of the most inhibiting forces in Western civilization. It is not only the power behind the adolescent flock urge, but a barrier to change and chance-taking in the adult life. There is not a single portrait or account of Christ laughing; he is always as solemn, serious, and gloomy as a prison guard. He is never seen laughing until tears roll down his cheeks like a plump cross-eyed Buddha laughing his fully-realized head off. In fact, the total absence of humour in the Bible is among the most peculiar things in all literature. Christian ministers would do their congregations infinitely more good if they stood up in their pulpits and said not "Let us pray," but "Let us laugh."

You are not angry with people when you laugh at them. A sense of humour is the perfect antidote for pride. Humour teaches tolerance. "You cannot make fun of the disabled!" says the moralist. Well, I put it to you that there are no serious subjects, only serious people. Why we laugh and the things we find humorous are in many ways descriptive of our personal values. I, for example, find *White Oleander* (2002) extremely funny—many other people do not. Some have a problem laughing at slapstick, because they think it is "beneath them." Tom Robbins called a sense of humour, when properly developed, "superior to any religion so far devised,"[16] but in actual fact, the root of comedy and the root of spirituality are one and the same. Slipping on a banana skin is destabilizing in the exact same way as having a spiritual experience is—the ego loses the wheel at that moment.

Freud may not have known it, but his *Jokes and Their Relation to the Unconscious* paved the way for the laugh tracks in American TV situation comedies. He saw laughter as an escape valve for pent-up emotions, ideas and inhibitions, and laugh tracks make use of exactly that principle, suggesting and triggering a release. Much as they have been criticized, laugh tracks are still used because they work. However, most laughter has little to do with humour: people laugh at funerals, they laugh when they are tickled; they laugh to belittle others, and they laugh because others are laughing. People use laughter to cover up their nervousness or embarrassment, or to secure a place in social pecking order. Both clinical and anecdotal evidence show

---

14. Epicurus, Letter to Menœceus.

15. 1924, 272.

16. 1984, 249.

laughter to be an essential element of good health, and people frequently laugh at things that are not, for any apparent reason, funny.

"The universe is the practical joke of the general at the expense of the particular," Aleister Crowley observed. "All individual existence is tragic. Perception of this fact is the essence of comedy. . . In love the individuality is slain; who loves not love? Love death therefore, and long eagerly for it. Die daily."[17] You cannot get rid of the ego permanently, except in "real" physical death. Siddharta taught us that the first principle of existence is impermanence—absolutely everything in this universe is impermanent. Impermanence, however, creates uncertainly, and humans have a particularly low tolerance for uncertainly. Uncertainty causes us discomfort, which causes us to do stupid things, which bring about unfortunate results; fortunately, these results are impermanent.

It is our clinging to impermanent things that causes our modern stress; it is our inability to enjoy these things, to let go, that causes our suffering. "The things you own end up owning you" and "it's not until you lose everything that you are free to do anything."[18] Stress and fear, or alertness, are both necessary, but only for a split second—before some mortal danger. When our emphasis is on stuff and getting stuff, more energy goes to concerns of safety and control, and less to concerns of freedom and creativity; comfortable and predictable consumption overrides our personal liberty and sovereignty. Life is not easy, but when we truly see this, we transcend it; once we truly know that life is not easy, once we truly accept it, life becomes easy—for once accepted, the fact that life is hard no longer matters.

"Fear leads to anger, anger leads to hate, hate leads to suffering."[19] Mind you, no-one is calling our fears groundless, or denying the threat of nuclear and biological war on our shores. There are militant factions within three world religions bent on fulfilling one or another prophecy of a final conflict between good and evil, certain that they and not their perceived enemies are the elect. Could there possibly be a greater threat? No, but that is exactly why it is necessary for us to live without fear. Of course we should protect ourselves from real danger, but at the same time, we must not heed the counsels of fear.

"There is nothing to fear but fear itself." Fear diverts one from the task at hand, breaks our concentration, and causes us to fail. If you think worrying about a problem is the same as solving it, you are obviously living in a universe where different laws prevail. What is more, we tend to worry about the wrong things; after all, we are not psychic. When the need arises, deal with it; as Emily Procter's character put it in an episode of *CSI: Miami*, "You're going to drive yourself crazy with hypotheticals."[20]

After 9/11, the number and size of government "watch lists" and other data programs aimed at early identification of potential terrorists ballooned. Current estimates say there are more than a million entries on the various lists, even though the U.S. Transportation Security Administration argues that only a few thousand

---

17. 1962, 39, 42; I Cor. 15:31.

18. *Fight Club*. Dir. David Fincher. Twentieth Century Fox, 1999.

19. *Star Wars: Episode I*. Dir. George Lucas. Twentieth Century Fox, 1999.

20. "Identity." CBS. February 14, 2005.

people are actually suspect. When everyone *is* out to get you, being paranoid is not going to help; nor can we ever be sure *anyone* is on our side—uncertainty is the name of the game. "What you don't know can't hurt you." You cannot know in advance what troubles you are going to face. God's freedom and His omniscience are incompatible attributes. Only a carnal person can be free, and a free person must be carnal. In other words: only mortal beings can be free.

The idea of "life management" is just a myth perpetuated by the media. Life can at most be guided and steered. You can only get things under control by striving against a force of nature that wants things disorganized. Scientists call it "entropy." Back in the early 19th century, Carl von Clausewitz, in his seminal work *On War*, called it "friction." He said you need to have a plan for the battle, but that the plan better include plenty of room for the absolute certainty that the plan will start to grow fur from the moment of its inception. We are all weak, but our illusion of control and false sense of security prevents us from living in the moment, resulting in mental trauma such as were caused by 9/11. Only an utter fool, for whom it comes as a complete surprise that he, too, can find himself in a crisis situation and his friends and loved ones can die, will benefit from crisis counselling. Tomorrow you might be dead, crossing the goddamn street.

Although chaos, disorder, change, and destruction are a necessary and integral part of life on this heavy-G planet, we abhor this realization, and worse yet, their existence. The whole terror threat existed long before September 11th of 2001, but until the United States got hit, it was off most people's radars. We systematically overestimate risks that viscerally strike us with awe, and underestimate risks that do not. Why else do we hear so much disquieting talk about "dirty bombs" when the experts agree it is panic rather than radioactivity that would kill people? Why else do we worry more about anthrax, with an annual death toll of roughly zero, than influenza, with an annual death toll of a quarter to half a million people.

If your world suddenly comes crashing down, there's obviously something wrong with your world. According to the U.S. State Department, deaths by terrorism have lately increased a bit, but the number still remains on the order of about a thousand deaths a year worldwide—a tiny fraction of the some 40,000 who die in car accidents each year just in the United States. The American mass media and the Bush administration did something that the terrorist never could have done: they legitimized terrorism. They made it bigger and scarier and more ominous, and made it appear far better organized and much more ubiquitous than it actually is. Do you feel safe going to your local mall? If you say yes, we are winning the war on terror. Until we stop living in fear, we are losing the war—regardless of the fact that the threat never really passes.

Since 9/11, we have been inundated with warning, predictions, and images of terror catastrophes. We have been so bamboozled by the hysterical imagery of the War on Terror that the absence of evidence for a truly serious terrorist threat is not even considered a viable topic of public discussion. Politicians, government agencies, defence contractors, lobbyists, the news media, and the entertainment industry vie with their competitors to increase revenues and boost reputations by affirming their commitment to winning the War on Terror. Frustrated by their inability to find any evidence of serious terrorist activities in the country, law enforcement and security agencies turn increasingly to pre-emptive prosecution and entrapment to justify their growing budgets.

Many argue that anti-terrorist measures are designed not to make us safer, but to make us *feel* safer; ironically, however, they often have the effect of making us feel even *less* safe. Spy satellites can help prevent large, organized groups from developing nuclear weapons, but no satellite will prevent a religious fanatic from building a cheap, home-made bomb and detonating it in the subway—there will always be angry and frustrated young men looking for excuses to kill. The bombings in the London Underground required no exit strategy and were carried out with simple devices made in a bathtub that were small enough to fit in backpacks. Why should the threat of terror be enough to make us sacrifice our civil liberties, when we would not even consider doing so for much higher risks, like getting run over by a car?

No terrorist attack has ever been stopped by airport security. Both the would-be "Shoe-Bomber," Richard Reid, and the "Underwear-Bomber," Umar Farouk Abdulmutallab, boarded their planes, and it was only the quick thinking of flight attendants and passengers that stopped them. They were taken down and the planes landed safely. Neither the passengers nor the cabin crew were terrorized, they were spurred into action when called upon, exhibiting courage and bravery. This has happened before, most notably on 9/11 itself, and will undoubtedly happen again. The headlines should have read "Passengers again prove stronger than al-Qaeda" and "Stewardess rebuffs terrorists, injuring attacker," but instead, American media and officials chose the victim route, and the cowering and scampering to get under the table began almost immediately. Passengers were turned into prisoners on flights, unable to move during the last hour, and having to ask permission like first-graders to go to the lavatory.

Meanwhile, the U.S. Congress questions intelligence officials on security failings that allowed a man whom they had been warned about, yet who had a valid visa, to allegedly smuggle explosives on board a trans-Atlantic jetliner. Despite rigorous employee training programmes and billions of dollars spent on new technologies, random tests show TSA screeners miss as much contraband as their minimum-wage rent-a-cop predecessors. After spending hours getting through security, most passengers are unaware that they are flying on planes whose holds contain tons of uninspected cargo. Seventy percent of all air cargo is shipped on passenger airlines and less than half of that is scanned. Under a system called "known consignor," parcels airmailed by companies which have been security vetted by the government are not subjected to any last minute security checks—if they were, air traffic would come to a halt. Since 9/11, at least two Americans have actually managed to post themselves home by airmail, this being cheaper than buying tickets.

To make things ever more absurd, large department stores, which attract huge crowds of shoppers, have no security procedures comparable to airports. Nor do movie theatres or concert halls. Yet airport security procedures have become routine, wasting hundreds of millions of dollars and further contributing to a siege mentality. That America has become increasingly insecure and paranoid is scarcely debatable: a recent study reported that in the summer of 2003, Congress identified 160 sites as potentially important targets for would-be terrorists; with lobbyist weighing in, by the end of the year, the list had grown to 1,849; by the end of 2004, to 28,360; by 2005, to 77,769. By November, 2006, the federal database of potential targets had some 300,000 items in it, including the Sears Tower in Chicago, but also an Indiana Apple and Pork Festival. The Los Angeles Police Department had eighty policemen detailed to counter-terrorism, NYPD had one thousand.[21] The public discourse focuses on whether the War on Terror suffers from insufficient resources and incompetent implementation, pre-empting any questions that might otherwise be raised about whether there really exists a sizeable terrorist threat and whether the War on Terror is truly a justified response.

Why are we so incapable of accepting our helplessness? Is the inability to accept impotence a survival trait or a cause of suffering? "Hitting bottom isn't a weekend retreat. It's not a goddamn seminar. Stop trying to control everything and just let go. Let go!"[22] All fear is fear of death, the ultimate unknown, and it is the ego that fears dying. Many people will tell you that they fear not death, but permanent injury. The truth is, this is how the brain works: "I'll be paralyzed, unable to move, unloved, I will die alone"; or, in some cases, "I'd rather die, so I will have to kill myself." Again, those who fear for their children, really fear for themselves, dying without progeny—the only physical immortality.

We all suffer from two basic forms of fear: fear of not getting what we want, and fear of losing what we have. Since both stem from actual or perceived threats to our actual or perceived survival, it follows that a good deal of our daily anxiety is a result of our faulty perception. This leaves us with two viable solutions: either change our perception or ignore our perception. In the ever-widening market of self-improvement, you never see ignoring yourself offered as a solution, yet it is the one thing that actually works. Of course, it is no longer advisable to ignore your fears, should you be boarding a metro train when the guy beside you has something hidden behind his unseasonably large overcoat and talks out loud to God.

Fear is not wicked; we are all afraid all the time. A soldier does not stop fighting just because he has a fear of bullets. Fear is necessary, if only for a split second, to warn us of danger: for example, all mammals have a natural fear of heights—otherwise, bungee-jumping wouldn't be such a rush. But isn't facing one's fears merely validating them? Courage is obviously overrated in the egocentric, Zen-challenged West. Courage is merely doing something while being afraid, of ***anything!*** Also, there is a fine line between a brave man and an adrenaline junkie. Rather than trying to conquer our fears, we should seek to transcend them. Simply relax and it is physically impossible for you to be afraid. Now, I am not saying you won't be startled when that bomb goes off, just that it is not physiologically possible to be both relaxed and afraid at the same time. Fear is not a nice feeling; people do not watch "scary movies" to be scared (those who are, don't watch them), but to be entertained.

"There are no atheists in the foxholes," and conversely, "The happy do not believe in miracles." Men whose past and future were threatened every day by extinction

21. Ian Lustick, et al. "Are We Trapped in the War on Terror," *Middle East Policy* 13(4), December 2006, 1–27.

22. *Fight Club*, op. cit.

thought it was by divine intervention that they survived at all. Interestingly, the saddest life, the vilest existence, is invariably attributed to God's will, while His respectability declines at the same rate as man becomes more healthy and prosperous. "People who rely most on God rely least on themselves."[23] Throughout the Christian Dark Ages, every great natural calamity that befell men, be it famine, plague, or flood, led to mass conversions; Christianity owes a great debt to the Black Death and the smallpox, no less than to earthquakes and tornadoes. The fearful are easy to manipulate by giving them hope of a better tomorrow—this is exactly how terrorism works. After promising freedom from fear, politicians can always invoke polls showing widespread fears to justify seizing new power; and the more people the government frightens, the more benevolent its dictatorial policies appear.

"I condemn Christianity," fumed Nietzsche. "Let anyone dare to speak to me of its 'humanitarian' blessing! To abolish any distress ran counter to its deepest advantages: it lived on distress, it created distress to externalise itself."[24] Christianity is the fix (grace) to the problem (guilt) that would not exist without it; the sole *raison d'être* for Christian clergy is administering penance, or giving absolution, the one sacrament that is neither a ritual nor a part of the original six "borrowed" from the ancient mystery cults, i.e. to make people feel so guilty that they just have to confess, and the only person they can confess to safely, in confidence, is the parish priest (or, in the case of a mediaeval monarch, his personal confessor).

This is what Marx meant when he said "Religion is the opiate of the masses," and why addictive personalities are such an easy prey for Christianity. Asserting that the believer is "happier" than the atheist is no more to the point than asserting that a drunken man is happier than a sober one. "The abolition of religion as *illusory* happiness of men, is a demand for their *real* happiness."[25] A person cannot be happy if he believes in Hell, any more than he can sweeten his drink with salt. "The happiness of credulity is a cheap and dangerous quality."[26]

Since we will never see the end of toil in this life, it is easy to perceive it as the punishment due for the Fall of Man; the ultimate emancipation from work can only be a postmortal condition. Christianity had to invent Hell, for the smarter Jews were beginning to realize what it would be like to spend eternity in Heaven with religious fanatics. Christians needed to invent some place worse—they failed. In exchange for obedience, Christianity promises salvation, but to elicit obedience through this promise, Christianity must first convince people that there is something to be saved from. It thus has nothing to offer a happy person living in a natural, rational universe, and to gain a motivational foothold, it has to declare war on earthly pleasure and happiness, which has been its exact historical course of action. "Just as Christianity must destroy reason before it can introduce faith, so it must destroy happiness before it can introduce salvation."[27]

---

23. Washburn, op. cit. 98.
24. *The Antichrist.* 1954, 655.
25. *The Basis of Religion.* Marx 1973, 14.
26. *Preface to Androcles and the Lion.* Shaw 1916, cxvi.
27. Smith 1979, 310.

H. L. Mencken defined immorality as the "morality of those who are having a better time."[28] The Puritans hated bear-baiting, not because it brought harm to the bear, but because it gave pleasure to the spectator. "Moral indignation," in H. G. Wells' definition, "is jealousy with a halo."[29] Thus the two most enduring Finnish sayings: "He who is happy should hide his happiness" and "Malicious pleasure is the greatest pleasure." A person who has no vices is bound to have some pretty annoying virtues: in fact, the people who tell me I am going to Hell, while they are on their way to Heaven, make me very glad we have separate destinations; they apparently talk to God only because no-one else will listen to them.

Nevertheless, saying "Faith is important to me" seems to have become the equivalent of "I'm a moral person." However, the percentage of religiously unaffiliated people has now skyrocketed to between 30 and 40 percent among younger Americans, and a rising number of them is more likely to call themselves "spiritual" than "religious," according to a 2009 *Newsweek* poll.[30] They have the same attitudes and values as people who go to church, but they grew up in a period when being religious meant being politically conservative. In the past two decades, many young people have begun to view organized religion as a source of "intolerance and rigidity and doctrinaire political views," and stopped attending services.[31] A genuine grass-roots spiritual renaissance simply cannot sustain itself in a corporate-controlled world, which has co-opted pieces of true spirituality and turned them—like everything else —into consumer commodities.

What passes as "spirituality" these days is not in the slightest a departure from the narcissistic culture of consumption, but rather an expression of it. Consumer materialism and spirituality co-evolved as on-going reactions against the seemingly repressive institutions of State and Church. Back in the 1893 Parliament of Religions at the World's Columbian Exposition in Chicago, the original practitioners of what we now call the "New Age" were all brought together for the first time: the Theosophist H. P. Blavatsky was there, alongside Mary Baker Eddy, the founder of Christian Science, and Swami Vivekananda, the founder of the Vedanta Society. The New Age movement strip-mined the esoteric traditions of ancient religions, took bits and pieces of them and turned them into marketable commodities for third-rate minds. By completely removing the traditional and institutional overtones from spirituality, it allowed its followers to embrace the here, the now, and most importantly, the self like never before, democratizing spiritual attainment. Despite their anti-authoritarian and self-affirming rhetoric, the New Agers did not offer a genuine alternative to American Protestantism; both movements focus on the salvation of the self, one through Divine Grace, the other through Positive Thinking.

The United States is home to just over a million Hindus, a fraction of the billion who live on Earth. Yet recent polls show that, conceptually, Americans are becoming more like Hindus and less like traditional Christians in their religious thinking.

28. 1916, 205.

29. 1914, 299.

30. Lisa Miller, "We Are All Hindus Now," *Newsweek*, August 31, 2009.

31. Robert Putnam, Remarks at the Faith Angle Conference, Key West, May 5, 2009.

According to a 2008 Harris poll, one-fourth of Americans say they believe in reincarnation. So agnostic are they about the ultimate fates of their bodies, that more than a third of the people in the United States now choose to burn them—like Hindus—after death, according to the Cremation Association of North America, up from a mere six percent of the population in 1975.[32] The Rig Veda, the most ancient Hindu scripture, says that "Truth is One, but the sages speak of it by many names."[33] The Hindus believe that there are many paths to God: Jesus is one way, Mohammed another, yoga a third—none is better than any other, all are equal. Traditional, conservative Christians do not think like this, however. They have been taught at Sunday school that their religion is the one true faith and that all others are false. Jesus said, "I am the way, the truth, and the life. No-one comes to the Father except through me."[34] But according to a 2008 Pew Forum survey, 70% of Americans now believe that "many religions can lead to eternal life."[35]

It is interesting that the movements with the greatest contradiction between profession and practice, i.e. with the strongest feeling of guilt, are the most fervent in imposing their beliefs on others. Consequently, no atheist can be elected to a public office in the U.S.—some states actually outlaw it—when in fact, religious people should never be made public officials exactly because they work for another boss. A University of Minnesota study undertaken between 2003 and 2004 found that Americans rank atheists as the single most disliked minority group in their country.[36] There are seven times as many atheists in Europe as in the United States, by percentage; but the second largest group, categorized by belief, is made up of those who call themselves "secular" or "non-religious"—and they make up 15% of the population. The Church has succeeded so well in guilting people for having a good time that most atheists remain members just because they do not want to appear uncharitable.

A tyrant "must be seen always to be exceptionally zealous as regards religious observances," wrote Aristotle in his *Politics*, "for people are less afraid of suffering any illegal treatment from men of this sort, if they think that their ruler has religious scruples and pays regard to the gods, and also they plot against him less, thinking that he has even the gods as allies."[37] Thus Polybius in the 2nd century BCE: "as the people universally are fickle and inconstant, filled with irregular desires, precipitate in their passions, and prone to violence; there is no way left to restrain them, but by the dread of things unseen, and by the pageantry of terrifying fiction. The ancients therefore acted not absurdly, nor without good reason, when they inculcated the notions

---

32. Miller, op. cit.

33. 1.164.46c.

34. John 14:6.

35. "August 2008 Religion and Public Life Survey," Pew Research Center for the People & the Press and Pew Forum on Religion & Public Life, Washington, D.C., July 31–August 10, 2008.

36. Penny Edgell, et al. "Atheists as the 'Other': Moral Boundaries and Cultural Membership in American Society," *American Sociological Review* 71(2), April 2006, 211–234.

37. V, xi, 1314b–1315a.

concerning the gods, and the belief in infernal punishments."[38] As Edward Gibbon, the most famous portrayer of the decline and fall of Rome, summarized it, "The various modes of worship which prevailed in the Roman world were all considered by the people as equally true; by the philosopher as equally false; and by the magistrate as equally useful."[39] In fact, the Russian anarchist Mikhail Bakunin reckoned that, "as long as we have a master in heaven we shall be slaves on earth,"[40] wherefore "if God existed, only in one way could he serve human liberty—by ceasing to exist."[41]

Britain is a secular country in many ways, for example, if measured by the number of people who go to church regularly. However, the United Kingdom has bishops who are members of Parliament as a right, which gives them a strong voice in the politics of the country. They are automatically elected to any kind of royal commission of inquiry, on any ethical issue, whether it be abortion or euthanasia. These days, there is also going to be a rabbi or an imam there, but religion is still a ticket to ride. The council seats in Finland's congregations are divided by political affiliation. In practice, the Church is led by the major parties, who have taken it upon themselves to dictate what true Christianity is. Thus Lutheranism has inadvertently become the spiritual wing of Social Democracy. Whenever Finnish society decides to draw a political outline concerning equality, labour law, etc., without fail a Christian version of it will also be made for the ministers to preach from their pulpits. "How can you have order in a state without religion?" asked Napoleon. "For, when one man is dying of hunger near another who is ill of surfeit, he cannot resign himself to this difference unless there is an authority which declares 'God wills it thus.' Religion is excellent stuff for keeping common people quiet."[42]

Atheists, on the other hand, are not joiners—which is not surprising, considering the only thing they have in common is their *lack* of belief in something. According to the *American Religious Identification Survey*, the U.S. citizens who answer "none" when asked to identify their religion numbered 29.4 million in 2001, more than double the number just a decade earlier; if unbelievers had their own state, it would be the second largest in the nation, with twice the population of New England's six states. The number of people willing to describe themselves as full-on atheists or agnostics increased three-fold from 1990 to 2008, from 1.2 million to 3.6 million—which is about twice the number of e.g. Episcopalians in the United States.[43] Yet the number joining atheists groups has hardly increased at all, the American Atheists, one of the several national atheist organizations, counting a dismal 2,200 members.

---

38. *Histories*, VI, 56, 10–12.

39. 1840, I, 18.

40. *State and Society*. 1973, 149.

41. *God and the State*. Ibid. 128.

42. As quoted in Wells 1920, II, 441.

43. Barry A. Kosmin & Ariela Keysar, "American Religious Identification Survey (ARIS 2008) Summary Report," Institute for the Study of Secularism in Society & Culture, Trinity College, Hartford, CT, March 2009.

"Fascism is a religious concept," declared Benito Mussolini.[44] One of Il Duce's greatest diplomatic triumphs was the conclusion of the Lateran Treaty, whereby the Vatican became a sovereign state and all Italian citizens were obliged to pay a tax to the Roman Church. The mandatory school prayer in Nazi Germany was: "Almighty God, dear Heavenly Father. In Thy name let us now, in pious spirit, begin our instruction. Enlighten us, teach us all truth, strengthen us in all that is good, lead us not into temptation, deliver us from all evil in order that, as good human beings, we may faithfully perform our duties and thereby, in time and eternity, be made truly happy. Amen."[45] Born and bred a Catholic, the Führer was raised in a religion and a culture that was anti-Semitic, and in persecuting the Jews, he repeatedly and consistently asserted that he was doing the "Lord's work"—"The work that Christ started but could not finish, I—Adolf Hitler—will conclude."[46]

In 1989, a 7-year-old American schoolboy, Ricky Sherman, urged his fellow students to refuse to recite the revised Pledge of Allegiance. "When kids are forced to say, 'under God,' it makes them think that atheists are bad people," he read from a note written in large block letters on composition paper. "Atheists are good people. We just know that God is make-believe."[47] Theism has imposed a false value on things: it calls a man good who attends church, prays in public, and accepts the Bible as the word of God; it calls a man bad who stays at home with his family on Sunday, who dines without asking a deity to bless his food, and who does not expect to climb the vicarious stairway to Heaven.

In any hierarchy, control is maintained by coercion, by the threat of negative sanctions of one kind or another: physical, social, economic, psychological, etc. However, such deterrent only works by fear of future punishment, which may be why some studies have linked fearlessness to crime. Parents of a chronically misbehaving child often intensify their reprimands, with the unintended result that the child is driven out into the street and becomes a delinquent. A 1996 study of youth homicide arrests found that, for example, 77% of youthful killers in Massachusetts had been arrested at least one before, with an average of 9.7 arrests each[48]; according to the 1988 statistics, over 89% of adult murderers in the U.S. had adult criminal records[49]—in the words of Sheriff Lucas Buck, "Conscience is just the fear of getting caught."[50]

We are unlikely to become more moral in our behaviour if the only incentive is that staying good will save us from punishment. Whatever good a believer would do out of hope of reward hereafter, the atheist would do simply because it is good; and being so, he will receive a far surer reward, springing from well-doing, which constitutes his pleasure and promotes his happiness. Coercion only makes people act

44. Bufe 1992, 177.

45. As quoted in *Liberty: A Magazine of Religious Freedom*, July/August 1995.

46. Toland 1976, I, 222.

47. *The Press Democrat*, June 15, 1989.

48. LaPierre 2003.

49. Lott 2010.

50. "Pilot." *American Gothic.* CBS. September 22, 1995.

as though they were highly ethical in public, when they privately harbour deep-rooted and suppressed desire for rebellion, if not revenge—a society that has too many laws unnecessarily restricting human liberty only drives many of its otherwise good members to criminal behaviour: "If laws worked, there would be no crime."

Many question whether relocating our valuing process within ourselves will result in widespread anarchy. The pioneering psychologist Carl Rogers (1902–1987) assures us that although this process of organismic valuing is entirely individual, the values that are created share a large degree of commonality across humanity. He asserts that "where individuals are valued, where there is greater freedom to feel and to be, certain value directions seem to emerge. These are not chaotic directions but instead have a surprising commonality. . . This commonality does not seem to be due to the influences of any one culture. . . I like to think that this commonality of value directions is due to the fact that we all belong to the same species. . . As a species there may be certain elements of experience which tend to make for inner development and which would be chosen by all individuals if they were genuinely free to choose."[51]

Man is from birth a social creature, and one of the preconditions of his development is the feeling of community. A newborn wants to belong, with his own family. Social skills and needs soon begin to expand, and even small children want child friends. "Morality is simply the attitude we adopt towards people we dislike." That is to say, you would never murder a loved one, now would you? While the FBI Uniform Crime Report (UCR) famously states that most homicides were committed by those who "knew" their victims, this category includes drug-dealers and clients, prostitutes and punters, rival gang-bangers involved in turf wars, and your garden variety of bar-room brawlers—in fact, the vast majority of murder victims themselves have prior criminal records.[52] Help people in need and they may one day reciprocate in kind; on the other hand, if you go around fighting and hitting people, they will fight and hit you back.

The play environment of American and European children has grown ever narrower over the last three generations, restricted by the fears of certain adults. In the upper middle-class, fairly affluent, suburban neighbourhoods where most of them live, there are no predators lurking on every street corner trying to kidnap their children, sell them drugs, or molest them. The suburbs are probably a lot safer than they used to be, but the perceived insecurity is growing, although without any grounds. Free play declined by at least a third between 1981 and 2003.[53] People are fearful of "stranger danger," because they don't know their neighbours and no longer live in such connected communities. Parents, who believe the outside world to be a dangerous place and project that onto their children, are doing them a disservice.

These children are not going to feel that the world is a place to be explored, they will not be able to make deep, long-lasting relationships with other children, or as they become adults, with other adults, since they have been brought up feeling that

---

51. 1969, 252.

52. Kleck & Kates 2001.

53. Szalavitz & Perry 2010.

people should not be trusted. Without unstructured time with playmates, children simply do not get to know each other very well. And you cannot learn to connect and care if you do not practise these things. Do you know how rare it is for a child to actually get snatched off the street? It is comparable to the number of people that get struck by lightning. Kidnappings and such are very marginal phenomena indeed, and have not increased at all according to statistics, but they get so much attention in the media, that people notice and remember them. In fact, people are hearing so many things so far removed from their local news about horrible things happening somewhere in the world that they have totally lost their perspective.

"Lots of men who would not associate with infidels for fear of contaminating their characters are not yet out of jail," quipped Lemuel K. Washburn.[54] Since a believer will always put God's law above man's law, "It is not disbelief that is dangerous to our society; it is belief."[55] In fact, statistics show convicts to be more religious than the general population; six of the seven U.S. states with the highest homicide rates in 2003 were "Red" in the 2004 elections, while the rate of murders in the "Blue" Northeastern States was well below the national average[56]: "A Christian is a man who feels repentance on Sunday for what he did on Saturday, and what he is going to do on Monday." Still, laws do not equal ethics; if the strict observance of a law leads to morally untenable results, then everyone's moral duty is to not obey the law—the whole idea behind civil disobedience is the discrepancy between the law and ethics. And "when freedom is outlawed, only outlaws will be free."[57]

The spirit of authority, law, tradition, and custom force us into a common groove and turn man into a will-less automaton without freedom or individuality. The "moral" man lives by the no-reason of laws, secular and spiritual, which is foolish and inadequate even when the law in question holds good; he is a mere mechanism, resourceless when any eventuality not already provided for in the original design arises. The habits we inherit from parents and through social conditioning provide a false sense of security while restricting conscious choice. By ignoring or sublimating individual volition, such ingrained habits destroy awareness and hinder growth and development. Once the fear of change, that is, the fear of the unknown, is overcome, the rewards are instantly realized.

The traditional man, or ***homo religiosus***, was conservative because keeping to the old was safe. Any kind of spontaneity or creativity spelled sudden change, which the small community struggling at the edge of survival could not sustain. The continuity of life depended on everything being done the way it had always been done, even if someone knew a better way. Common tradition, the knowledge about how things should be done, was what kept the community together. And like Suzanne LaFollette pointed out: "There is nothing more innately human than the tendency to transmute

---

54. Op. cit. 100.

55. Shaw, op. cit. lxvi.

56. Gregory S. Paul, "Cross-National Correlations of Quantifiable Societal Health with Popular Religiosity and Secularism in the Prosperous Democracies," *Journal of Religion & Society* 7, 2005.

57. Robbins 1980, 65.

what has become customary into what has been divinely ordained."[58]

Civilization naturally implies organization up to a point, and the freedom of any function is built upon system. Law and order are commendable as long as they make it easier for a man to follow his own way, but when the system is adored for it own sake, or as a means of endowing people with power over others, critical mass has been reached. "I have an almost complete disregard of precedent and a faith in the possibility of something better," declared Clara Barton, the founder of the American Red Cross. "It irritates me to be told how things always have been done. . . I defy the tyranny of precedent. I cannot afford the luxury of a closed mind. I go for anything new that might improve the past."[59] It is our duty as humans to carry the vision of future generations on our shoulders, by evolving.

"Quick to judge, quick to anger, slow to understand. Ignorance and prejudice and fear walk hand in hand."[60] Everything in the evolution of humanity has at first seemed impossible, be it the abolition of slavery, women's suffrage, or due process. To live is to change. All laws, all customs, all standards that produce uniformity are in direct opposition to Nature's imperative to change and develop through variety. The forces that resist change, resist life. "Progress is movement, and movement is life. To deny progress in to affirm nothingness, and to deify death."[61] Stability equals change. Rules are just things made up to justify everything that has been done before.

The instinct to rebel is just as important as the sex instinct for the survival of the species, for without rebellion from the "cult of adjustment" and domestication, nothing new would ever arise. "Society" hates the price of its own progress; its "representatives" claim to want the benefits of the sanctioned products of the "innovators" without the risk of the unsanctioned products of the "criminals." Almost all societies have mechanism to harness and take advantage of certain kinds of rebels: inventors, teachers, soldiers, priests, shamans. Physically active people are "encouraged" to become soldiers, police officers, and professional athletes; mystically inclined people become priests or monks; artistically creative people are "patronized." The rebels are thus made feel dependent on the social structure, and dependance breeds fear, and fear is control. Some societies—among them the feudal periods of Europe and Japan, and the grey futures of George Orwell's *1984* and Ayn Rand's *Anthem*—have, however, recognized that the attempt to harness a person of independent mind is inherently dangerous, and rather than risk change and their inevitable destruction, have opted for total stagnation.

Conservatism fears new ideas rightly from its point of view, because it has no distinctive principles of its own to oppose them. What is more, its lack of imagination beyond anything which experience has already proved deprives it of any weapons in the struggle of ideas. "Existing order thrives upon ignorance and lies," said legendary NFL coach Jimmy Johnson. "Objective truth and individual reason are feared above all." The Church will pardon murderers but not philosophers, and the government

58. 1926, 2.

59. As quoted in Buehrens & Church 1989, 41.

60. Rush. "Witch Hunt." *Moving Pictures.* Anthem Records, 1981.

61. Éliphas Lévi, *The Key of the Mysteries.* Crowley 1909–13, X, 55.

agencies "recapitulate the story of Christianity word for word, like the inevitable course of some unsightly disease: criminal ignorance, brutish stupidity, self-righteous bigotry, paranoid fear of outsiders. For the cultist, psychiatrists, the media, Government agencies have become Satan incarnate. Like the fundamental Christians, they have to be *right*."[62]

There is nothing more dangerous than making something "holy." "The idea of the sacred is quite simply one of the most conservative notions in any culture," asserted Salman Rushdie, "because it seeks to turn other ideas—uncertainty, progress, change —into crimes."[63] Thus: "All great truths begin as blasphemies,"[64] and "Every great advance in natural knowledge has involved the absolute rejection of authority."[65] The traditional man wanted to believe that there were people smarter than himself, and he wished to submit under their authority, be they priests, kings, fathers, or elder brothers. Hundreds of years after Aristotle's theorems had been disproven, they were still being presented as scientific truth, because people would rather believe an established authority than their own experience.

The Bible, the anthology of writings upon which Christianity is supposed to be founded, does not say what Christianity is, what a Christian is, or even what one must do in order to be a Christian. Nowhere in the Gospels is there a precept for confessions, oaths, dogmas, or the rest of nonsense that make up Christianity. "Jesus was all virtue, and acted from impulse, not from rules," observed William Blake.[66] "If thine eye offend thee" has been interpreted not as it stands, but as if it read: "If thine eye offend some artificial standard of morality, cut it out." Nor was Jesus' radical phrase "Let he who is without sin cast the first stone" some new moral-philosophical assertion. It was an act that opened up an alternative to the cycle of revenge and beyond the scape-goating, bringing a new truth to the world. This truth was not that "holy war is wrong" or that "fighting is wrong," but that the "sacred" of any community is always a sacrifice that forestalls the outbreak of violence, a religious H-bomb in the cold war within the community.

As G. B. Shaw declared, "No sooner had Jesus knocked over the dragon of superstition that Paul boldly set it on its legs again in the name of Jesus."[67] And the subsequent Synods made sure that the doctrines which were most opposed to common sense and individual liberty were confirmed. For whenever a competing group arose, the Church *had to* condemn its central doctrine, and thus confirm its opposite—no matter how intellectually or morally repugnant the latter might have been. Jesus was a rebel and a radical egalitarian; his best friends were dissidents and whores, unbelievers and rogues, artists of every shape and size. Were Jesus walking around today, he would undoubtedly be loathed and shunned by the Christian Right, if not literally crucified all over again.

---

62. William S. Burroughs, "Sects and Death." Stang 1990, 23.

63. 1991, 416.

64. *The Bolshevik Empress.* Shaw 1919, 289.

65. Huxley 1896, 40.

66. *The Marriage of Heaven and Hell*, pls. 23–24.

67. *Preface to Androcles and the Lion.* 1916, c.

Similarly, Islam totally revolutionized the nomadic tribal culture of the pagan Arabs, overturning its entrenched leadership and paving the way for a new social order. Buddhism revolutionized the yogic practices of the Indian subcontinent and South Asia by giving them transcendent purpose—rather than trying to secure a favoured position in the cycle of death and rebirth, Buddhists sought to escape it altogether. Sikhism revolutionized synergetic religion, by showing that different deities could be understood as different phases of the divine, that One could be Many could be One. Although all of these ideologies were co-opted by reactionary politicians, their distinctive revolutionary character cannot be denied. The Romans turned Christianity into a political tool, Islam became a form of nationalism, Buddhism's non-theistic character provided the gateway for communism in China and for ethnic chauvinism in Sri Lanka; Sikhism became a political ideology when the subcontinent was partitioned on ethnic and religious lines, with independent states for Hindus and Muslims and nothing at all for the Sikhs.

What passes for morality in today's Christian society was designed to keep people docile: "The clergy successfully preached the doctrines of patience and pusillanimity; the active virtues of society were discouraged; and the last remains of a military spirit were buried in the cloister: a large portion of public and private wealth was consecrated to the specious demands of charity and devotion; and the soldiers' pay was lavished on the useless multitudes of both sexes who could only plead the merits of abstinence and chastity."[68]

Each of the Seven Deadly Sins is a sin of excess: pride, envy, wrath, sloth, avarice, gluttony, and lust; and they are based not on the Bible, but the Greek golden mean. Yet it is precisely the road of excess that leads to the palace of wisdom. "Excess on occasion is exhilarating," wrote W. Somerset Maugham. "It prevents moderation from acquiring the deadening effect of a habit."[69] Respect for routine marks the second-rate man, and one should endeavour to break all customs or habits, of which ethics is just the social expression, just to break free from that form of slavery. Any habit is a bad habit, and a "person has not much excuse for living who can make no better use of life than passing it in a nunnery."[70]

The conditioning that took place in your past affects the belief you have about yourself in the present. The hopes and fears you base your life on stem from the authority figures of your youth and are predicated on the faith you put on those figures. Since your beliefs only allow you to give credence to information that support these beliefs and make you distrust information that does not, following the conditioning imposed on you by other people means you forfeit your own free will. And when people become convinced that their traditional customs are the right way to do things, they become equally convinced that other people's customs are wrong; they then begin imposing theirs, by force, if necessary—which applies to nations just well as to churches. "It is easier for a man to burn down his own house than to get rid

---

68. Gibbon 1840, II, 443.

69. 1938, 48.

70. Washburn, op. cit. 157.

of his prejudices,"[71] and "Most men would kill the truth if truth would kill their religion."[72]

What of the three Pauline virtues, Faith, Hope, and Charity? Believing in firemen will not salvage a burning building, believing in doctors will not make one well, but believing in a saviour saves men? As Voltaire put it, "The truths of religion are never so well understood as by those who have lost their power of reasoning."[73] Faith is deciding to believe in something your intellect would otherwise cause you to reject—otherwise there would be no need for faith. In order to test your faith, you are asked to believe in silly things like transubstantiation, that the communion wine turns into the blood of Christ; if this were an easy thing to believe, backed up by facts, then it would be no great achievement.

"Faith, indeed, has up to the present not been able to move real mountains," wrote Nietzsche. "But it can put mountains where there are none."[74] Every sect will gladly make use of reason as long as it well help them, but where it fails them, they declare the issue a matter of faith, above reason. But if faith is the only way by which you can accept an assertion, you are conceding that it cannot be taken on its own merits: "'Faith' means not wanting to know what is true."[75] The fiercest controversies are about matters of which no good evidence exists either way; persecution is used in theology, not in mathematics—"There is no sect in geometry; we never say,—An Euclidian, an Archimedian."[76] And whatever perpetuates the existence of ignorance or prevents the recognition of facts is a threat to the well-being of humanity: in the credulous Dark Ages, social life was cruel and treacherous; in the skeptical Modern Era, life became more humane—"There is no shame in not knowing; the shame lies in not finding out."[77]

And what of Hope? Ambrose Bierce defines "Religion" in *The Devil's Dictionary* as a "daughter of Hope and Fear, explaining to Ignorance the Nature of the Unknowable."[78] One only needs to glance over the world and contemplate the acts of Christians everywhere to be amazed at the singular inefficacy of their theology. One only needs to look back over past centuries at the iniquity of the populace, nobility, kings, and popes alike to see a near incomprehensible futility of the beliefs everywhere insisted upon. Hope and fear are the opposite phases of a single emotion; "Live in hope, die in despair," they say. "And then, something happened. I let go. Lost in oblivion. Dark and silent and complete. I found freedom. Losing all hope was freedom."[79]

And Charity? By taking pity, or sympathy, on someone you are actually declaring

71. Roger Bacon, attributed.

72. Washburn, op. cit. 80.

73. As quoted in McKinsey 1995, 276.

74. *Miscellaneous Maxims and Opinions*, Sec. 225. 1909–11, VII, 121.

75. Idem. 1954, 635.

76. Voltaire 1856, II, 296.

77. Russian proverb.

78. 1925, 283.

79. *Fight Club*, op. cit.

yourself superior to that person; at the same time, too much empathy can also be unwise: if you are taking on the suffering of another every day—if you work at a charity—you soon start to feel bad yourself and no longer care about the suffering of others; in fact, you may grow envious of the happiness of the "uncharitable." And if you really just want to be charitable, why flaunt the fact that you are also, first and foremost, a Christian? We all know that a person who slips a coin in the offertory bag thereby relieves his conscience; and such person has a guilty conscience about his "clear conscience." Does this mean charity is altruistic after all? No, because it is precisely the man with a guilty conscience who is considered a model specimen of a good person in our Christian culture. Of course the Church preaches charity—it subsists on hand-outs.

2

Prudens Quæstio Dimidium Scientiæ

Contrary to popular myth, perpetuated by Christian propaganda, monotheism is not the most evolved belief-system, but the most primitive. Each and every primitive divinity had for his or her sphere of beneficence the whole circle of human activities, for a primitive community cannot afford to departmentalize it deities. It is only the gradual dispersion of the tribes, together with their consequent isolation from one another, that favours differentiation in the ways of conceiving and worshipping the divinities whom they have brought with them from their original home. The eventual fusion of tribes then brings together a number of local divinities, which, if they are to stay together, divide their functions and attributes, taking their place side by side as departmental deities in the national pantheon.

The Judaeo-Christian deity had originally resembled the other divinities common in ancient days. Never had Yahweh been particularly kindly a god. When we first encounter him in the Bible, he is already, as the tribal god of the Hebrews, a mighty and sole god, and not merely a member of a group of gods competing with one another. Still, he is only the god of the Hebrews—the other tribes were presumed to bow down to other divinities. Among the most unattractive sections of the Bible are those which relate Yahweh's lengthy and triumphant struggle to defend himself and his people against the enticement of rival gods and goddesses. Yahweh was a jealous god who did not want his people to adopt any of the other tribes' deities. The struggle in Israel between Yahweh and various other divinities is a struggle between the centralized monarchy and priesthood in Jerusalem and the outlying communities.

There are no rules of ethics in the Bible. Sin equals breaking God's law, from which He is exempt, e.g. He gets to kill indiscriminately, just as any earthly tyrant. When asked to sacrifice his son Isaac, Abraham, the patriarch of Judaism, Christianity, and Islam, was fully prepared to do so until Yahweh let him off the hook. This may have been loyalty to his chosen divinity, but it would have been infinitely more moral for Abraham to defy and deny Yahweh for even asking him to do so. As a sign of their covenant, Yahweh instituted male circumcision, surgical removal of the foreskin, symbolic of castration, the apparent penalty for breaking the pact. The Israelites swore their oaths with their hand "under the thigh," that is, touching their testicles —whence our term "testimony."

Personal religious experiences, being individual and asocial, can never be national; in order to unite a nation, a religion has to consist of practices. The Ten—or however many—Commandments only applied to the tribe of Hebrews: as far as Yahweh was concerned, you could murder all the Gentiles you wished and have your way with all their women; in fact, were a man to follow the prescriptions of the Old Testament today, he would be a criminal. On the other hand, to "covet thy neighbour's wife" is not even considered adultery in modern civil law. And, in effect, the Ninth/Tenth Commandment only says that a Jewish man shall not sleep with a woman married to another Jew; plus he can fornicate with as many concubines and female slaves as he wants. Still, the number of stonable offences in the Law is astronomical; stoning was a natural part of the roving nomad culture, since stones are plentiful everywhere. The original Hebrew greeting was not ***Shalom***, but "Be fruitful and multiply!"[80]

"There is one notable thing about Christianity: bad, bloody, merciless, money-grabbing and predatory as it is—in our country particularly, and in all other Christian countries in a somewhat modified degree—it is still a hundred times better than the Christianity of the Bible," concluded Mark Twain.[81] The same, of course, applied to Judaism. "There are no witches. The witch text remains; only the practice has changed. Hell fire is gone, but the text remains. Infant damnation is gone, but the text remains. More than two hundred death penalties are gone from the law books, but the texts that authorized them remain."[82]

Forgiveness, be it of sin or anything else, implies debt. The whole of the Bible was written by slave owners, for slave owners. There is absolutely no criticism of slavery anywhere in the Scripture. Instead of objecting to the mistreatment of slaves, Paul indicated that selling of debtors into slavery would continue in the forthcoming Kingdom of Heaven, where masters would retain their right to beat and torture their slaves. "Sin" was actually the word for "debt" in all early Indo-European languages: ***Schuld***, the root of German ***sollen*** and English ***should***, and ***devoir***, the root of English ***debt***. It meant obligation, referring to the ancient practice whereby the offender was obligated to make good payment to atone for his offence. Now, while it is entirely possible to pay another man's debts on his behalf, it is quite impossible to make a

80. Genesis 1:28, 9:1.

81. 1983, 446.

82. Ibid. 422.

guilty man innocent by suffering in his place.

And this is the meaning of grace: "The whole point of Christianity is that everyone in the world, from Charles Manson to Mother Teresa, deserves to go to hell." The sense of guilt bears down on man more heavily than any other emotion. The burden of guilt has been placed on his shoulders by several authorities: parents, teachers, peers, and the media; governments, schools, and religious communities. This burden exists for two purposes: it can be used to both control and punish us. The person who gives in to his guilt is assailed by feelings of emptiness and a poor self-esteem, rendering him incapable of living in the present, much less to love himself or his fellow-men.

Christian salvation is, and must be, preordained, so that one cannot buy God's grace with good deeds; behaving morally guarantees nothing. However, there is no real world application for the Christian soteriology; on the contrary, "The doctrine of salvation by faith is a libel on justice and has done more to undermine the virtue of the world than vice itself."[83] Those who are quick to forgive others, often at the urging of a relative or a member of the clergy, tend to blame themselves for the bad things that have happened to them. Others forgive quickly because they are unwilling to acknowledge their general feelings of shame and anger, or simply because they do not feel worthy of better treatment. But forgiving an abuser does not make him any less of an abuser: "Fool me once, shame on you; fool me twice, shame on me." First someone screws you over, and then it's your fault that you don't want to embrace them in Heaven.

Abraham was prepared to sacrifice his only beloved son? God gave his only, grown son, albeit only to resurrect him three days later? To quote May Morrison in *The Wicker Man*, "You'll simply never understand the true nature of sacrifice."[84] The scapegoat was an animal on whose head the ancient Hebrews placed their sins, but "When men are hungry roast mutton is better than the lamb that taketh away wrath."[85] I should be thankful? For what? Being alive? It's the fear of death (or of the Lord?) all over again. Yes, one should be allowed to take things for granted! "Dear God. We paid for all this stuff ourselves, so thanks for nothing."[86]

Nobody died for my sins, thank you very much. I'll be damned if I'll let someone else eat my karma—those are my sins, I earned them! I do not need vicarious atonement, I do my own atoning. Even though I place Siddharta Gautama and Buddhism miles above Christianity or Islam, theirs is, at bottom, nonetheless just another "religion of suffering": you are going to suffer for the evil deeds you committed in your previous lives, even though you have no idea what you have done. This is a pretty bad motivator for cleaning up your act in anticipation of your next life, especially considering the fact that you can never know if one of your good deeds ultimately ends up harming someone else.

---

83. Washburn, op. cit. 161.

84. Dir. Robin Hardy. British Lion Film Corporation, 1973.

85. Washburn, op. cit. 43.

86. "Two Cars in Every Garage and Three Eyes on Every Fish." *The Simpsons*. FOX. November 1, 1990.

Innocence is not knowing right from wrong; or, rather, not thinking one does. "Ye shall not surely die"—who says the serpent didn't also lie about good and evil? Innocence is freedom from prejudice. God told Adam and Eve not to eat the fruit, but if this was the only way they could understand the difference between good and evil, how could they have known it was wrong to disobey God and eat the fruit? I put it to you that should we truly know right from wrong there would be no such trifles as moral codes; it is thinking that one does which constitutes the real "god-complex."

Guilt is an ego-trip; "hindsight is always 20/20." *A priori* moral knowledge is impossible—we can perhaps see a couple of steps ahead, but we have no more extensive perspective. This is exactly why man has thought that it is up to some power external to himself to decide what is good and what is evil; however, "We must question the story logic of having an all-knowing all-powerful God, who creates faulty Humans, and then blames them for his own mistakes." Or as Jack Nicholson put it in *The Witches of Eastwick*, "When we make mistakes they call it evil. When God makes mistakes they call it Nature."[87]

But what if one were to discard all definitions and just attempt to do good? Well, it is not that easy: one might for example invent the theory of relativity and later discover one has laid the foundation for the atomic bomb. "The road to Hell is paved with good intentions." Or to put it more bluntly, "Every religion in the world that has destroyed people is based on love."[88] All human actions have unforeseen consequences. Even if we wanted only good and had thoroughly thought out what we needed to do to accomplish this, unpredictable factors could thwart our goals. "We need not fear those who do evil in the name of evil, but Heaven protect us from those who do evil in the name of good," as Arthur C. Adams put it. "But I meant well." Well, some of the worst acts in history have been committed by men who meant well!

Moral good is not one but many. It can mean e.g. happiness, duty, profit, or pleasure. These are what a person aims at, sometimes more, sometimes less. There are bad deeds that are made necessary by ideals; deeds that seem bad to the outsider, but which mark an irreproachable fight for the ideal to their perpetrators. This kind of evil is as moral as it gets. It stems from morality; ethics is its precondition. The madmen who flew those planes into the Twin Towers were driven by visions of dancing girls in a milk and honey paradise; similarly, the Ashcroft response was actuated by a feeling that the last days predicted by the Book of Revelation were upon us. "Men never do evil so completely and cheerfully as when they do it from a religious conviction."[89]

Or as Stanislaw J. Lec wrote: "Woe to dictators who are convinced they are not dictators."[90] Of all tyrannies, a tyranny exercised for the good of its victim is the most oppressive. It is better to live under a robber-baron than under an all-powerful moral busybody. The robber-baron's cruelty will sometimes rest, his greed will eventually be sated, but those who torment us for our own good are going to torment us without

87. Dir. George Miller. Warner Bros. Pictures, 1987.

88. P-Orridge 2010, 253.

89. Pascal 2008, 206.

90. 1962, 125.

end, for they do so to appease their own guilty consciences.

Do you seriously think Hitler thought he was evil? That he wasn't doing the world a favour by ridding it of the Jews? This is what the Führer wrote in *Mein Kampf*, a book that is still banned in Germany: "I believe today that my conduct is in accordance with the will of the Almighty Creator. . . .the founder of Christianity made no secret indeed of his estimation of the Jewish people. When He found it necessary, He drove those enemies of the human race out of the Temple of God."[91] The German Christians were no counterforce to the Nazis, who murdered six million Jews in their country. Despite the Holocaust, many European Churches continued to support the anti-Semitic far-right after the War. When the Jewish genocide was revealed, many Christians had an excuse ready: the Jews killed Jesus. The same Jesus who said: "Forgive them Father, for they know not what they do."[92]

Nor is evil lunacy; otherwise every defendant could plead insanity. And what is there to stop the authorities from committing anyone who does not think like them? Before the advent of mental hospitals, heretics, prostitutes, madmen, and in general all "socially deviant" were "treated" by the Inquisition. Secularization has gone hand in hand with medicalization: after all, it is not that long ago that the "sin" of homosexuality was widely considered a "psychiatric disorder." In 1952, the United States passed the McCarran-Walter Immigration Act to keep communists, anarchists, and other "subversives" out of the country; the act also denied admission to aliens "afflicted with psychopathic personality."[93] The primary purpose of mental wards has always been to keep the "crazy" outside society, since they are deemed "dangerous." A recent study at Göttingen University shows that the number of people held in psychiatric clinics against their wills doubled in the last decade of the 20th century.[94]

However, habitual criminals are not, by and large, psychopaths—they are merely loyal to a different community than ordinary law-abiding citizens; whence the old reference to "honour among thieves." One only ever runs into intelligent murderers in fiction; the majority of murders and manslaughters are caused by mental breakdown. Murders are usually banal and sad: people often kill their loved ones because they are out of words. And even if Hitler was insane, as far as I know, he took but one life by his own hand—his own. How is it possible that the Germans fought for their Führer to his death, and then, in an historic nanosecond, became exemplary democrats?

Hannah Arendt's book, *Eichmann in Jerusalem*, tellingly subtitled *The Banality of Evil*, is essential reading for anyone interested in understanding the mind of the modern war criminal. Adolph Eichmann was a door-to-door vacuum cleaner salesman, who got a government job that sort of metamorphosed into middle management in a genocidal effort during the time of his employ. As a person, he was utterly disinterested in anti-Semitism and had no strong feelings about the whole

91. 1943, 65.

92. Luke 23:34

93. INA § 212(a)(4). 8 USC § 1182(a)(4).

94. Kirstin Inga Darsow-Schütte & Peter Müller, "Zahl der Einweisungen nach PsychKG in 10 Jahren verdoppelt," *Psychiatrische Praxis* 28(5), July 2001, 226–229.

National Socialist philosophy. The fact that he continued to do his job speaks to his stunning lack of individuality or personal will. As Arendt writes: "The trouble with Eichmann was precisely that so many were like him, and that they were neither perverted nor sadistic, that they were, and still are, terribly and terrifyingly normal. From the viewpoint of our legal institutions and of our moral standards of judgment, this normality was much more terrifying than all the atrocities put together, for it implied—as has been said at Nuremberg over and over again by defendants and counsels—that this type of criminal, who is in actual fact *hostis generis humani*, commits his crimes under circumstances that make it well-nigh impossible for him to know or to feel that he is doing wrong."[95]

In 1928, C. G. Jung accurately predicted the inhuman horrors of the Second World War in his critique of large organizations. He pointed out that here was "the tremendous heaping-up and accentuation of all that is primitive in man."[96] The person's individuality was submerged in the interests of the great monstrosity that is any big organization. So long as the majority resolutely believe in the righteousness of their cause, the greatest infamy on the part of the organization will not disturb the individual; and being a large organization, they can complacently reject the little doubt from the odd individual, his individuality being sacrificed to the organization as a whole. Man is sick, lame, addicted, and dangerous, needing constant supervision and protection by the state, insurance companies, and an endless parade of caring, licensed professionals. Over and over again, we are told that man's illnesses and addictions are costing *us* billions. Man is a resource that is causing *us* trouble, he is interfering with *our* plans. Those who question these "plans" or, indeed, the sanity of the metaphor, are diagnosed as either morally unfit or mentally ill. Yet as Nietzsche pointed out in *Beyond Good and Evil:* "Insanity in individuals is rare—but in groups, nations, and epochs, it is the rule."[97] Once you rile up people enough so they don't see reason anymore, they become slaves to the whims of the group. "It is no measure of health to be well adjusted to a profoundly sick society."[98]

The primary purpose of society, according to Dr. Robert Lindner, is "To bend the will of the individual to the will of the majority, to become as others are by accepting the illusions of the mass."[99] This being so, Lindner, author of the 1944 case history that was turned into the classic movie *Rebel Without a Cause* (1955), viewed psychological symptoms as protests against the surrender of individuality—never forget that "only dead fish swim with the stream."[100] He saw rebellion as normal and healthy, something that should be properly channelled, instead of being deemed as a problem for society, requiring either imprisonment or "treatment." It is curious that many psychiatrist today continue to believe that witches were "misdiagnosed," and that they were in fact suffering from "mental illness," not "demonic possession."

---

95. 1963, 276.

96. 159.

97. Verse 156. 1909–11, XII, 98.

98. Jiddu Krishnamurti, attributed.

99. 1962, 41.

100. Chinese proverb.

Psychiatrists alone don't buy the scapegoat theory, which all historians agree upon. Could this be due to the fact that the scapegoat theory also applies perfectly to the "mentally ill" of today?

"...psychiatry is appealing because it masks the necessarily evaluative dimensions of its activities behind a screen of scientific objectivity and neutrality... It was and is therefore, of great potential value in legitimising and depoliticising efforts to regulate social life and keep the recalcitrant and socially disruptive in line."[101] Lindner predicted that psychology and its associated disciplines would eventually become handmaidens of the State and Big Business. Both the government and the public would begin to believe that psychology had more to offer than it did, meaning that it would necessarily lose its value for those who needed it the most. Modern psychology is a traitor that doesn't help people, but takes part in their oppression. Central to this oppression is the psychologization of social and political issues. The collective solidarity is thus turned into nothing more than following other people's psychological reactions. The only possibility for change we are left with is the personal, inner change within each individual.

Lindner was speaking in the context of forced and coerced adjustment to the values of mediocrity, fate, and destiny as preached by educators, clinicians, and the clergy, but adjustment to culture and domestication is now practised by a great number of middle-class and "midzonal" professions. This fact alone may explain some of the "outrageous" acts of rebellion exhibited not only by young people, but by adults, whose rage seems to have no other place to go except towards self-destruction and "random" acts of violence. "Instead of removing the conditions that make people depressed, modern society gives them antidepressant drugs. In effect, antidepressants are a means of modifying an individual's internal state in such a way as to enable him to tolerate social conditions that he would otherwise find intolerable." Thus, Theodore Kaczynski, Ph.D., otherwise known as the "Unabomber."[102]

Barbed-wire camps were a very common sight all over the globe around the Second World War, though it must be emphasized that actual death camps only existed in the Soviet Union and in Germany. A plethora of different kinds of prison camps, quarantine camps, internment camps, and concentration camps were found in almost every country, although none like to recollect them in their own history books. We hear ***ad nauseam*** about what the Nazis did to the Jews, but we never hear of the 6.5 million German civilians and prisoners of war purposefully exterminated by the Americans at the end of WWII under the Morgenthau plan. Originally, Hitler merely wanted some slave labour in order to solve Germany's economic crisis; the "Final Solution," genocide and mass murder, was not a part of the plan from the beginning.

All in all, the number of Russian prisoners of war and gypsies killed in the Nazi death camps probably surpass the number of murdered Jews. In percentage terms, priests, freemasons, and homosexuals were perhaps exterminated the most. In terms of the war as a whole, it scarcely matters whether there had or had not been a

---

101. Scull 1993, 392.

102. *Industrial Society and Its Future.* 2010, 83.

Holocaust, though it did provide a splendid *ex post facto* justification for the war—even if its original causes lay solely in the Franco-British struggle for imperium. The Jews were somehow raised on a pedestal, for reasons that might have something to do with the Middle Eastern politics of the Cold War era. Defeated Germany was not just occupied, it was also re-educated: German schools and universities, under almost total government control, and the government-licensed mass media continue to proclaim to this day the official American view of history and, in particular, of the 20th century as a triumph of good over evil.

"Good" seems like such an everyday word, when in fact, there is no other word with as wide a conceptual horizon. The word "good" has two opposites: "bad" and "evil." And not only in English—the same duality is found in most languages. The two senses of good are distinguishable and yet intricately intertwined. Moral good is not an independent philosophical concept, but related to several forms of goodness. The many concepts have originally been one and the same; a good person in Neolithic times equalled a good hunter. There can be no horizontal good-evil axis, only a vertical one: "He who seeks the origin of evil, seeks the source of what is not. Evil is the disordered appetite for good, the unfruitful attempt of an unskilful will."[103]

Aristotle begins his ten-volume *Nichomachean Ethics* by declaring that every human pursuit is geared towards some good. He meant that we all try to do everything as skilfully as we can; it is philosophically a self-contradictory notion for us to seek to do something badly. On the other hand, the common Christian claim that "good cannot exist without evil" is pernicious nonsense of the worst kind. Sure, you have to tear down in order to build up, but that does not make the tearing down evil. Everyone but everyone aims to do good; even the person who aims to do evil—thinking that it is good to do evil. "The devil is a convenient myth invented by the real malefactors of the world."[104] Satanism is, after all, a Christian heresy; and one should "never attribute to devil-worshipping conspiracies what opportunism, emotional instability, and religious bigotry are sufficient to explain."[105]

When we realize that every act has a positive intention behind it, we can approach with positivity both our own and other people's seemingly strange, bizarre, wrong, or even crazy behaviour. If we separate the positive intention from the means to realize it, we will often gain useful results. For example, young people want to become independent, which is a positive intention. The means, however, can vary: one youngster starts using drugs, another fights with his parents, while the third begins taking responsibility for his own life. If we approach these young people on the level of means, we easily fall into the trap of deeming one bad, another good, instructing them, appraising them, judging them. Should we on the other hand converge with them on the level of their intentions, we can meet every one of them on the positive end, accept their goals, and begin negotiating on means that promote that goal even better.

However, good achievements are not proof of good intentions. General literacy is

---

103. *The Key of the Mysteries.* Op. cit. 31.

104. Wilson 1990a, 8.

105. Carlson & Larne 1989, 16.

held to be an achievement of the Reformation. But spreading literacy in itself was not the intention of the Protestants. They wanted to teach the people to read the Bible and to read it according to the Lutheran interpretation, in effect, to make them brainwash themselves. Which of course was a "good" intention from the Reformed point of view—just as the ultimate achievement was "bad." It is not a question of weak will, but unskilful will; it is the weaklings that are obsessed with strength. Our wills are anything but limitless. We can will ourselves to knowledge, but not to wisdom; to pleasure, but not to happiness; to diet and exercise, but not to good health. None of our deeper desires are attainable through the exercise of our wills.

Now, while evil is certainly incompetence, incompetence is not in itself evil. One should never demonize, for as Nietzsche put it, "He who fights with monsters should be careful lest he thereby become a monster."[106] President Bush might have waged war because he was an idealist, but then so were his left-wing critics. The problem Bush shared with Saddam is that they were incapable of admiring each other. According to the German philosopher, instead of considering the Trojans evil or unworthy, Homer admired them, his enemies. A balance of good and evil is only possible with absolute concepts. And there are no absolutes: "Quinine is 'good' for a malarial patient, but 'evil' for the germ of the disease. Heat is 'bad' for ice-cream and 'good' for coffee."[107] And while selfishness and laziness are undoubtedly negative qualities in a slave, it would be unwise for a hunter-gatherer to expend energy on activities unnecessary for his survival. If we think we know what is best for others, we are not a long way from accepting that maybe the government knows what is best for all of us.

The fundamental difference between the Shakespearean and the Greek forms of tragedy is that, in the former, the source of causal initiative is always a flaw in the protagonist's character, while in the latter, the source of causal initiative is circumstantial. Shakespeare paints his characters larger than life: they usually have political or social power, but are shown to be flawed and secretly weak despite their great power. This is popular in literature, because the idea that great men are flawed will always appeal to the masses. To see great men fall prey to their own flaws is very satisfying to the common man. In Shakespeare's plays, the characters always know what they "should" do, they just won't do it—in fact, they often do stupid things to make their problems even worse. In contrast, the characters in the Theban plays are sincerely doing what they think is right: they don't wind up in the situations they do because of some inner moral flaw; they go about their business, do their best, one thing leads to another, and they find themselves downhill from some shit—which we all know rolls downhill. As simple as that.

As Democritus pointed out in the 5th century BCE: "Sweet exists by convention, bitter by convention, colour by convention; atoms and Void (alone) exist in reality."[108] Images are formed in the brain, not in the eye, and "Many of the truths we cling to

106. *Beyond Good and Evil*, Verse 146. Op. cit. 97.

107. Crowley 1974, 93.

108. *Tetralogies of Thrasyllus*, III–VI, 9.

depend greatly upon our own point of view."[109] We all know that in order to fully understand a thing, one must become that thing, "walk a mile in its shoes" so to speak. The very act of believing in something causes us to separate ourselves from that thing, creating a duality: oneself and the thing in which one believes. Since the state of believing in something inevitably causes us to not understand the thing we believe in, believing in God always ends in variations of the Spanish Inquisition. If, on the other hand, you were one with God, you would act towards all beings as though they were your own creations; which, of course, they are. As Aleister Crowley put it, "The attempt to discover the nature of things by a study of the relations between them is precisely parallel with the ambition to obtain a finite value of Pi."[110]

Theories cannot be proven, only disproven; we cannot know anything for sure. Scientific hypotheses are always tentative; they are meant to be held only so long as they conform to the evidence. Proponents of the theistic hypothesis, on the other hand, are convinced that their assumption is correct, and only seek evidence to support a foregone conclusion. And if you think logic is not a good method for determining what to believe, try and convince me of that without the use of logic. Christians seem perfectly happy to use science to refute competing religions, but if you really want to look at things from the scientific point of view, you have to put Christianity on the same plane with the other faiths: "Religion is magic sanctioned by authority."[111] If you are not inclined to accept science as an authority when examining Christianity, you cannot appeal to it when assessing other religious traditions either.

"Generally speaking, the errors in religion are dangerous; those in philosophy only ridiculous," wrote David Hume in *A Treatise of Human Nature* (1739).[112] To paraphrase Voltaire, "as long as people believe in absurdities, they will continue to commit atrocities," and as the Rev. Donald Morgan famously opined: "The certainty with which a religious belief is held is usually in direct proportion to its absurdity." From time immemorial has God been the refuge of the incompetent, the helpless, and the miserable; even the weakest disputant is made so conceited by religion that he thinks himself wiser than the wisest who think differently from him.

"The fundamental cause of trouble is that in the modern world the stupid are cocksure while the intelligent are full of doubt," reckoned Bertrand Russell.[113] "The seeker after truth must," enjoined Descartes, "once in the course of his life, doubt everything, as far as possible."[114] W. B. Yeats observed that "The best lack all conviction, while the worst are full of passionate intensity,"[115] while G. B. Shaw declared martyrdom to be "the only way in which a man can become famous without ability."[116] Learned Hand defines the Spirit of Liberty as "the spirit which is not too

---

109. *Star Wars: Return of the Jedi.* Dir. Richard Marquand. Twentieth Century Fox, 1983.

110. Op. cit. 92.

111. Lévi 1922, Paradox I.

112. 1978, 272.

113. *The Triumph of Stupidity*, May 10, 1933. 1998, 28.

114. *Principles of Philosophy*, Bk. I § 1. (AT VIIIA 5).

115. *The Second Coming.* 2000, 158.

116. *The Devil's Disciple*, Act II. 1913, 58.

sure it is right."[117]

"To rebel against a powerful political, economic, religious, or social establishment is very dangerous and very few people do it," wrote Isaac Asimov, "except, perhaps, as part of a mob. To rebel against the scientific establishment, however, is the easiest thing in the world, and anyone can do it and feel enormously brave, without risking as much as a hangnail. Thus, the vast majority, who believe in astrology and think that the planets have nothing better to do than form a code that will tell them whether tomorrow is a good day to close a business deal or not, become all the more excited and enthusiastic about the bilge when a group of astronomers denounces it."[118]

"Mystical explanations are considered deep," remarked Nietzsche. "The truth is that they are not even superficial."[119] However, nor is science the key to infinite wisdom, but the guard against abysmal folly. A skeptic is not a person who doubts, but a person who researches and examines, as opposed to asserting and thinking he has found. According to Kierkegaard, "The self-assured believer is a greater sinner in the eyes of God than the troubled disbeliever."[120] Or as Oscar Wilde quipped: "Only the shallow know themselves."[121] People with high self-esteem think they make better impressions, have stronger friendships and more fulfilling romantic lives than other people, but research does not support their self-flattering views. On the contrary, people who love themselves too much tend to annoy others with their defensive know-it-all attitudes.

It is not low self-esteem that causes violence, but individuals, groups, and nations that think very highly of themselves. They become violent towards those who fail to give them the inflated respect they think they deserve. Still, "doubt is a good servant but a bad master; a perfect mistress, but a nagging wife."[122] Happiness, indeed, seems reversely proportional to one's intelligence, and "The richer your imagination, the poorer you feel."[123] But while doubt may not be a pleasant condition, "certainty is an absurd one."[124] Thinking is frightening, perhaps more frightening than anything else in life. The fragile security of everyday existence crumbles, which is why people will sooner be mere carriers and transmitters of memes than thinkers. "Uncertainty in the presence of vivid hopes and fears is painful, but must be endured if we wish to live without the support of comforting fairy tales."[125] Or, "if you wish to strive for peace of soul and pleasure, then believe: if you wish to be a devotee of truth, then inquire."[126] Ignorance is bliss.

So does a person always know what is good for him or her? Maybe not, but no-one

---

117. I Am an American Day Address, Central Park, New York City, May 21, 1944.

118. Asimov 1978, 234.

119. *The Gay Science*, Sec. 126. 1974, 182.

120. Untermeyer 1955, 10.

121. *Phrases and Philosophies for the Use of the Young.* 1916, 307.

122. Crowley 1962, 100.

123. Lec, op. cit. 93.

124. Voltaire to Frederick William, Prince of Prussia, November 28, 1770. 1919, 232.

125. Russell 1945, xiv.

126. Friedrich Nietzsche to Elisabeth Nietzsche, June 11, 1865. 1954, 30.

else sure as hell does; which is where the "golden rule"—itself but basic human empathy—gets it wrong. Christians will tell you that the golden rule is their invention, for Jesus said: "Do unto others as thou wouldst have others do unto thee."[127] He may have said it, but he was not the only one, and definitely not the first. Epictetus, too, declared in the first century that, "What you would avoid suffering yourself, seek not to impose on others."[128] The Talmud says: "What is hateful to you, do not to your fellow man. This is the law: all the rest is commentary."[129] The Mahabharata (c. 150 BCE) sums up duty as: "Do naught unto others which would cause you pain if done to you."[130] Five centuries before Christ, Confucius proclaimed that "What you do not want done to yourself, do not do to others."[131] And these are just a few examples.

Modern research points toward a neurological basis for empathy: the ability of our brains to mimic the internal bodily states of others. Every one of us understands a pantomime performed without words; every one of us can instinctively read the body language of friends and family. We know when someone is happy, excited, or sad, or even in love with a person in the room. In fact, when someone says, "I feel your pain," it may be literally true; the pain-sensing part of our brains switches on when we become aware that someone else is in pain. Our ability to empathize probably evolved from a system for representing our own internal body states, and the emotional representations we use to understand the feelings of others certainly reflect our own subjective feeling states.

Watching a consenting couple engage in a bit of S&M may be unbearable to some, but rest assured that the pair feels differently—and even they have to ask each other what they like and what they do not. "If I were you. . ." Remember Ace Ventura? "If you were me then I'd be you and I'd use your body to get to the top. You can't stop me no matter who you are!"[132] Abraham Lincoln wrote: "I am approached with the most opposite opinions and advice, and by religious men who are certain they represent the Divine will. . . I hope it will not be irreverent in me to say, that if it be probable that God would reveal his will to others, on a point so connected with my duty, it might be supposed he would reveal it directly to me."[133]

I put it to you that one cannot—and should not try to—change, or "grow spiritually," etc., one can merely be "true to himself" or not. In fact, I subscribe to the theory that every last one of us is a fully-realized being, but just does not know it yet. "It is impossible to alter the ultimate Nature of any Being, however completely we may succeed in transfiguring its external signs as displayed in any of its combinations."[134] If you are always doing what *you* think you should be doing, you

127. Luke 6:31.

128. *Fragments*, xxxviii.

129. *Shabbat*, 31a.

130. 5:1517.

131. *Analects*, 15:23.

132. *Ace Ventura: Pet Detective*. Dir. Tom Shadyac. Warner Bros. Pictures, 1994.

133. 1905, 250.

134. Crowley 1974, 225.

never have to—nor should—explain, complain, or apologize. "If you know your conscience is just an animal instinct, you don't need to follow it."[135] It is the thing that kicks in when there is no logical reason to behave the way other people want you to behave. In the classical sense of the word, a "virtue" refers to the qualities possessed by a particular object or event. Certain plants, for example, have the virtue of healing certain ailments, certain metals have the virtue of attracting certain forces, etc. Our virtues, then, seen in this light, are our own particular strengths, which, again, are naturally dependent on the conditions in which we find ourselves. It is a travesty to call anyone virtuous whose virtues do not result from the exercise of his or her own reason. "He noblest lives and noblest dies, who makes and keeps his self-made laws."[136]

Verily, "Rules are just helpful guidelines for stupid people who cannot make up their own mind."[137] You should never second-guess yourself, for: "Whenever man begins to doubt himself he does something so stupid that he is reassured."[138] Or as the Bard put it: "Our doubts are traitors, and make us lose the good we oft might win, by fearing to attempt."[139] Rationalization is trivialization. "Know thyself" and "To thine own self be true" are two very different exhortations. Since you cannot know, since there is always some factor you fail to include in the equation, why not go with what you will? "Act passionately; think rationally; be Thyself."[140] Emotions will cloud your judgement and reason only goes so far. "If Power asks why, then is Power weakness."[141]

It is the audience that decides the winner of a debate; thus, non-public debates are pointless, as is debating with someone dumber or less knowledgeable than yourself: to quote the first theorem of social cybernetics, "Communication is possible only between equals,"[142] or to paraphrase John Locke, "It is one thing to show that a man is in error, and another to put him in possession of the truth." You neither can nor need to answer nonsensical arguments. And if you get insulted by name-calling, you can be almost sure that you are not what you have been called; if you don't get insulted, you don't care if you are—you might even take it as a compliment. "It is said that the civilized man seeks out good and intelligent company, so that by learned discourse, he may rise above the savage, and be closer to God. Personally, however, I like to start the day with a total dickhead to remind me that I'm best."[143] It all depends on your point of view.

Everyone is the centre of the universe, quite literally, mathematically and astrophysically. In an infinite, expanding universe, where space and time are warped,

---

135. "Black Hole." *House M.D.* FOX. March 15, 2010.

136. *Kasidah*, xxxvii. Burton 1924, 91.

137. "Office Politics." *House M.D.* FOX. November 8, 2010.

138. Lec, op. cit. 125.

139. *Measure for Measure*, Act I, Scene 5.

140. *Liber Libræ*, 12. Crowley 1909–13, I, 19.

141. AL II:31.

142. Wilson & Shea 1983, 332, 499.

143. "Beer." *Blackadder II.* BBC. February 13, 1986.

every point is the centre. "Each man instinctively feels that he is the Centre of the Cosmos, and philosophers have jeered at his presumption. But it was he that was precisely right."[144] On the other hand, everyone is also a fly's fart when compared to the vastness of infinite space; no-one matters in the greater picture—human society itself is another fly's fart in the immensity of time. The latter fact causes existential crisis, while the former solves it. "The meaning of life is to give life a meaning."

We must accept the responsibility for ourselves and the fact that only by unfolding our powers, by living productively, can we give meaning to our lives. In the words of Sir Francis Bacon: "Half of science is asking the right questions." And, conversely, "Ask a stupid question, get a stupid answer." If you ask the wrong questions, you are going to get answers like "Forty-two" or "God." As humans, we are obsessed with purpose; the question "What is it for?" comes naturally to a species surrounded by tools, utensils, and machines. For artifact such as these, it is appropriate; but we have gone too far—we apply the same question to rocks, mountains, stars, and the universe, where it has no place. As Bertrand Russell put it: "The universe may have a purpose, but nothing we know suggests that, if so, this purpose has any similarity to ours."[145] Marquis de Sade declared anything beyond the grasp of human understanding to be either illusory or futile, and since God has to be one or the other, in the first instance one would be mad to believe in Him, in the second a fool.

Atheism is an absolute requirement for a complete human being. Deities are crutches that shackle us, ones that we never needed anyway, but were convinced by others that we could not live without. Once we realize them to be only an illusion, not even a real crutch, we cast them off gladly. "There is no God but Man." In quantum mechanics, observation of reality is different from things just interacting with one another to make reality. What we imagine to be particles bang into one another and give rise to waves of possibilities, such as when and where these particles will appear. These waves do not become real until a conscious observation occurs; only when you consciously observe a possibility does it become real.

Thus, unless some sort of awareness exists to perceive the universe, the universe itself does not exist. Or, to put it simply, when a tree falls in the forest and no-one is around to hear it, there is no sound. For a sound to be a sound, there has to be some sort of auditory organ linked to some sort of intelligence that says, "What was that?" Energy and mass only exist because of awareness—they have no inherent existence. "I am Omniscient, for naught exists for me unless I know it. I am Omnipotent, for naught occurs save by Necessity my soul's expression through my will to be, to do, to suffer symbols of itself. I am Omnipresent, for naught exists where I am not, who fashioned space as a condition of my consciousness of myself, who am the centre of all, and my circumference the frame of mine own fancy."[146] And this is the only way these qualities make any sense: for example, if God is all-powerful He can make a stone so heavy that even He cannot lift it; then there is something God cannot do, wherefore He is not all-powerful.

---

144. Crowley 1974, 84.

145. 1957, 73.

146. *Liber V vel Reguli.* Crowley 1961, 335.

"Obedience indeed is only the pitiful and cowardly egotism of him who thinks that he can do something better than reason," wrote Shelley.[147] Self-knowledge is the only worthy knowledge; and "Nothing that is worth knowing can be taught."[148] All our experiences contribute to making us complete in ourselves, and so long as we fail to recognize this, we perceive ourselves subject unto them. When we do recognize this, we realize that they are subject unto us. So whenever we try to evade an experience, whatever it may be, we are doing wrong to ourselves, thwarting our own tendencies. But, "Illusions die hard and it is painful to yield to the insight that a grown-up can be no man's disciple."[149]

Shaw's dictum that "Those who can, do; those who can't, teach" applies perfectly to morality: we would like to think that people who believe themselves to be devout Christians would behave in a manner consistent with Christian ethics; of course, we know this is not the case, and has never been: looking at facts rather than "values," you find, for example, that the substantially more secular U.S. Blue States also have substantially lower rates of homicide, STD, teen pregnancy, and abortion than the Bible Belt; globally, societies with larger percentage of atheists exhibit substantially lower degrees of social dysfunction than the highly religious United States.[150]

Humanity, as a race, has not grown smarter since ancient Greece, in fact, not since our days as hunter-gatherers; and our hunter-gatherer brains—designed to sort out where and when to eat, drink, and shit—are wholly inadequate for deeper philosophical speculation. However, "Faith is an absolutely marvellous tool. With faith there is no question too big for even the smallest mind."[151] The Truth is not meant for the masses—that was the flaw in Protestant thought. A quasi-Satanic hierarchy of tyranny, pain, and debauchery may have corrupted the Catholic Church, but at least she did not unleash the Bible on the common man. This is a rash act equivalent to a street person giving a precocious child a pack of matches and a bottle of vodka.

Now there is a grain of truth in every doctrine—otherwise no-one would believe in them. All religious tyranny stems from narrow-mindedness; "Whenever a theory appears to you as the only possible one, take this as a sign that you have neither understood the theory nor the problem which it was intended to solve."[152] The more convinced you are that a certain point of view is right, the more determined you should be to find proof that it is wrong. When you have done this thoroughly, these points of view will cease to trouble you; you will lose interest in controversies, be they religious, ethical, or political. As you advance in knowledge of your mind, you will come to understand that its structure is so faulty, that it is quite incapable, even in its most exalted states, of truth. "The greater our ignorance the more intense

147. *Notes on Queen Mab.* 2002, 92.

148. *The Critic as Artist.* Wilde 1997, 971.

149. Kopp 1980, 41.

150. Paul, op. cit.

151. Rev. Donald Morgan, attributed.

152. Popper 1972, 226.

appears the illumination,"[153] and conversely, "The higher we soar the smaller we appear to those who cannot fly."[154]

The modern mind has a tendency towards the illimitable. To make an absolute or objective statement about anything spiritual or philosophical is the height of blasphemy for the school of "everything is relative," because its members cannot distinguish between being objective and being dogmatic. When everything is relative, definition has no meaning. To define something is to set it apart from everything else, and thus provide a context to intellectually process that idea; to gather data, to form and test theories, to draw conclusions thereof—the scientific method—is an objective way of approaching spiritual attainment.

One should always examine also the opposite. There is a time and a place for *everything:* e.g. patience is not *always* a virtue, less is often more, reason only goes so far, "rain is 'good' or 'bad' for the farmer according to the requirements of his crops,"[155] etc. "Never say never." All Catholics should study Voltaire and Nietzsche, and all atheists should study Aquinas and Spinoza. It is the man who retains his skeptical attitude, the suspicion that what everyone in a new environment is telling him is not the full truth after all, who has the ability to ask the right questions. As Kahlil Gibran exhorted, "Say not, 'I have found the truth,' but rather, 'I have found a truth.'"[156] A truth differs from a fact in that a negation of a fact is a falsehood, while the negation of a truth may well be another profound truth; "Life is just as simple as it seems," for example, is just as true as "Life is not as simple as it seems." There is no dualism therein—truth is a paradox!

"The summit of Knowledge is knowing nothing." By clinging to every word and idea, you will only be caught in an endless circle of reasoning, "for there is a factor infinite & unknown."[157] Or, to put it another way, if you want to know the Truth, you need to make an infinite number of assumptions. The definition of a lunatic is a person who has lost everything *except* his mind; you should be wary not to make reason—or ego—your God. "Knowledge without understanding is static, understanding without wisdom is dangerous stupidity." Many things we do naturally become difficult when we try to turn them into intellectual subjects, and it is possible to know so much about a subject that you become totally ignorant. One should never confuse the map with the territory. We can use the rules of perspective to depict the world in a generally accepted fashion, but at the same time, we lose our direct connection to it. The world becomes a structural drawing, a chart projection, a flow chart. It is not the territory, the reality, that limits people, but the choices and options we deem possible based on our map.

We learn by doing. "Learning the hard way" is the only way to learn; repeating what you've been told is not knowing. Information has no endurance, it is constantly being replaced by updated information. One should thus strive to experience all

---

153. *The Sorcerer.* Crowley 1909–13, III, 142f.

154. *The Dawn of Day,* Verse 574. Nietzsche 1909–11, IX, 394.

155. Crowley 1974, 187.

156. 1923, 61.

157. AL II:32.

things rather than collect information. "To err is human," yet our culture better understands the person who says he only erred once—when he thought he was wrong. But if one has never erred spectacularly and thoroughly, one has never attempted anything worthwhile. The greatest of us make mistakes on a totally different plane from the rest of us. Allowing yourself to commit errors is a price you have to pay for high-level creativity. "Adversity is the first path to truth," wrote Byron.[158] New knowledge is sought at the fringes and boundaries, betwixt chaos and order, on the border of reason and imagination, where the risks are higher. Therein lay not only danger, but also progress.

The ability to adapt, to change one's mind, defines intellect. We all err in our turn, and it is precisely this ability that is one of man's most intriguing traits. A maggot cannot be wrong about the good of its kind; but when the organism becomes more advanced, its capacity for error grows to infinity. The more rational the person, the more choices and possibilities of mistake he sees; the "clothed animal" is both the wisest and the most fallible. Still, the vilest existence is the life lived without error, where the person does not stray one bit from the straight and narrow, even though he could use his own singular mistake for common good. Science approximates truth by constantly correcting errors, and a great part of our scientific belief system is always a mistake, more fiction than fact; when a theory becomes obsolete, science progresses —fact and fiction are intrinsically linked.

"There are no moral actions, only moral interpretations of actions." The only thing we know *for sure* about good and evil is that they are relative; we all need to use our individual judgement. "The doubter is the safe man, the man who can be depended upon. He does not build upon a foundation of guesswork, and the structure he erects will stand. Let us not fear doubt, but rather fear to have falsehood passed for truth."[159] We should always be ready to challenge even our own personal code of morality, and never ever impose it on others: "It is the scientific approach, the adventurous and yet critical temper of science, the search for the truth and new knowledge, the refusal to accept anything without testing and trial, the capacity to change previous conclusion in the face of new evidence, the reliance on observed fact and not on preconceived theory, the hard discipline of the mind—all this is necessary, not merely for the application of science but for life itself and the solution of its many problems."[160]

Only fundamentalists never question their values. What meaning does your life have? Consider you hopes and aims; are they really yours or somebody else's expectations? If they are not yours, could they possibly be placed upon you by some external authority, your parents, for example, or your church or school, your friends, teachers, or the media? Has their programming lead you to a different path than if you had been given the choice yourself? Ultimately, the only universally unethical thing is imposing your ethics on others: "In a sense, the religious person must have no real views of his own and it is presumptuous of him, in fact, to have any. In regard to sex-love affairs, to marriage and family relations, to business, to politics, and to virtually

---

158. *Don Juan*, xii, 50. 1943, 252.

159. Washburn, op. cit. 164.

160. Nehru 2004, 570.

everything else that is important in his life, he must try to discover what his god and his clergy would like him to do; and he must primarily do their bidding."[161]

Compulsory education never aided anybody. It is an inane presumption on the part of the intellectuals to think that a handful of mental acquirements has universal benefit, when the vast majority of people have no ambition in life beyond comfort and happiness. It is painfully obvious that the modern system of government-run public education is a colossal waste of time and money that does not prepare children for future adulthood. If we bought our food the way we buy our primary and secondary education, every community would have just one grocery store which would only offer the food government officials thought was best for everyone, and everyone would be forced to support it through taxes. There would of course be private stores that offered more and higher quality groceries, but few could afford them, since they were already paying taxes to finance the government grocery.

Most high school students in the West know that school is a joke. Those who study and learn would do so without any school at all, and those who slack around would slack around with or without school. Would rich children have advantage over poor children under a privatized educational system? Of course, but that is how life works. Efforts to eliminate unfairness may be morally appealing, but can only lead to economic collapse; the socialist theory has been thoroughly tested and has thoroughly failed. Many poor people leave their children better off than themselves, and their grandchildren better still. Such success has often been attributed to opportunities, hard work, genius, even luck, but never to public education. Since a function of the free market is to produce innovation, it is impossible to know in advance what kind of schools would be formed if the government educational monopoly were to be abolished; the only thing that is certain is that the quality of education would improve and that costs would go down.

Man is still an animal; the satisfaction of basic needs is alone sufficient for happiness. And our basic physical and mental needs have not changed a bit in the last 100,000 years—only the means to satisfy them have. With new ones constantly being developed, and marketed. "The feeling of happiness derived from the satisfaction of a wild instinctual impulse untamed by the ego is incomparably more intense than that derived from sating an instict that has been tamed. . . It was discovered that a person becomes neurotic because he cannot tolerate the amount of frustration which society imposes on him in service of its cultural ideals, and it was inferred from this that the abolition or reduction of those demands would result in a return to possibilities happiness."[162]

The modern problem is that our society assumes everybody wants the same things, thus artificially limiting the supply of those things; even when there exists a practically inexhaustible store of those benefits, like in the case of open air and bountiful nature. In Western society, these have become the luxuries of wealth and leisure, although they remain accessible to anyone with the sense to emancipate himself from the supposed advantages of urban life. There is no reason for cut-throat

---

161. Albert Ellis, "Sin and Psychotherapy." Ard 1975, 440.

162. Freud 2005, 49, 69.

competition in nature, but people have been purposely trained to wish for things they do not really want.

Counterintuitive as it may seem to Americans accustomed to bleak images of Africa, recent studies have documented the flight of immigrant professionals from the United States back to their home countries. Indian and Chinese workers increasingly see better opportunities—and lifestyles—at home. Diaspora associations of Nigerians, Kenyans, Ghanaians, and other Africans say their members, who mostly have middle-class backgrounds, are joining the exodus, choosing life in a land of slow internet connections and power outages over the pressures of recession-era America. Instead of running a dishwasher, they wash their plates by hand; instead of running an air conditioner, they open the windows; instead of shopping for groceries at Wal-Mart, they head to the local market and bargain for fresh produce, living on around $5 a day.

The widely-translated Finnish author Christer Kihlman lived in the South American slums for a long period in the early 1980s. The community was poor, but active, and attended to the civil rights violations directed at its members. After receiving the Nordic Literature Prize, Kihlman travelled North, where he was promptly asked if it was not horrible living in the ghetto. When he replied that many people were happier there than in the Northern welfare states, this was taken as blasphemy. If one does not own a summer home and a BMW, how can one possibly be happy? Our stress is a direct result of thinking too highly of ourselves, viz. "I'm not an animal." Thinking you are more than human is tantamount to a god-complex. "He who sits on a throne still sits on his ass," as Montaigne put it.

No-one is any "better person" than anyone else; more intelligent, maybe, physically stronger, more attractive—but no-one is superior to you at being human. When you compare yourself to someone else, your sense of self is inevitably impaired. The only valid comparison is that we are all equally human. Everyone has different attributes: all people are not short or tall, male or female, but each person is a human being—there is no competition; there are no means to enhance or lessen your status as a human. When you see people as just people, you realize that you can do things others cannot accomplish. You also realize that each and every one of them can do something that you are unable to accomplish yourself. Does this make other people better than you are? Maybe from their point of view, but from your point of view, they are just different.

Still, men are equal only "in the sight of God." Some are smarter, better looking, funnier; there is no "equality of endowment." Every individual has different needs, abilities, desires, and interests; there is no "equality of outcome." As soon as we have some frame of reference for comparison, it becomes impossible to assert equality. Greed is wanting more than *you* need. Ideological egalitarianism only leads to envy of the more fortunate and scorn of the less fortunate. We no longer have leaders, only people in leading positions. "The true man walks the earth as the stars walk the heavens, grandly obedient to those laws which are implanted in his nature,"[163] while "Much mischief has come from our ignorance in insisting, on the contrary, that each

163. Washburn, op. cit. 39.

citizen is fit for any and every social duty."[164] The modern man expresses himself without limits, when it is precisely the limits that make self-expression possible: "Liberty is not the freedom to do whatever we want, it is the freedom to do whatever we are able."

"And this is the Paradox, that there are Bonds which lead to Slavery, and Bonds which lead to Freedom. All we are bound in many Fetters by Environment, and it is for ourselves in great Part to determine whether they shall enslave us or emancipate us. . . This is also a general Law of Biology, for all Development is Structuralization; that is, a Limitation and Specialization of an originally indeterminate Protoplasm, which latter may therefore be called free, in the Definition of a Pedant."[165] It is from within constraints that the greatest originality can spring up. "Liberty is not licence, for licence is tyranny. Liberty is the guardian of duty, because it reclaims right."[166] Inner freedom manifests itself as self-discipline. "Every man has a right, the right of self-preservation, to fulfil himself to the utmost."[167]

---

164. Crowley, op. cit. 226.

165. Idem. 1991, 36–37.

166. *The Key of the Mysteries.* Op. cit. 23.

167. Idem. 1961, xx.

3

I Hope for Nothing, I Fear Nothing, I Am Free

The oft-repeated cliché is that freedom comes with responsibility, when in fact, freedom implies not knowing what comes next; and most people are terrified of the unknown. A much better byword is "embracing the uncertainty"—one cannot be both safe and free. "Eternal vigilance is the price of liberty." The difference between fear and danger would be too obvious to mention, if it was not so frequently overlooked. Fear is a product of the mind, and danger can be met without fear. Our society has become unwilling to face two inevitable facts of life: risk and suffering. And if you risk nothing, you risk even more. It is uncertainty and insecurity which drive us onwards and upwards. There can be no freedom without freedom from fear.

Our negative, superstitious determinism—"It wasn't meant to be"—is merely an excuse not to deal with unavoidable difficulties. Each of us is the creator of our own universe, we shape it, we mould it, and we make it what it will eventually become; if you stand idle, you are in effect letting others shape it for you. "There are many ways to victimize people, and one of the most insidious is to try to persuade them they are victims."[168] A person cannot see himself in the positive light, as a self-responsible individual, if he harbours resentment; if he blames some other person, society, or

168. James 1986, 24.

destiny for his lot in life. Responsibility equals control; only by taking responsibility for your problems will you have power to solve them. And herein lay the fatal flaw of Twelve-Step programs like Alcoholics Anonymous.

If someone tells you to go jump off a cliff and you do, it is obviously your fault. Neither can you be responsible for others—no matter what the guilt-ridden moralists claim. Responsibility is not the same thing as guilt, by the way. Guilt is self-reproach for something that has happened in the past or for something that might happen in the future. The past and the future have no physical existence, existing only in our heads—we cannot physically alter either. Nor is there any place for resentment: if someone hurt you and did nothing about it at the time, you are not permitted to collect on that imagined debt later. *Mea culpa.*

Avoiding responsibility sparks man's species-specific trait of inventiveness. Unhappy childhood, exorbitant taxes, Islamic hegemony, are all fair game. And one can always put the responsibility on God, who, after all, created everything and rules everything. You can also solicit the help of space aliens, pagan divinities, trees, or gnomes. The range of choices is vast in a world ruled by market forces. The Devil made me do it, God made me do it, the voices, the TV, etc. It's all about dodging responsibility. As Rush sang, paraphrasing Sartre: "You can choose a ready guide / in some celestial voice. / If you choose not to decide, / you still have made a choice. / You can choose from phantom fears / and kindness can kill; / I will choose a path that's clear / – I will choose Free Will."[169]

Public discourse today consists in television pundits asserting that we must understand the murderer, because he has had difficulties. His parents have neglected his needs and society, too, has evaded responsibility. We are all guilty and the killer is our victim. No-one cares if the killer has a narcissistic personality disorder or if he's simply an asshole by birth, because in the virtual reality maintained by the media, each and every one of us is born perfect and incredibly gifted. Calling him a disturbed bastard would have a completely different effect, but this cannot be done, because politicians and "experts" vie over who understands the killer the best and lay the blame on the contrarian masses, so that they would know to feel inferior to them. According to the media, nothing is more condemnable in the recent shooting incidents than the normal reaction to the news that depict them.

In the end, we all do exactly what we want; no-one can invade your brain and force your hand. Theism is wholly incompatible with human morality, because in theism, responsibility always falls back on the creator: "The original sin was not in eating of the forbidden fruit, but in planting the tree that bore the fruit."[170] Much of Western culture is embodied by the Cult of the Victim; elaborate systems have been erected to support us and reward us for our victimization: the typical American plaintiff holds some external moral force liable for every accident that befalls him. Should an alarm-clock fall on his head while walking down the street, the fault lay on the sleeper, the housing company, or the clockmaker. So sue!

Rather than changing ourselves, we prefer to blame others, and then we wonder

---

169. "Freewill." *Permanent Waves.* Anthem Records, 1980.

170. Washburn, op. cit. 98.

why this delegation of accountability results in increasing chaos, hardship, and malaise. We live by labels, thereby excising ourselves of the primary responsibility of being free—accountability. Accountability requires vigilance; it requires work; it mandates that we become involved and educate ourselves beyond what we are told. Accountability requires us to seek out opinions that are different from our own, to test them, to ponder over them, and to reach a conclusion; it means that we have the capacity to question, to compare and contrast, and when necessary, to admit our own misconceptions, misinterpretations, and ignorance.

Sovereign people who take the responsibility for their personal power are a threat to the Victim Cult. Like a bucket full of crabs pulling back any that try to escape, the victim culture acts reflexively to squash all acts of self-empowerment. Deep down everyone knows that they are responsible, but their denial requires them to eliminate anything that reminds them of what they are denying. When we help someone, we not only assume responsibility for him, but take power away from him—which is why some people are unable to ask for help and why "emancipated" women do not want doors opened for them.

This also applies to under-age children. How would you react if your pre-school daughter pulled a long knife from the kitchen drawer to carve the dessert cake? Yet teaching even young children to use sharp kitchen utensils safely is not that hard; is it not better to instruct them how to move safely in their environment instead of trying to create a safe environment for them? Building an elaborate fence around the wood stove may keep a child from burning himself, but it will also insulate him from the consequences of his choices. He is going to lack the skills to move responsively through an environment that has not been rendered secure in advance.

It was not until the 1970s that children became equal with adults in the eyes of the law. When we call a child "stubborn" are we not merely denying that he has free will? Rather than being kept in discipline—like in boarding-schools of the old or in modern military schools—children should be taught self-discipline. The idea of juvenile delinquency is a new and progressive one; but how can children learn responsibility if the parents, like drill sergeants, are forced to take responsibility? "Bad guys do what good guys dream,"[171] and go to prison where they learn even less about self-discipline than they did at home or school. Us humans have a much longer period of dependancy in our childhood than do any other species, and this can lead to sometimes quite extreme tendencies towards dependancy in adult life, making us susceptible to all kinds of gurus and totalistic movements.

"Just following orders" was an almost universal excuse with the Nazis. A broken soldier is a good soldier: he will obey orders without asking questions—soldier as hero is just a myth promulgated by the nation-state. When the eminent social psychologist Stanley Milgram examined how well people responded to authority, over 90% of his subjects obeyed his orders even when they thought it would cause physical pain on another. The essence of obedience is that one begins to see himself as a vehicle of the other person's wishes, and no longer realizes himself responsible for his own actions. How else would it be possible for ordinary people to have gotten mixed up with

---

171. "One." *Law & Order: Criminal Intent.* NBC. September 30, 2001.

genocide in Hitler's Germany of the 1930s and '40s? And this is a self-perpetuating phenomenon: "To give orders one must first learn to take orders." There is nothing commendable about being a "natural leader"—one leads a herd; an alpha male is always, and above all, a member of the pack.

The modern school, a Prussian invention, is little more than a jail for children, perfectly embodying the principle of "out of sight, out of mind." And whom do modern child labour laws actually serve? In the 19th century, children were expected to milk the cows and help in the fields, to contribute to the family like they have in all previous ages. Children like monotonous work; they love moving and stuffing envelopes. Children complain because they feel that they are not needed—when a person feels useful, he will not get anxious. "School is children's work"? I for one would much rather have worked than gone to middle school. By the early 20th century, notwithstanding all the past successes, parents were deemed too ignorant of child development to be trusted to raise children adequately. Power and authority over child rearing, which had previously been vested in the family, were usurped by government agencies.

Children's eagerness to learn is undermined above all by a phenomenon that is falsely called education—a common process in most homes and schools. The "educators" destroy most of the creative abilities of children by the things they themselves do and make the children do. These abilities are ruined by making children afraid of not doing what others expect of them, or fearful of not pleasing others, of making mistakes, of failing, or of being wrong. They thus learn to fear risks, experiments, and pursuit of anything difficult or unfamiliar. "Loser" is a common term of abuse even among preschoolers.

Losing is a taboo in our society; we have forgotten that losers changed the world—Columbus missed his target by thousands of miles. Failure is more an opinion than a result, and it is determined by attitude. A mistake is not just an error but information on how not to do things; an often mistaken man is well informed. When Edison failed to invent electric light on his 700th attempt, he was asked how it felt to have failed seven hundred times. The great inventor replied that he had not failed once—he had merely succeeded in proving that the above-mentioned 700 methods did not work. By ruling out the non-functioning methods in thousands of more experiments, he finally found a functioning one and invented electric light. "If you want to succeed, double your failure rate."[172]

Parents often let their children win at family games, ill-preparing them for the game of life. Some teachers today think that flunking a class is so detrimental to the child's self-esteem that they will just move him along to the next grade and onto bigger failures. Since corrections in exams seem so terribly judgemental when marked in red, pen and marker manufacturers have reported a surge in schools' demands for purple-ink pens. Because children are considered so fragile and vulnerable, such popular playground games as dodgeball are discouraged in favour of anxiety-reducing and self-esteem-boosting games like tag where nobody is ever "out." Yet extensive research indicates no correlation between high self-esteem and high achievement—or

---

172. Thomas J. Watson, Sr., attributed.

virtue.

Is not undeserved self-esteem a bigger problem? High self-esteem does not deter children from becoming bullies: it is a wholly unfounded assumption that beneath every detestable bully is an unhappy, self-hating child just in need of some sympathy and praise. Nor does self-esteem prevent youngsters from cheating, shoplifting, or experimenting with sex and drugs. If anything, children with high self-esteem are more prepared than average to try these things at a young age. It would be wiser to concentrate more on self-control and self-discipline, and forget about self-esteem. Winning is not always worth its weight in blue ribbons, while losing can be a positive and ennobling experience that makes us examine why we lost; it is, after all, how we learn. Otherwise, our society could be reduced to cowards; for what better way is there to avoid losing than to never enter the fray?

Several traditional schoolyard games formerly played during recess are now banned by American schools because they are viewed as dangerous. Recently, elementary schools in Wyoming and Washington state banned tag at recess, while a South Carolina school prohibited all contact sports, such as soccer and touch football. Principal Cindy Farwell of Freedom Elementary School in Cheyenne says tag was banned because it "progresses easily into slapping and hitting and pushing instead of just touching." Most educational associations, including the National School Boards Association, do not keep statistics on school games, but the National Program for Playground Safety confirms the trend toward schools increasingly prohibiting games that involve physical contact. At many schools, children are not even allowed to run on the asphalt during recess, and as Joe Frost, emeritus professor of early childhood education at the University of Texas–Austin, says, these restrictions on playground games are, in effect, "taking away the psychical development of the children. Having time to play is essential for children to keep their weight under control."[173]

"A man's got to know his limitations," enjoined Clint Eastwood in *Magnum Force.*[174] Some of our greatest strengths are the result of compensating for our weaknesses. However, "You never know what is enough unless you know what is more than enough."[175] In other words, there may be a fine line, but crossing it is the only way to find out where it lay. There has been a lot of concern in the media lately about the disappearance of childhood—ostensibly from parents nostalgic about their lost youth. But what exactly is "childhood"? And who will gain from it being prolonged? During various historical periods, no difference was made between a child and an adult. In fact, the child did not enter into the annals of Western history until the end of the European Middle Ages. The Child Jesus in the mediaeval Madonnas is a strange, often unpleasant-looking creature, something between an adult and a child. It was not that the old masters did not know how to paint a child—they just did not see a child as a child.

Juvenility is now generally considered a development phase characterized by absoluteness in thought and a clear separation of good and evil. Children are actually

173. Emily Bazar, "Tag! More Schools Ban Games at Recess," *USA Today*, June 27, 2006.

174. Dir. Ted Post. Warner Bros. Pictures, 1973.

175. *The Marriage of Heaven and Hell*, pl. 9.

the most ardent traditionalists in the world; they need to have things stable and categorized. They learn inductively, by example and by interacting with the environment around them, while adults tend to learn analytically and deductively. A child under six does not have enough knowledge, or reference points, to be able to trust his own judgement or reason; his critical ability—the capacity to question, value, analyze, estimate, and most importantly, to compare—has not yet developed. This is why so many people grow up to be like their parents, having been conditioned by incidents, opinions, and convictions that originate from the people and society around them, who in turn have been conditioned during their own formative years.

The infant wants and needs love, and tends to behave in a way that will bring a repetition of this desired experience. But this brings complications: each child is scolded for doing things the parents see as unacceptable and rewarded for things they view as acceptable; these various value judgements become adopted by the infant as if they were his own—a process known by psychologists as the "introjection of values." As Carl Rogers explains, "He has deserted the wisdom of his organism, giving up the locus of evaluation, and is trying to behave in terms of values set by another, in order to hold love."[176] Rogers writes that "because these [introjected] concepts are not based on his own valuing, they tend to be fixed and rigid, rather than fluid and changing. . . By taking over the conceptions of others as our own we lose contact with the potential wisdom of our own functioning, and lose confidence in ourselves. Since these value constructs are often sharply at variance with what is going on in our own experiencing, we have in a very basic way divorced ourselves from ourselves, and this accounts for much of modern strain and insecurity."[177] It is by questioning and discarding the values that we are enabled to move beyond psychological immaturity and become what Rogers calls the "psychologically mature adults." In this final approach to values, we bring our locus of evaluation once again within ourselves, relying on experimental evidence.

It would appear that as life-expectancy grew, so did the length of childhood, or rather, childishness. In pre-industrial society, which did not even have a word for "adolescence," post-pubescent teens were considered adults. In fact, by imposing all the restrictions it does on teenagers, modern society infantilizes them as a part of its grand scheme to extend childhood. Many say that the only solution to teenage angst and irresponsibility is to go to the opposite direction and treat them as grown-ups, yet today we actually have laws to protect grown people from themselves. Unfortunately, "The ultimate result of shielding men from the effects of folly, is to fill the world with fools."[178] Take childproof caps for example: the objective was to eliminate accidental child poisonings, but the actual result was a marked increase in poisoning. Parents either left the bottles around instead of putting them away since they were now safe, or just left the caps off because they were so difficult to remove.

Until pretty recently, people who had reached the age of thirteen—the traditional age of both the Jewish Bar Mitzvah and the Christian Confirmation—were not

176. 1969, 244.

177. Ibid. 245–247.

178. Spencer 1868, 349.

considered children at all. And once you had been Bar Mitzvahed or Confirmed, you could marry. We are, in fact, designed to breed in our youth. Not only is high maternal age recognized as being the main risk factor for birth defect, but mid-teens is physiologically the best time to give birth. Older mothers risk complications such as problems with blood pressure and poor circulation, which can cause the developing baby not to grow as well as it should. The number of Down's syndrome pregnancies has risen by more than 70% over the last two decades, which according to University of London researchers reflects the growing number of older women becoming pregnant.[179] As a species, our reasoning abilities peak at twelve and our brain size at fourteen; at sixteen, the brain and intelligence are fully developed, and growth in height stops. Yet voting age in most democracies is eighteen, whereas mediaeval kings' minority lasted only until puberty.

David Farragut took command of a captured British warship as a pre-teen, Thomas Edison published a broadsheet at the age of twelve, Benjamin Franklin apprenticed himself to a printer at the same age, then put himself through a course of study that would choke a senior at Harvard today. Dakota Fanning says she's glad she "sacrificed" a "normal" childhood to pursue her movie career; and she's also adamant that she has learnt more from her movie experiences than she ever would have done as an ordinary schoolgirl.[180] It may seem almost too obvious, but the object of childhood is to grow up! According to a 2003 study by the University of Michigan, the proportion of Americans still living with their parents in their twenties increased by half between 1970 and 1990. In Canada, 47% of twenty-something males lived with their parents in 2001, as compared to just 27% in 1981. In fact, according to a *TIME* Magazine survey, over a third of 18- to 29-year olds do not consider themselves grown up.[181] However, these "twixters" are of course great spenders—think a hundred percent disposable income!

Modern schooling has done a remarkable job of turning children into children, and this is hardly an accident. Theorists from Plato to Rousseau knew that if children were cloistered with other children, divested of responsibility and independence, and encouraged to develop only such trivial emotions as greed and envy, they would grow older but never truly grow up. Ellwood P. Cubberley, the longtime head of Stanford's school of education and a leading reformer of education in the early 20th century, praised the way the successive school enlargements had extended childhood by two to six years, and this was when mandatory schooling was still quite new. Nearly every aspect of our lives has now been stripped of maturity: easy credit has removed the need for fiscal self-control, easy entertainment has removed the need to entertain oneself, easy answers have removed the need to ask questions. Most of us are happy to surrender our judgement and will to political and commercial cajolery that would insult real adults.

Once we understand the logic behind modern public schooling, its traps become

179. Joan K. Morris & Eva Alberman, "Trends in Down's Syndrome Live Births and Antenatal Diagnoses in England and Wales from 1989 to 2008: Analysis of Data from the National Down Syndrome Cytogenetic Register," *British Medical Journal* 339, October 26, 2009, b3794.

180. WENN, December 2, 2008.

181. Lev Grossman, "They Just Won't Grow Up," January 24, 2005.

fairly easy to evade. Schools train children to be employees and consumers, so teach yours to be leaders and adventurers; schools train children to obey reflexively, so teach yours to think critically and independently. Today's high school students are so busy that they have no time to think. In fact, they are taught to feel guilty if they are thinking and not doing. I mean the kind of deep thinking that begins with daydreaming but turns to puzzling over a pivotal question until a Eureka moment arrives. Well-schooled children have a low threshold for boredom, so you should teach yours to develop a rich inner life so that they will never be bored. Encourage them to pick up the serious, grown-up works in history, philosophy, literature, and art; in other words, all the material their teachers know to avoid.

Some BlackBerry-tethered parents, who equate being constantly busy with being successful in their own lives, vie with each other to see whose children can cram in the most activities: ballet classes, Mandarin lessons, weekend soccer tournaments, PSAT tutoring sessions, pre-dawn swim practice. In the past twenty years, summer has become more an extension of the academic year than a respite from it. Unstructured time, which still remains essential to figuring out who one is and what one wants, tends now to be regarded as laziness or being unproductive. Did Albert Einstein, starting out as a lowly patent clerk, not have to just think for hours on end? If someone had passed his window as he sat thinking, they might have accused him of being a slacker. You should challenge your children with plenty of solitude, to teach them to enjoy their own company, to conduct inner dialogue. Many a college professor complains that his students cannot think critically, but how could they think critically if they have not learned how to formulate good questions, and then spent hours searching for good answers? Conditioned to dread being alone, well-schooled people seek constant companionship through television, PlayStation, internet, cell phones, and shallow, short-term friendships. Yet, "Everyone of us is alone."

Modern society has begun to look upon quietness and solitude as a problem. The strange demand of social activity has grown all the time. There is a lot of talk nowadays about the restless, disruptive, and inattentive children and their woes; yet these hyperactive children are better accepted than the quiet introverts. A "shy" person is fashionable neither in school nor in the workplace, even though he can be very social, i.e. get along well with other people. In his recent study, ***Shyness: How Normal Behavior Became a Sickness***, Christopher Lane, Ph.D., traces the metamorphosis of shyness from a character trait into a pathological condition dubbed "social phobia"—which the psychiatric bible DSM defines as "fears that he or she may do something or act in a way that will be humiliating or embarrassing."[182] With disorders so broadly drawn, the Northwestern University English professor wonders who among us is sane? A person should feel accepted and valued as he is from an early age; you are not going to make a bashful child more courageous by telling him to be brave and look at how the other children are playing while you are afraid to do anything—this will only make the child think that he is not as good as the other children in some indefinable way.

---

182. American Psychiatric Association 1994, 416.

Our society has a hysterical neurosis about its members being happy introverts. Extroverts tend to believe that the only good experiences are ones shared amongst the company of others, which of course is false. A person can obviously have fun with others, but not all the time. Extroverts are energized by social interaction, while introverts are wearied by it. Not everyone has a go-getting Type A personality, some people actually prefer calm and quiet. Extroverts are, by nature, nosy, and seem to be downright offended when introverts want to keep to themselves. "How can you possibly be happy, if you're inside by yourself all the time?" We're going to drag you kicking and screaming into the outside world, whether you like it or not, because that's what we think is best for you. The truth is that the quiet, intelligent, and introspective introverts find most extroverts loud, stupid, and boring.

It is not like the typical introvert speaks, acts, or dresses like the common herd, so in the back of his head, he may be thinking that most people don't really like what they see or hear; trying to "fit in" is not an option for him, any more than getting the vast mass of people to switch over to his way of thinking—so he prefers to keep to himself or among those with whom he is already familiar. It should be noted that all animal species have naturally shy members among them. Shy animals have a better chance at survival, since their timidity shields them from danger. In humans, shyness can make it harder for one to be a part of society, but it also provides an immense opportunity to develop one's inner abilities, to which others who are too busy socially have no time to pay attention.

Do you listen to heavy metal, progressive rock, or some other type of music that the record companies and radio stations consider marginal and advertisers shun as an unsuitable environment for commercials? Do you think that there are better movies than the overhyped Hollywood blockbusters that are billed as hits even before they premier? Do you often buy products that are not advertised on TV, but which require your own effort and initiative to find? Do you find that the news just serve as superficial airtime fillers that generally only deal with peripheral issues which the talking heads have not even bothered to properly read up on? Did you choose your trade on the basis of your own preferences, instead of what was at the time considered a good profession? Do you find it difficult to find a political candidate for whom you could be bothered to vote, even though the parties try their best to rustle up a group of candidates that appeals to most of the voting public? Congratulations, you are disenfranchised. There is no group of people in the world more tedious and helpless than those who think that they've got it all going on.

Modern people often criticize monasticism as a form of escape, seeing it as a way to shut out the cares of the world. Yet the concept of escapism is ambivalent: the escapist supposedly flees from everyday life, but is everyday life not itself, if understood as series of daily routines, precisely an escape? Instead of calling things into question, we fall back on our habits, never facing the great questions. In the monastery, there is nowhere to hide, no TV, no magazines, no toys, no pills; you are basically alone with your own mind. Now compare that to the average living room, where the TV is on for six and a half hours every day. How many adults depend on Valium to get through the night? How many children are hooked on Ritalin? How much time do they spend shopping? With nothing to divert you, you will only have what you have been ignoring until then: the contents of your own mind.

Remember *Star Trek*'s "prime directive of non-interference"?[183] Everyone makes his own destiny, and one can only learn from one's *own* mistakes. "Helping is the same as messing around with someone," as Nastassja Kinski put it.[184] If you save a guy's life, *you* owe him! When your advice is solicited, of course you should offer it. But when it is not, you should remain quiet, even if, in your experience, the person's choices are about to get painful for them. You must respect the individual's learning process and not interfere. You are not responsible for them, but should you impose your unsolicited advice you will share responsibility for the fruit of their actions.

"No good deed goes unpunished," as they say. A "selfless" deed usually interferes with the will of another; as long as you do not interfere, selfishness has no adverse consequences: in fact, the only way you can better society is by bettering yourself. Why is it then that people who cannot control the universe or be dictators of their own banana republic or get through a dinner party without alienating everyone end up fronting groups that are meant to make you a better person? When a plane loses cabin pressure, you are supposed to put an oxygen mask on yourself first, and then help your child; of course, it is easier to help someone you are not close to, someone you have never met, say, some anonymous children in Africa, than someone very close, like your own child, wife, mother, etc. That is to say, "random acts of kindness" are the easiest. So, by all means, engage in them, but please don't pat yourself in the back for doing so, and above all, don't be surprised or dismayed if people do not always thank you for it. In most cases, international aid workers are perceived negatively by at least one party where there is a conflict that has raised the need for aid; they are seen as interfering, neo-colonialist, or at the very least, politically biased. The only truly humanitarian work is to let everyone carry out their own will in peace: "Live and let die!"

Buddhists believe that there is no such thing as a truly selfless act: if someone strives to be totally altruistic, he only does so from the egotistical need to achieve an altruistic state of being. People who think they're making the world a better place violently dislike having this belief challenged, because their motivator is feeling good about themselves. Even mother's love has been proven selfish by modern science; after all, it is the protection of what one definitely knows to be one's own DNA. But just how meaningful is a concept of selfishness that will have us believe that the mugger who stabbed us, the passer-by who gave us first aid, and the factory that produced the knife are "at bottom" the same? Selfishness does not equal wickedness; nor is true selfishness possible for anyone but God, eternal and omniscient. "Selfishness is not living as one wishes to live, it is asking others to live as one wishes to live."[185]

And what is all this talk about "innocents"? We are all guilty of something. Yes, even women and children: both the bully and his spineless victim, and their clueless mothers. "There are no saints, only unrecognized villains." In other words, people

183. "The Return of the Archons." NBC. February 9, 1967.

184. *Terminal Velocity*. Dir. Deran Sarafian. Hollywood Pictures, 1994.

185. *The Soul of Man under Socialism*. Wilde 1997, 1063.

"should always be judged guilty until they are proven innocent."[186] Countless additional lives were lost on 9/11 due to the incompetence of the "heroic" firemen, who e.g. told people to get back to the South Tower which had not yet been hit; in the end, they got more people killed than they saved. Tens of thousands of tsunami victims would have survived in December of 2004 had there only been a warning system: at one stage, monitors in the Pacific and a meteorologist in Thailand knew what was happening but not who to call. One reason for the magnitude of that disaster was overpopulation, in addition to which the tourist season was at its peak. And I do not even want to ponder how many dead sex tourists got the national hero treatment when their caskets were shipped back to Sweden draped in the flag of the mourning nation.

As most dictionaries will explain, true heroism involves "extraordinary courage, fortitude, or greatness of soul." A firefighter who takes unusual risks to save others can legitimately be called a hero, but just showing up for work and turning on the water hose when required is hardly enough. It is a big mistake to confuse the idea of service—or the idea of sacrifice and suffering—with the idea of heroism. We should vehemently resist the Lake Wobegon effect, where all or nearly all of a group claim to be special, because in a world where "all the children are above average," the truly extraordinary child gets no recognition, and genuine acts of exceptional courage are trivialized. As modern technology shifted the balance of power in the West, we have come to see the square-jawed warrior slowly but surely replaced by variations on the theme of Mickey Mouse: the hero triumphs against impossible odds, not through his strength, but in spite of his weakness. For a chilling account of another society in which "the devaluation of the concept of heroism" was "proportional to the frequency of its use and abuse," see the *Encyclopedia of Soviet Life* by Ilya Zemtsov.[187] In 1938, the Soviet Union instituted the title 'Hero of Socialist Labour'—"Thousands of those heroes emerged... The hero was supposed to die in the name of Stalin during wartime [and] give his or her all in labor on communist constructions... [but] a person upon whom the title 'hero' is bestowed has often performed no heroic deed whatsoever, but may receive the title . . . merely in return for displaying loyalty and/or diligence."[188]

What makes the tsunami that killed about 225,000 people in Southeast Asia such an exceptional disaster is that, compared to the dead, only few people were injured, so there was not much for relief workers to do. Local affected people saved virtually every life that was to be saved before international rescue teams arrived. In fact, foreigners were warned to stay out of the worst-hit areas, so as not to place a fresh burden on the victims, since there was not enough food to support everyone. Not only did well-meaning donors clog the supply lines with non-essential goods, but the Doctors Without Borders organization was forced to return part of the money donated towards the tsunami victims, since it could not use anywhere near the whole sum in the area. At the same time, a week after the October 2005 flooding in Guatemala, which received comparatively little attention in the international media, the UN

---

186. George Orwell, "Reflections on Gandhi," *Partisan Review*, January 1949.

187. 1991, 150.

188. Ibid. 149.

appeal had managed to raise only one percent of what was needed.[189]

On the other hand, the lack of coordination between the relief agencies following the December 2004 disaster was largely due to the immense scale of aid raised. Three to five hundred charities arrived in Sri Lanka following the disaster, many with little or no experience. The glare of public attention pressured the agencies to spend quickly and visibly, rivalries between hundreds of often faith-based groups leading to both duplications and delays in aid reaching the affected. Far from requiring foreign aid, Thailand needed very much for the tourists to return. Most of the Thai resort island of Phuket survived the tsunami unscathed, and even the affected areas like Patong Beach were cleared up so quickly that no-one going there for the first time the summer after the disaster could notice anything had happened. The Thais, dependent as they are on the tourism industry, usually save enough money in the high season to carry them through the low season, but as the tsunami happened at the very beginning of the peak, they had no savings to last them through the quieter period.

The tsunami also led to a drop in piracy in the Asian waters from January through most of February of 2005. This was not entirely because the tsunami put some smaller pirates out of business, but due to the presence of large number of military vessels delivering aid in the area. Since then, there has been a notable increase in highjackings in the Malacca Strait, through which between a quarter and a third of the world's sea trade goes, and fear-mongers warn it could become the target of terrorists hoping to paralyze global trade. The way in which Somalia is portrayed in the Western media makes it appear like the whole country is a humanitarian disaster in desperate need of U.S. or UN intervention. Yet Somalia's current crisis in security, food shortages, and internal displacement results largely from the U.S.-backed and coordinated invasion and occupation. Violence in Somalia is grossly exaggerated and focuses mainly in Mogadishu, as opposed to the rural areas, which never depended on state institutions in the first place, and to whom the collapse of the government in 1991 simply meant less taxes and murder-rape raids.

Strategically located near the Indian Ocean, where the transport of minerals and oil makes it valuable to the multinational corporations that dominate the commerce of the region, Somalia also has seen European ships loot its seas of their greatest resource—seafood. Its nine million people are teetering on starvation, as more than $300 million worth of tuna, shrimp, and lobster are being stolen every year by illegal trawlers. This is the context in which the "pirates" emerged: starving Somalian fishermen took speedboats to try and dissuade the foreign trawlers and toxic waste dumpers, or at least levy a "tax" on them. They call themselves the Volunteer Coastguard of Somalia, and the independent Somalian news organization WardheerNews (WDN) found 70% of Somalis "strongly supported the piracy as a form of national defence."[190]

Meanwhile, the *New York Times* ran a piece, the title of which read "Standoff with Somali pirates shows limits to U.S. power." The opening paragraph sums up the whole situation pretty well: "The Indian Ocean standoff between an $800 million U.S.

189. "2005: Year of Disasters," Oxfam International, Oxford, October 2005.

190. Johann Hari, "You Are Being Lied to About Pirates," *The Independent*, January 5, 2009.

Navy destroyer and four pirates bobbing in a lifeboat low on fuel showed the limits facing the world's most powerful military."[191] Yet the story of the 2009 war on piracy might be best summarized by another pirate, one who lived and died in the 4th century BCE. He was captured and brought before Alexander the Great, who demanded to know "what he meant by keeping hostile possession of the sea." The pirate smiled and answered with bold pride, "What thou meanest by seizing the whole earth; but because I do it with a petty ship, I am called a robber, whilst thou, who dost it with a great fleet art styled emperor."[192] Great imperial fleets sail again—but who is the robber?

In the Aceh province of Indonesia, which bore the brunt of the 2004 tsunami, 170,000 people were killed, far outstripping the casualties in three decades of armed conflict between the Acehnese rebels and the Indonesian government. The waves and water accomplished what years of political negotiations had not, leading to a peace deal in August 2005. However, Aceh remains the most corrupt province in one the world's most corrupt countries, and there is not much chance that the more than $6 billion that the global community pledged to this disaster-struck region will be honestly spent. For many low-paid employees, bribery is seen as part of their regular income, and without it, there is little incentive to work. As one local told BBC News, "corruption does not interfere with the system here; it is the system here."[193]

In March 2005, the Indonesian government estimated that 100,000 new houses would be needed for those left homeless along Aceh's battered coastline, yet when the rainy season started in October, more than 400,000 people were still living with relatives or in rubble-stewn refugee camps.[194] Which may be for the best, since that scale of construction poses a major threat to the ravaged tropical forests of the region, where 70% of annual timber output is already cut illegally, largely for export. Aceh's extensive rainforest on the northern tip of Sumatra is full of diverse habitats and rare animals, including 4% of all known bird species. Logging was banned in Aceh back in 2001, but unlicensed cutting persists, taking place mostly inside the Leuser Ecosystem, a 2.6 million hectare natural reserve that is home to the endangered Sumatran tiger and rhino.[195]

In Sri Lanka, dense mangrove and shrub forests actually saved lives in the tsunami disaster, according to the World Conservation Union. It compared the death toll from two local villages that were hit by the giant waves, and while 6,000 died in the vegetation-free village, only two people perished in the one with healthy forests. Though no reliable data exists on how the trees mitigate the impact of a tsunami, research shows that mangroves are able to absorb up to 90% of the energy from a regular wave.[196] In all, the tsunami killed many fewer people in Sri Lanka than in

---

191. Mark Mazzetti, April 10, 2009.

192. St. Augustine, *The City of God.* Schaff 1887, 66.

193. Lucy Williamson, "Indonesia Corruption Drive Breeds Fear," August 11, 2009.

194. "UN Relief Chief Bemoans Slow Aceh Reconstruction," Reuters, October 16, 2005.

195. Simon Montlake, "Aceh Regeneration Fuels Logging Threat," BBC News, March 28, 2005.

196. "Mangrove Forests Saved Lives in 2004 Tsunami Disaster," IUCN, Bangkok, December 19, 2005.

Indonesia, but the damage to the former may prove more long-lasting: the disaster exposed the fragility of the cease-fire between the government and Tamil rebels, who are squabbling over how the generous foreign aid that poured in should be divided.

Of the countries around the Indian Ocean rim, Malaysia escaped most unscathed. Protected from the main waves by the island of Sumatra, fewer than 10,000 Malays were affected by the disaster, the country's death toll reaching only 68. What is more, by the standards of the region, Malaysia is relatively wealthy, its income per capita being almost five times that of Indonesia, and four times that of Sri Lanka. Yet six months on, many Malaysian villages were still struggling to get back on their feet. Aid was slow in coming, some had received no aid at all; somewhere along the line, middle men were helping themselves to money meant for tsunami victims, the generous donations often going no further than the village headman.[197]

The Asian Tsunami received huge media attention compared for example to the three million people who had died over the last decade in the Congo, or the children abducted every day in Uganda, or the hunger crisis in Niger. While the international community sent millions of dollars to Haïti in earthquake relief efforts, in a country with 80% unemployment, where UN and relief workers have frequently been involved in drug trade and gang wars, where the children eat mud and rape is commonplace, you have to ask: wasn't the situation already so awful, desperate, and shameful, that it's as though Haïti has been in a state of perpetual emergency for more than half a century? The globe is always filled with great disasters and wars, but no-one can be bothered about slowly unfolding tragedies that are ever present. At all the Asian resorts, wealth increased exposure to the Tsunami rather than impeding it; most of the poor were farther inland, the rich Western tourists being right on the sand. Many Western insurance companies were hit by the financial fall-out of the disaster, and the insurers are in turn an important player on global capital markets.

Grieving is inherently selfish; no, not "evil," not unnatural, but selfish: we say "we lost somebody," not "somebody lost their life." Now how many Thais did you see grieving in those ubiquitous newsreels? None, and it actually makes no sense from the Christian point of view either, geared as it is toward an afterlife; in fact, early Christians treated funerals as joyous occasions. However, a whole industry of credentialed—which is not the same as competent—"caring professionals" has a financial stake in the myth that people are too fragile to cope with life's many vicissitudes without professional help. Trained grief "counsellors" assume that everyone should grieve the same way, while a failure to manifest grief is construed as alarming evidence of repression, and possibly even a precursor of "delayed onset" PTSD. All this despite the voluminous research that indicates reticence and suppression of feelings to be perfectly healthy.

Because Vietnam was supposedly an unjust war, the theory held that it would produce an epidemic of post-traumatic stress disorders. A study released in 1990 claimed that half of Vietnam veterans suffered from some form of PTSD—notwithstanding the fact that only 15% of them had served in combat units.[198]

---

197. Jonathan Kent, "The Mystery of Malaysia's Tsunami Aid," BBC News, June 20, 2005.

198. Sommers & Satel 2005.

Unsurprisingly, 9/11 became another excuse for branding healthy human reactions as pathological. Did terrorist attacks make you nervous and angry? Must be PTSD. 9/11 also gave rise to what Sommers and Satel call "diagnostic mission creep" in their book *How the Helping Culture Is Eroding Self-Reliance:* the idea of trauma has been expanded to include watching a disaster on television. There is simply no authentic human experience that doesn't somehow and in some way affect, stain, taint, or scar the human animal. But people recover from negative events very quickly: studies show that people who became paraplegic had similar levels of happiness a few years later to those who had not been affected this way. Physical, emotional, and spiritual scarring and discolouration is, after a manner, what we do. Drama is exactly what we are designed for; our spirits are here to experience and taste and immerse in it all. The only sensible worry is that this "commodification of grief" will destroy the very virtue on which the United States was founded, namely, personal independence.

All sorrow is selfish. The feeling of sadness is so bad that people have the tendency to feel anger whenever sadness threatens, for the simple reason that sadness feels worse. Anger at least can flow outwards, but sadness invariably flows in. However, anger causes road rage and similar phenomena that can get you and others killed, while sadness inspires you to engage in activities that distract you from your feelings. Both sadness and anger stem from fear: fear of losing what we have or fear of not getting what we want. And fear stems from our tightly-held belief that what we have or want is even remotely important. To be fearless is to be free from desire, and that includes desire for one's own life.

You can never really know another person. Other people, as you know them, exist only in your head; you cannot get into theirs any more than they can get into yours. Insisting otherwise and trying to get someone else to understand you or trying to understand someone else only leads to sorrow. Thinking that others are deeply aware of you, your work, your relationships, problems, thoughts, attitudes, tastes, etc. will only produce a state of constant low-grade anxiety. Other people, as kind and considerate as they may be, do not really care about your life; they care about theirs. You thus need not concern yourself about what others think of you. The opposite of love is not hate, or even apathy, but envy.

The problem with having idols is that you cannot surpass them; children getting disillusioned with their role-models is called "growing up." Plus how many of us would *really* want to be a sports hero or movie star anyway? To put it bluntly, adoration is no better than envy; "Don't dream it, be it!" Or as Lord Henry said in *The Picture of Dorian Gray:* "There is no such thing as a good influence. . . All influence is immoral. . . The aim of life is self-development. To realize one's nature perfectly—that is what each of us is here for."[199]

The "do nots" of yesterday have transformed into norms. Norms guide the in-itself justified pursuit of happiness. They have three sources and three basic elements: health, rights, and fashion. Since everyone has an equal right to happiness, we need to make sure that our own pursuit of happiness does not cause unhappiness in others. The norm of fashion, on the other hand, implies that he who does not want the same

---

199. Op. cit. 15–16.

things as others, will fall off. As the norms thicken, we eventually realize that practically everything is either dangerous to oneself or objectionable to others. Unhealthiness is close to sin, fashion resembles morality, norms are almost taboos.

I say: "Do what thou wilt," anything short of that is hypocritical. Why in the world would you want someone you don't like to like you? For fear of confrontation? "Always be ready to speak your mind," wrote William Blake, "and a base man will avoid you."[200] Aristotle put it thus: "to conceal one's feelings, i.e. to care less for truth than for what people will think, is a coward's part."[201] And Harry S. Truman: "I never did give anybody hell. I just told the truth on 'em, and they thought it was hell."[202] John F. Kennedy: "Let us never negotiate out of fear. But let us never fear to negotiate."[203] Fearful people always react aggressively and try to attack first.

"When we are at odds with ourselves, we are at odds with the whole universe."[204] And "a city divided against itself cannot stand."[205] Mahatma Gandhi, perhaps the world's most renowned pacifist, declared that: "A 'No' uttered from deepest conviction is better and greater than a 'Yes' merely uttered to please, or what is worse, to avoid trouble."[206] It is the nice guys who have the most issues, inspiring the Backyard Babies to sing: "Making enemies is good."[207] Besides, one does not really ever make enemies, one just runs into them. By all means "love thine enemy," but don't fear him, don't be mad at him, don't hate him. Should your foe be strong enough to deserve the title of "enemy," they also deserve your respect.

"He makes no friend who never made a foe," scribbled Tennyson.[208] Antisthenes, the founder of the Cynic school of philosophy, reckoned that there are only two people who can tell a person the truth about himself—an enemy who has lost his temper and a friend who loves him dearly. Therefore, "You shall judge a man by his foes as well as by his friends."[209] People invariably mirror themselves in their enemies: the juxtaposition of Islam and the rest of the world was not created until after the end of the Cold War, as a response to the absence of an enemy. Nothing unites people like a common foe; "The enemy of my enemy is my friend."

The idea of enduring political peace is a relatively new concept. For the first time since a furless biped grabbed a stone in anger, the UN Charter seeks to eliminate war and to help the nations of the world to "live together in peace with one another as good neighbours,"[210] despite the abysmal failure of millennia of philosophical and religious teaching to accomplish anything of the sort. Talking as a means of resolving

---

200. *The Marriage of Heaven and Hell*, pl. 9.

201. *Nichomachean Ethics*, IV.3.28.

202. As quoted in "Television: First Draft of History," *TIME*, February 10, 1958.

203. The Inaugural Address, Washington, D.C., January 20, 1961.

204. Johann Wolfgang von Goethe, attributed.

205. Matthew 12:25.

206. 1935, 119.

207. "Brand New Hate." *Making Enemies is Good*. RCA Records, 2001.

208. *Idylls of the King*. 1898, 396.

209. Conrad 1905, 304.

210. *Preamble*, June 26, 1945.

conflict actually goes against every biological instinct that we have; we feel threatened, so we fight, or if we don't have the stomach for that, we run. People go out of their way to get along, because they've been trained to go out of their way to get along since they were little kindergarten students; at some point, a person has to have personal principles, because otherwise he can get talked into anything. Accepting an external code of behaviour is likely to cause internal conflict, and it is the inner peace that matters; conflict is constant in nature, since one man's gain is always another man's loss. "All life is conflict. Every breath that you draw represents a victory in the struggle of the whole Universe. You can't have peace without perfect mastery of circumstance."[211]

Conflict is a natural state at every level of human existence. Outward peace involves structures, organizations, and laws which exist to manage that conflict over many years. Far from being a natural condition, peace is something that always develops only over long periods of time with a great deal of hard work and much backsliding. It is no more a natural state of society than war is. Conflicts are perpetual, and during peacetime, boil up until they explode into open warfare. "To allow oneself to be carried away by a multitude of conflicting concerns, to surrender to too many projects, to want to help everyone in everything is to succumb to violence. More than that, it is cooperation in violence," wrote Thomas Merton. "The frenzy of the activist neutralizes his work for peace. It destroys his own inner capacity for peace."[212]

Oscar Wilde had it right: "It is absurd to divide people into good and bad. People are either charming or tedious."[213] Just as a happy and fulfilled individual is pleasant and refreshing to be around, a repressed and self-loathing person makes for tiring and irritating company. From the smallest acts of petty insult to criminal acts of physical violence, the ill will that builds up between people comes from this frustration. I say "ill will" and not "conflict," because happy people will still come into conflict with each other due to competing desires; they will still verbally fight with each other over conflicting values; and they will still physically attack each other at times. Now, these conflicts can be viewed in a sporting sense if one diminishes the sense of threat. We are accustomed to identifying with our bodies, but we also identify with numerous ideas, images, and representations, and we react to attacks on those abstract things in the same way we would to personal attacks on ourselves.

We are not all supposed to get along; in fact, paraphrasing Dante, "The hottest places in hell are reserved for those who, in times of great moral crisis, maintain their neutrality."[214] However, nor should we demonize our enemies: "To be good is to be in harmony with one's self. Discord is to be forced to be in harmony with others."[215] Peace means the absence of war, that people are not fighting one another, but it does not mean that they are not likely to start fighting at any moment. A situation where

---

211. Crowley 1954, xiv.

212. 1966, 73.

213. *Lady Windermere's Fan.* Op. cit. 490.

214. John F. Kennedy, Remarks on the establishment of a West German Peace Corps, Bonn, June 24, 1963.

215. *The Picture of Dorian Gray.* Op. cit. 56.

there is no probability of conflict, where people do not have to prepare for it or think about it, where there is no need nor inclination to resort to violence, is and will always be a mere fantasy—"Sooner or later, Mr. Fowler, one has to take sides, if one is to remain human."[216]

"You can have Peace, or you can have Freedom," declared Robert A. Heinlein. "Don't ever count on having both at the same time."[217] Without the capacity to defend our rights, we have no real liberty. The irony is, if you are willing to kill your assailant, you probably will not have to. Violent crime is practicable only when its targets are cowards. A mark who fights back renders the whole business impractical. It is true that one may suffer for fighting back, but if one does not fight back, one will certainly suffer. The stated objective of gun control is usually to reduce accidents and deaths involving the use of firearms; its actual result has invariably been a marked increase in hot burglaries (i.e. ones where the owners are at home), rapes, assaults, and assaults with a deadly weapon.

At the turn of this century, the UN Interregional Crime and Justice Research Institute reported that Australia and England led the seventeen nations of the industrialized Western world in violent crime.[218] In 1997, England did not have a gun problem; the year after its nearly complete ban of firearms in 1997, English armed crime rose by 10 percent—it is no exaggeration to say that the English model took the guns away from the shooting ranges and put them onto the streets. Home Office figures for April of 1999 through March of 2000 show a 16% increase in violent crime, 26% increase in street robberies (making it the highest rate on record), 28% increase in muggings, and 40% increase in London-area robberies. Nearly all of the detected, worsened problems were the same that the extremely strict gun laws were supposed to erase. Even as the overall crime rate fell from 1996 to 2000, violent crime more than doubled.[219] By June of 2001, police and customs had identified a vast and organized network of illegal gun smugglers. The number of knife deaths in areas targeted by UK anti-knife schemes rose in a similar manner. The British government's Tackling Knives Action Programme was launched in July of 2009 in ten police districts in England and Wales: in the first nine months alone, 126 people were killed with knives or other sharp objects—seven more than in the same period the previous year.[220] In the UK and Canada, almost half of all burglaries take place when the occupants are at home, whereas only 13% of the burglars in the heavily-armed United States are foolish enough to take that risk.[221]

Yet, increasingly, we are being taught to seek help, not to self-defend, to give our responsibility over to others. Let us, for example, look at criminal law and the use of

216. *The Quiet American.* Dir. Phillip Noyce. Miramax Films, 2002.

217. 1988, 244.

218. John van Kesteren, et al. "Criminal Victimisation in Seventeen Industrialised Countries: Key Findings from the 2000 International Crime Victims Survey," NSCR, The Hague, 2000.

219. Malcolm 2002.

220. Liz Ward & Alana Diamond, "Tackling Knives Action Programme (TKAP) Phase I: Overview of Key Trends from a Monitoring Programme," UK Home Office, London, July 2009.

221. Lott 2010.

"excessive force." Everything except asking for help can, if so desired, be interpreted as excessive, and thus punishable by law. Most private security guards refuse to interfere in violent situations outside of work, because it is easier to tell the police that they were afraid for their own lives and tried but failed calling in the law as they fled the scene. And why is this? For the simple reason that the defendant will be provided with the names and addresses of the witnesses and the plaintiffs no later than the day of the trial. What is the difference between a person who assaults you and the person who ties your hands so that you can be assaulted? Whoever wishes to deprive us of our ability to defend ourselves needs to be defended against. Liberalizing concealed-carry laws will not takes us back to the Wild West, though it would not be bad if it did: in the 19th-century cattle towns, homicide was confined to transient males who shot each other in saloon disturbances; the per capita robbery rate was 7% of modern New York City's; the burglary rate was 1%.[222]

The traditional function of a firearm is to procure food and to defend one's life. Recreational and target shooting are a much later invention, conceived only after the security brought about by guns. It is quite lamentable that people who practise shooting have to stoop to explanations and invent all sorts of excuses how shooting is a sensible hobby that, for example, helps develop coordination. No-one dares to confess that they just like shooting, because there has to be something very wrong with you, if you enjoy a hobby without any scientific and medical rationales. Crazy people should not be allowed to carry firearms, but the trouble is, a perfectly trustworthy and sane person can turn into a lunatic without any warning. Most of firearm homicides are committed in anger or frustration, when a drinking buddy has, for example, taken a sip out of the wrong glass. Most homicides, in general, are committed under the influence of alcohol in the company of friends or family, but these incidents are too everyday to make the news. However, according to the FBI, people have ten times greater chance of being killed by a knife or a blunt object than by any kind of rifle, including an "assault rifle."[223] The plain old fist is just as common a murder weapon, but it is hard to turn this into news. A man can kill a woman with whatever he has at hand, but in most cases, she can resist him successfully only with a gun.

The conclusion Prof. John Lott drew from his monumental study of gun ownership that covered all 3,054 U.S. counties from 1977 to 1992 was that: "Of all the methods studied so far by economists, the carrying of concealed handguns appears to be the most cost-effective method of reducing crime."[224] He quotes surveys which indicate that 98% of the time when people used guns defensively, they merely needed to brandish them before a criminal to stop the attack. The effect of reducing violent crime was particularly significant for women who carried guns. During the late 1960s, an Orlando Police Department program trained women in firearm safety as an anti-rape measure; in the year following the initiative, there was a dramatic decrease of 88% in rape cases in Orlando, while rape statewide had increased 5% and 7%

---

222. McGrath 1984.

223. Federal Bureau of Investigation 2011, Expanded Homicide Data Table 8.

224. 2010, 21.

nationwide.[225]

According to the National Self-Defense Survey conducted by Prof. Gary Kleck in 1993, 2.5 million crimes were thwarted each year by gun-owning Americans. The survey excluded cases where people grabbed a gun to investigate suspicious noises and the like, focusing on actual confrontations between the offenders and their intended victims.[226] According to the National Center for Injury Prevention and Control, the total number of U.S. gun deaths (accidents, suicides, and homicides combined) account for less than 25,000 deaths per year.[227] This means that, each year, firearms are used more than 100 times more often to protect the lives of honest citizens than to commit murders. In 2002, five years before the Virginia Tech massacre—the deadliest school shooting in U.S. history—another shooting took place in Virginia at the Appalachian School of Law, where a failing student killed three and wounded another three. According to the media, the killer was "subdued" by fellow students; of the 280 news stories reporting the incident, only four mentioned that the deadly attack had been stopped by a student armed with a handgun.[228] After he had run to his car to get his pistol, the killer dropped his and surrendered; no doubt lives could have been spared had only law-abiding citizens been legally able to carry weapons in the school.

Some say violence is categorically wrong; even between consenting adults—I have to disagree. "Hate itself is almost like Love! Fighting most certainly is Love! 'As brothers fight ye!' All the many races of the world understand this."[229] And as the Narrator observed in *Fight Club:* "After fighting, everything else in your life got the volume turned down. . . No fear. No distractions. The ability to let that which does not matter truly slide." The first major movie with violent content to be released after the Columbine incident, it was scapegoated by the moral pundits, even though only one person died in the entire film, an unarmed man shot—off camera!—by police officers.

It is rudimentary psychology that violence in movies, TV, and video games reduces violence, not increases it. A desire to watch such things is a healthy, normal human function, and there is no evidence to suggest that seeing violent images would desensitize people to death or suffering. Indeed, if watching violent entertainment "desensitized" people to violence, why on earth would they want to continue watching it? After all, they would have become indifferent to its selling point. However, the daily news footage we get from Iraq and Afghanistan is so sanitized and bloodless that we might assume no-one is actually getting hurt over there. Obviously, the newscasters inform us that so-and-so many people were killed, but "a picture is

---

225. Gary Kleck & David J. Bordua, "The Factual Foundation for Certain Key Assumptions of Gun Control," *Law & Policy* 5(3), July 1983, 271–298.

226. Gary Kleck & Marc Gertz, "Carrying Guns for Protection: Results from the National Self-Defense Survey," *Journal of Research in Crime and Delinquency* 35(2), May 1998, 193–224.

227. Debra L. Karch, et al. "Surveillance for Violent Deaths—National Violent Death Reporting System, 16 States, 2008," *Morbidity and Mortality Weekly Report* 60(SS-10), August 26, 2011, 1–54.

228. LaPierre, op. cit.

229. *Liber II: The Message of the Master Therion.* Crowley 1919, 43.

worth a thousand words."

There are, of course, children *and* adults whose ability to differentiate between reality and fantasy is impaired, but that constitutes a mental disorder, the origin of which lay not in movies or video games. The human mind is not a blank slate, onto which all external influences are drawn as such and result in direct action. It is the smoking-gave-me-cancer/McDonald's-made-me-fat argument all over again. The moralist out there, ask yourself, does seeing violence on TV make you want to engage in it? Because if it does, it is you who is disturbed. Case in point: Japanese entertainment is perhaps the most violent in the world, yet Japan has the lowest rates of violent crime in any industrialized nation. And since bloody "first-person shooter" games were first introduced about 15 years ago, violent crime in the United States has dropped by nearly 30%, youth crime dropping even faster than adult crime.[230]

In fact, the last ten years has not only seen the phenomenal rise of violent games such as "Quake" and "Grand Theft Auto," but also the most dramatic drop in violent crime in recent memory. According to the Child and Youth Well-Being Index (CWI) produced by Duke University researchers, children are less violent today than they have been at any period since the study began in 1975.[231] Yes, appalling deeds have been committed by children who played video games, but also by children who did not. The last thing we need is having the police waste their resources putting careless electronics store clerks in prison for selling games to underage kids.

Everyone of us kills millions of micro-organisms with every breath. The human body maintains a high level of alert, with T- and B-cells, macrophages, and natural killer cells roaming the body, searching and destroying cellular threats. Gandhi observed that a mouse cannot be non-violent with a cat, because a mouse does not have the potential to be violent with a cat. Non-violence is only possible from a position of power, where there is the choice, the tools, and the opportunity to be violent. In other words, if you are not fit enough to fight off an attacker, you definitely are not fit enough to run to safety from one. "It is better to confront the aggressor head-on than delay conflict."[232] There is no place for revenge.

"Violence begets violence"? That is like saying "you need money to make money" —neither against nor for. Besides, scars from physical violence heal a lot faster than those from mental violence; yet those who oppose physical violence usually have no qualms whatsoever about using mental violence. Which latter is also harder to prove in court: when the EU pressured Turkey to abolish torture, psychological torture —which leaves no physical evidence—skyrocketed; since the use of violence was prohibited, guards began using humiliation—as if that was not the whole point of torture. Plus if you apply a Bunsen burner to a prisoner's genitals, he will confess to just about anything, which would be pointless. Can you say "passive aggression"?

"I got in everyone's hostile little face. Yes, these are bruises from fighting. Yes, I'm

---

230. Federal Bureau of Investigation 2006 & 2011, Table 32.

231. Kenneth C. Land, "The Foundation for Child Development Index of Child Well-Being (CWI),1975–2003 with Projections for 2004," Duke University, Durham, NC, March 30, 2005. Available online at <www.soc.duke.edu/~cwi/>.

232. Steve Andreasen, "Bush's Passive Appeasement," *Los Angeles Times*, May 31, 2005.

comfortable with that. I am enlightened."[233] Sticks and stones may hurt our bones, but bones heal relatively fast, while one critical peer or parent can cripple you forever. A Chinese proverb declares that, "The man who strikes first admits that his ideas have given out," but the Asians always were adept at psychological warfare; besides, I have a feeling the proverb is more about keeping your calm: after all, beating your opponent to a pulp without losing your temper is what Chinese martial arts are all about. "Don't slander your enemy, as the newspapers would have you do; just kill him, and then bury him with honour. Don't keep crying 'Foul' like a fifth-rate pugilist. Don't boast! Don't squeal! If you're down, get up and hit him again! Fights of that sort make fast friends."[234] Incidentally, physicality is not the same as aggression; sometimes a slap in the face is the fastest way to get the message through, viz. "Snap out of it!"

"Violence never solved anything." No? I put it to you that it is the only thing that ever has. Just look at the government, the police, the military, etc. For once, Blaise Pascal hit the nail on the head when he said that, "Force without law is tyranny, and law without force is impotent." One of the most powerful elements in nation building has always been the people's fight for their independence, not least in the United States. The Republic of Ireland gained independence from Britain in 1922, because it fought for it. Britain gave India and Pakistan independence in 1946 and 1947 respectively, because otherwise it would have been stuck with an endless war which it was unlikely to win. After that, the British Empire decided that the moment any of the colonies starts demanding independence, it would pre-empt them by granting it to them. Similarly, if the Russians had not given Finland independence in 1917, the Finns would have fought for it, like they did when Russia tried to retake their country during WWII.

It is interesting that somehow advocating non-violence makes it all good, when in the case of the Dalai Lama, for example, there is reason to believe that he has actually made things worse for the Tibetan cause. A review of Tibetan history shows that the control of Tibet by the Chinese has been among the gentlest régimes under which the country has lived in several centuries. On the 28th of March, 1959, the Chinese Communist Party announced the dissolution of the existing local government in Tibet, following the Dalai Lama's escape a few days earlier. China asserts, quite accurately, that this move freed about one million Tibetans from serfdom and slavery. Tibetan Buddhism, with its institutionalized child abuse and brainwashing techniques, makes Jesus Camp look like a picnic, but is alright, because its despotic, homophobic leader happens to preach non-violence.

For most of history, either you conquered or you were conquered. Fighting was not only deemed natural, but necessary, and even desirable. Men—and it was a male-dominated society—found their greatest fulfilment and justification in fighting. They saw peace as a bad thing; in peace, people rotted and became decadent while societies degenerated. Indeed, mediocrity, such as in a democracy, appears to be a prerequisite of peace; both are, and have always been, stumbling-blocks to progress. As Orson

233. *Fight Club*, op. cit.

234. Crowley 1974, 291.

Welles put it in *The Third Man*, "In Italy for 30 years under the Borgias they had warfare, terror, murder, and bloodshed, but they produced Michelangelo, Leonardo da Vinci, and the Renaissance. In Switzerland they had brotherly love—they had 500 years of democracy and peace, and what did that produce? The cuckoo clock."[235]

The notion that society could even be organized without war, or the possibility or probability of war happening, was only developed with the 18th-century Enlightenment, and it took quite a long time for it to become the accepted view of Western societies. As late as 1933, Wilhelm Reich attested that, "We are confronted with the incontrovertible fact: At no time in the history of human society did masses of people succeed in preserving, organizing, and developing the freedom and peace they had achieved by bloody battles. We mean genuine freedom of personal and social development, the freedom to face life without fear, freedom from all forms of economic suppression, freedom from reactionary inhibitions of development; in short, the free self-administration of life."[236]

---

235. Dir. Carol Reed. British Lion Film Corporation, 1949.

236. 1980, 331.

4

He Who Is Unable to Live in Society Must Be Either a Beast or a God

Why is murder illegal? Governments have long had the right to take a life; capital punishment is still used in countries that consider themselves civilized. Murder, then, is illegal, not because it is immoral, but because it is vigilante justice, usurping the prerogative of the State to punish the wrongdoer—and to define what is wrong or unlawful. "Vengeance is mine!" sayeth the Lord.[237] The only law to be found in all five books of the Torah is the one that puts murderers to death. Nor can there be an ethical objection to death sentence; the objection is to government: "It is forbidden to kill; therefore all murderers are punished who kill not in large companies, and to the sound of trumpets."[238]

I used to think the only excuse for the existence of the state of Israel was that God had promised the land to the Jews. I then realized that it is the only excuse for *any* state: if "all men are created equal" then God is the *only* thing that can justify one man's power over another. This is one of the reasons why socialism failed, if also one of the reasons it came into being. All early governments were theocracies; that is, there was no separation, nay, difference between the State and the Church. The

237. Deuteronomy 32:35.

238. Voltaire 1856, II, 275.

secular rulers were the religious rulers—and vice versa. Monarchy was the preferred political ideal for millennia precisely because the monarch's legitimacy came from God and he was thus seen as entitled to monopolize the initiation of force.

Why do you think there are so many all-but-in-name republics where the head of state is still a monarch, viz. the United Kingdom. Or republics where the president has only nominal authority, viz. Germany? How is "God bless America" any better than "God save the Queen"? "Remember, the German people are the chosen of God. On me the German Emperor, the spirit of God has descended. I am His sword, His weapon, and His vice-regent." (Kaiser Wilhelm II, August 4, 1914.)[239] Have you ever met a nationalist who did not believe in God? "No, I don't know that atheists should be considered as citizens, nor should they be considered as patriots. This is one nation under God." (George H. W. Bush, August 27, 1987.)[240]

The movement to get "under God" inserted into the Pledge of Allegiance started with the Knights of Columbus, a Catholic benefit society, and was pushed by various religious organizations until Congress respected it through an unconstitutional law at the height of the Second Red Scare. Now the "under God" part is not what Americans should be upset about; it is the outrage that children are being coerced into reciting a loyalty oath, to a flag of all things—no other modern democracy has such a thing. It was written by a Christian socialist in the late 19th century to celebrate Columbus Day, and was only officialized as the national pledge during World War II, as part of the effort to instill—for the first time—national feeling in the disparate peoples of a federal republic. Early on, the pledge was started with the right hand over the heart, and at the words "to the flag," the hand would be extended towards the flag; this practice, known as the Bellamy Salute after the author of the pledge, was stopped during the War, because it resembled the Nazi salute—both were based on the salute used in ancient Rome.

As David Starr Jordan remarked: "When a dog barks at the moon, then it is religion; but when he barks at strangers, it is patriotism!"[241] It maddens me to no end when politicians quote George Santayana out of context and say that "those who cannot remember the past are condemned to repeat it," for the inability to forget is the prime requisite of national consciousness. It is, of course, those who do not *learn from* the past who are condemned to repeat it. A good American friend of mine once quipped that the United States has the best 18th-century justice system in the world; trouble is, modern egalitarianism has made a mockery of the "jury of peers," a development of feudal England.

A State, according to commonly accepted terminology, is defined as a compulsory territorial monopolist of law and order—an ultimate decision maker, if you will. Feudal lords and kings did not generally fulfill the requirements of a State in that they could only levy a tax with the consent of the taxed, and on his own land, every free man was as much a sovereign as the feudal king was on his. Over the course of

239. George 1918, 284.

240. Flynn 2007, 12.

241. As quoted in Edward Tenner, "Citizen Canine," *Wilson Quarterly* 22(3), Summer 1998, 71–79.

centuries, however, these originally stateless societies gradually transformed into absolute, statist monopolies. Initially acknowledged as judges and protectors, European kings ultimately succeeded in establishing themselves as hereditary heads of state. Opposed by the aristocracy, but supported by the "commoners," they became absolute monarchs with the power to tax without consent and to make ultimate decisions regarding the property of free men. Far from letting the inherited royal institutions of colonies and colonial governments fade into oblivion, the Americans reconstituted them within the old political borders in the form of independent states, each equipped with its own coercive taxing and legislative powers.

Columbus' voyage made its way into the annals of history because it was the first voyage of discovery made in the name of a king, as an official expedition of annexation—the islands thus became the property of the crown. It was not quite this simple, however. That would not have been legally possible, since any old mariner could claim previously undiscovered islands as his own, which is what Columbus did. To his misfortune, Columbus was a Jew, and a royal edict barred Jews from owning anything, so the king was allowed to repossess Columbus' claims. Since the Antilles were now legally the king's property, this particular voyage was turned into the one and only voyage, and all the previous expeditions were quietly discarded. Unlike the settlers' founding of private property, and their voluntary and co-operative production of security and administration of justice, the establishment of the royal colonies and administration was not the result of original appropriation and contract, but of usurpation and imposition; in fact, no European king had ever set foot on the American continent.

In the U.S., a nation built on land stolen from Indians, "property rights" are take very seriously. No-one can doubt that "property is theft," as Proudhon famously declared. Everything, including the land of all other sovereign countries, used to belong to someone else. It was conquered, and made subject to laws—"Property does not exist because there are laws, but laws exist because there is property."[242] The laws prohibiting theft are necessary for a well-ordered society—itself predicated on the very same thing it forbids. This is the Catch-22 of socialism. In *Lost Rights* (1994), James Bovard reminds us that, "Private property marks the boundary between the citizen and the State. The degree of respect the State shows for property rights will largely determine how much privacy, autonomy, and independence the citizen has."[243]

As Jan Švankmajer contends, "Sooner or later, everyone is faced with the same dilemma—either to live their life in conformity with the misty promises of institutionalised 'happiness,' or to rebel and take the path away from civilisation, whatever the results. This second path always ends in individual failure, while the first ends in the failure of humanity as a whole. Or is it the other way round? The ambivalence makes no difference when it comes to the tragedy of human fate."[244] Whatever the driving forces, we all are trying to strike the same balance as everyone

242. *Property and Law.* Bastiat 1968, 97.

243. 1995, 10.

244. Hames 1995, 114.

else, namely, between the two powerful, universal human needs for attachment and independence.

"Penitentiary" (from "penance") is a Christian concept. Surely there were prisons before Christianity, you say? Sure, but not that many: prisons were reserved for important felons—others were either executed, banished, or sold to slavery. Of course, a sentence of "banishment" nowadays violates the constitutional rights in most of the democratic countries, but no-one seems to mind using prisoners as slave labour: the goods and services produced by prisoners in the United States amount to about two billion dollars a year; one out of every five office chairs and desks made in America is made by convicts—and those jobs are not going overseas. Then there is public humiliation, which was common in the Middle Ages and is apparently making a big comeback in the West, and flogging and mutilation, which are still used in some Arab countries, to the horror of "human rights" activists everywhere.

The early modern man put the demands of society ahead of his own wishes. He was ready to live his life according to the principle of "what other people think," in order not to be excluded from the community. He did not want to look or act different from its other members, for to do so would have placed him in an economically and mentally untenable situation. This innate solidarity was essential for the survival of the community as a whole. We are still intrinsically social creatures: the worst punishment for any human being to suffer is solitary confinement, or total exile from communication with other people. We need each other to be both mentally and physically healthy: normal people kept in complete isolation can become psychotic in as little as a few days; in the long term, solitary isolation can lead to permanent insanity—this would not be true if most people were happy without social contact.

The etiquette-obsessed Japan has one of the lowest rates of incarceration among developed nations, though the numbers have risen at an alarming rate even as Japanese society has become Westernized. Recent statistic show Japan has 63 inmates for every 100,000 people, compared with 153 in the United Kingdom, and 756 in the United States.[245] We need not look as far away as Iraq to see how prisons develop perverse internal culture: California prisons have of late been rife with accusations of excessive force by guards and lack of basic medical care, not to mention their utter failure to rehabilitate criminals.

Associations only form among peer groups; prison guards, corrupt or not, can no more control inmate relations than school teachers can control student relations, e.g. bullying. A Harvard task force set up in the wake of an agreement between MySpace and all 50 of the state attorneys general examined the safety of children who venture online and came to the same conclusion as other recent studies: "cyberbullying" does happen, but generally simply as an extension of the child's offline social circles, rather than as a distinct internet phenomenon—much of the bullying children suffer online differs from their real-world experiences only in the terms of the medium. And when it comes to sexual solicitation, the fraction of underage children targeted by adult strangers is quite small, most of the youth targeted being older adolescents; rather

245. Roy Walmsley, "World Prison Population List," International Centre for Prison Studies, King's College, London, 1999–2009.

than the internet being a means by which children are in constant danger from predatory paedophiles, it appears that they are more at risk from each other—of consensual sexual contact.[246]

Children are "innocent" only from the adult point of view, prison gangs "guilty" only from the correctional officers'. Everybody wants to feel important, and that is what gangs are about—mattering. Children have similar hierarchies, and both form a society within society, with its own rules and a strict code of honour. Bullying has to do with the internal power dynamics of a closed group: the bully is attempting to gain power for himself. In primary school, pupils bully other pupils who are different and everyone thus learns that they have to dress alike and act alike in order to gain the acceptance of the group. Telling on a fellow student is a violation of the code and exposes oneself to being bullied. You can be a member of a different social group, but you cannot be unique, since this would mean you are not a member of any group and you would be socially ostracized. In order to become a member of a group, you would have to purchase the apparel, music, and other products that one needs to be a street-credible member of the group. All of this applies to prisoners just the same.

The low rate of violence in Finnish correctional facilities is credited to their policy of giving the convicts as much contact as possible with other people, both inside and outside prisons. Frequent visits from friends and family are encouraged, and at Hämeenlinna Central Prison, male and female prisoners live together. Occasionally they fall in love and get married in the prison, but there are also conjugal visits and even home leaves. After having served six months, any prisoner can apply for leave to return to their home town for periods up to six days every four months. Ninety percent of these leaves take place without the slightest difficulty, but if a prisoner is misbehaving or considered likely to re-offend, he is likely to be turned down for one.[247] In any case, locking people up is always just a temporary solution, since more than 95% of prisoners will eventually be released back into the community.

For decades, the U.S. policy has been driven by the emotional response of the American public to criminals. People are mad at them and frightened by them, so the typical response has been very punitive; we need to stop arguing what criminals deserve and start thinking long-term. By allowing inmates the chance to return briefly to the real world, home leaves help to maintain relationships and prevent the atrophy of social skills. Similarly, Finland's extensive use of parole and early release creates transition periods where released prisoners are supervised while they get established in legitimate society. If the prisons did not encourage these relationships, released convicts would be met on the outside by a gang or friends involved in crime, as they are in many other countries. As George Jung commented on a Connecticut penitentiary, "Danbury wasn't a prison, it was a crime school. I went in with a Bachelor of Marijuana, came out with a Doctorate of Cocaine."[248]

Most modern prisons are perfect networking opportunities for criminals, forming

---

246. "Enhancing Child Safety & Online Technologies: Final Report of the Internet Safety Technical Task Force," The Berkman Center for Internet & Society at Harvard University, Cambridge, MA, December 31, 2008.

247. Dan Gardner, "Why Finland Is Soft on Crime," *Ottawa Citizen*, March 18, 2002.

248. *Blow*. Dir. Ted Demme. New Line Cinema, 2001.

a complete antithesis to the ancient practice of "ostracism." Free room and board plus regimented, almost monastic conditions mean that ex-convicts are unable, and even unwilling, to return to society; "Prison life consists of routine, and then more routine."[249] The prison system, partly justified by the growth of general population, is now dysfunctional because of the growth of prison population. Even before the fall of the Soviet Union, the United States, "the land of the free," had the largest percentage of imprisoned citizens in the entire world. Three-strikes laws and other get-tough policies enacted in the 1980s and '90s swelled the prison inmate population to a record 2.3 million in 2007.[250] The U.S. accounts for only five percent of the world's population, but a quarter of all prisoners; every year, hundreds of thousands of Americans are sent to jail for crimes that pose little if any danger or harm to society.

Finland's incarceration rate is just 64 per 100,000 people, about half of the Canadian rate of 116 per 100,000, and just a tiny fraction of the U.S. rate of 756.[251] Back when Finland was still a province of Russia, crime and punishment were governed by the harsh Russian justice system, which the Finns inherited after independence. Until the 1950s, Finland's incarceration rate was 200 per 100,000, a normal rate for Eastern Bloc countries like Poland and Czechoslovakia, but four times the rate in the other Nordic countries.[252] In the '60s, Finland began a cautious prison reform, using its Scandinavian neighbours as a model: during the next two decades, imprisonment was reduced by both diverting offenders to other forms of punishment, such as fines, probation, and community service, or reducing the time served in prison. Never before or since has any country so completely shifted from one philosophy of justice to its opposite.

From the late 1960s to the early '90s, crime rose sharply in Finland, while imprisonment declined rapidly, suggesting that going "soft" fostered crime. However, crime rose during that period in all the other countries in the developed world as well, regardless of their criminal justice policies. One of the reasons for this was the huge bulge in young males, always responsible for most crime, produced by the post-war baby boom; another reason was the near worldwide criminalization of recreational drugs in the mid-20th century. Ultimately, Finland's choices about how to punish crime had little or no effect on the national crime rate. After more than 30 years, the Finnish prison reform has yielded one clear conclusion: high incarceration rates and austere prison conditions do not control crime.[253] So should people be allowed to "get away with murder"? In my book, if you manage to murder someone in the first place, you have already gotten away with it!

In 1979, the head of the California Corrections Department warned that the prison population could shoot out of control, to 27,000 by 1986, from about 20,000. By 1986,

---

249. *The Shawshank Redemption.* Dir. Frank Darabont. Columbia Pictures, 1994.

250. Walmsley, op. cit.

251. Ibid.

252. Tapio Lappi-Seppälä, "Regulating the Prison Population: Experiences from a Long-term Policy in Finland," National Research Institute of Legal Policy, Helsinki, 1998.

253. Ibid.

there were 54,000 prisoners in California, and the state never caught up.[254] The huge increases in federal and state prison populations during the 1980s and '90s were mainly for drug convictions. Those sentenced solely for the sale or possession of drugs made up 55% of federal inmates in 2003. The number of drug offenders in prisons and jails has risen from a little over 40,000 in 1980 to nearly half a million in 2005.[255] According to FBI figures, nearly three times as many American were arrested in 2010 on drug charges than for murder, manslaughter, forcible rape, and aggravated assault combined.[256] Consequently, U.S. prisons now hold nearly twice the number of inmates they were designed for, meaning that areas such as gymnasiums and classrooms have been converted into dormitories.

The other major cause of overcrowding in Californian prisons is a parole system that sends 70% of parolees back to prison within 18 months of their release. The nation's highest return rate, more than twice the national average, rests on the state's decision to de-emphasize rehabilitation programs, lengthen parole periods, and send parole violators back to prison instead of giving them treatment. California keeps most released inmates on parole for far longer periods than any other state, and sends parolees back to prison even for relatively minor offences such as missing meetings or failing drug tests. Parole can also be violated for things like possessing a kitchen knife in a room other than the kitchen or having "too much" cash in your pocket. So many parole violators return to prison that they make up more than one-third of all inmates.

According to the Little Hoover Commission, ten percent of the inmates who do make it back home are homeless, and as many as 90% are unemployed.[257] Another 80% are drug users—and the numbers are similar in other countries: even in the otherwise exemplary Finland, two-thirds of convicts are addicts.[258] The incarcerated disproportionately come from, and return to, the same neighbourhoods. When the addict is released from prison, he goes straight back to his old surroundings, with the forces and pressures which led him into addiction unchanged. Prison has only made things worse, ruining the prospects of the young person who will have little reason to finish school or take an entry-level job, and of the older person who finds himself virtually unemployable. Sending addicts to prison simply ensures the problem will continue.

Because of substance abuse problems, violence, and often impoverished backgrounds, prison inmates are among the sickest people in the U.S. They have high levels of chronic diseases like diabetes, asthma, and hypertension, and near epidemic levels of infectious diseases such as hepatitis C, and suffer violent injuries as prison crowding raises tensions. The average sentence was seven months longer in 2005 than

---

254. James Sterngold & Mark Martin, "Hard Time: California's Prisons in Crisis," *San Francisco Chronicle*, July 3, 2005.

255. Marc Mauer & Ryan S. King, "A 25-Year Quagmire: The War on Drugs and Its Impact on American Society," The Sentencing Project, Washington, D.C., September 2007.

256. Federal Bureau of Investigation 2011, Table 29.

257. 2004.

258. Tomi Lintonen, et al. "The Changing Picture of Substance Abuse Problems among Finnish Prisoners," *Social Psychiatry and Psychiatric Epidemiology* 46, 2011, 390.

in 1995, resulting in an ageing inmate population with much more expensive medical needs; according to an internal California Corrections Department report, the cost of an elderly inmate is three times that of a young one.[259] However, the level of medical care in Californian prisons is so poor that U.S. District Judge Thelton Henderson has said it violates the constitutional right against cruel and unusual punishment.[260] The vacancy rates are high for doctors, nurses, therapists, and pharmacists, who have to work under deplorable conditions. And when inmates are not properly treated, they return to society with costly ailments, often carrying communicable diseases.

Laws are necessary in order for organized society to function at all. We cannot co-exist without rules: it is a very good idea for all the road users to agree on which side of the road to drive. However, the decision-makers should make sure that each regulation is necessary, that it is more useful than harmful, and that society has a legitimate interest in enforcing it. The police are given more and more responsibilities and tasks, but no new resources to carry them out. The main role of any State is to include as many people as possible in its "social contract," meaning that citizens promise not to kill or rob in exchange of being provided with the means to live with dignity; crime is usually an event that occurs when a member of society finds that his own selfish needs overcome his contractual considerations. The price of justice has risen astronomically, while the quality of law has steadily deteriorated to the point where the idea of law as a body of universal principles of justice has been replaced by the idea of law as government legislation.

We seem to have lost sight of the fact that laws are in essence no more than generalized statements about prevailing customs. It is common for us to say that something is right or wrong just because some statute so decrees. Yet the abstract ideas of justice have little to do with legislation, whose idea is only to enforce compliance with current conventions. One does not receive justice from a court of law, only the application of government-made law. Nor does formal fidelity to the law guarantee that your actions are morally acceptable. At worst, the mixing of law and morality can lead to a situation where only the formal rules are abided by: should a pedestrian violate a red light, the motorist is not required by law to stop, because the light is green for him; even if one did wrong, one would be right, as long as one did not break the law.

Modern legislation has broken its banks; it has become a thing-in-itself that has claimed for itself the right of revolutionizing the habits of people in accordance with abstract ideals which take no account of prevailing conditions. The criminalization of recreational drugs is of course the most glaring example of this inhuman tyranny, but all such deviations from common sense defeat themselves in the long run. One side of this argument wants to convince us that if something is legal, it is also condoned or encouraged; but saying we should not send people to prison for doing something is not the same as saying that it is a good idea to do that thing. Many things can be made to work only if the superfluous and unreasonable rules are appropriately broken. Modern trade union activists have developed a type of strike where, rather than to

259. Sterngold & Martin, op. cit.

260. *Madrid v. Gomez*, 889 F. Supp. 1146 (N.D. Cal. 1995).

walk off the job, they pull out the procedural manuals and follow every single rule to the letter.

One effect of this is that the only things that get done are those strictly defined in the job description of a worker: for example, nurses will refuse to hook up intravenous drips, take blood, assist with ECGs, or perform any clerical duties, including answering telephones, basically grinding the hospital to a halt. Another example is the stretching out of the line of cars and trucks at the border to several miles should the customs officials begin to meticulously inspect every single detail according to the guidebook; at the same time, they would also overlook all unforeseen methods of smuggling. Suddenly, the utter inadequacy of "comprehensive guidelines" becomes clear, as does the value of seasoned and intelligent human presence. Called "work to rule," this type of strike both brings attention to the flaws in the system and makes the company rules seem stupid—which they usually are.

The ever-growing system of regulations teaches citizens to act in a certain way. This development has been dubbed the "tyranny of small steps"; in other words, while every individual step is justifiable, the whole becomes too complex. Even the most honest man cannot invariably be sure that he is not violating one or another statute. Federal laws, state laws, municipal laws, and police regulations clash at every turn. Not even the greatest legal mind can pretend to know what the law is until the case in dispute has been thrashed out and the decision established as a precedent. While "ignorance of the law excuses no man," one is bound to risk peril which he cannot but ignore, causing the law to fall into disrespect; censorship, licensing, and tax codes are arbitrarily invoked against people who have no idea that they are doing wrong in doing exactly as their neighbours do—and the only winners are lawyers!

In the ideal situation, law would be restricted to regulate only the larger structures and absent itself from the realm of private life—except for violent offences taking place within that realm. There should be no laws on morals, no laws that cannot be enforced, and no laws on victimless crimes. By forcing non-criminals, including the victims of crime, to pay for the imprisonment of criminals, rather than making criminals compensate their victims and pay the cost of their own incarceration, crime will only increase. I cannot find a section of the U.S. Constitution or the Bill of Rights that allows government to imprison people who have not committed crimes against others; on the contrary, the First Amendment guarantees free expression, the Fourth Amendment guarantees privacy, and the Ninth and Tenth Amendments tell the government exactly where it must stop. Every decent parent knows that if you treat a child like a half-wit, the child will act like a half-wit. A normal child can take responsibility for his actions, within the constraints of his age of course. The same principle applies to adults. We should trust the judgement of the private citizen whenever possible; in the end, everybody is an expert on their own life.

There is a common misconception that the heavily publicized American trials have brought Big Tobacco to its knees. Bans on smoking and the damages won from the tobacco companies have not killed the industry. It has managed to turn the bans into its advantage in the courts and transfer the damages into its prices. Smoking may be on the wane in the developed countries, but it is growing that much more in the developing world. The tobacco companies have consolidated their positions with a federal settlement that has in practice closed the markets. The settlement guarantees the federal government so much income tied to the cigarette sales that it does not wish to actually curtail smoking. The problem is the same as with the excise on tobacco in the EU: no chancellor of the exchequer in any member country is prepared to raise the tax to a level that would fulfil the stated aim of health policy, that is, reduce the demand substantially. Similarly, alcohol is quite the gold mine for governments: there is, of course, the tax benefit, but also the holier-than-thou benefit, where the powers that be alternately raise and lower the price of spirits, giving the citizens an impression that something important is being done. Ironically, deaths from alcohol are on the rise at a time when researchers and public authorities know more about the prevention of alcohol abuse than ever before.

"When fantastic restrictions disappear, the greater freedom of the individual will itself teach him to avoid acts which really restrict natural rights. Thus real crime will diminish dramatically."[261] Many of our secular laws—such as traffic regulations—are predicated on the Christian doctrine of man's innate evil. In 1974, 120 people died in traffic accidents in Dutch Friesland. In 2001, there were only 45 fatal accidents. There might of course be several reasons for the stunning improvement of road safety, but all the statistics indicate a pivotal role of the radical traffic experiment implemented in the area. Not one person died that year in the traffic of Drachten, a city of 40,000. In the last year before the experiment, there were five traffic deaths in the city.[262]

The idea behind the Frisian experiment is simple: they have stopped controlling the traffic by the usual medley of lights and signs. Roundabouts have been built in the intersections. The responsibility for safety has been transferred to the road user himself. The thought of no traffic lights may sound strange and even dangerous, but all the effects have been positive. The attentiveness of drivers has increased as they can no longer blindly trust the lights. The average situational speed in intersections has dropped to half, increasing safety. Yet the travel times have not grown much at all, since all the idle time spent sitting at lights has been eliminated.

Speeding by and in itself has never caused a single accident; wrong situational speed, whether too high or too low, has—and no amount of traffic signs will change that. German car makers, such as Audi, BMW, and Mercedes-Benz, take pride in their high-performance models, seen as symbols of the mighty German export industry; unlike its EU neighbours, Germany has motorway speed restrictions only near road work, in traffic bottlenecks, and at junctions. Speed limits were first instituted when cars were considerably less safe, yet the authorities keep bringing them down: it is disingenuous to blame "reckless drivers" when the modern vehicles can safely do 120 mph but the speed limit is 30. In fact, the only way to further improve road safety is to make cars *less* safe again; should their air-bags be disconnected, the drivers would be sure to maintain a safe distance on wet highways.

Laws, regulations, rules, guidelines, and directives are sort of invisible traffic lights that steer our actions. Most people obey the law most of the time, not because they fear they will be punished if they don't, but because they believe in the system. No

---

261. *Duty.* Crowley 1998, 142.

262. Eero Hämeenniemi, "Lupa ajatella," *Helsingin Sanomat*, July 17, 2002.

law should rest on myth or be tied to any authority, lest doubt about the myth or about the legitimacy of the authority imperil sound judgement and action; e.g. "This crime called blasphemy was invented by priests for the purpose of defending doctrines not able to take care of themselves."[263] The prestige of government was undoubtedly lowered by the passing of the Prohibition Law in the 1920s, "For nothing is more destructive of respect for the government and the law of the land than passing laws which cannot be enforced."[264] What followed was not only the criminalization of millions of Americans and a general loss of respect for law, but the creation of organized crime and the invention of the drive-by shooting; without prohibition, there could never have been an Al Capone.

The subsequent "War on Drugs" has had similar results: children are being recruited as runners, mules, and lookouts; innocent bystanders are getting shot in firefights between rival drug-dealers; dedicated narcotics officers are being tortured and killed in the line of duty; prisons are filling up with non-violent drug offenders. Every legal scholar knows that punishment does not reform anybody: if prison changes a person in any way, it changes him for the worse; yet we still want to put the offenders there—we think criminals should "pay their debt to society." But what authority empowers the government to imprison people who have not committed crimes against others? In a totalitarian state, something is a crime just because the government or the esteemed leader so decides. However, in a free country, the government has the burden to prove something ought to be considered a crime. Some things are obviously criminal, such as causing physical harm to another; other things are less so, and must be carefully evaluated. Marijuana, in particular, has not been—it is against the law because the government says so.

Whom exactly do these laws protect? You can put two kilos of heroin on my living room table and I won't touch it; if someone else wants to be a moron and take it, let them—it is the quintessential victimless crime. When you criminalize a drug for which there is a large market, it does not disappear; the trade is merely transferred from pharmacists and medical professionals to armed criminal gangs. And the more you criminalize, the more the criminals can profit. While imposing its prohibitionist policies on the rest of the world for nearly a century, the United States has created a network of treaties and international agreements requiring universal drug prohibition. According to the UN, the number of people taking illegal drugs worldwide rose by over 14% in 2005. The value of the global narcotics trade, which the 2005 UN drug report says was about $320 billion, is higher than the gross domestic product of 90% of the world's nations. Drug syndicates control 8% of global GDP, meaning that they have greater resources than many national armies.[265]

The cartels control tax-exempt networks that multiply by thousands the value of simple raw materials, and are so profitable that they can bribe, intimidate, or kill public servants of countries rich and poor. They own helicopters and submarines, and they can afford to spread the rot of corruption through developing nations, right to

---

263. *An Interview on Chief Justice Comegys.* Ingersoll 1901, VII, 466.

264. *The World as I See It.* Einstein 1954, 6.

265. United Nations Office on Drugs and Crime 2005.

the top. In fact, drug money saved several banks from collapse at the height of the global financial crisis, according to Antonio Maria Costa, executive director of the UN Office on Drugs and Crime. Apparently, proceeds from the drug trade and other illegal activities were the "only liquid investment capital" available to some banks on the verge of collapse in the second half of 2008. As a result, a majority of that year's $352 billion in drug profits was absorbed into the regular economic system, in effect laundering it.[266] An old Chinese proverb says that the best ruler is one of whose existence the people are barely aware; "When laws are unjust, monstrous, ridiculous, that same average man, will he-nill he, becomes a criminal; and the law requires a Tcheka or a Gestapo with dictatorial powers and no safeguards to maintain the farce. Also, corruption becomes normal in official circles; and is excused."[267]

"Of all the strange 'crimes' that humanity has legislated out of nothing, 'blasphemy' is the most amazing—with 'obscenity' and 'indecent exposure' fighting it out for second and third place," protested Robert A. Heinlein.[268] Recently, a private television channel in New Delhi aired grainy hidden-camera footage of Hindu holy men sexually abusing female devotees, politicians having sex with prostitutes, and Bollywood actors propositioning an undercover journalist in exchange for film roles. The Indian public expressed outrage, not at the public figures implicated, but at the upstart TV channel. The Ministry of Information and Broadcasting declared that the footage "offended good taste and decency" and "was obscene and likely to corrupt public morality."[269] The biggest dilemma facing American filmmakers, both in the adult world and mainstream cinema, is the U.S. government's restrictions on sexually explicit imagery. There are several producers of consensual, adults-only pornography still serving prison sentences for violating the Comstock Act of 1873 (otherwise known as 18 USC 1461), which was made the top priority for the Justice Department during the presidency of George W. Bush, even above prosecution of terrorists.

Due to the rapid growth of internet pornography, stamping out obscene material became a major concern for the Bush administration's powerful Christian conservative supporters. Federal and local authorities launched a manhunt for someone peddling a dozen pictures of Britney Spears, her teenage sister Jamie Lynn, daughter Maddie and the father, Casey Aldridge. One of the pictures showed Jamie Lynn, a minor, breastfeeding her daughter, sparking a nationwide child pornography investigation. More recently, a Los Angeles-based clothing firm was banned from publishing a "provocative" advertisement in a UK magazine using a model who *looked* under 16. The UK Advertising Standards Authority ruled the shot of the then 23-year-old model "could be seen to sexualise a model who appeared to be a child."[270] Another content that has fallen under government ban is small-breasted porn, and an appeals court judge in Australia ruled an internet animation depicting cartoon

---

266. Rajeev Syal, "Drug Money Saved Banks in Global Crisis, Claims UN Advisor," *The Observer*, December 13, 2009.

267. Crowley 1954, 345.

268. Op. cit. 242.

269. V. Venkatesan, "Public Interest vs. Privacy," *Frontline*, May 6, 2005.

270. "ASA Adjudication on American Apparel (UK) Ltd," September 2, 2009.

characters from *The Simpsons* engaging in sexual acts to be child pornography.[271] In fact, the Australian federal government plans to introduce a mandatory internet filtering system in 2013 that will block all web sites it finds obscene and make Australia one of the strictest internet regulators among the world's democracies.

In most Western countries, pictures of naked children are only considered child pornography if they depict sexual acts; in Russia, only depictions of sexual acts with minors under the age of 14 are illegal. The Nordic censors could care less about nudity or profanity, but take exception to graphic violence—the kind you see daily on American network television. The UK DVD release of the first season of the U.S. series *Angel* (1999) was rated "18 and over" because of a blink-and-you'll-miss-it head butt in one episode. Until recently, cockfights, being illegal in Britain, had to be cut out of all foreign films released in the UK. Bestiality will land you in jail in some U.S. states, but is rarely prosecuted in most, being a felony in 16 and a misdemeanor in 14 states. The FCC prohibits the public broadcast of the words "fuck," "cunt," "cocksucker," and "asshole," but allows the terms "damn," "shit," "dick," and "bitch." If we are to believe the U.S. Solicitor General, loosening indecency standards could lead to "Big Bird dropping the F-bomb on Sesame Street."[272]

Swearing is effective as a means to vent aggression, and thereby forestall physical violence: "Barking dogs never bite," but no man is deadlier than one too enraged for expletives. But why exactly is "fuck" considered a dirty word? Or "cunt"? Or, indeed, "bloody" and "bleeding"? It is the same source as "hell" and "damn," namely Christianity. What counts as taboo language in any given culture is a mirror into the fears and fixations of that culture. The word "golly," which sounds almost comically wholesome these days, is actually a contraction of the phrase "God's body," and, thus, was once a strong profanity. In a society where the purity and honour of women is of the highest importance, it is not surprising that many swear-words are variations on "bastard," an insult directed at a person's mother, not his father.

Generally speaking, the people who crow loudest about being politically correct are white, college-educated, and generally come from one or more levels of privilege. People who do not have those opportunities and are thus less likely to be aware of the need for political correctness—or busy working three jobs to keep the babies fed—are looked down upon as a result. Yet children will invariably memorize the common vulgarities long before they can grasp the sense, and literary giants have always built their work on profanities; as any English professor will tell you, there is not a single piece of work we consider "literature" that would meet the 21st-century standards of political correctness. Shakespeare himself could scarcely pen a stanza without the likes of "'Zounds" and "'Sblood"—offensive compactions of "God's wounds" and "God's blood," respectively. The title of his play "Much Ado about Nothing" is a pun on "Much Ado about an O Thing," a reference to the female genitalia.

Pornography is, by definition, that sexual material which is offensive to most people. In other words, porn is in the eye of the beholder, or, to paraphrase Alfred C. Kinsey, "it ain't filth if everyone's buying it." Hard-core pornography, once confined

---

271. *McEwen v Simmons & Anor* [2008] NSWSC 1292.

272. Oral Argument of Gen. Gregory G. Garre on Behalf of the Petitioners, *FCC v. Fox Television Stations*, 129 S. Ct. 1800 (2009).

to seedy theatres and shops, is nowadays purveyed by upscale hotels and most cable and satellite television companies. "Adult entertainment" is a profit maker for such large corporations as General Motors, Time Warner, News Corp, and the Hilton, Sheraton, Marriot, and Hyatt hotel chains. A study by the Kaiser Family Foundation found that 70% of the 15- to 17-year olds in the United States have "accidentally stumbled across pornography online"[273]; and the average porn site can generate as many sexual images in a minute as an entire issue of *Hustler*, and is usually much more explicit than the centerfolds that their fathers and grandfathers used to stash under the mattress.

Exploring sexuality is an important part of a healthy adolescence, but the common outlets for that are not what they used to be. Yet for all the sex and nudity in their sight, pregnancy and abortion rates for minors are the lowest in decades. Personally, I never understood the X rating, i.e. "no-one under 18 admitted." Would not "no-one between 12 and 18 admitted" make more sense? A younger child will warp his fragile little mind watching violence (such as one sees on the evening news), not sex. The older "children" will masturbate anyway—to a Victoria's Secret catalog if nothing else is available—or have sex instead! The age of consent varies from 12 to 18 in the Western countries, and up to twenty for homosexual acts; many Eastern countries still ban the latter altogether, some even treat them as capital offences. Of course, these laws do not apply if the lovers are married, and the age of consent for marriage, especially with parental permission, is generally lower than the age of sexual consent.

Many U.S. states still have different ages of marital consent for young women than they do for young men, and that age is always lower for girls than it is for boys. According to Finnish sociologist and MP Anna Kontula, child protective services monitor the chastity of girls more vehemently than that of boys. She worked at the City of Tampere Board of Child and Youth Services between 2007 and 2008, and her finding was that the forced custody cases of girls often cite their sexual activity. Boys' custody petitions do not mention risky sexual behaviour at all, even though studies show that boys encounter just as much sexual harassment as do girls. In the case of girls, the grounds for forced custody included interest in men, acting older than ones' age, using oversexed language, and fraternizing with older men—sexuality did not raise any flags with boys.[274]

Statutory rape is the only felony a minor can willingly take part in with an adult and not suffer any legal repercussions; which makes me wonder when Levi Johnston will be charged with raping Bristol Palin? When two teenagers engage in consensual sexual intercourse, they are not considered victims, but when a teenager knowingly consents to sex with an adult—typically while lying about their age—they are viewed as a victim by the U.S. legal system. Funnily enough, the United States can have an administration that gets away with violating the Constitution and destroying the economic infrastructure, but a seventeen-year old who has oral sex with her fifteen-year-old boyfriend stands to lose everything because of a few moments of mutually

273. Victoria Rideout, "Generation Rx.com: How Young People Use the Internet for Health Information," Keiser Family Foundation, Menlo Park, CA, December 2001.

274. Venla Pystynen, "Tyttöjen huostaanottojen perusteita ovat varhaiset seksikokemukset ja rivo kielenkäyttö," *Helsingin Sanomat*, June 27, 2009.

consensual pleasure. Maybe the country should stop spending taxpayer money making sex offenders out of college kids because of their high-school lovers, and start using that money to educate them on the values of safe sexual practices?

We should be very suspicious of parental perception and motives; older generations always think newer generations are worse than they were, or more sexually promiscuous; yet most of the measures of that are at all-time lows. "All children alarm their parents, if only because you are forever expecting to encounter yourself."[275] According to the Church, even unmarried cohabitants are committing adultery. On the other hand, mediaeval marriages were often between rather young children, who frequently did not even meet each other until later. And although sexual relations would usually not begin until the pair was somewhat older, the standards were still quite different from ours. What would now be considered paedophilia, or child-abuse at the very least, used to be the common, Church-endorsed practice. Parents had their daughter married off and churning out babies at thirteen, if only because average life-expectancy was about twenty-eight.

Sexual relations between an unmarried man and woman, or "fornication," did not cease to be a criminal offence in the West until the early decades of the 20th century; homosexual couples had to wait about half a century longer. Any sex act other than vaginal intercourse can and has been considered "sodomy," and there are still state laws in America that make all acts of sodomy illegal, even among married couples; oral sex, for example, used to be a chargeable offense in many states and grounds for divorce in others, because it was deemed unnatural. Before Kinsey pioneered sex research in the 1940s and '50s, the only sexual act sanctioned by society was vaginal intercourse between a legally married couple. Based on personal interviews with more than 18,000 people, the Kinsey Report revealed that Americans of both genders—in substantial numbers—not only engaged in premarital and extramarital sex, but had homosexual sex as well, and most shocking of all, had had sex with animals.[276] Before the internet, many vendors of mail-order erotica feared criminal prosecution and local sanctions, but the World Wide Web opened the door for a flood of cheap content, much of it produced outside U.S. jurisdiction; and any vestige of self-censorship vanished with the corner adult bookstore.

In his more than a decade in the Washington state legislature, Rep. Mark Miloscia had supported all manner of methods to fill the state's coffers, including increasing taxes on alcohol and cigarettes, most of which passed, he says, "without a peep." In 2009, he decided he might try to "find a new tax source," namely, pornography. However, when he proposed an 18.5% sales tax on items like adult magazines and sex toys, people, as he puts it, came down on him like a ton of bricks. He also received criticism from a vast array of residents and business owners from his suburban district between Tacoma and Seattle, who accused him of attacking the First Amendment and other sacred institutions. In fact, his constituents were calling him up saying their marriages would fall apart—"Apparently, porn is right up there with Mom and apple

275. Gore Vidal, attributed.

276. Kinsey, et al. 1948 & 1953.

pie," he concluded in a *New York Times* interview.[277]

Much of both straight and gay porn in Europe is produced in the extremely conservative Eastern Bloc countries. In the summer of 2009, Ukraine criminalized all pornographic material and its possession—the only exception being its use for "medical purposes." Prostitution is also illegal in Ukraine, but that does not prevent it from being the principal means of livelihood for many Ukrainian women. With Russia and Belarus, Ukraine remains one of the main sources of employment for European porn actors, and it is the Draconian blue laws that have made this possible. In order for the system to work, society ironically needs to have a particularly dim view on pornography. The risk of locals seeing the girls next door doing porn on the internet is extremely low; the strict blue laws ensure that friends, relatives, teachers, etc. do not have access to porn, so they cannot identify the women—secrets will remain secret.

It is important to clarify the ethical issue involved in the production of pornographic material: conditions under which people are being coerced, pressured, threatened, manipulated, or actually forced to participate in the production of such material against their will cannot be excused. The trouble is, these conditions are not necessarily identifiable merely by examining the final product; a photo spread or video depicting gruesome sexual torture could be compeletely simulated, totally safe, and wholly consensual, while a video or photo series depicting nothing more than a little nudity and perhaps some suggestive poses could be a heinous crime against humanity if the subjects were being coerced.

A hundred years ago, part of the women's movement put out the claim that prostitution represents male dominance, and that women, especially prostitutes, are victims. The prostitutes' own interest groups, however, emphasize that society should treat their occupation as any other source of livelihood; Carol Leigh, a veteran activist, is credited for coining the term "sex worker" as an anti-euphemism. Sex workers should not be branded as victims, because wardship undermines their right of self-determination. Where prostitution is legal, there is no need for the protective services of a pimp. If we want to oversee their working conditions, all laws and practices that make sex workers unable to avail themselves of health care and social services need to be overturned. State systems of control and prohibition of brothels can lead to illegal employment relationships and, at worse, to slave-like working conditions. History shows that criminalization only increases crime by driving the illegal acts under ground, and people who wish to keep prostitution illegal usually use as their rationale a laundry list of problems created by the black market nature of the sex trade.

Decriminalization, on the other hand, gives authorities greater control over activities that take place regardless. After the Netherlands overturned its widely-ignored 1912 ban on brothels in 2000, these businesses became taxpaying establishments with the standard employee benefit requirements. The new law is also hoped to weed out illegal immigrants, forced prostitution, and underage girls. In Amsterdam, people going to an organ concert in the spired 14th-century Old Church

277. Jesse McKinley, "Struggling States Look to Unorthodox Taxes," March 1, 2009.

have to walk through the heart of the city's red light district, with its live shows, gay bars, unabashed store fronts, and the famous picture-window prostitutes. Yet it has almost none of the seediness of such districts elsewhere in Europe, as tourist boats glide through the canals past notorious sex clubs, and middle-aged couples walk hand in hand along the cobbled streets.

Studies have shown, again and again, that sex workers are less likely to spread STDs or get unwanted pregnancies than other sexually promiscuous people; however, laws legalizing prostitution do not remove the social stigma that still surrounds their job. The sex worker frequently tells her family, friends, and neighbours that she is working in a different field. Sometimes she will tell her husband that she is working in an office or in a restaurant, which can make life very complicated for her; but should she be open about it, her husband and her children will likely be discriminated against. Many sex workers even keep regular part-time jobs to avoid leaving suspicious gaps in their CVs. Most of the prostitutes in Western Europe are part-timers anyway, and include students, the unemployed, pensioners, and short- and part-time workers; only a few are underaged, and most of them are local natives.[278]

Working abroad can often be the ideal option for a prostitute, for it enables her to lead a respectable life in her home country. The visits can last up to a couple of weeks, but are usually only for a few days. In the worst position are the paperless immigrants, who turn to the local authorities only in extreme distress. The term "white slavery" is highly insulting to anyone with the slightest sense of history. Not only are there still millions of the traditional kind of slaves around the world, but racial slavery itself is a relatively new phenomenon. An estimated 27 million people worldwide are living lives of exploitation without basic human rights—a larger number than at any other point in history.[279] And though women from Albania, for example, are known to be trafficked to southeastern Europe as prostitutes, 70% of Albanians trafficked for work or begging are male.[280] In 2010, the first time the United States was included in the state department's human trafficking report, forced labour in areas including agriculture and manufacturing was identified as the biggest problem in the country.[281]

There are also many signs of consumer culture-based prostitution, where young women in particular obtain money to buy luxury items through soft-core erotica, such as selling used underpants online. It is far more commonplace than once believed for teens to be paid at parties to strip, give sexual favours, or have sex. Nine percent of students at the University of Michigan, an affluent place of education, say they have "initiated an attempt to trade sex for some tangible benefit," such as money, clothes, or even homework.[282] According to a recent study by the Swedish National Board for

278. Anna Kontula, "Prostituutio Suomessa," Sexpo-säätiö, Helsinki, May 26, 2005.

279. Bales 1999.

280. Sarah Stephens & Mariska van der Linden, "Trafficking of Migrant Workers from Albania: Issues of Labour and Sexual Exploitation," International Labour Organization, Geneva, September 2005.

281. "Trafficking in Persons Report: 10th Edition," U.S. Department of State, Washington, D.C., June 2010.

282. Meston & Buss 2009, 168.

Youth Affairs, 200,000 young people have sold their bodies in a nation of 9 million.[283] Both male and female students prostitute themselves to pay for their bills. Whether people become sex workers due to circumstances or of their own free will is a complex question. Most students have the choice to get by with less money, and it appears to be the prettiest girls from the wealthiest families who are most at risk. Back in the late '60s, a prostitution ring was broken up at the exclusive River Oaks Country Club in Houston, Texas. The girls, twelve to eighteen years of age, were all from the best families and the operation had apparently been going on for over a decade. However, the families did not want their daughters' names exposed, so only minor charges were ever pressed.

But what do laws against "soliciting" actually prohibit? One cannot discuss something honestly, if one cannot call it by its real name. So does it include stimulating dance and sensual massage? And perhaps also sexual counselling and therapy? The only way you can prove soliciting, or solicitation, is by engaging in either. Equal enforcement of such a law is impossible and only sends out a moralizing message. Or have you ever heard of a police officer impersonating a high-class call girl, who goes straight to the punter's apartment or hotel room? You can always bug the room, but this type of escort knows that accepting gifts of money is not illegal. A rich man can also afford to fly to another country, or state, where prostitution is legal. And it is perfectly legal to pay for sex almost anywhere if you are filming it.

Craigslist erotic services section transformed both the meaning and means of being a sex worker. Such online services provide those who would do sex work a different kind of venue than the streets and brothels that had been the norm for so long. On the street, the sex worker is subject to constant harassment and a myriad of dangers, in a brothel at the mercy of pimps and madams. On the internet, one can open a virtual lemonade stand that operates according to self-imposed rules and regulations. Anonymity is almost guaranteed. The internet made sex work accessible to people who would never have considered it otherwise. It affords the ability to screen potential clients and, indeed, to be very discriminating if one wants to be. Many treat it as an extention of dating—getting financial benefits is just an added bonus.

One after another, the traditionally liberal Scandinavian countries have recently made the purchase of sex illegal. According to the Finnish law, purchasing sex from a victim of human trafficking is a crime. Even the attempt to purchase is punishable. The penalty for breaking the law is a fine or at maximum six months in prison. This new legislation has increased the risk of prostitutes becoming victims of violence by scaring away the good customers—the nasty clients will not go away. Procuration and human trafficking remain hidden, since the punters cannot risk telling the police about their suspicions. For law enforcement to be able to intervene, there has to be proof of procuration or human trafficking, and that is for the courts to decide, not the police. Criminalization has merely made the activity covert, which in itself is a threat to the security of the sex workers. The seller and the customer may be left with a differing impression of the sort of service and price they have agreed to. Putting the customers under the threat of penalty only makes the investigation of serious cases

283. "See Me," Stockholm, 2010.

more difficult, since it is no longer safe for them to share what they have seen with the police. Enforcing the law is also difficult, because cops cannot stand in the doorways ticketing people who have just bought sex.

Besides, as they say, "one always pays for sex." In the name of consistency, we should also outlaw marriages for money. In Victorian times, one was supposed to "lie back and think of England." Reciprocal sexual enjoyment with your loved one should be a goal, but the law cannot put every citizen under an obligation to always enjoy sex. Or maybe the police can spare the resources to monitor this with psychrometers and commando raids. Philosophers like Michel Foucault have pointed out that the easiest way to control a society is to convince each of its members—usually through taboo, legislation, or publicized threats of eternal damnation—to restrict their sexual power; as Wilhelm Reich made clear in *Die Massenpsychologie des Fascismus* (1933), if you control a person's sexuality, you control the whole person!

Government has no business in the bedroom, and indeed, moved there only after the Church-State controversy. The Church used to govern marriage, the most important step in life, and through it a wide social sphere. Nowadays, you are not supposed to marry for money or status, although we all know that some people do. Part of our culture says weddings are about true love, while another part says they are about toasters. A sham marriage is a legal term for pretending to be a couple in order to get an immigration visa, but it is hard to prove that any marriage is for real. People in general marry for lots of different reasons, such as love, security, and even money. If you married someone just so he could remain safely in the country, would that not be a marriage of love?

Spain's streamlining of its divorce laws in 2005 seems to have resulted in a fake divorce phenomenon in the country. Under the new regulations, couples could officially separate within three weeks, and Spanish family court judges soon began complaining that parents were divorcing to increase their children's chances of gaining admission into their preferred state school—a child receives extra points if they live in a single parent home. Each year during March, the cut-off month for entry into state schools, the number of official separations apparently rises by half compared to other months. Court officials claim to have seen couples who have recently divorced back in court seeking reconciliation after the school entry date. While the officials say they are now investigating whether the separations were genuine, faking divorce is not a criminal offence in Spain.[284]

In Italy and other European countries where large Muslim communities have settled, some officials favour recognizing polygamous marriage in order to ensure the wives' access to pensions, medical care, and other state benefits. Official estimates put the number of polygamous families in Italy at 14,000, but the number may be even higher. Many European Muslims take advantage of the so-called *'urfi* marriage, a less formal union performed by an imam that does not carry the same legal or social standing as regular marriage. In Islamic countries, the husband can by law marry no more women than he can adequately and justly care for, but the polygamists in the West are practising a more fundamentalist and abusive form of plural marriage. Since

284. Danny Wood, "Fake Divorce to Get School Places," BBC News, April 9, 2008.

they feel threatened by the Western culture around them, they often imprison their wives and confine them to a life of solitude completely dependent on the husband.[285]

People say that minority rights are important, but it is the individual rights that matter—a collection of individuals is a mob. Government does not grant rights, it can only regulate rights that we are all born with. Legalizing alternatives to traditional marriage is just another step in acknowledging that the right to marry is a state-granted privilege. Supporting it means you accept that the State has power to dictate hospital visitation and medical decisions, rights of survivorship, and filing joint tax returns. When Canada legalized same-sex marriage in 2004, its lawmakers forgot to make the necessary amendments to divorce law. The first couple to marry under the new law became the first to file for divorce, but had to wait for the Ontario Supreme Court to find the divorce law unconstitutional. In British Columbia, the definition of adultery was limited to extra-marital sex between a man and a woman, until a woman won a case in the state supreme court in 2005, allowing her to divorce her husband for having an affair with another man.

Marriage, as it exists in the West today, is essentially a Christian institution. Divorce, with its waiting period etc., stems from the Protestant tradition, not the ancient, secular one. The Reformer Martin Luther deemed divorces acceptable only if one spouse committed adultery or abandoned the other, and secular laws were enacted to buttress the inviolability of marriage. In England, adultery was the sole grounds for divorce until 1937. This led to the situation where even the amicably divorcing couples had to stage separate visits to Brighton or other disreputable coastal towns. Today, you only need to show that your marriage no longer has the means to continue, though marital infidelity still constitutes such a proof.

The legal consequences of marital infidelity have typically always been more severe for women than for men, an injustice that traces back to when the wife was the property of the husband. The lawmakers have essentially been interested in controlling women's behaviour: Luther concluded that men's broad shoulders and narrow hips tell about their spirituality, whereas women's narrow shoulders and broad hips betray carnality and lust. In France, a wife could be sent to prison for adultery until 1975. A man could only be fined, and only when the act of adultery had taken place at the family home. It has also been historically easier for men to divorce their wives for infidelity than vice versa. In the devoutly Catholic Ireland, divorce did not become legal until as late as 1997, and getting one still takes four years. During the previous decades, Irish judges deliberated on the separated parents' moral suitability for guardianship of their children.

In Italy, the family court judge still assesses the moral welfare of the child. The Italian family has the role of protecting its members, which impedes the family from breaking down, but also slows change. Like much of the Mediterranean region, Italy lags behind northern Europe in incorporating women into the workforce, and in social policies that support working mothers. Protecting the family is the most common grounds for condemning divorce and marital infidelity. In practice, the criminalization of adultery has always worked precisely against women and families.

285. Tracy Wilkinson, "Italy Grapples with Polygamy," *Los Angeles Times*, July 15, 2008.

Convicting a woman for infidelity can label her as a "whore" and seclude her from normal society.

In Poland, the adulterous party in a divorce case cannot apply for alimony. In fact, the adulterer cannot even get a divorce if the innocent party does not consent to it. Women's growing level of education and the means to earn their own living that come with it has led to states having less and less ability or interest to control people's private lives. The worst female employment rate in Europe is in Turkey, exacerbated by female illiteracy and poor education; one in every eight Turkish girls is out of school, often pushed into arranged marriages at an early age. In highly-educated Scandinavia, the courts no longer look at adultery or guilt; marital infidelity has no bearing on the granting of divorce, the division of property, or the custody of children—it is distinctly a private matter.

The number of women in U.S. prisons has increased fivefold in the last two decades, but the reason has nothing to do with some modern-day gender equality in crime. Female convicts remain as different from male ones as they were twenty years ago: whereas 50% of men were imprisoned for violent offences, more than two-thirds of women were convicted of non-violent drug or property crime. And although women accounted for nearly one in four arrests, they still made up only 7% of all inmates in state and federal prisons in 2005. However, women's imprisonment numbers have been growing at nearly twice the rate of men's because of rising substance abuse rates and tougher sentencing policies prompted by the War on Drugs. In California, women are often housed together regardless of the seriousness of their crimes. The vast majority of female offenders are parents of minors, and of those, nearly half are single mothers; yet most of the children never get to visit their mothers because the prisons are hundreds of miles away and they cannot travel so far.[286] Using the policies, practices, programs, and facilities designed for violent male offenders means missing out on cheaper, more successful methods of incarcerating and rehabilitating women.

The imprisonment of women for drug use only causes further detriment to them and their families. The increase of fatherless and motherless homes, which the current policy causes, is extraordinarily disruptive to the family unit and usually those harmed the most are the children. The long-term separation of children from their primary caretakers often results in a marked decline in the quality of shelter, nutrition, medical care, and emotional nurturing. Studies show that children whose primary guardian has spent significant amounts of time in prison are more likely to manifest behavioural difficulties and juvenile delinquency, often followed by adult criminal activity.[287] Moreover, a combination of mandatory reporting requirements and the child abuse and neglect laws serve to deprive drug-addicted mothers from access to medical services, pre-natal care, and even abuse counselling. They face criminal prosecution on serious charges, including drug distribution, assault, and murder, upon a legal theory that drug use while pregnant constitutes "delivery" of drugs to the unborn baby. This presents a novel category of penal sanctions, from which men are

---

286. Little Hoover Commission, op. cit.

287. Ludwig F. Lowenstein, "Recent Investigations into Criminality," *Criminologist* 15(2), Summer 1991, 97–106.

entirely excluded.[288]

Why is it illegal, but not uncommon, for adults to use certain narcotic substances in the privacy of their own homes? "Substance abuse" is not a pharmacological but a legal concept; "controlled substances" are those psychotropic drugs that have been criminalized. These prohibitions are a matter of public policy, though not necessarily of health policy. The vast majority of the millions who die through drug use, die through the use of legal drugs. Tobacco causes 40% of all hospital illnesses, while alcohol is blamed for more than half of all visits to emergency rooms—it is the single biggest preventable cause of death, killing one in every twenty-five people in the world.[289] In Russia alone, 40,000 people die from alcohol poisonings every year,[290] but in 5,000 years of recorded use, there are no known cases of lethal poisoning from cannabis anywhere. Quite the opposite, specific medical benefits of its active ingredients, tetrahydrocannabinol (THC) and cannabidiol (CBD), such as dimming pain and helping cancer patients combat nausea, have been thoroughly established in clinical trials.[291] What is more, while cannabis does contain carcinogens as potentially harmful as those in tobacco, the most heavily subsidized crop in the EU's Common Agricultural Policy, THC actually kills ageing cells, keeping them from becoming cancerous.[292] There is also growing evidence that CBD may stop cancer from metastasizing, or spreading throughout the body, offering a non-toxic alternative to chemotherapy.[293] And unlike prescription pain-killers like Vicodin® or Valium™, cannabis does not induce lethargy, but only relaxes the pain sufferer and lets him get on with his life; then again, you cannot patent a plant. Indeed, the main funders of the Partnership for a Drug-Free America are alcohol, tobacco, and pharmaceutical industries.

By prohibiting cannabis, we are steering people towards a substance that far too many people already abuse, that is, alcohol. There is no need for bouncers in Dutch coffee-shops; alcohol, however, is known to induce violence, towards one's self and others—about one-third of all violent crimes in the United States are committed

288. Alan B. Fischler, et al. "Report and Recommendations of the Drug Policy Task Force," New York County Lawyers' Association, New York, October, 1996.

289. David Nutt, et al. "Development of a Rational Scale to Assess the Harm of Drugs of Potential Misuse," *The Lancet* 369(9566), March 20/24, 2007, 1047–1053; Jürgen Rehm, et al. "Global Burden of Disease and Injury and Economic Cost Attributable to Alcohol Use and Alcohol-Use Disorders," *Ibid.* 373(9682), June 27/July 3, 2009, 2223–2233.

290. A. V. Nemtsov, "Alcohol-Related Human Losses in Russia in the 1980s and 1990s," *Addiction* 97(11), November 2002, 1413–1425.

291. C. Alvin Head, at al. "Use of Cannabis for Medical Purposes: CSAPH Report 3-I-09," AMA Council on Science and Public Health, Chicago, November 2009.

292. Donald P. Tashkin, et al. "Marijuana Use and Lung Cancer: Results of a Case-Control Study," American Thoracic Society International Conference, San Diego, May 24, 2006.

293. Sean D. McAllister, et al. "Cannabidiol as a Novel Inhibitor of Id-1 Gene Expression in Aggressive Breast Cancer Cells," *Molecular Cancer Therapeutics* 6(11), November 2007, 2921–2927.

under the influence of this perfectly legal substance.[294] Ask any police officer if they would rather arrest someone who is drunk or someone who is high on weed; their very jobs depend on a steady stream of arrests and prosecutions, and as long as the marijuana arrests keep coming, so do their paychecks. Drunk drivers kill more people each year than all the wars in the world put together, but according to the EU drug agency, there is no evidence that cannabis has any effect on a person's driving ability.[295] And not only is nicotine more addictive than heroin, but tobacco has a far higher death rate than either heroin or alcohol, and yet is sold alongside candy for children. Cocaine, on the other hand, is not physically addictive at all, and in moderate doses has similar effect as Ritalin, i.e. increased attention span, less impulsive behaviour, and better ability to focus, but prescription drug abuse is much more common. The greatest danger associated with smoking pot appears to be jail time. Almost half of all federal drug arrests are for possession of marijuana.[296] Nearly 100 million Americans have tried it, and some 15 million use it regularly.[297] In fact, cannabis is the most widely used drug worldwide, being consumed by 160 million people according to the 2005 UN drug report.[298]

Yet we should not speak collectively about "drugs," since illegal narcotics have no common effect that legal narcotics would lack. Cannabis and heroin are as different from each other as coffee and alcohol. The fact that the general public is led to think that all drugs are similar in effect has unfortunate and dangerous consequences: someone who smokes one or two joints every now or then might assume that heroin and crack cocaine are equally harmless. The effects also vary from person to person, those of methamphetamine, for example, ranging from increased focus through heightened libido to homicidal mania. Older people tend to avoid morphine-based drugs, because they fear that they will need higher and higher doses as they build tolerance and will become addicted. However, older patients develop tolerance very slowly, with patients under 50 requiring medication twice as strong as those over 60.[299] Opiate drugs in moderate doses have less-serious side effects than other painkillers: the primary side effects of opioids are nausea and constipation, while anti-inflammatory agents such as COX-2 inhibitors can induce both heart and kidney damage and gastric ulcers.[300]

A person can now be arrested for driving while intoxicated if they have any drugs or their metabolites in their bloodstream. The list of controlled substances is long, and

---

294. Lawrence A. Greenfeld, "Alcohol and Crime: An Analysis of National Data on the Prevalence of Alcohol Involvement in Crime," Bureau of Justice Statistics, Washington, D.C., April 28, 1998.

295. "Literature Review on the Relation between Drug Use, Impaired Driving and Traffic Accidents: CT.97.EP.14," European Monitoring Centre for Drugs and Drug Addiction, Lisbon, February 1999.

296. Federal Bureau of Investigation 2011, Arrests Table.

297. Substance Abuse and Mental Health Services Administration 2005.

298. United Nations Office on Drugs and Crime, op. cit.

299. Chante Buntin-Mushock, et al. "Age-Dependent Opioid Escalation in Chronic Pain Patients," *Anesthesia & Analgesia* 100(6), June 2005, 1740–1745.

300. David Spurgeon, "Older Patients Are at Smaller Risk of Opioid Tolerance Than Younger Patients," *British Medical Journal* 330(7502), May 28, 2005, 1230.

for the most part, there is no evidence that they lower the capacity to operate a motor vehicle. In fact, some of these substances are banned in professional sports because they *enhance* performance. Air force pilots and long-haul truckers have long used amphetamines to ward off drowsiness. What is more, the inactive metabolites of cannabis can stay in the blood for up to two months after it was taken, meaning that one is punished not for DWI, but for having smoked pot previously—something which carries its own, lesser penalty. The person may have also consumed the substance in a country or jurisdiction where it is legal. In 2008, the California Supreme Court poked another hole in the state's 1996 medical marijuana law, when it ruled that the voter-approved measure does not protect users from being fired for testing positive for cannabis at work.[301]

Would it not be silly to talk about a workplace alcohol problem, if some of the employees consumed alcohol in their free time? Funnily enough, this is precisely the logic on which workplace drug tests are founded. The effects of marijuana are temporary and go away after you stop using it. Unlike alcohol, it does not make people prone to do things they would not ordinarily do. It is singularly different from nearly all other drugs in the fact that, taken alone, it does not cause violent behaviour, nor does it permanently alter one's brain or otherwise have a lasting physical impact. Alcohol is a toxin, marijuana is not; that's why the latter does not give you a hangover. If the use of drugs or alcohol does not affect one's work, why would the employer have any right to interfere in it? The employer is not the police or government authority; its power over the employee is limited to the working hours. Or should private companies also keep tabs on their workers' traffic violations and obedience to the law in general outside the workplace? In any case, users have proven persistently creative at cheating on non-random drug tests, rendering the whole concept impracticable.

The demand for illicit drugs is as strong today as the thirst for bootleg liquor was during Prohibition. People throughout the millennia have turned to mood- and mind-altering substances, and they are not about to stop, no matter what anybody else says or does. In the preface to his book, *Ceremonial Chemistry* (1973), Dr. Thomas Szasz, M.D., wrote that he wished "to identify the moral and legal implications of the view that using and avoiding drugs are not matters of health and disease but matters of good and evil; that, in other words, drug abuse is not a regrettable medical disease but a repudiated religious observance."[302] The ritual consumption of hallucinogenic drugs was part and parcel of nearly every ancient religious tradition, but an hierarchical Church has no interest in granting its rank-and-file members genuine spiritual experiences, much less the means to independently reach them. The nature and content of the experiences that these substances induce are not artificial products of their pharmacological interaction with the brain, but authentic expressions of the human psyche revealing its functioning on levels ordinarily unavailable for observation and study; that is, a person who has "dropped acid" does not have an "acid trip," but a journey into deep recesses of his own mind. "Pursuing the religious life

301. *Ross v. RagingWire Telecommunications, Inc.*, 42 Cal. 4th 920 (2008).
302. 2003, xii.

today without using psychedelic drugs is like studying astronomy with the naked eye," as the '60s LSD guru Timothy Leary put it.[303] In 1993, after the U.S. Supreme Court had ruled that states could criminalize the use of peyote, a bitter-tasting cactus which contains mescaline, Congress changed the law to allow its sacramental use in Native American tribal services.

On the other hand, the New York Supreme Court has twice ruled that Twelve-Step Programs are inherently religious and that mandating attendance is a violation of constitutional rights; in fact, God is mentioned at least seven times in the twelve steps, whereas only one of them has anything directly to do with stopping substance abuse. More to the point, repeated studies have shown that the average person with a substance abuse problem will discontinue use on their own 20–30% of the time, whereas those enrolled in the AA have a dramatically decreased chance of achieving sobriety, with only 3–8% "making it."[304] In fact, the only form of organized rehabilitation that has been shown to work to any reasonable degree is substitution treatment; unfortunately, methadone has already proved more dangerous than heroin (which may explain why the Swiss have opted for a nationwide heroin maintenance programme). "Never trust anyone who doesn't drink." The only two reasons to refrain from alcohol are alcoholism and blind faith—both imply the lack of self-control.

There are, of course, more drug users than there are addicts—many more in fact—just as of the many who drink alcohol, only a few are alcoholics. Most consumers of illegal drugs, including crack cocaine and heroin, take them only occasionally. Teetotalism is decidedly a new thing: according to the Bible, Noah was the first brewer and Jesus turned water into wine. Monks used to brew beer and make wine, such as the famous Dom Perignon, for the longest time. Elizabethan statesmen were drunk from morning to night, if only because water was not safe to drink back then and tea had not yet been introduced to England. During the Renaissance, the typical English breakfast included a mug of ale or wine, and did so for the upper classes well into the modern age. In the warm south, where food goes bad quickly, there are still no underage drinking laws, or indeed, much alcoholism. There has been a lot of talk about the health benefits of red wine, even if excess use of alcohol is not considered beneficial. (Some studies show that, when consumed in moderation, alcohol can reduce the risk of heart attacks; Spain, a country with relatively high rates of alcohol consumption, has low rates of coronary disease.) The fact remains, intoxicants are good for your health—your mental health.

However far back in history you go, men and women have always used substances such as fermented grapes, plant juices, and hallucinogenic fungi to help them escape from their day-to-day worries and find peace and temporary contentment, to excite and stimulate themselves when they feel bored, and to give themselves energy when they feel tired. Primitive peoples chewed nuts and leaves and ate mushrooms to energize themselves; ancient priests used herbs in order to sway the mood of the congregants and to enter mystical states in which they communed with the gods.

---

303. 1998, 44.

304. Linda C. Sobel, et al. "Recovery from Alcohol Problems with and without Treatment: Prevalence in Two Population Surveys," *American Journal of Public Health* 86(7), July 1996, 966–972.

Opium was first used 7,000 years ago, alcohol was first brewed 5,000 years ago. The use of drugs to alter perception is older than industry, older than the law, older than medicine, and older even than agriculture.[305]

A physician will tell a drinker that it is dangerous to use alcohol to relieve real life problems, yet the same medical professional is ready to prescribe drugs for patients with physical or mental symptoms caused by social problems. Trouble is, it is impossible to produce effective relief from anxiety without producing an addiction to the agent responsible for providing that relief, for as soon as the person stops taking the substance, his original, unpleasant symptoms will recur. Thus any drug used to treat anxiety must—if it works—be addictive. But since therapeutic prescribing is clearly not recreational drug abuse, the term "dependence" is preferred to addiction, and the abstinence syndrome is dubbed a "discontinuance syndrome."[306]

The sales of prescription medication in America have grown nearly 400% in the last 15 years, and nearly half of all U.S. consumers are now on at least one prescription drug. At the same time, prescription medication has become the fastest-growing category of abused drugs, the biggest growth of abuse being among persons aged twelve to twenty-four.[307] In 2004, a federal study on teen drug abuse found that teenagers were, for the first time, more likely to have used a prescription painkiller to get high than they were to have experimented with any of the wide variety of illegal narcotics.[308] In other words, more adolescents had abused a legal prescription drug in 2004 than ecstasy, cocaine, crack, or LSD. Apparently, while overall drug use among young adults has declined slightly, abuse of prescription drugs among the "Ritalin generation" has been growing and will no doubt grow further as drug sales continue to increase.

Statistics show that a full third of teenagers abusing prescription drugs obtained them at home or from their parents.[309] Pills are overall more seductive to younger people because they see them as safer and less illegal. Girls in particular appear to perceive pills as "cleaner" than other narcotics: they are less likely than boys to use marijuana or cocaine, but equally likely to take prescription drugs. Pills are also often more attractive than other drugs because they lack the telltale signs of use, such as the distinctive smell of marijuana, or the disoriented state of drunkenness. Prescription pills can further be less expensive than other illegal drugs, methylphenidate or Ritalin, for example, selling for one or two USD a pill on the black market, though the street price rises before mid-terms and finals, when students use them to cram.

Many underage users do not even know what many of the pills are for or which are more addictive than others. Nor are they aware of how separate drugs interact or what constitutes a dangerous dose. The leading cause of acute liver failure in the

---

305. Coleman 1992.

306. "Benzodiazepine Dependence, Toxicity, and Abuse," American Psychiatric Association Task Force on Benzodiazepine Dependency, Washington, D.C., 1990.

307. Substance Abuse and Mental Health Services Administration, op. cit.

308. Partnership for a Drug Free America 2005.

309. "National Survey of American Attitudes on Substance Abuse XIII: Teens and Parents," The National Center on Addiction and Substance Abuse at Columbia University, New York, August 2008.

United States today, according to a landmark study published in the *Annals of Internal Medicine*, is not alcohol or hepatitis, but overdose of acetaminophen (paracetamol), the number one over-the-counter analgesic; in fact, Aspirin kills more people in the U.S. every year than does heroin.[310] According to the Drug Abuse Warning Network, visit to hospital emergency rooms increased significantly nationwide from 1994 to 2002 for overdoses of prescription medication: e.g. overdoses of OxyContin, or oxycodone, increased by 450%, those of Lortab, or hydrocodone, by 170%, and those of benzodiazepines such as Valium and Xanax by 41%; the data also shows that many overdose patients were using more than one drug.[311] Federal law prohibits the possession of controlled substances without a prescription and many schools forbid students to carry unprescribed medication, but enforcement has proven difficult. An arm's length relationship has existed between colleges and police since the 1960s, as law enforcement has largely turned a blind eye to drugs on campus.

Today, public figures justify past drug use as "youthful indiscretions" and the matter is dropped. Drugs are bad, because if you take them, you might become President of the United States or win the Olympics. Among the large population of rich white people, who have smoked pot and not been arrested for it, is Michael Bloomberg, the current Mayor of New York City, and once the 8th richest person in the country. Asked during his 2001 mayoral campaign by *New York* Magazine if he had ever smoked it, Mr. Bloomberg, a Johns Hopkins *and* Harvard graduate, replied: "You bet I did. And I enjoyed it."[312] But after he was elected and his remarks were used by advocates of marijuana legalization, Mayor Bloomberg said his administration would vigorously enforce the drug laws. Nor does Obama want to expend his political capital on this issue: he may be the third consecutive President to have used recreational drugs in his youth, but far from scaling back funding for drug interdiction and law enforcement, his administration's 2010 budget increased the levels established under George W. Bush. Will any police department in the United States conduct a systematic raid of a college dorm at a prominent university with the goal of arresting anyone in possession of marijuana? Of course not—if such an action were to take place on any broader scale, the arrests would be in the thousands. Will poor non-Caucasians continue to be arrested by local law enforcement for possession of small amounts of pot? You can bet your black ass they will.

"Ok, right now, all over this great nation of ours, 'hundred thousand white people from the suburbs are cruisin' around downtown asking every black person they see 'You got any drugs? You know where I can score some drugs?' *Think* about the effect that has on the psyche of a black person, on their possibilities. I—God, I guarantee you, bring a hundred thousand black people into your neighborhood, into fuckin'

310. George Ostapowicz, et al. "Results of a Prospective Study of Acute Liver Failure at 17 Tertiary Care Centers in the United States," *Annals of Internal Medicine* 137(12), December 17, 2002, 947–954; Alvin C. Bronstein, et al. "2009 Annual Report of the American Association of Poison Control Centers' National Poison Data System," *Clinical Toxicology* 48(10), December 2010, 979–1178.

311. "Trends in Drug-Related Emergency Department Visits, 1994–2002 At a Glance," *The DAWN Report*, November 2003.

312. Meryl Gordon, "Citizen Mike," April 16, 2001.

Indian Hills, and they're asking every white person they see 'You got any drugs? You know where I can score some drugs?,' within a *day* everyone would be selling. Your friends. Their kids. Here's why: it's an unbeatable market force, man. It's a 300% mark-up value. You go out on the street and make $500 in two hours, come back and do whatever you want to do with the rest of your day and, I'm sorry, you're telling me that—you're telling me that white people would still be going to law school?"[313]

It has been said that modern Hollywood is a factory where people high on cocaine make movies about people high on heroin, and the audience wants to see the movies even when they make the drugs look awful. No amount of didactic condemnation from the silver screen has ever slowed down the trade or done anything to persuade the corner boys that they would be better off trying to improve their grades. Charlie Parker, the legendary jazz saxophonist who ruined his life with drugs, tried to tell his fellow musicians that they were fooling themselves, if they thought they could play better when they were high. Not many listened to him, so why would anyone listen to Nancy Reagan, when she told Americans to "Just say no"?

Each generation usually has its own drug of choice: LSD was it in the '70s, cocaine in the '80s, and ecstasy and crack in the '90s. Today, it seems to be crystal methamphetamine, a chemical variant of amphetamine with much more powerful effects. The dirty little secret about Silicon Valley is that the IT business demands more of you than you can produce: the only way to continually work 60 or 70 hours a week is to stay lit. The "soccer moms" have a similar agenda, with the added incentive of losing weight. Typically a friend gives a housewife a few lines of meth, and she finds that not only has she energy to burn, but the pounds just seem to melt away. And every time she begins to gain weight, she goes back to it. Cue the public service announcement on the dangers of methamphetamine and everyone just rolls their eyes—remember when pot was the gateway to heroin?

Potent, accessible, and cheap, crystal meth is more addictive than heroin or crack cocaine, and can be purchased for as little as twenty bucks a pop. What is more, cooking meth is as simple as a trip to the local supermarket. Sometimes dubbed "ghetto prozac," it has overtaken cocaine as the biggest drug problem in the U.S., prompting many states to try and limit the sales of the over-the-counter decongestant pseudoephedrine that is commonly used to make it in small, home laboratories. However, it is also easy to produce from chemicals found on farms, and the homemade labs are less easy to detect in the countryside. Since the DEA has shut down many of the American mom-and-pop labs that generated an uneven, impure product, meth is now coming from major suppliers in Mexico; which only means that the quality is better—and the price even lower.

If there ever was a case where the cure was worse than the disease, the War on Drugs has to be it. War, noun: a conflict carried on by force of arms, as between nations or between parties within a nation; drug, noun: any substance, other than food, intended to affect the structure or any function of the body. In declaring a war on drugs, the United States has declared war on its own citizens. As the nation's longest running armed conflict, the drug war has been waged with equal

---

313. *Traffic.* Dir. Steven Soderbergh. Initial Entertainment Group, 2000.

determination by both Republican and Democratic administrations. How much they hate those evil terrorists! How much they decry corrupt dictators and brutal governments! Meanwhile, their drug-related foreign policies have fostered political instability, wreaked environmental and health disasters, and made life even harder for indigenous subsistence farmers in places like Latin America and Central Asia.

Between 2000 and 2005, the U.S. spent about $4.5 billion of taxpayer money on "Plan Colombia," a six-year effort to fight drug trafficking and to train the Colombian army to battle insurgents—the largest amount of U.S. aid outside the Middle East.[314] The centrepiece of the initiative formulated by President Bill Clinton in 1999 has been the aerial spraying of country's coca plantations, which yield the raw material for 80% of the world's cocaine and help finance rebels in the civil war. According to U.S. and Colombian officials, they eradicated a record-breaking million acres of coca plants in 2004, yet the price and purity of the cocaine on sale in America remained stable. Whereas annual cocaine production fell 11% in Colombia, it rose 23% in Peru and 35% in Bolivia, according to the 2005 UN drug report. Overall, coca cultivation in the Andean region increased 3% in 2004, the UN study says.[315] Colombia remains the world's top cocaine producer and is reportedly still the source of 90% of the drug in the United States.

The price of an illegal substance is determined more by the cost of distribution than of production. The mark-up between the coca field and the consumer is more than a hundredfold. Even if dumping toxic chemicals on the crops of peasant farmers quadruples the local price of coca leaves, this has little impact on the street price, which is set mainly by the risk of getting cocaine into the United States. Consequently, there has been little interruption to the export of cocaine, which U.S. authorities estimate to be as high as 1,000 metric tonnes a year.[316] Nor is the decades-long armed strife in Colombia any closer to an end; the human rights record of the Colombian army has only worsened since 2000, with reports of collaboration between the army and the paramilitaries accused of civilian massacres. For every capo captured, another five are waiting to take his place.

More than 30,000 paramilitaries were demobilized in 2006 and many of their leaders extradited to the U.S. to face drugs charges. However, extraditing the militia leaders to another country means that they will not face justice at home or reveal their alleged links to government figures. Investigations have linked dozens of current and former politicians to the paramilitaries, while the UN High Commission for Human Rights says Colombia's U.S.-backed security forces are engaging in "systematic and widespread" executions of civilians as part of their counter-insurgency campaign; more than 2,300 members of the security forces are under investigation for such extrajudicial killings.[317] Colombian opposition groups reacted angrily after details of a

---

314. Connie Veillette, "Plan Colombia: A Progress Report," Congressional Research Service, Washington, D.C., June 22, 2005.

315. United Nations Office on Drugs and Crime, op. cit.

316. John A. Glaze, "Opium and Afghanistan: Reassessing U.S. Counternarcotics Strategy," Strategic Studies Institute, U.S. Army War College, Carlisle, PA, October 2007.

317. "U.N. Says Colombian Military Executing Civilians," CNN, November 1, 2008; "Colombian Army Commander Resigns," BBC News, November 4, 2008.

military deal with the United States to help rid Colombia of drug gangs and left-wing rebel groups were made public in 2009. Under the ten-year deal, the U.S. military will not only have access to seven Colombian army, navy, and air force bases, but will also be able to use civilian airports under conditions that have still not been made clear.

For decades, the opium poppies that feed the world's drug pipeline have been harvested by poor farmers in the mountain valleys of Afghanistan trying to fend off starvation. The trade is booming partly as a result of the U.S. overthrow of the fiercely anti-drugs Taliban régime: in 2001, opium prices surged tenfold from 2000, to a record high, after the Taliban all but eliminated opium poppy cultivation across the Afghan territory under its control. Despite U.S.-sponsored eradication efforts, opium production in Afghanistan broke all records in 2007, reaching an historic high. According to the Afghanistan Ministry of Counter Narcotics, opium trade employed some 3.3 million Afghans, while the opium crop constituted nearly 477,000 acres of cultivated land in the country. At approximately 8,200 metric tonnes, it amounted to more than nine-tenths of world production, making it the biggest narco-crop in history.[318] Afghan opium, morphine, and heroin feed the habits of about 10 million people, or two-thirds of the world's opiate users.[319] Not only that, but drug lords seem to actually pose a bigger threat to Afghanistan's emerging democracy than terrorists.

At the urging of the U.S. and other Western allies, President Karzai continued to accommodate former warlords in the central government in hope that they would be easier to control inside the halls of power. On the contrary, they have taken advantage of drug trafficking and are protecting it: militia fighters have followed their commanders into the local police force, turning it into a private army in police uniform; a key link in the trafficking network is formed by the national highway police, largely made up of former mujahedin trained to protect the main road linking Afghanistan's regions. At the same time, money generated by trafficking—which the UN estimates is worth $3 billion a year—funds attacks by the resurrected Taliban fighters who used to ban opium as un-Islamic.[320] The warlords who once fought them collect a tribute on drug shipments headed to Pakistan, Iran, and Tajikistan; as long as the Taliban pay cash, bygones are considered bygones.

Until the U.S. invasion, Afghanistan was known only as an opium exporter, not as a major heroin producer. After the post-Taliban instability, small heroin labs sprang up in hundreds of Afghan villages. Even if the authorities should find them all and put a stop to poppy cultivation altogether, there is enough opium stashed in village wells and other caches to keep labs and smugglers working for 10 to 15 years. Consequently, in 2008, the worst drought in a generation left millions of Afghans starving, but barely dented the world opium supply.[321] The drug cartels have a much bigger budget than the elected government, so they have left the police force and army riddled with corruption and virtually useless. NATO military units largely overlook the huge, openly-run drug bazaars in fear that cracking down on traffickers might alienate the

318. United Nations Office on Drugs and Crime 2009.

319. Idem. 2005.

320. Ibid.

321. Idem. 2009.

Afghan tribesmen in the south and increase popular support for the insurgents. Drug crops like poppies and coca are vastly more lucrative than wheat or barley, and the poverty-stricken tenant farmers depend on the little money they receive from them to eke out a miserable living. However, should opium be made legal, it would boost Afghanistan's legitimate economy by an estimated 60%.[322]

Smaller harvests will only push prices up and encourage more planting and trafficking. A government crackdown cuts competition, meaning that only the professional dealers will remain. The more restrictions, the more their business will boom. Arrests and seizures just tell you how busy the police are, they tell you nothing of the impact they have. The truth is that big drug busts do nothing to stem the flow of drugs or change the complexion of the culture, except for making a handful of uninformed citizens and concerned parents feel better for about two minutes, while the street price of the drug in question jumps 20% for a week. By for example reducing purity, dealers are able to adapt quickly to interruptions in availability, enabling them to maintain their profit margins. The rules of supply and demand apply to the drug trade as well: the bottom line is not how much is produced or how much is eradicated, but that there will always be enough supply to meet the demand in the United States and elsewhere.

All the War on Drugs has accomplished is to make the drugs cheaper and purer than ever before. Nor do the dealers go around killing each other when business is good, i.e. when the police is not interfering; and if you take out one dealer, you help another, meaning that narcotics officers are *ipso facto* working for drug dealers. Since the legal drinking age is 21 in the U.S., it is easier for American youth to get drugs than to get alcohol; yet far more teens die in alcohol-related incidents than in those caused by all the illicit drugs combined. Despite the easy availability of drugs in the Netherlands, a 1997 study by the Centre for Drugs Research at Amsterdam University found that marijuana use is twice as high in the U.S. as in Holland.[323] Embarrassed drug warriors blame this on alleged cultural differences, but harsh rules make little difference to the number of addicts even in fairly similar countries: tough-on-drugs Sweden and more liberal Norway have precisely the same addiction rates; in the UK, the temporary downgrading of cannabis offences to a lesser status was also accompanied by a drop in use.[324]

In 2001, Portugal began a remarkable policy experiment, removing criminal penalties for possession of all drugs, including heroin. Many predicted disastrous results, soaring addiction rates, and the small European country turning into a haven for "drug tourists." The UN drug czar even suggested that the Portuguese policy was in violation of international treaties, which prevent countries from legalizing drugs. Now that ten years have passed, policy experts can study the results: the doomsayers were wrong and there is a widespread consensus in Portugal that decriminalization has been a success. In its 2009 *World Drug Report*, the UN had little but kind words

---

322. Ibid.

323. Manja D. Abraham, et al. "Licit and Illicit Drug Use in the Netherlands, 1997," Centrum voor Drugsonderzoek, Amsterdam, 1999.

324. United Nations Office on Drugs and Crime, op. cit.

for the country's radical approach.[325] The debate in Portugal itself has shifted quite dramatically to minor adjustments in the existing arrangement, with no real debate on whether drugs should once again be criminalized.

A post-enlargement crime explosion was feared when the EU opened up its borders to ten new countries in Eastern Europe. One concern was that the open borders would increase the flow of illicit drugs from the East to Western markets. However, the reverse has turned out to be true: while drug use has settled down in the West, it is rising noticeably in Eastern Europe. New EU member states have transformed from drug transit routes to major consumers of synthetic drugs like ecstasy and amphetamines. The communist governments considered narcotics an "imperial scourge" of the West, another way to degrade the worker's soul. Since the salaries in Slovakia, for example, have soared, the use of synthetic drugs almost doubled in the first two years following its accession to the EU. Even the Slovakian police admit that it would be a waste of resources to try to stop the influx of drugs from the West into their country: the national drug consumption is gradually reaching Western levels and there is absolutely nothing they can do about it.[326]

In fact, drug use has already exploded in Russia; and in Russia, "drugs" does not mean marijuana, but heroin. Even President Medvedev acknowledges that it is such a big problem that it threatens national security. In a couple of years, the country has gained two million new intravenous drug users. Most of the young addicts are members of the Russian middle class, i.e. the part of the nation on whose relative prosperity Prime Minister Putin's power rests. One does not need a tin foil hat to see that the stigmatization of drug use is an effective means of maintaining order, fear, and discipline. It is not that the Kremlin was genuinely interested in fighting the drug problem; if it were, it would do all it could to help the West succeed in Afghanistan, for during the last few years, Russia has become the principal transit route and market for Afghan heroin. Even so, alcohol remains a bigger problem for Russia than drugs, and although both of its leaders are teetotallers, weeding out alcoholism could prove risky: Russia adopted a prohibition act in 1914 and it led to a revolution; Gorbachev embarked on a large-scale abstinence campaign by, for example, restricting the sale of alcohol, and that led to the fall of the Soviet Union.

By criminalizing a basic human behaviour, we have done nothing but allow vast criminal conspiracies not only to flourish, but to take over the governments of countries like Afghanistan and Colombia, while more than 140,000 Americans are arrested every month in an unending procession of prisons and jails.[327] "Well, in all honesty, I don't feel that what I've done is a crime. And I think it's illogical and irresponsible for you to sentence me to prison. Because, when you think about it, what did I really do? I crossed an imaginary line with a bunch of plants."[328] As an illicit commodity, narcotics cost and generate extravagant sums of untaxed money, a powerful incentive for dishonest police officers. Just as sure as the Pope is Catholic,

325. Ibid.

326. Tamsin Smith, "EU Status Raises Slovak Drug Woes," BBC News, May 4, 2005.

327. Federal Bureau of Investigation, op. cit. Table 29.

328. *Blow*, op. cit.

law enforcement in Mexico is corrupt, but there is not a major police force in the world that would have evaded the problem: corrupt law enforcement officers everywhere are confiscating and converting drugs to their own use, robbing and extorting pushers, taking up dealing themselves, planting dope on suspects, intimidating or murdering witnesses.

The U.S. Border Patrol is now the nation's largest law enforcement agency, and the stepped-up border security only makes corruption all the more necessary to smugglers. In 2005, a federal sting operation exposed the shocking openness to bribery among American military and police on the U.S.-Mexico border. Uniformed national guardsmen used their official vehicles to carry hundreds of kilos of cocaine into the U.S., while a federal inspector waved trucks he knew to be carrying drugs safely across the border. The defence lawyers for the dozens of guardsmen, immigration agents, Air Force personnel, and prison guards who were charged or pled guilty described their clients as only "the bottom tier"—a federal grand jury indicted a former IRS intelligence chief in San Diego on charges of covering up a drug and immigrant smuggling ring. Even if just a tiny fraction of border officials is corrupt, it only takes a few to help move large amounts of drugs or illegal immigrants.

The War of Drugs and the clampdown on immigration from Mexico form a highly volatile mixture: would-be immigrants put themselves in greater physical and legal danger by muling drugs for smugglers who promise to see them safely across Arizona deserts; when the security on the U.S.-Mexico line was tightened in 2005, attacks on American Border Patrol agents doubled—which was inevitable, since neither human nor drug traffic have diminished, and the desperation of those trying to get in is no lower than it has ever been.[329] The income gap between the United States and Mexico remains the widest between any two contiguous countries in the world, and raising the costs and risks of undocumented entry has only discouraged illegal immigrants from going back home; having faced the hazards of border crossing, they prefer not to do so again, instead staying longer and increasingly sending for their families. Not only that, but the tightened security has also convinced many Mexican drug cartels that it is easier to grow marijuana in the States than to smuggle it across the border. With scant demands for cultivation, watering, or fertilizing, marijuana can be easily grown almost anywhere; as a hardy perennial, it needs no year-after-year replanting, nor pesticides or herbicides. In fact, the value of U.S. marijuana crops was estimated at around $36 billion in 2005, making it more valuable than the country's largest legal crop, maize, which produced only some $23 billion in revenue.[330]

One consequence of tightening border control is that the excess supply of Colombian cocaine and Asian heroin gets backed up and bartered in Mexico, the world's most lucrative border smuggling corridor. A trade that once bypassed Mexico is now taking root there too, as the carters have opened up local markets to avoid risking the tightened border control and to take advantage of growing Mexican affluence. Street-level drug dealers are rarely prosecuted in Mexico, since federal courts are saturated with bigger cases and local judges cannot interfere. Yet the

329. Richard Marosi, "Violent Border Clashes Surging," *Los Angeles Times*, October 31, 2005.

330. Jon Gettman, "Marijuana Production in the United States," *The Bulletin of Cannabis Reform*, December 2006.

country's corruption-prone police often shake down casual users, threatening long jail sentences if people do not pay. Meanwhile, the army-backed crackdown on gangs has forced cartels to seek new ways of making money to fund their operations and extortion and protection rackets are suddenly becoming common. In fact, according to national media, Mexico has overtaken Colombia and Iraq in the number of kidnappings.[331]

Ciudad Juárez has been called "the most dangerous city on earth." Felix Batista, a U.S. anti-kidnapping expert, who has negotiated the release of dozens of hostages in Latin America, was himself abducted by gunmen in Mexico. A Cuban-American from Miami, he was kidnapped in 2008 as he stepped outside a restaurant to answer his cell phone in the northern Mexican city of Saltillo. So we have kidnappings, extortions, murders, and skyrocketing addiction rates that are beginning to match those in the United States. The rising drug addiction in Mexico helps the international drug trade by making it easier to find "mules," people so desperate for quick cash that they are willing to smuggle drugs into the U.S. At the same time, the talk among better-off Mexicans is whether they should try to leave the country rather than risk their children getting kidnapped.

Washington made Mexico vulnerable by cracking down on the Colombian cartels, which then turned to Mexican crime organizations to move their drugs to the United States. When cocaine consumption first took off in the U.S. during the 1970s and '80s, the cartels' principal smuggling route involved island-hopping across the Carribean in a light aircraft. It was precisely the success of American drug warriors in shutting down this route that brought big-time organized crime to Mexico. Small gangs had long run marijuana and heroin across the Mexican border, but the move into cocaine made them far more powerful; they gained control of retail distribution in many American cities, allowing them to dictate terms to the Colombians—seventy percent of the cocaine that enters the United States passes through Mexico first.[332]

In 2000, the Mexican government disturbed this hornets' nest, when it began arresting and prosecuting major domestic drugs distributors, who had previously relied on bribes and corruption to maintain their peaceful co-existence with the government. The move to crush the cartels, which for many years had operated with minimal government interference, unleashed a brutal underworld war. The latest escalation in violence began after the high-profile arrests early last decade of several cartel bosses, including heads of the Arellano-Félix family, which had long controlled trafficking through Tijuana, opening the field for the brutal Sinaloa and Gulf cartels to push their way in. The cartels are now engaged in a fierce war as they compete for lucrative trade routes and try to fill power vacuums left following the extradition of several major cartel leaders to the United States.

In Mexico, Guatemala, and other countries in the region, drug traffickers have not only gunned down rivals, but killed scores of public officials and journalists. Former Drug Czar General McCaffrey testified in 2009 that "squad-sized units of the police and [Mexican] army have been tortured, murdered, and their decapitated bodies

331. "Mexico Prepares for Mass Protests Against Insecurity," AFP, August 30, 2008.

332. United Nations Office on Drugs and Crime, op. cit.

publicly left on display."[333] Beheadings, bodies burned alive in acid, faces sliced off and sewed to a soccer ball are just some of the gruesome terror tactics copied from the brutal conflict in Iraq; the death toll in Tijuana is now higher than in Baghdad. Mass graves are commonplace, and the terror the cartels sow has silenced the media in several Mexican towns along the border with the United States. Border towns in both countries have seen their economies disappear. It used to be common for borderlanders on both sides to cross over to shop, dine, visit family and friends, or just soak in a different atmosphere. Today, from the Gulf of Mexico to the Pacific coast, shopkeepers on the U.S. side see only a trickle of Mexican customers. Similarly, arrests of illegal immigrants on the border have fallen to levels unseen since the 1970s as the ailing U.S. economy appears to be deterring people from trekking north. The average annual inflow of illegal immigrants has tumbled from 425,000 in 2000 to 150,000 in 2009. Exits have outnumbered arrivals since 2007, with the total population of illegals falling from 12 million to 11.1 million.[334]

Mexican President Vicente Fox had taken a relatively soft approach to fighting the drug cartels, but all that changed when Felipe Calderón took office in December 2006. Politically weak after winning a disputed election, Calderón chose a popular issue by taking a tougher approach to drug trafficking after two decades during which Mexico's war on drugs had been crippled by corruption and incompetence. Mexico's disadvantage, compared with Colombia's centralized police service, is a disjointed system of local, state, and federal forces. All three are notoriously corrupt, so President Calderón sought to bypass them using the military. In what is one of the largest domestic deployments in Mexican history, Calderón has sent more than 45,000 soldiers across the country since taking office in response to drug-related violence that has killed more nearly 50,000 people since 2007 and shows no signs of abating any time soon. In a setback to basic democracy, civilian authorities have essentially been supplanted by the army.

In nearly every Mexican state where the army has been deployed, residents have accused soldiers of numerous grave human rights violations. According to Human Rights Watch, the armed forces are involved in rape, murder, and torture. The abuses go unpunished because the military handles all allegations of crimes under its own justice system. According to the HRW report, "None of the military investigations . . . has led to a criminal conviction of even a single soldier."[335] The cartels are also breaking with their tradition of avoiding civilian casualties in order to put pressure on Calderón, who has begun a massive police recruiting and training effort to reduce his dependence in the drug war on the military. With the police strained and outgunned, the crisis created an opening for a motley crew of private security companies and contractors that offer services not only to wealthy individuals and corporations, but also to local governments and municipalities.

---

333. Barry R. McCaffrey, "Narco-Violence in Mexico: A Growing Threat to U.S. Security," *American Diplomacy*, November 25, 2008.

334. Jeffrey S. Passel, et al. "U.S. Unauthorized Immigration Flows Are Down Sharply Since Mid-Decade," Pew Hispanic Center, Washington, D.C., September 1, 2010.

335. "Uniform Impunity: Mexico's Misuse of Military Justice to Prosecute Abuses in Counternarcotics and Public Security Operations," Human Rights Watch, New York, April 2009.

In 2008, President Bush signed a three-year $400-million package to help Mexico fight the cartels, who control both the internal market and the lucrative flow of drugs across the border, which is estimated to bring in more than $14 billion a year. In fact, the U.S. Drug Enforcement Agency estimates that the cartels are spending hundreds of millions just in bribes each year, while the Mexican government forces will continue to be undertrained, under-equipped, and outgunned even with U.S. aid.[336] And this aid was held up for years, mostly because U.S. legislators were concerned that the money might end up in the hands of corrupt Mexican officials. Every major human rights group opposed releasing the money and most of the funds earmarked for Mexico have yet to find their way there. Instead, they are funding American defence and security contractors, who have refused to disclose how exactly the money is being used.

The cartels offer Mexican police and politicos a choice: *plato o ploma*, "silver or lead"—take a bribe or take a bullet. Increasingly, people in Michoacan, the home state of President Calderón, pay protection money to *La Familia* in lieu of taxes to the government. Brusing aside domestic considerations, Señor Calderón has stepped up the extradition of traffickers to the United States, sending hundreds north so far. Yet a Senate committee in Washington was told that the presence of the Mexican drug cartels in the U.S. has more than quadrupled between 2006 and 2009.[337] In its 2010 *National Drug Threat Assessment*, the Justice Department said that Mexican groups were active in every region of the U.S. The bloodshed has spread to American cities, even into the heartland.[338]

U.S. officials are faced with the choice of either walking away or supporting the Mexican President's strategy, even with the risk that counter-narcotics intelligence, equipment, and training could end up in the hands of cartel bosses. Cartel operatives have infiltrated Interpol, the U.S. Embassy in Mexico City, and even DEA operations. The Bush measure, known as the Merida Initiative, was pushed through by lawmakers who were impressed by the Mexican President's commitment to working more closely with U.S. law enforcement. But by 2009, Mexico was named by the U.S. Joint Forces Command as the most likely place after Pakistan to suffer a "rapid and sudden collapse."[339] In response, Felipe Calderón told the press that the main cause of Mexico's drug gang problems was "having the world's biggest consumer [of narcotics] next to us."[340] He rejected U.S. concern that his country could become a failed state, while pointing out that it was impossible to smuggle tonnes of cocaine into the United States without the complicity of some American authorities.

The U.S. Justice Department pronounced the Mexican drug cartels "a national

---

336. "National Drug Threat Assessment 2009," National Drug Intelligence Center, Washington, D.C., December 2008.

337. "Law Enforcement Responses to Mexican Drug Cartels," Subcommittee on Crime and Drugs and Senate Caucus on International Narcotics Control, Washington, D.C., March 17, 2009.

338. "National Drug Threat Assessment 2010," National Drug Intelligence Center, Washington, D.C., February 2010.

339. "Joint Operation Environment 2008: Challenges and Implications for the Future Joint Force," Suffolk, VA, November 25, 2008.

340. "US Corruption Fuels Drug Trade: Mexican President," AFP, March 4, 2009.

security threat"[341] even as law enforcement officers on both sides of the border have never seen anything like the flood of money and guns now surging into Mexico. Except for occasional random inspections, the American border authorities do not make exit inspections of people and vehicles when they leave the country. The Mexican police estimate that 100% of drug-related killings are committed with smuggled U.S. weapons.[342] Mexico is a rich market for gun smugglers because it bans high-caliber automatic weapons, even in law enforcement, and has strict gun control laws that make it extremely difficult for members of the public to buy handguns. In August 2009, Mexico replaced all 700 of its customs officers with new recruits and doubled their number to 1,400—to little avail. Meanwhile, the U.S. military is already employing border security techniques mastered in the war zones of Iraq and Afghanistan, including unmanned aerial drones.

President Calderón's March 2010 speech in Juarez calling for the United States to share more responsibility in the battle against drug traffickers was greeted with hundreds of demonstrators demanding the withdrawal of Mexican troops from the town. Protesters frustrated with unrelenting violence held up signs reading "government assassins" and accused the President of living "on another planet."[343] A poll in the Mexican newspaper *Milenio* a few days later found 59% of respondents thought the cartels were winning the drug war, compared with just 21% who thought the government was.[344] Political analysts say Calderón's campaign has only succeeded in pushing violence from one region to another, without uprooting the cartels that challenge the power of the Mexican state. It could take decades and billions of dollars more to establish the corruption-resistant criminal justice institutions necessary for eliminating the cartels and their government benefactors. As Colombia and Mexico become more effective at targeting trafficking, the fear is that the burden may shift to other, even less equipped Latin American countries and the entire process will begin anew.

By prohibiting drugs, society is dodging responsibility; if drugs are illegal, people take them at their own risk, and will not get treated for abuse, but get jailed even for recreational use. Crack cocaine, heroin, and amphetamines can be highly addictive and harmful, both physically and psychologically; but prohibition only makes those dangers worse, unleashing chemicals of unknown content and potency on the vulnerable, while deterring addicts from seeking help with their dependency. The United States does not have a lot of problems with violence among alcohol dealers—the very thought of rival gangs from Miller and Budweiser having deadly gunfights in the streets sounds absolutely ridiculous to us now; but back in the '20s, when alcohol was illegal, that is exactly what we had. Regulated legalization would remove the

341. "Attorney General Holder Holds a Justice Department News Conference on a Drug Enforcement Issue," Political Transcript Wire, February 25, 2009.

342. Manuel Roig-Franzia, "U.S. Guns Behind Cartel Killings in Mexico," *Washington Post*, October 29, 2007.

343. Julian Cardona, "Protests Greet Mexico's Calderon After U.S. Killings," Reuters, March 16, 2010.

344. Ken Ellingwood, "U.S. Pledges More Help in Mexico Drug War," *Los Angeles Times*, March 23, 2010.

obscene profits from modern drug dealing that attract the needy and greedy and breed armed violence.

When alcohol was criminalized in the U.S., the murder rate soared; the year it was made legal again, the number of murders fell off a cliff—and continued its drop for the next ten years. Rates of alcoholism did remain the same, but deaths from alcohol poisoning declined dramatically as beer replaced moonshine.[345] Just as Al Capone was bankrupted by the legalization of alcohol, so could we bankrupt the Mexican cartels and the Taliban, before they cause the total collapse of two large countries. In 2006, President Calderón's predecessor, Vicente Fox, actually proposed drug legalization, and the Mexican Congress voted in favour of it—but the Bush administration went ape-shit. They applied so much pressure that, at the last minute, President Fox vetoed his own proposal. Meanwhile, Joaquín "El Chapo" Guzmán, the alleged head of the ruthless Sinaloa cartel, was named by *Forbes* Magazine as one of the world's top billionaires.

Spraying crops, seizing shipments, and arresting dealers can drive up prices and create temporary shortages, but it does not stop drug use. Addicts will simply have to pay more for an inferior product or switch to other, often more harmful substances. Cocaine users might move to powder amphetamine or crystal meth, while heroin addicts try out oxycodone. Dozens of studies from around the world suggest that inexpensive needle exchange programs not only reduce HIV, but attract addicts to recovery. Substance abuse treatment programs, on the other hand, have cost California taxpayers more than $1 billion since 1989, but have had no effect on keeping people off drugs so that they do not end up back in prison.[346] The privately-owned U.S. prison industry charges American taxpayers approximately $22,000 a year per prisoner, making it the single greatest expense of the War on Drugs—one which most Americans mistake for just about the best thing the government does for them.[347]

Private prisons are like the hotel business: they live and die on occupancy. Pot smokers make much more amenable lodgers than do crazed murderers and there is a huge Washington lobby that makes sure that the sentencing guidelines reflect this preference. There is a company called the Corrections Corporation of America listed on the New York Stock Exchange, which is convenient, since that is where all the real crime is taking place anyway. Prison spending in the U.S. is now greater than that for any other major program, except for public schools and health care. And prisoners are, by definition, outside society, and contribute nothing to it. They will not be reformed, nor will they be cured; quite the contrary, they tend to continue their life of crime from within the prison walls. Despite prisons crowded with inmates, massive amounts of illegal drugs continue to flow into the country. Harvard economist Jeffrey A. Miron has calculated that drug prohibition costs the U.S. government $41.3 billion a year in

345. "After the War on Drugs: Tools for Debate," Transform Drug Policy Foundation, Bristol, November 2007.

346. Matthew L. Cate, "Special Review into In-Prison Substance Abuse Programs Managed by the California Department of Corrections and Rehabilitation," Office of the Inspector General, Sacramento, February 2007.

347. David Jay Brown, "Liberty & the Pursuit of Forbidden Fruit." Hyatt 2000.

wasted cash, whereas if drugs were subject to the same taxes as alcohol and cigarettes, it would raise another $46.7 billion in revenue on top of that.[348] The only reason to put drug offenders in jail is the moralistic stance that "they are guilty and need to be punished." It is a policy backed by the Christian Right, who see the War on Drugs purely as one predicated on religious values.

If a hundred and fifty years ago the U.S. government had tried to regulate what substances its citizens can or cannot ingest, the effort would not only have been rejected as unconstitutional, but ridiculed as absurd. If seventy-five years ago the U.S. government had tried to regulate what crops farmers in foreign countries can or cannot cultivate, the effort would have immediately been rejected as colonialism. The War on Drugs cannot be conducted without massive invasions of liberty and property. The single most important right implicated, and endangered, is the Fourth Amendment, which forbids unreasonable searches and seizures. A new body of law rose out of the Prohibition that is today driven by drugs. Modern drug prohibition is much more popular than alcohol prohibition ever was, and the rights of every citizen are now defined by the rights the judiciary grudgingly grants to drug offenders. The minute trivial offences were turned into felonies, this magic word "felony" became a perpetual depriver of rights and privileges enjoyed by citizens since the signing of the Magna Charta.

As always, the question to ask is: *qui bene?* The truth is, the drug war has grown into an immensely successful capitalistic enterprise, benefiting the privately-owned prison industry, the military-industrial complex, the urine testers, manufacturers of surveillance equipment, public prosecutors, defence attorneys, politicians and police officers, as well as the alcohol, tobacco, and pharmaceutical companies, while scapegoating racial minorities, inner-city youth, left-wing intellectuals, and rebellious government protesters. Because it is a phony war, the War on Drugs is fiscally manageable: i.e. the government can spend as much or as little as it likes, since the results will always be the same. Even the out-of-pocket costs are concealed, being divided among federal, state, and local governments, and confused with funding for law enforcement.

Financed to the tune of about $70 billion a year, virtually every U.S. government agency has a piece of the drug war, from the Pentagon and the Coast Guard to the National Park Service and the Bureau of Indian Affairs.[349] Yet unlike a real war, the War on Drugs has no central command, no coordinated intelligence effort, and very little accountability. The need for illegal labour started increasing as the drug laws were enforced, giving pot smokers felonies and keeping them from working when they return to society. Millions of Americans—mostly young people under the age of 30—have been busted for pot. Thousands have been disenfranchised, tens of thousands have been unnecessarily sent to "rehabilitation," hundreds of thousands have lost their eligibility for student aid, and perhaps an entire generation has been alienated to believe that the police are an instrument of their oppression rather than their protection. Laws deny almost 500 federal benefits to pot offenders, including

348. Miron & Waldock 2010.

349. Robert Dreyfuss, "The Drug War: Where the Money Goes," *Rolling Stone*, December 11, 1995.

small business loans, professional licenses, farm subsidies, and food stamps, while asset-forfeiture programs enrich police departments and divert the focus of law enforcement from violent and other predatory criminal activity. It is all so depressing and messed up that it makes you want to tear your hair out and scream—or, you know, start doing drugs.

5

When You Divide Responsibility, You Make It Disappear

It was Benjamin Franklin who declared in 1759, "They that can give up essential liberty to obtain a little temporary safety deserve neither liberty nor safety."[350] The very fact that man has the ability to choose, to decide for himself, is what distinguishes him from the animal, and from anything below the animal. Animals cannot choose, they have to obey their instincts, the only motivating forces at their level of evolution. The great dignity of man, his uniqueness, emerging from the evolutionary stream that goes back hundreds of millions of years, derives from the fact that he does not have to obey. Since humans are thinking creatures, to deny them the liberty to choose is to deny them the opportunity to think for themselves, which is to deny their very existence as humans.

We should never forget that whatever power we give to the good cops, goes to the bad ones as well. Police, as workers, are notoriously difficult to manage, because they tend to go out by themselves, unsupervised. Up to a point, police shakedowns of drug dealers, pimps, bookmakers, and other businessmen who operate outside the law are beneficial to the State; the more the officers collect in bribes and confiscations, the less they have to be paid in salaries. "Crime does not pay," not for the police at least:

350. 1972, 289.

why do you think you always get pulled over for speeding when there is an armed robbery taking place somewhere else? The latter could get them killed, of course, while the former pays their salary! President Yushchenko, who came to power after the Orange Revolution, disbanded Ukraine's traffic police when it proved impossible to stamp out corruption. Like in other former communist countries, the police routinely imposed on-the-spot fines and demanded bribes from the motorists. "If you bring in the cops, you will also bring in the robbers."

This all boils down to a misconception about just what the product of the criminal justice system is. It is *not* crime control, since even if that could be measured with any accuracy, there is no evidence that law enforcement in general reduces crime. The product is crime rates, which are a function, not of the amount of crime, but the amount of law enforcement. The authorities can manufacture a "crime wave," if they want more money, or ease up on enforcement, if they want to take credit for doing exactly the opposite; it is a no-lose situation for them. Just as mediaeval armies used to subsist by "living off the land," i.e. pillaging the villages they passed through, so the modern drug warriors fill their coffers with booty from forfeitures—and that's just on the legal level.

The occasional polls conducted among law students reveal a horde of delinquents: every aspiring lawyer admits to once having committed an act that would have necessitated police intervention and criminal sanction if they had been caught. How is it possible that the justice system has not been shaken by these criminals, and why are the police not using their resources to apprehend them? One reason is that they represent the system, the powers that be, or at the very least their children, and we know that they will be the public authorities of the future. No system would remain standing if its most powerful advocates were locked up in a correctional facility. The State needs the police for a modicum of selective law enforcement, but more importantly, for social control: to break strikes, evict squatters, quell riots, silence dissidents, and to keep the traffic moving.

The reason the State is eager that its citizens are not robbed is the same reason the Mafia or any other protection racket would generally like to "keep the peace"—from other criminals unaffliliated with its organization. Such competition serves against its own interests, disturbing the conditions that make its own collection of income as efficient and peaceful as possible. Given that in preserving law and order, the State is really only interested in protecting "vital interests," it is generally not able to effectively tackle and convict the criminals who pursue crime on a small scale. With the police concentrating mainly on limiting only heinous crimes like murder and victimless crimes like the possession of drugs, the citizens are expected not to waste their time, having paid for services the police cannot sufficiently provide.

The imposition of a government tax on property or income violates the rights of the property owner or income producer just as much as theft does. In both cases, the owner-producer's supply of goods is diminished against his will and without his consent. Government money creation or "quantitative easing" involves no less a fraudulent expropriation of private property-owners than the operations of an illegal counterfeiting organization. Beyond the rule that no-one may physically damage the property of others and that all exchange and trade be voluntary and contractual, any government regulation as to what an owner may or may not do with his property implies the taking of someone's property and is at a par with extortion, robbery, or vandalism. Yet unlike their criminal equivalents, taxation, quantitative easing, and government regulations are considered legitimate, but unlike the victim of a crime, the victims of government interference are not entitled to physically defend and protect their property.

To quote the German philosopher Max Stirner, "The State's behaviour is violence, and it calls its violence 'law'; that of the individual, 'crime.'"[351] And because it is illegitimate, crime occurs only intermittently; that is, the robber disappears from the scene with his loot and leaves his victim alone—governmental property violations, in contrast, happen continually, because they are legitimate. Violent attacks, whether with guns, knives, gasoline, or explosives, are symptoms, effects of an underlying cause; and as long as we only address the symptom and not the cause, its effects will get more intense and persistent. Fired during the first battle of the American Revolution, the "shot heard round the world" was aimed at British soldiers seeking to confiscate the weapons and gunpowder belonging to the citizens of Concord, Massachusetts. The Second Amendment of the U.S. Constitution would subsequently postulate gun-ownership as "the right of the people"; and as Thomas Jefferson himself reportedly asserted, "The strongest reason for the people to retain the right to keep and bear arms is, as a last resort, to protect themselves against the tyranny in government."

Some people assert that we do not need guns because the police are there to protect us—"When seconds count, the cops are just minutes away." In the United States, civilians shoot and kill at least twice as many criminals as police do every year. And only 2% of civilian shootings involve an innocent person mistakenly identified as a criminal; the "error rate" for the police is 11%, i.e. more than five times as high.[352] However, law enforcement officers have no duty to protect any individual, their duty is to enforce the law in general—as confirmed by the U.S. Supreme Court in 1856.[353] More recently, the Seventh Circuit Court of Appeals held in 1982 that "there is no constitutional right to be protected by the state against being murdered by criminals or madmen. It is monstrous if the state fails to protects its residents . . . but it does not violate . . . the Constitution."[354] In fact, police and human rights are historical opposites: the police force has been the iron fist of every tyrannical régime, of which the rising bourgeois society defended itself by creating an area bounded by the separation of powers, constitutional state, and civil liberties, where the government could intrude only in the democratically enacted order.

Yet kings—even absolute kings—had never been considered the makers, but only the interpreters and executors of pre-existing and immutable law. It is absurd to believe that an agency with legislative powers can preserve law and order, and the

---

351. 1971, 133.

352. John R. Lott, Jr. & David B. Mustard, "Crime, Deterrence, and Right-to-Carry Concealed Handguns," *The Journal of Legal Studies* 26(1), January 1997, 1–68.

353. *South v. Maryland*, 59 U.S. (18 How.) 396, 15 L.Ed. 433 (1856).

354. *Bowers v. DeVito*, 686 F.2d 616, 618 (7th Cir. 1982).

constitutionally provided separation of powers makes no difference in this regard; two—or even three—wrongs do not make a right. To the contrary, they lead to the accumulation, proliferation, reinforcement, and aggravation of error: legislators cannot enforce their will on the citizens without the co-operation of the executive branch, and the President in turn will use his position and resources to influence legislators and legislation; and although the Supreme Court may disagree with the particular acts of the legislative or the executive branch, its judges are nominated by the President and confirmed by the Senate, not to mention dependent on them for funding. As an integral part of the government, they have no interest in limiting, but every interest in expanding the government's—and thereby their own—power.

Sir Winston Churchill famously argued that "democracy is the worst form of government except all the others that have been tried," but even if that were true, the least of all evils is still evil. "Government is not reason, it is not eloquence," wrote George Washington, "it is force! Like fire it is a dangerous servant and a fearful master."[355] From the ability to enforce compliance with traffic lights and speed limits, to impose and collect taxes, punish thieves and murderers, and to wage war with vast armies and destructive weapons, government is force. By its definition alone, government is therefore a potential threat to anyone who falls within its sphere of influence. The U.S. Founding Fathers recognized this truism when they set to protect themselves and their progeny by severely limiting government. The Second Amendment says "people," not "law-abiding citizens," or "goodie-two-shoes," or what have you. Every man has the inherent right to protect himself, his family, and his home from lethal force; to acknowledge that right is to acknowledge the need for an effective response—one cannot acknowledge a right and at the same time deny the means to exercise it.

The liberties guaranteed by the Bill of Rights can only be held by a citizenry willing and able to protect its freedom from those who would attempt to seize it. As Noah Webster noted in 1787, "Before a standing army can rule, the people must be disarmed; as they are in almost every kingdom of Europe. The supreme power in America cannot enforce unjust laws by the sword; because the whole body of the people are armed, and constitute a force superior to any bands of regular troops that can be, on any pretense, raised in the United States."[356] Just because weapons have been used, mainly by the State against its own citizens, to destroy people, does not mean that it is the only use for firearms; crying "Get rid of guns" does not equal "Get rid of war, hate, and suffering."

When there is no more need for violence, when that awareness is shared among all sovereign beings, it will not matter if anyone is carrying a gun or not. "For it is true now, as it always was and always will be, that to be free is the same as to be pious, to be wise, to be temperate and just, to be frugal and abstinent, and to be magnanimous and brave; and to be the opposite of these is the same as to be a slave."[357] But this is a task of the heart, not a task given to government legislators. A political system that

355. Sprading 1913, 53.

356. *The Constitution Defended.* Wootton 2003, 132.

357. *The Second Defence of the People of England.* Milton 1806, VI, 445.

seeks to maximize individual liberty must retain enough discipline to meet the needs of human survival; and in a free society, the required discipline is self-discipline.

Society is not sentient; it has no rights—rights belong to the individual. Government can only be imposed and perpetuated by force, whereas liberty, by its very nature, cannot be given. An individual cannot be freed by another, but must break his or her own fetters through their own effort. "The man who is set free is nothing but a freed man . . . a dog dragging a piece of chain with him."[358] Many who support gun control travel with their own armed bodyguards or police protection. When we support gun control, we support the one thing that made every genocide and massacre of civilians throughout history possible.

On the 12th of April, 1928, the German Republic enacted the Law on Firearms and Ammunition, which required registration and renewable permits for firearms and ammunition, and that all firearms were stamped with model and serial numbers by their manufacturers. When the Nazis came to power in 1933, they had access to the name and address of every legal gun-owner in Germany, along with a description of his weapons. On the 18th of March, 1938, they enacted the Weapons Law which guaranteed that only "persons of undoubted reliability," that is, friends of the Nazi Party, were able to own and carry firearms. From 1933 to 1945, the Nazis killed 13 million German Jews, gypsies, and enemies of the Party.

In 1926, the Soviet Union enacted gun control law, articles 59 and 182 of the penal code; from 1929 to 1953, 20 million Russian anti-Stalinist and anti-communists were killed in the Soviet Union. In 1935, China enacted gun control law, articles 186–87 of the criminal code, followed in 1957 by article 9 of the security law; from 1949 to 1952, China killed her communists, from 1957 to 1960, she killer her farmers, from 1966 to 1976, she killed her reformers: in all, China killed 20 million Chinese.[359] An estimated 38 million people died in all the international and civil wars from 1900 to 1987; over the same period, a minimum of 169 million were starved, gassed, and otherwise slaughtered by their own government during peacetime—which means a person was four times more likely to get murdered at the hand of his government than be killed by its enemies.[360]

But that could never happen in America, right? It did happen in America! Hitler admired how the United States had cleared the continent of Native Americans, and used the 19th-century U.S. policies that e.g. prohibited slaves and freed former slaves from owning handguns as a model for his own policies of clearing ***Lebensraum*** for the German people. Conversely, the U.S. Gun Control Act of 1968 was modelled nearly word for word on the German Weapons Law of 1938.[361] So has every country whose citizens allowed themselves to be disarmed suffered slaughter from their government? Not yet. Has any country whose citizens have kept their guns ever been massacred by their government? Not once.

When the political leadership does not enjoy popular confidence, the leaders try to

358. Stirner 1971, 123.

359. Zelman & Stevens 2001.

360. Rummel 1994, Table 1.2.

361. Zelman 1993.

justify their actions under the guise of national security. When security becomes the highest value of society, we are dangerously near to a militaristic state. At the same time, values the leaders pretend to be defending, such as freedom and privacy, begin to crumble. We start to hear such claims as "al-Qaeda is arming itself with weapons bought at U.S. guns shows." A more likely source of terrorist arms was seized by Israelis in January of 2002, when they intercepted a shipment of 50 tons of weapons being smuggled from Iran by the PLO. The .50 caliber heavy sniper rifles were purchased directly from the American manufacturer by the CIA during the 1980s, and turned over by the U.S. government—the world's largest arms dealer—to its mujahedin allies in Afghanistan.[362]

While the Clinton administration boasted that half a million people were stopped from illegally purchasing a weapon by Brady Law background checks, there were less than a dozen arrests for this federal offence in the first 17 months after the law was passed.[363] As if criminals had ever had any difficulty in obtaining weapons or as though a person contemplating a mass murder without an escape plan would be deterred by the possibility of getting fined for possession of an unlawful handgun. In Germany, home to the infamous "Hamburg cell," everyone over the age of sixteen is required to carry an ID card at all times. However, even terrorists have legitimate identification documents or can forge them—the problem is knowing who is planning an attack. Nor are ID cards of any use in tracking down illegal immigrants, unless you live in a police state that carries out constant identity checks on the entire population. Nearly half of the estimated 12 million illegal immigrants in the United States entered the country not by sneaking across the border, but by evading detection at one of the 326 legal ports of entry, or by simply overstaying their visas.[364] And what ever happened to freedom of movement within the EU? You may not need a valid travel document, but you do need an internationally recognized ID—such as a passport!

"Most people do not really want freedom," as Freud famously asserted, "because freedom involves responsibility, and most people are frightened of responsibility." People who have not accepted the responsibility of their own personal power and the results of their choices are not ready to accept it in others. It may be that people who have not dealt with their own personal demons think everyone else is like them, ready to explode at the next insult; however, misuse of firearms by the millions of carry permit holders in the U.S. is virtually nil. Normal people do not turn into homicidal maniacs when a gun is placed in their hands, any more than guns levitate from holsters or closets to discharge themselves, killing innocent people. The oft-quoted statistic that a gun in the home is 43 times more likely to kill a family member than an intruder is a purposeful distortion of the truth: 37 of the 43 deaths are suicides, and while there are countless other ways in which a person can commit suicide, only a gun allows a small woman a realistic chance to fend off a large male

---

362. Wasserman 2004.

363. Ibid.

364. "Modes of Entry for the Unauthorized Migrant Population," Pew Hispanic Center, Washington, D.C., May 22, 2006.

attacker.[365]

"The fact is that the average man's love of liberty is nine-tenths imaginary, exactly like his love of sense, justice and truth. He is not actually happy when free; he is uncomfortable, a bit alarmed, and intolerably lonely. Liberty is not a thing for the great masses of men. It is the exclusive possession of a small and disreputable minority, like knowledge, courage and honor. It takes a special sort of man to understand and enjoy liberty—and he is usually an outlaw in democratic societies."[366] A free person with a gun is perceived as a threat to the State, whether he is or not; free and independent enough to not run reflexively to the State for his safety, he and his kind must be made to see the light. A functional authority requires that making trouble can always be blamed on the trouble-maker: if everybody plays by the rules, no-one will suffer; all would be fine if that one person would just shut up.

As Jack Nicholson put it in ***Easy Rider***, "They'll talk to ya and talk to ya and talk to ya about individual freedom. But they see a free individual, it's gonna scare 'em."[367] Every aspect of the ironically named Patriot Act was fully drafted, and rejected by Congress, in the decade before 9/11. Special counter-terrorism legislation, introduced for a short-term emergency, can all too easily become entrenched and has an insidious impact on the rule of law in general. The executive branch accrues more power, to the detriment of the legislature and the judiciary, which are supposed to act as bulwarks against the excessive centralization of power. Yet the number of Americans who trusted the federal government to do the right thing more than doubled in the weeks after September 11th, 2001. By the end of September, almost two-thirds of Americans said they "trust the government in Washington to do what is right" either "just about always" or "most of the time"—"follow the leader" has often been a recipe for national suicide.[368] The United States stands in danger of repeating the fate of the ancient democratic empire of Athens: "In the end, more than freedom, they wanted security. They wanted a comfortable life, and they lost it all—security, comfort, and freedom. When the Athenians finally wanted not to give to society but for society to give to them, when freedom they wished for most was freedom from responsibility then Athens ceased to be free and was never free again."[369]

If it feels like you cannot do anything these days without someone looking over your shoulder, you are not just being paranoid. With the advent of cheap computers and super-fast networks, engineers are finding more and more ways to keep tabs on our movements and our purchases, and are even getting better at guessing what we will do next. We love convenience, we love service, but at the same time, we instinctively feel that there is a dark side to all this. As homeland security and law enforcement are rushing to take advantage of this wealth of information ostensibly to

---

365. David Kopel, "An Army of Gun Lies: How the Other Side Plays," *National Review* 52(7), April 17, 2000.

366. H. L. Mencken, *Baltimore Evening Sun*, February 12, 1923.

367. Dir. Dennis Hopper. Columbia Pictures, 1969.

368. Virginia A. Chanley, "Trust in Government in the Aftermath of 9/11: Determinants and Consequences," *Political Psychology* 23(3), September 2002, 469–483.

369. Edith Hamilton, "The Lessons of the Past," *The Saturday Evening Post*, September 27, 1958.

protect the country, every move you make is becoming part of your permanent record. Collecting every bit of communications information on a person is no different than if someone was physically following him—where he moves, who he talks to, what he reads, what services he uses—and recording this information in a file. This is just an electronic version of the surveillance policies of already dead and buried police states: information is being collected not merely about suspects but of everyone.

In a police state, the persons watched over could assume that the state was interested in them; the others believed they were outside the constant surveillance. The system under development would enable panoptical surveillance, meaning that everyone can assume they can be monitored anywhere and anytime. The securocrats insist that installing cameras everywhere will make you safer, but the evidence is far from conclusive. The best empirical studies of CCTV cameras show that they do reduce crime in private premises such as parking lots, but have little effect in city centres and mass transit systems. The huge public investment in CCTV technology failed to cut the crime rate in the United Kingdom, with only 3% of the street robberies in London being solved using security cameras.[370] Although Britain has more cameras than any other European country—there are more than 5 million cameras in the UK—the problem remains that criminals are not afraid of cameras. Terrorist, in particular, are very unlikely to be deterred by surveillance equipment; quite the contrary, suicide bombers want their martyrdom to be recorded.

Security is not necessarily improved even if there was an immense database on every communicator and network user. Data mining has never proven a result, and remains more or less a voyeuristic tool; after all, has Amazon ever really given you a product referral you could use? Announcing the conclusions of a review of intelligence failures exposed by a White House inquiry, President Obama said the U.S. government "had the information scattered throughout the system to potentially uncover" the Christmas Day bombing plot and disrupt the attack. But the information was never pulled together to present a coherent picture of the threat. Instead, there was a "series of human errors," which culminated in someone apparently misspelling Umar Farouk Abdulmutallab's name when they entered it in a database.[371] Of course, Obama's retort that everyone needs to play better together is as pathetic as the 9/11 Commission's final conclusion that everyone is at fault and therefore nobody is at fault.

The Bush administration had one clear, unambiguous message after September 11th, 2001—"Everything has changed." The underlying message of that mantra was that the attacks did not represent a failure of the government to connect the dots, to be alert to and correlate the "fusillade of warnings" that was famously setting terrorism advisor Richard Clarke's "hair on fire" in the summer of 2001, and that John Ashcroft's reported statement to the interim head of the FBI about not wanting to hear any more warnings did not reflect a systematic failure. In the post-9/11 world,

370. Leon Hempel & Eric Töpfer, "The Surveillance Consensus: Reviewing the Politics of CCTV in Three European Countries," *European Journal of Criminology* 6(2), March 2009, 157–177.

371. "Remarks by the President on Strengthening Intelligence and Aviation Security," State Dining Room, Washington, D.C., January 7, 2010.

the gloves had to come off: the fault was in the silly restrictions that prevented tough-minded people from doing what had to be done. If the criticism from the 9/11 Commission was that dots had not been connected, in this brave new world we would connect anything that even bore a resemblance to a dot, and where there were no dots, we would create some. "You want dots? We got 'em."

In addition to the cost of storing such a vast quantity of information, the problem is there are no absolutely secure data systems. Increasingly, people are wondering if the organizations that gather sensitive personal information can be trusted to keep it safe. Identity thieves are rarely prosecuted, even though they cost the United States alone an estimated $47.6 billion each year.[372] In Europe, the United Kingdom has taken the lead on losing data, starting with the disappearance of disks containing personal details of 25 million people in November 2007. And how might a person's psyche be affected by the knowledge that his acts and thoughts can be traced without him knowing who is watching, when, and why? Monitoring may or may not prevent unlawful acts, but it can also keep people from exercising their rights. People will avoid electronic communication and the use of internet services, because they do not want everything to be recorded, even if they have nothing criminal to hide; "we all have our secrets." According to a 2006 House report, former Secretary of Defense, Donald Rumsfeld, and current Secretary of Homeland Security, Michael Chertoff, opted not to use e-mail on the job, while President Bush himself cited personal privacy issues for his decision to forgo e-mail.[373] While courts have extended lawfulness to private acts of all kinds, fewer and fewer people are able to cultivate this privacy.

From the start, President Bush made it seem like freedom was the central issue in the 9/11 attacks. He said of al-Qaeda members just nine days after the attack: "They hate our freedoms—our freedom of religion, our freedom of speech, our freedom to vote and assemble and disagree with each other."[374] But in truth, the attacks on the World Trade Center and the Pentagon had nothing to do with these so-called democratic freedoms. Osama bin Laden hated the United States because of his own fundamentalist religious views, which he effortlessly linked to U.S. foreign policy. The attacks would have not been averted if the Constitution and Bill of Rights had been abolished years before.

How can the democratic freedoms, or more accurately the liberties associated with modern liberal democracy, even be considered real freedoms? They are certainly not freedoms in the sense of "freedom of thought," more rights in the vein of "right to vote." Speech regarding political and religious issues is thought to present the strongest case for protection, but because of its practical effects, such speech could be treated as action; by establishing what beliefs and opinions are publicly acceptable, the State creates the social environment where we live. There is no real freedom of speech, no real freedom of the press, and certainly no real freedom of association in

372. "Federal Trade Commission—Identity Theft Survey Report," Synovate, McLean, VA, September 2003.

373. Davis, et al. 2006.

374. "Address to a Joint Session of Congress and the American People," U.S. Capitol, Washington, D.C., September 20, 2001.

any society, democratic or otherwise; the phrase "freedom of association" does not even appear in the U.S. Constitution, although the First Amendment protects the right to "peaceably assemble"—you need a permit or legal registration for almost any kind of public assembly.

They say that "knowledge is power," and that we live in an "information society," but if our freedom of speech was not restricted, if documents would not be classified, neither assumption would be correct; it is knowing what others do not know that is power. The strongest argument for protection of speech is that it acts as a safeguard against government abuse, but there is nothing unique about speech as a check on government. At various times and places, a similar role has been proposed for other restrictions on government power, such as hereditary privilege, private property, limited government, municipal liberties, direct democracy, and the right of the people to keep and bear arms. Such arguments lost respectability with the rise of liberal democracy, which created state control of our rights in the form of licensed privileges: the right to travel became a driver's license, the right to marry became a marriage license, the right to self-defence became a concealed-carry permit.

Having the right to free speech means everyone has the right to free speech; if I have the right to assemble, you have the right to assemble; my rights do not lessen or negate your rights. Privileges are another thing entirely: if people have the privilege of free speech, the government can tell them not to say things that bother it; if a person has the privilege of privacy, the government can perform "sneak and peak" secret searches, or inform him that since he lives in public housing, or is driving his car on a public road, the police can search his apartment or vehicle anytime they want. True freedom, on the other hand, is an inner quality: "freedom of thought" cannot be taken away any more than "freedom of conscience" can be granted. "Man is free at the moment he wishes to be."[375] Our freedoms are like our muscles; we must exercise them or we will lose them. "The most common way people give up their power is by thinking they don't have any."[376]

The Universal Declaration of Human Rights presents a laundry list of "rights," among which are the right to paid vacations and the right to hold opinions, effectively diluting the meaning of the word to the point of it becoming meaningless. What is more, every "right" promised by the United Nations can be taken away at the will of the member government; as the International Covenant on Civil and Political Rights clearly states: "The above-mentioned rights shall not be subject to any restrictions except those which are provided by law, are necessary to protect national security, public order, public health or morals."[377] There is no individual right of self-defence anywhere in the UN plan; in fact, the only armed people in the United Nations vision are the police, select bureaucrats, and the military.

As Kierkegaard observed, "People hardly ever make use of the freedom which they have, for example, freedom of thought; instead they demand freedom of speech as

375. Voltaire, attributed.

376. Alice Walker, attributed.

377. Part III, Article 12, December 16, 1966.

compensation."[378] Because of laws that ban spitting gum on the streets and its caning sentences for vandalism, Singapore has an autocratic image in the West, yet Western scientists have discovered a more open scientific environment there than at home. While U.S. science is being undermined by post-9/11 visa curbs on foreign scholars, sweeping new lab security rules, federal limits on stem-cell research, and a bioscience funding squeeze, Singapore has risen to the forefront of the industry. The "autocratic" state has welcomed with open arms and pocket books the thousands of Asian experts and trainees that the United States has turned away, not one of whom considers the right to spit gum any kind of a priority.

However, "most people would die sooner than think—in fact they do so."[379] And as Oscar Wilde pointed out, "A thing is not necessarily true because a man dies for it."[380] The only way you can topple a democracy is by getting elected—which is exactly what Hitler and Mussolini did. "Totalitarianism" is not even possible without the democratic notion that the people are the source and justification of power. Totalitarianism is therefore not the denial of democracy, but the radicalization of democracy: a totalitarian leader speaks directly and without mediation from the mouth of the people, its nature or history. The only difference between these conditions and the modern Western society is that there is no leader who interprets the "common will." Instead, we have a corporate-owned and operated mass media that creates the idea of common will in its depiction of "the people." Totalitarianism wishes to create a new man, to make him "the person he really is"; which is another difference from the authoritarian states of the old, where the citizen did not need to change, only to clean up his act and mouth a little. In totalitarian conditions, on the other hand, man's freedom of speech is greater than his freedom of thought.

It is important to realize that the ultimate power of any government—whether of kings or parliamentarians—rests solely on opinion and not on physical force. Any government can be brought down just by a change in public opinion, that is, by withdrawal of the public's consent and co-operation. It is likewise an error to assume that totalitarianism manifests its real character only when it employs crushing coercion. As history has demonstrated, there can exist a "clean" totalitarianism, which, in a "soft" manner, yields the same consequences as the classic kinds of totalitarianism; the "happy robots" of *1984* live under no more enviable conditions than prisoners in the camps. The central mystery of modern political life is: why are people prone to think that politicians and governments are more trustworthy than they appear? The question is not, "Why do people distrust government?" The question is, "Why do people follow and applaud politicians who they know are lying to them?" It is not astonishing that politicians lie, but that citizens believe.

We have come to the point where the citizens, confident that their democratically elected rulers will behave virtuously, have granted them a *de facto* "right to lie for 72 hours." "As long as the lies are not exposed in the same news cycle," explains James Bovard in his book, *Attention Deficit Democracy*, "the refutations may as well be

378. 1952, 28.

379. Russell 1925, 166.

380. *The Portrait of Mr. W. H.* Wilde 1997, 231.

done in a different century."[381] Blind trust in government has resulted in far more carnage than distrust of government. Docility is a far greater danger than blind fanaticism, at least in Western societies. In fact, it is mass docility that permits fanatics to seize power. The more people there are who unconditionally trust the government, the more atrocities the government can commit. It was people who followed orders who carried out the Nazi Holocaust and all the other war crimes that characterize conflicts around the globe. To say that people should not blindly trust the government is not a call for anarchy or for violence in the streets or the torching of city halls across the land. Nor is it a choice between trusting the government and refusing to drive on the right side of the road.

It is clear that, historically, the selfish impulses of man constitute a much smaller danger than his integrative tendencies: the individual who indulges in an excess of aggressive self-assertiveness invariably outlaws himself, contracts out of the hierarchy, incurring the penalties of society; whereas the true believer becomes more closely knit to it, entering the womb of his church, or party, or whatever the social group to which he surrenders his identity. All heretics of history have been virtuous men: they need the virtue of fortitude, without which they cannot dare to own their heresy; nor can they afford to be deficient in any other virtue, as that would lend advantage to their countless enemies—unlike orthodox sinners, heretics have no great number of friends to excuse or justify them. They are honest men not because of their heresy, but are heretics exactly because of their honesty.

"Disobedience, in the eyes of anyone who has read history, is man's original virtue. It is through disobedience that progress has been made, through disobedience and through rebellion."[382] The essence of power is impenetrability, while the subjects of power are controlled. The perhaps greatest achievement of bourgeois democracy is to turn this arrangement on its head: the private autonomy of the citizen was guarded with civil liberties and the exercise of power was made as transparent as possible. However, as Robert A. Heinlein observes, "Democracy is based on the assumption that a million men are wiser than one man. How's that again? I missed something. Autocracy is based on the assumption that one man is wiser than a million men. Let's play that over again, too. Who decides?"[383]

Aristocracy originally signified the rule of the best (Gr. *aristos*)—hereditary aristocracy was a much later development. It was largely the inflated price of justice and the perversion of ancient law by the kings that motivated the historical opposition against monarchy. Yet there was confusion as to the causes of this phenomenon: some recognized correctly that the problem lay with monopoly, not with élites or nobility; but they were far outnumbered by those who instead erroneously blamed it on the élitist nature of the ruler, advocating to maintain the monopoly of law and law enforcement, and merely to replace the king by the "people." The rise of democracy made it much easier for politicians to convince people that government posed no threat, because they controlled its actions. The result was

---

381. 2006, 91.

382. *The Soul of Man under Socialism.* Op. cit. 1043.

383. Op. cit. 246.

that the brakes on government power became weakest at the exact time when politicians were most dangerous. The normal defences people have against outside authority were undermined by a chorus of politicians and government officials continually reminding them that government is themselves. Fear of government became portrayed as a relic of less civilized times, and there is a concerted effort today to make distrusting the government intellectually unacceptable, a sign of ill breeding.

"To be governed is to be watched, inspected, spied upon, directed, law-ridden, regulated, penned up, indoctrinated, preached at, checked, appraised, seized, censured, commanded, by beings who have neither title, nor knowledge, nor virtue," wrote Proudhon in *General Idea of the Revolution*. "To be governed is to have every operation, every transaction, every movement, noted, registered, counted, rated, stamped, measured, numbered, assessed, licensed, refused, authorized, endorsed, admonished, prevented, reformed, redressed, corrected."[384] Did you know that modern Germany has banned more books than did Nazi Germany? The Nazis removed the banned books from public distribution, but left copies for the universities etc. to study. Modern book burning constitutes an absolute prohibition where even scholarship does not protect one from prison. Common sense tells us that more laws equal less freedom, and there tends to be exponentially more laws under democracy than under any other form of government.

"It is proof of a base and low mind for one to wish to think with the masses or majority, merely because the majority is the majority. Truth does not change because it is, or is not, believed by a majority of the people." Thus Giordano Bruno, who was burned at the stake in 1600.[385] Socrates thought along similar lines—and died for his beliefs at the hands of democracy. The will to power is fundamentally different from the will to enlighten; whoever is at the wheel, the thinkers are *ipso facto* the opposition. However, it was only when power came into the hands of the majority that further limitations on the power of government was thought unnecessary. The steady erosion of individual liberties and the erection of the so-called "welfare state" was made possible by convincing people that democracy is an unconditionally good thing. Any act of prohibition is thus all right, as long as it is the result of democratic decision-making; after all, it was you who voted those 200 people into the parliament. Nobody is qualified to wield unlimited power, and there is no reason why we should not limit the scope of majority rule as well as that of any other form of government.

During the age of monarchy, there was a clear-cut distinction between the ruler and the ruled, and the king and his parliament were held to be under the law. They only applied pre-existing law as judge and jury—they did not make the law. George III had very limited powers in Britain, where the supremacy of parliament, albeit with limited suffrage, was established as early as 1688—a hundred years before the signing of the U.S. Constitution. In fact, one of the reasons the American Revolution took place was that King George attempted to exercise power in the colonies that he could not back home. Both the United Kingdom and the United States were equally undemocratic at the time: voting rights in both countries were determined by

---

384. *Epilogue*. 1923, 293–94.

385. Bufe 1992, 128.

property ownership, not by universal suffrage, which neither introduced until the late 19th century. Neither was democratic by today's standard, but both were more democratic than most other 18th-century régimes in the Western world.

The U.S. Founding Fathers were well aware of the dangers of democracy, the anti-symbol of which is the lynch mob, an apotheosis of unrestrained majority rule; they purposely set up an inefficient government, "bound by the chains of the Constitution," as Jefferson put it.[386] It is necessary to remember that neither the American Revolution nor the American Constitution was the result of the will of the majority of the population. A full third of the American colonists were actually Tories, and another third were preoccupied with daily routines and cared little either way. No more than a third of the colonists were committed to and supportive of the revolution, yet they won the day. What is more, as far as the Constitution is concerned, the overwhelming majority of Americans were actually opposed to its adoption, so its ratification represented more of a minority coup than the will of the people. The Founders considered themselves to be members of a "natural aristocracy," and rather than democracy, they advocated an aristocratic republic.

"The beauty of the Constitution is that it can always be changed. The beauty of the Constitution is that it makes no set laws other than faith in the wisdom of ordinary people to govern themselves... Our 'founding parents' were pompous, white, middle-aged farmers, but they were also great men. Because they knew one thing all great men should know: that they didn't know everything. Sure, they'd make mistakes, but they made sure to leave a way to correct them. The president is not an 'elected king,' no matter how many bombs he can drop. Because the . . . Constitution doesn't trust him."[387] Still, any form of organization that is based on the delegation of power always forms a threat to the liberty and dignity of the people subjected to that power; the Founding Fathers intended that the United States be composed of self-reliant individuals, who would not hesitate to pull the reins in on their rulers.

"Never doubt that a small group of thoughtful, committed citizens can change the world," as the renowned American anthropologist, Margaret Mead, famously said. "Indeed, it is the only thing that ever has." In politics as in nature, evolution depends on the fortunes of the singularly successful, not the majority. What Napoleon, Conqueror of Europe, failed to appreciate was the extent to which his mass conscription of ordinary citizens promoted national consciousness. And it was only modern technology that made democracy as we know it and its attendant, nationalism, possible. Detailed maps of conquered and held territories consolidated national identity, spread to even the farthest corners of each rising nation by the mass media; industrialization not only led to the abolition of slavery, but made luxury goods everyday—there can be no *de juri* democratization without there having been a *de facto* democratization first.

Already during the late Renaissance period, surveyors and map-makers began to dissolve the service and respect that a landlord owed a king. The mapping of Europe allowed the Europeans to see their countries in a way never before possible, showing

386. Mayer 1994, 129.

387. *With Honors*. Dir. Alek Keshishian. Warner Bros. Pictures, 1994.

royal authority to be merely an ornamental adjunct to the nation to which they belonged. Modern cartography thus unveiled a conceptual divide between the land and its ruler, a divide that would soon span battlefields. The good of the country, often deemed as the aim of political activity, is a mythical concept. All groups are made up of individuals, so the notion that men should sacrifice their individuality for the "greater good" of any given group is nonsensical. Since the interests of individuals and groups contradict each other, there is no "common good" that political decisions could serve. Even the good of the individual is a problematic concept, seeing that each and every person has several contradictory values and goals. It does not take a rocket scientist to figure out that democracy works the poorer the more voters there are and the more diverse they are.

Only when they have a common goal or a common enemy do human beings work together effectively. Democracy requires that representatives of various different regions and interests co-operate to govern, yet it lacks the sort of goal-oriented framework that would actually enable such co-operation. At best, the mandate of a democratic government is to protect the State and take care of social problems, but politicians cannot even agree what the real threats to the State are, or which social problems should be addressed. Regardless of the branch or department, when you have a new boss every two to six years—and possibly a new mandate altogether should a different party win the elections—the strategy is constantly changing. Political careers are built on short-term plans, leading to a series of cosmetic changes over time that have no real impact. An individual or an institution acting according to a plan moves toward a goal one step at a time; but in a democracy, where political institutions change direction every few steps, they end up going in circles without really ever getting anywhere.

In ancient Athens, the world's first and some would argue best democracy, voting rights were limited to 10% of the population, with only the top 1% (male citizens over age 30) being eligible to run for office—and there were only about 400,000 Athenians even at the height of its empire.[388] Not only did Athens have a highly monolithic culture, but the ruling classes all went through the same regimented existence before dying at the age of 40 on the average.[389] The modern middle classes, on the other hand, are but a shared illusion, built on what we think other people reckon as the prerequisite of the "good life." No-one is directly middle-class; the critic of the bourgeoisie has precisely the same image of the average person as do the middle classes, he just does not identify with it.

Most people who find their way into party politics today thus represent a caricature of an ideology. The rest are populists whose principal message is along the lines of "stop animal cruelty," and who buy all the other tenets of the party in order to proclaim it. In party politics, embracing one opinion means adopting a whole host of others, with no logical connection. It seems impossible for a politician to form an opinion on the basis of an issue, instead of party tradition; as Mark Twain once remarked, "In religion and politics, people's beliefs and convictions are in almost

388. Noble, et al. 2011.

389. Gallant 1991.

every case gotten at second-hand, and without examination."[390] Never mind that the media demand superhuman consistency from the candidates: God help the vegetarian nominee who dons leather shoes. The biggest problem arises when the party line takes over reality: a Republican candidate cannot admit to having taken drugs in college, as this might show that a few puffs of pot does not ruin a person. People in groups tend to agree on courses of action which they as individuals know to be stupid.

"Politics is the art of compromise," which means, among other things, that democratic process is slow and expensive. This, not the "lack of education" or some such, is also the main reason poor countries are non-democratic. Taxes were considerably lower before industrialization, and are still quite low in Third World "dictatorships." In small towns, where the candidates in municipal elections are able to meet virtually every eligible voter, printing up campaign posters is still a big deal. But in big cities, mass media advertising is the primary and most efficient way to reach voters, meaning serious candidates need to be able to raise significant sums of money to pay for TV spots. As Gore Vidal wrote in *The Decline and Fall of the American Empire*, "Every four years the naive half who vote are encouraged to believe if we can elect a really nice man or woman President everything will be all right. But it won't be. Any individual who is able to raise $25 million to be considered presidential is not going to be much use to the people at large. He will represent oil, or aerospace, or banking, or whatever moneyed entities are paying for him."[391]

"It makes no difference who you vote for—the two parties are really one party representing four percent of the people."[392] The central principle of the system originally conceived by the ancient Greeks was giving the voters concrete political alternatives from which to choose. But a multi-party system is often no better: in the so-called rainbow coalition, you have parties from the left and the right, who despite their opposite ideologies should find a joint course to follow until the next election. In practice, this means that the parties frame their pre-election programs in such a way that they will be able to join the government even if they lose the election, resulting in an innumerable amount of compromises, slipping and sliding from the declared goals of the party. It has been argued that the function of extremism is to determine limits for the majority; the trouble is, as Barry Goldwater famously put it, "The truth is extreme." Advocates of the middle way, on the other hand, have no goal, opinion, stand, or spine of their own to begin with—or have you ever heard of "angry moderates"?

Another basic principle of the Greeks was that power should come with accountability. In a rainbow coalition, the political accountability is divided between several different parties, completely watering down that idea. When the ruling parties are not directly accountable for their actions, the position of the opposition is also compromised. It becomes difficult for the latter to hold the former responsible for anything, because all the government policies are compromises between several party lines. Thus the status of the opposition does not necessarily improve even if the

390. 1990, 369–70.

391. 1992, 65.

392. Idem., attributed.

incumbent government fails in its task: in Germany, for example, the Christian Democrat Party has lost power only twice since 1949.

However, the greatest problem for democracy as a governing philosophy arises from the democratic rejection of any authority that is not based on consent. When democracy acts as a critic of established power, that rejection can lead to demands that government justify its rule by obtaining popular support; but as soon as democrats themselves become the authorities, they need the governed to consent to their rule: people who reject democracy philosophically are considered an immediate threat to a democratic society, because they have no evident reason for accepting the binding power of the law. Once established, the democratic state therefore lays great stress on state indoctrination of the young, and becomes as intolerant as any theocracy, a "despotism of the multitude" that demands not only obedience to its laws, but acceptance of its principles as well.

"The surest way to corrupt a youth," in the opinion of Nietzsche, "is to instruct him to hold in higher esteem those who think alike than those who think differently."[393] Democracy does not equal freedom: "Giving every man a vote has no more made men wise and free than Christianity has made them good."[394] Even if the world at large did desire democracy such desire does not automatically render it beneficial. Each person is equally important, but that does not mean that the opinion of each person would be equally valuable or important. Everyone's opinion is not equal, nor does it need to be. It is no great exaggeration to say that the majority is always wrong; as Harlan Ellison complained, "The two most common things in the universe are hydrogen and stupidity."[395] In his decision overturning Arkansas Act 590, which required public schools to teach Creation Science, Judge William R. Overton concluded thus: "No doubt a sizeable majority of Americans believe in the concept of a Creator or, at least, are not opposed to the concept and see nothing wrong with teaching school children about the idea. The application and content of First Amendment principles are not determined by public opinion polls or by a majority vote. . . No group, no matter how large or small, may use the organs of government, of which the public schools are the most conspicuous and influential, to foist its religious beliefs on others."[396]

"One of the proofs of the immortality of the soul is that myriads have believed it," wrote Mark Twain, "they also believed the world was flat."[397] Any opinion, in order for it to have any value, needs to be based on factual knowledge and different people simply have different amounts of knowledge on different subjects. The existing democracies would not survive a day without a division between expert bodies and the "will of the people": technical and economic issues fall into the domain of experts, while the people with their dreary opinions can complain about other issues. In California, for example, the state legislature sends the governor over 1,000 bills to sign

393. *The Dawn*, Axiom 297. 1954, 91.

394. Mencken 1956, 394.

395. *Omni*, February 1987.

396. *McLean v. Arkansas Board of Education* 529 F. Supp. 1255 (E.D. La. 1982).

397. Notebook 346, 381, 236, 344, 379. 1935.

each year, so you can rest assured most lawmakers did not read much of what they voted on, relying instead on advice from trusted sources. Thus, in practice, representative democracy is only a means of politically legitimizing the decisions of bureaucrats, things that cannot in fact—or so we are told—be done any other way. "Democracy is a device that ensures we shall be governed no better than we deserve"[398]—in this, and this sense only, can democracy be considered the "most ethical form of government"; but it is ethics of the eye-for-an-eye kind.

We are products of our evolutionary history, and the reason John Edward's marital infidelity garnered more attention than a dry policy dispute that could end up costing American taxpayers billions of dollars is that the human brain evolved in a period when there were significant survival advantages to knowing the secrets of others. Because humans lived in small groups, the things they learned about other people's character could tell them whom they could and could not trust in a tight spot. We may consciously know that we no longer live in small hunter-gatherer groups, and it no longer makes sense to judge someone like Edwards as we might a friend or lover, but our reptilian brain does not realize this. In the Pleistocene era, there was no survival value in being able to decipher a health care initiative, but there was significant value in information about who is trustworthy, who is a liar, who is available sexually, who is guarded by a jealous partner, who is likely to abandon a family. The human brain does not have a special module for evaluating welfare or immigration policy, but it has modules for evaluating people on the basis of character. Verily, "politics is just show business for ugly people."[399]

Trouble is, in politics, cynical realists and selfish opportunists can often achieve better and even more just results than well-meaning fools. It is no joke to say that in today's politics, if you can fake sincerity, you have got it made. Honest candidates, who will not abuse their office, cannot sell favours, and thus have fewer resources to campaign with, leaving them at a huge disadvantage in an election. If people vote against their own interests, it is not because they do not understand what is in their interests, but because they resent having their interests decided for them by politicians who think they know best. By constantly telling us that every vote counts and that everyone's voice is equally important, democracy generates undeserved interest in everyone's opinion. Our cognitive bias is to assume that we have a voice equivalent to an individual in a Pleistocene hunter-gatherer tribe, and so we comment on nationwide events with a passion to match, even thought no-one is really listening. When we hear in the evening news that we are footing the bill for another bank bailout, we react by complaining to a few of our close friends and discussing alternatives, when success requires the agreement of tens of millions. Direct democracy frequently means that many poor but optimistic people vote for tax cuts for the few rich, who neither need nor want any.

By wide margins, Americans think referendums and initiatives are a good idea, and that having choices is important; they "find themselves" in the car they drive, the job they have, the school they went to, the clothes they wear, the music they listen to,

398. George Bernard Shaw, attributed.

399. Jay Leno, attributed.

and the movies they watch. But research on 401(k) retirement savings plans shows that, as the number of choices that people are offered goes up, the number of choices they make goes down. People say they want more choice, but when they are given it, they get overwhelmed and opt out of deciding; in the 2005 November elections, the California referendum boasted as many as eight initiatives, every last one of which got turned down by voters. Our society is arranged in such a way as to ensure that our choices will not effect change. Young peole are typically stuck in low-income jobs simply because they fear making the wrong choice of career; professors at liberal arts colleges even joke that they take students who would have been stuck working at McDonald's and turn them into people who are stuck working at Starbucks.

The by-and-large blue collar citizens of Kansas are certain to be a "Red" state in any election, holding a deep animosity toward the left. This is pretty much a self-defeating phenomenon, since the policies of the Republican Party tend to benefit the wealthy and powerful at the expense of the average worker. Regardless of the facts, the Kansans continue to buy into the right-wing rhetoric that the Republicans are the party of values, in touch with the working-class way of life. At the same time, jobs are flying out and standards of living are falling, but the blue-collar worker finds solace in knowing he that represents real America, where Superman grew up and where Dorothy wants to return. He views the cosmopolitan world as being against him, fiercely protecting his home from outside influences, albeit with no little hypocrisy: he rails against the Hollywood culture, but has a satellite dish bringing in MTV; he will challenge anyone mocking his choice of small town life, but is equally willing to travel 100 miles to Wal-Mart to get groceries, rather than supporting his local, independently-owned market.

Like supermarkets, all governments require some type of support. The strength of any government rests not with itself, but with the people. It is possible for a great tyrant to be a fool instead of a superman, if the superstition of the people makes them think it is right to obey him. As long as the superstition exists, it is patently useless for any outside liberator to end the tyranny, for the people will create another, having accustomed to relying on something external to themselves. Nor can any government fully conform with the will of the people, whatever that is taken to mean. Governments may be deemed representative, but they and the people are never the same. These facts apply to both autocratic and democratic states, the only difference is between the mechanisms which protect the will of the people from itself.

There appear to be three historic options: first, the ruler is the highest subject of the people, which makes the opposition his rivals; second, the ruler embodies the supreme will of the people in everything he does, making the opposition enemies of the people; third, the ruler knows better than the people, meaning the opposition are populists. The first option is represented by the traditional monarch and the second by the totalitarian leader. The third is represented by the democratic government, for despite all its loathing for élitism, it is exactly the democracy where the rulers "know best." And, unlike all the other forms of government, democracy has—or is—a value system, and cannot be challenged; you often hear about "anti-democratic element," but only ever of "rebels" in a non-democratic system. To sum up, in a democracy, the people oppose the rulers but support the system; in an autocracy, the people support the ruler, but oppose the system—and the system, being an abstract construct, can neither help nor harm the people.

Historically, democracy is the only form of government that has tried to impose itself on others; by referring to "democracy deficit" in foreign cultures, the West makes its own artificial, slowly-evolved system sound like the natural state of things. As recently as 25 years ago, only a minority of the world's countries held multi-party elections, while about 140 do so today. On the face of it, the over one billion votes cast worldwide each year seem to indicate a triumph of the Western ideal, but closer scrutiny reveals many of those countries are not "free" by any other measure. Most countries of the former Soviet Union and the Arab Middle East still lack, for example, a free press, a viable opposition, an active civil society, an independent judiciary, and minority rights legislation. In these conditions, elections are merely *pro forma* exercises that seek to help legitimize the incumbents rather than to hold them accountable to the electorate. So long as totalitarianism cloaks itself in the garb of individual choice, it can operate as it always has; as long as the choices it offers remain meaningless, it will avoid serious disturbance. As a famous anarchist graffiti says, "If voting could change anything, it would be illegal."

"Freedom of the press" is not a threat to the democratic system: frequent elections coupled with free press means that the voters have the memory of a goldfish, while democratic leaders get away with stuff that would get a dictator toppled in a New York minute. In a democracy, the media are presumed to help people make informed voting decisions; however, media are businesses, and I am not referring to the fact that rich candidates get more screen time, but the fact that sensation sells: people only get to see the exception to the rule, never the bigger picture, rendering them actually unable to make informed decisions. It is precisely the news, not entertainment, that is making modern people dumber: the news can never give you all the necessary facts, or the whole background; with entertainment, people at least know it is not intended to be taken seriously. Nor did earlier forms of totalitarianism try to convince their subjects that they were free.

True power is always hard to identify. Power does not climb the platform, but pulls the strings in the background. If some issue is hotly debated in the media, it cannot be very important, for the really important decisions are never immediately brought into the limelight. Some of the media gnaw at the respect of politics by bringing out trivial issues and capitalizing on populist opinion polls. When the American republic was formed, ordinary citizens had little formal education, and with communications moving at the speed of a man on a horse, even a literate person had to struggle to be informed. Under these conditions, it was perfectly reasonable to appoint a group of educated representatives to meet in the state capitals to conduct the public's business. Now that 84% of Americans have high school diplomas and more than a quarter boast college degrees, they no longer see their representatives as having a monopoly on knowledge or wisdom; there is nothing today's voters hate more than having things explained to them as though they were idiots. The disregard and even contempt for politics erodes the interest of capable individuals in the profession, and

"Incompetence," as Det. Harve Poole pointed out, "is the worst form of corruption."[400]

Of course, you cannot vote against democracy, or for monarchy or anarchy. However, election violence in such diverse countries as Jamaica and Iraq shows that democracy can become a focus for terrorism as armed groups "try to influence elections." Across Latin America, elected governments have been toppled by angry protesters in recent years. In Bolivia, for example, a citizenry outraged by Washington Consensus-inspired reforms brought down two presidents in as many years. Expectations that democracy would improve security, employment, health care, and housing have consistently been dashed, leaving the electorate angry and disenchanted. Many now argue that elections may not even be appropriate for the poorer countries, especially if they are just emerging from conflict, on account of the demagoguery and jostling for position they inevitably encourage. In fact, Paul Collier, professor of economics at Oxford University, calculates that elections are not of any use until the gross domestic product per capita exceeds $2,700 a year. In conditions poorer than that a dictatorship functions better; instability begins to grow in a dictatorship only after the GDPpc surpasses the $2,700 limit.[401] To quote U.S. Defense Secretary Robert Gates, "Afghanistan is the fourth or fifth poorest country in the world, and if we set ourselves the objective of creating some sort of Central Asian Valhalla over there, we will lose."[402]

Even established democracies are invariably plagued with "election-year policies"; in a representative democracy, the candidates are *perforce* more interested in the votes than listening to the voters. And that, my friends, is the best argument for hereditary rule—a king rules out of duty, whereas a politician is purposely seeking power. Voter turnout is seldom more than 50%, something conventional wisdom would blame on voter apathy, i.e. the assumption that low turnout is reversely proportional to the confidence the voters hold in the integrity of elected officials. However, a 2004 survey by the California Voter Foundation (CVF) found that the main reason why voters stay away from the polls is because they are "too busy." More than half of infrequent voters and non-voters in California work more than 40 hours a week, while trying to maintain some semblance of family and social life. Many of them do not even know that their employers are obliged to give them time off to vote, or are afraid that exercising this right might jeopardize their jobs.[403] Absentee ballots are no help when people do not know about them or how to get one.

And that is just the way political strategists, campaigners, elected officials, and aspiring candidates like it; after all, they make a living off "voter apathy." Elections are a billion-dollar industry, and the main tool of the trade is known as targeting. It allows political operatives that are working with limited resources in regions with over a million registered voters to carve out smaller, niche groups of voters, who, based on their past voting habits, are considered the most likely to vote for a particular candidate or ballot measure. Once a target is acquired, they employ the

---

400. *Electra Glide in Blue.* Dir. James William Guercio. United Artists, 1973.

401. 2010.

402. Testimony before the Senate Committee on Armed Services, January 27, 2009.

403. "California Voter Participation Survey," CVF, Davis, CA, March 2005.

latest in communication and data manipulation technologies to pommel those voters with persuasive pitches at the door, in the mail, and over the phone. In truth then, it is only these votes that they actually care about.

Within the EU, the most active voters reside precisely in countries where voting is mandatory. Among these countries are Belgium, Cyprus, Greece, and Luxembourg. In Greece, however, there is no penalty for not voting, unlike, for example, in Belgium. Italy gave up mandatory voting in 1992. Not everyone has the strength to keep up with politics. Most American voters do not even know the name of their own Congressman, the length of terms of House or Senate members, or what liberties the Bill of Rights guarantees. In fact, most Americans cannot name a single Supreme Court justice or a single cabinet department in the federal government. If voting was made mandatory in the United States, even these people would vote. And their votes would lessen the weight of the vote cast by a voter who actually knew something about politics. The ability of citizens to assess the political situation and political trends has deteriorated considerably: only about ten percent of the people have this ability any more and the percentage is decreasing as we speak; in a few years, no-one will have any idea what is going on in politics.

There is, of course, no real difference between parties; both the Democrats and the Republicans support a democratic republic, and the same is true in any Western country. The central principle of democracy—giving clear political alternatives—remains everywhere unrealized. Parties automatically gravitate towards the middle, because that is how you get the most votes. Since you cannot argue with facts, political debates will never be based on facts. Politicians avoid making specific statements to the public about the issues they are advocating. Party platforms are invariably perfunctory and vague. They concentrate more on "values" and down-home qualities than with how the party stands on hard questions of policy. They advocate such abstract causes as responsibility, caring, solidarity, fairness, freedom, or security. They might make isolated, less important proposals on concrete issues, but do not always even mention how they would finance these or how they affect the whole. So, to quote Gore Vidal, "a democracy is a place where numerous elections are held at great cost without issues and with interchangeable candidates."[404]

In the United States, unassuageable cultural grievances are elevated over solid material ones, with provocative myths of national authenticity and righteousness wronged eclipsing basic economic self-interest. "The American Republic will endure," in the famous words of Alexis de Tocqueville, "until politicians realize they can bribe the people with their own money." A recent Public Policy Institute survey found that 72% of Californians believe that voters, rather than legislators, should make budget decisions; the annual budget process in California has been turned into an annual budget crisis by direct democracy.[405] However, "The genius of our ruling class is that it has kept a majority of the people from ever questioning the inequity of a system where most people drudge along, paying heavy taxes for which they get nothing in

404. 1991, 201.

405. Mark Baldassare, "PPIC Statewide Survey: Special Survey on the California State Budget," Public Policy Institute of California, San Francisco, May 2005.

return."[406] The only real difference between this and slavery is that the masters lack the authority to beat, sell, or kill the people who are forced to labour for them.

"The art of government," declared Voltaire, "is to make two-thirds of a nation pay all it possibly can pay for the benefit of the other third."[407] Have you ever wondered why, if both the Democrats and the Republicans are against deficits, the United States still has massive deficits? Have you ever wondered why, if all the politicians are against inflation and high taxes, the U.S. still has inflation and high taxes? We have to face the fact that elections are typically decided by old people, not only because senior citizens historically swing elections with their votes, but because they also have the most money to stuff the campaign coffers. Baby boomers do not dominate the country in size alone; having lived through various employment and housing booms, they are the richest and most powerful generation that has ever lived. Certainly McCain and Obama were painfully aware of this during their presidential campaigns, or how else do you explain their deafening silence on the nation's biggest fiscal nightmare: that more and more of the federal budget goes to subsidizing old people, with Medicare, Medicaid, and Social Security spending expected to double over the next ten years. Is a single member of Congress willing to cut entitlements or increase taxes in order to avert a crisis that will culminate only when today's babies retire?

Because the U.S. Constitution provided for an explicit "open entry" into government, because anyone could become a member of Congress, a Supreme Court judge, or even President of the United States, resistance to State property invasions declined. By freeing up entry into government, the Constitution permitted anyone to openly express his desire for his neighbour's property; indeed, owing to the constitutional guarantee of "freedom of speech," everyone is protected in so doing, and what is more, everyone is permitted to act on this desire, provided that they gain entry into government. Of course, there are people who have no desire to enrich themselves at the expense of others or to lord over them, people who wish only to work, produce, and enjoy the fruits of their labour. But in order to defend themselves against attacks on their liberty and property, even the honest, hardworking people must become politically active, which means spending more and more of their time and energy in developing political skills.

As Lew Rockwell explains, while competition in the marketplace improves quality, competition in politics does exactly the opposite: given that the traits and talents required for political success—sociability, oratorial skills, charisma, etc.—are unevenly distributed among people, those with these particular traits and skills have a sound advantage in the competition for this scarce resource as compared with those without them; the only improvements that take place are in the process of doing bad things—lying, cheating, stealing, and killing. The price of political service is constantly increasing, whether measured in tax dollars or bribes, otherwise known as campaign contributions. Given that there are more "have-nots" of everything worth having than "haves" in every society, open political competition clearly favours the politically talented with little or no inhibition against taking other people's property

406. Vidal 2001, 993.

407. As quoted in Laing 1850, 184.

over people who respect the rights of others. It leads to the cultivation of the peculiar skills of demagoguery, deception, opportunism, and corruption, whereby entrance into and success within government becomes increasingly impossible for anyone who has a problem with lying and stealing. While the electorate recognizes that they are electing, at best, incompetents, and at worst, crooks, the constant mantra of pro-democracy is that "we just need to elect the right people"—as if there was any chance of the "right people" ever running for office.

Only a sovereign ruler can make smart decisions, an elected leader must make popular decisions, otherwise he won't get re-elected. Even in the U.S. House of Representatives, the more honest Congressmen decry the "permanent election" mentality, which has them spending more time to raise money for the next go-round than to actually do the job they were sent to Washington to do. In ***The Decline and Fall of the Athenian Republic***, Sir Alexander Fraser Tytler observed that: "A democracy cannot exist as a permanent form of government. It can only exist until the voters discover they can vote themselves money from the Public Treasury. From that moment on, the majority always votes for the candidate promising the most benefits from the Public Treasury with the result that a democracy always collapses over loose fiscal policy always followed by dictatorship."[408] A UN report shows that, after two decades of democratic government offset by dismal growth and persistent inequality, nearly half of all Latin Americans would welcome a return to authoritarian rule if it guaranteed greater economic benefits.[409]

Frequent elections make any truly long term decisions impossible—"A politician . . . thinks of the next election; while the statesman thinks of the next generation."[410] Unlike democratic "caretakers" of "public goods," kings, as proprietors of these same goods, take a long-run view and are interested in the preservation or enhancement of capital values. As the late Anarcho-Capitalist theorist and polemist Murray N. Rothbard explained, "while a private owner, secure in his property and owning its capital value, plans the use of his resource over a long period of time, the government official must milk the property as quickly as he can, since he has no security of ownership. . . .government officials own the use of resources but not their capital value (except in the case of the 'private property' of a hereditary monarch). When only the current use can be owned, but not the resource itself, there will quickly ensue uneconomic exhaustion of the resources, since it will be to no-one's benefit to conserve it over a period of time and to every owner's advantage to use it up as quickly as possible."[411]

Democracies have historically been short-lived, whereas the Roman Empire lasted 1,500 years, falling not to a democracy, but to another conquering empire, namely that of the Ottomans. The longest-lived republic in history, Venice, was hardly democratic. If by the oldest democracy in the world we mean, "Which country has ensured that all adult citizens, regardless of sex, race, or creed, may choose

408. As quoted in Krug 1969, 48.

409. United Nations Development Programme 2005.

410. J. F. Clarke, "Wanted, A Statesman!" Hale 1870, 644.

411. 1977, 188–89.

representatives to exercise the power of government longest?" the answer is not the United States, but New Zealand—universal adult suffrage was first established there as late as 1893. We should never forget that Hitler was elected, thanks in large measure to the financial crisis in which the German government had found itself. The fact that so few Americans believe a domestic dictatorship to be possible is exactly why it is becoming likely. Let us not kid ourselves: if tyranny is a breeding-ground for democracy, then democracy is a breeding-ground for tyranny. In democracies, the minorities are politically active, or have something to gain, and vice versa for tyrannies. But the amount of power is constant: when one person has it, another lacks it; only in exceptional circumstances does it ever stop at the hands of the people.

As Einstein put it, "Politics is a pendulum whose swings between anarchy and tyranny are fueled by perennially rejuvenated illusions."[412] Mass revolutions have been commonplace since Parisians stormed the Bastille in 1789, lynching the governor of the massive state prison and his guards. Although, in reality, they found only seven prisoners to release, and none of them political, the image of masses storming government buildings and toppling a tyrannical régime has haunted public imagination for over two hundred years. Indeed, Burke demostrated that such unbridled orgies of destruction did away with more liberty than they created, throwing out the good with the bad, leading inexorably towards violence and dictatorship, for which France suffered for many decades to come. The basics of ascending to power have not changed since the days of Montaigne any more than since those of Plutarch: the key is how to get the people on the move and then to calm them down again. Or as Gilbert Keith Chesterton phrased it: "You can never have a revolution in order to establish a democracy. You must have a democracy in order to have a revolution."[413]

If the collapse of the Soviet Union and the liberation of its satellites in Eastern and Central Europe, the Baltics, and Central Asia could be described as the first act in a perceived process of global democratization and liberalization, the so-called "colour revolutions" were seen in Washington as the second act in this historic epoch. Mikhail Saakashvili in Georgia, Viktor Yushchenko and Yulia Tymoshenko in Ukraine, Kurmanbek Bakiyev in Kyrgyzstan, and even Ahmed Chalabi in Iraq proved to be as greedy and power-hungry as their predecessors, discarding democratic principles in favour of nationalism and chauvinism, while exploiting American diplomatic and economic support as part of their effort to contain domestic and foreign threats. And as soon as being "pro-American" became less cost-effective, each of them hedged their bets by allying with countries like Russia and Iran.

"The natural progress of things is for liberty to yield and government to gain ground," wrote Jefferson.[414] "Men fight for freedom; then they begin to accumulate laws to take it away from themselves." In most societies at most times in history, people have had plenty of reasons to be discontent. The modern idea of "People Power" as the solution to corrupt and incompetent government is only liable to

412. 1979, 38.

413. *The Wind and the Trees.* 1909, 94–95.

414. To Edward Carrington, 27 May 1788. Mayer 1994, 145.

promote an endless cycle of upheaval. People Power can always oust one set of rulers and replace it with another, but it can never guarantee an honest or competent government. The cold cynical reality that inevitably follows the short revolutionary ecstasy can only be erased with another fix of revolt—resulting in a twisted caricature of Trotsky's "permanent revolution." "When smashing monuments, save the pedestals," suggested Stanislaw J. Lec, for "they always come in handy."[415] Of course, there are no great leaders anymore: the fact that we need to have a vote on "The Greatest American" proves that we no longer have great Americans; the first prerequisite of a symbolic authority is that everyone knows—and knows that everyone else knows—who holds that status. But even though anyone can become a celebrity these days, celebrities are still so revered that they are asked for their take on all sorts of political issues.

But if politics is the management of the public affairs, then what difference is there between a civic activist and a politician? Civic organizations have begun to patch the leaks in our society. Year after year, they take on a larger share of the burden that used to belong exclusively to the public sector. Government officials and politicians have reduced, both during recession and recovery, the amount and quality of public services. So what is the difference between an activist and a politician? Or an NGO and a government organization? Well, the politicians usually get paid—and ensure their income through electoral politics. The political enthusiast has become a wage-conscious professional. The civic activist helps others, but the professional politician only helps himself.

The so-called intrusion of politics into everyday life is interestingly linked with the talk about growing political passivity. People are not interested in politics and do not vote, but if their daily lives are filled with politically important decisions, even the small things count; the fact is, we vote more with our dollars than we do at the ballot. Foreclosures, lay-offs, bank failures and bailouts may dominate the headlines, but the decisions that will make or break the economy are not made on Wall Street; they are made on Main Street, where American consumers contribute 70 cents of every dollar spent in the U.S. economy. Consumption is really the least conspicuous form of power that the ordinary citizen has today. Wall Street may set the course of politics, but the consumers react quickly to decisions that are not to their liking. Inexpensive groceries and reasonably priced gasoline hold more interest than stuffy old ideologies. For a party to really do well in elections, it needs to promise cash for clunkers, or better yet, free Ferraris for everyone.

The definition of politics is itself a political definition. Today's politics are no longer for the enthusiast but for experts and professionals. Politics is a profession and a career, but therefore also the art of covering one's own behind. Ayn Rand defined a man of greatness as someone who is independent and uncompromising, who derives his self-respect from his accomplishments and integrity rather than from the approval of others. A man of mediocrity, by contrast, is someone who does not actually care about being competent and upright so long as he appears that way to others. Referred to as a "second-hander," he is perfectly embodied in the elected official, who is totally

415. Op. cit. 50.

dependent on the approval of those around him. By voting, you can only show that you support the system, that everything is fine, instead of actually asking whether things should be done differently. Voters will tell the non-voters: "If you don't vote, you can't complain"—even though settling for this is what really sounds nihilistic and apathetic.

An authority is he who is able to declare: "This is the way it is, because I say so." The present-day exercise of power is no longer based on such a master. He has been replaced by a manager, who says: "This is the way it is, because it is beneficial and profitable and convenient for all the parties involved." According to the liberal ideology, this signals the disappearance of power and its substitution by efficient management. But the exact opposite is actually true: only in conditions of equality can there be power as such; only a self-justifying power, which tries its best to act like a friend, appears as a "mere exercise of power." It is only today's fair and reasonable power that enables us to differentiate between the position of power and its justification. In President Clinton, you really had someone who nailed the central purpose of public confession in the 20th century; such confessions are a very powerful way for a leader to lay down power and say to the people: "I know I am no better than you are. I know I am just one of you. I am just a sinner like you."

"I am humbled," the favourite phrase of today's politician, is actually the antithesis of humility. Yet, as Orson Welles pointed out, "Nobody who takes on anything big and tough can afford to be modest."[416] And democratic accountability is clearly a joke: "If something goes wrong, it is more important to talk about who is going to fix it, than who is to blame."[417] Of course, "People find it far easier to forgive others for being wrong than being right."[418] But apologizing is not the same as admitting you are wrong. "When we blame ourselves, we feel that no one else has a right to blame us. It is the confession, not the priest, that gives us absolution."[419] And you know who are always apologizing? Abusive husbands and boyfriends, that's who! It is infinitely more important to stop doing what you are doing wrong than to apologize for it.

"In science it often happens that scientists say, 'You know that's a really good argument; my position is mistaken,' and then they actually change their minds and you never hear the old view from them again. They really do it. It doesn't happen as often as it should, because scientists are human and change is sometimes painful. But it happens every day. I cannot recall the last time something like that happened in politics or religion."[420] The productivity of public services is at the same level it was fifteen years ago, even though the rest of society has experienced massive innovation and rise in productivity. Since non-governmental organizations tend to be more efficient and less bureaucratic than the public sector, state and local governments are allocating more and more of the workload and responsibility to volunteer associations.

But this is always the case; the better you perform, the more work you will be

416. Welles & Bogdanovich 1998, 36.

417. Francis J. Gable, attributed.

418. Rowling 2005, 96.

419. *The Picture of Dorian Gray.* Op. cit. 68.

420. Carl Sagan, "The Burden of Skepticism," *Skeptical Inquirer* 12(1), Fall 1987.

assigned. If a unit improves its return, its budget is lowered, so the most rational course of action is not to improve anything. Every time a new employee goes to his workplace bursting with fresh ideas and suggests a novel and superior way to do things, the old employees take a look at each other and say, "just you wait and see." Talented people are divested of the passion and courage to realize their own concepts in an instant. It is incredible to how large a degree people accommodate themselves to the existing conditions and learn not to make waves. Conway's Law states that: "In any organization, there will always be one person who knows what is going on—this person must be fired."[421]

"All the problems of the world could be settled easily if men were only willing to think," insisted Thomas J. Watson. "The trouble is that men very often resort to all sorts of devices in order not to think, because thinking is such hard work." And it was Ralph Waldo Emerson who defined a "party" as "an elegant incognito devised to save a man from the vexation of thinking."[422] Today's political debates are not unlike barroom conversations, where everyone agrees with each other, and should anyone express a novel opinion, it is dismissed only because it differs from the consensus. Still, we should really be glad that our local, state, and national government officials are not terribly efficient: we now have the technological ability to make *1984* a reality, but scarcely anyone even cares what non-celebrities say or do.

421. Bloch 2003, 45.

422. June 20, 1831. 1982, 78.

6

If It Moves, Tax It; If It Keeps Moving, Regulate It; If It Stops Moving, Subsidize It

"Sometimes the only way to win is to lose."[423] Or as Sun Tzu put it, "Never fight a battle, unless you know you will win." It has been said that the moral arc of a political career can be divided into four parts: idealism, pragmatism, ambition, and corruption. You go into politics with a passion for a cause, determined to challenge the system; you then learn to work for your cause within the system; then advancing in the system becomes your cause; and, finally, you begin exploiting the system for personal profit. If we, as individuals, are to regain our personal sovereignty, it will not happen by fighting the system—that only reinforces and justifies it. And even if an external revolution does occur, without a corresponding change in our inner awareness, we shall soon find ourselves back in the same unsovereign muddle.

Picture if you will an inmate in a mental asylum, who stops taking his drugs and begins to see clearly, realizing that he is the prisoner of an institution. It is better for him to go about his daily routine as if he is none the wiser than to start storming the gates. While it serves no purpose to scream at the guards, there is a great difference

423. "Legs." *Oz.* HBO. July 28, 1999.

between the person who abides by the regulations from a consciousness of sovereignty and the one who abides by them because that is what you are supposed to do. "The true perfection of man lies, not in what man has but in what man is. Nothing should be able to harm a man but himself. Nothing should be able to rob a man at all. What a man really has is what is in him. What is outside of him should be a matter of no importance."[424] Society does not equal the world; the universe is within you, not without you.

"The only person who has more illusions than the dreamer is the man of action."[425] Those who try to "change the world" do not understand even the rudiments of evolution: evolution is a very, very long process and it takes a cataclysmic event to alter its course—like when the dinosaurs were wiped out by a comet (or an ice age), or in human history, the agricultural and industrial revolutions, the conquests of Alexander and Napoleon, the atomic bomb. The population growth that followed industrialization led to horrible sanitary and social plight. A series of cholera epidemics in the mid-19th century compelled the erection of sewer and water systems and the development of construction legislation. Still, humans have only tilled the land for a few thousand years, while we have been hunter-gatherers for hundreds of thousands of years—even the few cataclysmic events our species has experienced have not changed the fact that man is still, at bottom, very much a hunter-gatherer.

"The charm of history and its enigmatic lesson," noted Aldous Huxley, "consists in the fact that, from age to age, nothing changes and yet everything is completely different."[426] The human brain is first and foremost an economic engine forged by evolution through countless millennia of scrounging for scarce resources. The ability to trade things of value is the keystone of human character. Trade preceded agriculture, it preceded cities, it is the defining characteristic of human sociality and explains our success as a species. The same reward circuitry activated in the brain by cocaine, fast cars, and sexual attraction is activated by hard currency, be it in the form of paper, plastic, or animal skins. In fact, the prospect of gaining money activates specific brain regions in a way that the threat of losing it does not.[427] Animals have been known to develop addictions to mind-altering substances like catnip, but you are not going to see a leopard at Gamblers Anonymous any time soon.

As long as people could continue their free hunter-gatherer life, they were not interested in heavy and monotonous cultivation of the land. Studies indicate that the average proto-human spent only fifteen to twenty hours a week actually "working," while the rest was spent playing or relaxing.[428] The kind of society we have today has only existed for about five thousand years, having appeared with the first primitive states based on conquest, where the labour of slaves created a surplus that supported the ruling class. Until very recently, all farmers were slaves of varying degree—serfs,

---

424. *The Soul of Man under Socialism.* Op. cit. 1045–46.

425. *The Critic as Artist.* Ibid. 979.

426. 1965, 259.

427. Brian Knutson, et al. "Anticipation of Increasing Monetary Reward Selectively Recruits Nucleus Accumbens," *The Journal of Neuroscience* 21(16), August 15, 2001, RC159.

428. Sahlins 1972.

tenant-farmers, etc.—and slavery continues to exist today in West African and South American lands. For millennia, it was viewed as a normal consequence of military defeat, economic deprivation, or the vicissitudes of power. In Aristotle's mind, every worker was a slave; the only real change brought about by industrialization is that the slaves get paid—more.

Work is not distasteful to man only because of the physical exertion it requires, but because it has to be done for someone else. And it is not that the someone else is getting more than you are, but that he is not just another captive but the captor. Everyone who has expropriated our means of enjoyment is a captor: God, State, employer. Every time we try to acquire a means of enjoyment, the captors demand their lawful share—in the form of sacrifice, taxes, or work. "There is not one verse in the Bible inhibiting slavery, but many regulating it," observed the Rev. Alexander Campbell in the early 19th century. "It is not then, we conclude, immoral."[429] At the end of the 6th century *anno Domini*, Pope St. Gregory the Great became perhaps the greatest slave-owner in the world by convincing wealthy landowners and slave-owners that their heirs would not live to enjoy their property. The Protestant Church did not oppose slavery for the slaves, but because slavery guaranteed its rivals, the Catholics, free labour.

Since capitalism emerged out of the contradictions of feudalism, there has never been such a thing as "pure competition" as described in the textbooks. Nor has there ever been true *laissez-faire* or unregulated capitalism. Ever. Under modern corporate capitalism, workers are driven by economic necessity to sell their labour, and so liberty, to those who own the means of life. In effect, they are only free to the extent that they can choose whom they will obey. To mean anything, freedom must imply more than just the right to change masters—voluntary servitude is still servitude. Portraying the parties of an employment contract as free and equal to each other ignores the serious inequality in bargaining power that exists between the worker and the employer. To go on and portray the relationship of subordination and exploitation which inevitably results as the epitome of freedom is to make a mockery of both individual sovereignty and social justice.

If you ignore the hierarchical nature of an association, you can end up supporting organizations predicated on the denial of freedom, all because they are "voluntary." You cannot demonize state authoritarianism while ignoring identical albeit contract-sanctified subservient arrangements in private corporations. Most factories are run like military dictatorships, with privates at the bottom, supervisors acting like sergeants, and on up through the hierarchy. The company can dictate everything from your clothing and hair style to how you spend a large portion of your life, working. It can suppress freedom of speech, press, and assembly; it can use ID cards, closed-circuit cameras, and armed security guards to watch us. We are forced, by circumstances, to accept much of this, or join the millions of unemployed; in nearly any job, you have only the "right" to quit. People know that the corporations they work for do not really value them, and they will undermine the institutional structure of that corporation for their own personal interests—this is not a system that can sustain

429. Pillsbury 1883, 441.

itself.

In pre-industrial society, taxes over 10% were considered extortionate. While the English king's power to tax without consent was only assumed and thus in dispute, the U.S. Constitution explicitly granted this very power to Congress. At the outset of the American "experiment," the tax burden imposed on citizens was light, almost negligible. Modern income taxes, if merely at 0.001%, mean that the person does not own the fruit of his own labour, which is a human rights violation comparable to slavery. The incredible growth of the U.S. federal government over the course of the 20th century would have been impossible without the bountiful confiscations of all-encompassing, progressive income taxation. After the Sixteenth Amendment was ratified in 1913, expenditures of the federal government grew from 3.6% to 25.6% of national income. By the end of the century, income taxes provided 80% of federal revenue, making even the economic burden imposed on slaves and serfs seem moderate in comparison.[430] All confiscatory taxation, no matter at how low a percentage, denotes socialism; just because we are taught at school that only Soviet-style communism is "socialism," it does not change the facts.

Until the very end of the 19th century, government employment rarely exceeded 3% of the total labour force. In late 1992, for the first time in U.S. history, more Americans were employed by various levels of local, state, and federal government than were employed by private industry.[431] In other words, the United States now has more people paid to monitor its citizens, than it has people producing money to pay the monitors. The sheer bulk of tax laws and regulations render compliance arbitrary and enforcement selective, superceding the rule of law; it allows government to seize the assets of its citizens without obtaining court judgments; the assumption that taxpayers are guilty until proven innocent evades due process, while the requirement of taxpayers to admit under penalty of perjury how much they have earned violates the Fifth Amendment guarantee against self-incrimination. Complying with the tax system means a lack of privacy; the government needs to put a price tag on every thing and person in your life—unless you are a church.

At a time when most non-homeland security agencies were taking cuts, the Bush administration asked for a budget increase for the Internal Revenue Service. The White House budget office noted that tax work "towers over the entire paperwork burden for the rest of the federal government," accounting for some 80% of the whole.[432] The tax code is extremely complex partially because rates have gotten so high that people cannot function unless there are deductions and credits. Most U.S. senators and congressmen derive much of their power precisely from inventing and defending the complexities of the tax code in the form of special breaks for favoured voting blocks and fashionable public causes: there were an astonishing 15,000 changes in tax provisions between 1986 and 2006. The power to tax is with Congress, and its focal point is the Ways and Means Committee, where all tax bills begin. As soon as you become a member of this committee, you will be told that this lobbyist for that

430. David Hartman, "Dr. Pangloss on Taxation, " *Chronicles*, October 2002.

431. James Wasserman, "The Price of Freedom." Hyatt 2000, 57.

432. Office of Management and Budget 2004, 17.

corporation wants to meet with you. Capitol Hill is an institution overrun with registered lobbyists—their numbers roughly tripled just between 1997 and 2005, from 11,000 to 33,000.[433]

No Washington lobbyist will tell a congressional committee member that they want some special interest favour; they walk in and they say they have been looking at the rules and have found something that just isn't fair and what they are seeking is fairness. Unfortunately, "fairness" for the banking industry and the pharmaceutical industry and every other special interest results in unfairness for the rest of us. Lawmakers are so inundated with special-interest demands, Robert Reich writes in *Supercapitalism: The Transformation of Business, Democracy, and Everyday Life*, that "our voices as citizens—as opposed to our voices as consumers and investors—are being drowned out."[434] One of the reasons tax policy in the U.S. looks worse than it might look if we just had a bunch of trained monkeys design a tax system is that Congress is full of people with divergent interests who steer tax policy towards rewarding their own favourites. Before you know it, the tax bill will have hundreds and hundreds of special lines and special giveaways in it. At present, the U.S. tax code runs more than 60,000 pages—a tangled web of loopholes and exemptions that is all but incomprehensible to the ordinary taxpayer. In fact, the tax law has become so complicated that not even IRS workers understand it; figuring out the tax code forms a huge dead-weight burden that threatens to turn the United States into a paper-shuffling nation where no-one actually gets anything done.

There is only one legitimate reason for the government to levy a tax, and that is to raise money; anything they try to accomplish with taxes other than raising money is corruption. The U.S. Constitution gives the federal government the right to tax for the "common Defense" and "general [not specific] welfare," as in the case of the Centers for Disease Control and Prevention; however, many of the current government departments, such as the Departments of Housing, Energy, Education, and Health and Human Services, seem to lack any constitutional basis. Nowhere does the Constitution give the federal government the power to engage in income redistribution or, indeed, social engineering; yet Congress uses the tax code to affect all sorts of human behaviour: citizens are encouraged to get married, they are encouraged to buy houses, they are encouraged to save for their retirement, and discouraged from drinking alcohol or smoking cigarettes. Progressive taxation is just another way of the government imposing its values on the people—flat-rate tax is the only morally neutral form of taxation.

It was Adam Smith who said that, "The tax which each individual is bound to pay ought to be certain, and not arbitrary. Where it is otherwise, every person subject to the tax is put more or less in the power of the tax gatherer."[435] Having a government that is reasonably sized and finances itself with a reasonable tax code is something we should all demand. It is kind of puzzling that the code has evolved to the extend it has without people getting really upset. One of the many paradoxes of the United States

---

433. Reich 2007, 134.

434. Ibid. 163.

435. 1804, II, 259.

is that it fought for its independence from the British Crown to escape unfair taxes, yet it now has one of the most complicated tax codes in the world. Two hundred years ago, America had real freedom: if you never hurt, robbed, cheated, or slandered anyone, you had nothing to fear from the government. But now, largely because of the complexity of the tax code, there is no-one in the U.S. who can say beyond a shadow of a doubt that they are innocent; and when no-one is sure they are innocent, no-one can speak out.

Less taxes mean less government and that means more privacy and more freedom. Even after adjusting for differences in the cost of living and the population in each country, total U.S. government spending per capita in 2009 exceeded that of all but eight nations in the world. Canada, which most Americans view as much less free than their country, spent 14% less per capita than the United States; Japan 32% less, and New Zealand about 40% less.[436] If federal spending follows the pattern of the last forty years, the government will spend almost one-third of the gross domestic product by 2050. To cover all the additional spending with income taxes alone, they would have to be more than tripled from the 2005 levels—which would not work because the top rate would exceed 100%. And economists generally agree that even 60% tax rates would discourage people from working and saving, leading to a flood of new, unproductive tax shelters. Should the share of tax revenues in the economy return to and stay at the historical average, the public debt would swell to almost four times the GDP by 2050—the interest on a debt load that size would exceed all tax revenues. The only way out is to reduce runaway government spending.

It is quite hard, administratively, to reduce the budget of a government bureau, but it is quite easy to increase it. Bureaus are fiercely resistant to zero-based budgeting, i.e. starting from scratch every year and having to annually rejustify every line of the budget request. It is also difficult for higher-level authority to identify areas for cost reduction, since the very *raison d'être* of a bureaucratic organization is deference to institutionalized expertise. The easy way is to take the previous budget and treat it as the next one—with adjustments for inflation and annual increases, of course. It is only departures from the *status quo*, not the *status quo* itself, that require justification. Staffed with supposed experts, the bureau itself is usually the source of justification for departures—and these departures are always in the direction of more money and more power for the bureau. What goes for one bureau goes for all of them, and thus government grows. By compelling private property-owners and market-income earners to subsidize politicians and civil servants, there will be less wealth formation, fewer producers, less productivity, and ever more waste and parasitism.

When private-sector workers' 401(k)s and IRAs plummeted in value due to economic collapse and endemic, Wall Street-orchestrated market manipulation, government "defined-benefit," lifetime-cost-of-living-adjusted pension plans, despite already being underfunded by $2 trillion, were made richer than ever. When more than seven million American workers lost their jobs and were subsisting on unemployment benefits and food stamps, federal government employees—who now earn double what private-sector workers make—were given another round of pay and

436. "The Welfare State of America," *Washington Times*, April 16, 2010.

benefit increases. The federal work force is older than the private-sector work force; the seemingly guaranteed and ever-escalating monthly pension benefits of retirees who were once state or municipal workers are breaking local budgets nationwide. It is adding insult to injury to let those living off of other peoples' taxes have a say in how high those taxes are; no government employee or anyone who receives government benefits, whether they are welfare recipients or government contractors, should have the right to vote—the conflict of interest is glaring.

For the last thirty years, American corporate taxes were the lowest in the world; now the United States has the second highest corporate tax rate of the industrialized countries.[437] The problem is, you cannot tax corporations in the sense that you cannot tax a piece of paper—you can only tax people. A tax on a corporation is really just a tax on people, specifically the people who do all the hiring. How exactly are you supposed to create jobs by taking money away from those who do the hiring? The sales of the world's top 200 companies make up 27.5% of global economic activity, but they employ only under one percent of the world's workforce, having outsourced their manufacturing, their research and development, their back-office work, and even much of their logistics coordination.[438] As the New York real estate mogul Leona Helmsley famously exclaimed, "Only the little people pay taxes." Entities are created so that profits appear to be earned where taxes are low, while losses are borne where taxes are high. At the same time, tax-breaks for such pursuits as flying in private jets help minimize the burden at the top. What is more, the IRS continues to focus on large manufacturing companies, while mostly ignoring the big financial service companies, which represent only a small fraction of all corporate filings, but control 72% of all large corporate assets and receive 46% of all large corporate income.[439]

Equitable tax enforcement is crucial to overall compliance, due to the fact that humans tend to obey in direct proportion to the chance of getting caught. No-one likes to be the sucker who pays taxes while his neighbour gets round them. The problem occurs when the government divides us into different groups, taxes us at different rates, or different times, or different ways, and we do not know whether we are paying more than our neighbour. Politicians love that, they want everyone to think that somebody else is getting away with murder, so we should raise their taxes, but since you are getting away with something, you should stay out of the conversation. The flat tax is the only tax that could even remotely be considered fair: everyone pays the same rate regardless of their race, creed, sex, income, or wealth. And although a simpler tax code would not eliminate the temptation to cheat, it would provide fewer means to do so. A flat tax would actually represent a tax increase for wealthy people who have established elaborate tax shelters or who reap the

---

437. "National and State Corporate Income Tax Rates, U.S. States and OECD Countries, 2011," The Tax Foundation, Washington, D.C., January 17, 2011.

438. Sarah Anderson & John Cavanagh, "Top 200: The Rise of Corporate Global Power," Institute for Policy Studies, Washington, D.C., December 4, 2000.

439. "Large Financial Service Corporations Dominate the Corporate World: But Internal Revenue Service Allocates Only a Small Proportion of Its Corporate Auditors to the IRS Group Policing These Companies," Transactional Records Access Clearinghouse, Syracuse University, April 6, 2009.

benefits of large deductions. It would also eliminate the need for a dysfunctional bureaucracy to administer it, saving billions of dollars of federal money each year. In the meantime, tax avoidance and tax evasion remain growth industries; accountants have now even been compelled into coining the term "tax avoision" to describe the grey areas in between. The old libertarian argument that all taxes are just a form of theft from hard-working individuals suddenly has new credibility.

At the same time that Congress has put more Americans on the dole than ever before, it has also exempted vast numbers of people from any federal income tax obligation whatsoever. According to the Tax Foundation, more than 52 million tax filers had zero tax obligation in 2008. The Tax Policy Center says that, as of 2009, roughly 47% of households, or 71 million, will not owe any federal income tax.[440] In the past 75 years, the soaring number of government dependents has made it far more difficult to curb politicians' power. As H. L. Mencken quipped during the New Deal, federal policy is dividing society between "those who work for a living and those who vote for a living."[441] The sheer number of hand-out recipients has transformed the purpose of government from maintaining order to confiscating as much as possible from vulnerable taxpayers. Instead of a vote on what government should do, elections have become referendum on how much it should take.

Work has, of course, become the modern golden calf: work hard and the world will respect you; work hard and you can have anything you want; work extra super hard, ignoring your family while spending 14 hours a day at the office, and you will make a few hundred grand a year, which you will never have the time to spend, and can buy a nice eight-bedroom mansion you never spend any time in. Work is the one thing really worth doing and if you are not working that makes you either a slacker or a leech. Our jobs have become synonymous with our identities, yet quitting a job is the most liberating act there is—well, after renouncing God, anyway. "You're not your job. You're not how much money you have in the bank. You're not the car you drive. You're not the contents of your wallet. You're not your fucking khakis. You're the all-singing, all-dancing crap of the world."[442]

However, if you live in a stooped position long enough, you can easily mistake it for an upright stance. We frown at people who decide to "give it all up" and start exploring something radical and independent, something more attuned with their passions, whilst secretly envying them. We are both infuriated and enchanted by the idea that someone can just up and quit their jobs, and give up certain "mandatory" lifestyle accoutrements in order to dive into some seemingly random creative or spiritual endeavour that has nothing to do with boosting the gross domestic product. We are taught from day one to be productive members of society, and are guilted into believing that this has to involve some type of repetitive, dress-coded, cubicle-based work for a larger corporate or consumerist cause.

Commoners were either serfs or independently wealthy before industrialization; however, there was no separation of work and leisure even then. During imperialism,

440. "Tax Units that Pay No Individual Income Tax by Cash Income Level, 2009," April 9, 2010.

441. As quoted in Bovard 2000, 125.

442. *Fight Club*, op. cit.

the necessary manpower was taken by force; today, the democratic lectures about "individuality" and against "authoritarianism" are a much better way to turn people into an obedient workforce. "Listen up, maggots. You are not special. You are not a beautiful or unique snowflake. You're the same decaying organic matter as everything else."[443] A receptionist used to be called a receptionist, now she is known as "director of first impressions"; school bus drivers have become "transporters of learners"; cleaning ladies are "sanitation technicians." But "there is nothing more debasing than the work of those who do well what is not worth doing at all."[444] The irony is, modern automation was supposed to *free* us from work.

Nowadays, people have only time and energy to work and rest, not to reflect and create. And harried schedules, international competition, and unrealistic expectations are not just for adults anymore. Children as young as seven or eight have stress caused by having to choose school subjects that will fit their future professions; before, a carpenter's son simply went on to become a carpenter. There is a palpable fear among schoolchildren yet to reach double digits that the wrong curriculum will condemn them to a no-name university and a second-class life—even the rich kids are now expected to undergo intensive training to prepare for life in our brutally competitive modern economy.

The tougher the economic times, the more employers need to know what they are getting when they hire someone. When job applications pour in by the buckets, each and every one padded with degrees and trying to appear as impressive as possible, what matters is what the person can do for the company. Unfortunately, many young people cannot get jobs because they have no work experience, having been wildly misled all their lives about the great glories that await anyone who "stays in school" and gets good grades. There are numerous engineers, mathematicians, and even lawyers in this situation, to say nothing of historians, sociologists, and people with degrees in communications or marketing. Adding to the predicament is the burden of student loans: today's college graduates can be six figures in debt and are immediately forced to service it if they accept employment; with no opportunities outside McDonald's or Wal-Mart, they often opt to stay in school and get another degree in hopes that the labour market will eventually turn around.

Young professionals wish to work in a more free and independent fashion, and to live in more individual settings. Many modern individualists abhor the 9-to-5 routine, making no clear demarcation between work and leisure. Especially in "creative professions," work and non-work time are intertwined in the same manner as in family farms of the old. And just what is considered creative today? Investing. Consulting. Marketing. Polling. The modern tragedies are self-employment and the exercise of "free" professions. We try to get rid of the boss but end up bossing ourselves. The truth about the present situation is that everyone is a worker—except for the handful of large investors who hold both labour and management in a stranglehold.

443. Ibid.

444. Vidal 2001, 65.

"The trouble with being in the rat race is that even if you win, you're still a rat."[445] At the moment, the globalizing labour market can run riot without fear of revolt; no CEO, answerable to shareholders and fearful of competitors answerable to theirs, would dare give his employees a raise. This might go some way towards explaining the anomalies of the last couple recoveries, where profits have soared but wages have stagnated and few new jobs have been created. There has been zero net job creation in the United States since December 1999; no previous decade going back to the 1940s had job growth of less than 20%.[446] "Jobless recovery" is a recovery for economists, corporate balance sheets, and investors only, not for the millions out of work. In our society, the unemployed lack basic human dignity, but the powers that be do not even want full employment—what they want is a labour reserve in a poor bargaining position. The military machine needs poor people to enlist, which they will not do if they can easily find gainful employment elsewhere; aided by the bleak job market, the U.S. military met all its recruitment goals in 2008 for the first time since becoming an all-volunteer force in 1973.[447]

Corporate profits today accrue less from innovation than from squeezing costs. The American consulting firm Booz Allen Hamilton found that the rate of turnover in the world's 2,500 largest corporations increased from 9% in 1995 to 15.3% in 2005.[448] Now, efficiency in general is a good thing. If you have several ways in which to reach the same goal, surely it is best to use the least wasteful one? Most businesses spend a lot of resources to improve their efficiency and there is nothing wrong with that. For example, an efficient process is bound to be more environmentally friendly, resulting in less depletion of natural resources and less pollution. If we can keep the world going with fewer resources/employees, why is that suddenly a bad thing? It is not immediately obvious why full employment should be a goal in itself. The aim of every employer is to gain more value from his employees than he pays in wages; otherwise, there is no growth, no advance, and no gain for the company. Conversely, the aim of each employee should be to contribute more to the company than he receives in wages, thereby providing a solid rationale for getting raises and promotions.

An increase in salaries, without a corresponding increase in productivity, only means more expensive labour, and hence lower demand for labour. The real problem is the massive public sector, whose labour force does not compete in free markets at all. We are now in the situation where the public sector offers better salaries, bigger pay hikes, faster advancement, and larger pensions than the private sector. If we had genuine economic growth and real productivity gains, there would also be increases in real wages. When companies fire their native workers and import stuff they used to make, it appears like productivity—the value of the goods and services produced per hours worked—has increased. But it is the trade deficit that has increased: the

445. Lily Tomlin, attributed.

446. Neil Irwin, "Aughts Were a Lost Decade for U.S. Economy, Workers," *Washington Post*, January 2, 2010.

447. Ann Scott Tyson, "A Historic Success in Military Recruiting: In Midst of Downturn, All Targets Are Met," *Washington Post*, October 14, 2009.

448. Reich 2007.

United States has replaced much of its domestic labour force with foreign labour, and American workers are not benefiting from the economic growth because it does not really exist; it only looks like the economy is growing, because the U.S. dollar is losing its value, thanks to massive fiscal stimuli, quantitative easing, and government borrowing. A notable portion of American workers are struggling under long, stressful workdays, while others are out of work.

Ask yourself, which is worse, honest Graeco-Roman slavery or modern wage-slavery—indentured servants slaving away to pay off their student loans, mortgages, and credit card debt? Slaves of antiquity were often educated people, frequently more so than their masters—many were employed as teachers or scribes. They could not only amass money and property, including slaves of their own, but purchase their freedom, conjuring up comparisons to modern retirement. However, the notion of public pensions is predicated on the Protestant work ethic. How often do you hear the hard-working man say "I'll do it when I retire"? In other words, people will do something they do not really like doing for their whole lives, and when they are done, it's like getting out of prison, they finally get to do what they actually like doing? This is no more rational than the Puritan version of the final reward: "No, I don't think people really give a shit about [meeting their maker] unless they're completely bamboozled by religious superstition—to live your life in planning for this good time you're going to have in the sky."[449]

It is clear that work is the measure of human dignity for the American male. If you have no job, you must become an alcoholic, beat your family, and commit suicide with the help of a thick rope and a roof beam. A combination of benzodiazepines and a 12-gauge can also be recommended, since no-one has a chance of surviving in this world without a job. A working man has to bear in mind that vacations are not meant for holidaymaking. They entail careful plans with precise goals and tasks. It is necessary to see every sight and visit every landmark, so that one can return to work to rest after such a labourious project. One's back yard is a perpetual construction site that grows weeds, unsightly trees, and even rocks. One is reminded of Robinson Crusoe, who even on a desert island builds a farm, filling his days with trimming the hedges and carrying water, not thinking for one moment that he could just as easily be relaxing under a palm tree and letting fruit rain on him from above. He manages to turn even paradise into a labour camp.

The pathological workaholic, who sacrifices his wive and children on the altar of his livelihood, appears as a righteous and selfless person in the eyes of society, one who toils and toils and works his fingers to the bone for the welfare of his loved ones. On the other hand, a person who neglects his family in order to booze and whore in the local tavern is viewed as a complete asshole. The motives of the two may differ, but the end result is the same: Dad does not come home. By appealing to work, one can even avoid family life altogether: a woman who does not want to have children can invoke her career. And what about the saying "work hard, play hard"? An alcoholic is always viewed with suspicion, but as long as the lush "puts food on the table," no-one is allowed to interfere with his self-destructive habit. Only when he

449. Frank Zappa, Interview by Bob Marshall, October 22, 1988.

fails to do his job is his family or employer allowed to intervene. In other words, work can be used to justify just about anything—today's "I just work here" rhetoric bears an uncanny resemblance to Eichmann's mantra of "just following orders."

The International Labour Organization estimates that approximately two million workers are killed annually due to occupational injuries and illnesses, with workplace accidents causing at least 350,000 fatalities a year. According to the ILO, half of the deaths are avoidable. And for every fatal accident, there are an estimated 1,000 non-fatal injuries, which often result in lost earnings or permanent disability. The death toll at work is the equivalent of 5,000 workers dying each day, three persons every minute—more than double the figure for deaths from warfare. In fact, work kills more people than alcohol and drugs put together.[450] And although blue-collar workers face a lot of the most obvious dangers, those slaving in offices and stores must contend with e.g. toxic air, workplace violence, and transmittable diseases. Sitting down is hard work when you do it all day long. A Japanese labour bureau recently ruled that one of Toyota's top engineers died from working too many hours in 2008, just one case in a string of such findings in a nation where extraordinarily long hours has been the norm. He was only 45 years old, but had been under immense pressure as the lead engineer in developing a hybrid version of the popular Camry line. Known as *karoshi* in Japan, "deaths from overwork" have steadily increased since the country's health ministry first recognized the phenomenon in 1987.[451]

Even so, people today live longer, are healthier, and have less gruelling jobs than ever before. Until relatively recently, most people only lived for a few years after retiring; now they can easily hang on for another thirty or forty years. People in the West live to have very expensive treatments for cancer and heart disease, because they no longer routinely die of measles or tuberculosis. Retirement is not some moral reward or recompense you get for "doing the right thing," but something necessitated by our eventual inability to work—all pensions used to be disability pensions. The whole idea of the pension was to provide public servants with decent old-age benefits, not to make them wealthy, to allow them to retire younger and with more money and be able to go play golf while the rest of us support them. The classic dilemma of democracy is that too many people benefit from the *status quo* to change it, but the *status quo* is not sustainable. Even modest efforts in Europe to curb social benefits and raise retirement age have triggered backlashes. All industrial societies are getting steadily older: in 1935, 6% of Americans were 65 and older; they are now 12% and by 2030 are projected to constitute 20%.[452] The question is how generous a "safety net" for retirees can our society afford without overtaxing the young or bankrupting the economy.

Americans tend to view "earned benefits" and "welfare" differently, thinking the first a right and the second a privilege. But, in theory, welfare should serve some

450. Sameera Al-Tuwaijri, et al. "XVIII World Congress on Safety and Health at Work, June 2008, Seoul, Korea: Introductory Report," International Labour Organization, Geneva, 2008.

451. Sunichi Araki & Kenji Iwasaki, "Death Due to Overwork (Karoshi): Causation, Health Service, and Life Expectancy of Japanese Males," *Japan Medical Association Journal* 48(2), February 2005, 92–98.

452. Schieber & Shoven 1999.

public purpose and not just profit the recipient. We cannot ask the relevant questions if we refuse to admit that Social Security and Medicare are welfare. Ida May Fuller, the first U.S. retiree to receive benefits, paid $24.75 and got $22,888.92—almost a thousand times her contribution. That was in 1940, but throughout the '50s and '60s, many beneficiaries continued to receive ten times or more the amount their payroll taxes would have returned if invested in treasury bonds, which they were not. In fact, most beneficiaries still receive a surplus in benefits over what their taxes would have returned if invested in such a manner.[453] Of course, government bonds themselves are based on a similar pyramid scheme: in order for the government to be able to pay interest on its bonds, future taxpayers need to come up with the money. Every rate of interest implies a doubling time, and no "real" growth of any economy has ever been able to increase exponentially at a fast enough rate to pay the debts that keep accruing interest. As early as 1967, economist Paul Samuelson wrote that "a growing nation is the greatest Ponzi game ever contrived."[454]

With the huge stock market losses in 2009, public pensions in the United States are now underfunded by more than $1 trillion. This lack of funds explains why dozens of American retirement plans have issued more than $50 billion in pension obligation bonds during the past quarter of a century—more than half of them after 1997.[455] The quick fix for pension funds becomes a future albatross for taxpayers, who may have to cover what fund administrators had hoped to get from investment returns. In 1978, when Congress amended the Internal Revenue Code to include Section 401(k), it saw the provision as a way for workers to supplement their employer's traditional defined-benefit pension plans and Social Security, although it also provided a nifty hideaway for highly paid executives to shelter income from taxes. However, no-one at the time envisioned 401(k)s as something on which people would have to rely for their retirement, as 60% of all U.S. workers do today.[456] Essentially, millions of regular Americans have been conscripted into the equities markets, where they have helped fuel stock prices and provide a bonanza for the financial services sector that manages and sells investment funds. American workers have locked themselves into the stock market to such a degree that they will allow nearly anything to happen on Wall Street as long as their pension funds and invested savings recover. Every cent of the bailout money that the banks "pay back" is made up of interest margins, the difference between the interests of deposits and loans, or to put it simply, value taken away from society, which each of us in the end has to produce with our own labour.

Yet the national debt represents only a relatively small portion of the government's total financial obligations; the far greater bulk is made up of long-term liabilities inherent in entitlement programs. For more than two decades, regardless of which party was in power, Congress has raided the Social Security trust funds to pay for other programs, thus masking the actual size of the budget deficit; this means that

---

453. Ibid.

454. "Social Security," *Newsweek*, February 13, 1967.

455. Alicia H. Munnell, et al. "Pension Obligation Bonds: Financial Crisis Exposes Risks," Center for Retirement Research at Boston College, Chestnut Hill, MA, January 2010.

456. Idem. "An Update on 401(k) Plans: Insights from the 2007 Survey of Consumer Finances," CRR Boston College, Chestnut Hill, MA, November 2009.

every single government entitlement program in the United States is now bankrupt. Social Security, Medicare, and Medicaid together constituted more than half of all federal spending by 2009. The Congressional Budget Office has estimated these entitlement programs will grow by two-thirds or more between 2005 and 2030, on account of the baby boom, longer life expectancies, and rising health care costs. If the Congress wishes to cover these expenses, it will have to do one of the following: a) raise all federal taxes by 50%; b) triple annual budget deficits; c) eliminate defence spending plus one-third of other federal spending, excluding interest payments.[457] According to some scholarly research, the low birth rates are partly explained by high old-age benefits: if the State pays for old age, why go to the trouble of raising children, who at least used to return the favour by acting as caregivers? At the same time, the resultant high taxes are discouraging young couples from assuming the added cost of children.

Having a child is practically a luxury in a consumer economy—a tremendously expensive investment of time and energy. Couples with the most intellectual prowess, and thus the aptitudes to help the country maintain a competitive position in a technologically complex world, are having the fewest number of children. The economic consequences of having a child today are pretty much the exact opposite of having one in the feudal or agricultural societies of the past, where children constituted a huge economic advantage. Birthrates will only decline as a result of the ironically named Social Security system, because in subsidizing retirees out of taxes imposed on current income earners, the institution of a family is systematically weakened. The intergenerational bond between parents, grandparents, and children is broken as the old no longer need rely on the assistance of their children. The young, who typically have less accumulated wealth, must support the old, rather than the other way around, as was once typical within families. Family breakups and dysfunction are on the increase, and provisionary action—saving and capital formation—is falling, while consumption rises.

Western culture affords practically no room for creative breaks between kindergarten and retirement. There is little tolerance for seeking out a different kind of work, the type that does not involve cubicles and paid health care. "You are what you do. If you do boring, stupid, monotonous work, chances are you'll end up boring, stupid, and monotonous. Work is a much better explanation for the creeping cretinisation all around us than even such significant moronising mechanisms as television and education. People who are regimented all their lives, handed to work from school and bracketed by the family in the beginning and the nursing home in the end, are habituated to hierarchy and psychologically enslaved. Their aptitude for autonomy is so atrophied that their fear of freedom is among their few rationally grounded phobias."[458]

Leave an "honest job"? Have no reliable source of income for months on end? Trade stability for risk and blind chance? No way, most of us would say. However, intense competition and technological advancements have made jobs less secure, and

---

457. Robert J. Samuelson, "AARP's America Is a Mirage," *Washington Post*, November 16, 2005.

458. Black 1986, 22.

as parents work longer hours, they put their children in more scheduled activities. The schedule of the typical middle-class child begins at 6 a.m. when he starts "lugging body-bag sized equipment valises from the SUVs into the [hockey] rink," as *New York Times* columnist David Brooks put it, and continues after school with debate team, volunteer work at a retirement home, and then studying for the math quiz.[459] We have been taught to think of "success" as dependent upon, or even synonymous with, "schooling," which is historically untrue in both an intellectual and a financial sense. Even today, the self-made millionaires are often high school or college drop-outs.

Advocates of "free" or public education promote a view that a system based on fees would cause many children to forego an education; literary rates would decline and the country would slide down towards low economic growth and stagnation. In 1650, male literacy in the United States was 60%. Between 1800 and 1840, literacy in the North rose from 75% to 90% and in the South from 60% to 81%. These increases took place before the Common School Movement led by Horace Mann even began. Massachusetts had reached a level of 98% literacy by 1850, two years before the state's compulsory education law was enacted. According to Senator Edward Kennedy's office, the literacy rate of Massachusetts was only 91% in the 1980s. Some people might wonder exactly what literacy entailed during the early 19th century, so here are some numbers: Thomas Paine's *Common Sense* (1776) sold 120,000 copies to a population of three million, the equivalent of over twelve million copies today; Noah Webster's *Spelling Bee* sold five million copies to a population of less than twenty million in 1818; and Walter Scott's novels sold the same number between 1813 and 1823—the equivalent of almost eighty million copies today.[460]

A considerable number of well-known Americans never went through the system of compulsory secondary schools that quite often resemble prisons. Washington, Franklin, Jefferson, and Lincoln have countless public schools named after them, though not one of them ever "graduated" from one. Alexander Inglis, for whom a lecture in education at Harvard is named, makes it perfectly clear in his 1918 book, *Principles of Secondary Education*, that compulsory schooling in the United States was intended to be exactly what it had been for Prussia a century earlier: a fifth column in the burgeoning democratic movement that threatened to give the peasantry and the proletariat a voice at the bargaining table. Dividing their children by age-grading, subject, constant rankings on tests, and other, subtler means, meant that the likelihood of the ignorant masses ever re-uniting into a dangerous whole was radically reduced.

It has always been in the interest of economic and political leaders to dumb people down, to demoralize them, to divide them from one another, and to discard them if they refuse to conform. The captains of industry and government explicitly wanted an educational system that would maintain social order by teaching the masses just enough to get by but not enough so that they could think for themselves, question the socio-political order, or communicate articulately. In the late 19th century, the Senate Committee on Education was getting worried about the localized, non-standardized,

---

459. As quoted in Kay S. Hymowitz, "Great Expectations: Life Among the Sushi Generation," *In Character*, Fall 2004.

460. Richman 1994.

non-mandatory form of education that was actually teaching children to read at advanced levels, to comprehend history, and what is worse, to think for themselves. The committee stated in its 1888 report that, "education is one of the principal causes of discontent of late years manifesting itself among the laboring classes."[461] By the turn of the century, America's new educrats were pushing a new form of schooling with a new mission—and it had nothing to do with teaching or learning.

The famous American philosopher and educational reformer John Dewey wrote in 1897: "Every teacher should realize he is a social servant set apart for the maintenance of the proper social order and the securing of the right social growth."[462] As Woodrow Wilson, the president of Princeton University, said to the NYC School Teachers Association in 1909: "We want one class of persons to have a liberal education, and we want another class of persons, a very much larger class, of necessity, in every society, to forgo the privileges of a liberal education and fit themselves to perform specific difficult manual tasks."[463] But the motives behind this need not be class-based, but can stem purely from fear, or from the modern belief that "efficiency" is the highest virtue, and above all, they can stem from simple greed: there were vast fortunes to be made in an economy based on mass production and thus organized to favour the large corporations rather than the small business or the family farm.

Mass production requires mass consumption, but at the turn of the 20th century, most Americans considered it both unnatural and unwise to buy things they did not actually need. Men like George Peabody, who only had four years of formal education but sufficient financial success to fund the cause of mandatory schooling throughout the South, saw the usefulness of the Prussian system in creating not only a servile labour force but also a herd of mindless consumers. Eventually, a great number of industrial tycoons from Andrew Carnegie to John D. Rockefeller came to recognize the enormous profits to be had by tending such a herd via public education. There was no need for schools to teach children to think they should consume non-stop, because they did something ever more devious: they encouraged their pupils not to think at all, leaving them sitting ducks for another great invention of the era, that is, marketing.

Consumer, from consume, "to eat immoderately" or "to destroy completely," used to be a negative term; but in advanced manufacturing societies, the production of consumption has become more important than the production of goods. During the Cold War, the more liberal baby boomers could express their youthfulness through the same marijuana leaf T-shirt for decades on end, now they fall apart in a few months. Before, the life span of refrigerators could be used as a geohistorical measure, while the new models break down every couple of years. Cars made in the early '60s lasted a quarter of a century, the modern ones barely make it home from the dealership. The culprit is naturally consumerism, in whose interest it is to make products obsolete as fast as possible. As a perhaps more alarming example, DuPont manufactures both body armour and armour piercing bullets.

461. As quoted in Gatto 2009, 15.

462. "My Pedagogic Creed," *The School Journal* 54(3), January 16, 1897.

463. 1974, 597.

American pseudo-capitalism, in general, worked badly and posed no threat to communism; it takes an average of 3 years for a private company to start making profit, and even then, 9 out of 10 businesses fail within the first 5 years. But consumerism has corrupted everyone: people everywhere want cars, clothes, and gadgets. We basically work jobs we do not like to make things nobody needs, so we can buy things we do not need ourselves: "Home was a condo on the fifteenth floor of a filing cabinet for widows and young professionals. . . I flipped through catalogs and wondered: What kind of dining set defines me as a person? . . . I had it all. I had a stereo that was very decent, a wardrobe that was getting very respectable. I was close to being complete. . . It's just, when you buy furniture, you tell yourself, that's it. That's the last sofa I'm gonna need. Whatever else happens, I've got that sofa problem handled."[464]

And when one seeks redemption or deliverance through these means, one only ends up in perpetual procrastination: I will really start "living" when my need has been fulfilled—when my problems have been solved, when I have money, a spouse, or a new car. Instead of living, you will just perform or accomplish goals you have set for yourself. In the modern world, we define ourselves through our professions, yet our homes and workplaces are strictly separate. Suburbs are planned for habitation alone; sleeping, watching TV, walking the dog. You cannot do much besides that where we live. We need to take the train or the car to the industrial and office blocks several miles away; and we tend to meet our friends "on the way home," at the movies, at the mall, at a restaurant—anywhere other than at our houses or apartments.

Even though our society is designed to provide its productive members with the maximum amount of leisure time, the full force of herd mentality is focused on filling that leisure time with banal distractions. American popular culture has produced some amazing pieces of art, but for the most part, they repeat the same naïve, moralistic, and emotional themes with only minor cosmetic changes in tone, character, and plot. The identity of the modern secularists is wholly founded on the fiction, music, and art they consume. This consumption devours a lion's share of their free time, leaving them little time to really think about what they have consumed. So although most social activities revolve around the consumption of art, it very seldom amounts to anything deeper than flag waving. Deep thought requires time, specifically, leisure time, during which there are no serious distractions to one's attention and concentration.

The British author Tom Hodgkinson rose to international fame with his book *How to Be Idle* (2004), which was a humorous and erudite attack on career thinking. In his 2009 parenting guide, *The Idle Parent*, he instructs people to be idle also as parents. Many a parent say they slave away at work in order to give their children a good life, but all too often that means toys and hobbies. Why are the children in Africa not screaming all the time? The abundance of things and choices makes children lose their temper. If you take a child to a forest, he will start playing happily; but if you take a child to a department store, he throws himself on the floor screaming. African villages

464. *Fight Club*, op. cit.

have fewer things for the children to squabble about. Overbearing, competitive, working parents, who fill the world of the child with "activities," make children nervous. If their parents are constantly hovering over them, children are unable to act independently. Whiny children are clingy children and their only weapon is whining.

The number of first babies born to mothers over thirty is currently at 38%, more than double what it was just a generation ago. Many of these mothers have built up a bank account before they got married, and a half of them continue working after the children are born. And partly because the mothers are older, the families are smaller.[465] These older, richer mothers are ready, willing, and able to indulge their one or two children. The 76% drop in the birth rate for women of childbearing age translated to a 76% increase in per capita family spending. And when both of your parents are rushing to the office while you are waiting for the school bus, they are likely to slip you twenty bucks and tell you to order out for dinner. Then when you do go grocery shopping with your guilt-ridden mother, she is likely to get you a frozen pizza or chicken nuggets since you will probably have to microwave the food yourself.

The toy industry was once a largely Christmas-time business; until the late '70s, two-thirds of all toys were sold in the six weeks before the winter holidays. Now that industry brings in about $30 billion, and kids are getting showered with toys all year round. By the time we are a few months old, we already have more stuff and entertainment than even Uncle Walt dreamed possible. In the past, children's TV shows might be so popular that they spawned merchandising; now we merchandise first and then make the TV show. According to marketers, fast food comes next in the things children pester their parents for. Over 70% of mothers work and are too busy or tired to cook dinner, but even if parents were able to eat every single meal with their children, they still could not compete with the modern advertising industry. Operating on the tried and tested sales principle that it is easier to keep an existing customer than it is to convert a new one, advertisers are eager to implement new cradle-to-grave marketing strategies.[466]

What is more, today's parents think it is a good thing for their children to have more say over money. Younger parents, in particular, are letting their children control even the household purchases. They want them to be "empowered," to "make their own decisions," to choose their own clothes. They want decisions about the next car or house to be a family affair. At the turn of this century, children twelve and under spent $27.9 billion of their own money in the United States alone, and influenced an estimated $300 billion of their parents' spending; marketers expect this "kid-fluence" to continue growing at a rate of 10 to 20 percent a year.[467] Children today are no longer treated as future consumers, like they were a generation ago—they are just consumers, plain and simple.

Americans have been liberated from their Puritan ethic of frugal saving to enjoy spendthrift consumption by the negative incentives of multi-layered, progressive

465. Hymowitz, op. cit.

466. Ibid.

467. McNeal 1999.

taxation of savings and investment. As the "minimum wages" keep on rising, "poverty rates" also remain high: according to the U.S. Census Bureau, almost a half of those classified as "poor" in 2005 had their own homes; more than two-thirds of those homes had three bedrooms and one and a half bathrooms, thus being larger than the middle-class home of 1950s.[468] Every U.S. President since Carter could utter one phrase in his annual State of the Union address: ". . .and I'm proud to say that more Americans own their own home today than at any time in history. . ." However, the term "homeowner" may soon become obsolete: while the average '50s family owned three-quarters of their house, today the lender owns half.[469] The whole attitude of paying off the mortgage and owning one's home free and clear is disappearing from the country. For the first time in history, Americans owe more money than they make. No longer a nest egg whose equity should never be touched, a home is increasingly a magical pouch that enables the owner to spend wantonly.

The phenomenon during 2000 and 2007, where the American economy grew, even though employment shrunk, was due to the fact that consumption was financed with debt. This was made possible by the constant appreciation, until 2007, in the prices of the real property that acted as the collateral for the credit cards. The U.S. housing bubble both caused, and was enabled by, a nationwide boom in indebtedness. Total household debt in the United States rose a whopping 117% from 1999 to its peak in early 2008, as Americans borrowed to buy even more expensive homes and to support their consumption in general.[470] The conventional expectation is that people will borrow—and banks will make loans—only for sound investments, ones that are capable of making a profit, thus enabling the debtor to pay back the lender with interest. The financial crisis of 2008 was not the result of deregulation or market failure: the real reason for the crisis was that American banks issued loans to people who could not afford them.

The U.S. mortgage system encourages people to take on enormous debts, because the debtor is not personally responsible for his debts; if you cannot pay back what you owe, you simply return the house keys and that's that. American legislation has further obligated banks to give out loans to poor people, so that the United States would become an "ownership society." The roots of all this stretch back to a program initiated by President Carter known as the Community Reinvestment Act of 1977. Banks were forced to open branches in areas that would produce low-balance accounts characterized by high overdraft and default activity. When they complained that they were forced to issue mortgages and finance small businesses that were not creditworthy, the government responded by forming Fannie Mae and Freddie Mac, forcing the banks to seek out even less creditworthy individuals and businesses. About 90% of home loans in the U.S. are now backed by government-controlled entities, meaning the government "has done more than simply support the mortgage market, in many ways it has become the mortgage market, with the taxpayer shouldering the

468. "American Housing Survey for the United States: 2005," U.S. Census Bureau & U.S. Department of Housing and Urban Development, Washington, D.C., August 2006.

469. Ibid.

470. Neil Irwin, "Aughts Were a Lost Decade for U.S. Economy, Workers," *Washington Post*, January 2, 2010.

risk that had once been borne by the private investor."[471] The sub-prime market tapped a section of the American public that did not typically have anything to do with Wall Street: lenders were making loans to people who, based on their credit ratings, were less creditworthy than 71% of the population.[472]

The only problem in the fractional reserve system, where money is debt, i.e. a promise to create value, is that the cessation of real growth results in inflation and, through the rise in interest rates, in the contraction of the money supply precisely through credit defaults and bankruptcies. Debts grow by purely mathematical principles, but real economies taper off in S-curves; by leaving less revenue available for direct investment in capital formation and to sustain rising living standards, interest payments end up plunging economies into recession. In other words, the GDP has to grow, or else part of the people will be pushed into excessive indebtedness and a circle of misery. If we had a stable population engaged in sustainable activities using non-debt-based money as a freely circulating medium of exchange, there would be no need for economic growth; but what we have is a growing population and debt-based money, so we are stuck with the political necessity of growth in the economy—even though this "need" is self-inflicted by our political decisions and not due to some fundamental law of the universe like gravity. The trouble is, there is no such thing as "long-term sustainable growth." In fact, in the long run, there is no such thing as "sustainable growth." Nothing grows forever, everything has a limit.

Bankruptcy may sound horrible, but it is actually a wonderful and orderly process. It fixes the balance sheets quickly and provides an opportunity to replace the owners and administrators who operated the business in a risky fashion. Some bankrupt companies will go completely out of business and their resources will be auctioned off to other entrepreneurs at greatly reduced prices. Other firms will remain in business with most of the employees keeping their jobs, but bankruptcy reduces debt and cost, while providing an opportunity to renegotiate contracts and wage rates. The result of a bankruptcy is often one of new owners and operators with far less debt and therefore lower cost structures. Some consumers would be flush with saved money and have an opportunity to make purchases at much lower prices. The economy thus quickly enters recovery and soon attains full employment, but more importantly, by not bailing out the failures, the moral hazard of being able to rely on bailouts in the future is eliminated.

In order to prevent the immediate creation of asset bubbles, the interest rate must *always* be greater than the risk-free rate of return, that is, the growth rate. Yet this guarantees, as a direct consequence of the laws of exponential growth—a fundamental mathematical concept—that debt defaults and, thus, clearance of the system, along with the contraction of GDP and the economy, and failure of both lenders and borrowers, must on occasion occur. We know exactly why the bubble happened. Call it Greenspanism: central banks, taking cue from the U.S. Federal Reserve, rescued assets every time there was a hiccup, but let booms run unchecked. They pulled real rates even lower, creating an addiction to monetary stimulus. Larger doses were

471. "Quarterly Report to Congress," Office of the Special Inspector General for the Troubled Asset Relief Program, Washington, D.C., January 30, 2010.

472. Michael Lewis, "The End," *Condé Nast Portfolio*, December 2008.

required with each cycle, until the rates hit zero, and they still were not low enough. By making sure that traditionally safe investments like CDs and savings accounts earned basically zero interest, investors were forced to go elsewhere to search for money-making opportunities. Recently, the UK Financial Services Authority said they did not want the banks to lend any money against property, but the problem is, they have so much tied up in unproductive assets that if they cannot to lend against property, they will never get them off their books and will never be able to lend productively again.

During World War II, U.S. manufacturing was entirely directed by war; no cars, for example, were manufactured for the domestic market, but the big automakers built military planes and ships. The workers got money with nothing to spend it on—buying liberty bonds was not merely patriotic, but about the only thing one could do with the money. Bankrupt and homeless people today have less money to invest than their WWII grandparents, but electronics are now so affordable that a large majority of American poor have air conditioning and colour televisions with cable or satellite service; a full quarter of them even own cellular phones.[473] Rapture is no longer tied to the meaning given to it by religion. The result is a workaholic, who makes money by any means necessary in order to purchase ever diminishing experiences with ever growing sums. "We are by-products of a lifestyle obsession. Murder, crime, poverty, these things don't concern me. What concerns me are celebrity magazines, television with 500 channels, some guy's name on my underwear. Rogaine, Viagra, Olestra."[474] Our children are being brought up in a world where the meaning of life has been reduced to shopping at the mall and where entertainment is the sole salvation.

Marketers spend over $4.5 billion a year promising to make the child consumer the coolest kid on the block by selling him the right sneakers or offering sugar heaven through the latest designer soft drink.[475] "I see all this potential, and I see squandering. God damn it, an entire generation pumping gas, waiting tables; slaves with white collars. . . We're the middle children of history, man. No purpose or place. We have no Great War. No Great Depression. Our great war's a spiritual war; our great depression is our lives. We've all been raised on television to believe that one day we'd all be millionaires, and movie gods, and rock stars. But we won't. And we're slowly learning that fact. And we're very, very pissed off."[476]

The Western way of life, creating values as it does only through money and consumption, requires an ever more intensive resource management in order to continue as the growth machine it is today. Due to the limited amount of natural resources and the environmental damage caused by their exploitation, the present economic phase can drag on for no more than four generations—which is about as long as it has lasted. The modern lifestyle is just another transitory stage in the history of man: "In the world I see, you are stalking elk through the damp canyon forests

473. Robert Rector, "How Poor Are America's Poor?: Examining the 'Plague' of Poverty in America," The Heritage Foundation, Washington, D.C., August 27, 2007.

474. *Fight Club*, op. cit.

475. McNeal, op. cit.

476. *Fight Club*, op. cit.

around the ruins of Rockefeller Center. You'll wear leather clothes that will last you the rest of your life. You'll climb the wrist-thick kudzu vines that wrap the Sears Tower. And when you look down, you'll see tiny figures pounding corn, laying strips of venison on the empty car pool lane of some abandoned superhighway."[477]

However, the view that "developing" countries are victims of Western exploitation is highly patronizing. Third World poverty is not caused by the ill will of Westerners. There are no forces that would expressly aim at making the poor poorer. In fact, many of the world's poorest countries are kept afloat only through massive amounts of foreign aid and debt relief. But businesses are not charities and "ethical" investments do not make very good ones—"People used to think that to mix religion with business spoiled the religion, now they think it spoils the business."[478] Ironically, job contracts, minimum wages, and unions not only prevent employers from adjusting wages according to the performance of their economy, industry, or business, but induce them to hire as little as possible and automate as much as possible; and if hiring women or minorities leads to increased risk of lawsuits, then companies are less likely to hire women and minorities.

With high unemployment benefits, almost half of Western Europe's jobless had been out of work a year or more in 2004 at the peak of the last recovery; the U.S. figure was only about 12 percent.[479] The Catch-22 is that high benefits require a strong economy, while the sources of these benefits—high taxes and rigid regulations —weaken the economy. Our prosperity is the result of the toil and success of working people, businesses, and their owners. The State collects half of this in taxes to provide for services, but it does this poorly. It does not do it on purpose, but because it is in a monopoly position and monopolies always do things poorly. Queues are formed, the services are expensive, and nothing much gets done. Subsidies always create more of whatever is being subsidized: subsidize the ill and diseased and you end up promoting carelessness, dependency, and indigence; eliminate such subsidies, and you will strengthen the will to live healthy lives and to work for a living.

Since we create prosperity through our labour, should we not be able to keep the fruits of that labour and decide for ourselves how to solve our problems? Instead of the government appropriating a good portion of our hard-earned money to give us poor services, we could be buying the services we want. Think, for example, of the widespread practice of "free" university education, whereby the working class, whose children rarely go to universities, is made to pay for the education of the middle classes. A voluntary welfare insurance or sickness insurance would guarantee freedom of choice. The service providers would have to compete for clients and provide better services than public options ever could. Finland has universal health care, but uses a smaller tax percentage to achieve it than the U.S. uses for its limited medical aid.[480] I have heard this used against the American system countless of times, but never against the high taxes of the Nordic welfare state—all that tax money still has to go

477. Ibid.

478. Washburn, op. cit. 80.

479. Robert J. Samuelson, "The End of Europe," *Washington Post*, June 15, 2005.

480. World Health Organization 2011.

somewhere!

While the Scandinavian countries have extremely high taxes, their saving grace is their relatively lower amount of regulation. This puts Scandinavia on a level playing field with other developed countries, and helps explain why it enjoys an equal or higher living standard. As the Heritage Foundation's annual *Index of Economic Freedom* shows, Sweden, Finland, and Denmark have more economic freedom than most of their Continental counterparts, including Germany, France, Spain, Greece, and Portugal.[481] Another measurement that reveals a similar pattern is the World Bank's *Ease of Doing Business Index*, which measures the amount of bureaucracy and regulation one has to put up with when starting and running a business. Here, too, the Nordic countries uniformly score in the top 10s and 20s, their biggest burden typically being their rigorous labour laws.[482] While Scandinavia has higher taxes and government spending than the rest of Europe, the other European countries tend to have more regulation and less efficient and transparent legal systems, which cancel out the positive effects of the lower taxation.[483]

As Margaret Thatcher famously put it: "No-one would have remembered the good Samaritan if he'd only had good intentions. He had money as well." Charities are businesses too; in fact, they are among the fastest growing businesses in the world. The purchase, transport, and delivery of food aid gives work to hundreds of thousands of paid employees and civil servants. The mediaeval Church, convinced that "the love of money is the root of all evil,"[484] prohibited usury, the lending of money at interest; the 13th-century Churchmen treated usury as theft and hence considered it a violation of the Eighth Commandment. In other words, money could only be loaned within Christendom at the risk of incurring disgrace in this world and damnation in the next. As a result, there was little capital and few lenders; the rates of interest grew enormous, as high as 10% per month in Italy and Spain; commerce, manufacture, and enterprise in general were dwarfed, while pauperism ran rampart.

The mediaeval prohibition of usury not only discouraged economy, but promoted luxury: since the rich found no easy way of employing their incomes productively, they ended up spending them in ostentation and riotous living. Everything is driven by profit—monetary or otherwise—and not to admit this reality is to distort the market and leave everyone worse off. When a younger woman marries an older man, she gains money and status, while he gets sex. If you do me a favour, you expect me to return it, otherwise you are not likely to do me any more favours. In her seminal study of the Renaissance, *Worldly Goods* (1996), Lisa Jardine discovered that the engine behind its vast cultural accomplishments was materialism and greed and the international trade of luxury goods.

A country will not be stronger if it produces everything itself. Economics 101 teaches us that everyone benefits when people who are good at one thing can

481. Miller, et al. 2011.

482. Devan, et al. 2011.

483. "Persistently High Corruption in Low-Income Countries Amounts to an 'Ongoing Humanitarian Disaster,'" Transparency International, Berlin, September 23, 2008.

484. I Timothy 6:10.

exchange it with people who are good at something else. Even if the United States cuts down on imported oil, it will still be dependent on other nations. The U.S. imports electricity from Mexico and Canada. It imports 20% of its natural gas and 80% of its uranium. If being independent from foreign oil is good, so would being independent from foreign fish, foreign beer, foreign cars, and foreign movies. Do Americans really want to live without Spanish mackerel, Corona, Toyotas, or James Bond? Energy interdependence makes the United States more secure, not less. When Hurricanes Katrina and Rita hit in 2005, for instance, the U.S. got oil to the ravaged Gulf Coast by buying extra from Venezuela and the Netherlands.

The entertainment industry is just the latest in many where the idea of vertical integration failed to live up to its promise. Consider the past experiences of the auto industry: Henry Ford was a firm believer in the concept, his River Rouge plant having its own electricity plant and its own mill for turning iron ore into steel. Most of the components that went into the Model A were made on site, but over time, this soup-to-nuts strategy proved inefficient; car makers could obtain better prices and more flexibility by dealing with a competing array of outside suppliers. Eventually, once vertically-integrated companies like Ford and General Motors spun off their internal supply divisions to form stand-alone companies, in an attempt to compete with the leaner, more flexible supply chains of Toyota and Honda.

"There is perhaps no single factor contributing so much to people's frequent reluctance to let the market work as their inability to conceive how some necessary balance, between demand and supply, between exports and imports, or the like, will be brought about without deliberate control. The conservative feels safe and content only if he is assured that some higher wisdom watches and supervises change, only if he knows that some authority is charged with keeping the change 'orderly.'"[485] However, the daily behaviour of buyers and sellers is so complex that even experts in chaos theory have failed to discern a predictable pattern; we have no idea why stocks go up and down, why savings rates are so different in different parts of the world, or why there is labour market discrimination. At one point, Palm, Inc., a maker of personal digital assistants, had a larger capitalization than the computer company 3Com; but this was mathematically absurd since 3Com Corporation owned 95% of Palm's shares.

The idea that mathematical models could somehow reveal universal truths, in both business and science, has been successfully promoted, despite strong historical evidence to the contrary. ***Rolling Stone*** Magazine's Matt Taibbi neatly sums up the situation that led to the financial meltdown of 2008: the mess had it roots in an investment boom fuelled in part by a relatively new type of financial instrument known as a collateralized debt obligation; to get AAA ratings, the CDOs relied not on their actual underlying assets, but on crazy mathematical formulas cooked up by the banks to make the investments appear safer than they actually were. "They had some back room somewhere where a bunch of Indian guys who'd been doing nothing but math for God knows how many years would come up with some kind of model saying that this or that combination of debtors would only default once every 10,000 years,"

485. Hayek 2011, 522.

said one CDO trader interviewed in the article.[486]

In a nutshell, the "financial entrepreneurship" of recent years—credit default swaps, CDOs, and so on—has undermined all notion of true value. According to Paul Volcker, former chairman of the Federal Reserve, the entire modern financial system is based on derivatives, and as such, entirely different from the traditional American financial system because these derivatives now underlie the entire fabric of the system.[487] No-one knows what their own derivatives assets and liabilities are, let alone anybody else's; which is why Lehman Brothers' CDSs caused so much anxiety, and why lending ground to a halt. The largest U.S. banks remain the largest holders of financial derivatives, which suggests that they may hold liabilities far in excess of what can be paid or bailed out if significant losses occur; the CDS market, the single largest class of financial derivatives, represents over $600 trillion, or roughly ten times world GDP—once that bubble pops, there will not be enough money in the whole world to fix it.[488]

"When an accident is waiting to happen, it eventually does," economists Carmen Reinhart and Ken Rogoff wrote in their 2009 book, ***This Time Is Different: Eight Centuries of Financial Folly***. "But the exact timing can be very difficult to guess, and a crisis that seems imminent can sometimes take years to ignite."[489] Efforts to set interest rates, police the sale of securities, revise pensions and health insurance, all rely to some degree on the ability of our economists to make reliable predictions about the choices people will make. The trouble is, many of our choices originate in the subconscious, as emotional responses to the stimuli around us, and are not well thought out and logical decisions. A growing body of research shows that millions of taxpayers fail to get even the most elementary investment decisions right. When analysts examine the actual behaviour of individuals, as opposed to what most economic theories predict, they find it seldom to be very rational at all.

Harry M. Markowitz won the Nobel Prize in economics as the father of "modern portfolio theory," the idea that instead of putting all our eggs in one basket, we should diversify our investments. Yet when it came to his own retirement investments, Markowitz simply split his money down the middle, putting half in a stock fund and the other half in a conservative, low-interest investment. Some economics Nobel laureates have even confessed to missing the mark in how they invested their prize winnings. Just because we have an economic self-interest to do something, or even if we are given a strong incentive to do so, does not mean we are going to do it, much less do it right—not even if we are highly educated Nobelists.[490]

Only a tiny fraction of Americans is interested in preserving a high price for sugar. The immense majority of the American public are buyers and consumers, not producers or sellers, of sugar. Yet the U.S. government is firmly committed to a policy of high sugar prices, by restricting both the importation of sugar and domestic

---

486. Matt Taibbi, "The Big Takeover," ***Rolling Stone***, April 2, 2009.

487. ***Charlie Rose***. PBS. March 18, 2008.

488. Rick Schmitt, "Prophet and Loss," ***Stanford Magazine***, March/April 2009.

489. Reinhart & Rogoff 2009, xliii.

490. Peter G. Gosselin, "Experts Are at a Loss on Investing," ***Los Angeles Times***, May 11, 2005.

production. It has adopted similar policies with regard to meat, bread, butter, eggs, potatoes, cotton, and many other agricultural products. However, less than one-fifth of the U.S. population is dependent upon agriculture for a living, and the interests of these people with regard to the prices of various agricultural products are dissimilar. The dairy farmer is not interested in a high, but in a low price for fodder and wheat. The poultry farmers are hurt by high prices of any agricultural product except chickens and eggs. The growers of cotton, oranges, apples, and grapes are obviously prejudiced by a system that raises the price of staple foods. Most of the items in the "pro-farm" policy favour only a minority of the total farming population at the expense of the majority of both farmers and non-farmers.

In the mid-1980s, New Zealand decided to stop all subsidies for its farmers. At the time, the farmers naturally thought the effects would be disastrous, but far from destroying New Zealand's agriculture, this "radical" action revived it. Two decades after the removal of subsidies, agriculture contributes more to the total economy of the island than it did before that, and the land is being farmed more creatively. The wine industry used to be too small to measure, now grapes have replaced sheep in some areas as the main source of revenue. In fact, sheep have been supplanted by dairy farming as the country's biggest foreign exchange earner, and more than two million deer are farmed across the nation.[491]

Back when there still was government cash on offer, many farmers conducted their business less than honestly. What was officially known as the "livestock incentive scheme," a direct payment to encourage farmers to increase the size of their flocks, got nicknamed the "skinny sheep scheme." One farmer even named his new boat SMP, after the "supplementary minimum prices" subsidy, the backbone of the whole system. These and several other subsidies provided some New Zealand farmers with up to 40% of their income in the late '70s and early '80s. Today, most farmers are thriving despite the fact that government financial support now amounts to less than 1% of average farm income in the country.[492]

Globalization, free trade and competition neither cut the agricultural production nor "steal the bread from the mouth of labour." Quite the opposite, they increase production, which has to be constrained through treaties so that the subsidized overproduction does not prevent Third World producers from competing with their more ecologically friendly products. Big corporations, which may have held a monopoly position in the country, are often actually against free trade. According to a 2005 Oxfam report, thirty-eight developing countries have suffered from unfair competition as a result of illegal subsidies in the West.[493] The U.S. and EU governments spend approximately $20 and $23 billion per annum respectively to subsidize agriculture, artificially forcing down global crop prices and thereby depriving the world's poorest farmers of the money they need to survive. Until 2006, the American cotton industry got 20% of its income in subsidies from the

491. *From Our Own Correspondent.* BBC Radio 4. October 16, 2004.

492. Ibid.

493. "Truth or Consequences: Why the EU and the USA Must Reform Their Subsidies, or Pay the Price," Oxfam International, Oxford, November 2005.

government, meaning that the United States spent almost three times as much on subsidies for cotton as it did on aid for the whole of the African continent, cancelling out any benefits that might derive thereof. At the same time, the impoverished sub-Saharan West Africa is only getting deeper into debt, while its 20 million cotton farmers cannot afford basic things like health care or even food in some cases.[494]

Globalization is an objective phenomenon and the world leaders could not halt it even if they wanted to. Nor is globalization a conspiracy by the rich to humiliate the poor, but a result of technological advancement and the more efficient trade and communications that it enables. Globalization is simply another economic step, like industrialization before it. The fact that global corporations benefit more from it than the weaker companies is unavoidable. Businesses inevitably turn to cheaper workforce for production and services, bringing instability to the country that is losing jobs. Yet it helps the developing countries, for not only do they receive major international investments, but also competition on the world market. What we tend to forget is that the investment and income streams created by globalization are a much larger—dozens of times larger—form of development aid than the official development aid could ever be. It is the selfish actions of multinational companies that have been the driving force behind Third World growth. And the fastest growth in the world is occurring in the some of its poorest countries, notably China and India.

Should a company stop using Third World child labour because of a consumer boycott, the children have to earn their living through some other means, like begging or prostitution. Although 250 million children are forced to work in appalling conditions, two billion children live in even worse conditions. In lieu of Western consumer boycotts, it might be better not to interfere too much with the development of poor nations, seeing that reducing legal child labour does not necessarily improve the situation for the children. Many cheap-labour countries are at a stage of development the Western countries were at earlier. During the early stages of industrialization, Western workers also had poor working conditions and there was no labour legislation yet. In early 19th-century England, it was considered a major step forward when the minimum age of children working in factories was set at nine years and their working hours to twelve, not counting overtime.

One could say that the people who work for multinational corporations in developing countries and produce our shoes and clothes are the victims of Western oppression. If this is true, then the problem is that there is too little oppression. It is precisely those who obtain such a job that make the most money and have the best terms of employment. Foreign companies pay double what the domestic companies in the same field do. The foreigners are not more generous, they are simply more globalized and advanced. They have developed new technologies and equipment that they bring with them to these countries. The locals can thus produce more and, at the same time, earn more. It is this sort of investment that has lifted up East Asia and is making China richer and richer. The problem with Africa is that foreign corporations have not invested there. If we wish to help poor African countries to rise from poverty, we must invest in Africa and bring as many multinational corporations there

494. "Finding the Moral Fiber: Why Reform Is Urgently Needed for a Fair Cotton Trade," Ibid., October 2004.

as possible.

It was capital investment that dramatically increased the productivity of Western labour following the Industrial Revolution, allowing the working hours to decline from an average of 61 per week in 1870 to 48 by 1929.[495] Higher productivity also made it less necessary for families to force their children to work. Child labour was on the wane for decades before governments got around to regulating and finally outlawing it. And when they did so, it was to protect unionized labour from competition, not to protect children from hazardous working conditions. Similarly, the current economic crisis is blamed by American politicians on too much economic freedom and not enough regulation, despite the fact that there are a dozen executive-branch cabinet departments, over one hundred federal agencies, more than 85,000 pages in the Federal Register, and dozens of state and local government agencies that regulate, tax, and control every aspect of every business in the United States—and they have been doing so for decades.

The question that policy-makers have not faced honestly is: why do illegal immigrants come to our country? The answer is not that they are lured in by jobs and government benefits, but that they are pushed away by the abject poverty that their families face at home. While that may seem like semantics, the difference is huge when you are trying to develop a policy that will stop the flood of illegals across the border. The North American Free Trade Agreement, or NAFTA, inundated Mexico with cheap, subsidized U.S. agricultural products that displaced millions of Mexican farmers. The United States is the only country in the world permitted to protect its agriculture by import quotas, having "grandfathered" these into world trade rules half a century ago. Between 2000 and 2005, Mexico lost 900,000 rural jobs and 700,000 industrial ones, resulting in steep unemployment throughout the country and forcing millions of Mexican workers north in order to feed their families.[496] You never hear it mentioned in debates on the issue, but you might want to start with this reality: most Mexicans would prefer to live in their own country. Their family, language, culture, and identity is Mexican; it is sheer economic survival that requires so many of them to abandon the place they love.

But illegal immigration is not caused only by the fact that poor countries have an excess of poor people. It is also caused by the demand in developed nations for cheap labour that does not worry about its rights. The demand for undocumented labour in the Western economy is structural; it is not just a few companies seeking to cut corners or jobs that native workers refuse to take. Grey economy constitutes an estimated 27% of GDP in Italy, and the bulk of the illegal labour is done by immigrants.[497] The Italian manufacturing industry need not invest in countries with cheap labour, for the cheap labour comes to Italy. The industry not only saves in investments, wages, and social security costs, but gets to keep production near the market. And so the Tunisians pick the vegetables of Southern Italy, while the

495. DiLorenzo 2004.

496. Laura Carlsen, "Migrants: Globalization's Junk Mail?" *Foreign Policy in Focus*, February 26, 2007.

497. Friedrich Schneider, et al. "Shadow Economies All over the World: New Estimates for 162 Countries from 1999 to 2007," World Bank, Washington, D.C., July 2010.

Filipinos and Ukrainians clean up the homes of the Romans; the Chinese pedal the sewing-machines of the murky textile factories in the suburbs of Milan and Rome, the Turks and Iraqis work at the building sites by day, the Africans and Bangladeshi tidy up the restaurants at night. All the low-skill jobs in the West are increasingly being done by immigrants. They work in nearly all low-paying occupations and have become essential to the Western economy in the age of global competition.

However, it is not only the dismal jobs anymore that are subject to domestic outsourcing; and it is also worth noting that the West does not always need to look abroad to find cheap labour, as such companies as Wal-Mart in the U.S. and Lidl in Europe make clear. Thousands upon thousands of immigrants are taking every advantage to gain the skills and experience they need to get a foothold in the Western economies. In Virginia, the largely immigrant-driven need for technical skills has turned Northern Virginia Community College into the largest institution of higher education in the state, and the second-largest community college in the nation.[498] The mom-and-pop convenience stores in New York that were run by Jews a generation ago, were sold in turn to Chinese, Korean, and other Asian entrepreneurs, and are now increasingly run by Africans.

The outcry in the United States about the "invasion of immigrants" has been long and loud. As one complainer put it, "Few of their children in the country know English. . . The signs in our streets have inscriptions in both languages. . . In short, unless the stream of their importation could be turned . . . they will soon so outnumber us, that the advantages we have will . . . be not able to preserve our language, and even our government will become precarious." Now, that is not a diatribe from one of the conservative talk show hosts, but the wail of Benjamin Franklin, deploring the wave of German immigrants pouring into the British colony of Pennsylvania in the 1750s.[499] So the anti-immigrant rhetoric is, in fact, older than the nation itself, and at one point or another, the Irish, French, Italians, and Chinese have felt the sharp end of that stick. There is absolutely no way the U.S. government can expel all the 12 million or so illegal immigrants who are now in the country. Immigrants—legal or otherwise—are statistically less likely than white Anglo-Saxon Protestants to commit violent crimes or obtain state services fraudulently. But you would never know this, because no cable network has given a Native American a nightly program to call for the deportation of all white folks.

Even common concerns about the negative effects of migration on employment are often unfounded. Rather than taking jobs from local workers, a major study by the International Organization for Migration says that migrants tend to fill spaces mainly at the poles of the labour market, that is, working both in low-skilled, high-risk jobs and in the highly-skilled, well-paid ones.[500] The reality is that, in the increasingly globalized world, we can no longer depend on domestic labour markets alone. If managed properly, migration can bring the West more benefits than costs. In a flexible labour market such as that of the United States, immigrants play a central

---

498. William Raspberry, "Outsourcing at Home," *Washington Post*, May 23, 2005.

499. Letter to Peter Collinson, May 1753. Abbott 1969, 415–416.

500. Omelaniuk, et al. 2005.

role. In ageing societies like those of Western Europe, immigrants are sorely needed. A more liberalized global labour market would boost economic growth all round, while restrictions can only cut it. To jeopardize the benefits of globalization just to protect the employment prospects of high school dropouts does not make any sense. "U.S. citizens" can stoop over a field of crops and pick them all day long, but then Americans would be paying $20 a pound for strawberries.

Migrants also make a significant contribution to the economies of their home countries, for returning cash flow often exceeds official development assistance, and is far more effective, because it is direct people-to-people aid. It is going directly to starting up businesses, to buying food and medicines, to building clinics and schools. Brazilian workers in Japan send home more than $2 billion each year, out-grossing Brazil's coffee industry. Foreign remittances bring in more than tea exports do in Sri Lanka or tourism does in Morocco. Remittances rank along with oil as Mexico's biggest currency earner. In Jordan, Lesotho, Nicaragua, Tajikistan, and Tonga, they make up more than a quarter of the gross domestic product. Remittances are, in fact, the largest, fastest-growing, and most reliable source of income for developing countries.[501] And although many skilled workers abandon their home countries to seek higher pay abroad, many will return home bringing acquired skills and experience, a phenomenon otherwise known as "brain gain."

It is nearly impossible to discern between the industrial and the developing nations a similar exploitation mechanism as Marx saw in the management-labour relationship. The *Communist Manifesto* (1848) itself had a positive attitude towards the slowly globalizing economy, which would draw "even the most barbarian nations into civilization."[502] What Marx might see as a problem is the fact that there are many regions in the world into which international capital does not reach. After the fall of the Soviet Union, many concluded that Marxist philosophy had failed. But Marx was writing in the mid-19th century on what he perceived as being wrong in the industrializing West at the time; he might think differently of modern capitalism, which is very different from that of his day, when there was no governmental control. Marx could not possibly foresee the vast developments in capitalistic societies over the last century. In fact, the Scandinavian welfare states are now closer to the socialism which Marx had in mind that Soviet Russia ever was.

Marx was among the first to call for "a heavy progressive or graduated income tax," at a time when the flat rate was the norm across the early industrializing countries.[503] The Western tax codes were designed to promote "social justice" and reduce the burden of the poor precisely by redistributing income through progressive taxation. In practice, however, the redistribution of income has failed to materialize: while the share of income taxes on the top ten percent has risen 15% over the past 40 years, the after-tax income share of the remaining ninety percent has declined 13%, leaving the less wealthy only worse off.[504] Yet, income disparity has not grown in all countries.

---

501. Maimbo & Ratha 2005.

502. Marx & Engels 1998, 39.

503. Ibid. 60.

504. Hartman, op. cit.

The disparities have grown in about half of the world's nations, especially in the former socialist countries and post-socialist China, where the distribution of income used to be more even than under other systems.

Yes, free-market economy does increase income disparity, but that is a good thing. Income, after all, is the compensation we get for the work we do or the products we make. If your contribution is valuable, you will be well compensated; if you no nothing but sleep at work, you might not get paid too much. Most Americans do not stay in the same income bracket throughout their lives. Millions of working people move from one bracket to another within a few years. If you compare the top income bracket with the bottom bracket over a period of years, the resulting statistic tells you nothing about what is happening to the actual flesh-and-blood people who are, in fact, moving between the brackets. Many such statistics are about households or families, whose sizes vary over time and between one racial or ethnic group and another, and, indeed, between one income bracket and another. Thus, for example, differences in the number of people per household explain why Hispanics have higher household incomes than blacks, while blacks have higher individual incomes than Hispanics.[505]

Government income transfers are a really bad idea. They remove the motivation from entrepreneurship and promote freeloading, thus driving the economy into a deadlock before long. They also violate our collective sense of justice, unless you think that it is okay for the government to use its monopoly on violence to confiscate your neighbour's property. All wealth redistribution, regardless of the criteria on which it is based, involves taking from the original owners and/or producers and giving to non-owners and non-producers. The incentive to be an original owner or producer of the thing in question is thus reduced, while the incentive to be a non-owner and non-producer is raised. Accordingly, subsidizing individuals because they are poor will only result in more poverty; and subsidizing people because they are unemployed will only create more unemployment.

The countries where income disparities have increased are very different from each other. There is no one common factor, such as globalization. In Russia, the high tax rates which followed the Soviet collapse encouraged tax evasion on a huge scale, with the shadow economy at least twice as large as the state budget. The greatest single factor in the distribution of income seems to be technological advancement, which has increased the demand for skilled labour and thus the wages of skilled labour everywhere. The impact of this technological advancement is dependent on the policies—especially the education policies—practised by the individual countries. It defines how large a portion of the population gains from the demand for education. The effects of globalization on income distribution are unclear, and ultimately even it is largely influenced by local policies. In the end, the problems of local development can only be solved by local measures, which is why individual nations need to take and have the responsibility for it.

Overseas outsourcing generally has two explanations: the first is that competent and reliable overseas workers are willing to work for less than domestic employees

505. Sowell 2011.

would demand for the same job, often less than the minimum wage the latter would have to be paid; the second, which also applies to domestic outsourcing, is that it is increasingly difficult to find competent and reliable workers at home to begin with. Young people all around the United States are leaving high school every year with neither diplomas nor any marketable skills. Free public education was born in the country when the early Puritan capitalists realized that in order to be productive, they needed a literate, numerate, and articulate work force for even the most menial jobs. However, these capitalists needed to teach their own children how to be leaders, so they founded what remain the most-esteemed private schools to this day. The disparity in earnings, social standing, and comfort between Americans with a university degree and those with only a high school education has nearly doubled over the last generation.[506]

Thanks to laws requiring attendance in secondary school, 84% of American adults now have a high school diploma, up from mere 63% in 1975.[507] However, over a twenty-year period beginning in the early 1970s, the average SAT scores fell by 35 points, while the number of high school seniors with an A or B average jumped from 28% to a stunning 83%, as teachers felt increasingly pressured to adopt more "supportive" grading policies.[508] American education is so expensive today largely because the nation pays for it twice: children are sent to high school to pick up the knowledge and skills they should have learned in primary school; they go to college to acquire a passable secondary education. It has been said that "the bachelor's degree is the new high school diploma," because everybody has one; the average student now takes five years to get a four-year degree. Should an employer actually need someone with an education, he is likely to look for people with post-graduate degrees.

Since governments guarantee student loans, it does not matter whether you major in engineering or computer science, or art history or sociology, nobody cares whether you will be able to earn enough money to pay back what you owe. Just as the government pressured Fannie Mae and Freddie Mac to open mortgage doors to unqualified applicants, the same political dynamic causes higher educational institutions to graduate people who do not deserve college degrees. Just as Moody's and Standard & Poor's inflated their ratings for Wall Street's loan securitizations, the American educational accreditation services are only starting to recognize what is wrong with the product generated in educational enterprises. Essentially, college credentials for the bottom third of students graduating from many U.S. schools are now as worthless as liar loans. If public education did what it says on the tin, fewer people would feel compelled to attend college since fewer employers would require college degrees, confident that a high school diploma testified to a full measure of basic knowledge and skills.

Just a generation ago, only half of all American high school seniors went to university; the other half had good options, not dead-end jobs. In 1965, one of three

506. Jennifer Cheeseman Day & Eric C. Newburger, "The Big Payoff: Educational Attainment and Synthetic Estimates of Work-Life Earnings," U.S. Census Bureau, Washington, D.C., July 2002.

507. Ibid.

508. Salerno 2005.

payroll jobs was in manufacturing, mining, and construction; in 2005, it was only one in six.[509] But who can say whether this is the cause or effect of increasing college applications? Two-thirds of high school seniors today go to college. A generation ago, the Ivy League schools accepted 20% of applicants, now just half of that number. Since perfect grades come easy, everyone is expected to show some extraordinary community service or such, except maybe the 15% admitted in medallion schools as legacies.[510] This is of course the time-honoured tradition by which applicants with average grades, but with money and family ties to the school, are accepted ahead of the smart kids with no connections. Harvard University, the wealthiest institution of higher education in the world, gets about a third of its operating funds from endowments.[511]

Universities in general have not traditionally been good at cutting; they just add, and rising tuition and income from endowments have made this possible. But the unique structure of colleges has also made it inconvenient to do otherwise. In many ways, higher education is closer to a political environment than the management of a private corporation. Except that, thanks to tenure, it is hard to vote anyone out of office. Alienating the faculty members is something a college administrator will try to avoid at all costs. The political challenges with faculty make something as simple and obvious as cutting expensive and undersubscribed academic departments extremely difficult, if not impossible. Many colleges now spend more on non-faculty salaries than on pay for the teachers, the evolution of career counselling being a prime example. There were few placement offices thirty years ago, but today all colleges are expected to help students in entering the workplace. And these are just some of the reasons why it is so hard to make significant cuts to a college's budget and thus reduce tuition.

Student lending is a big business, one that has become the subject of many complaints over the past few years, after revelations of questionable ties between lenders and colleges' financial aid officers. For most students, loans have gone from being the exception to being the norm. Two-thirds of college students now borrow to pay for college, with their average debt load being in excess of $23,000 by the time they graduate. Only a dozen years earlier, 58% of students borrowed to pay for college, and the average amount borrowed was just over $13,000.[512] The rising levels of borrowing may ironically be contributing to the accelerating cost of higher education, since guaranteed loans mean that universities are free to charge more per pupil than if their customers paid out of pocket. This phenomenon is playing a big role in why tuition grows at about twice the rate of inflation. Tough loan payments now affect major life decisions by recent graduates, forcing them to postpone

---

509. Robert J. Samuelson, "Our Entitlement Paralysis," *Washington Post*, December 28, 2005.

510. "America's New Class Division." *Letter.* BBC World Service. February 21, 2005.

511. Peter Coy, "Academic Endowments: The Curse of Hoarded Treasure," *Business Week*, March 1, 2009.

512. Anne Marie Chaker, "Students Borrow More Than Ever for College," *Wall Street Journal*, September 2, 2009.

traditional milestones from buying a first home to marrying and having children.[513] At the time they graduate from college, almost everyone is technically eligible for bankruptcy, because their debts exceed their assets.

In 2010, after years of subsidizing loans originating in private banks, Congress decreed that all loans would henceforth originate directly from the federal government. A narrow partisan majority effected the drastic policy change: Democrats want to reduce the cost of providing student loans by taking the profits out of the industry. According to President Obama, student loans are too expensive because banks profit from issuing them; by nationalizing the function, the government will be able to bring down costs by eliminating the profits. Of course, if this were true, it would apply to all industries, not just banking; states like Cuba and North Korea would be the envy of the world, prohibiting as they do all profits. This is the process by which markets shrink, choice is curtailed, and government dependency grows. It is profits, earned from free-market competition, that keep cost down. By taking the profits out and putting the bureaucrats in, any incentive to provide better service or lower costs is eliminated. Student loan costs are thus set to rise faster than ever.[514]

At the same time, however, the advantages of a college degree are being erased: the same thing that happened to non-college-educated workers during the 1990–91 recession is now happening to college-educated employees. Rather than the usual ups and down of the business cycle, the 2001 recession involved concrete structural changes in industries. Educated people have not only become subject to the same job insecurities that used to plague only the blue-collar labourer, but different factors also make it even harder for them to return to the workforce once laid off. The number of long-term unemployed with college degrees tripled in the five years following the bursting of the tech bubble in 2000. Should a college graduate lose a job, he is statistically more likely to be chronically unemployed than a high school dropout. At the same time, wage differences between those with and without degrees are at record highs. The traditionally well-paid professionals take longer to find work partly because they are reluctant to accept a lower-paying job, even if many ultimately do.[515] With jobs so hard to find in this market, a lot of college graduates would gladly settle for an unpaid internship, but even then, they are competing with laid-off professionals with far more experience.[516]

Circuit City is gone. Macy's is laying people off. So is Home Depot, Sears, even Starbucks. Google, Microsoft, Kodak, Boeing—all of these companies are letting people go. Guess who is not? Wal-Mart. Wal-Mart is one of the few retailers that posted positive sales in 2009 as the newest recession hammered away at consumer spending. In January, sales at stores open at least a year rose 2.1% compared with the same month in 2008, exceeding the company's expectations. Wal-Mart has 1.4 million

513. Ibid.

514. Peter Schiff, "The Fed's Last Hurrah," Euro Pacific Capital, Westport, CT, April 1, 2010.

515. Nicholas Riccardi, "Long-Term Jobless Find a Degree Just Isn't Working," *Los Angeles Times*, March 11, 2005.

516. Gerry Shih, "Unpaid Work, but They Pay for Privilege," *New York Times*, August 9, 2009.

employees at its 4,000 U.S. locations, and these employees have one thing in common: a job.[517] It may not be the most rewarding job in the world, but it is a job nonetheless. Meanwhile, Wal-Mart's critics continue to argue that the company should increase wages from its $10 per hour average. If the economy were at full employment, the argument might make sense, but when jobless claims for Americans are hitting records, the only important fact is that Wal-Mart employees are among the few not drawing unemployment.

Although Western capitalism is largely taking the blame for global capitalism, the Franco-German model of society with a high social wage is altogether uncompetitive in the 21st century. It is threatened neither by Great Britain nor the United States, but by the rapidly industrializing Southeast Asia and South America, which threatens the Anglo-Saxon standard of living just as much as it does the Continental one. The industrial revolution gave the Western nations a long, artificial boost in economic influence, which is now being reversed to the historical situation where the world trade giants are the most populous countries. Less than two centuries ago, pre-communist China accounted for a third of global total value of goods and services, and we are now witnessing its re-emergence as an international economic power. For almost all of the past two thousand years, China and India were the largest economies in the world. To think that the Westerners who have lost their jobs to "globalization" deserve their income more than a Chinese or Indian person is racist and arrogant. By knitting together global markets for goods, capital, and labour, we have raised the material standard of living significantly for the majority of the world's population.

At current rates of growth, the Chinese economy will not surpass that of the U.S. until sometime in the 2040s.[518] But it will keep on growing, because it will still be much smaller in terms of gross domestic product per capita. As for India, it has a younger population than China with its one-child policy, and may thus exceed China in population and growth terms. However, it is quite possible that China and India will end up like Japan, not seeing their economic growth accompanied by extended geo-political power or influence; indeed, America's chief competitors remain far too busy with problems at home and along their borders to bear heavy international burdens. Yet even the people who were not alarmed when Japanese companies started taking over famous American businesses in the 1990s seem worried about Chinese companies doing the same today. The Japan scare was characterized by xenophobia, and racist analogies between Japan's military imperialism during WWII and its so-called economic imperialism half a century later. Its strange and alien forms of organization, the ***keiretsu***, were said to combine the wicked qualities of socialism and corporate capitalism into a super-efficient production machine that somehow overrode the basic laws of economics.

Today's growing anti-Chinese sentiment has the same fundamental causes: the resentment we feel at another country's economic success and the fear we have about its impact on our own economy. There is really only one clear difference: the Japanophobia of yesterday and the Sinophobia of today draw from different themes of

517. Ron Galloway, "We're All Wal-Mart Shoppers Now," *Huffington Post*, February 5, 2009.

518. Thomas Renard, "A BRIC in the World: Emerging Powers, Europe, and the Coming Order," Egmont, Brussels, October 2009.

historical Western prejudice against the East. If Japan was the crafty Oriental with his knavish plots, then China is the Asian hordes. It is not that they work hard and save while we spend and borrow, but it is simply that there are just so many of them. The Communist Party has Chinese peasants pouring into huge factories where they work 20 hours a day for half the U.S. minimum wage and produce enough stuff to fill an entire Wal-Mart every few minutes. And like idiots, we buy their products.

How often do you hear comments about the Chinese taking our jobs and stealing our intellectual property? What the two million American workers who have lost their manufacturing jobs fail to realize is that ten times as many Chinese have lost theirs over the same period, in large part due to the restructuring of state-owned enterprises.[519] Similarly, U.S. media companies upset over piracy in China seem to have forgotten the time when piracy laws were flouted in Japan, and more importantly, how things got better as soon as Japanese companies grew and needed these same protections themselves. Intellectual property violations have been a problem in all countries at some point in their history, and some level of piracy is always endemic in developing countries, which have an interest in spreading products cheaply rather than rewarding foreigners for inventing them. This makes the fact that China actually has decent anti-piracy legislation even more surprising: to meet the terms of it accession to the World Trade Organization in 2001, China has abolished or amended thousands of statutes and regulations, so much so that the United States has brought fewer WTO cases against China than it has brought against Europe.[520] According to the UN intellectual property agency WIPO, China has seen a sharp increase in request for patents in recent years, and is set to take first place in patent applications worldwide in 2011.[521]

China's political system may be abominable, its arms build-up may be frightening, but its economic performance is far from sinister: between 1981 and 2001, a period when the net progress against poverty in the rest of the world was zero, China lifted 400 million people above the poverty line.[522] Despite minuscule return, the Chinese middle class keeps on saving, at the highest savings rate of any country, amounting to almost 40% of income.[523] Their incentive to save lay not in high interest rates, but in the fact that the largest socialist country in the world no longer offers its citizens a viable social safety net. China has a population bulge similar to the Western baby boom generation, which means that if the world's most populous nation does not grow rich before it grows old, it may witness the greatest demographic time bomb in all history. And China also suffers from a severe brain drain: about two-thirds of the Chinese who have studied abroad since the 1980s have chosen not to return home. This ratio, according to the Academy of Social Sciences in Beijing, is the highest in the

519. Lyric Hughes Hale, "It's a Juggernaut . . . Not!: The China of Our Imagination Bears No Resemblance to Reality," *Los Angeles Times*, May 22, 2005.

520. Neil C. Hughes, "A Trade War with China?" *Foreign Affairs*, July/August 2005; Sebastian Mallaby, "Trade and the China Card," *Washington Post*, March 6, 2006.

521. Eve Y. Zhou & Bob Stembridge, "Patented in China: The Present and Future State of Innovation in China," Thomson Reuters, New York, August 2010.

522. Sebastian Mallaby, "China's (Petty) Fiscal Crimes," *Washington Post*, June 6, 2005.

523. Hale, op. cit.

world.[524]

Ironically, the best possible thing for the American consumer is for China's economy to keep growing at its current high rate. Globalization has allowed the United States to suck up the savings of the rest of the world and consume more than it produces. When individuals or society consume more than they produce, they go into debt, while others hold their IOUs. In international trade, the American IOUs are known as "dollars" and are ultimately good for just one thing: buying stuff from the U.S. So the Chinese middle class works and saves in order that the Chinese government can buy billions of dollars worth of U.S. treasury bonds, which in turn support the spending habits of both the U.S. government and the American consumers, who can buy more Chinese-manufactured goods at low prices. The two countries have an absolute co-dependency predicated on the modern consumer addiction to plastic money.

Before the "Great Recession," foreigners were buying more treasuries than the government was issuing, enabling Americans to reduce their treasury holdings even as the government borrowed hundreds of billions of dollars. Foreigners seemed endlessly willing to hold American bonds, allowing the U.S. government to run budget deficits while still enjoying high growth, something no developing country could get away with. By 2009, however, the Federal Reserve "purchased" the vast majority of new government debt.[525] The U.S. financial meltdown created a worldwide crisis, but worldwide scared money is still flowing into U.S. treasury bonds as a safe haven; this allows for more U.S. borrowing, but by drying up credit overseas, it creates financial crises in other countries. Should other countries stop accumulating or spending dollars, then the United States would be in trouble.

Never in the history of the world has an advanced economy been as reliant on the inflow of foreign capital as the United States is today. Yet when the foreigners spend their dollars instead of just accumulating them, Americans are shocked at what they are able to buy: established brand names, high-tech patents, oil companies. The U.S. government is complaining how China discriminates against foreign investors, even though China took in 10 times more foreign investment between 1980 and 2005 than Japan did between 1945 and 2000.[526] At the same time, the United States retains antiquated limits on foreign ownership in several sectors of the economy, notably broadcasting and aviation. Not only are most of the goods that China sells abroad made with some imported components, but half of China's exports are actually made by foreign subsidiaries, so much of what the United States is buying "from China" was produced by American companies there.[527] Those who think China discriminates against imports should consider the fact that in 2004, China imported 60% more

---

524. "On the Development of Chinese Talent in 2006," Chinese Academy of Social Sciences (CASS), Beijing, May 30, 2007.

525. Jon Harooni & Ravi Tanuku, "Who Is Really Lending the U.S. All This Money?" *AR Magazine*, October 20, 2009.

526. Mallaby, op. cit.

527. "The Chinese Invasion," *Los Angeles Times*, July 3, 2005.

American goods than France, although the latter had a bigger economy.[528]

One factor in America's success after World War II was the fact that almost all manufacturing plants in the producing and exporting countries had been bombed to smithereens. In 1945, Europe, Russia, and Asia lay in ruins. The United States was the sole manufacturer left intact, and it took years and years, not to mention a great deal of financial aid from the U.S., for the economies of Western Europe and Japan to return to competitive large exporter status. By the 1970s, the U.S. saw jobs vanish in key industrial sectors and, to stop the rot, a new engine of growth had to be found—enter the financial sector. Wall Street began moving away from what it was always meant to be: a conduit between the holders of capital and those who wish to deploy it in productive economic activity. By the '80s, financial markets started to become globalized and the U.S. began to run a current account deficit; the over-valued dollar made American goods uncompetitive internationally by raising the price of U.S. exports to foreigners and lowering the price of foreign-made goods to Americans.

Bankers and multinationals were not too bothered about the U.S. trade deficit, because much of the U.S. trade was big corporations buying from their overseas subsidiaries which sold to them on credit. However, contrary to popular opinion, the trade balance—deficit or surplus—barely affects total employment over long periods. From 1991 to 2006, the U.S. trade deficit rose from $31 billion to an incredible $759 billion; in the same period, payroll jobs increased by 28 million, while the unemployment rate fell from 6.8% to 4.6%.[529] Still, the Fortune 500 companies have generated net negative job growth over the last thirty years; it is the start-ups, which constitute just 0.2% of GDP, that have generated 17.8% of economic output[530]—this goes a long way to explain why the U.S. keeps losing jobs even as its GDP is apparently expanding. Start-up companies are where the country should be investing; they are the only part of the economy that generates new output. But unless you are dealing with the stock of a major, publicly traded company, or the bonds of a large corporation, or anything else that can be rapidly traded back and forth in huge numbers by big banks, you are not on Wall Street's radar.

Over 99% of businesses in the United States are small businesses. In the last truly serious downturn, the 1970s, Microsoft, Apple, and Intel were all "small." Once upon a time, Marks & Spencer only had a barrow in a market and Walgreens made do with just one store. Similarly, the global successes of tomorrow are somewhere in the small business landscape of today. None of them has gone bust in the present crisis, much less needed a government bailout. They are individually so small as to be invisible to the powers that be, yet they are where innovation inevitably comes from. Small businesses are forced to innovate, because they cannot compete with established businesses unless they have an edge. The only competitive advantage of large corporations is their size; they tend to breed weak managers who throw money at problems and use pools of resources to sink competitors. Yet the corporate sector has

528. Mallaby, op. cit.

529. Robert J. Samuelson, "Globalization to the Rescue?" *Washington Post*, October 23, 2007.

530. Steve Rosenbaum, "'Stimulus? The Dollar Is Toast' Says Harvard MBA Juan Enriquez," *Huffington Post*, February 7, 2009.

received the largest cheque ever written, because they employ such huge numbers that politicians naturally think of saving them first; they would rather prop up zombie corporations than risk alienating such large electoral blocs.

During the over-optimistic '90s, many economists argued that as an economy becomes more sophisticated, it can abandon its manufacturing component altogether and simply move into a variety of service sectors. In a country with over 300 million people and the staggering diversity that the United States has, there will always be people who are ill-equipped for service labour, which was supposed to replace the manufacturing that went overseas. And although an economy may cease to produce industrial goods, it will continue to consume them; indeed, as an economy becomes wealthier and more developed, it may consume even more industrial products than it did before, and these products have to be imported. These imports have to be paid for with exports, which now have to come in the form of services; but only some services are exportable—or "internationally tradable"—of which finance is the most important.

Finance has become the largest single economic sector, along with being the most profitable and prestigious one; thus it is not surprising that it is now the most politically influential sector as well. This is why the U.S. response to the current economic crisis has been finance-centred and why it has emphasized bailouts of "too big to fail" financial institutions, along with the manipulation of interest rates and monetary policy. But as long as the government props up failed companies, soaks up all available investment capital, discourages savings, and chases capital out of the country, jobs will continue to be lost. When a factory shuts down in a factory town, all the service businesses shut down too. There are quite simply too many people employed in the financial sector today. There was a time when a 10-million share day on the New York Stock Exchange would have brought everything to a one or two day halt; with today's electronic settlement procedures, the NYSE handles billions of shares a day without a hiccup.

During the '90s, inflationary Federal Reserve policies fuelled a tech stock bubble. When that bubble burst, the Fed inflated an even larger one in real estate. And now that the real estate bubble has burst, the U.S. central bank is inflating the biggest bubble of them all: a bubble in government. Why government spending is included in the GDP is a mystery to me. It makes up nearly 25%, but because no-one buys them, no-one can actually demonstrate that government goods and services are worth their costs, or if, in fact, anyone attaches any value to them at all. Yet because government spending makes up a big part of GDP, cutting spending shrinks the GDP. The more spending is cut, the more GDP shrinks, making the deficit ratio less favourable. And since government revenues expand and shrink in proportion to GDP, cutting spending actually leads to reduced revenues, which lead to higher deficits, which lead to more cutting, and so on and so on. One might just as easily assume that government goods and services are worth nothing, and that the cost of politicians and the entire civil service should be subtracted from the total value of privately produced goods and services; in fact, to assume this would be more justified.

There is no way the record $800-billion U.S. current account deficit (2006)—the combined balances on trade in goods and services, income, and net unilateral current transfers—can be blamed on the Chinese surplus, which was only $230 billion in 2006; on the contrary, China's exports have soared mainly at the expense of other developing countries, and China itself has a significant trade deficit with some other nations. World leaders have spoken out against rising protectionism, which is blamed for sparking the global trade wars in the 1930s that deepened and prolonged the Great Depression. A host of nations are now adopting protectionist measures, including the United States. After "Buy American" provisions won support in Congress as part of the initial $787-billion stimulus package, Indonesian authorities fired back, ordering all civil servants in Southeast Asia's largest economy to only consume food, clothing, shoes, and other products made in Indonesia.

By artificially restricting e.g. the supply of Chinese textiles, Western governments will only drive up their prices and boost profit margins. Quotas also tend to create an incentive for fancier, higher-profit products; in other words, precisely the market niche that the West's own apparel industry fills. When the United States imposed quotas on Japanese automobiles, Toyota created the Lexus line, while Nissan came up with the Infiniti series. In September 2009, the U.S. trade deficit surged by 18.2%, the largest gain in ten years; much of the record deficit resulted from Americans spending Cash-for-Clunkers stimulus money on imported cars—or "American" cars loaded to the sunroof with imported parts.[531] Just how you define an American car is one of the greatest conundrums of our time: e.g. fewer than half of the parts on some Big Three vehicles are made in the United States, while Toyota's Camry, Sienna, and Tundra lines are composed 80% of parts made in America.

Foreign car manufacturers generate billions of dollars in jobs and community infrastructure in both the U.S. and Europe. Even if it is unilateral, free trade is beneficial; the West gains from being open to anything the poorer countries wish to sell it, whether or not they reciprocate. But the public discourse tends to focus on the lost jobs, rather than the cheap shirts, shoes, and electronics, which are about the only thing that has raised the standard of living for the poorer Westerners since the '90s. The much smaller number of Western people who are hurt by trade should perhaps receive help from the vast majority who benefit from it, but restricting trade to help those few only harms the many. Ultimately, politicians, governments, and public authorities are afraid of people gaining too great a freedom of movement and capital movements, because they are afraid of losing control.

531. Peter Schiff, "Job Losses Demystified," Euro Pacific Capital, Westport, CT, November 13, 2009.

7

Foreign Aid Is a Process by Which Poor People in Rich Countries Help Rich People in Poor Countries

Back in the 18th century, the famed Scottish economist Adam Smith wrote a book on why some nations are rich and other nations are poor: according to him, economic growth depends on free markets, limited government, and a system of natural liberty. The most important thing is to keep the poor countries involved in the world economy and have their governments running so that foreign investors are not afraid to invest in them. Foreign aid only tends to drive up the exchange rate for poor countries, harming domestic exporters who represent the surest long-term route out of poverty. "Charity sees the need, not the cause," says a German proverb.

Trade, not aid, has always been the biggest enemy of poverty in the developing world, India being the best contemporary example. World trade has freed up a lot during the last few decades, and is the reason why the absolute number of poor has dropped by 3 billion people in thirty years. The fastest climb above the poverty line has taken place in Asia, which used to have the most poor people in proportion to population, but then decided to abandon central planning. Trade in Africa has not opened up in a similar fashion, so it remains poor. Poverty has been substantially reduced only in countries such as India and China, which have gained momentum for structural change and the modernization of their economies by joining the globalization process.[532]

In poor countries, it costs more to enforce contracts and gain access to capital than it does in richer countries. When regulations are simplified, the number of new businesses skyrockets. The UN Millennium Development Goals seem to be only further away for most of the poorer regions of Africa and Asia, even when they have followed the prevailing doctrines of international development and poverty reduction. The sad reality is that most reforms are happening in richer countries. Less than a third of the 58 countries that the World Bank listed as having improved regulatory environments in 2004 were identified as poor or lower-middle-income nations. At the same time, many of the world's poorest economies—mainly in sub-Saharan Africa—failed to show any improvements at all.[533]

It is in the interest of Western businesses that they be able to do business with as many countries in the world as possible. The wealth of other nations is good for us in the narrowest selfish terms. We not only need access to raw materials, we also need people who are able to buy our products. When you go into another country in order to do business with it, you become aware of the things going on around you, and feel a certain obligation to prevent the local régime from committing atrocities. But if you do not have any business interests in that country, you may not even care what is going on there. The complete indifference of the West to what has been going on in central Africa for the last two decades can be largely attributed to the fact that, apart from some mines in Congo, we have no financial or economic interests in the vast expanse of equatorial Africa. Nor will any rational investor put his money on a dictator that can take away his investment.

Half a century ago African countries like Zambia and Tanzania were equally as poor or rich as South Korea or Taiwan in East Asia. The latter gave their citizens the right to invest in agriculture or business, and in ten to twenty years, the wait bore fruit: the two countries started trading with the rest of the world. These liberal reforms brought prosperity to the Asian countries; the Africans never gained the same freedoms. They could not own property, and if anyone gained success in farming and invested, for example, in irrigation, the bureaucrats, administrators, and politicians took their share. They could not trade with the rest of the world, because the African system was so protectionistic that they were not given a chance. Naomi Klein disagrees. Ms Klein, like every civilized person, wants poor countries to prosper. But she and her followers do not want it to happen with the help of free-market economy. Unfortunately, she has not managed to come up with anything that would raise the standard of living faster than deregulation, freedom of choice, and free enterprise.

The annual $23 billion in aid to Africa is twice is much as the Asian countries get, although Asia has four times as many people as Africa. One reason for this disparity is that many Asian countries simply do not wish to receive foreign aid. India, for example, was not willing to accept any emergency aid following the 2004 tsunami. African governments, on the other hand, have no qualms about begging for

---

532. Gill, et al. 2009.

533. Djankov, et al. 2005.

development assistance. Many of the African countries in fact see the ability to garner aid from abroad as a measure of success. Some sub-Saharan countries get most of their state budget from foreign donors, instead of domestic revenue. In Kenya, the budget has been financed with domestic funds only recently, while the neighbouring Uganda and Tanzania still finance their budgets with charitable donations from other countries.[534]

There is a lot of campaigning in the West to help Africa, even though the decades-long aid and development programs have not yielded the desired results. Essentially, eight times the amount of the original Marshall Plan has already been swallowed up by the continent, but where has this investment gone? More often than not, the answer is Africa's ruling kleptocrats, who just want another Mercedes 600 to add to their fleet of luxury sedans. The greatest obstacle to progress in Africa is its own political culture, a culture of corruption, mismanagement, waste, and war. People do not easily give up customs that have brought them wealth and power. Public indignation focuses on the bribe-taking head of state, but without the bribe-paying businessman, domestic or foreign, massive corruption cannot take place. And while ordinary people may resent the corrupt police, how many of them have not given a bribe to a traffic cop to get off a charge?

We all know that cultural change is an excruciatingly slow process, and there is a danger that by offering more aid and debt-relief we are only encouraging the behaviours that are holding Africa back. This is a game where the real obstacles to the economic emancipation of the African people—their rulers—are indulged at every opportunity, while ordinary Africans become increasingly poorer. In fact, no impoverished African has ever asked anyone for aid. Africa existed long before the birth of the international aid industry, and even before the colonial period; the notion that Africans can only stay alive with the help of international aid is clearly baseless. However, the funding by the international financial institutions usually covers the lion's share of the supply of public services and investments. If it were to be cancelled, a disaster would undoubtedly follow. The decision-makers know this, making the open misappropriation of funds possible. But the failures of the international effort go much deeper than this.

A study from the World Bank's independent evaluation unit shows that health, education, and other projects in a given country may all be rated "successful," yet poverty in that same country may show no sign of falling.[535] And even actual "reduction" of poverty would hardly solve the developmental problems of the world: statistical crossing of the poverty line has no impact on the life of a poor farmer or slum resident, nor does it automatically add to the general security. Promises to "eradicate" poverty by increasing the aid are based on confused concepts and shaky calculations. Treating the poor as wards of the global economy ignores the fact that the 4 billion people who live on less than $2 a day make up a vast, untapped market, which companies can profit from right now by serving its needs. We should stop thinking of the poor as victims and start to make and distribute inexpensive products

534. Rasna Warah, "The Development Myth." 2008.

535. Carvalho, et al. 2002.

for these potential consumers; the profit margins might be low for each unit of product, but what we are talking about here is volume—on an unprecedented scale.

It is an idle hope that development assistance will confine the development problems in developing countries. Many countries are poor because they lack skilled people, which means they cannot administer aid programs effectively. A big part of outside resources go into project management, since the sponsors usually demand detailed reporting, even if there are no consequences for breaking the terms. The "administrative costs" can take anywhere from 2% to 50% of the total expenditure.[536] Generously financed aid experiments like the Gates Foundation HIV/AIDS program in Botswana show that even when money is abundant, progress can still be difficult because health care workers are scarce. Nor is training more workers an effective solution, because many will emigrate to the West, where their skills are in demand and salaries are much higher. Sub-Saharan Africa is short of one million health workers, Ghana having only 1,500 doctors for a population of 22 million, since two-thirds of the young doctors leave the country within three years of graduation.[537]

However, assistance can also take the form of research in rich and middle-income nations: e.g. finding new drugs for tropical diseases and developing new seeds that could boost agricultural gains. Malaria alone kills 1 to 3 million Africans each year. But the research commitment behind any new drug or vaccine is immense, with it taking anywhere from 7 to 20 years to produce one, at a cost of up to $1 billion. Since many leads do not ultimately pan out, drug companies take a great financial risk every time they fund research into a new product: if they want to keep making the kind of profits they do today, they have to focus on ailments for which people are willing and able to pay substantial amounts of money. Ninety percent of those who die of malaria live in sub-Saharan Africa, and most of them are children under five, whose parents typically make less than $1 a day.[538] That is not exactly an alluring market for Big Pharma, which explains why out of 1,233 new medications licensed worldwide between 1975 and 1997, only 13 were for tropical diseases, and five of those for veterinary purposes.[539]

The March of Dimes raised a lot of money, which—or what was left of it after most of it was spent on administration and advertising—financed research on a polio vaccine. Then disaster hit: Jonas Salk found a vaccine for polio. So, with its goal accomplished, the March of Dimes probably went out of business? Not quite. The organization turned to a more amorphous task, i.e. to fight "birth defects," of which there are so many varieties that it can count on doing business for years and years to come. The Jesuits may or may not have believed that "the ends justify the means," but the March of Dimes has transcended the contradiction; for them, the means justify

---

536. Nirmala Ravishankar, et al. "Financing of Global Health: Tracking Development Assistance for Health from 1990 to 2007," *The Lancet* 373(9681), June 20, 2009, 2113–2124.

537. J. B. Eastwood, et al. "Loss of Health Professionals from sub-Saharan Africa: The Pivotal Role of the UK," *The Lancet* 365(9474), May 28, 2005, 1893–1900.

538. Jeffrey Sachs & Pia Malaney, "The Economic and Social Burden of Malaria," *Nature* 415(6872), February 7, 2002, 680–685.

539. "Genomics and World Health: Report of the Advisory Committee on Health Research," World Health Organization, Geneva, 2002.

the end. Sting took a lot of flak in 2008, when Charity Navigator, an independent watchdog organization, rated his Rainforest Foundation as one of New York's worst charities, because only 41% of the almost $2.2 million raised at one of its concerts made its way to projects on the ground; yet many of the better-known mega charities spend a shocking amount of donations on fundraising, image building, and fancy offices—they just are not subject to the same public scrutiny as organizations set up by celebrities.[540]

Vaccines for diseases like polio, yellow fever, and hepatitis B have been around for decades, but poor countries cannot afford to buy them, so most manufacturers have quit producing them; when aid organizations raised money for vaccines in the 1990s, they had trouble finding suppliers. About 6.5 million people in poor countries, where 90% of the world's AIDS patients live, are at risk of imminent death if they do not receive ludicrously expensive anti-retroviral therapy.[541] Since poor countries buy almost none of the required drugs anyway, it would not hurt the drug companies to give up patent rights in those markets. But the companies apparently fear that if Africans were allowed to get cheap pills, these would somehow find their way back onto the Western markets. In much of the developing world, 70–95% of the people still rely on traditional plant-based medicine as their primary form of health care.[542] For the vast majority of human history, the thought that anyone owned an idea or technique was laughable. Gone is the spirit of Jonas Salk, who refused to patent the polio vaccine, because "it would be like patenting the sun."[543] Drug companies wish to suppress all thought of weaker intellectual property rights, even when these rights have no business value. The above-mentioned Gates Foundation derives its money from Microsoft's intellectual property, so it has no interest in challenging this policy.

Another common complaint is that the foundation's fund-raising arm—which operates independently of the charitable side—is known to invest its assets in companies that pollute the environment, exploit poor workers, and distort the global financial system.[544] Its wealth and image also lures health workers and medical resources away from less glamorous areas of need. In the last two decades, the international community has spent almost $200 billion trying to save people from death and disease in poor countries. When the World Health Organization examined the impact of various global health initiatives during the last twenty years, they found some benefits, like higher vaccination rates and increased diagnosis of tuberculosis cases; but they also concluded that some UN programs actually hurt health care in Africa by disrupting basic services and leading some countries to slash their health

540. Jonathan Foreman, "Taking the Private Jet to Copenhagen," *The Sunday Times*, November 29, 2009.

541. "Progress on Global Access to HIV Retroviral Therapy: An Update on '3 by 5,'" World Health Organization, Geneva, June 29, 2005.

542. Molly Meri Robinson & Xiaorui Zhang, "The World Medicines Situation 2011: Traditional Medicines," World Health Organization, Geneva, 2011.

543. Smith 1990, 338.

544. William Langley, "The Billionaire Boys: Beware of Geeks Bearing Gifts," *Sunday Telegraph*, August 8, 2010.

care spending.[545] Foreign money often only destroys local initiative and props up dysfunctional health care systems. If you have a corrupt government, no amount of development aid is going to fix that.

In his book, ***Small Change***, Michael Edwards, a former World Bank advisor, asks: "Why should the rich and famous decide how schools are going to be reformed, or what kinds of drugs will be supplied at prices affordable to the poor, or which civil society groups get funded for their work?"[546] Some countries fail to get more donations even if they are in worse shape than others. The predominantly Christian Ethiopia and Uganda both receive more money than the predominantly Muslim Nigeria, Pakistan, or Bangladesh, though the latter have bigger health crises.[547] Funds tend to go to whichever lobby group shouts the loudest, HIV/AIDS being a case in point. According to World Bank figures, two-thirds of the people below the poverty line live in Asian countries and Asia has three times as many people living in absolute poverty than Africa, but most of the global development aid goes to Africa, albeit much of it to foreign campaign planners, consultants, coordinators, publicists, and other PR personnel.[548] The public health community has convinced the public that the only way to improve health in poor countries is by throwing a ton of money at it; it may or may not be coincidental that thousands of highly paid jobs also depend on that. Most development aid professionals cannot see that their own careers and the surrounding institutions only serve themselves.

Large organizations, UN bodies, international financial institutions, national foreign aid bureaus, and professional non-profit organizations have been created over the course of decades in the name of development assistance. They employ hundreds of thousands of people all around the world, the vast majority of whom manage, classify, and evaluate various technical and economic statistics, on the basis of which individual aid decisions are made. Massive streams of money naturally require an immense administrative apparatus. But over the years, these bureaucracies have become an end in themselves, and no longer have much to do with helping poor people in poor countries. As opposed to regular businesses, development aid is probably the only form of economic activity where results have no bearing on the continuation of operation. Despite forty years of continual aid, the UN development organization, UNDP, reports that African countries are now poorer than they were in 1980.[549] Development assistance has been around a long time, but it has not made the poor any better off than Mother Teresa did; however, at least Mother Terasa had the decency to admit that her purpose was only to help the poor endure God's will.

Nor do things appear to be changing, although the GDP in many African countries is now growing at an annual pace of 5%. In spite of economic growth, the number of people living in poverty and in the dismal conditions of big city slums has only

---

545. Badara Samb, et al. "An Assessment of Interactions between Global Health Initiatives and Country Health Systems," *The Lancet* 373(9681), June 20, 2009, 2137–2169.

546. 2010, xiii.

547. Ravishankar, et al. Op. cit.

548. Gill et al. Op. cit.

549. United Nations Development Program 2010.

increased year by year. The Kenyan capital, Nairobi, has seen its slum population triple since the 1970s. The most modern metropolis in East Africa has two million people, over half of its population, living in Kibera or other unofficial provinces.[550] As it happens, Nairobi is also the headquarters to HABITAT, the UN agency responsible for helping governments address the problems of human settlements and urban development. The agency estimates that today over half of the urban populations in Africa live in slums.[551] Without the slums, most African cities would grind to a halt. The urban metropolises of the continent are completely dependent on the cheap labour provided by the slum dwellers, who ultimately keep the factories running, the construction sites operating, the streets clean, and the economic growth going. However, growth and prosperity are two entirely different things, and in a world of limits, one steals from the other; it might be better for most if prosperity were the thief and growth the victim, but our political leaders desire just the opposite.

It is easier to deal with results than to affect the causes; it is easier to give money for the treatment of AIDS victims than to prevent HIV from spreading; it is easier to distribute food provisions than to eradicate famine. What we have won in the rise of employment, we have lost in the rise of AIDS cases and starving populations. According to the UN, family planning programs have worked relatively well in Asia, the Arab nations, and Latin America, but in the poorest parts of Africa their success has been modest.[552] Aid campaigners work hard to get funds for distributing condoms to as many Africans as possible, while the Catholic Church spends vast amounts of money and missionary power to prevent the use of contraceptives all around the world. In a continent with the world's highest rates of infant and maternal mortality, less than half of the pregnancies and births result in both a live mother and a live baby. The Church is growing the fastest precisely in Africa, where the rate of HIV infection has jumped sharply and the number of AIDS orphans has escalated dramatically.[553] This appalling fact is well known to the aid workers, who are afraid to say it out loud because the Catholic Church is a major financial contributor to several other relief efforts.

With the help of social conservatives in the U.S. Congress, the Catholic Church continues to dictate sexual morés to the world at large, often at the expense of public health. For example, American groups working to combat the HIV epidemic need to comply with a 2003 law that requires them to have "a policy explicitly opposing prostitution and sex trafficking" before they can even be considered for federal grants.[554] It is patently absurd to think that any of the groups providing health services in the Third World would support prostitution, but a big part of fighting sexually-transmitted diseases inevitably involves working with prostitutes. Aid workers are doing their best to give these women better options, not through moralizing or coercion, but through literacy programs, job training, and STD counselling.

---

550. Warah, op. cit.

551. United Nations Human Settlements Programme 2010.

552. United Nations Fund for Population Activities 2004.

553. Erlandson, et al. 2004.

554. 22 USC § 7631(f).

In 2005, the Pope was granted immunity for any liability in sex abuse cover-ups in the U.S. by President George W. Bush. In 2006, USAID declared Brazil ineligible for a renewal of a $48 million AIDS prevention grant, because it refused to emphasize abstinence as the basis of prevention efforts. The following year, Brazil's president authorized the country to bypass the patent of an AIDS drug manufactured by Merck, a U.S. pharmaceutical giant. The country will henceforth import a cheaper, generic Indian-made version of the drug, but it also produces generic versions of eight other drugs that have no patents. What is more, the Brazilian government says it is the world's largest single buyer of condoms, having purchased more than a billion of them in recent years to give away free as part of the national program to fight AIDS. According to Brazilian health officials, a working partnership with prostitutes is a key reason that the country's AIDS prevention and treatment programs are considered by the UN as the most successful in the developing world.[555] Pamphlets distributed by the Health Ministry advertise a character called "Maria Without Shame," a cartoon prostitute who flaunts her cleavage and exhorts sex workers to take pride in their jobs —and tells the people of the world's most populous Catholic country that condoms should be used without guilt.

Being a non-Catholic today is more and more like being a non-American; important, historic decisions are being made without you having any say in the matter: the United States chooses a president who decides to invade Iraq and a large part of the world goes to war; the College of Cardinals choose a pope whose actions affect an even bigger part of the world. And what do we hear from the mouth of free market critics? That the chief problem today is the trampling of values and people under commercialism. Yet infinitely more people have recently been blow up in the name of values than in the name of commerce. Human rights are a value. The freedom and independence of the United States are values. The statehood of Israel is a value. Allah Himself has got to be a value. Religion is increasingly filling the void left by the failure of secular politics to explain, restrain, or contain the forces of change unleashed in the super-connected world of globalization.

As George Soros pointed out, "There is a serious mismatch between current political and economic conditions. We have a global economy but our political arrangements are still firmly grounded in the sovereignty of the state."[556] Many citizens feel powerless in a situation where they have to try to influence global policy decisions via national politics and local elections. The nation-states were formed with the industrial revolution, and they have become obsolete as we are entering a new social phase. "Nations have to disappear. There is no need of any nations; the whole earth belongs to the whole of humanity. There is no need of any passports, there is no need of any visas. This earth is ours, and what kind of freedom is there if we cannot even move? Everywhere there are barriers, every nation is a big imprisonment."[557]

The central thesis of Thomas P. M. Barnett's work of strategy, called *The*

555. Monte Reel, "Where Prostitutes Also Fight AIDS: Brazil's Sex Workers Hand Out Condoms, Crossing U.S. Ideological Line," *Washington Post*, March 2, 2006.

556. Speech at the State of the World Forum 2000, September 5, 2000. *World Affairs* 5(1), January–March 2001.

557. Bhagwan Shree Rajneesh, "Rebellion is the Biggest 'YES' Yet." Hyatt 2001, 128.

Pentagon's New Map, is that the world is now divided into two categories: the "Functioning Core" is constituted by nations that are connected to the global economy and prospering as never before, while the "Non-Integrating Gap" is made up of countries that are disconnected from the matrix of wealth and progress, and thus spinning towards chaos. Though the vast majority of the military interventions by the United States in recent years have been in the Gap, the West has failed to realize that it faces a common enemy there. According to Barnett, this enemy "is neither religion (Islam) nor a place (the Middle East), but a condition—disconnectedness."[558]

"If disconnectedness is the real enemy, then the combatants we target in this war are those who promote it, enforce it and terrorize those who seek to overcome it by reaching out to the larger world."[559] Peace groups tend to be on the left of the political spectrum and thus oppose free trade and free markets, but in so doing, they are actually working against peace, since they are undermining one of the most powerful forces for promoting peace today. Free trade and globalization are knitting countries together and making war less likely. The secret to world peace is not love, but money, trade, and financial interdependancy. For eight centuries, the French and the English made war with each other about every five minutes, now they are both trading peaceably in the European Union. They still pretty much despise each other, but they have stopped trying to gouge each other's eyes out. In matters of war and peace, how you feel is of no consequence; what matters is whether or not you swing the axe. Thus far the only proven long-term solution has been letting people buy and sell from each other. And if we trade long enough and respect each other's property rights long enough, we may start to give ourselves the chance to be friends.

World trade has quadrupled since 1982, but some see that exponential growth as just another part of the largest credit bubble in history, a bubble that is now bursting.[560] The old type of globalization may well be dead in the water: it is founded on cheap oil which could rapidly be coming to an end, and for which there is no replacement in sight. Its premise is that production can be concentrated in a few places at great distances from consumption, which requires that the cost to transport products is not adverse to the economics of the transaction. At the same time, the old capitalism of buying and selling objects fashioned by human hands is also at an end. Investment markets and the "new economy" are the engines of modern finance; but the labour of a consultant, innovator, broker, agent, or PR person does not usually produce a three-dimensional object.

The renowned American economist Dr. Paul Zane Pilzer, who famously predicted the "dot-com" boom, contends that the wealth of nations no longer depends on its physical resources. If it did, the former Soviet Union with its oil, gas, and gold would be the richest region in the world. But it is not, because today's wealth is predicated on technology and innovation.[561] The white-collar workers are the ones most

---

558. 2004, 49.

559. Ibid.

560. Anthony Faiola, "A Global Retreat as Economies Dry Up: As World Trade Plummets, Bustling Ports Stand Idle and Foreign Workers Track Back Home," *Washington Post*, March 5, 2009.

561. Pilzer 1990.

vulnerable to change in the globalized economy; they are the people whose jobs are going to be under threat of outsourcing. Information requires no physical transport and not only does but must move at the speed of light. The internet has made secrecy impossible, both in the world of business and in the world of politics—a perfect example of the democratizing effect of technology.

"But, unlike authoritarian regimes, democratic governments hold secrets largely because citizens agree that they should, in order to protect legitimate policy."[562] Which has got to be among the biggest crocks of shit in modern history. The fact is that WikiLeaks is doing more to promote self-government than the vast majority of the liberal press that kowtows to government cover-ups. The Obama administration fulfills even fewer FOI requests than its predecessor—wouldn't it be ironic if the administration that promised and was elected on transparency turns out to be the most secretive of all?[563] Secrecy can be harmful to national security as well as to democratic values, because it can impede the flow of information to those who need it. Should the United States tighten its law against classified leaks, presidential aides would be unable to properly brief the press since a huge amount of important information is classified and much of it involves no risk to national security. Historically, leaks from anonymous sources have been crucial to informing the public. Without anonymity for sources, a free press would lose its ability to act as a check and balance against the power of government. However, a government that cannot hide a blowjob cannot hide much else either; most people are constitutionally unable to keep a secret, which fact alone makes the notion of giant "conspiracies" patently ludicrous—it is not a "secret organization" if people know about it.

The effect on society of the evolution of digital photography is profound, from changing the way people record their daily lives to making it more difficult to trust the images we see. The value of the image is no longer what it once was: without the cost of film and processing, there is little to stop people from photographing everything in sight; and thanks to e-mail, you can instantaneously share the photo you took with your cell phone camera with friends and family around the world. Almost all digital cameras will connect to your personal computer and many come with software to retool images, something that used to be the exclusive purview of professionals. In fact, the more elaborate desktop animation and editing programs now allow any teenager to blow up a CGI spaceship on a garage-band budget.

The mass consumer has at his or her disposal ever more gadgets with greater capacity to record, store, and share content. Digital photos play a powerful role in shaping the news and the political agenda today. The incredible spread of broadband internet connections means that a movie does not have to open to 3,000 screens to get seen by the millions. Wireless networks enable video and audio to be moved around the home and enjoyed on the most convenient device. Fast wireless data networks have spurred deals between content providers and mobile companies that let people turn to their cell phones for news and entertainment. The ubiquitous digital cameras, cellular phones, and portable game consoles effortless connect both to each other and

562. Raffi Khatchadourian, "No Secrets: Julian Assange's Mission for Total Transparency," *The New Yorker*, June 7, 2010.

563. "Promises, Promises: Little Transparency Progress," Associated Press, March 14, 2011.

to the internet.

Not long ago, you could take an album or two—of music, not photos—and copy a bunch of different songs to a cassette and give the resulting "mix tape" to a friend. If you do the same thing today with online tools, it is called "file sharing" and it may get you sued. It also used to be easy to take a polaroid of your naked body and hand it to a friend. That friend might pass the picture around without you knowing it, but this was a risk you were willing to take. It was not uncommon for persons under the legal age to do this, with their teenage hormones raging and all, and they would be in a lot of trouble if they got caught—mostly from their parents. Today, if a person under the age of eighteen does the same thing with a cell phone and the internet, they will be charged with trafficking child pornography and have to register as sex offenders, even if they have taken the photos themselves.

Despite all the fancy closed-circuit cameras and all the idealistic talk about thwarting gun crimes and drug dealers and paedophiles and homosexuals kissing in public, the bottom line remains that cameras simply do not work as a deterrent. When most people see the cameras, they just shrug. And then smile. And maybe fix their hair. And hope the camera catches their good side and does not make their ass look big or their double chin too obvious. Surveillance society, you say? Nah, it's a celebrity society. Everybody wants to be on television—no matter what kind of television it is. A nobody can become a somebody at a moment's notice, just because everybody is always watching everything. Popular websites such as MySpace and YouTube, in which the user is effectively turned into a star, get more hits than concerts and movies get audiences. According to *Fortune* Magazine, MySpace had more than 100 million users worldwide by August 2006, and 54 million of them spend, on average, 124 minutes on the site for each visit, more than the length of the average studio album. YouTube's most popular videos attract more than 40 million views, a substantially larger number than all but very few Hollywood movies.[564]

It has become unbelievably easy to get and leverage attention. We are on our way to a world in which everyone has the right and opportunity to use their freedom of speech. Not long ago, very few writers got their work published, and they were often paid for it; now anyone can type anything about any subject online. While newspapers continue their seemingly unending decline and publishers cut their costs, degrees in journalism and creative writing have never been more popular. People used to read when they arrived first at a meeting or waited at the doctor's office—now they type. The distinction between a note left on the counter and a publishable work has been erased. Our notes are being blasted to everyone we know and everyone they know as we are using some of the most advanced technology in history to provide the type of entertainment last enjoyed by the Waltons. The world has never had more communication and yet produces little understanding or dialogue.

A camcorder held the Los Angeles police accountable by capturing the beating of Rodney King. Photographs of American soldiers returning in coffins from the Persian Gulf exposed the cost of the Iraq War. Without the omnipresent digital camera, the torture of inmates at the Abu Graib prison might never have seen the light of day. It

---

564. Patricia Sellers, "MySpace Cowboys," *Fortune*, September 4, 2006.

is nearly impossible to stop illicitly taken pictures or video circulating online; every attempt to get material removed only alerts a new audience to the existence of the footage. Far from producing Orwell's "1984," the intrusiveness of modern technology into daily life is everywhere undermining the power of, and respect for, the government and politics in general. Thanks to YouTube, blogging, instant fact-checking, and viral e-mails, it is getting harder and harder for politicians to get away with repeating brazen lies, or to run baseless smear campaigns without being exposed. Governments may be watching their citizens, but the citizens are watching right back.

China has the most sophisticated internet filtering régime in the world, which involves Microsoft altering the local version of its blog tool at the behest of the Chinese government. Eloquent as he is on the subject of Third World poverty, Bill Gates seems less worried about Third World free speech. None of this can "alter the fact that the ideas which are changing our civilization respect no boundaries."[565] Despite the power of the search engine giants, few say Google strikes as much fear in them as Microsoft did during the 1990s, when its *de facto* monopoly on computer operating systems earned it the nickname "evil empire." No-one can own the ideas on the internet; if you have an idea, its value is not reduced if you share it with a friend, quite the opposite: the technical superiority of the Linux operating system is predicated on the fact that its source code is open and can be improved upon by anyone with the will and ability.

Although many governments have infiltrated the activities of the internet to varying degrees, it remains the closest thing to a genuinely free economy in the modern world. Given that the State neither inhibits the activities of the internet nor props up or favours any particular actors or individuals, we may actually be witnessing the closest thing to a free market that has ever existed. It can be argued that humanity has seen more progress and innovation through the use of the internet in the past twenty years than through the use of any other innovation in recorded history. We have seen entrepreneurs from all kinds of economic backgrounds making full use of their skills, ideas, and passions. Some very young people have been able to generate massive wealth, while providing cheap, convenient, and valuable new tools for everyone across the globe to enjoy. Information that used to cost individuals and companies exorbitant fees can now be found online for free, thus allowing them to spend that money elsewhere. This is the beauty of a system free from government intervention, and as we have seen throughout history, when companies become threatened by competition, they do whatever possible to squash that competition—more often than not through the force of government.

All so-called "intellectual property" is a government-created right adopted quite recently in economic history to further a public policy goal. "Illegal downloading" is not the same as stealing, either legally, practically, or morally. If you have something valuable, and I steal it, then I have something valuable and you do not. That's the definition of stealing: taking someone else's property and depriving them of its use. It is predicated on the "scarcity of resource": stealing your food would mean you go

565. Hayek 2011, 527.

hungry and stealing your money would mean you cannot afford to buy more food. Digital information, by virtue of being infinitely replicable for negligible cost, cannot—by definition—be stolen. Anyone who claims that copying their intellectual property is the same as stealing money out of their pocket either does not understand the facts or is deliberately obscuring them for profit. Writing in the *New York Times*, Bono called internet service providers "reverse Robin Hoods," who benefited from the music industry's lost profits, and hinted that China's efforts prove the tracking of online content possible.[566] But U2 topped the list of top-grossing live acts in 2009, whereas, in the words of Cory Doctorow, "For an indie artist, the big problem isn't piracy, it's obscurity: no one even cares enough about your tunes to steal 'em."[567]

The old industrial logic was based on the large corporation feeding consumers with commodities it had developed and whose value derived from their limited availability. In the internet age, however, even distributing the commodities for free becomes profitable, and the surplus value comes from more and more consumers using the product and developing it further. "But refusal to acquaint one's self with new ideas merely deprives one of the power of effectively countering them when necessary. The growth of ideas is an international process, and only those who fully take part in the discussion will be able to exercise a significant influence."[568] However, as political leaders around the world become more connected with the global economy, they also become more disconnected from their own cultures.

As social and economic change becomes more pronounced, intrusive, and unpredictable, people seek out "eternal verities." The role of religion in political speeches has only grown, although globalization and information technology were supposed to make religions redundant. Indeed, religion in its many forms has become the principal force of political backlash in the era of globalization. Yet for most of history, cultures and civilizations *have* been interdependent, flowing into and out of each other, and the exclusive ethnic and religious identity of modern nation-states suppresses that reality. We now know that man is naturally multilingual, but when the "confusion of Babel" first got challenged in early the 19th century, European countries were in the midst of inventing their national dresses and composing their national anthems.

During the age of imperialism, French was the dominant language the world over, but today, people all over the world resent the dominance of the English tongue because it is associated with a nation; and that nation is not England, but the United States—which itself ironically has no official language. Susan Sontag wrote that "America was founded on a genocide, on the unquestioned assumption of the right of white Europeans to exterminate a resident, technologically backward, colored population in order to take over the continent."[569] Paradoxical as it seems at first, anti-internationalism is often associated with imperialism: the more a person dislikes the unfamiliar and thinks his own customs superior, the more he tends to see it as his

566. "Ten for the Next Ten," January 2, 2010.

567. 2008, 116.

568. Hayek, op. cit.

569. "What's Happening in America," *Partisan Review*, Winter 1967.

mission to "civilize" others; not by free and voluntary intercourse, but by bringing the blessing of efficient government to all the world—and this, not poverty or poor education, is the root cause of terrorism.

This is also the core paradox of Europe. The Nazis brought it to a head: universalism became a racial characteristic of the Aryans. But whereas the West views the Second World War as a global conflict, Russia sees it merely as a "national crusade to repel the invader." German forces suffered 93% of their casualties on the Soviet front, which might suggest it was the Russians, not the Allies, who defeated Hitler.[570] The subsequent fall of communism proved for the West that corporate capitalism and representative democracy were the final truth, and needed to be disseminated everywhere. However, in the eyes of Russia, the collapse of the Soviet Union was "the greatest geo-political catastrophe of the 20th century."[571] For Russia's greatest generation, the one which defended their country in WWII, the rampant inflation and capitalist oligarchy that supplanted communism were a disaster that wiped out their savings and stole their patrimony.

For many East Europeans, the 9th of May, 1945, only meant the transition from one totalitarian occupation to another, but for Russia it marked the end of the Great Patriotic War, when the Red Army almost single-handedly liberated most of Europe from fascism. The fact is, we should not really talk about the Second World War, but about the Second World Wars, a plural that applies inside as well as between countries. Only a great collective effort of national myth-making has enabled the French to combine the resistance France of Charles de Gaulle and the collaborating France of Marshal Petain into a single, coherent memory. The Algerians mark the 8th of May, 1945, as the anniversary of the Setif massacre, when a V-E Day demonstration turned into a protest for Algerian independence, which was brutally suppressed by French security forces. As Orwell wrote: "Who controls the past controls the future,"[572] and the memory wars began the day WWII ended.

To many Americans, it seemed obvious that the A-bomb ended the War, "saving" millions of lives that might have been lost if the United States had been forced to invade mainland Japan. This powerful myth took root quickly and is deeply embedded in how Americans today see themselves as a nation. We were told that the use of the bombs "led to the immediate surrender of Japan and made unnecessary the planned invasion of the Japanese home islands."[573] But as Tsuyoshi Hasegawa has established in his book, ***Racing the Enemy*** (2005), and as many other historians have long argued, it was the Soviet entry into the Pacific war on the 8th of August, two days after the Hiroshima bombing, that provided the final impetus for Japan's capitulation. The second bomb was dropped, as J. Robert Oppenheimer, scientific director of the Manhattan Project, said, on "an essentially defeated enemy."[574] It was plainly meant

570. Konstantin Rozhnov, "Who Won World War II?" BBC News, May 3, 2005.

571. Vladimir Putin, Speech before the Russian Duma, April 25, 2005.

572. 2003, 35, 255.

573. The Enola Gay Exhibit, the Smithsonian Institution, Washington, D.C., June 28, 1995.

574. "Atomic Weapons and the Crisis in Science," ***Saturday Review of Literature***, November 24, 1945.

to prevent the Soviets from sharing in the occupation of Japan, which had announced its readiness for peace already at the Potsdam Conference on August the 3rd.

During both world wars, Hollywood studios produced propaganda for the U.S. government, in exchange for government aid in opening resistant foreign markets. For the Russian novelist Vasily Aksyonov, the VOA jazz broadcasts were "America's secret weapon number one," a glimpse of "the inaccessible but oh so desirable West."[575] All through the Cold War, Washington boosted the commercial export of popular culture in accordance with the view set forth in a State Department memo from 1948: "American motion pictures, as ambassadors of good will—at no cost to the American taxpayers—interpret the American way of life to all the nations of the world, which may be invaluable from a political, cultural, and commercial point of view."[576] During the 1970s, this effort to pry open world markets to American entertainment caused UNESCO to mount a backlash against "U.S. cultural imperialism," which led President Reagan to withdraw the United States from the organization in 1984.

With all the talk about "soft power" and the attractiveness of American popular culture to the rest of the world, the Western political commentators usually forget that popular culture is chiefly popular with the young—people who are still irresponsible, rebellious, and apolitical. Popular culture tends not to attract the mature, particularly those mature enough to be leaders of their families, communities, or countries, the people responsible for the security and welfare of those around them. To put it bluntly, American popular culture is a culture for children, not for adults. Instead of being the beacon of freedom to huddled masses in closed societies it once was, American popular culture has become a glut on the market, and in the absence of any counterbalancing cultural diplomacy, it is the nation's *de facto* ambassador to the world.

Protesters in Lebanon, Syria, and Palestine may burn the U.S. flag during street demonstrations, but in their free time they go see the latest American films in theatres. The very word "freedom" has so many different meanings to so many people that it has ceased to have much collective significance. It can alternately be used to describe the right to free speech or the availability of fifty different types of toilet paper; or the right to stand in the middle of the street, or the right not to have your day disrupted by such public disturbance. To some, freedom means that everyone is given the basic necessities of life, while others reckon that it guarantees the individual's right to personal gain, even at the expense of the disadvantaged. Meanwhile, the perplexed West cannot comprehend why the glad tidings of freedom, materialism, and democracy—carried partly on the point of bayonets—would get such a hostile reception.

The conventional wisdom that terrorism is rooted in poverty and lack of education does not fit in with data showing, for example, that Palestinian suicide bombers are wealthier and better educated than the general population. Neither bin Laden nor the 9/11 hijackers were poor, nor is Saudi Arabia, where most of them were from. Dr.

575. 1987, 18.

576. As quoted in Fraser 2003, 55.

Reuven Paz, an Israeli expert on terrorism, notes that among those who blew themselves up in Iraq over a six-month period were engineering students and English majors, and a handful of Europeanized Arabs.[577] Many of these bombers were married, well-educated, and in their late twenties, traits they shared with the 9/11 hijackers. A number of top figures in al-Qaeda have academic backgrounds in science. The proselytizing does not take place in mosques, but in schools and universities. Campuses already have an anti-government atmosphere, a left-wing tradition, and freedom of speech. It is easy to set up an Islamic colloquium, and no-one will interfere if radicals are invited to speak there. Successful terrorist plots of the above magnitude require big money to succeed, and are driven by religio-political ideology, not poverty. "The mind of the fundamentalist is like the pupil of the eye: the more light you pour on it, the more it will contract."

While there is a lot of illiteracy and what we perceive as a lack of democracy in the Arab countries, that does not mean that the ordinary citizens would consider their social structure any worse than that of the West. The status of women is very strong in Arab societies, even though they do not yet have the right to vote in all countries—neither do many men in Kuwait. The popular management of public affairs has been realized in the large Arab families and the *diwaniya* system long before Western democracy. The distinctive features of each political system are explained by their ancient family and marriage systems. Many also argue that globalization, through the spread of planned parenthood and literacy, is slowly but surely leading the whole world towards democracy, so there is really no need for any American sermons on popular rule.

However, democracy calls for a *demos*, a "people," and the Arab countries were not formed on basis of common nationality or language, but are former colonies of the great European powers. Consequently, national slates in the Middle East tend to bolster religious and sectarian parties, while medium size districts, at the provincial level for instance, favour tribal identities; when Jordan increased the number of voting districts, the vote for the Muslim Brotherhood fell by half.[578] Yet it seems pretty futile to instruct "non-democratic" countries on party politics: if the Democrats and the Republicans are like Coca-Cola and Pepsi respectively, how do you explain this difference to someone from a different culture? In times past, the left-right dichotomy was an instrument of clarification; today, no other definition causes more confusion.

Was Boris Jeltsin a right-winger or a lefty? He set himself against socialism, so he must have been a rightist; on the other hand, he was a radical revolutionary, who sought to liberate the people from the control of stagnant tyranny, so maybe he was a left-winger after all. We also tend to view avant-garde artists as leftist, fighting as they do on side of the New against the Old. But is this not the same path as that of money? All the old is sacrificed on the altar of new market areas and technologies. And the champions of capital are of course right-wing. Thus one might say the

577. "Arab Volunteers Killed in Iraq: An Analysis," *PRISM Series on Global Jihad*, No. 1/3, March 2005.

578. David Schenker, "Jordan's New Election Law: New Tactics, Old Strategy?" *PolicyWatch* 546, July 26, 2001.

Republican Party is radical, because it is conservative. And the new economy has not even found its political expression yet: it poses a dilemma for the left, which has modelled itself on the old economy; and although the new economy with its industrious workers labouring without overtime pay is a godsend to the right, that is exactly why they do not want to politicize it.

One of the things the West wishes to export under the guise of "freedom and democracy" is consumerism. There were battles over the oil of the Middle East to perpetuate the untenable and spendthrift consumerism of the West as early as World War I. Today, the United States is the largest per capita consumer of fossil fuels on the planet.[579] It is oil that drives the military machine of every country, providing the fuel for the aircrafts, battleships, tanks, and trucks. Control of oil is imperative: if you run out of it, your army comes to a halt. For modern Iraq, oil has always been at the heart of everything—its very existence as a unified state is largely the product of oil. In 1920, under the aegis of the League of Nations, Britain patched together the Kingdom of Iraq from the Ottoman provinces of Basra, Baghdad, and Mosul, in order to better exploit the holdings of what was then known as the Turkish Petroleum Company.

There is a direct connection between the War in Iraq today and events that took place more than half a century ago. In 1953, Mohammed Mosaddegh, Prime Minister of Iran, became frustrated with the way that Britain was pilfering his country's national resources, and demanded a greater share in it. The British asked for the help of U.S. President Eisenhower, who immediately declared Mosaddegh to be a communist, and send the CIA to overthrow him. Not only did the Americans not support democracy, they actively opposed it and were responsible for the overthrow of a freely elected government. By bringing the Shah into power, the United States created an extremely repressive régime that within twenty years led into a violently anti-American revolution by Ayatollah Khomeini.

The U.S. government then made a puppet out of Saddam Hussein in Iraq, because he was anti-Iranian and feared that the revolution in Iran would spread into his country. He started an extremely bloody war with Iran that went on throughout the 1980s. And, unfortunately, Saddam began losing the conflict, at which point Ronald Reagan sent Donald Rumsfeld to tell Saddam the United States would supply him with the weapons he might need, "under the rose" of course. This is why cynics in Washington say, "We know Saddam had WMD. We have the receipts." In fact, the U.S. continues to sell billions in conventional weapons to its friends in the United Arab Emirates and Saudi Arabia, for example, régimes second only in oppression to the Taliban. It is all a part of the arms export boom started by George W. Bush: according to Vice Admiral Jeffrey Wieringa, director of the Defense Security Cooperation Agency, the 2009 export figures were more than four times as high as those of the record low year of 1998.[580]

OPEC, founded in Baghdad in 1960, agreed to price oil exclusively in U.S. dollars for all worldwide transactions. This gave the almighty buck a special place among world currencies and in essence backed the greenback with oil. In return, the United

579. International Energy Agency 2010.

580. "Arms Sales Hit Record in 2009," Reuters, November 7, 2009.

States promised to protect the various oil-rich kingdoms in the Persian Gulf against threat of invasion or coup d'état. Saddam remained an American ally right up to his invasion of Kuwait in 1990. The U.S. government became alarmed that he could go on and invade Saudi Arabia itself, with the largest reserves of oil on Earth. However, the stationing of American troops in Saudi Arabia was a big mistake. Osama bin Laden, another former ally trained by the CIA, would soon voice his resentment of the Saudi government for using foreign infidels to defend the holiest Muslim land.

The events of September 11th, 2001, can be understood without any deep analysis by anyone who is least aware of the background of the terrorists. The hatred Arab terrorists have for the United States is obviously tied to the political history of the Middle East. There is no need for a minute breakdown of historical details. Or do you think all terrorists have delved deep into the archives before making their choice of career? It is more an emotional choice, predicated on personally experienced or historically manifested injustice. But despite the Crusades, and the 19th- and 20th-century colonialist meddling and betrayal by the West, Muslim culture itself bears the brunt of responsibility for its current predicament. After all, it is the corrupt Arab oligarchies, who control the vast oil revenues and receive protection money as "foreign aid," who are to blame for the poverty that fuels the rage of the Arab people.

According to World Bank estimates, excluding oil, the total exports of the entire Arab world amount to less than those of Finland, a nation of five million on the periphery of Europe. While trillions and trillions of dollars have flown into the coffers of the oil sheikhs, the majority of the Arab population lives in squalor. Extremists scream colonial oppression, but what jihadists call "rape of resources" might be dubbed "commerce" by other cultures. Colonization was not evil; in fact, it was almost inevitable: if it was not going to be done by governments, it was going to be done by businessmen. The average Kuwaiti retiree has witnessed a greater increase in standard of living than any other person anywhere on the globe before. Though it has only been a little over half a century since the oil was discovered, the money has already transformed Kuwait into an outward duplicate of America.

The all-pervasive American popular culture also lay at the heart of terrorism. At a time when Washington radically decreased its funding for cultural diplomacy, Hollywood aggressively expanded its exports. According to the Yale Center for the Study of Globalization, the fees generated by the export of filmed and taped entertainment rose from $1.68 billion to $8.85 billion between 1986 and 2000—a more than four-fold increase. Foreign box-office revenue has grown much faster than domestic, approaching a 2-to-1 ratio, and the same holds true for music, television, and video games.[581] "So much in Denmark is American. We are a nation under influence," declared Danish director Lars von Trier in his exasperation. "America fills about 60% of my brain. So, in fact, I am American. But I can't go there to vote and I can't change anything, because I am from a small country. So that is why I make films about America."[582]

"A nation where part of the population couldn't name a foreign language, never

581. Martha Bayles, "Now Showing: The Good, the Bad and the Ugly Americans—Exporting the Wrong Picture," *Washington Post*, August 28, 2005.

582. Remarks at the Cannes Film Festival, May 18, 2005.

mind speak one (and even the President appears to struggle with English.) Where TV news stations and documentary makers have their own, splendidly subjective, versions of the truth happily consumed by partisans of each shade."[583] It is exactly the news that embody what media critique has said again and again about entertainment —they have a passivating effect: every news category always gets filled, teaching us day after day that the world cannot be changed. The national political reporters generally come from the same cultural and class background as the people they are supposed to be holding to account. They inhabit the same suburbs, frequent the same cocktail parties, and are in debt to the same large business interests.

The Western news networks are owned by giant corporations, whose executives the politicians rely on to fund their election campaigns across the nation. And because the media rely on government "news" hand-outs, they in turn ignore most official abuses and focus instead on the perils of citizens distrusting their leaders. Who needs al-Jazeera when you have CNN? The subliminal purpose of the news is to make the impression that nothing has again happened; no miracles, no revolutionary practices, not one attempt to do things any differently—only when these fail do we get to hear about them. The news do not keep us informed about the world, but replay it each day just the way we have become accustomed to knowing it from the news. "Who is more to be pitied," asked Kurt Vonnegut, "a writer bound and gagged by policemen or one living in perfect freedom who has nothing more to say?"[584]

For more than 500 years, the Ottomans ruled with a gentle hand over an empire that stretched across three continents, and never felt any need to force the conquered peoples into adopting their religion and language. The Ottoman rule over North Africa lasted longer than the United States has existed, but the first post-French President of Algeria had to address his fellow Algerians in French, because they could no longer speak their native Arabic. Kemal Atatürk, the founder of modern Turkey, dissolved the Ottoman sultanate and imported from France the notion that religion has no place in public life. But the secularized Turkey of Kemal remained just a dream, for in its hearts the nation held on tight to its religious identity. And, unfortunately, modernization was also connected to the idea of a nation-state, that miserable European invention which embittered the lives of Armenians, Kurds, Greeks, and other Turkish minorities.

Only homogeneous societies can be truly democratic, others are invariably dictatorships of some sort, where a united minority rules over the fragmented majority, or rather, over several disunited minorities. In homogenous societies such as those of the West, political minorities find majority rule acceptable because they have a prospect of becoming majorities, while political majorities are restrained in the exercise of their power by their temporary status. This equation does not apply in societies where minority status is permanently established by religious or ethnic background. In such circumstances, majority rule is just another version of the oppression of the weak by the powerful, and democratic elections will only lead to the most populous group gaining and maintaining power at the exclusion of the

---

583. Aubrey Day, "Team America," *Total Film*, July 2005.

584. 1987, 176.

seriously marginalized minorities.

No-one doubts that getting 8.5 million Iraqis to vote was a great achievement—but it is also the primary reason why the people of Iraq, a country stitched together by British colonialists in the 1920s from three disparate provinces of the Ottoman Empire, now perceive their identity through an ethnic and sectarian prism. After the parliamentary elections, more and more of the minority Sunnis began to endorse armed resistance. Since the summer of 2003, several mosques have been bombed, numerous people have been kidnapped and executed, and previously mixed districts of Baghdad, such as Doura and Ghazaliya, have slowly but inexorably been cleansed of Shiites through intimidation and violence. Similar pressure has been exerted on Sunnis in Shiite-dominated villages in south Iraq, and on Arabs and Turkmen in Kirkuk. In the biggest wave of displacement in the Middle East since the creation of Israel in 1948, millions have either been displaced internally or fled to neighbouring countries.[585] As one 19-year-old Iraqi put it in a *Los Angeles Times* interview, "My father is Sunni and my mother is Shiite. I never knew the difference between these two sects before the occupation started."[586]

International law requires occupying powers to respect existing laws in the occupied country "unless absolutely prevented."[587] When an authoritarian government collapses, such a geographically ill-defined country as Iraq may no longer be secular and harmonious. Elections are not only empowering, but can act to sharpen the social divisions and to increase the political instability. Warnings like this were trampled under President Bush's neo-conservative mission to topple Saddam and bring democracy to the Middle East: the theory was that the authoritarian régimes in the area would tumble like dominoes after the fall of Saddam. Balance of power, deterrence, and punitive action were abandoned in favour of a scheme to recast the entire political culture of a vast region, something that would have been prohibitively difficult even with a flawless rationale, since not even the most powerful country on the globe can transform the world at will.

Democracy promotion seemed also to be the sole and defining element of Bush's long-term counter-terrorism approach, but does democracy even matter in the war on terror? The Iraq War was supposed to make the world a safer place—this is at least how the invasion was justified. Now Iraq is known as the greatest training ground for terrorists in the world. However, the IRA in Northern Ireland and the Basque militants in Spain and France show that terrorism can infest even well-established democracies. The history of the Ku Klux Klan and the case of Timothy McVeigh likewise suggest that democratic societies are not immune to home-grown terrorism. According to the U.S. State Department records, between 2000 and 2003, India, the most populous democracy in the world, had 203 terrorist attacks, while China, the world's most populous authoritarian state, had none. The fact is, most terrorist incidents occur precisely in democracies, and generally both the victims *and* the

585. "Iraq Situation Response," Office of the United Nations High Commissioner for Refugees, Geneva, July 2007.

586. Megan K. Stack, "A Nation Teeters on Brink of Civil War," February 25, 2006.

587. Hague Convention No. IV, Section III, Article 43, October 18, 1907.

perpetrators are citizens of democracies.[588]

President Bush consistently linked the building of democracy in Iraq and the broader Middle East with the defeat of the insurgency there, despite the phenomenal failure of the democratic process to accomplish anything of the sort. "Nation building" almost inevitably entails some violence. The Middle Eastern countries are stable exactly because they are ruled in an authoritarian manner. When the statue of the Iraqi dictator fell, the Americans thought they had won the hearts and minds of his people, not realizing that liberation from tyranny does not make up for the lack of food, water, electricity, jobs, and safety. In spite of what Bush called "incredible political progress,"[589] the Iraqi insurgency grew in strength and sophistication. From about 5,000 Saddam loyalists in 2003, the insurgency mushroomed after the parliamentary elections into a disparate force of 20,000, engaged in a deadly struggle whose battle lines were drawn by the highly polarized vote results.[590]

Neither has the balloting in Afghanistan done anything to stop the killing, with each passing year being declared the bloodiest thus far since the United States ousted the Taliban from power. More U.S. soldiers are killed in Afghanistan than in Iraq, there are more civilian victims, and more of them are killed by the Americans. The insurgency has spread to previously secure areas, including parts close to the capital, Kabul. The government is regarded as weak, corrupt, and ineffective by most Afghans. During her confirmation hearings, even U.S. Secretary of State Hillary Clinton called Afghanistan a "narco-state" that was "plagued by limited capacity and widespread corruption."[591] It is an under-developed, socially-conservative country traumatized by three decades of war and civil conflicts, where most of the population live in isolated, rural regions. A cursory look at history shows that there are no guarantees that political progress will diminish political violence. Colombia, Sri Lanka, and the Philippines are examples of countries where insurgencies have survived for decades in functioning democracies; in the former Yugoslavia, majority voting in the provinces of the federal republic led not to a democratic agreement but to war. The idea that voting automatically eliminates the need for violence is highly suspect.

Numerous polls show the wars in Afghanistan and Iraq have not only increased antipathy toward Americans, but also boosted solidarity among Muslims. According to a 2006 survey, over 80% of the 1.5 million British Muslims consider themselves Muslims first and foremost, not Brits.[592] After the 9/11 attacks, however, the popular opinion demanded a greater and greater affection to one's country of residence, and a number of Islamic schools in Britain were closed because of fears of an anti-Muslim backlash. But when a government decides to expel a radical imam, many mainstream Muslims regard this as an attack on all Muslims. European Muslims already suffer

---

588. F. Gregory Gause, "Can Democracy Stop Terrorism?" *Foreign Affairs*, September/October 2005.

589. Speech at the National Endowment for Democracy, October 6, 2005.

590. John Daniszewski, "Iraqi Civil War?: Some Experts Say It's Arrived," *Los Angeles Times*, January 1, 2006.

591. Hearing before the Committee on Foreign Relations, January 13, 2009.

592. "The Great Divide: How Westerners and Muslims View Each Other," Pew Research Center, Washington, D.C., June 22, 2006.

from socio-economic disadvantages and discrimination that create a hospitable environment for radical Islamic recruiters. Yet the problem is not so much social deprivation as lack of a clear cultural identity; democracy ceases to function the moment a critical mass of citizens no longer feel part of the *demos*.

The 7/7 London bombers were third-generation British Muslims, so the deadliest terrorist attack in history on British soil could have nothing to do with porous borders, an influx of counterfeit asylum seekers, or weaknesses in British deportation laws. In fact, they embody a variation on the greater theme recurring from Paris to Milan to Amsterdam: young, inexperienced extremists with no criminal records from "well-integrated" families who radicalize fast and strike out of nowhere. When young Muslims raised in European cities largely without religious instruction begin asking questions, radical groups have answers ready. The young men who carried out the London bombings did not see themselves as members of the Pakistani community, but as members of a radical Muslim Ummah.

However, Western governments are wrong to regard the global *jihad* as a religious phenomenon—youths who before would have become criminals or gangbangers are now increasingly attracted to radical ideologies like Salafism. In the 1970s, they would have joined the radical left; today they join radical Islam, because it is the main violent ideology available for young men with Muslim roots. The European fighters who have travelled to and survived Iraq return as seasoned urban guerillas, whose skills make the German Red Army Faction and the Spanish ETA look like amateurs. Al-Qaeda were nowhere near Iraq until after the U.S.-led invasion and the disorder that ensued from it. None of Washington's Arab allies—such as Egypt, Saudi Arabia, or Jordan—have made official visits to Iraq, or even maintain active embassies there, because their natural allies, Saddam Hussein's Sunni community, were the losers. The only country that has actually benefited from the invasion is the increasingly radical Iran: it now knows that the United States lacks both the military resources and the political will to attack it; and it has found an obvious ally in the new, democratic, predominantly Shia Iraq.

In Nigeria, the most populous country in Africa, the end of military dictatorship and the return to elections and civilian government brought numerous liberties. But the freedom of opinion also led to the expression of religious opinions becoming more and more radical. Islamic politicians boost their vote by allying themselves with Muslim conservatives, while Christian politicians get more votes by opposing the enforcement of the Shariah. In homogeneous societies, it does not matter if the State is influenced by religion or not. It is only when there are other faiths, or other interpretations of the same faith, that the State can become an instrument of oppression in the hands of the majority. On the other hand, people can also use religion to fight oppressive secular nationalism, such as that implemented in the Egypt of Gamal Abdel Nasser or the Iraq of Saddam Hussein.

In the West, the best examples of freedom and protection of religious minorities have come under secular democracies, but in the Arab world the same has been accomplished under the reign of Islam. Religion acts as a critic of modern society, blaming it for the widespread poverty and unemployment, political corruption, and human rights violations. In such societies, religion alone seems to speak for human dignity, self-respect, and aspiration, and if we fail to recognize this, we will never understand the power of the Muslim reaction against secularized governments. However, in a language reminiscent of Cold War rhetoric, President Bush cast the conflict in Iraq as the pivotal battleground in a greater contest between the advocates of freedom and those who seek "to establish a totalitarian Islamic empire that reaches from Indonesia to Spain."[593]

A poll by Gallup of more than 50,000 Muslims in 35 countries—the largest survey to date of Muslims worldwide—suggests the vast majority want democracy and freedom. "Radical" Muslims believed in democracy even more than many of the moderate Muslims polled. In fact, the radicals appear to be better educated, to have better jobs, and be more hopeful with regard to the future than mainstream Muslims.[594] The groups that would be most likely to benefit from abrupt democratization are those that are the best organized and that have the strongest claims to "authenticity." In societies where the only relatively free spaces have been mosques, these will perforce be Islamist groups like the Muslim Brotherhood in Egypt or the Supreme Council of Islamic Revolution in Iraq. In many Arab countries, Islamist parties hostile to Western interests would undoubtedly sweep the board. In fact, this is already happening: Hezbollah, which advocates the establishment of an Islamic republic, got 14 seats in the Lebanese parliament through completely democratic means, and most notably, Hamas, whose charter calls for the destruction of Israel, won a clear majority of seats the first time it was included in the Palestinian parliamentary elections.

The same of course applies also to our allies: the more Kuwait has democratized, the more Islamist it has become, prompting its government to erect a fence along the Iraqi border to prevent its youth from joining the insurgency. There is a good chance that a democratic Saudi Arabia would choose to no longer sell its oil to the West. A democratic Egypt might start developing nuclear weapons. A democratic Jordan might start a new war with Israel. The more Turkey and Pakistan approach the genuine democracy to which U.S. policy directs them, the more Islamist they become and the more they do exactly the opposite of what the United States desires. One can point to a whole list of cases around the globe where the power of the U.S. was brought to bear in support of oppressive régimes and in opposition to democratic movements. But in order to justify their imperial ambitions to the voting public, democratically elected leaders must proclaim their commitment to democracy and declare to be working to advance the cause of that ideology.

President Bush often stated, as if it were a self-evident fact, that "democracies are peaceful countries." This claim, which has been advanced in the past in regard to both Christianity and socialism, is the postulate on which U.S. foreign policy now rests. But even though Americans may not like to see themselves as a militant nation, the "world's leading democracy" is, and has always been, an exceptionally militant and militaristic nation. Or what is one to make of the Mexican and Spanish-American wars, in which the United States moved to war on the flimsiest of pretexts? And then

---

593. Address to the Midshipmen at the U.S. Naval Academy, November 30, 2005.

594. Esposito & Mogahed 2007.

there is the most destructive war in American history, which arose entirely from within, four score and five years after the nation's founding, in a belated fulfilment of the U.S. Constitution and Declaration of Independence, themselves documents universally considered as the guiding lights of democracy.

In addition to the run-of-the-mill subversion and overthrow of governments in competition with the Soviet Union during the Cold War, the United States has resorted to political assassinations, surrogate death squads, and unseemly freedom fighters, not the least Osama bin Laden. The U.S. government has put up with the most heinous human rights abuses in "friendly" countries, and even trained them how to commit more human rights abuses. Washington masterminded the killing of Lumumba and Allende, and unsuccessfully tried to put to death Castro, Gaddafi, and Saddam. "Although we regularly stigmatize other societies as rogue states, we ourselves have become the largest rogue state of all," asserts the great American writer Gore Vidal. "We honor no treaties. We spurn international courts. We strike unilaterally wherever we choose. We give orders to the United Nations but do not pay our dues. We complain of terrorism, yet our empire is now the greatest terrorist of all. We bomb, invade, subvert other states."[595]

595. 2002, 158.

8

Fighting for Peace Is Like Fucking for Virginity

The Arabic for secular is *la-diniyya*, "godless," so when Islamic fundamentalists hear the West advocate secularization, they think it is advocating the renunciation of God. It cannot be denied that even in the relatively religious United States, the Sunday morning Mass has increasingly been replaced by Sunday night football. Bread and circuses were instituted by Cæsar as an alternative method of crowd control at a time when Roman religiosity was waning, and religious devotion has always characterized both totalitarian ideologies and competitive sports. Today, sports figures are more revered than ever before, with athletes seen as role models and visions of purity. This despite that fact that there has been "doping" in one form or another as long as men have competed in physical games, and there will always be.

Sports Illustrated gets on its high horse about sports remaining "natural," although its highest selling issue is the swimsuit edition, filled with silicone, collagen, botox, and everything from diet pills and diuretics to low doses of anabolic steroids to produce a leaner, harder body. Testing for steroids is, of course, a farce—some of them only have a half-life of 24 hours. The arms race between the drug takers and the drug testers leads to more sophisticated drugs and drug tests. The drugs testers are five years away from catching the drug takers; and always will be. Doping cannot be contained and it will never be controlled. Moralists like to speak out against steroids as being killer drugs, but hundreds of thousands of Americans use steroids each year, and the grand total of steroid-related deaths to date is zero.[596] As with any drug, there is use, and there is abuse: e.g. amateur bodybuilders using a hundred times the usual therapeutic dosage. But why are people so concerned about what millionaire athletes do?

As every Little Leaguer knows, you sacrifice what you have to for the good of the team. You play injured if necessary, and you take your advantages where you find them. Gaylord Perry threw spitballs for twenty years, and he got into Cooperstown. John McGraw tripped so many runners that baseball was forced to introduce an infield umpire—and he made it to the Hall of Fame. Babe Ruth himself was caught corking his bat. These and hundreds of other incidents of ball scuffing, bat tippling, sign stealing, etc. are staples of baseball lore, lovingly recounted by generations of after-dinner speakers and broadcasters across America. Cheating is as much a part of Major League Baseball as the ground-rule double, bench jockeying, and alcoholism.[597]

And just how can an individual victory be a victory for the whole nation? There are entire towns in America clinging to their high school football teams as if these could bring back their glory days and crush years of decline and disappointment under the feet of athletic victory. The jocks are the favourite sons of these small communities, fragrantly indulged by the parents, the teachers, and even the police. A member of the team caught driving drunk? The town sheriff lets him off with a fatherly reprimand. Gifted athletes are given second, third, and 14th chances solely because of their talent, and many of them come to believe that the rules do not apply to them. Neither do professional sports teams care if their new recruit has been stopped a hundred times for traffic violations, stomped on a dozen opponents' legs, or been to jail—all they care about is if he can play.

True athletes compete only with themselves; and so do all the others when they are in training. As Steve Courson, a Superbowl winner who confessed to using steroids, told a Congressional hearing: "How can coaches teach valuable lessons about preparing youth for life when their value is based only on wins and losses?"[598] It has long been known that eating disorders are most common among athletes, but pressure to succeed—and not only in sports—is now driving a growing number of children to abuse steroids. The sports medicine division at the Oregon Health & Science University recently found that two-thirds of high school girls who admitted using steroids were not athletes, but young women looking for ways to get thin.[599] Overall, the number of high school students who had tried the body-altering drugs was nearly

596. Charles E. Yesalis, et al. "Anabolic-Androgenic Steroid Use in the United States," *JAMA* 270(10), September 8, 1993, 1217–1221.

597. Zev Chafets, "A-Rod, Get Back on the 'roids," *Los Angeles Times*, February 12, 2009.

598. "Performance-Enhancement and the Future," Statement to the House Committee on Government Reform, Washington, D.C., April 25, 2005.

599. Diane L. Elliot, et al. "Cross-sectional Study of Female Students Reporting Anabolic Steroid Use," *Archives of Pediatrics & Adolescent Medicine* 161(6), June 2007, 572–577.

six times the number a decade earlier.[600] Anorexia is intimately connected with the "swifter, higher, stronger" accomplishments familiar from professional sports, but which are increasingly sought also in school life, studying, jobs, hobbies, and personal relationships.

After-school sports have gotten more intense and time-consuming; rather than being an educational function, youth athletics have become a screening function. Children are being pushed harder and younger than ever before, playing team sports in the U.S. by the age of four. The early exposure facilitates the acquisition of the motor and cognitive skills required for high-level performance, but everyone cannot end up as Magic Johnson or José Canseco. A small child can find it hard to understand why the score was so important to the coach, when everybody was having a good time. The weekly training schedules are hard, but you need to train if you want to stay in the team. Not that it is uncommon for a child to be dropped from the starting line-up for an easy mistake. The problem I always had with team sports is that, "The weakest link in the chain is also the strongest. It can break the chain."[601] Each year, a great number of children quit sports—and exercise—altogether.

By the time they reach the age of 10, other children may already be in élite competitions. If children are often made feel guilty for not having the strength to live out their parents' dreams, it is not fair to call it "only a game" either, after thousands of dollars and hours spent at the sports hall. The fact remains, no-one will remember the junior league champions after a few years. The players that get the trophies in adult leagues are frequently the persevering athletes who were seen as mediocre or untalented when they were young, and who are used to doing a good job without pressure or expectations. They have learned a relaxed attitude towards losing, and their parents' dollars have not necessarily been wasted in anything unessential, but been aimed at long-term quality training. Conversely, "A fencer afraid to lose almost always loses."[602]

At top high school level, many athletes are practically professional sports stars facing huge pressure to perform, both for their communities and to win college scholarships; of course, these days many kids go professional straight from high school. The fear of losing has become a bigger force than the will to win. People today are seeking perfect success in all life's arenas, for the regular average is no longer enough. Nowhere is winner-worship and loser-loathing more evident than in sports—except in the field of democratic politics. No loser suffers more acutely than the defeated candidate. After his landslide loss to Ronald Reagan in 1980, Jimmy Carter all but vanished from the national political scene. He took no part in the 1984 presidential campaign, even though his former vice president, Walter Mondale, was running against Reagan. When Mondale was asked several years later how long it took to recover from his loss, he famously replied: "I'll let you know when the grieving ends." And as the 2000 Nader campaign so aptly demonstrated, this winner-

600. Charlene Rosenfield, "The Use of Ergogenic Agents in High School Athletes," *The Journal of School Nursing* 21(6), December 2005, 333–339.

601. Lec, op. cit. 159.

602. Wolfgang Agotta. "Local Body Reports," *Agapé* 7(2), August 1, 2005.

take-all electoral system makes the formation of a third party futile.

Under an authoritarian rule, dissidents are the ones persecuted; the demand for equality brings with it racism. When a person's social status "should" no longer be relevant in his classification, it is his actual physical attributes that become the basis for discrimination. Switzerland is the only country in the world with direct democracy, but it also has the world's strictest citizenship rules. The Swiss system of direct democracy means that the people have the last word on every political decision, from the appointment of teachers in the local school to whether the government should cut interest on state pensions. However, direct democracy does not come with the usual checks and balances of the legislative process that protect the rights of the minority from a "tyranny of the majority."

There are seven million permanent residents in Switzerland, and 1.5 million of them—more than 20%—are not Swiss. Switzerland has one of Europe's highest number of foreigners, because being born in Switzerland carries no right to be Swiss, nor are the children and even grandchildren of foreign immigrants entitled to citizenship. Foreigners usually have to live, work, and pay taxes at least 12 years before they can apply, and the fee can amount to tens of thousands of dollars. In many Swiss towns, applicants with any connection to the Balkans or to Africa are summarily rejected, even if they meet all the legal requirements for naturalization. Switzerland's direct democracy means that referendums need to be held several times a year, and their turnout seldom exceeds fifty percent. But when the tough citizenship policy was challenged in 2004, 53% of the country's 4.7 million voters were drawn to the polls. Needless to say, the policy was not relaxed.[603]

In a republic, there is no monarch, but more importantly, representatives elected by the people enact laws on their behalf. It is not a stretch to say that "referendums are undemocratic." Propositions are often long and complicated, and all the surveys show that most voters fail to read them in detail. Instead, voters rely on what political scientists term "information cues," that is, advice from trusted sources, including friends and family, the media, and political leaders. Case in point: 55% of French voters turned down the new EU constitution—which only 2.5% of the French had ever read—for being too "Anglo-Saxon," which it was not. Its adoption would not have much altered everyday life in France, but it symbolized change, thus becoming a lightning rod for many local sources of discontent, such as poor economic growth.[604]

In Europe, nationalism has historically been based on language, and multilingual countries such as Switzerland and Finland tend to be "neutral." In the former, the political divide lay between the more liberal French-speaking areas and the conservative German- and Italian-speaking regions. In the painstakingly-constructed federal state of Belgium, the Dutch-speaking and French-speaking communities have traditionally kept themselves to themselves, and any attempt to change the linguistic balance is hotly disputed. The recent immigration of many French speakers into the Dutch-speaking suburbs has enraged the Flemish parties, because foreign immigrants have to learn the local language, but the French speakers do not. The argument is as

603. Jonathan Fowler, "Swiss Voters Reject Loosening of Tough Citizenship Rules; OK National Maternity Leave Plan," Associated Press, September 26, 2004.

604. Robert J. Samuelson, "The End of Europe." Op. cit.

old as the country, and violent clashes were not uncommon in the years following WWII.

"Good fences make good neighbors," as Robert Frost famously put it in 1914, as nationalism and ethnic rivalries were tearing Europe apart.[605] The test scores of Catholic, Muslim, and Jewish schools have consistently been found better than those of mixed schools. But where the grades improve, tolerance dissipates, which can be a real problem when the school is located in a mixed neighbourhood. Schools, probably more than any other institution, are intimately involved in their local communities. American "political correctness" means that public school teachers have to be really careful about teaching U.S. history, lest they offend or disturb any minority student. Otherwise known as "dead white men," the nation's Founding Fathers have been turned into untouchables, solely because many of them were at one point slave-owners. However, a citizenship with no sense of history or national identity is unlikely to be a patriotic one.

Switzerland, whose neutrality stems from centuries of infighting, is not pacifistic: every adult Swiss male is required by law to have a loaded assault weapon at his residence. The fact is, no country has even been neutral on ideological grounds; besides, during peace time, a nation can merely be non-aligned. Thanks to its "neutrality" during WWII, Sweden was never bombed or invaded, though in reality, the Swedish government quietly sided with Germany and allowed the Nazis to make use of the Swedish railroad network and natural resources in order to avoid an armed occupation. Historically, great powers dominant in their particular regions have been generally satisfied with having their security interests preserved—along with some economic presence—while allowing a large amount of political autonomy within the smaller states. It was thus the Soviet relationship with Finland that fits the traditional norm, rather than its relationship with those neighbours on which it had imposed communist régimes; in fact, the current Russian relationship with the former Soviet republics in Central Asia largely fits this pattern as well.

As Einstein once declared, "All of us who are concerned for peace and the triumph of reason and justice must be keenly aware how small an influence reason and honest good will have upon events in the political field."[606] War has been the main engine for the extension of State power in Europe for a thousand years—and not only in Europe. Because governments can externalize the costs of their own actions onto hapless taxpayers, they are always prone to become aggressors and warmongers. War enlarges the State and increases its wealth and powers. It promotes obedience and justifies the repression of dissent, or "disloyalty" as it is rebranded during wartime. War relieves social tensions by redirecting them outwards at an enemy government which is, of course, doing exactly the same thing with all the same consequences. War is usually well worth the risk; not to the combatants or the civilians, mind you, but to the State. From the State's perspective, there is only one thing wrong with wars: they end.

There has been overall peace in Europe for a hundred years since 1815, when the major powers of the Continent emerged from the Napoleonic wars with an artificial

605. *The Mending Wall.* 1914, 12–13.

606. 1954, 147.

balance negotiated between them. The Europeans wanted peace, not because they were peace-loving people, but because another major war would likely have resulted in another major revolution—peace was simply in the interest of the rulers of every European nation. The balance was disturbed with the first unification of Germany in 1871. In the 20th century, the Cold War did not go hot because neither side really wanted to fight, both having had very disagreeable experiences in World War II. According to the renowned German legal theoretician Carl Schmitt, a body politic is born when it identifies its enemies, and until now, Western politics has been predicated on the exclusion of the strange and foreign.

A régime may artificially prolong the wartime climate of repression and sacrifice, as the United States did by building up the Red Scare after World War I, but soon the people will demand what Warren Harding promised them, a "Return to Normalcy." In the U.S., there is still a very strong feeling of patriotism and willingness to serve the country, but the people in countries like Germany and Italy that suffered so terribly from the world wars no longer feel that the youth of the nation should be trained for war. At the same time, globalization is playing down the whole concept of the nation-state, leaving a vacuum of loyalties on the part of the global citizens. This is a sharp change in attitude from a hundred years ago, let alone two centuries ago, when it was regarded as the duty of every young man to fight and die for his country and the right of government to ask him to do so.

But after having consistently lied to its citizens in every military escapade over the last 50 or 60 years, the United States is catching on the trend. Memorial Day, which began after the Civil War and was adopted nationally after World War I to honour all those lost to war, has become just another commercial holiday. Not only do department stores compete over who has the best "Memorial Day Sale," but some people actually wish each other a "Happy Memorial Day." Armistice Day, which used to mark a real event—the end of the WWI—has morphed into "Veterans Day," and is increasingly seen as just another day off work. The celebration of "veterans" is so amorphous that no-one can tell who or what is being celebrated. The term can equally apply and not apply to war heroes, combat experience, a lifetime of military service, and anyone who was ever in the armed forces for any reason.

The euphemisms fed to the media by the government have transformed negative expressions into positive ones: war is only peace enforcement or crisis management. This is a dangerous proposition—you can either condemn all violence or recognize that violence is a useful and important moral option. "Thus, the Romans, observing troubles from afar, always found remedies for them and never allowed them to develop in order to avoid war," wrote Niccolò Machiavelli, "for they knew that war does not go away, but is merely deferred to the advantage of others."[607] The technological advancements of the last few decades have increased the wealth and military superiority of the West in a way that allows it to once again meddle in the world's affairs without having to pay too high a price. The United States can fire off cruise missiles with a range of thousands of miles without the faintest possibility of anybody getting back at them.

---

607. *The Prince.* 2003, 14.

It was Clinton and Kosovo, rather than Bush and Iraq, that opened the period we are now living in. The eleven weeks of NATO bombings on the former Yugoslavia from March through June 1999, a supposed exertion of humanity in the cause of a beleaguered people, was also a test of strategy and weapons. It was a public war—legal and just, as far as the Western media could see—a war organized in the open and waged with a glow of conscience, radiant on the face of Tony Blair. It was the Kosovo War, more than any other military engagement of the past fifty years, that prepared an American consensus in favour of serial wars against transnational enemies of whatever sort.

We were told that the Serbs were oppressors while Albanians were victims—a mythology that bears a striking resemblance to the later black and white reports of the guilty Sunnis and innocent Shiites of Iraq. But the Kosovo Liberation Army had a record of viciousness and racism that differed little from that of Serbian leader Slobodan Milosevic's forces. It was not the evil Serbs, but the "freedom fighters" of the KLA that, in 1998, broke the terms of the peace agreement negotiated by Richard Holbrooke and made a war inevitable. Far from preventing mass killings, NATO's "surgical strikes" only increased them. The total number killed on both sides before the war was about 2,000; after the bombings, about 10,000 people were killed in revenge by Serbian security forces alone.[608] And the deeper one digs the less tenable the Kosovo War seems as a precedent for future "humanitarian interventions."

An entirely new attitude toward war has been created, one that fits in with the general development in Western society of risk avoidance—the undesirability of death or of being wounded and the notion that governments have the duty to protect their peoples from risk and save them from death. But this is exactly what makes the West so vulnerable: "America is a great power possessed of tremendous military might and a wide-ranging economy, but all this is built on an unstable foundation which can be targeted, with special attention to its obvious weak spots. If America is hit in one hundredth of these weak spots, God willing, it will stumble, wither away and relinquish world leadership." Thus Osama bin Laden in 2003.[609] The goal of any organized terrorist attack is to goad a vastly superior enemy into an excessive response. And over the past ten yeans, the United States has fallen into the 9/11 snare with one overreaction after another. The U.S. military is so overstretched that defence contracting—from interrogation through security to intelligence gathering—remains one of the country's few growth industries.

Ironically, civilian casualties are characteristic of ***modern*** conflicts, smart bombs notwithstanding. In 1991, when the bombardment in Operation Desert Storm began, a CNN correspondent commented on the "sweet beautiful sight" of U.S. bombers leaving runways in Saudi Arabia. Jim Stewart from CBS told his viewers about "two days of almost picture-perfect assaults." At the same time, the Iraqi Scud missiles were termed "an evil weapon" by NBC reporter Arthur Kent, while CNN's Richard Blystone called the enemy armament "a quarter-ton of concentrated hatred."[610] In

608. Gibbs 2009.

609. As quoted in Pape 2006, 123.

610. As quoted in Solomon 2005, 187.

certain conditions, bombardments can be the best way to force the two sides of a conflict into peace. However, in poor countries, there is little to bomb besides people. But the image of a "smart" missile going down a chimney in the first Gulf War sold thousands upon thousands of those missiles to nations all over the world.

In the wars of the 1990s, civilian deaths made up between 75 and 90 percent of all war deaths.[611] After more than five years of increasingly intense fighting, the conflict in Afghanistan reached a grim milestone in the first half of 2007: more civilians were killed by American troops and their NATO allies than by insurgents.[612] Yet as late as 2010, Gen. Stanley McChrystal admitted that he knew of no case when "we have engaged in an escalation of force incident and hurt someone has it turned out that the vehicle had a suicide bomb or weapons in it."[613] "Collateral damage" may be an inevitable result of going to war, but it does not matter to bereaved parents whether their child was killed deliberately, as the result of the callous indifference, or of a utilitarian calculation of the "greater good."

Starting with the Vietnam War, and again with the wars in Iraq and Afghanistan, the United States has been confronted with a new problem. Neither its advantages in massive industrial-age armies, nor in nuclear weapons, nor even in state-of-the-art information-age weaponry, have been effective in subduing a determined and sustained insurgency by a pre-industrial adversary. The use of overwhelming force has not only lost its utility in today's warfare, it has become counterproductive: the Taliban found it hard to recruit a few years ago, now they have significant influence across the Afghan countryside, although not the main roads and towns of Afghanistan. An expanded Western military footprint might only galvanize new armed opposition to the U.S. and its allies, and draw their forces into a conflict not unlike the guerilla war against the Soviet Union in the 1980s.

However, to honour his pledge to disown Iraq, President Obama felt obliged to adopt Afghanistan. On taking office, Obama gave Gen. David Petraeus three months to come up with a new Afghan strategy. To no-one's surprise, his advice was for a "surge," with more troops and airstrikes, creating more violence, more casualties, and more anti-American sentiment. The northern provinces, long considered one of the most stable and peaceful parts of Afghanistan, have seen rising violence as heavy insurgent activity has spread to 80% of the country.[614] What had begun as a punitive raid on the Taliban for harbouring Osama bin Laden morphed into a campaign of régime change, counter-insurgency, and nation-building—never mind the absurdity of imposing electoral democracy on a tribal society. The parcelling out of reinforcements is driven in part by the country's lack of infrastructure, which cannot immediately support a larger military force. As the U.S. Senate Committee on Foreign

---

611. Hedges 2003.

612. Laura King, "Errant Afghan Civilian Deaths Surge: U.S. and NATO Troops Killed More Noncombatants in the Last Six Months than Did Taliban Insurgents, Several Tallies Indicate," *Los Angeles Times*, July 6, 2007.

613. As quoted in Richard A. Oppel, Jr. & Taimoor Shah, "Civilians Killed as U.S. Troops Fire on Afghan Bus," *New York Times*, April 12, 2010.

614. "Afghanistan Map: January–August 2009," International Council on Security and Development, London, September 2009.

Relations stated in a 2009 report, "Unlike Iraq, Afghanistan is not a reconstruction project—it is a construction project, starting almost from scratch in a country that will probably remain poverty-stricken no matter how much the U.S. and the international community accomplish in the coming years."[615]

Many of the tribes living in rural, isolated, and sparsely populated provinces of Afghanistan have little interest in co-operating with "foreigners"—a relative term considering the limited contact they have with their country's own central government. The United States is effectively defending a government that is weak, ineffective, and as corrupt as the Saigon régime that the U.S. failed to prop up during the Vietnam War. The dreams to install technocrats or elevate women or eradicate poppies have vanished in a morass of corruption and aid extravaganza. U.S. envoys took a huge gamble by rescuing Hamid Karzai from exile and political obscurity, installing him in the palace, and ousting a legitimate monarch whose family had ruled the country for more than two centuries. Ever since Washington flew Karzai back to Kabul in 2002, he has received billions of dollars in aid money, which he has craftily used to barter deals with tribal chiefs and provincial commanders. With his volatile mixture of dependence and independence, President Karzai is an archetype of all the autocrats the U.S. has backed in Asia, Africa, and Latin America since European empires began disintegrating after WWII: torn between pleasing their foreign patrons and their own people, they end up pleasing neither.

The rigging of the August 2009 presidential elections was assured months before, when Karzai began allying himself with regional warlords, drug traffickers, and top provincial officials terrified of losing their jobs and their lucrative sinecures if he did not win. Transparency International, a non-governmental organization based in Berlin, ranked Afghanistan 176 out of 180 countries on its Corruption Perceptions Index (CPI) the year before; by 2009, Afghanistan was ranked as the world's second most corrupt nation, just a notch below Somalia.[616] Inherent in the unequal alliances between Washington and its puppet régimes is a peculiar dynamic that makes the eventual collapse of these régimes almost inevitable: Washington initially selects a client who seems pliant enough to do its bidding, and the client, in turn, opts for Washington's support exactly because he is weak and needs foreign patronage to gain and hold office. Apart from its warlord allies, the power of the Karzai government does not extend a rifle shot beyond Kabul.

It took 25 years longer than George Orwell predicted for the slogans of *1984* to become reality: "War is Peace," "Freedom is Slavery," "Ignorance is Strength." The Nobel Committee claimed that during Obama's short period as president, the United Stated was already "playing a more constructive role in meeting the great climatic challenges the world is confronting. Democracy and human rights are to be strengthened."[617] If the Taliban cannot be eliminated, if the troops cannot be brought home, if victory cannot be declared, then Western leaders must find some reason for soldiers to die; and in this case, that reason is the franchise. But as Boston University

---

615. Kerry 2009a, 2.

616. Doren, et al. 2009 & 2010.

617. "The Nobel Peace Prize for 2009," The Norwegian Nobel Committee, Oslo, October 9, 2009.

professor Andrew J. Bacevich argues: "For those who, despite all this, still hanker to have a go at nation building, why start with Afghanistan? Why not first fix, say, Mexico? In terms of its importance to the United States, our southern neighbor . . . outranks Afghanistan by several orders of magnitude. . . Yet any politician calling for the commitment of sixty thousand U.S. troops to Mexico to secure those interests or acquit those moral obligations would be laughed out of Washington—and rightly so."[618] If Nobel Peace Prizes are being handed out to people for simply making flowery speeches about hope and change, even the dictatorial leaders of China and North Korea deserve one.

Catastrophically enough, the foreign troops are in Afghanistan under the UN banner, even though it is not a case of keeping two hostile parties apart, but one of intervention, peace enforcement, and violation of national sovereignty in a country over the control of which people have fought for centuries. It is understandable for two neighbouring countries to have conflicting interests, but the overlordship of Afghanistan has been in the sights of not only all its immediate neighbours, but also of e.g. the Indians, Russians, Arabs, Mongols, and most recently, the Americans. Each time, the Afghans wore down their invaders with weary fatalism, remaining essentially unchanged and reverting to their ancient tribal squabbles after briefly uniting to expel the aliens. While all the invaders have thought they were sincerely trying to free the Afghans, the country has dozens of languages and ethnic groups, the representatives of which have all in their turn allied with the invaders they have liked. Just imagine what the political field might look like in a situation where each and every party had taken part in a different invasion of the country by a different foreign power.

A peculiar, well-established fact underlies the current conflict in Afghanistan: the United States sponsored both sides. In fact, the U.S. is still funding both sides of the conflict, indirectly through its military-industrial complex, and directly through a system of payoffs to Taliban commanders, who charge protection money to allow convoys of military supplies to reach NATO bases in the south of the country. The Western military imports virtually everything it uses in Afghanistan—including water, food, fuel, and ammunition—by truck through Pakistan or Central Asia to distribution hubs at Bagram Air Base north of Kabul and a similar base outside Kandahar. U.S. military officials in Kabul estimate that a minimum of ten percent of the Pentagon's logistics contracts, hundreds of millions of dollars, consists of payments to insurgents.[619] In Pashtun-speaking Afghanistan, the war is largely between armies run by heroin merchants, some aligned with the Taliban, others with the Americans. U.S.-allied drug dealers are put in charge of the police and border patrol, while their rivals are marked for death or capture. Sending in tens of thousands of new U.S. troops will only push America's drug-dealer partners into the arms of the Taliban.

Obama has been suckered into a mendacity that is well beyond the scale of Iraq's weapons of mass destruction. "Afghanistan," according to Obama, "is a war of

618. "The War We Can't Win: Afghanistan & the Limits of American Power," *Commonweal* CXXXVI(14), August 14, 2009.

619. Aram Roston, "How the US Funds the Taliban," *The Nation*, November 30, 2009.

necessity. . . If left unchecked, the Taliban insurgency will mean an even larger safe haven from which al-Qaeda would plot to kill more Americans."[620] Such explanations are an insult to public intelligence: the essence of global terrorism is that it does not need bases—9/11 was planned in Germany and the United States by Saudis and Egyptians. Just as the government of Vietnam was never a puppet of Communist China or the Soviet Union, the Taliban is not a surrogate for al-Qaeda. Both cases involved an American intrusion into a civil war whose causes and parameters were never fully grasped by Washington and which it could not control militarily. The Taliban, the Haqqani network, and other jihadi movements indigenous to this region have no shadowy global mission. Its ethnic Pasthun population, divided arbitrarily by a porous 1,500-mile border, is only fighting against what they see as a hostile foreign occupation. Taliban members were never agents of al-Qaeda; on the contrary, the only three governments that financed and diplomatically recognized the Taliban—Saudi Arabia, the United Arab Emirates, and Pakistan—were all targets of bin Laden's group.[621]

The stepped-up U.S. air strikes in Pakistan's tribal belt have only radicalized the tribes along the Afghan border, strengthened the Taliban, and weakened Pakistani state institutions. The border region between Afghanistan and Pakistan has become the "world's largest free-trade zone in anything and everything that is illicit."[622] Not only drugs, but bomb-making equipment, chemicals, money, and even people are traded there.[623] Yet the dominant political force within Pakistan is not radical Islam, but a desire for basic security and a sound economy. Most people in Pakistan's tribal areas see the U.S. drone attacks in very much the same light as Americans saw the destruction of the World Trade Center in New York. The collateral damage unleashed by such heavy-handed measures could very well unify the different extremist groups in this nuclear-armed Muslim-majority country. Pakistan has lost more soldiers in fighting the Taliban and al-Qaeda on the Afghan border than all the NATO forces combined, with hundreds of thousands of unarmed civilians caught in the middle.[624] But for all of Washington's talk about the "Af-Pak" border, some eighty percent of Pakistan's military still sits on the border with India, not Afghanistan, and dialogue between the two countries has been halted since the 2008 attacks in Mumbai.[625]

Several independent analysts have publicly warned that the presence of foreign troops in Afghanistan is probably the single most important driving force in the expansion of militancy. If you place troops in another country, that is called

---

620. Speech at the Veterans of Foreign Wars Convention, Phoenix Convention Center, August 17, 2009.

621. Scheer 2008.

622. "UNODC Reveals Devastating Impact of Afghan Opium: How the World's Deadliest Drug Feeds Addiction, Crime and Insurgency," United Nations Office of Drugs and Crime, Vienna, October 21, 2009.

623. "Addiction, Crime and Insurgency: The Transnational Threat of Afghan Opium," Idem., October 2009.

624. Barnett R. Rubin & Ahmed Rashid, "From Great Game to Grand Bargain: Ending Chaos in Afghanistan and Pakistan," *Foreign Affairs*, November/December 2008.

625. Leo Shane III, "Pakistan Focuses on India, Despite Taliban," *Stars and Stripes*, May 1, 2009.

"occupation." And if you occupy 150 countries, that is called "empire." In every empire, from the Persians through the Romans to the British, occupation has produced rebellion. Naturally the occupiers themselves disagree; for example, the actions of the Nazis in France, the Soviets in Eastern Europe, and the Americans in Vietnam and Afghanistan have all entailed the demonization of the resistance as terrorists and saboteurs, and involved excessive counteractions and the murder of civilians. Thus, for instance, the Fallujah massacre carried out by U.S. forces in Iraq is very similar to the Srebrenica massacre carried out by the Serbs, only the Western media do not wish to advertise and reminisce the former. One of the challenges of "peace enforcement" is to explain how encroaching on matters traditionally falling under national sovereignty, such as civil wars, is any different from the colonial powers carrying out their self-imposed "white man's burden."

However, history has shown that stopping war crimes and punishing those guilty of them always requires an armed intervention of some sort. Those who protest against any and all forms of armed intervention may not realize that their actions are more likely to cost innocent lives than to spare them. As Benjamin Franklin famously observed, "People who beat their swords into plow shares usually wind up plowing for the people who kept theirs." All the compassion and understanding in the world will only result in letting the enemy get close enough to slit your throat. However, after 9/11, the most unpatriotic act imaginable in the United States was to denounce President Bush's claim that the attackers were "cowards." Yet as Susan Sontag wrote in *The New Yorker*, courage is a morally neutral virtue, and "whatever may be said of the perpetrators of [the] . . . slaughter, they were not cowards."[626] What flabby Western cowboy would have had the stomach to pull off such an attack? And, at the same time, you hear complaints about the lack of morality, selfishness, and unwillingness of people to sacrifice themselves for the common good.

The West is now in what Sir Michael Howard calls a Post-Heroic Age. Unlike in World War II and all the previous conflicts, there is no longer practically any face-to-face combat as modern weaponry enables us to fire at a distance. People think children are being corrupted by imitation violence in video games, when this is exactly what has happened to modern Western politicians. They believe they can murder others in faraway lands without the fear of reprisal, or indeed, without any moral suffering on their part. Do our governments really expect us to believe that such brutal indifference to other people's lives has nothing to do with the recent spate of suicide attacks against the West? In a poll of 17,000 people in 15 countries between March and May of 2006, the Washington-based Pew Research Center found more people concerned about the U.S. presence in Iraq than about Iran's alleged nuclear weapons ambitions. According to the poll, people worldwide see Washington as a bigger threat to world peace than Tehran, and the survey also records a large drop in support for the U.S.-led "War on Terror" even in countries such as Spain, where the Madrid bombings just two years before left 192 people dead.[627] If Iran builds a nuke, it will do so for one reason: because there is already a nuclear-armed state in the

626. "The Talk of the Town," September 24, 2001.

627. "The Great Divide." Op. cit.

Middle East, by which it feels threatened.

Western media have devoted countless pages and hours to wondering what would drive a seemingly normal Muslim youth to kill himself and others. Not a paragraph or minute has been wasted asking what would cause a seemingly normal Christian youth to climb into a warplane and drop bombs on a village full of civilians as well as enemy forces. Because of the Christian taboo on suicide, we tend to view suicide bombings as incomprehensible, although they are at bottom merely a tactic used by those who lack other means of delivering explosives. Surely, "War is terrorism with a bigger budget." Since 2005, the Taliban insurgents have increasingly turned to Iraq-style suicide strikes, a tactic previously unknown in Afghanistan, because they lose only one person in such an attack, not ten or fifteen as they would in battle.[628] Instead of confronting U.S. firepower head on, they are attacking more exposed targets, such as government buildings, police stations, and unarmoured vehicles belonging to the Afghan army. And, with the exception of WMD, there is no type of attack more effective than suicide terrorism, which has proven near impossible to guard against.

The dirty little secret in the war on terror is that terrorism is not going anywhere, even if our governments are unwilling to admit that. Rather than a movement, terrorism is a method, and not even a new one at that. Those who lack armies but not enemies have always resorted to surprise attacks on civilians and other soft targets. The origin of the word "zealot" is in 1st-century Jews who committed terrorist acts against the Roman occupiers and their Jewish collaborators, while an "assassin" originally signified a member of the 11th-century Islamic sect famous for its covert attacks. In WWII, Japanese ***kamikaze*** pilots sought to cause maximum damage by crashing their planes into enemy ships. For centuries, any attack on military or political leaders was a *de facto* suicide strike, since it had to be done at close quarters, ensuring certain death for the killer.

But why is everyone so afraid of these people? The government would have us to believe that terrorists are some sort of supermen sent in by evil masterminds that have us by the short hairs, when, in fact, they are just a bunch of primitive nomads with nothing but antiquated strategies living in the caves of Afghanistan and Pakistan. Every person in every nation of the world will always be at some risk from terrorism: it is probably one of the oldest forms of warfare. The idea that the government is going to "defeat" terrorism and make us "safe" is complete and utter nonsense. The "War on Terror" is nothing more than just another "War on Drugs"—just a slogan to keep people scared and money flowing into government programs and ultimately to government contractors. We keep hearing that the Taliban are powerful, organized, and even sophisticated, but the reality of the matter is that the West has imposed such a corrupt and incompetent government on Afghanistan that it cannot defeat a bunch of illiterate mullahs.

States have always used war analogies as a way of securing public support for dramatic measures. There have been wars not only on drugs, but on organized crime, and even on poverty and global warming, but the terminology has invariably served a rhetorical purpose. The word "terrorism" itself has been so overused that it has lost

---

628. "Afghanistan: All Who Are Not Friends, Are Enemies," Amnesty International, London, April 2007.

some of its meaning. When peaceful Tibetan demonstrators are called "terrorists" for expressing anger at Chinese repression, or when Uighurs who refuse to be silenced or forced into relocation are executed for "terrorist" activities, the language loses its legitimacy, as does anyone who uses it. To put it simply, terrorism is the use or threat of indiscriminate violence to advance a political cause, conditions met by neither Tibetans nor the East Turkestan Islamic Movement. Indeed, the United States' listing of ETIM as a terrorist organization was widely seen as a political move by Washington to enlist China's help in passing a UN resolution on Iraq in 2002.

However, the description of the current counter-terrorism efforts as a "war on terror" differs in one way from the rhetorical flourishes of the past. The United States, in particular, expects the war paradigm to provide a legal justification for setting aside criminal law and human rights safeguards, and replacing them with the extraordinary powers supposedly conferred under international laws of war. Over the last decade, this rhetoric has done immense damage to a previously shared international consensus on the legal framework that underlies both human rights and humanitarian law, while giving a spurious justification to a range of serious human rights and humanitarian law violations. The war paradigm, as applied by the U.S., has had a detrimental impact around the globe as governments everywhere appear to relativise or justify their own wrong-doing by comparisons with the U.S. Both the European Union and Canada have been complicit in practices such as extraordinary renditions. Other states, such as Colombia, have even sought to redefine long-standing internal conflicts as part of the global war on terror.[629]

The *Human Security Report 2005* found a decline in all other forms of political violence besides terrorism since the end of the Cold War. But although the death toll has jumped sharply over the past few years, terrorists still kill only a fraction of the number who die in wars. The number of international conflicts is ever fewer, with most armed conflicts now being civil wars; historic nation-state wars, though always plausible, are declining, but a great number of civil wars have involved foreign intervention. On the whole, civil wars since 1945 have been more deadly than wars between countries, claiming as they have more than 16 million lives and devastating the economies of the war-torn nations in the process.[630] Large-scale wars between huge armies with heavy weaponry have been replaced by low-intensity conflicts that pit weak government forces against ill-trained rebels. Most "conventional" insurgent groups, including the IRA, did not, as a rule, deliberately target civilians. Al-Qaeda's justification was simple: "You kill our innocent civilians in Iraq and Afghanistan, now see how it feels when we kill yours." In geo-politics as in physics, there is no action without reaction.

Yet we were told after 9/11 that even to ask whether U.S. government actions might have sparked antagonism against America was unpatriotic. How could anyone be upset with Washington for imposing deadly sanctions, unseating democratically elected leaders, supporting dictators, and backing another country's Apartheid-like

629. "Accessing Damage, Urging Action: Report of the Eminent Jurist Panel on Terrorism, Counter-Terrorism and Human Rights," International Commission of Jurists, Geneva, 2009.

630. James D. Fearon & David D. Laitin, "Ethnicity, Insurgency, and Civil War," *American Political Science Review* 97(1), February 2003, 75–90.

system? How could anyone anywhere end up disliking the U.S. government or seek to strike back? Robert Pape, Lindsey O'Rourke, and Jenna McDermit of the University of Chicago studied suicide terrorists in Lebabon, the West Bank, Iraq, Afghanistan, Sri Lanka, and elsewhere. Few had religious motives, rather suicide terrorist campaigns were almost always a last resort against foreign military occupation.[631] Terrorist strikes cannot be justified, whether committed by al-Qaeda, Palestinians, Iraqi or Afghan insurgents, Tamil Tigers, the Irish Republican Army, or Chechen militants; but terrorism can be explained and understood.

It is not out of the ordinary in today's "peace rallies" for the protesters to demand the execution of the warmongers, and some demonstrations for peace have even been labelled expressions of hatred. "War is peace" appears to now be the position of the formerly antiwar organization, Code Pink, which has decided that women's rights are worth a war in Afghanistan. "Impartiality is not neutrality," wrote Stanislaw J. Lec, "it is partiality for justice."[632] There are things that are not just by anyone's standards: within society, for example, it is not just that part of the population is dispossessed, while another part is merely partying and having fun; and globally, it is not just that 50,000 people die each year of easily treatable diseases, while a part of the globe is "gettin' jiggy wit it." Global social justice is theoretically a self-evident goal, but in practice, it is largely a Utopia. "Life is never fair," said Oscar Wilde. "And perhaps it is a good thing for most of us that it is not."[633]

In the words of Susan Sontag, "the truth is that Mozart, Pascal, Boolean algebra, Shakespeare, parliamentary government, baroque churches, Newton, the emancipation of women, Kant, Marx, Balanchine ballets, et al., don't redeem what this particular civilization has wrought upon the world. The white race is the cancer of human history; it is the white race and it alone—its ideologies and inventions—which eradicates autonomous civilizations wherever it spreads."[634] Western culture has extended its conquests to foreign continents in the name of religion and civilization since the Age of Discovery. Western-centric values were also the basis for 19th-century imperialism, and at the same time the West secured the supply of natural resources for its technologically superior commodity and growth culture. Nor did the exploitation of the former colonies by the rich West cease with the end of the colonial period. The difference is, of course, that during Britain's century of dominion, the self-confident "servants of empire" ruled much of Asia and Africa through a system of protectorates, indirect rule, and direct colonial rule, while in the succeeding American half a century of hegemony, Washington has had to carry the burden of global power without a formal colonial system, substituting "military advisors" for imperial viceroys.

Modern political philosophers are seeking the possibility of a community that is not based on exclusion, but is still political. They are also trying to find a way to supercede violent appropriation of land as the basis of law and order. While this type

631. "What Makes Chechen Women So Dangerous?" *New York Times*, March 31, 2010.

632. Op. cit. 60.

633. *An Ideal Husband.* 1997, 615.

634. 1969, 203.

of universal *nomos* was already known to the ancient Stoics, it excluded everyone who did not meet their criteria of "right reason." A true non-exclusive community would have to be an unprincipled community, since a principle in itself always excludes, be it universal or particular. It would also require the renunciation of judgement, that is, distinguishing between good and evil in every situation. The *nomos* should not be destroyed, but made unnecessary, which would require it to become weak. Every large organization takes on a life of its own, independent of why it was created. It seeks to grow and ensure its survival, which it does by amassing control and eliminating threats to its survival. Perhaps a truly non-exclusive political community can only be possible on the global level, where it cannot have an outside, or conquer land from itself.

International, however, is the opposite of universal: "The trouble is that most international institutions don't work well. This is because they are associations of states and, as Cardinal Richelieu said, states have only interests, and no principles. This finds expression in their behavior within international organizations. Whatever the faults of a state bureaucracy, they are multiplied in an international bureaucracy. The United Nations is ill-suited to safeguard universal principles because it is subject to the whims of its members. This can be seen in the record of the UN in protecting human rights from Bosnia to Rwanda and Sierra Leone."[635] There is no real international consensus on what constitutes a crime against humanity. Some think Argentina and Chile are better off without the left-wingers who disappeared in the 1970s. Others reckon that people like President Mugabe, General Mladic, and the Janjaweed of Darfur have merely gotten bad press. Conversely, the African National Congress (ANC) was designated as a terrorist organization by South Africa's Apartheid régime. The international community cannot agree on a common definition of terrorism, or even on whether such a definition is needed in the first place. The fact is that the UN cannot deal effectively with crimes against humanity because few subjects have more political resonance.

The knowledge about the scarcity of natural resources has, at least temporarily, replaced the traditional competition between Western nations with such concentrations of power as the European Union. The United States alone is any longer able to take advantage of resources that lay under foreign feet. Its wars in Iraq and Afghanistan are a global anomaly: in 2002, the average number of people killed per conflict was just over 600.[636] Since the Cold War ended, resource-rich Russia has become crucial to European countries wary of the chaotic politics and unpredictable markets of the Middle East. About 25% of Russia's GDP and 40% of its government revenue come from the energy trade. Russia lacks the rule of law, transparent markets, and a solid economic foundation, but as long as energy prices stay high, they will protect the country against any sudden shocks in the international marketplace.[637] Exploiting its control of oil and gas is a part of Russia's foreign policy,

---

635. Soros, op. cit.

636. Human Security Centre 2006.

637. Eugene B. Rumer, "Russia: For Real Results, Let's Get Real," *Los Angeles Times*, May 10, 2005.

and far more effective than its nuclear weapons were during communist times.

By no traditional measure does Russia deserve to be in the G8, a group meant to include the leaders of the major industrial democracies. Russia's economy is smaller than those of Holland, Mexico, and Brazil, for example, its per capita income lower than that of Malta, Chile, and Uruguay, among others. Even in conventional military power, Russia is nothing like the behemoth it once was. Its clout lay not in its political beliefs and practices, or in its economic model, but in its reserves of oil and naturals gas, on which Europe in particular is dependent.[638] National oil companies have been with us for decades, but they now control more than 75% of the world's crude oil reserves.[639] In its ability to manipulate European suppliers of natural gas, Russia is approaching superpower status. George Soros has called the formation of unholy alliances between government and business the greatest threat to freedom and democracy, finding it "particularly disturbing that the collapse of communism in the former Soviet Union has lead not to democracy and open society but to robber capitalism."[640]

In resource-poor countries, where the state has limited funds at its disposal, the most efficient way to attract votes is to promise public goods—rule of law, low inflation, healthy infrastructure—so elections theoretically promote pro-growth policies. In oil-rich societies, by contrast, the simplest way to get votes is to buy them, making a transparent government, an independent public prosecutor, and a separation of power over the public purse essential to counter corruption. However, it is the considered opinion of Gore Vidal, among others, that: "Our Congress has been hijacked by corporate America and its enforcers, the imperial military machine. We the unrepresented People of the United States are as much victims of this militarized government as the Panamanians, Iraqis, or Somalians. We have allowed our institutions to take over in the name of a globalized American empire that is totally alien in concept to anything our founders had in mind."[641]

More and more experts now assert that the aggressive policies of the Bush administration were predicated on its desire to do whatever it takes to protect the value of the U.S. dollar—it is a currency that is "too big to fail." There is such an abundance of dollars in the world due to the fact that, since the Nixon days, when the dollar was detached from the gold standard, an excess amount has been printed to finance American consumption. It is this money that has allowed the United States to build its superior war machine. And until late, oil has always been traded in dollars, but recently certain countries have sought to withdraw from this established practice. When President Bush proclaimed his "Axis of Evil," it was made up of Iraq, Iran, and North Korea—all countries that had just switched their foreign trade, including that in oil, from dollars to euros. If such a change were to spread globally, it would erode the interest in dollars, which all countries need to keep in reserve precisely due to oil trade. If the world's dependency on dollars were diminished, their value would

---

638. Anne Applebaum, "Playing Politics with Pipelines," *Washington Post*, January 4, 2006.

639. Bremmer 2010.

640. Op. cit.

641. 2002, 159.

plummet because so much U.S. currency has been put into global circulation with nothing to back it up.

So far, however, countries of the world have been powerless to defend themselves against the fact that a compulsory financing of the U.S. military machine is built into the global financial system. Keeping international reserves in dollars means foreign central banks are forced to recycle their dollar inflows to buy U.S. Treasury bills—U.S. government debt issued in large measure to finance the military. This is effectively "taxation without representation," since governments around the world are forced to fund U.S. military policies which they have no say in formulating, and which threaten them more and more belligerently. The only way a nation can block capital movements is to withdraw from the IMF, the World Bank, and the WTO, and for the first time since the 1950s, this looks like a real possibility. However, from the U.S. vantage point, this would be nothing less than an attempt to curtail its global military program. And if its economy can no longer rule over the world markets by sheer size alone, it will be tempted to use its military power for this purpose. Afghanistan is regarded by Pentagon as highly strategic: it is a platform from which the U.S. military could directly threaten not only Iran and other oil-rich Middle Eastern countries, but also the only two powers that could conceivably pose a challenge to America's sole superpower status—China and Russia.

Much of what we have been told about the threat of international terrorism is a fantasy that has been exaggerated and distorted by politicians. Neither the 9/11 Commission nor any court of law has been allowed to take evidence directly from the key terror detainees held by the United States. Everything we know comes from the two sides that profit from the exaggeration of the threat posed by al-Qaeda: the terrorists themselves and the Western security services. During the 1990s, the espionage community atrophied by 40 percent; in the words of the former U.S. Director of National Intelligence, J. Michael McConnell, "we lost a generation."[642] Since then, American intelligence agencies have seen their roles and authorities altered by legislation and are turning to unprecedented numbers of outside contractors to perform jobs traditionally the exclusive domain of government employees. The number of civilian contractors at the CIA, for example, nearly doubled between 2001 and 2006, surpassing the full-time workforce of about 17,500. Meanwhile, intelligence budgets have swelled by more than $10 billion a year, with contractors typically paid 50% to 100% more than staff officers for comparable work.[643]

Around a third of the initial $87-billion Iraq reconstruction package set out in 2003 was earmarked for security, turning the country into a gold rush for private security contractors such as the notorious Blackwater—subsequently re-christened Xe Services and now doing business as Academi.[644] The U.S. military relies on private contractors (read: mercenaries) to offset chronic troop shortages; handing their tasks back to

---

642. Remarks at the Excellence in Government Conference, Washington Convention Center, April 4, 2007.

643. Greg Miller, "Spy Agencies Outsourcing to Fill Key Jobs," *Los Angeles Times*, September 17, 2006.

644. Ashcroft 2006.

American troops would further overstretch a military that is already "dangerously overstretched."[645] When your work is dangerous, big wads of cash and a possible future as a rich playboy is more tempting than ending up an unknown soldier. Government officials are able to misuse classified contracting to evade accountability and reduce transparency—contractor deaths are not even counted in the official toll. Privatization may evade the Hatch Act and secure large contributions to the political parties, but it is also the most expensive way to do anything.

More than 160,000 for-hire personnel were working in Iraq in 2007, a greater number than the total amount of uniformed military personnel even at the height of the surge.[646] These private forces perform all sorts of key functions, such as moving fuel, food, and ammunition, as well as guarding bases and protecting top U.S. officials. They are, in essence, a private army with no clear chain of command and no clear rules of accountability. When the Iraqis banned Blackwater in 2007, it was not just the firm that stopped operations for five days; so did all U.S. diplomatic and intelligence efforts in Iraq, because they were completely reliant on Blackwater guards to leave the Green Zone. And instead of simply providing security for CIA officers, Blackwater personnel have at times become partners in missions to capture or kill militants in both Iraq and Afghanistan. In all, the U.S. government's 10 million-strong "hidden workforce" absorbs nearly $400 billion in federal contracting funds and $100 billion in federal grants a year.[647] It is effectively a fourth branch of the government, theoretically under executive control, but in practice, independent and not subject to the usual checks and balances or to the democratic process.

Before dismissing 9/11 conspiracy theories, we ought not forget that the official story about "Osama and the Nineteen Thieves" is technically also a conspiracy theory. According to a Senate Foreign Relations Committee report, U.S. forces had bin Laden "within their grasp" in Afghanistan in late 2001. Apparently, calls for reinforcements were rejected, allowing the al-Qaeda leader to "walk unmolested" into Pakistan's unregulated tribal belt.[648] Petty dictators like Saddam Hussein and the persistent Taliban rebels are at bottom welcome phenomena for the West, because they make it easier for the Western governments to justify the imposition of their hegemony all over the globe. Rather than being the vanguard of the Muslim people, however, jihadis everywhere are rebelling both against the West and their own community. In their talks with the Americans, Russian and Israeli leaders can hardly utter a sentence without using the "T" word. At the same time, they seek to transform the U.S. War on Terror into a common battle against their own particular Muslim neighbours. This of course applies also to the Western allies of the United States and their non-Muslim renegades: not only the stock of the Basque separatists, but also that of the Irish Republican Army, has been on the skids lately. Many Irish-Americans working in the New York Fire and Police Departments were killed during 9/11. They were the ones

---

645. Robert Gates, as quoted in P. W. Singer, "Sure, He's Got Guns for Hire: But They're Just Not Worth It," *Washington Post*, October 7, 2007.

646. Ibid.

647. Paul C. Light, "The True Size of the Government," The Organizational Performance Initiative, NYU Wagner, New York, August 2006.

648. Kerry, et al. 2009b, 2–3.

who had traditionally supported the IRA's fight for independence against Great Britain. When terrorism became a brand to be avoided, the money taps suddenly dried up.

Russia's interests are nowadays compatible with Western cultural imperialism. Europe is Gazprom's most lucrative market, and Russia needs European energy revenues as much as Europe needs Russian gas. Instead of taking over countries, the United States has developed a better way: it just goes in and has "free markets," whether it is trying to sell its products to foreign citizens or to mine their resources. If it needs to have a presence in a foreign country for some reason, it will talk about free markets and free trade, but what it really wants is for its companies to get rich in that country. This is also exactly what is happening in today's "expanded Europe": post-Soviet economies have met with disastrous results after joining the European Union; instead of helping them industrialize and become more efficient, the Lisbon Treaty simply handed matters over to EU bankers, who looked at the new member countries simply as credit customers to be loaded with debt—not for loans to build up manufacturing and sorely needed infrastructure, but loans against existing real estate and infrastructure collateral.

The United States, the European Union, and the International Monetary Fund are couching their demands for "austerity" policies in the language of capitalism. But what the global investment community is actually promoting is a financial system that threatens to end in debt peonage, not a democratic market economy. It has already destroyed the industrial capacity of debtor nations subjected to the austerity programs imposed by the IMF. In order to handle the cost of servicing their debts, the debtor nations are forced to sell raw materials at a discount, while their governments are kept in the tight political control of industrial nations. Of course, this only repeats what the British did in India, Turkey, and Egypt. Industrial growth has been replaced with a financialized real estate bubble and the final stage of this dynamic is to foreclose and sell off the debtors' assets at giveaway prices. The struggle for hegemony can only allow one truth: the idealistic message of "freedom," "democracy," and "market economy" hides behind it the distinctive features of a totalitarian régime: the critics of the official truth are silenced, while the government spies on its own citizens and NGOs.

The International Criminal Court at The Hague was set up to investigate and prosecute people for genocide and war crimes. When the ICC was established by an international conference in Rome, only seven countries voted against it, among them Saddam Hussein's Iraq, Israel, and the United States; but the United States is the only nation in the world that is actively opposed to it. By trying Saddam in Iraq, Washington has effectively ensured that all the facts will never come out. In February of 2002, President Bush decided to set aside the Geneva Conventions as well as standing U.S. regulations for the handling of detainees. Al-Qaeda militants could have been denied prisoner-of-war status and held indefinitely even under the Geneva Conventions; they could also have been interrogated and tried, either in U.S. courts or under the military system of justice. Instead, not a single al-Qaeda leader has been prosecuted since 9/11, the first direct attack on the continental United States since the British burned the White House in 1814.

The 9/11 Commission report says that "the American homeland is the planet."[649] In 2001, the American military budget was equal to the combined military budgets of the next twenty-four most powerful nations in the world. To defend its "homeland," the United States spends six times as much on its military as China, the next highest-spending nation, funding more than 730 military bases in more than 130 countries—two-thirds of the states belonging to the UN—aided by more than a hundred military satellites and more than 250,000 seaborne battle-ready forces; this makes it by far the greatest military colossus ever forged.[650] Who could forget one of the most glaring hypocrisies of all time, Bush's pathetic wail that the development of weapons of mass destruction must be stopped in countries the United States does not like, when the U.S. owns more WMD than all the other nations on the planet combined?

Not to worry: numerous studies show a link between hegemony and decline. For example, in *The Rise and Fall of the Great Powers* (1987), Yale historian Paul Kennedy recounts that decline has been the fate of all would-be hegemons from Habsburg Spain, through Bourbon and Napoleonic France, to liberal Britain. The basic reasons for this are similar in each case: burdened by heavy military spending and debt, the hegemonic power becomes overstretched. It neglects and thereby weakens its economy and society, ultimately undermining its military strength as well; as they say, Rome did not fall to the barbarians, all they did was to kick in the rotting gates.

With its military resources tied up in Iraq and Afghanistan—rightly called "the Graveyard of Empires"—the United States is rendered impotent to counter any unforeseen military threat: by the end of 2006, all combat units of the U.S. Army were either deployed, returning from deployment, or preparing to deploy, leaving none to prepare for other contingencies.[651] Never in the history of the United States has war been considered the normal state of things. For two centuries, Americans were taught to think of war as an aberration, and "wars" in the plural could only have seemed doubly aberrant. In fact, Congress still does not even put these wars on the budget; they are funded through an "emergency supplemental"—a decade-long "emergency." Younger generations of Americans are now being taught to expect no end of war: as early as the primary campaign of 2007, Obama assured the military and political establishments that withdrawal from Iraq would be compensated for by a larger war in Afghanistan and Pakistan. The United States has come to a point where a new president is expected never to give up one war without taking on another. We can debate whether or not all or some of the wars are good, but what cannot be debated is that the U.S. wages war more than any other country, basically continuously.

Obama promised transformative "change"—but as some critics pointed out during his campaign, he left the direction of "change" so vague that voters of various stripes could read into it whatever they wanted. In his *Washington Post* column entitled "Obama in Command," David S. Broder pointed out that Obama is "continuing, with

649. Kean, et al. 2004, 362.

650. Ibid. 9.4.

651. Kevin Ryan, "Stretched Too Thin: We Don't Have Enough Troops to Meet Defense Demands," *Washington Post*, December 18, 2006.

minor modifications, the policies and practices of his Republican predecessor. . . Obama's liberal critics are right. He is a different man now. He has learned what it means to be commander in chief."[652] There is no such thing as an American President who is not also a "War President." That is why saying that things are different when "America is at war" is so manipulative and misleading. The U.S. never goes more than a few years without some kind of a direct war, and is always waging covert and indirect ones. War has become a permanent feature of America's social landscape, so much so that no-one really notices it anymore. To vest a specific power in a President on grounds that he is a "War President" is to vest that power in the executive branch generally and permanently. America's allies can easily become its enemies and its enemies can just as easily become its allies, but what never changes is its status as a war-fighting nation.

"War," as the radical intellectual Randolph Bourne famously explained, "is the health of the state."[653] It benefits state officials and their dependants, clients, and other sycophants at the expense of the rest of society. It keeps "the wheels of industry turning without increasing the real wealth of the world."[654] Since the United States' fateful decision not to demobilize after Word War II, excessive U.S. "defense" spending has steadily misallocated capital that could have been invested in productive capacity. The beneficiaries of what the Marxist sociologist Alvin Gouldner termed the "Welfare-Warfare State" are the growing congressional, industrial, and military bureaucracies that oversee America's ever expanding global presence—in effect, a colonial class. Democracy has succeeded where monarchy only made a modest start: the ultimate destruction of natural élites. The fortunes of great families have dissipated, their tradition of economic independence and intellectual farsightedness has been lost and forgotten. Rich people still exist today, but more often than not they owe their wealth directly or indirectly to the State. These new plutocrats are what Ayn Rand referred to in her famous novel *Atlas Shrugged* as the "aristocracy of pull," corrupt businessmen who succeeded on account of their political connections, rather than their entrepreneurial skill; hence, they are often more dependent on the State's continued favour than people of far lesser wealth.

The costs of war have been rendered invisible. There is no draft; instead, the most vulnerable elements of the population are given a choice between unemployment and gun fodder. Government deficits conceal the need to pay for war. "Every gun that is made, every warship launched, every rocked fired signifies, in the final sense, a theft from those who hunger and are not fed, those who are cold and are not clothed. This world in arms is not spending money alone. It is spending the sweat of its laborers, the genius of its scientists, the hopes of its children." So which left-wing hippie pacifist said this? Dennis Kucinich? Noam Chomsky? Jane Fonda? Nope, it was Gen. Dwight D. Eisenhower, Supreme Commander of the Allied Forces in Europe and President of the United States.[655] During WWII, thousands of peacetime

652. May 20, 2009.

653. 1964, 69, 71, 77, 84, 92.

654. Orwell 2003, 195.

655. Speech to the American Society of Newspaper Editors, April 16, 1953.

manufacturers were turned by government fiat into arms producers for the war effort. Factories that once made automobiles and home appliances were retooled to churn out weapons. In the present recession, market forces appear to be doing the same thing, threatening to throw what remains of American manufacturing into the war business.

The U.S. automakers are losing to foreign competition, but Pentagon policy ensures that it has to spend its billions at home; in today's desperate economic times, such protectionist practices can proudly paint themselves as "recession-proof" devices of recovery. One of the steadiest hopes of America's founders—manifest not only in the scores of pamphlets they penned against the British Empire but the checks against war powers built into the U.S. Constitution itself—was that a republic like the United States would lead irresistibly away from the conduct of wars. They saw wars as an affair of kings, waged in the interest of aggrandizement, or an affair of the hereditary landed aristocracy, in the interest of augmented privilege and unaccountable wealth. Four of the first seven Federalist Papers offer, as a principal reason for the founding of the republic, the belief that, by so doing, the United States would more easily avert the infection of the multiple wars that had desolated monarchical Europe.

A king's motive for war is typically an ownership or inheritance dispute. The objective of his wars is tangible and territorial: to gain control over a piece of real estate and its inhabitants. To reach this objective, it is in the king's interest to distinguish between combatants and non-combatants and their property. It is democracy that has transformed the limited wars of kings into total wars. The motive for war has become ideological—franchise, liberty, humanity. Its objectives are both intangible and elusive: the conversion of the losers to the democratic ideology. Similarly, the distinction between combatants and non-combatants becomes fuzzy and ultimately disappears, since one can never be certain about the sincerity of conversion. At the same time, mass involvement in war—conscription and popular war rallies—along with "collateral damage," become part of war strategy.

The historian, anthropologist, political scientist, and demographer Emmanuel Todd—as a French intellectual he is perfectly capable of being all these at the same time—claims in his bestseller *Après l'Empire: Essai sur la Décomposition du Système Américain* (2002) that the decayed American Empire will crumble and fall during the course of this decade, after which Europe will once again be the economic power it in fact already is. What makes his assertions so compelling is that in 1976, Monsieur Todd correctly predicted the fall of the Soviet Union in his work *La Chute Finale*, almost to the year. His conclusions are largely based on statistics.

One would be excused for drawing a different conclusion from watching the news or reading the papers following the so-called "Operation Iraqi Freedom." They told of a crushing victory by U.S. armed forces of a sizeable Middle Eastern nation. According to Todd, however, this does not allude to the strength but to the weakness of the United States. Iraq is a metaphor, a demonstration of American theatrical micromilitarism: the United States is seeking conflicts with militarily weak enemies like Iraq in order to show its own power, to mislead the uncontrollable world. The only successful wars fought by the First World in the Third World have been short and decisive, like the Falklands conflict and the first Gulf War.

The dreary U.S. experience with counterinsurgency in Vietnam at the height of the American century convinced the U.S. military for more than a generation that counterinsurgency warfare was incompatible with any version of the American way of war. According to the Army and Marine Corps field manual, written by none other than General Petraeus himself, counterinsurgency operations require, at minimum, twenty counterinsurgents per 1,000 residents.[656] In Afghanistan, this would mean combined forces of 640,000 troops, perhaps for a decade or more. Villages would have to be taken from the Taliban and held, not merely taken. It was easy to walk away from Vietnam and leave a few million locals in re-education camps, but leaving Iraq will not be as easy, because it sits atop or adjacent to the world's largest oil supply.

Speaking on the eighth anniversary of the 9/11 attacks, the then top U.S. commander in Afghanistan, Gen. Stanley McChrystal said that he saw no indication of any large al-Qaeda presence in Afghanistan.[657] Most of the few American successes against terrorists, such as the snatch-and-grab operations that bagged Khalid Sheikh Mohammed and Ramzi bin al-Shibh, and even the black op that finally located and killed Osama bin Laden, have not relied on large number of U.S. troops, but look a lot like good old-fashioned police work. "As soon as we became an empire," Gore Vidal says, "we stopped teaching geography in the schools, so nobody would know where anything is."[658] But the neo-con idea that the defence of the United States—with two giant oceans to protect it—requires an overseas presence that surpasses the British Empire at its zenith is proving far more costly than advertised.

In the words of Dr. Ron Paul: "As the war in Iraq surges forward, and the administration ponders military action against Iran, it's important to ask ourselves an overlooked question: Can we really afford it? If every American taxpayer had to submit an extra five or ten thousand dollars to the IRS this April to pay for the war, I'm quite certain it would end very quickly. The problem is that government finances war by borrowing and printing money, rather than presenting a bill directly in the form of higher taxes. When the costs are obscured, the question of whether any war is worth it becomes distorted."[659] Some American commentators now argue that the worst thing that ever happened to the United States was for its currency to become the world's only reserve currency. This has allowed American politicians to indulge in the worst vice of any democracy: making promises without paying for them.

Never in history has any bankrupt nation defended or preserved the freedoms of its citizens; in fact, they have usually done the exact opposite. More often than not, bankrupt governments impose totalitarian controls and plunder their citizens' wealth in desperation. The weak European economy is one of the main reasons why the world economy is so shaky and dependent on American growth. However, the United States is falling apart, not figuratively, but literally: the rotten flood defences of New Orleans are a symbol of failed infrastructure across the nation. Hurricane Katrina hurt the U.S. economy more than 9/11, and most of the damage was caused not by high

656. Petraeus & Amos 2006.

657. Remarks at the Netherlands Ministry of Defence, The Hague, September 11, 2009.

658. Johann Hari, "Gore Vidal's United States of Fury," *The Independent*, October 7, 2009.

659. "Inflation and War Finance," *Texas Straight Talk*, January 29, 2007.

winds, but by massive flooding that resulted from the breach of the city's poorly-constructed levees. Rather than there being a few breaks in the levees caused by water going over the top, there were dozens of major breaches across the entire system, sending the water surging across 80% of the city and swamping an estimated 100,000 homes in "the single most costly catastrophic failure of an engineered system in history."[660]

Long before the hurricane hit, the report card on U.S. infrastructure issued by the American Society of Civil Engineers gave the nation's physical plant a D.[661] Nor have the grades improved since then, according to the society's newest report, published in 2009. According to the ASCE, the infrastructure has deteriorated to what often seems like Third World standards, and sometimes, is even below Third World standards. The U.S. power grid is outdated and vulnerable, and not just to local thunderstorms but to widespread blackouts as well, whereas most developing countries manage to keep the power on during the occasional electric storm. The nation's roads are deteriorating rapidly, even as mass transit has to accommodate more riders while having to make do with less money for maintenance. The highways are so clogged that there are no longer fixed "rush hours," just random times when the roads are at a standstill.[662]

More than one in four of the some 590,000 bridges in the U.S. are either "structurally deficient or functionally obsolete," and in urban areas, that figure rises to one in three. The number of unsafe dams rose a full third between 1998 and 2005. The ASCE report estimates that it would take half a decade and $1.6 trillion to repair all this, not counting the destruction caused by Katrina or post-9/11 security improvements.[663] The price of steel, concrete, and oil are all up, partly driven by demand for raw materials in China, where the government is busy laying out a national highway system of its own. Meanwhile, asphalt roads are being ground up and replaced with gravel all over the United States, because it is cheaper to maintain. At the same time, the government focus on the war on terror has diverted funds from health care, resulting in many avoidable deaths. Prof. Erica Frank estimates that while 3,400 died in the 9/11 attacks, around 5,200 American died the same day from common diseases—and have done each day since.[664] Between collapsing bridges, exploding pipes, and sweltering heat in a jammed subway car, some Americans are beginning to wonder whether they should be more worried about death by failed infrastructure than terrorist attacks.

The creation of the Department of Homeland Security in 2002 represents the largest restructuring of government in modern American history. However, in a time

---

660. Raymond B. Seed, et al. "Investigation of the Performance of the New Orleans Flood Protection Systems in Hurricane Katrina on August 29, 2005," Independent Levee Investigation Team, University of California, Berkeley, CA, July 31, 2006.

661. "1998 Report Card for America's Infrastructure," American Society of Civil Engineers, Reston, VA, March 5, 1998.

662. "2009 Report Card for America's Infrastructure," Idem., March 25, 2009.

663. Ibid.

664. "Funding the Public Health Response to Terrorism: Thoughts on the Fourth Anniversary of 9/11," *British Medical Journal* 331(7517), September 17, 2005, E378–E379.

of crisis, it is hardly advisable to undertake a major reshuffle of the intelligence community, and one should rather consolidate the existing structure. At least 263 organizations have been created as a response to 9/11. Thirty-three new building complexes, occupying 17 million square feet, have been built for intelligence bureaucracies alone. The new system produces 50,000 reports a year, or 137 a day, so few ever get read.[665] Lack of coordination, not lack of resources, was at the heart of both the Fort Hood shooting that left 13 dead and the Christmas Day bomb attempt thwarted not by the thousands of analysts employed by the DHS, but an alert passenger who saw smoke coming from his seatmate.

When the law enforcement resources, be they FBI or Customs, are focused on terrorism, conventional crime gets ignored: 2005 saw a 2.5% jump in homicides, assaults, and other violent offences, the largest increase in 15 years, followed by an unprecedented 4% surge the year after.[666] The FBI and its parent agency, the Justice Department, are supposed to police the illegal activities of bankers and other financial professionals. But since they were focused on national security and other priorities, they paid little attention to white-collar crimes that may have contributed to the lending and securities debacle, and ultimately the global mortgage meltdown. The fall in the stock market did not create the recent surge in financial crimes; mortgage fraud was perpetrated in good times, although no-one saw it. However, the recent addition of economic news to the daily White House intelligence report reflects a growing belief among intelligence officials that the economic meltdown is now pre-eminent among security threats facing the United States.[667]

The world has come to rely on the United States to drive economic growth, but both the U.S. government and American consumers have borrowed to spend lavishly. Of course the global economy tanked with the Americans—their personal debt being traded around was supporting everything! U.S. consumers continue to spend much more than they produce, which means they need constant financing from the rest of the world. It took the U.S. government over four decades, from 1940 to 1982, to run up its first trillion dollars of debt. The second and third trillions were racked up much more quickly, each in just four years. And it only took from 1990 to 1992 for the national debt to hit $4 trillion. On the day George W. Bush was sworn in, the debt stood at $5.7 trillion. Eight years later, it had swelled another $4.9 trillion on his watch—an embarrassing milestone for a president who considered himself an advocate of fiscal discipline.[668]

The U.S. trade deficit is around $800 billion each year, the highest level for any country in history, and it has transformed the United States from the world's largest creditor to the world's largest debtor.[669] Much of the U.S. budget deficit is now

665. Dana Priest & William M. Arkin, "A Hidden World, Growing Beyond Control," *Washington Post*, July 19, 2010.

666. Federal Bureau of Investigation 2006.

667. Joby Warrick, "CIA Adds Economy to Threat Updates: White House Given First Daily Briefing," *Washington Post*, February 26, 2009.

668. Office of Management and Budget 2010.

669. "Hyperinflation Special Report: Issue Number 41," Shadow Government Statistics, San Francisco, April 8, 2008; Hartman, op. cit.

structural, meaning that it sits in the "mandatory" column, as opposed to the "discretionary" column.[670] This makes the country dependent on other nations—that is to say, weak. In the words of Gore Vidal: "On 16 September 1985, when the Commerce Department announced that the United States had become a debtor nation, the American Empire died."[671] Those who govern, live off government, or oversee the service sector are able to enjoy cheap imports and low-cost services provided by displaced workers, but only until the credit runs out.

Marx may have gotten it wrong on most other issues, but his analysis of money and credit, and how the credit system can bring an otherwise well-functioning market economy to its knees, was spot on. For Adam Smith and other classical economists, a free market was one free of debt—especially foreign debt. And even Keynes believed that the proper task of governments was to prevent over-indebtedness from leading to economic depression. But today's politicians seem to assume that if we just bail out the banks, add a modicum of regulation, and get the economy going, we can go back to business as usual. Yet that is neither possible, nor desirable. Wall Street now controls Washington, and its unproductive trading is extracting billions of dollars from the economy with a lot of pointless speculation in stocks, bonds, and derivatives. Economies do not run on money, they run on physical production and consumption; the strength of an economy lay not in its banks, but in its physical plant—its infrastructure, its agro-industrial base, and ultimately, in the creative potential of its people.

The old economy was founded on stagnant incomes and unsustainable debt. The United States basically only has two profitable branches of industry left: Wall Street and War. American families struggle to keep their heads above water by taking money out of their homes and assuming ever higher levels of credit card, student, and consumer loans. The U.S. has served as the consumer of last resort for the world by borrowing staggering sums—$2 billion a day—mostly from creditors abroad, as a result of negligible domestic saving.[672] The U.S. is mired in debt to countries that now produce what it once did, because production is more profitable where labour costs are low and governments cannot enforce the few regulations they have. The U.S. economy was floated on asset bubbles like that in housing which has now burst. The delusion that a crisis of excess debt can be solved by creating more debt is at the heart of the global downturn, yet it is precisely what most governments currently propose to do.

Exactly the same debt instruments that triggered the crisis are in play today: the banks' balance sheets still hold over $1 trillion in toxic assets and nothing has been done to reduce financial sector debt.[673] What is more, it is now mathematically impossible for the U.S. government to pay off the national debt. That is to say, the U.S. government now owes more dollars than actually exist. Even if the government

---

670. Office of Management and Budget, op. cit.

671. 1992, 7.

672. Robert L. Borosage, "Get Ready to Rumble: The Fight for the Next Economy Begins," *Huffington Post*, January 27, 2009.

673. Mike Whitney, "Is the Fed Juicing the Stock Market?" Information Clearing House, Imperial Beach, CA, January 3, 2010.

took every single penny from every single American bank, business, and taxpayer, it still would not be enough to pay off the debt. Even if the government were to nationalize all the private wealth accumulated by U.S. citizens since the nation's founding 235 years ago, it would still remain totally bankrupt.[674] We cannot resuscitate the old economy, nor should we want to. You can regulate the Wall Street casinos all you want, but as long as there is too much surplus capital around, new casino games and assets bubbles will always be created. Government-created inflation reduces the debt burden—but only as long as wages and other income rise in tandem.

The finance-led economy, where the share of the financial sector in GDP grew constantly and veraciously, is not coming back. The financial sector will shrink, and several more of the inefficient and corrupt behemoths are going to shrink, merge, or simply disappear. And so will other sectors that have come to rely on government hand-outs for survival since their business models are clearly unsustainable, the automobile and airline industries being two obvious examples. Despite expensive and sophisticated propaganda campaigns from Washington claiming that the United States can "grow" out of its debt and deficits, it is arithmetically impossible for the country to do so. You can be absolutely certain that any Ph.D. in economics, including Dr. Ben Bernanke, is well aware of this reality, regardless of what he might say in his speeches to Congress. So, in fact, are Chinese schoolchildren, who laughed Timothy Geithner off the podium when he patronized them about "strong dollar."[675] "The Americans," Churchill famously remarked, "will always do the right thing. . . .after they've exhausted all the alternatives." As Adam Smith explained in *The Wealth of Nations*, no nation has ever repaid its debts. Any attempt to add more debt to the system, instead of clearing it through defaults and bankruptcies, will precipitate not only an economic depression, but a full-on monetary collapse.

After the Cold War, the Western nations thought history had ended in the victory of the West. But this was not so. After a short interim period, the world saw the rise of Asia. The triumph of the West lasted only for a decade or so. The current financial crisis is less likely to cause a global recession than a radical realignment of the global economy, with the relative decline of the U.S. and the rise of China and other countries in the developing world. It marks a global economic role reversal of sorts. When financial crises hit the Asian markets in the 1990s and Argentina in 2001, the aftershocks spread to other emerging economies, plunging several of them into recession, while the wealthy countries remained relatively unscathed. Rather than taking its toll on the people of developing countries, the current economic downturn may cause the greatest damage to those living in the wealthiest parts of the planet.

While Chinese GDP continues to grow at double digits, this is based on output; in the West, GDP growth is based on spending—it is like comparing apples and oranges. The financial crisis of 2008 is rooted precisely in these global imbalances, where the West borrowed too much, funded by Asian savings. The 48 hours that brought down Lehman Brothers and AIG, and would have done away with Merrill Lynch, Morgan Stanley, and Goldman Sachs within a week if Washington had not stepped in, marked

674. Stewart Dougherty, "America's Impending Master Class Dictatorship," Kitco Metals Inc., Montréal, January 23, 2010.

675. Ibid.

the inevitable exhaustion of a global order where the West chokes in debt, while the East chokes on export capacity. Globalized financial markets then transmitted the American-led crisis around the world. The global credit bubble was complete when long-term rates collapsed as a result of Asia accumulating $5 trillion in reserves, a side effect of holding down currencies to gain export share.

Resolving this crisis, in the least painful manner, will require a thorough rebalancing of the global economy. China and rising Asia have reached the point where they can no longer keep holding down their currencies to boost exports, because this is causing problems within their own economies, propping up asset bubbles. What is taking place is a pivotal loss in the relative wealth and economic power of the G10 bloc of rich countries in comparison to rising regions of the world. The euro, sterling, Swiss franc, and other mature currencies will be relegated in this epochal process of global rebalancing, though the U.S. dollar will undoubtedly bear the brunt. The dollar could eventually be replaced as the world's reserve currency by the Special Drawing Right, or SDR, which was created as a unit of account by the International Monetary Fund in 1969.

The location of the 2009 meeting of the IMF in Istanbul was symbolic in that it paid homage to emerging markets, but also because history has always put Istanbul as the gateway between East and West. The United States must now deal on more equal terms with a rising China and India, a united Europe, and a powerful block of Asian manufacturing nations. Even Latin America, traditionally the underperformer in the global economy, is beginning to flex its muscles. The ability of the U.S. to shape the global markets through trade pacts, the IMF, and the World Bank is starting to diminish, along with its financial resources. In many parts of the world, American ideas, advice, and even aid is less welcome than it once was. The West as a whole is not the power it used to be: its debt-fuelled consumers are not the source of demand they once were, its financial system is not the source of credit it once was, nor is the integration of economies the driving force of growth it was over the past three decades.

Leaders of the world's major economies, both advanced and emerging, must co-operate and institute sweeping reforms if the world economy is not to suffer further calamities in years ahead. If the West is wise, it will greet the inevitable rise of Asia with joy and welcome it as a partner in both politics and economy. The East-West co-operation should prove easy, because the rise of Asia is based largely on wisdom learned from the West. However, much of America seems blissfully unaware of their diminished role in the world, and this distorted self-image, along with a reluctance to admit the deep-seated nature of the problems, make a happy resolution unlikely. Global trade talks collapsed in the summer of 2008 because China and India believed the proposed agricultural import rules would imperil their farmers. When the Doha Development Round began in 2001, it was inconceivable that the negotiations could be derailed by non-Western powers, but by 2008, it was clear to the world that the "American Century" would not lap over from the 20th into the 21st.

Capitalism is now global, democracy is not. America must disenthral itself from one of its most cherished myths: that capitalism and democracy go hand in hand and the spread of markets inevitably means the dawn of democracy. China's stability has belied the hopes and expectations of Western leaders that growing prosperity would significantly alter the country's political system. The Chinese Communist Party, arguably the most successful political organization in history, has now had decades of experience in economic management. It is not a four-year administration that is never in power long enough to get anything major done; it takes a very long-term view and knows what it is doing. The Chinese version of economic stimulus centres on large infrastructure projects like highways, railroads, bridges, dams, and rural electricity grids. These projects not only provide stable markets and continuing employment for such basic industries as steel, heavy machinery, and construction, they also bring long-term productivity gains to the national economy.

All the great undertakings that transformed the United States into a world power started out as government initiatives. The government paid for the initial costs and private industry did the rest. This is how both the American airline and space industry were formed, as were the great research institutes and universities. It was the Pentagon that created the internet, it was the National Institutes of Health that began the research on the human genome, the U.S. Air Force that launched the GPS satellites into outer space, and the list continues. Precisely this sort of collaboration of the public and private sectors was typical of the 20th-century America of large factories and broad sidewalks. In contrast to both the Roosevelt administration in the 1930s and the Chinese government today, the Obama administration is spending little on new infrastructure; most of its stimulus programs are directed at maintaining existing assets and employment in selected service sectors, particularly state and local governments.

The democratic dilemma is that human beings find it extremely difficult to deny themselves today in favour of a safer and calmer tomorrow. Westerners are thinking one to two years ahead, while the Chinese tend to think ten to twenty years ahead, and by then, the world will be a very different place. Should New York City need a new bridge or tunnel from Manhattan to Long Island, it will take at least twelve years before all the appeals have been exhausted and the bulldozers can get to work. When China decides to embark on a similar project, the bulldozers are ready to roll the very next day. In China, the government gets things done, but in the United States, it just goes back and forth and back and forth. We are moving towards one unified world market that is home to democratic and authoritarian systems alike; global opinions will no longer be dictated by 900 million Westerners, who are only 15 percent of the population. And China has a unique advantage—a capitalist economy not being run by elected drones.

The Chinese model of Leninist capitalism poses a systemic challenge to the democratic capitalism that the West espouses. We have to grudgingly applaud the long-term tenacity of the Chinese communists, whose domestic and foreign policy decisions are not hampered by unnecessary elections. Their model of government promises continuing power and greatly increased wealth to the ruling élites of developing nations. We are used to thinking of China as an economic miracle, but it is also becoming a political model. Beijing has shown dictators around the world that they need not choose between power and profit—they can have both. America's power and influence rested not just on its bombs and dollars, but on the fact that most people found its form of self-government attractive and wanted to reshape their own societies along the same lines. When China posted the greatest and fastest economic growth in history, it proved that market economy works perfectly well without democracy.

By making democratic reform a component in the "war on terror," which many Muslims see as a war against Islam, the United States alienated and isolated scores of potential reformist allies. As Aleister Crowley pointed out in the early 20th century, "the original brand of American freedom—which really was Freedom—contained the precept to leave other people severely alone, and thus assured the possibility of expansion on his own lines to every man."[676] There is, believe it or not, a lot more respect for individual liberty and private property in Communist China than there is in the United States today. Not everyone believes in the benevolent intentions of democratic countries; Iraq and Afghanistan have led to the phenomenon that the most active exponent of democracy, the U.S., has attracted the greatest criticism. Democracy has had its weaknesses exposed, and for the leaders of today's developing nations looking for models of political stability, the world's largest free-market democracies have little to recommend them.

Democracy sometimes breaks down by not offering stability, order, and security. Many societies, in the Middle East in particular but the People's Republic of China as well, rate these values higher than the political freedoms exercised in the West. In Singapore, where Lee Kuan Yew's thirty-year reign as prime minister spawned an authoritarian régime that combined strong economic growth with endless petty encroachments on personal liberty, the government has almost completely repressed political opposition. When journalists criticize the government, they are bankrupted by a flood of defamation suits; people confide only in their good friends; meaningful opinion polls do not exist; but as long as the economy has boomed, there has been little or no resistance to authoritarianism. In China, ordinary people are sometimes more sensitive than state officials to opinions they do not like to hear, forcing the government to take a tougher stance internationally.

It is difficult to find many proponents of democracy in the history of political theory. Since its inception in Greece a couple of millennia ago, it took more than a thousand years for democracy to gain a tenuous foothold in Europe. Almost all major thinkers had nothing but contempt for democracy. Even the Founding Fathers of the United States—now considered the model of a democracy—were strictly opposed to it; without a single exception, they thought of democracy as nothing but mob rule. And even among the few theoretical defenders of democracy such as Rousseau, it is almost impossible to find anyone advocating democracy for anything but extremely small communities, i.e. towns or villages. Today's China demonstrates that a nation's élite can be kept happy with comfortable apartments, clothes, entertainment, the chance to make money, and significant advances in personal, non-political freedoms. The ruling party allows urban élites the freedom to wear and buy whatever they want, to travel the world, to have affairs, and perhaps most importantly, to invest and profit. In return, the élites refrain from challenging the Communist Party's hold on

---

676. 1974, 122.

power.

Iraq and Afghanistan have shown that you cannot simply impose outside values on a society. The United States helped liberate Morocco, Algeria, and Tunisia seven decades ago and they have yet to opt for democracy. The U.S. liberated Kuwait twenty years ago and it has yet to opt for democracy. Just maybe China as a state would not benefit or survive the introduction of so-called Western democracy. Any régime, even that of Kim Jong Il, rests on approval of the people. This approval takes many forms, but the most usual in the West is something halfway between resignation and hunger for the dole. To many people around the world, American rhetoric about democracy sounds a lot like an excuse for furthering U.S. hegemony.

If majority decisions are "right," then the largest of all possible majorities, a world majority and a democratic world government must be considered the ultimate "right." The gradual expansion of the franchise and the eventual establishment of universal adult suffrage did within each country in Europe what a world democracy would do for the entire globe: it put in place a seemingly permanent policy of wealth and income redistribution. Imagine a world government, democratically elected according to the principle of "One Person, One Vote" on a global scale. We would probably have a Chinese-Indian coalition government that, to satisfy its supporters and secure re-election, would probably decide that the West had too much wealth and the rest of the world, in particular China and India, too little, and that a systematic wealth and income redistribution was in order.

The fact is that the democratic nation-state can no longer convincingly meet the challenges posed by economic, scientific, and technological advances and the global problems. When Charlemagne managed to unite Western Europe in the 8th century, he prefigured the EU. But this unification was by the sword, and the empire collapsed like a house of cards on his death. The European Union was formed voluntarily, and several countries are still lining up to join it. For the first time in history, a great power is expanding on public demand; instead of menacing its neighbours, it is irresistibly attracting them within its sphere. At the same time, however, Europe is depopulating itself in numbers greater than any since the Black Death in the 14th century.

The birthrates in Europe have dropped well below the replacement rate of 2.1 children for each woman of childbearing age. The rate for Western Europe as a whole is 1.5, and in Germany and Italy it is lower still, or 1.4 and 1.3 respectively.[677] If these rates continue—and there is no reason to suppose otherwise—there will not be many Germans left in Germany or Italians in Italy before the century is done. Europe's population growth is already coming entirely from immigration. A population explosion in the Middle East and North Africa means that, by 2030, the region is forecast to have 104 million people in their twenties, many of whom are likely to leave for Europe, with or without permission.[678] Fortunately, Europe has always been anything but traditionalistic: in fact, the only great European invention is the

677. Samuelson, op. cit.

678. Philippe Fargues, "Emerging Demographic Patterns across the Mediterranean and their Implications for Migration through 2030," Migration Policy Institute, Washington, D.C., November 2008.

separation of truth and tradition. Socrates called into question the mythic violence of ancient tragedies, the Renaissance challenged the Middle Ages, the new science contravened Aristotelianism.

Europe exists only the moment the preceding tradition is questioned, especially if that tradition is European. That is why the critics are the more European the more they criticize Europe. And the further East they travel to find themselves, the more typical European romantics they prove themselves. How many Tibetan monks do you know who have travelled to Germany, the birthplace of the Reformation, in order to find a new perspective for their world view? Euro-sceptics should never be called that, since no-one calls the U.S. congressmen who criticize the administration "America-sceptics." A person can perfectly well be critical of every single action of the European Union and still fully support its existence.

We should not forget that the Western world did not begin with the birth of Christ. "Western values" are not Christian, and Christianity is not Western now, nor was it when it was founded. The principal early bishoprics were those of Jerusalem, Antioch, and Alexandria, not Rome. Today, Africa and Asia are by far the fastest growing regions for Catholicism, while the number of faithful—and more importantly, the number of clergy—in Europe and America is dwindling.[679] In the ancient world, Graeco-Roman religion represented the exceptional case of a religion where the function of social control was largely absent. Since religion was not used to cement the social order and the position of those in power, it did not assert monopoly control over the way people conducted their lives.

Not least owing to the lack of sacred scriptures, the Hellenic priesthood was relatively weak. It was not priests but philosophers who served the function of providing ethical guidance, a guidance that was secular, pluralistic, and never instrumentalized for the purposes of social control. As John Leland concluded in his ***Short Essays on Government*** (1820): "The liberty I contend for is more than toleration. The very idea of toleration is despicable; it supposes that some have a pre-eminence above the rest to grant indulgence; whereas all should be equally free, Jews, Turks, Pagans and Christians. Test oaths and established creeds should be avoided as the worst of evils."[680]

The ancient Roman Republic was for centuries polytheistic, with no single person wielding absolute power. The Empire brought with itself absolutism, and soon also its spiritual parallel of monotheism. However, history shows how difficult it is to effect real change: the new has to always be dressed in the garb of the old. This was exactly what happened when Christianity was Romanized and Romanism was Christianized. The common people saw Christ as the Emperor of Rome—which by that time had been physically moved to Constantinople in Asia. Much of Western culture owes its existence to Emperor Constantine's merger of Christianity and the State. Our laws, marriage, family structures, and many of our cultural values go back in some way to this period in history.

The ancient pagan festivals were painlessly replaced with Christian holidays,

---

679. Erlandson, et al. Op. cit.

680. Stokes 1950, I, 355.

which took over not only the date but the customs of celebration. If a change in mentality takes four generations, the rites and feasts of old religions endure even longer. Europe is in any case more than just a "Christian club," with not only Jerusalem but also Athens having shaped its particular nature. From Plato on, dialogue has been a part of the European way of life, one that has no parallels in other cultures. If you add to this the struggle against religious and political oppression during the Enlightenment and the demand for "liberty, equality, and fraternity" during the French Revolution, you get a good idea of what values ultimately bind modern Europeans together.

In common parlance, the very word "paganism" may elicit some derision and laughter. Who would want to be associated with witches and warlocks, sorcery and black magic? In an era of cable television and smart weapons, worshipping plants or animals and chanting hymns to Zeus or Wotan does not inspire confidence in one's abilities as a serious academic or intellectual. Yet, paganism is not just anthropomorphic deities and witches' brew; paganism also means Seneca and Tacitus, Julius Cæsar and Marcus Aurelius, the Italian Renaissance, Richard Wagner, Friedrich Nietzsche, and Paul Gauguin. Two millennia of Judaeo-Christianity have not erased pagan thought from the Western cultural heritage, even though it has constantly been blurred, stifled, and persecuted by monotheistic religions and their secular offshoots.

The Western cry for "human rights" is not a Christian cause, quite the opposite. The savage rise of Christianity made free thought, atheistic expression, and anything remotely heretical dangerous, whereas—to quote Robert G. Ingersoll—"Infidels in all ages have battled for the rights of man, and have at all times been the fearless advocates of liberty and justice."[681] The most famous American of the post-Civil War era, Ingersoll explained that the word God does not appear in the U.S. Constitution because the Founding Fathers "knew that the recognition of a Deity would be seized upon by fanatics and zealots as a pretext for destroying the liberty of thought. They knew the terrible history of the church too well to place in her keeping, or in the keeping of her God, the sacred rights of man."[682]

There have always been, in every place and at every time, massacres and crimes against humanity. But it is difficult to find in the pagan texts, sacred or profane, the equivalent of what one so frequently encounters in the Judaeo-Christian scriptures: the idea that these massacres could be morally justified, or deliberately authorized and ordained by a deity, "as Moses the servant of the Lord commanded."[683] Yahweh Himself was responsible for a genocide in unleashing the Deluge on the humanity that had sinned against Him. While residing with the Philistine king Achish, David also practised genocide.[684] Moses organized the extermination of the Midian people.[685] Joshua massacred the people of Hazor and the tribes of Anakim.[686] For the

681. *The Gods.* 1901, I, 86.

682. *Individuality.* Ibid. 201.

683. Joshua 11:12.

684. I Samuel 27:9.

685. Numbers 31:7.

686. Joshua 11:11, 15:21.

perpetrators of these horrible crimes, good conscience continued to rule, not in spite of these massacres, but entirely because of the massacres.

In every Western country, it was mainly a band of freethinkers who fought for human rights. Until the mid-19th century, every major Christian denomination was either indifferent or hostile to education reform, industrial betterment, child labour laws, universal suffrage, women's rights, and so on. As Lemuel K. Washburn put it, "The church wants us to believe that God will go out of his way to strike a blasphemer and work a week to save the soul of a murder."[687] Never before has there been more concern in the world for peace and freedom, for social justice and equality, and it is precisely this sentiment that has caused the majority of Christendom to abandon the two principal dogmas of Christianity, those of eternal damnation and the atoning death of Christ.

Through his 1993 essay "The Clash of Civilizations?" Harvard professor Samuel P. Huntington introduced to politicians and the media the tempting idea of three great cultures fighting for power—and how Islam and Confucianism supposedly threaten the Christian West.[688] The world has indeed been divided into mutually hostile groups, but the division does not run between cultures or civilizations, but within them. On one side are the religious fundamentalists of every culture, whose world views are quite similar despite their hostility towards each other. On the other side are those who believe in a dialogue between cultures and nations, and recognize the fact that no culture is free of foreign influences. The great divide in values is not between those who believe in God and those who do not, but between those who believe in scriptural inerrancy and those who do not.

There is a tendency to focus on the most vocal members of any religious tradition, who often happen to be the most orthodox, or the most traditional, or the most observant, while largely ignoring the more moderate believers and especially those who are nominal in their religiosity. A massive survey of religion in America released by the Pew Forum on Religion & Public Life in 2008 found that 70% of Americans, and even 57% of evangelical Protestants, believe that many religions can lead to eternal life, while 68% say there is more than one true way to interpret the teachings of their religion.[689] There is not one pro-life group in the United States that supports contraception, yet the vast majority of pro-life Americans, 80%, support contraception. What is more, 90% of Catholics, followers of the only religion to officially oppose artificial contraception, support it. And although the Catholic Church is known for its ardent opposition to abortion, Catholics are almost evenly split on the issue, with 48% saying abortion should be legal in most cases, and only 45% saying it should be illegal.[690] Some U.S. bishops made opposition to abortion the one and only criterion for who the faithful were supposed vote for in a recent election, but its outcome showed that the majority of American Catholics have greater moral discernment than their shepherds.

---

687. Op. cit. 117.

688. *Foreign Affairs*, Summer 1993.

689. Op. cit.

690. Ibid.

The West has long attached an image of depravity and diabolical violence to the Ottoman Empire. Yet the Ottomans never introduced artificial divisions in local communities and regions with arbitrary ruler-edge boundaries and entirely novel puppet states with extreme imbalances in access to natural resources and trade routes. Quite the opposite, the Ottomans respected traditional, natural, geographic, and cultural boundaries, and maintained historical continuity. Many in the Balkans benefited from *Pax Turcica;* the sense of security was in fact so strong that cities did not require walls around them. Roman—or what we now like to call "Western"—values underlie "Islamic," or more precisely Arab, civilization as well. Both the Judaeo-Christian and the Muslim religion are patriarchal, monotheistic faiths of Levantine origin. And the most warlike religion of all history is undoubtedly Christianity. In India, Hindus, whose caste system has always included a warrior class, or *satria,* have begun a persecution of Muslims; the country's democratic pretensions have not stood in the way of horrific attacks on minority Muslims by Hindu mobs, sometimes aided and abetted by the Indian police.

The responsibility for associating war and Islam falls squarely on the Western media. God being referred to as "Allah" (definite article *al* + the word *ilah,* god) when discussing Muslims does not build any bridges either—the media do not speak of "Yahweh" when talking about Jews. Incidentally, the West is also responsible for exporting anti-Semitism to the Muslim East. (Though the term is rather inaccurate here: Arabs are a Semitic people themselves.) The famous Ottoman tolerance was especially beneficial to the Jews who had been expelled from Catholic Spain in 1492. They found a new free city in Turkey and Istanbul alone soon boasted 44 synagogues. Unlike in Christian Europe, no law precluded them from gainful employment or public office. At a time when Jews were treated like animals in the West, the "barbaric" Turks represented the true humanitarians in the Jewish Question.

The colonial period played a big role in the poverty of the Third World, and this, not Islam, is the reason for low education of girls in Muslim countries. It is a cause for much social discontent, which again is a fertile breeding ground for religious fundamentalism. However, female circumcision is an African tradition, while the *hijab* is an Arabian one—neither have anything to do with Islam. The Palestinian problem is not a Muslim one: many of the most important and prominent Palestinian leaders and activists have been Christian, and during the Cold War, Arab Socialism occupied the same position in the Middle East as radical Islam does today. The Middle Eastern terrorist movement came to world attention on September 5th, 1972, through the murder of eleven Israeli athletes during the Munich Olympics. This action was taken under the Marxist banner of the PLO, which at its core was secular and atheistic, as a nationalistic protest against the state of Israel. The ideologies change, but the underlying causes remain the same.

Some Western commentators have put forth the claim that political terrorism is an inevitable consequence of the Islamic value system. Others have rushed to point out that the Koran does not condone violence against the innocent, and the terrorists' interpretation of Islam is either completely wrong or at the very least extremely narrow. As BBC reporters found, many young people in the British Muslim community simply refused to believe there was any connection between Muslims and the London subway bombings.[691] And if you went to the Middle East and asked "Where in the world is Osama?" the majority would answer: "Back home in the U.S.A." The Dubai-based Gulf News made this discovery, when they had a survey on the subject a few years ago and the most popular answer was not even among the given choices.[692] There are more Muslims in Indonesia and Malaysia than in the entire Middle East, but they appear to have little impact in shaping American perceptions of Islam. However, I would be very surprised if such a rich and multifaceted religion either forced people to take up violence or rendered it impossible. Let us not forget how many good and evil deeds have been justified throughout the centuries with Christian arguments.

The Islamic or Christian or Western set of values contain within them a possibility for almost any kind of acts imaginable. Violence stems from concrete, social reasons, not from abstractions about the nature of a Muslim or a Westerner—both can be almost any kind whatsoever. The difference is, Western politicians try to couch their religious motivations in secular terms when advocating certain policies. A good example is the unyielding support for Israel and its occupation of West Bank and Gaza among some American politicians. In Muslim countries, legitimacy comes from Islam and thus many Muslim politicians on the contrary justify material motivations through an Islamic cover. There are 1.7 billion Muslims in the world, and if all of them are terrorists, the world is doomed. Fortunately, according to EU law enforcement officials, only one of the 294 "failed, foiled, or successfully executed terrorist attacks" in Europe was committed by Islamists in 2009.[693] So it is not only that a tiny minority of Muslims are terrorists, but that a tiny minority of terrorists are Muslims.

The often-used term "moderate Muslims" implies that moderation is the exception to the norm, when in fact, the vast majority of the world's Muslims are moderate. Hundreds of millions of ordinary Muslims demonstrate their rejection of extremism by simply going about their everyday lives. At his inauguration, President Obama said: "To the Muslim world, we seek a new way forward, based on mutual interest and mutual respect."[694] Substitute "Jewish" or "Christian" where Obama said "Muslim," and you begin to see the problem. It makes no sense to speak of a "Christian world" as though it were possible to extrapolate from their religious affiliation the shared values of all Christians everywhere. There are more Muslims in Germany than in Lebanon, and more in Russia than in Jordan and Libya put together; more than 300 million Muslims live in countries where Islam is not the majority religion—many have fled to the West precisely in order to escape a radical Islamist régime.[695]

691. BBC Radio 1, July 9, 2005.

692. Mahmood Saberi, "Gulf News Survey: People Believe Bin Laden 'Probably Back Home in US,'" May 13, 2006.

693. "TE-SAT 2010: EU Terrorism Situation and Trend Report," Europol, The Hague, April 1, 2010.

694. The Inaugural Address, Washington, D.C., January 20, 2009.

695. "Mapping the Global Muslim Population: A Report on the Size and Distribution of the World's Muslim Population," Pew Forum on Religion & Public Life, Washington, D.C., October 2009.

There are millions of Muslims who admire America and who would love nothing more than to have economic partnerships with the United States. They would love to learn business leadership skills and to know what makes a successful entrepreneur. In fact, the vast majority of people in the world of any religion want a decent life, want to send their kids to school, and want to be at peace. Terrorists and extremists are as much a threat to these people as to anyone else. If President Obama is really looking for mutual interests, then it is at this level that he must pitch his policies, rather than at the level of the mutual political interests of the United States and the Egyptian and Syrian police states, or the web of economic, political, and military interests that link the U.S. with the archetype of oppressive and undemocratic rule, Saudi Arabia.

It is worth remembering that the 9/11 terrorists were not religious fanatics, but secular men. The attacks on New York and Washington were political. It was the United States that masterminded the use of an armed political Islamic movement as a counter for godless communism; it was the U.S. that bankrolled the *jihad* against Soviet troops occupying Afghanistan. And once the Cold War was over, these former mujahedin turned against the Western infidels whom they had never trusted—the Soviet-Afghan war was the crucible from which emerged al-Qaeda. The terrorism that wells forth from radical Islamic sects is nothing more than desperation. Islamic fundamentalism has already proven impracticable in the modern world. The modern Islamists argue that Islam is not a religion, but a world view at par with capitalism and communism. However, unlike Arab Nationalism or Socialism, over which one might argue at the dinner table, criticizing the distorted teachings of a radical mullah could be considered anti-Islamic apostasy. Yet if you go to the majority of Islamic mosques in the world today, you will hear people calling for peace and denouncing violence.

The same message echoes through conferences in Muslim countries. This is not surprising when you consider the fact that Muslims are the ones paying most heavily for terrorism. By ratio of 10 to 1, the people who have died in the Iraq War are Muslim. Not only those dying in the daily bombings in Iraq, but in the bombings that have hit Riyadh, Istanbul, Casablanca, and Sharm el-Sheikh, are overwhelmingly Muslim. Indeed, some of the London subway victims came from the British capital's large Muslim community. It is simply in the best interest of Muslims all over the globe to denounce violence. Even Hezbollah—the "Party of God" considered a terrorist organization by the United States—has publicly denounced the "mass murder attacks against innocent people" and called for a "decisive stance by Muslim clerics" against violence.[696] Two decades after al-Qaeda was founded in the Pakistani border city of Peshawar by a former CIA asset named Osama bin Laden and a handful of veterans of the U.S.-backed war against the Soviets in Afghanistan, the group is more famous and feared than ever; but its grand design—transforming the Muslim world into a militant Islamist caliphate—has been a complete and utter failure.

Islam was a religion that united disparate ethnic groups that had previously been fighting with the ruling empires and with each other, by displacing the cultural norms that had kept various nomadic tribes from working together. There is, to this day, no Muslim world, only a variety of nations with Muslim majorities. Some of

---

696. Charles Levinson, "Muslims Feel Strain of Global Terrorism's Grip on Their Faith," *San Francisco Chronicle*, August 1, 2005.

these call themselves Islamic states, but the extent to which they are governed according to Islamic principles and under Islamic law is a matter of debate. Pakistan, for example, declares itself to be an Islamic nation, yet it has no clear legal definition of what that means. We must understand that Islamic extremism is a distinctly modern movement, a radical response to the challenges of the industrial, globalized world; it fuses modern Western ideas of the role of the State and Law with radical rereadings of old religious texts and traditions to create an ideology that is specifically tailored to the world of today. It is traditional religious authorities that therefore constitute the strongest bulwark against Islamism. Those who insist on blaming Islam have unwittingly rejected the West's best allies, the traditional Muslim clerics, often in favour of secular authoritarians like Musharraf and Mubarak, whose oppressive policies only drive people into the arms of extremism. The Islamophobes say Islam and the West are incompatible; the Islamists say Islam and the West are incompatible —to reject the attitude of the latter while embracing the attitude of the former seems a little strange to me.

There is a tendency in the West to think that it is Islam that prohibits women from driving a car, for instance, even though women drive cars all over the world except in one country. Many Saudis also drive over to Dubai on the weekends to drink alcohol and act like pigs, and then return to home to practise Islamic teaching like a good Muslim. Although the Taliban banned television when they were in power in Afghanistan, they now use video recordings that contain messages and footage of their attacks on foreign and local security forces—Taliban anthems are even used as cellular ringtones in some areas. Mecca, which is the centre of the Islamic world and the worst tourist trap in the known universe, probably has more fast-food restaurants per square mile than any other place on the globe. And in some parts of Turkey, it is deemed perfectly acceptable for a Muslim to eat pork.

The Shariah is systematically distorted and misinterpreted in the West. While the focus on sensational stories about amputations and stonings is partly justified, it obscures the fact that Shariah courts deal mainly with family and merchant law. These Islamic courts aim at swift resolutions, which increased their popularity in countries such as Nigeria where the otherwise poorly-run courts process cases slowly, if at all. Indeed, even some Nigerian Christians like to bring their cases before Shariah courts, because they tend to focus less on the technical details of the legislation. As an example, a Christian who had been defrauded by a Muslim car dealer made the local news when he sued in an Islamic court, won his case within a few weeks, and had to pay no legal fees.[697] Nor were Islamic financial institutions hit as hard by the global banking crisis as their Western counterparts, because they did not and could not invest in toxic assets.

However, when religion is disguised as national interest or secular reason, it can seriously undermine minority rights. As a faith grows more assertive, and its zealous advocates become skilled at "playing the system," constitutional guarantees are rendered meaningless. Fanaticism is wanting one's enemy to lose utterly—not just to lose the war, but to vanish from the face of the earth. This cannot happen in any

697. Ali Ahmad, "In Defense of Sharia," Project Syndicate, August 20, 2002.

other conflict save the Final Battle, which constitutes a sort of a prelude to the Last Judgement. The U.S. War on Terror of course shows all these distinctive characteristics. Any political issue that is important eventually affects individual and collective identity, and in doing so, triggers religious sentiments; as long as religion plays a role in people's identities, it will continue to play a role in politics—and it is religious devotion that sets the United States apart from its closest Western allies.

According to Ipsos, the people of Western Europe are the least devout among the 10 nations covered by its 2005 survey. The polling was conducted in the United States, Britain, Australia, Canada, France, Germany, Italy, Mexico, South Korea, and Spain. Nearly one-fifth of the French consider themselves atheists, a figure surpassed only by that of South Korea. In Spain, where the Catholic Church receives government subsidies, and in Germany, where the government collects a religious tax on behalf of its Churches, people are evenly divided over whether they consider faith important.[698] The results are similar in Britain, a country where the State Church headed by the Queen is struggling to fill pews. Tony Blair said that his decision to delay converting to Catholicism until after he had resigned as prime minister was prompted by fear that talking about his religious beliefs while in office would have led to people dismissing him as a "nutter." Europeans, especially North Europeans, have difficulty understanding the power of religion. They have inherited an exceptional history, whose roots stretch back to the centuries-long religious and political conflicts between the Catholics and the Protestants.

The wars of religion began with the Reformation in 1517 and ended with the Peace of Westphalia in 1648. The memory of these wars guided the intellectual and political history of Europe for over three centuries: natural science and the nation-state evolved, the independence of universities was reinforced, the culture grew more secular, and religion had to forgo the inroads it had made into temporal power. However, the secularization was not a result of people giving up their belief in God. It was the result of the fact that Europeans no longer had faith in the ability of competing religions to exist peacefully alongside each other. The United States chose another route entirely: the first amendment to its secular constitution separated Church and State.

Secularism, like atheism and agnosticism, is as American as cherry pie. One of the pivotal works of the 18th-century Enlightenment was *The Age of Reason* by Thomas Paine. The United States was the first and only country to adopt a constitution that specifically excludes any and all references to a higher power. Ironically, the refusal to establish any particular religion opened the door for free competition between faiths, giving birth to one revivalist movement after another. If modernity meant the damping down of religious fervour for Europe, in the United States it signified the admission of same into secular politics, enabling American lawmakers to invoke the blessing of Heaven on whichever cause they happen to favour.

Secularism, in any form, is a device meant to protect politics from becoming usurped by religion and religion from being corrupted by politics. It rests on the assumption of pure religion and pure politics—the naïve belief in, not the separation

698. AP/Ipsos Religious Attitudes Poll, May 13–26, 2006.

of Church and State, but the separability of Church and State. In the secular West, religious beliefs are seen as personal and private, and it is considered in poor taste to question them too deeply. There are also few topics that elicit more hypocrisy than the relationship between religion and politics. American politicians habitually welcome religion into politics when it helps their side and see "a Church-State problem" if it helps the other side. Conservatives tend to praise religious activism on abortion and homosexuality, but summarily dismiss liberal clerics who comment on economics or social spending.

It was paradoxically the separation of Church and State that made possible the observance of Christian ethics—until then compromised by the Constantinian tradition. Religion, when incorporated into a political structure, inevitably becomes diluted and distorted, ultimately losing its most essential power. European Christianism is slowly losing all the characteristics of a religion: the Finnish parliament does not see the traditional recital of Hymn No. 571 at public school closing ceremonies as an infringement on religious equality, since it has become so routine that it holds an historical and not a religious meaning. Despite the Italian constitution supposedly separating Church and State, it is customary to see crucifixes in Italian public buildings, including schools. Meanwhile, polls show that the voters in the U.S. Presidential Elections of 2004 were more concerned about the erosion of Christian values than about the nation's economy, terrorism, or the war in Iraq.[699] And that is a problem, because many Christians believe that Jesus will come again after nuclear Armageddon, and the U.S. nearly had such a person a heartbeat away from having her finger on the button in 2008.

Ultimately, the religious wars of the 16th and 17th centuries were responsible for both Europe's secularism and America's religiosity; as Frank Zappa so eloquently articulated it, "America was founded by the refuse of the religious fanatics of England, these undesirable elements that came over on the Mayflower. Ignorant, religious fanatics who land here, abuse the Indians, and then go to bed with a board down the middle, you know, the bundling board, so they don't have sex. That's how we got started."[700] In the Ipsos poll, only Mexicans came close to Americans in embracing faith, but unlike Americans, they objected strongly to clergy lobbying lawmakers. Eighty percent of Italians said religion was significant to them, but even in the home of the Catholic Church, only 10% thought the clergy should try to influence government decisions.[701] If Pakistan had a clearly defined political notion of Islam, Maulana Maududi and his Deobandi fundamentalists could never have exercised the influence they did, in much the same way as the secular quality of the United States allowed Christian fundamentalists to slip under the radar and take the White House.

It is important to realize that rather than killing religion, science boosted religion —by admitting that it could not explain everything. In 1776, church membership in

---

699. "National Election Pool (NEP) Exit Poll 2004," Edison Media Research & Mitofsky International, November 2, 2004.

700. Interview by Bob Marshall, op. cit.

701. Op. cit.

the United States was at mere five percent.[702] Today, as the British actor Liam Neeson noted after starring in the American movie *Kinsey* (2004): "There is just incredible schizophrenia in this country about sex. You have shows like *Sex And The City* winning Emmy awards every year, millions of people watching a bunch of women sitting around talking about blow-jobs, *Queer Eye For The Straight Guy*, *The L Word*. And yet you show footage of two guys who've just got married holding hands outside City Hall and there's fucking outrage."[703] While it may be true that they make pornographic films in Los Angeles and there are probably some prostitutes in Las Vegas, American attitudes towards social and sexual matters have more in common with the thinking in Tehran than Paris. A bunch of top Bush administration officials may have committed war crimes for which they will undoubtedly never be prosecuted, but a love child, now that's a career killer!

Fundamentalism is not some relic from the days of the old; it is a thoroughly modern phenomenon, in two senses: firstly, it is a reaction against the modernization of society and its byproducts; secondly, it presupposes, at least in its Christian incarnation, a scientific world view, an unintentional parody of which it offers in its "literal" interpretation of the holy scriptures. The great theologians of old, like St. Thomas Aquinas, never believed in taking the Bible literally, but saw it—or at least the Old Testament—as a metaphor. Fundamentalists are thus a perverted, latter-day product of the modern world. They "leap up and down in apoplectic rage and joy. Their worst fantasies are vindicated, and therefore (or so they like to think), their entire theology and socio-political agenda is too. . . The born-agains are ready to burn again, and not just books this time."[704]

Perhaps the most valuable thing in the West is its certain amorality, the faded conception of what is actually unique to it. For, at bottom, all codes of ethics are really only justifications of one's own customs versus foreign ones. When the French parliament approved a ban on religious symbols in public schools, every single party represented in the National Assembly voted in favour; of course, not a single member of parliament from mainland France is of Arab or African origin, although 10% of the people are.[705] In my humble opinion, Muslims and Christian should be *obliged* to wear veils and crosses in public, not the other way around—the Holocaust and the Inquisition notwithstanding. They should do this as a warning: it is not like they can actually turn off their religious identity while going about their everyday business; it is what they are.

Blacks are not made to hide their racial identity, nor are gays made to hide their sexual identity—or at least they should not be. Prohibiting Muslim families from sending their girls to school in head scarves does not stop those families from wanting to cover the hair of their female offspring. For the last 30 years, political correctness has dictated that the French should not acknowledge the existence of cultural and religious differences. It is against the law in France to keep statistics based on race or

702. Robertson 1987.

703. As quoted in Simon Braund, "The Sex Inspector," *Empire*, April 2005.

704. Gregory Krupey, "The Devil You Say!" Hoy 1990, 291.

705. *Le Figaro*, November 18, 2005.

ethnicity, so according to the French government, ethnic or religious enclaves do not exist in the country. In 2005, those nonexistent slums were consumed for several weeks by very real flames. National rioting was sparked in 300 or more ***zone de non-droit*** or "lawless areas," immigrant suburbs of Paris and other large cities, where police do not venture as a matter of policy.

You cannot make differences and disparities disappear just by ignoring them. Religion should be a mandatory subject in all public schools; had it not been in Finland when I went to school, I am not sure I would be an unbeliever today. As Morton Downey, Jr. put it: "If they teach Greek and Roman mythology, they should also teach Middle Eastern mythology." In the Christian West, it is not customary to treat the story of Jesus as a myth, maybe because a comparison to other heroic tales would open up revealing insights into Christianity. I very much suspect that the European clergy, schooled as it is in theology and comparative religion, has a bigger portion of atheists than the general population. In the United States, however, partly because of its frontier history, most of the Protestant churches are congregational, i.e. they are free to create their own Bible colleges for training ministers. And if you send people to a Bible college that teaches only the Bible, they will come back preaching only the Bible. On the other hand, a 2010 Pew Research Center survey found American atheists and agnostics to be more knowledgeable about religion than either the Catholic or Evangelical laymen in the country.[706]

"If the liberties of the American people are ever destroyed," Marquis de Lafayette reputedly asserted in 1789, "they will fall by the hands of the clergy." In the United States, people do not pay a church tax, but they just as well might: "Church tax exemption means that we all drop our money in the collection boxes, whether we go to church or not and whether we are interested in the church or not. It is systematic and complete robbery, from which none of us escapes."[707] However, keeping a giant space open for a couple of hundred people to attend two or three services a week with pay-what-you-can entrance fees does not exactly cover the electric bills, much less the mortgage. Thus, many of the most historic places of worship in the West boast gift shops and speakers' series, and are used extensively as secular performance venues.

I have never been convinced by any of the arguments for using public funds to preserve "religious landmarks." The Spanish Inquisition was a religious landmark, as was the persecution of witches and the burning of heretics. The low position women occupied for centuries in Western society was mostly due to Christianity. "The church has contributed nothing to civilization. It has progressed somewhat, and it has become a little more decent, in reflection of the movements of civilization that have taken place outside of the church and usually in the face of the strong opposition of the church. But the church has always resisted the process of civilization. It has struggled to the last ditch, by fair means and foul, to preserve as long as it could the vestiges of ancient and medieval theology, with all the puerile moralities and harsh

---

706. "U.S. Religious Knowledge Survey," Pew Forum on Religion & Public Life, Washington, D.C., September 28, 2010.

707. Emanuel Haldeman-Julius, ***The Church Is a Burden, Not a Benefit, in Social Life.***

customs and medieval styles of belief."[708] Or to quote Frank Zappa once more: "The only difference between a cult and a religion is the amount of real estate they own."

708. Ibid.

9

Anyone Who Goes to a Psychiatrist Ought to Have His Head Examined

I have never understood Christian politicians defending "home and country." It would be difficult to come up with a more un-Christian concept than family; or nation—statehood seen through the family metaphor, forming the core of bourgeois heathenism. The so-called "traditional family," or nuclear family, did not come about in the West until the secular times of the Enlightenment. One's family evokes the most beautiful and compelling feelings of love and intimacy, but it is precisely because of this that it also has to be defended with any and all forms of violence when necessary. There is no paradox in the fact that many of the Nazis working at the concentration camps during the day were good and loving fathers in the evening. Or that today's neo-conservatives are affectionate caregivers to their families and pets. On the contrary, this is exactly what is to be expected.

Jesus, the proper sectarian that he was, withdrew himself from his family before doing anything else, and repeatedly made discipleship contingent on the total renunciation of all family ties. Nor was Paul a strong proponent of marriage, advocating celibacy instead as spiritually superior. Cults use social frameworks to control the minds of their members: the social environment is made such that it forces the person to relinquish his former identity and adopt the identity of the group. Christian sects today thrive in China precisely because they are being persecuted, and thus driven outside society at large. The whole force of the Gospels was aimed at a tribal deity sustained by sacrifice, an archaic model of the family structure. Shared guilt, self-imposed austerity, penetrating honesty and authenticity, the glimmer of grace unconcerned with communal boundaries and roles are the forces in which Christians put their hope—but one cannot build a society on them.

As they say, "You can pick your friends, but you cannot pick your family." No-one asks to be born—"Life is a sexually transmitted terminal disease." Only the parents have any choice in the matter, so should they not at the very least try to make sure their child will be born healthy? Recent studies have disproved the long-held assumption about a harmonic relationship between the pregnant mother and the unborn child. Today, pregnancy is understood as a conflict between the mother's and the father's genes. According to the Australian biologist David Haig, this explains morning sickness, miscarriages, and elevated blood pressure of the expecting mother.[709] Of course, "Jesus loves the little zygotes / All the zygotes in the world / Jesus gives them birth defects / Missing fingers, crooked necks / Jesus loves the little zygotes of the world."[710]

I never understood the great outcry over infant euthanasia. Aren't the poor little bastards supposed to be tainted with Original Sin? Which kind of is the whole point of infant baptism. Christians now talk about "rights of the unborn," whereas, until the secular 20th century, the idea of a child as an individual being was so vague that it was common practice to give a new child the name of its deceased sibling, in effect replacing the dead baby with the new one. During the devout Middle Ages, infants were buried in any convenient place: the parents rested in a consecrated crypt, the little ones somewhere in the church yard, or even in a mass grave. The names of the dead children were carved neither on the headstones nor on the family trees.

Childbirth is not only painful to the human female, but positively dangerous and sometimes lethal, because the human birth canal is too small for the head of a full-grown foetus. Why would God, when He was designing the exit for a baby, engineer a route that passes through the narrow confines of the pelvic bones? Anyone looking at a skeleton can see right away that there is plenty of room for even the most large-brained foetus to be easily delivered anywhere in the large, non-bony region below the ribs. In fact, this is the exact route obstetricians use when performing a Cæsarean section. It is thanks to modern technology that there are so few post-partum deaths and newborns receive proper and competent care.

The human species evolved from four-legged mammals who carried their spines parallel to the ground. Unfortunately, when we developed an upright posture our pelvic girdles had to be rotated and thus narrowed, turning what for other mammals is an easy passage into a constricted space. The creationist will of course argue that the dangers and discomforts of childbirth were intelligently designed as punishment for Eve's disobedience: "in sorrow thou shalt bring forth children."[711] A traumatic

709. "Genetic Conflict in Human Pregnancy," *The Quarterly Review of Biology* 68(4), December 1993, 495–532; "Altercation of Generations: Genetic Conflicts of Pregnancy," *American Journal of Reproductive Immunology* 35(3), March 1996, 226–232.

710. Frank Zindler, Dial-an-Atheist Ohio.

711. Genesis 3:16.

birthing experience can easily lead a woman to depression and a heightened fear of new pregnancy and childbirth. Nor should children have to die to uphold the religious beliefs of their parents. Surely the purpose of the First Amendment was not to allow believers to inflict their views upon their children and let them die from such things as infections, which can be quickly and easily treated by any medical professional?

It is the parents who should respect their children, not the other way around; in a way, it is their purpose in life—"We do not own the land, we rent it from our children." This is the moral difference between those who acknowledge evolution and those who subscribe to creationism. And as Aristotle pointed out in his *Politics* around 350 BCE, neglect of an effective birth control policy "is a never-failing source of poverty," which, in turn, "is the parent of revolution and crime."[712] The best contraceptive is prosperity, in that people have sexual intercourse for pleasure, instead of deriving all their pleasure from begetting children. The wealthy classes in particular have always practised birth control, even through the centuries when the Church sternly condemned it, *coitus interruptus* being the historically most common method.

Even today, teenage pregnancies are connected with social disadvantage and poverty. In Britain, they are ten times more common in the families of unskilled workers than in those of the middle classes.[713] An impoverished, poorly-educated girl seldom cares about contraception, and an adolescent who becomes pregnant is more likely to drop out of school altogether, leading again to a low-paying job. Young mothers are also less likely to marry, meaning their children will be raised in a one-income household. All of these factors conspire to make sure that teenage mothers and their infants do not find their way out from what is usually a low-income community to begin with. "If the art of conversation stood a little higher we would have a lower birthrate," as Stanislaw J. Lec put it.[714]

In times past, women were much more scared about getting pregnant than they are today. There were no contraceptives and abortions were illegal. In fact, all Christian denominations remained categorically opposed to contraception until the Church of England took a brave stand in 1930 by declaring birth control allowable under certain circumstances. And as the contemporary journalist H. L. Mencken observed, "It is now quite lawful for a Catholic woman to avoid pregnancy by a resort to mathematics, though she is still forbidden to resort to physics or chemistry."[715] In analyzing reports by the National Center for Health Statistics, Prof. James Trussell from Princeton University found that half of all intended pregnancies in the United States occur among the more than 95% of women who use some type of contraception, meaning that the other half came from the tiny minority not using any

712. Bk. II, Sec. 6. (1265b10–1265b12).

713. "Teenage Pregnancy: Report Presented to Parliament by the Prime Minister by Command of Her Majesty," Social Exclusion Unit, London, June 1999.

714. Op. cit. 53.

715. 1956, 52.

birth control at all.[716]

Accidents do happen, and by that I do not mean only that contraception is never 100% effective, but that people do not always act rationally. They forget; they can't control themselves; they get too drunk to think. But that someone would consciously and deliberately say that they have not even considered birth control is strange indeed. In the past, pregnancy was a source of anxiety for women. A child born out of wedlock was a disgrace. The poor did not have the means to support their children. Pregnancy was an immense risk to a woman's health, economy, and social status. During the mid-19th century, 32,000 children were still abandoned each year in France alone.[717] This was not only a sign of poverty but a sign of indifference and outright hostility towards unwanted children. The advent of modern contraceptives was a great relief.

A decisive improvement in infants' chances of survival into adulthood took place with advances in hygiene and medicine at the end of the 19th century. However, 15–20% of clinically recognized pregnancies still result in miscarriage even in the developed countries; in fact, up to half of all fertilized eggs are aborted spontaneously before the woman even knows she is pregnant. There are an estimated 6.4 million diagnosed pregnancies every year in the United States and approximately 2.3 million of those end without a live birth.[718] Despite the approval of the birth control pill half a century ago and the subsequent development of new and superior forms of contraception, half of all pregnancies in the U.S. are unplanned.[719] But if a teenage girl has an "accident" and decides to keep the baby, modern secularized society will support her financially and guarantee her an education if she desires one—society, of course, meaning you and your tax dollars. It costs far less to supply birth control than it does to help raise a child, and in countries where women have control over their own bodies, they choose not to be perpetually pregnant. The United Nations Population Fund has calculated that 350 million women in the poorest regions of the world did not want their last child, but had no means to prevent it.[720] Curiously enough, the same people who oppose birth control are also against abortion, sex education, and planned parenthood.

Suicide, Latin for "self-murder," is a Christian concept; the ancient Romans considered taking one's own life acceptable and, in some cases, commendable—much like many Asians still do today. The Christian rationale against abortion and euthanasia is the same: God has given life, only God can take it away—through an anti-abortionist bombing a clinic for instance. The irony is, abortion would cease to exist if sex education and birth control technology were not obstructed by these same religious zealots. And while politicians on both sides of the abortion debate offer

716. James Trussell & Barbara Vaughan, "Contraceptive Failure, Method-Related Discontinuation and Resumption of Use: Results from the 1995 National Survey of Family Growth," *Family Planning Perspectives* (31)2, March–April 1999, 64–72+93.

717. Alphonse Esquiros, "Les Enfans trouvés," *Revue des Deux Mondes* 13, 1846.

718. Stephanie J. Ventura, et al. "Estimated Pregnancy Rates by Outcome for the United States, 1990–2004," *National Vital Statistics Reports* 56(15), April 14, 2008, 1–25+28.

719. Trussell & Vaughan, op. cit.

720. United Nations Fund for Population Activities, op. cit.

adoption as a better alternative, the patients themselves rarely consider it an option. For example, a high school senior cheering in a championship drill team is hardly prepared to give up her body for nine months. Also, giving away a child would mean having to wonder every day if he were loved. Ending the pregnancy just seems easier.

It is the emphasis on the "willingly" or "choosing" to have a baby part of the anti-abortion rhetoric that befuddles me—why praise someone for simply choosing not to commit an act you believe to be murder? Which is more irresponsible, getting an abortion or continuing to live the same way without giving one's pregnancy any thought? If you don't take care of birth control, and you don't take care of abortion, you probably will not take care of the child either. Childbirth should be joyous—no woman should ever have to consider it a punishment or an obligation. In absence of Virgin Birth, mother is the creator of life, not God. Of course, although Christians often call themselves "pro-life," they are not the least bit interested in saving lives; what they care about is saving souls. But until recently, the Catholic Church did not even consider a foetus less than 3 months old to have a soul; and most women seek abortion much earlier in pregnancy, over 90% of them in their first trimester.[721]

"Only by the most tortured exegesis and in the most tenuous theologizing can anything resembling an anti-abortion position be ripped from the scripture."[722] Or have you ever heard of Jewish anti-abortionists? Although all life is considered sacred in Judaism, the health of the mother always comes first, before the life of a potential child. The Mishnah clearly states that a woman is required to have an abortion if her life is in danger.[723] However, essentially all rabbinical figures agree that a woman is prohibited from abortion at any stage if the sole purpose is convenience. But another point agreed upon by rabbis in all forms of Judaism is that a foetus only becomes a human being after its head emerges from the mother's womb.

That truth is, the Christian activists who preach the "sanctity of life" are about as concerned about this life as your friendly neighbourhood suicide bomber. Health is a central value for a secularized society, one not concerned about the life hereafter. Today, people's anxiety about themselves is pointedly somatic and concerned with this world, whereas it used to be more spiritual and metaphysical and otherworldly. Since the Age of Enlightenment, the health of the population has been a subject of political interest and a target of positive measures. The projects of public hygiene and health care have become public undertakings that bear upon political order and power structures. Today's morbid respect for life is a throughly modern phenomenon: a "liberated" person no longer fears punishment in the next world, but that the reward in this one will be too short.

Yet without death, life would have no meaning. Human life is a result of sexual reproduction, which makes evolution possible. Primitive organisms, such as bacteria, multiply by dividing; viruses mutate because they are barely life forms at all. But us humans "must die to be reborn." Even on the cell level, catabolism is an absolute

721. Karen Pazol, et al. "Abortion Surveillance—United States, 2007," *Morbidity and Mortality Weekly Report* 60(SS-1), February 25, 2011, 1–39.

722. Delos B. McKown, "What Does the Bible Say about Abortion?" *Free Inquiry* 11(4), Fall 1991, 29–34.

723. Ohalot 7:6.

prerequisite for anabolism; in other words, we need to tear down the old before we can build the new. Neither death, nor destruction, nor even extinction is evil. As Proudhon noted, "All progress begins by abolishing something; every reform rests upon denunciation of some abuse; each new idea is based upon the proved insufficiency of the old idea."[724]

Life span is just another evolutionary adaptation. If a mouse were built to live as long as a man, it would not—it would get killed. So rather than making a mouse that can live to eighty, nature had the little rodents take the energy needed to repair ageing cells and invest it in food gathering and reproduction. Evolution clearly did not care to guarantee a long life to any species. Instead, this grand architect only made sure that the members of the species would reach sexual maturity. Our bodies were not designed for long-term use. We drag on with a living machine, even though its warranty expired years ago. Aged organs wear out; they experience malfunctions, just like any old gadget. We would die even if science conquered all diseases: "Health is merely the slowest possible rate at which one can die."

Modern biology explains that the mortality of all creatures is due to a built-in degeneration program. In fact, only cancer cells never die. Most normal, healthy cells stop growing after they have divided about 50 times, but cancer cells are immortal, capable of dividing and growing forever. When Henrietta Lacks died of cervical cancer in 1951, a researcher harvested cells from her tumour; subsequently christened HeLa cells, they are now studied in petri dishes all over the world, dividing as vigorously as ever. There are two ways in which any cell dies: it is either killed by injurious agents—such as the toxins used in chemotherapy—or it commits suicide, through a natural process known as *apoptosis*, or programmed cell death. The latter is essential to a healthy immune system, and its impairment is associated with autoimmune disorders.

Discovered in 1961 by Leonard Hayflick, the limit to which normal cells can divide is known as the "Hayflick limit." Cancer is by and large a disease of ageing, whether its ultimate cause is random internal damage or cigarette smoke. It comes about when a cell accumulates so many harmful mutations, or "genetic lesions," that the cell eludes the body's intricate control mechanism, allowing it to grow wildly. Until now, the group of cells that forms a human being has been able to survive for no more than 120 years. The Old Testament notwithstanding, this upper limit has remained unchanged throughout history. The longest-lived person in the world was the Frenchwoman Jeanne Calment, who died at the age of 122 in 1997.

In the future, the rise in life expectancy will be measured in days or months, not years. When the life expectancy is at 50 years, it rises by a year if the mortality rate is reduced by 4.1 percent. But in order to raise it by a year from 80 requires a reduction of 9.1% in mortality. Moreover, the whole concept is no longer a reliable measure of national health in today's ageing countries. In the West, life expectancy can now be lifted further only by extending the lives of those over 70. In the younger age groups, the mortality rates are already quite low. There is a new, better measure that is known as "health-adjusted life expectancy," or HALE. It has shown us that age-related

724. *The Principle of Authority*. 1923, 101.

disabilities strike at the same time in both sexes—women are merely willing to bear their illness longer. Should a man live to be ninety, he will likely be in better health than women of the same age. Four-fifths of 90-year olds are women, but the few men are by every measure in better condition than the women.[725]

Breast and prostate cancer rates have doubled around the globe over the last three decades, and much of the growth is due to more people living longer. In Africa, only 7% of deaths are due to cancer, compared to 23% in Europe. People tend to blame air pollution and the Western way of life, but if you eliminate the age factor, cancer has not increased in the West at all.[726] Cancer is one of five age-related diseases that accounts for the vast majority of deaths for persons aged 50 to 85. The other four are diabetes, Alzheimer's, stroke, and heart disease.

Unlike other tissue, the heart muscle does not regenerate, and diabetes increases the risk of a stroke, but how is it possible that 30% of Americans are apparently born with a specific mutation that predisposes them to Alzheimer's? At the beginning of the 20th century, the average life span in the United States was 49; now it is 77. Genetic variations that used to be inert or innocuous make a great difference when people start living past 60. Natural selection could not eliminate these variants simply because humans did not use to live long enough to get these diseases. For the first time, we have extended our lifespan so much that we have outpaced our genome.[727] Or to put it in simpler terms, we were not designed to live this long, as evidenced by the five major age-related diseases.

Each year, approximately half a million people around the world die of the common cold.[728] This may seem like a large figure, but a lot of people die from various causes every year. If a moribund, demented elderly person dies while battling a cold, the primary cause of death will be flu. This is how the statistics are created. Vaccinating the elderly against influenza is not very effective, since people older than 65 do not respond well to the flu vaccine—or indeed to most other vaccines. Their immune systems are not as efficient at generating antibodies as those of younger people. A 2005 study of three decades of mortality data, reported in the *Archives of Internal Medicine*, indicates that widespread use of vaccines may not have reduced death among the elderly at all. Back in 1989, only 15% of people over the age of 65 were vaccinated against flu in the United States and Canada; today, more than 65% are immunized, yet death rates among the elderly during flu season have increased rather than decreased.[729] Another study in the same journal found vaccination to be highly effective for young people, reducing deaths by 78% and hospitalizations by

---

725. S. Jay Olshansky, et al. "Prospects for Human Longevity," *Science* 291(5508), February 23, 2001, 1491–1492.

726. "CancerStats: Cancer Worldwide," Cancer Research UK, London, September 2011.

727. Tanzi & Parson 2000.

728. Mark Schoofs, "How Genetics Is Changing Our Lives," *Village Voice*, September 30–December 30, 1997.

729. Lone Simonsen, et al. "Impact of Influenza Vaccination on Seasonal Mortality in the US Elderly Population," 165(3), February 14, 2005, 265–272.

87%.[730] Indeed, the most effective way to protect the elderly is to give the vaccine to the people who work around them and to school-aged children, the most common carriers of the disease; multiple studies suggest that vaccinating more than 70% of school children would eliminate the need to vaccinate the elderly altogether.[731]

In the past, population growth was mainly and severely checked by plagues and famines—or God as believers were wont to say—factors over which man had no control. Many women stayed unmarried, many others were barren due to disease or difficult births. When the great epidemics and hard years of famine ended during the 18th century and the productivity of labour increased, the population began an unprecedented growth. With the rise of the nation-states during the 17th and 18th centuries, governments started paying more and more attention to the population. It became a part of the national reserve as it were. It was important to have a lot of population, the idea being that a bigger population equalled a larger labour force and also a more powerful military. All the great demagogues of our age appear to be greatly worried about the health of their subjects, and none more so than Adolf Hitler. His racist rhetoric was the last word in "biological" demagoguery; it was very effective in terms of political results due to its emphasis on health and virility. According to a 1943 committee report on health insurance to the Canadian House of Commons, "During the early years of Hitler's regime, the government's medical program was looked upon by many observers as one of the greatest props of the totalitarian state."[732] Surprise, surprise: when the State declares its concern for your health, it is not concerned about you, but about your contribution to the common good. Certainly, a healthy worker is a better worker, and a more efficient worker. The European marriage pattern, characterized as it was by late marriage, few children, and many single people, served the Western form of economy well.

During the last three decades, the average number of children per woman has decreased from six to three, but the poorest fifth still give birth to about twice as many children as the richest fifth. In the same period, economic growth has been most marked in those developing countries where the rates of birth have been the lowest.[733] Although the proportion of hungry people in the world is shrinking, overall population increase means the actual number continues to climb. And though the proportion of people living in poverty is continuing to fall, the absolute number keeps on rising, because their fertility rates far outstrip the efforts of the international community to improve their lives. To put it bluntly, six billion people inevitably translates to 800 million starving.

The results of the United Nations' long campaign against famine and for the improvement of economic conditions in the poor countries are slim at best. All food aid does is to put local farmers out of work by making food too cheap to compete

---

730. Eelko Hak, et al. "Clinical Effectiveness of Influenza Vaccination in Persons Younger Than 65 Years With High-Risk Medical Conditions: The PRISMA Study," Ibid. 274–280.

731. Gilbert Ross, "Vaccinate Schoolchildren to Reduce Influenza Toll," *Archives of Internal Medicine* 165(17), September 26, 2005, 2038.

732. Heagerty, et al. 1943, 108.

733. United Nations Fund for Population Activities, op. cit.

with. The worst results are found in regions where foreign aid has enabled the population to stay put and have more children. The extra food has made the increase of family size possible, and thereby only perpetuated both overpopulation and poverty. Ethiopia, for example, has doubled its population since Live Aid, but is no richer. While celebrity do-gooders like Bob Geldof repeat the familiar refrain, "if aid efforts are not producing the desired result, then redouble those efforts," many experts conclude that even a complete discontinuation of aid would yield better results. Food aid should only be given in emergencies, i.e. in situations when people would otherwise go hungry.

But are high infant mortality rates the result or cause of children's lives being less valuable? Global under-one mortality has dropped roughly a third from the figures in 1960, while the under-five death rate has declined by almost two-thirds. Ninety-nine percent of the unnecessary deaths occur in poor or middle-income nations, mostly in sub-Saharan Africa and South Asia. One woman dies every minute due to complications from pregnancy or from birth, which amounts to the population of Charleston, Portland, or Des Moines, every year.[734] No new inventions are needed to save the mothers and the babies: infants die from diarrhea, measles, malaria, and pneumonia; mothers from unsafe abortions, high blood pressure, infections, and bleeding. According to a recent report by the United Nations Population Fund, donors of development aid would do well to invest in health care and family planning services for the poor women of the world.[735]

Ultimately, the most important mechanism regulating the number of children is the length of the time between fertile age and menopause. The menarche, or the onset age of menstruation, is a measure of societal well-being. The higher the standard of living and the better nourished the population, the earlier girls have their first periods. In the hundred years between 1850 and 1950, the onset of periods in the West was pushed forward by three years; since then, the average age at first menstruation has fallen little, if at all.[736] Before industrialization, few women lived old enough to reach menopause. In the early modern era, the average European woman gave birth to her last baby at the age of 40.

When the fertile age is over, the strict regularity in human biology wanes. From an evolutionary standpoint, the exact order of ageing is of no consequence. The early human communities had next to no old people—ageing is a result of social development. By analyzing how much people are willing to pay for various life-extending precautions, health economists have concluded that modern society values an extra year of life at about $75,000. According to a Harvard study, American oncologists are perfectly willing to prescribe medications costing more than $300,000 for every extra year.[737] At the same time, the cost of treating dementia in the 5-million nation of Finland stood at 3.4 billion euros annually, accounting for nearly a

734. World Health Organization 2005.

735. United Nations Fund for Population Activities, op. cit.

736. Paul Kaplowitz, "Pubertal Development in Girls: Secular Trends," *Current Opinion in Obstetrics and Gynecology* 18(5), October 2006, 487–491.

737. Eric Nadler, at al. "Do Oncologists Believe New Cancer Drugs Offer Good Value?" *The Oncologist* 11(2), February 2006, 90–95.

fourth of all health care spending.[738] On a global scale, the costs associated with dementia amount to more than one percent of the world's gross domestic product. The *World Alzheimer Report 2010* concluded that dementia poses the most significant health and social crisis of the century as its global financial burden continues to escalate.[739]

Only two generations ago, cancer was a death sentence, an ailment that dare not speak its name. The same was true for AIDS a generation ago. Today, the number of people living with HIV is rising across the globe, though the rate of new infections is decreasing in only a few countries.[740] There has been an overall devaluation of terms like tragedy and catastrophe: no civilization got wiped out by the Asian Tsunami. When the Bible tells people to "multiply and replenish the earth,"[741] the inevitable consequence is a spiralling death toll in all natural disasters. Modern New Orleans suffered more damage than was ever done to old New Orleans because the wetlands that used to absorb storm surges were drained for human habitation.

There has also been a similar devaluation of "heroism" in our society. Good soldiers live, not die; as Gen. George S. Patton put it, "No poor bastard ever won a war by dying for his country. He won it by making other bastards die for their country."[742] Thanks to modern medicine, most wounded soldiers no longer die, but are crippled for life. Only 10% of American soldiers injured in Iraq have died from their wounds, the lowest casualty rate ever. By contrast, a fourth of those wounded in Vietnam or in the first Gulf War did not survive. However, half of those wounded in Iraq have been unable to return to duty, spawning a generation of severely disabled young veterans with such injuries as lost limbs and sight.[743] By almost every measure, returning vets are in worse shape from Bush and Obama's wars (sorry, "Overseas Contingency Operations") than perhaps vets of any U.S. war since 1865.

Whereas 5% of the victims of civilian violence perished in the past, now the figure is less than 2%. According to Prof. Anthony Harris of UMass Amherst, people who would have ended up in the morgue twenty years ago are today treated in hospitals and often discharged in just a few days. There have been vast advances in emergency care, and these days a victim of violence can be quickly stabilized. Also, more hospitals and emergency rooms have been built. Without these preventive steps, 45,000 to 70,000 Americans would die from violent crime each year instead of the current number of 15,000, say Harvard researchers.[744]

---

738. "Health Expenditure and Financing 2009," National Institute of Health and Welfare, Helsinki, April 5, 2011.

739. Anders Wimo & Martin Prince, "World Alzheimer Report 2010: The Global Economic Impact of Dementia," Alzheimer's Disease International, London, September 21, 2010.

740. Joint United Nations Programme on HIV/AIDS 2010.

741. Genesis 1:28, 9:1.

742. *Patton*. Dir. Franklin J. Schaffner. Twentieth Century Fox, 1970.

743. Atul Gawande, "Casualties of War: Military Care for the Wounded from Iraq and Afghanistan," *New England Journal of Medicine* 351(24), December 9, 2004, 2471–2475.

744. Anthony R. Harris, et al. "Murder and Medicine: The Lethality of Criminal Assault 1960–1999," *Homicide Studies* 6(2), May 2002, 128–166.

This has profound implications also for organized religion: in past centuries, a sick pope either recovered or died quickly, and the tradition throughout the centuries has been for popes to die in office, rather than retire. With all the advances in medical science, the Catholic Church faces the situation where the pope becomes very sick and unable to function, but remains in power; he might fall into a coma, or even become mentally unbalanced, but he will still be formally in charge—his office is for life. The fact that there is no procedure for dealing with a pope who has become incapacitated could cause the next major constitutional crisis in the Church, since modern medical technology can keep a person alive well beyond the point of functioning.

Some countries practise coercive treatment, but the Utilitarian philosopher John Stuart Mill defended the right of adult individuals to hurt themselves if its does not injure others. Secularized society is unequipped to criticize the decision by an octogenarian to start using hard drugs. If no-one believes in life after death any more, why could a person with nothing to lose not inject himself with a daily dose of euphoria? We need not worry about setting a bad example to the youth, for no modern teenager will take cue from a geriatric grandfather. Besides, the use of heavy narcotics by the terminally ill is already a reality in hospitals around the world.

But when does life begin, and when does it end? Individual organs are living things, as are cells and parasites; a decomposing organism has a wealth of life running through it. Menstruation is the human female body's way of disposing of live unfertilized eggs. According to the narrowest definition, a human being is a human being immediately after conception. However, Monty Python sang in *The Meaning of Life* that "Every sperm is sacred, every sperm is good,"[745] and this is still the view of many Christian denominations. Others conclude that even a week-old embryo is not human, but just a cluster of cells. It has about 150 of them, while an adult human has trillions of cells. According to one definition, the embryo becomes human only after it has developed a nervous system.

Even then, foetuses cannot feel pain until the last few weeks of a pregnancy. Pain requires the conscious recognition of an unpleasant stimulus, which cannot happen until the brain structures connecting the thalamus and the cerebral cortex develop during the third trimester of pregnancy. A review of medical evidence published in the *Journal of the American Medical Association* in 2005 shows that these connections are not generally apparent until the 23rd week and may not begin to be made until the 30th. What is more, it takes several additional weeks for the brain circuitry of a foetus to start functioning in such a way that allows pain signals to reach the brain.[746]

Stem-cells are the "first" cells of a human embryo. They transform into the approximately 250 different cell types of an adult human during embryogenesis, fashioning the liver, muscular system, bone structure, teeth, the brain, and so on. There are three different types of stem-cells: the ones adults produce in their bone marrow are not as versatile as those of the embryo; the umbilical cord also yields

---

745. Dir. Terry Jones. Universal Pictures, 1983.

746. Susan J. Lee, et al. "Fetal Pain: A Systematic Multidisciplinary Review of the Evidence," *JAMA* 294(8), August 24/31, 2005, 947–954.

stems-cells, but they are more difficult to harvest that those from a week-old blastula. Describing the destruction of a blastocyst as the dismembering of a human being conjures propagandistically expedient images of a grisly procedure in which unborn babies are torn apart. However, it is hard to dismember something that has no limbs—a cluster of a couple of hundred non-differentiated cells.

These cells have no consciousness, they are not aware that they exist. Nature herself creates and destroys million of them each year. No-one mourns, no-one objects; in most cases, no-one even knows. But in the anti-abortion circles, this is considered murder. All the world over, millions of legal and illegal abortions are performed when the embryo is several times older. Every fertility clinic routinely creates many test-tube embryos for every human baby that is produced. Some of them are destroyed because a microscopic examination reveals a defect or abnormality; some will be discarded, or frozen for future attempts, or frozen indefinitely—some do not even survive the freezing process. The vast majority will never be needed or used.

Some Catholic theologians encourage married couples to adopt unwanted embryos from fertility clinics—something evangelical Christians dub an "embryo adoption"—while others are vehemently opposed to the idea, calling it a grave violation of the principle that procreation should occur naturally. Not only would embryo adoption make Catholics complicit in test-tube fertilizations, which the Church still considers illicit, but artificially implanting an embryo in a Catholic woman's womb would violate the sacred nature of marital sexuality. At present, there are so few such adoptions that thousands of embryos will simply be discarded if they are not used for research. And even if the practice were to increase a thousandfold, it would not save the embryos that die in other stages of the process. What is more, the recipients of donated embryos themselves usually have to have several implanted in order that one will survive. So ironically, an adoption will result in the deaths of fertilized eggs that would otherwise stay frozen.

Of course, we all start dying before we are even born; "For every change that involves a thing outstepping its own limits," wrote Lucretius, "means the instantaneous death of what previously existed."[747] Contrary to popular belief, death is not a specific moment; it is a process that begins when the heart stops beating, the lungs stop working, and the brain ceases to function. The legal definition of dead still varies in different countries and jurisdictions, but generally brain death is now considered to take precedent over cardiac death. Human life is obviously precious, but what is not so obvious is why it is precious. People who request their physician's help in hastening their deaths cite a decreasing ability to do the things that make life enjoyable, loss of autonomy, and loss of dignity as the reason they wish to stop living. To be clear, everyone dies; there are no life-saving medications, only life-prolonging ones. An elderly person or their family may have to choose, for example, between dialysis and death, or a feeding tube and death. Without a safe, legal way to end their suffering, patients often hoard pills for a much less certain suicide, starve themselves to death, or kill themselves by a violent method. Men over the retirement age commit suicide with greater frequency than either sex in any other demographic group,

---

747. *On the Nature of Things*, Bk. I, 670–671, 792–793, Bk. III, 519–520.

usually with a firearm.[748]

According to a 2009 study published in the *Journal of the American Medical Association*, terminally ill cancer patients who drew comfort from religion were far *more* likely to seek aggressive, life-prolonging care and want doctors to do everything possible to keep them alive than were less religious patients. The devout patients were three times as likely as less religious ones to be put on a mechanical ventilator to maintain breathing during the last week of life, and were less likely to do any advance care planning, such as signing a Comfort Care/Do Not Resuscitate (CC/DNR) order, preparing a living will, or creating a health care proxy.[749] Similarly, a 2003 study conducted by researchers at the Medical University of South Carolina found that cancer patients listed their faith in God as a more influential factor in their decisions about medical care than the recommendations of their doctors, spouses, and children, and even information about whether treatment would cure the disease.[750] Aggressive life-prolonging care comes at a cost, however, in terms of both public money and human suffering: Medicare spends about a third of its budget on people who are in the last year of life, and much of that at the very end.[751]

A century ago, when average life expectancy in the United States was 47, people who fell ill either got better or died quickly. Now that life expectancy is 77, dying has become a difficult and often excruciatingly slow process with most Americans spending at least two years of their lives too disabled to care for themselves without help and the very old looking forward to ten years of chronic illness.[752] All of them may not end up on a feeding tube, but they will almost certainly be hospitalized or in a nursing home. Many are going to be surrounded by strangers and hooked up to machines, even ones who have living wills saying that they wish not to be. Through our own indecision and fear of death, we are continually allowing extreme medical methods to perversely prolong the dying rather than the living of our loved ones. We are constantly bombarded with commercials for personal maladies from incontinence to erectile dysfunction, yet when a family member is diagnosed with a serious illness, we fail to ask how they would like to be treated near the end, for fear of insensitivity or appearing defeatist. Usually the healthy are the only uncomfortable ones, for advance discussion actually tends to afford the dying a sense of control and peace.

With nearly 7,000 Americans dying on an average day, death is the most normal of occurrences next to birth.[753] A dead person does not immediately turn white as a ghost, nor does the body start decomposing rapidly. Provided that measures are taken within the first 6 to 12 hours, a body can lay in state at home for up to three days,

---

748. Arialdi M. Miniño, et al. "Deaths: Preliminary Data for 2008," *National Vital Statistics Reports* 59(2), December 9, 2010.

749. Phelps, op. cit.

750. Gerard A. Silvestri, et al. "Importance of Faith on Medical Decisions Regarding Cancer Care," *Journal of Clinical Oncology* 21(7), April 2003, 1379–1382.

751. Steve Calfo, et al. "Last Year of Life Study," Office of the Actuary, Centers for Medicare & Medicaid Services, Baltimore, MD, 2004.

752. Anne Applebaum, "How We Die: Choice and Chance," *Washington Post*, March 30, 2005.

753. Miniño, et al. Op. cit.

maybe longer. It was only during the Civil War that formaldehyde as an embalming agent was first used and non-family members were paid to undertake the job of transporting the bodies of soldiers killed far from home. Being present for the transition from life to death, feeling the body lose its warmth, seeing the tension leave the face, helps us accept that the person is really gone. This way, there is no escaping, no pretending it did not happen or getting busy doing something else.

We think we are not emotionally or even physically capable of carrying this out, yet it was only a hundred years ago that we started routinely handing over our dead to the undertakers. Soon after, the terminally ill, too, were deemed too frightening, and moved from our homes to die in hospitals. In a few decades, what had for countless millennia been familial responsibilities were appropriated by a multi-billion dollar industry. Dying in the U.S. now involves Blue Cross, health care delivery systems, the Centers for Medicare & Medicaid Services (CMS), terminal patient wards, undertakers, cemeteries, and large formal funerals. And this modern "death-denying tradition" is not just costly but detrimental to body and spirit, not to mention the environment and communities.

Half of modern burial expenses are made up of things people falsely think are required by law, like caskets and embalming fluid. Shroud burials are not only a part of the Jewish tradition, but the way most cultures buried their dead until the late 19th century. Nor does embalming fluid serve any purpose, but is an extremely toxic substance to which no-one should be exposed, and which certainly should not be put in the ground. It is like we are trying to protect the corpse from a direct nuclear attack, but to what end? Nature's original plan was that we fall down somewhere in a field and become soil, but apparently we do not wish our bodies to be violated by natural processes. As a bizarre remnant of ancestral worship, we erect monuments to our deceased relatives whom we then visit as if they were not really dead, unable to let go. What ever happened to "rest in peace"?

Starting from the early 1980s, medical professionals have gained a lot of say in the day-to-day lives of ordinary people. The behaviour of individuals was medicalized, and medicine suddenly had a say and a role in everything. What was new in the '90s is that people medicalized themselves: looking after one's own health became a trend and there can be no fashionable health before it is created. Yet the best "medicine" may be inexpensive low-tech measures such as small modifications in diet or exercise patterns, or indeed, simply waiting and giving the body's own healing mechanisms a chance to find equilibrium. Instead, people spend billions of dollars and countless hours on health and beauty "care"—and reveal their veiled despair and helplessness in the process.

"Non-toxic," "natural," and "fragrance free" are particularly misleading claims, because governments have never set a precise standard for personal care products to meet. Yet the only active ingredient in any moisturizer is urea, the chief solid component of mammalian urine, not vitamin E or some other healthy-sounding additive. Similarly, almost every perfume contains a substance called "musk," otherwise known as the odour of feces, the only scent proven to be sexually appealing to primates. A generation or two of Western children were taught to brush their teeth too hard and it turns out flouride is a nerve toxin with no salutary effect on dental health. All shampoos rob hair of body, and hair, being dead tissue, has no use for vitamins or proteins. The wealth of minerals in bottled water is not necessarily beneficial, nor can distilled water, with no impurities at all, be considered any healthier, since humans do need a trace amount of minerals, such as found in plain tap water. In its favour, bottled water is not subject to contamination from lead in residential pipes, but it may contain chemicals that leach out of plastic bottles, often made of polyethylene terephthalate (PET) which can cause birth defects and hormone abnormalities.

We should drink when we are thirsty, but the prescription to drink several litres of water a day is just plain silly: much like our bodies, most solid foods are over 50% water—drinking excessive amounts of water will only flush salt out of your body, which can actually kill you. Everyone assumes that caffeinated beverages dehydrate, but even if you had a really strong cup of coffee, which is actually quite hard to make, you would still have a net gain of fluid. Americans now drink more bottled water than any other commercial beverage apart from carbonated soft drinks—more than milk, more than coffee, more even than beer.[754] And this despite the fact that, priced by the gallon, the water in those single-serve bottles is more expensive than today's high-priced gasoline. In a triumph of marketing by powerful beverage companies like Coca-Cola and Nestlé, people are being sold a ubiquitous commodity that they can easily and safely obtain from their faucets.

When nothing in this world seems controllable, people figure they can at least control what they put in their mouths. Ask anyone these days about food and no matter what their gastronomic predilections are, they will likely speak of them with a fervour bordering on religiosity. But how can anyone, and especially someone interested in their so-called spiritual growth, be so self-centred in a world where people die of hunger and thirst every day? To the average Westerner, food no longer means nourishment, our deepest bond with the communion of life, after air, water, and heat. It has transformed into one of the instruments of our imagined life management. I can imagine knowing the separate facts about human anatomy and physiology by heart, but to think that one could comprehend the totality of the parts and functions of the organism is just as absurd as to think that one could comprehend the universe.

All ascetic religions of the past have considered some foods polluted while others are permitted, and one of the newest additions to disorder classification is *orthorexia* —the compulsion to "eat right." The vastly influential 2nd-century physician Galen believed that all bodily ailments could be righted by balancing bodily humours with the rights foods, blood-letting, and herbs. Hitler and the Nazis promoted this idea, with the SS farms at Dachau being billed as the "largest research institute for natural herbs and medicines in Europe."[755] Such is also the function, if not the stated purpose, of the modern focus on finding and popularizing perfect dietary content. Knowledge about the content and effect of foods has increased exponentially in the last two decades, and no-one is any longer able to memorize the list of beneficial and harmful

754. "2007 HOD & Filtered Water Market in the U.S.," Beverage Marketing Corporation, New York, November 2007.

755. Proctor 1988, 250.

substances. It is difficult to choose what to eat when the information we have is often contradictory and the experts disagree with each other.

Meanwhile, the creation of government dietary guidelines remains political from start to finish. The first federal nutrition pamphlets came out in the United States at the beginning of the 20th century, courtesy of the Department of Agriculture, and were aimed more to promote the agricultural industry than to educate citizens about food. At the time, the main concern was poverty and malnutrition; today, the national Centers for Disease Control and Prevention counts that two-thirds of Americans are overweight, and half of those obese. A century ago, the best advice the government could give was to eat widely and plentifully, but the message has changed through the years.[756] Because food choices influence and are influenced by economic, social, and political institutions, it is difficult to alter individual dietary behaviour without also changing the economic, social, and political environment within which individuals make food choices.

The food groups numbered five in 1917, twelve during the Great Depression, seven, eight, or eleven during World War II—depending on which pamphlet you consulted—and four in the '50s. By the '60s, both the economic and the medical landscape had thoroughly changed: Americans were not only living longer, but increasingly contracting chronic diseases like cancer and heart conditions. Consequently, the message gradually shifted to eating less, be it fat, sugar, salt, red meat, or eggs.[757] This is when the trouble started: after a Senate committee report suggested that citizens should cut back on saturated fats, sugar, cholesterol, and salt, the influential cattle, dairy, egg, and sugar industries launched a protest. Needless to say, the report was revised, with the phrase "reduce consumption of meat," for example, being replaced with a vague "choose meats, poultry and fish which will reduce saturated fat intake."[758]

As a result, the average American eats about 90 lbs. of chicken a year, more than twice as much as in the '70s, but roughly a third of the fresh chicken sold in the United States is "plumped" with water, salt, and sometimes a vaseline-like food additive called carrageenan that helps it retain the added water. The USDA says chicken processed this way can still be labelled "all natural" or "100% natural," because those are all natural ingredients, even if they are not naturally found in chicken.[759] Meanwhile, confined feeding operations of both chicken and pork overburden the ability of land and water to absorb the waste products. Overfishing has already led more than 75% of the world's fisheries near the point of collapse, meaning not only that entire species are in danger of extinction, but also that food for much of the world's population may vanish unless people eat less fish. The proposed solution to this problem is fish farming, which creates water pollution, spreads marine diseases, and—ironically—requires catching large numbers of wild fish to use as

756. Rosie Mestel, "Nibbling at the Pyramid," *Los Angeles Times*, March 22, 2005.

757. Ibid.

758. As quoted in Nestle 2007, 42.

759. Melinda Beck, "The Fine Print: What's Really in a Lot of 'Healthy' Foods," *Wall Street Journal*, May 5, 2009.

feed.[760]

Thanks to USDA policies, the U.S. food supply provides a whopping 4,000 kcal per day for every man, woman, and child in the nation. Although this level is nearly twice the amount needed to meet average energy requirements, Congress continues to subsidize the production of commodity crops such as maize, wheat, and soya. This promotes the production of processed foods made with subsidized ingredients, e.g. corn sweeteners, wheat starch, soy oils. Subsidized maize and soy are also fed to farm animals and reduce the cost of meat, encouraging people to eat more.[761] Americans have been scolded for eating too much fat and salt for decades, and as a result, they have switched to margarines and other diet products. Yet cardiovascular diseases have not been reduced, because the real reason for their prevalence is the calcium contained in milk.[762] The U.S. is the world's largest consumer of dairy products—the USDA's pyramid recommends drinking three glasses of milk per day.[763] Celebrities, athletes, and even the Clinton administration's head of Health and Human Services, Donna Shalala, proudly wear the white "milk moustache." However, most scientists agree that it is better for us to get calcium, potassium, protein, and fats from other food sources like vegetables, fruits, beans, whole grains, nuts, seeds, and seaweed.

Even as America fattens up, no-one is ever instructed to eat less of any specifically identified foodstuff, including candy bars or soft drinks. Americans get a fifth of their daily calorie intake in a liquid form, and nearly half of all public schools in the country have exclusive contracts with beverage companies, who supply the students with overpriced sugared water.[764] Is it any wonder that the number of overweight children in the U.S. has nearly tripled in the past two decades? Public health experts have been very concerned about the soda issue of late, and the National Dairy Council spends $100 million a year to promote the idea that milk can help people lose weight. However, a nationwide study of 12,000 children found that replacing soda with milk yielded no benefit. In fact, those who drank more than three 8 oz. servings of milk a day over a one-year period gained more weight than subjects in any other group. Drinking low-fat milk interestingly made no difference in the result, and the research took into consideration factors such as physical activity, growth, and other dietary habits.[765]

It is impossible for anyone to know for certain what they should eat to remain

---

760. "State of World Fisheries and Aquaculture 2006," Food and Agriculture Organization of the United Nations, Rome, 2007.

761. Pablo Monsivais & Adam Drewnowski, "The Rising Cost of Low-Energy-Density Foods," *Journal of the American Dietetic Association* 107(12), December 2007, 2071–2076.

762. D. Feskanich, et al. "Milk, Dietary Calcium, and Bone Fractures in Women: A 12-Year Prospective Study," *American Journal of Public Health* 87(6), June 1997, 992–997.

763. "Dietary Guidelines for Americans 2005," U.S. Department of Health and Human Services & U.S. Department of Agriculture, Washington, D.C., January 2005.

764. Kiyah J. Duffey & Barry M. Popkin, "Shifts in Patterns and Consumption of Beverages Between 1965 and 2002," *Obesity* 15(11), November 2007, 2739–2747.

765. Catherine S. Berkey, et al. "Milk, Dairy Fat, Dietary Calcium, and Weight Gain: A Longitudinal Study of Adolescents," *Archives of Pediatrics & Adolescent Medicine* 159(6), June 2005, 543–550.

youthful and healthy forever, but common sense suggests that if you feed your children cow's milk, meant for calves to put on three tons of weight, they are going to get fat. On the other hand, there is no better sports drink than whole milk—GatorAde® claims notwithstanding; why do you think protein shakes are supposed to be mixed in milk, otherwise know as "liquid meat"? In the prosperous West, the relationship to food has changed rapidly and reflects the brutalization of our commercial culture. Big Money somewhere out there increasingly decides what the little people put in their mouths: "Early don't eat breakfast. He thinks it's a conspiracy put together by the cereal people."[766] Television has taught us to think that breakfast is the most important meal of the day, even though the metabolic system, which slows down when we sleep, does not speed up until long after we wake up. The USDA guidelines from the early '90s promoting the daily consumption of 6 to 11 servings of bread and cereal led to the pasta, carbohydrate, and sugar generation and the largest epidemic of obesity in the history of our species.[767]

A drink of milk was off the menu for Europeans until only a few thousand years ago. Analysis of Neolithic remains suggests no European adults could digest the drink at that time. The genetic mutation that allowed the digestion of milk arose at some point after dairy farming began. For most mammals, the normal condition is to stop producing the enzymes needed to properly digest and metabolize milk after they have been weaned. The majority of humans naturally stop producing significant amounts of lactase, the enzyme needed to break down the lactose in milk, sometime between the ages of two and five. Lactose, a milk sugar, is made up of two sugars, glucose and galactose; the latter has been identified as a causative factor in heart disease, cataracts, and glaucoma. Since most adult humans "lack" the lactase enzyme, lactose is broken down by bacteria in their lower intestines instead—their own body wastes combine with those sugars to ferment into toxins causing bloating, stomach cramps, and diarrhoea. Today, more than 90% of people of northern European origin have the gene that produces lactase, but intolerance to milk remains common in modern times. "Lactase deficiency" affects about 5% of white Britons, and a larger portion of those from some ethnic minorities. In some part of the world, such as Asia and Africa, the vast majority of people are lactose intolerant to some degree. All in all, about 75% of the world's population is genetically unable to properly digest milk and other dairy products.[768]

As early as the 1930s, the U.S. government began requiring dairy producers to fortify milk with vitamin D, a substance that promotes the absorption of the milk's calcium and which our skins synthesize naturally when exposed to the sun. Since then, the assumption has been that the citizens are getting all the vitamin D they need, but recent studies have shown most Americans to actually be undernourished in the "sunshine vitamin." It is not found naturally in any food, and it is difficult to

---

766. *Kalifornia*. Dir. Dominic Sena. PolyGram Filmed Entertainment, 1993.

767. Mark Hyman, "Dairy: 6 Reasons You Should Avoid It at All Costs or Why Following the USDA Food Pyramid Guidelines Is Bad for Your Health," *Huffington Post*, May 1, 2010.

768. P. M. Brannon, et al. "NIH Consensus Development Conference Statement: Lactose Intolerance and Health," *NIH Consensus and State-of-the-Science Statements* 27(2), February 2010, 1–27.

get enough of it from fortified milk alone, nor do supplements help much. Most multivitamins contain the nutrient in an old form, D-2, which is far less potent that D-3, and they usually also contain vitamin A, which offsets the benefits of D. Calcium and vitamin D are needed in the constant remodelling our bones go through, and were long recommended for post-menopausal women as a way to fend off osteoporosis. However, American women have been consuming an average of two pounds of milk a day for their entire lives, yet 30 million of them have osteoporosis. Drinking milk obviously does not prevent bone loss: countries with the highest rates of osteoporosis, such as the United States, Britain, and Sweden, consume the most milk; China and Japan, where people digest much less calcium and dairy food, have low rates of osteoporosis.[769] The Women's Health Initiative, a 15-year American study, also found that taking supplements did nothing to decrease hip fractures in the elderly.[770] The fact is, with age, bone breakdown eventually exceeds formation, resulting inevitably in bone loss.

Osteoporosis is not caused by the lack of calcium in diet, but by the loss of calcium in bones. It is a metabolic disturbance, not a mineral deficiency. Osteoporosis is caused when the skeletal structure cannot renew itself due to the lack of protein. Bone is formed by erecting a protein frame first, which the minerals then harden. A high carbohydrate, sugar-laden diet inhibits the secretion of growth hormones, which are essential to bone health. Unfortunately, the ageing population has been brainwashed into eating margarines and nutrient-free refined carbohydrates. Meanwhile, the diagnostic criteria for osteoporosis are left purposely vague in order to get as many people as possible into medical treatment. Bisphosphonates will soon be prescribed to anyone anywhere near the risk group. The European Medicines Agency, responsible for the scientific evaluation of medicines developed by pharmaceutical companies for use in the EU, called attention to the negative side effects of the osteoporosis drugs as early as 2005.[771] In North America, nearly 5% of femur fractures are deemed a result of bisphosphonate use, and it is especially alarming that the drug-induced fractures occur in young, working-age people.[772] In reality, osteoporosis causes much fewer problems than the hype would suggest. Usually, it progresses slowly without symptoms and very few patients experience pain. Even though inexperienced physicians tend to label every ache an elderly patient complains about as osteoporosis, the disease is really quite inconspicuous.

Our bodies make vitamin D from sun's ultraviolet B waves, but unfortunately sunscreen blocks its production. Dermatologists and health agencies have long preached that such lotions are needed to prevent skin cancer from UVA exposure, but most sunscreens only protect against the shorter-wave UVB radiation, which merely causes sunburns. At the same time, several unrelated studies have found that vitamin

---

769. Ji-Fan Hu, et al. "Dietary Calcium and Bone Density Among Middle-Aged and Elderly Women in China," *American Journal of Clinical Nutrition* 58(2), August 1993, 219–227.

770. Rebecca D. Jackson, et al. "Calcium plus Vitamin D Supplementation and the Risk of Fractures," *New England Journal of Medicine* 354(7), February 16, 2006, 669–683.

771. "Fosavance: EPAR," EMA, London, October 21, 2005.

772. Elizabeth Shane, et al. "Atypical Subtrochanteric and Diaphyseal Femoral Fractures," *Journal of Bone and Mineral Research* 25(11), November 2010, 2267–2294.

D protects us against many types of cancer, including, ironically, that of the skin. According to a study published in the *Archives of Internal Medicine*, between 50 and 75 percent of Americans get suboptimal levels of vitamin D. Seven out of every ten American children have low levels.[773] As long as humans lived close to the equator and spent a lot of time outdoors, they were okay; but that is not the case today. Like all primates, man is a tropical animal; but before the 20th century, only poor people were tanned in the West—thus the disparaging terms "farmer's tan" and "redneck." Tanning did not become popular until the early 1920s, when the tanned look became a sign of leisure time, hinting at yacht clubs, lawn tennis, and afternoons by the pool. Much more than being just a matter of fashion, it actually enjoyed an initial boost from the medical establishment. The same establishment that began warning against the hazards of overexposure to the sun by the mid-1940s, and helped launch a large new industry—sunscreen.

However, there is no known nutrient that has such consistent anti-cancer properties as vitamin D. Lab and animal studies have long shown that vitamin D stifles abnormal cell growth, helps cells die when they are supposed to, and curbs formation of blood vessels that feed tumours. More recently, scientists have been uncovering its effects elsewhere, including the production of peptides to fight microbes in the skin, the regulation of blood pressure and insulin levels, and the maintenance of the nervous system. There is not one nutritional supplement that has the power to affect human health as much as vitamin D. This is because vitamin D is not actually a vitamin—it is a hormone that regulates more than 2,000 different genes governing virtually every tissue in the body. It appears to have a positive effect on nearly every chronic disease or the risk of getting one, with ample vitamin D levels putting off prostate cancer, for example, by a couple of years. The skin makes less vitamin D as you age, and cancer is more common the older you get. Black people have more UV-blocking pigment in their skin than Caucasians, and higher rates of cancer. Obese people have lower blood levels of vitamin D, which gets trapped in fat, and high cancer rates. The kidneys of diabetics have trouble converting vitamin D into a form the body can use, and are also prone to cancer. People in Scandinavia and other northern regions of the globe have higher rates of cancer than those who get year-round sunshine.

Taking too many vitamin D supplements can cause a dangerous build-up of calcium in the body, whereas it is almost impossible to overdose on vitamin D from sunshine; once the body has made enough, it will produce no more. However, it is also impossible to give a fixed "safe sun" recommendation, as the amount needed depends on the season, time of day, where you live, your age, your skin colour, and several other factors. While wearing sunscreen with a high SPF factor, sunbathers have been able to stay in the sun for much longer periods without getting the natural warning sign of a red skin. But they have still been exposed to dangerous UVA rays, and in the end, obtained a much higher dose of radiation. The rate of skin cancer is holding steady and the International Agency for Research on Cancer warns consumers not to depend on sunscreen for primary protection from the sun—hats, clothing, and shade

---

773. Adit A. Ginde, et al. "Demographic Differences and Trends of Vitamin D Insufficiency in the US Population, 1988–2004," 169(6), March 23, 2009, 626–632.

are still the most reliable sun protection available.[774] More than one million milder forms of skin cancer occur each year as a result of chronic or prolonged suntanning. Repeated sunburns have also been linked to melanoma, but there is no evidence that moderate sun exposure causes it. Skin can handle a bit of sun every now and then, just like the liver can handle a few shots of alcohol. And even melanoma, the deadliest form of skin cancer, accounts for less than one in 73 cancer deaths in the United States.[775]

In the mid-1990s, every third product was advertised as being low-fat.[776] You could find a low-fat alternative for any food: potato chips, mayonnaise, peanut butter, ice cream, candy bars. However, the brain is made of fat and body cells have saturated fat in them, and now that we have been scared off fat, problems such as allergies and intestinal symptoms have increased. In 2005, a huge new study sponsored by the National Heart Lung and Blood Institute challenged for good the long-held notion that a diet low in fat can cut the risk of cardiovascular disease and cancer. Some 50,000 women took part in the $415 million study, with 20,000 embarked on years of low-fat dieting, and the rest being allowed to eat as they pleased. After an average of eight years, the women on the low-fat diet fared no better than the others in rates of colorectal cancer, heart disease, or stroke.[777]

Today, only one in ten food products has a low-fat label.[778] But perhaps the principal reason for the displacement of non-fat products is their lack of taste. In many products, fat had been replaced with various substitutes and sugar to preserve flavour, yet consumers still missed the taste of real fat. And even though the taste did not meet their expectations, dieters received no compensation for their sacrifice: most diets yielded no results, because the fat had been replaced with sugar, which meant that the products still packed a huge amount of calories. If you were not careful, you might get 15 teaspoons worth of sugar with one cup of fat free yoghurt. When people started to get their calories from carbohydrates, which do not satisfy like fat, they began to overeat. Between 1970 and 2005, consumption of added sugars in the typical American diet increased by 19% to a total of 140 lbs. per year.[779] Many dieters also thought that they could eat as many low-fat cookies as they wanted without gaining any weight. The trouble is, marketers use a complicated terminology, while people want black-and-white answers. "Light" or "diet" is not the same thing as low-calorie

---

774. "IARC Handbooks on Cancer Prevention, Volume 5: Sunscreens," IARC Working Group on the Evaluation of Cancer Preventive Agents, Lyon, 2001.

775. Marilynn Marchione, "Scientists Say Sunshine May Prevent Cancer," Associated Press, May 21, 2005.

776. Bruce Horovitz, "Low-Fat Industry Loses Out as Consumers Favor Flavor," *USA Today*, October 15, 2001.

777. Shirley A. A. Beresford, et al. "Low-Fat Dietary Pattern and Risk of Colorectal Cancer," *JAMA* 295(6), February 8, 2006, 643–654; Barbara V. Howard, et al. "Low-Fat Dietary Pattern and Risk of Cardiovascular Disease," Ibid. 655–666.

778. Horovitz, op. cit.

779. Rachel K. Johnson, et al. "Dietary Sugars Intake and Cardiovascular Health: A Scientific Statement from the American Heart Association," *Circulation* 120(11), September 15, 2009, 1011–1020.

or low-fat; what is more, common wood alcohol-based sweeteners like aspartame strain the liver, the organ responsible for fat burning, actually causing more fat to be stored by the body than usual.

Studies also show that drinking an artificially sweetened beverage can whet the appetite and cause people to eat more in a subsequent meal—an effect a sugared beverage or glass of water does not have.[780] This suggests that artificial sweeteners may stimulate brain areas that create appetite, but not those that provide satiation, thus triggering people to eat a bigger lunch. The mere taste of sugar is shown to improve endurance in athletes who have fasted for several hours: when cyclists rinsed their mouth with sugared water, but did not swallow any, the apparent promise that sugar will soon reach the bloodstream provoked their brains to drive their legs harder; tasting artificial sweeteners did not improve cycling speed, even though they tasted sweet.[781] Both sugar and non-caloric sweeteners activated a brain region called the amygdala, which signals sensory pleasure, but only the sugared drink turned on a cherry-sized nugget of brain tissue in a region called the caudate. That little nugget, the study concluded, seemed to represent an unconscious perception of calories, which appears to be assessed quite separately from the sweet taste.[782] Like many other mammals, humans are hooked on sugar because it is packed with energy and our bodies have evolved ways of encouraging us to consume more of it.

Calorie-only messages may compel people to choose smaller portions of less nutritious food; and in general, less nutritious foods encourage overeating, while more nutritious foods fill us up on fewer calories. The average American gets 10% of their calories from fructose.[783] Sweeter than cane sugars, fructose was once thought to be a possible diabetic-friendly sweetener, because it did not cause spikes in blood sugar. The rub is that fructose-sweetened foods tend to have adverse effects on lipids like cholesterol and triglycerides.[784] There is no glycogenic intermediate as with glucose: if you fail to burn the calories immediately, fructose is directly stored as fat along with the biosynthesis of LDL cholesterol as a transport medium. According to a study of more than 6,000 adults by Emory University and the CDC, people who received at least 25% of their daily calories from any type of sweetener had more than triple the

---

780. Richard D. Mattes & Barry M. Popkin, "Nonnutritive Sweetener Consumption in Humans: Effects on Appetite and Food Intake and Their Putative Mechanisms," *American Journal of Clinical Nutrition* 89(1), January 2009, 1–14.

781. E. S. Chambers, et al. "Carbohydrate Sensing in the Human Mouth: Effects on Exercise Performance and Brain Activity," *The Journal of Physiology* 587(8), April 15, 2009, 1779–1794.

782. P. A. M. Smeets, et al. "Functional Magnetic Resonance Imaging of Human Hypothalamic Responses to Sweet Taste and Calories," *American Journal of Clinical Nutrition* 82(5), November 2005, 1011–1016.

783. Miriam B. Vos, et al. "Dietary Fructose Consumption Among US Children and Adults: The Third National Health and Nutrition Examination Survey," *Medscape Journal of Medicine* 10(7), 2008, 160.

784. J. E. Swanson, et al. "Metabolic Effects of Dietary Fructose in Healthy Subjects," *American Journal of Clinical Nutrition* 55(4), April 1992, 851–856.

normal risk of having low HDL levels than those with a portion of less than 5%.[785] The best way to address your cholesterol is not necessarily a low-fat diet, but a low glycemic load diet, which keeps your blood sugar even. Wholesome, highly nutritious foods are often high in calories, but they tend to induce a lasting feeling of fullness that helps control total calorie intake in the end.

The introduction of cheap and abundant high-fructose corn syrup to a wide variety of foods and beverages in the early '70s coincides with the rise of obesity levels in the United States, casting suspicion on the sweetener as a possible cause of the national weight gain. The country's huge agricultural subsidies make prices for corn products such as HFCS artificially low, and as a result, they show up in a dizzying array of processed foods in America. For good or bad, high-fructose corn syrup is considerably cheaper than sugar and has thus become the nation's sweetener of choice.[786] Now, it does not start off as something sweet like cane sugar: corn starch is chemically changed into HFCS-55 by using caustic soda, hydrochloric acid, alpha-amylase, gluco-amylase, isomerase, filter aid, powdered carbon, calcium chloride, and magnesium sulphate—sometimes with mercury added for good measure. In spite of the extensive chemical work involved, federal tax subsidies make this artificially created product cheaper to produce than regular sugar. The average American consumes an obscene amount of added sugar each day—almost 22 teaspoons—driving the "diabesity" epidemic and promising to make this generation of children the first in U.S. history to die sooner than their parents.[787]

Those extra sugar calories are due in part to the addition of high-fructose corn syrup to many foods that were not always sweetened, such as crackers, mustard, peanut butter, and bread. You will be surprised to find HFCS in just about everything: sodas, canned soups, cereals, chips, and most sliced breads; salad dressings, condiments, cakes, and even dried fruits. Fast food does not make you fat only because it has so many calories. According to a recent study, high-sugar foods alter the make-up of the gut flora in such a way that makes weight easier to gain. Bacteria belonging to the Firmicutes phylum seem to increase the tendency to gain weight by breaking down food passing through the intestines more efficiently than the bacteria of the Bacteroidetes phylum.[788] However, it is difficult to blame the obesity incidence on any particular sugar; the best advice is to cut down on sugars of all kinds. The combination of fructose and glucose simultaneously elevates insulin levels while overloading the liver with carbohydrates.[789] Through their direct effect on insulin secretion, and thus the hormonal regulation of homeostasis—the entire harmonic ensemble of the human body—refined carbohydrates, starches, and sugars are the dietary cause of coronary

785. Jean A. Welsh, et al. "Caloric Sweetener Consumption and Dyslipidemia Among US Adults," *JAMA* 303(15), April 21, 2010, 1490–1497.

786. Pollan 2006.

787. Welsh, op. cit.

788. Ruth E. Ley, et al. "Microbial Ecology: Human Gut Microbes Associated with Obesity," *Nature* 444(7122), December 21, 2006, 1022–1023; Peter J. Turnbaugh, et al. "An Obesity-Associated Gut Microbiome with Increased Capacity for Energy Harvest," Ibid. 1027–1031.

789. Robert H. Lustig, "The Fructose Epidemic," *The Bariatrician* 24(1), January–February 2009, 10–18.

disease and diabetes, and the most likely dietary cause of cancer, Alzheimer's disease, and other chronic diseases of modern Western society.[790]

One reason for the recent re-emergence of high-fat foods is the Robert C. Atkins diet, popularized by American celebrities. Its idea is to reduce carbohydrates, i.e. sugars, to a minimum, forcing the body to use the extra fat as fuel. The bankruptcy of Atkins Nutritionals, Inc. in 2005 did nothing to dissuade millions of Americans from high-protein diets rich in meat and cheese and low on carbohydrates from grains, fruits, and vegetables. In order to grow, muscles need protein, but a high-carbohydrate diet causes proteins to be also used as fuel; extra protein does not translate to more muscle any more than dietary fat translates to body fat. If what ultimately matters for weight control is the amount of calories ingested, not whether you get them from proteins, fat, or carbohydrates, then Weight Watchers™ would work. Perhaps one reason the multi-billion dollar weight-loss industry is aimed almost exclusively at women is that it is more difficult for them to shed pounds than men, because women's bodies are simply more efficient at storing fat. If you merely reduce the amount of calories you ingest, your metabolism will soon adjust, opting to store more fat and start using your muscle-tissue as an auxiliary source of energy. Even at rest, muscles require more calories than body fat, so dieting without anaerobic muscle-building exercise is utterly pointless. However, since anaerobic exercise does not burn fat, some aerobic or cardiovascular exercise is also required.

Too much body fat accelerates ageing, by speeding the unravelling of crucial genetic structures inside cells that wither with age. Fat cells churn out a host of substances that can be toxic to the body, and many health problems associated with being overweight appear to result from fat cells hastening the natural ageing process. The more a person weighs, the older his cells are on the molecular level, with obesity adding nine years to a body's age.[791] In fact, an alarming number of obese children around the world are now developing the form of diabetes previously known as "adult-onset" diabetes, because it used to be seen only in adults.[792] Over-consumption of calories has been found more likely to increase the risk of cancer than trace levels of carcinogens in food.[793] The truth is, anything will kill you, or give you cancer, or what not, if consumed in too large quantities—"Nothing to excess" as the Greeks said.

However, the classical notion of dietary moderation has been overwhelmed in the West by three socio-economic forces: the food industry, which has learned to retool its products quickly to use any new dietary guidelines to its benefit; the academic community, which receives grants to research specific foods, avoiding the issue of dietary restraint in the process; and the health media, which would have little to write about were it not for the latest dietary villain. The newest group of problem eaters is formed by health enthusiasts, who spend their days planning their meals and

790. Taubes 2007.

791. A. M. Valdes, et al. "Obesity, Cigarette Smoking, and Telomere Length in Women," *The Lancet* 366(9486), August 20–26, 2005, 662–664.

792. George Alberti, et al. "Type 2 Diabetes in the Young: The Evolving Epidemic," *Diabetes Care* 27(7), July 2004, 1798–1811.

793. Michael S. Donaldson, "Nutrition and Cancer: A Review of the Evidence for an Anti-Cancer Diet," *Nutrition Journal* 3, 2004, 19.

canvassing the supermarkets for everything "organic" and "natural." They cannot eat out, which Americans do about four times a week on the average, because restaurants are thankfully not yet required to post nutritional information about the foods they serve.

The general guidelines to a healthy life apply to the elderly only in part. The dietary guidelines are meant for middle-aged people, who in particular need to avoid obesity, because it will cause serious ailments over the years. An elderly person, however, will not live long enough to develop these ailments. Not only do seniors not need to lose weight, but dieting can cause them more harm: they may start losing muscles and fall into a cycle of debilitation. The production of vitamin D is retarded in the elderly, reducing muscle mass as it is. They should thus attempt to slim down only by increasing exercise. It is even advisable for octogenerians to begin eating more fat, since calorie absorption is reduced by a full fifth between the age of seventy and eighty. Low cholesterol levels in the elderly are often a sign of undernutrition or, indeed, cancer.

In the United States alone, people spend $23 billion on tablets that they think will prevent or cure diseases in a natural way. Millions of Americans eat vitamin tablets every day, because they believe in their health-sustaining power.[794] The scientific community, however, is beginning to worry that the liberal use of vitamins might have the very opposite effect. Vitamins are substances that regular food contains, and their vital significance was uncovered about a century ago. They are essential for a healthy body—we simply cannot exist without them. In the early 20th century, scientists discovered that not all illnesses were caused by pathogens, but by the simple absence of a single substance from our diet, a vitamin; that a vitamin deficiency could cause disease and even death. The disorders known today as deficiency diseases were eradicated simply by ensuring the supply of the relevant vitamins.

Physicians agree that a balanced diet containing fruits, vegetables, grain products, and fats is perfectly adequate to maintain the necessary amount of vitamins. Vitamin A, which affects vision and growth, is found in dairy products, liver, and fish. Vitamin C, which has wiped out scurvy, is peculiar to citrus fruits. Vitamin D is found in fish, and has in turn wiped out rickets. Scientists have formulated the recommended daily dosage of vitamins, the exceeding of which is recommended only in specific circumstances, such as during pregnancy. Folic acid, a form of vitamin B, is important in preventing birth defects, and it is thus essential for a woman considering pregnancy to take a folic acid supplement before getting pregnant and during the first twelve weeks of pregnancy. (However, taking high doses of vitamin C and E has been found to raise both the risk of pre-eclampsia in pregnant women and the likelihood of low birth-weight in babies.)

In the late 1960s, a scientist by the name of Linus Pauling changed our view on vitamins. He pursued his research on the formation of chemical bonds between atoms in molecules and crystals, paving the way for Crick and Watson's discovery of the structure of DNA. The only double Nobelist, with both the chemistry and the peace

---

794. NIH State-of-the-Science Panel, "National Institutes of Health State-of-the-Science Conference Statement: Multivitamin/Mineral Supplements and Chronic Disease Prevention," *American Journal of Clinical Nutrition* 85(1), January 2007, 257S–264S.

prize, Pauling enjoyed such great authority that vitamins were moved from doctors' offices to millions of homes and supermarkets. Not only did Pauling have incredible scientific credibility, but he was also an extremely charming and charismatic man. He was convinced that the effect of vitamins was not limited to merely preventing deficiency diseases; he firmly believed that vitamins would also prevent diseases that had nothing to do with deficiencies, that vitamins would fend off cancer and coronary disease, that they would even slow down ageing. Pauling though they would just need to be ingested in massive doses.

When Pauling announced his ideas to the public, people were immediately attracted to them. It was the swinging '60s, and vitamins appeared to be a safe and convenient remedy against common maladies. People knew that drugs had side effects, and vitamins seemed a better, more natural way to fight disease. Pauling's belief in large vitamin dosages has created a whole new trade of health promotion. Together with nutrition gurus, he dreamed up a very profitable business. Vitamin supplements are now sold in markets, health stores, and pharmacies. They are universally marketed as a safe, natural way to stay healthy and fit.

Of all the vitamins, the most popular is C. To eliminate scurvy, 10 mg of vitamin C was needed, the amount contained in one slice of orange; but a thousand-fold dosage —or a hundred oranges—was even better, because, according to Pauling, it would prevent one from catching the common cold. (Cold, incidentally, is no better attribution of the cause for viral flu than is *influenza coeli*, "the influence of the stars.") Based on clinical research on thousands of subjects around the world, there may be a role for vitamin C in alleviating and shortening the duration of cold symptoms for some people. However, even the Linus Pauling Institute at Oregon State University concedes that there is no evidence that vitamin C can lower the incidence of the common cold for the general population or prevent it in the first place.[795] Vitamin C is a water-soluble molecule, and unless you have a deficiency, you cannot use more than a given maximum amount at any given time—take extra to prevent a cold and you will pass it out in your urine.

There are of course other reasons to take vitamin C supplements. The vitamins that act as antioxidants (A, C, E) seem to have amazing effects. Antioxidants neutralize free radicals, which help fend off infections, but also accelerate the ageing process. Many, extensive studies have shown that people who get plenty of antioxidants from fruits, vegetables, grains, and fats live longer and are healthier than others. Millions of people around the world take vitamin E supplements as a potential cure-all; however, vitamin E is a fat-soluble substance, so taking it in the pill form on an empty stomach is the same as taking nothing at all. Another popular antioxidant is vitamin A, of which scientists are much more skeptical. Beta-carotene is the precursor of vitamin A that the body turns into the vitamin itself. It is found in carrots and green vegetables, and research has shown that people who get a lot of beta-carotene from their diet have lower rates of cancer than those who do not.[796]

However, studies also show that in pill form, antioxidants provide no protection

795. "Vitamin C and the Common Cold," *LPI Research Newsletter*, Spring/Summer 2006.

796. NIH State-of-the-Science Panel, op. cit.

against cancer, and in high doses, can even increase the risk of cancer. In one study, 15,000 subjects were fed beta-carotene pills in doses equal to eating six carrots. All subjects were smokers, and thus already prone to lung cancer. The study was halted after eight years, because the group taking beta-carotene was discovered to have a whopping 18% more lung cancer than the control group.[797] Half a year later, another study showed a 28% increase in the number of lung cancers among those taking the supplement.[798] These results were confirmed in later studies, prompting British drug safety officials to issue a warning against smokers taking beta-carotene and against anyone taking it in large daily doses.[799]

Some researchers also warn against another form of vitamin A, retinol, which has been linked to liver disease. If you consume more vitamin A each day than your body needs, the vitamin will accumulate in your liver, because there is no easy way of excreting it. In Sweden, the only country with vitamin A fortified milk, the vitamin intake has been linked to high incidence of osteoporosis. With an intake of 1.5 mg per day, which is approximately twice the recommended daily dosage, but less than the strength of many over-the-counter supplements, there was a reduction in bone density of about 10% while the risk of hip fracture had doubled.[800] In the United States, the sunscreen industry includes vitamin A in its formulations, because it is an antioxidant that is thought to slow skin ageing. While that might be true for lotions and night creams used indoors, the U.S. Food and Drug Administration recently conducted a study into vitamin A's photocarcinogenic properties, i.e. the possibility that it results in cancerous tumours when used on skin exposed to sunlight.[801]

Another study conducted in Sweden found that women who routinely took a multivitamin were 19% more likely to be diagnosed with breast cancer after adjusting for other potential explanations.[802] The fortification of the U.S. food supply with folic acid in 1998 reduced certain rare birth defects by 15%, but it may have also caused an additional 15,000 cancer deaths a year.[803] These studies are a reminder of the fact that

---

797. Demetrius Albanes, et al. "Effects of α-Tocopherol and β-Carotene Supplements and Lung Cancer Incidence in the Alpha-Tocopherol Beta-Carotene Cancer Prevention Study," *American Journal of Clinical Nutrition* 62(6), December 1995, 1427S–1430S.

798. Gilbert S. Omenn, et al. "Effects of a Combination of Beta Carotene and Vitamin A on Lung Cancer and Cardiovascular Disease," *New England Journal of Medicine* 334(18), May 2, 1996, 1150–1155.

799. Expert Group on Vitamins and Minerals, "Safe Upper Levels for Vitamins and Minerals," Food Standards Agency, London, May 2003.

800. Håkan Melhus, et al. "Excessive Dietary Intake of Vitamin A Is Associated with Reduced Bone Mineral Density and Increased Risk for Hip Fracture," *Annals of Internal Medicine* 129(10), November 15, 1988, 770–778.

801. National Toxicology Program, "NTP Technical Report on the Photococarcinogenesis Study of Retinoic Acid and Retinyl Palmitate," U.S. Department of Health and Human Services, Washington, D.C., January 26, 2011.

802. Susanna C. Larsson, et al. "Multivitamin Use and Breast Cancer Incidence in a Prospective Cohort of Swedish Women," *American Journal of Clinical Nutrition* 91(5), May 2010, 1268–1272.

803. Young-In Kim, "Will Mandatory Folic Acid Fortification Prevent or Promote Cancer?" *Ibid.* 80(5), November 2004, 1123–1128.

vitamins are not just a harmless natural remedy—in large doses they may have unexpected and damaging side effects. Tumours grow less well when certain nutrients are in rate-limiting supply and taking a multivitamin just might feed cells in a tumour.[804] However, every nutrition expert agrees that antioxidants found in fresh fruit, vegetables, and other whole foods are essential to our health, and vitamin-rich food should form the core of any diet.

People in the West are healthier and live longer than ever before. Yet only a small portion of us can be considered healthy—if we use recommended blood pressure and cholesterol levels as a criteria. If the patient is doing well, it has traditionally been considered unethical to start treating them solely on basis of a laboratory value; this time-honoured policy has now been turned on its head. Even though average levels have dropped during the last few decades, the recommended levels have been lowered so much that fewer and fewer people are able to reach them without the help of medication. So are we to conclude that it is the pharmaceutical companies that decide who is healthy and who is not? In Finland, deaths from cardiovascular diseases in men of working age have gone down since the 1970s, when a public education campaign was launched in the country. During this thirty-year period, the average blood cholesterol levels fell by 20%, a drop comparable to putting the whole nation on cholesterol medication, yet one that was accomplished almost solely through a change in diet.[805]

In the period that saw the greatest drop, the cholesterol-lowering statins had not even been invented yet. Today, statin drugs are the single best selling pharmaceuticals in the West. More than 13 million Americans take statins regularly, and worldwide sales total more than $22 billion a year.[806] In Finland, their use has increased more than that of any other drug. They are usually first prescribed to a middle-aged patient, who then continues to take them for the rest of his life, that is, for several decades. The international recommendations are based on gigantic studies funded by the pharmaceutical industry, studies so broad that they can make even minute differences between the treated and the untreated appear statistically significant. According to the Norwegian Institute of Public Health, nine-tenths of all middle-aged citizens in Norway have cholesterol or blood pressure levels higher than the established norm.[807] So in a country with one of the highest average life expectancies in the world, the healthy would actually form a small minority.

What is more, there is no evidence that low blood pressure and cholesterol reduce the incidence of fatal cardiac episodes—about half of heart attacks occur in patients with normal cholesterol levels. In fact, a long follow-up study of Finnish male

---

804. Cornelia M. Ulrich & John D. Potter, "Folate Supplementation: Too Much of a Good Thing?" *Cancer Epidemiology, Biomarkers & Prevention* 15(2), February 2006, 189–193.

805. Tiina Laatikainen, et al. "Explaining the Decline in Coronary Heart Disease Mortality in Finland between 1982 and 1997," *American Journal of Epidemiology* 162(8), October 15, 2005, 764–773.

806. Mike Mitka, "Expanding Statin Use to Help More At-Risk Patients Is Causing Financial Heartburn," *JAMA* 290(17), November 5, 2003, 2243–2245.

807. Sidsel Graff-Iversen, et al. "Risikofaktorer for hjerteinfarkt, hjerneslag og diabetes i Norge," *Tidsskrift for Den norske lægeforening* 127(19), October 4, 2007, 2537–2541.

executives published in 1990 concluded that preventive treatment only increased deaths. Half of the men, all at risk for heart disease, were given medication and advice, half of them were not. While blood pressure and cholesterol were indeed lowered in the medicated group, the incidence of deaths from heart attacks was twice as high as in the untreated group.[808] To determine what the target blood pressure should be, the Hypertension Optimal Treatment Study looked at 18,790 patients in 16 countries between 1992 and 1997. Published in the British journal *The Lancet*, the principal results of the HOT Study demonstrated the benefits of lowering blood pressure to 140 mm Hg systolic and 85 mm Hg diastolic. However, using medication to lower blood pressure further, down to 120/70, appeared to give no additional benefit.[809]

A year's worth of statin medication costs about $1,000, so preventing one heart attack costs at least $500,000. Since we know that only 30% of heart attacks are fatal, preventing one death with this method sets us back by around $1.7 million. And for every heart attack prevented by statins, two or more people suffer liver damage, kidney failure, cataracts, or extreme muscle weakness as a side effect.[810] The pharmaceutical industry naturally focuses its research and development on drugs for middle-aged people who are afraid of dying and can afford to pay for this type of faith healing. Heart disease is the biggest killer of men and women in the rich world, but cholesterol is just one risk factor among many, and there are over 60 known risk factors at the moment. Turning cholesterol into the cause of the disease is not science, but business. Arterial inflammation, ironically caused by a no-fat or low-fat diet, is considered another explanation for heart disease alongside the cholesterol theory. Researchers critical of statins generally consider the little benefit the drugs have to lay in their anti-inflammatory properties.[811] Since every physician knows that life never boils down to just one factor, the whole cholesterol hysteria is, in any case, tantamount to medical malpractice.

The obsession with cholesterol has drastically changed the dietary fat profile of Americans with at best no apparent benefit. The Swiss have the highest cholesterol levels in the world, yet they have the fewest heart attacks. In the early '90s, Italians ate 70% more animal fat than 25 years earlier, yet cardiovascular deaths in Italy fell by 61%. In Japan, known for its low-fat national cuisine, the consumption of animal fats has increased considerably over the last 40 years, yet fatal heart attacks have

---

808. Timo E. Strandberg, et al. "Long-term Mortality After 5-Year Multifactorial Primary Prevention of Cardiovascular Diseases in Middle-aged Men," *JAMA* 266(9), September 4, 1991, 1225–1229.

809. Lennart Hansson, et al. "Effects of Intensive Blood-pressure Lowering and Low-Dose Aspirin in Patients with Hypertension," 351(9118), June 13, 1998, 1755–1762.

810. Julia Hippisley-Cox & Carol Coupland, "Unintended Effects of Statins in Men and Women in England and Wales: Population Based Cohort Study Using the QResearch Database," *British Medical Journal* 340, 2010, c2197.

811. Paul M. Ridker, et al. "Rosuvastatin to Prevent Vascular Events in Men and Women with Elevated C-Reactive Protein," *New England Journal of Medicine* 359(21), November 20, 2008, 2195–2207.

declined in all age groups.[812] An extreme example is the Australian aborigines, who have the world's lowest levels of cholesterol, but the highest incidence of fatal cardiac events.[813] Statins come with many side effects, among them memory disorders. The cholesterol molecule is essential for brain function and a part of the memory mechanism. Since cholesterol cannot penetrate the blood-brain barrier, the brain produces its own cholesterol. Nor can you increase your cholesterol by digesting cholesterol: if your diet is high in cholesterol, the production of cholesterol in the liver is reduced. The liver produces three to four times as much cholesterol each day as you would normally get from food; and if you get too little cholesterol in your diet, its production will increase. One can only venture a guess as to what happens when blood cholesterol levels are lowered artificially.

Is the triumph of modern medicine not simply spectacular? Just look at the rise in average life expectancy. Who could doubt the power of drugs, surgery, and injections when hundred-year olds will soon swarm the earth? A closer look at the numbers shows that medicine has nothing to do with it. A member of the British upper class lived easily as long in the 19th century as they do today, whereas a coal miner only lived 18 to 29 years, or in the case of child miners, somewhere between nine and twelve. If we are to be honest, we need to admit that medical science has only marginally raised our life expectancies, whereas the increase in our standard of living has made us all live long lives. And we would do well to remember that sometimes taking medications may shorten our life spans instead of lengthening them. The elderly are given drugs that have only been tested on otherwise healthy young people, although their metabolism, elimination, etc. tend to be completely different. Needless use of antipsychotic drugs to manage aggression in dementia patients is widespread in care homes and hospitals, contributing to the death of many elderly people.[814] The United States is next to Cuba in life expectancy, yet the latter spends less than $700 per capita a year on health care while the former spends over $7,000.[815]

Preventive care should comprise of daily exercise and a healthy diet, not visits to the doctor's office to prevent this or that. It should also be noted that doctors do *not* receive nutritional training in medical school. Over the past decade, drug companies have spent more than $3 billion on lobbyists and political contributions in the United States alone.[816] They have not only taken over the strategies of the health care sector, but also play a major role in the national economy on account of their magnificent profits. Yet, according to a recent study by the University of California, the elderly spend their retirement in a worse and worse condition: those born between 1930 and

---

812. "Rasvainen kupla." *MOT.* Yle TV1. September 13, 2010.

813. Zhiqiang Wang & Wendy E. Hoy, "C-Reactive Protein: An Independent Predictor of Cardiovascular Disease in Aboriginal Australians," *Australian and New Zealand Journal of Public Health* 34(S1), July 2010, S25–S29.

814. Sube Banerjee, "The Use of Antipsychotic Medication for People with Dementia: Time for Action," UK Department of Health, London, 2009.

815. World Health Organization 2004.

816. "The Other Drug War 2003: Drug Companies Deploy an Army of 675 Lobbyists to Protect Profits," Public Citizen's Congress Watch, Washington, D.C., June 2003.

1944 are in much worse shape than previous retirees.[817] The major reason why people get sick today is a combination of old age, cancer, and what they do to themselves, and these three factors are, of course, interrelated. The problem is created when a sick person frequently relies upon a drug to provide temporary relief, instead of seeking real healing. Doctors and drug companies tend to minimize the problems of suppressing the disease by referring to the "side effects" of a drug. However, any pharmacologist will tell you that determining a drug's "effects" and its "side effects" is completely arbitrary—both are the direct effect of the drug on the human body.

Rarely do drugs accomplish anything more than allowing the patient's body a little more time to heal itself. The three most significant medical discoveries of the last hundred years are: 1) The development of the sterile technique; 2) antibiotics; and 3) vaccines. It is only in the last century that microscopic pathogens were identified as the cause of disease, yet cultures as far back as thousands of years ago have had prescriptions as to what is and is not clean. We congratulate ourselves and proudly state we now know of viruses and bacteria and how to deter their spread, but is there really a significant difference between this and what "primitive" cultures did? Western aid organizations and charities recently made the catastrophic error of attempting to supplant local tribal customs and impose modern medical practices on certain African populations in order to prevent the spread of infectious diseases. These organizations completely misunderstood the way in which local practices were actually efficacious in helping prevent the spread of disease, despite being justified on grounds that were absurd and superstitious from a scientific viewpoint. Isolating the "cursed" individual from the rest of society and restricting the use of the water supply in order to "repent" for collective sins certainly sounds like a bunch of nonsense, yet the actual practices adopted on the basis of this reasoning had been quite effective at preventing the spread of illness.

Getting rid of an infection will not influence the immune factors that led the person to be susceptible to infection in the first place. In fact, antibiotics are known to disrupt our inner ecology, hamper the assimilation of nutrients, and even make the person more susceptible to infection in the future. It is well established that germs are fast becoming resistant to antibiotics, thanks to the overuse of the latter. About a billion people around the world are estimated to take penicillin every year. According to an EU report published in 2009, new antibiotics need to be developed as soon as possible, because tens of thousands of Europeans die each year from diseases caused by antibiotic-resistant bacteria.[818] More than half of all the antibiotics in the U.S. are used in animal agriculture, which has led to a proliferation of bacteria resistant to common anti-microbial agents.[819] And did you know that anti-bacterial soaps are

817. "Disability Trends Among Older Americans: National Health and Nutrition Examination Surveys, 1988–1994 and 1999–2004," *American Journal of Public Health* 100(1), January 2010, 100–107.

818. "The Bacterial Challenge: Time to React," European Centre for Disease Prevention and Control, Stockholm, September 2009.

819. Pew Commission on Industrial Farm Production, "Putting Meat on the Table: Industrial Farm Animal Production in America," The Pew Charitable Trusts & Johns Hopkins Bloomberg School of Public Health, Baltimore, MD, 2008.

actually less effective than regular ones?

A 2005 study by infection control specialists shows that the best way to get rid of germs is with plain old soap and water. Researchers at UNC Hospitals tested 14 different hand hygiene agents plus regular tap water against specific bacteria and viruses applied to the hands of 62 volunteers. After just one wash, hand gels and soaps worked about the same, removing 99% of the infectious agents, but after multiple washes, regular soap and warm water worked the best.[820] Since the germs used in the study were much hardier than the flu virus, soap and water are almost certainly adequate to fend off the flu. Many common diseases are viral in nature and thus unaffected by anti-bacterial products. However, soap and regular cleaning products get the job done, whereas if you kill all the susceptible bacteria, the more resistant bacteria only become stronger. In fact, all this cleanliness could do a lot to weaken your immune system, making it easier for you to get sick, thus making you more dependent on other products that companies will be more than happy to sell you.

Allergists also advise against making your bed in the morning. When the bunk starts to dry out and cool down during the day, dust mites begin looking for a more welcoming environment somewhere else. If you absolutely must arrange the bed covers, you are better off postponing it until the evening. Nor is there any such thing as a sterile kitchen, Lysol® advertisements notwithstanding. There are an estimated hundred trillion microbes living on or inside the human body. In fact, our bodies have ten times more bacteria than body cells; we need microbes as much as microbes need us. They are thought to play a key role in many physiological functions, from the development of the immune system through digestion of key nutrients to deterring potentially disease-causing pathogens. Children should be allowed to get dirty, if only because being too clean can impair the skin's ability to heal. Normal bacteria living on the skin trigger a pathway that helps prevent inflammation when we get hurt, dampening down overactive immune responses that can cause cuts and grazes to swell. And should our deposit of intestinal bacteria begin to wane, we would literally get sick in the stomach. Excess hygiene puts children at risk of allergies and asthma by denying their bodies the opportunity to develop natural resistance. This is known as the "hygiene hypothesis" and it is almost certainly the reason there is so much autoimmune disease in the developed world and almost none in developing countries.

Rates of allergy have tripled in the UK just in the last decade—one in three Britons now has some kind of allergy.[821] Several studies suggest that exposure to animals and the bacteria they carry, during the early years of life, could cut the risk of allergic diseases. And a study of more than 1,000 farmers' children goes even further, suggesting that this protection could start building even before birth. New Zealand researchers writing in the *European Respiratory Journal* say exposure before and after

820. Emily E. Sickbert-Bennett, et al. "Comparative Efficacy of Hand Hygiene Agents in the Reduction of Bacteria and Viruses," *American Journal of Infection Control* 33(2), March 2005, 67–77.

821. "Allergy: The Unmet Need—A Blueprint for Better Patient Care," Royal College of Physicians, London, June 2003.

birth halved the risk of the child developing asthma, eczema, or even hay fever.[822] Our mammalian disaster plan is a solid one: every child is supposed to receive antibodies against countless infections from his mother through the placenta and then from breast milk; with that protection, the infants can take their time to develop their own antibodies. However, these days, mothers have scant immunity because they too were raised in a plastic bubble.

The World Health Organization recommends nursing for the first two years and beyond. In fact, it recommends that babies be exclusively breast-fed until they are six months old, but only about one out of four mothers in the UK follows that advice.[823] In *Breastfeeding: Biocultural Perspectives* (1995), Dr. Katherine A. Dettwyler discussed the natural age of weaning for humans, or the length of time humans would likely nurse if cultural expectations did not interfere. By comparing humans to other primates, researchers were able to deduct that our natural age of weaning is a minimum of two and a half years and a maximum of between six and seven years. They compared such things as the length of gestation, the age of sexual maturity, the age of the eruption of permanent molars, and the time when children quadrupled their birthweight. In all other primates, nursing continues for years, not just months.[824]

Our food is hosed and boiled and rinsed and frozen and salted and preserved. Recently, we have begun to irradiate it as well, just in case. As a result, when our bodies finally encounter the occasional inevitable bug, we are not happy campers. Our century-long program of winnowing out all the muck has turned us into pathetic little sissies and withered the substantial part of the immune system mediated by our intestinal tract. Whereas the "friendly bacteria" in DanActive® have mainly been shown to fight diarrhea in people taking antibiotics, children who attend daycare or playgroups cut their risk of most childhood leukaemia by around 30%. Contracting some childhood infections—which are readily spread in environments where children are in close contact with each other—appears to prime the immune system against leukaemia, the most common cancer found in children in the industrialized world.[825] But most of our children have zero experience with routine gut infections and when they encounter one that has slipped past our funnels and filters, the results can be catastrophic.

Humans continue to evolve in response to diseases, diet, climate, and other factors. But technological advances have rendered natural selection a much less potent force on us than it was in the past. Modern medicines also may have reduced the pressure for the gene pool to create and spread mutations that would protect us against new

822. J. Douwes, et al. "Farm Exposure *In Utero* May Protect Against Asthma, Hay Fever and Eczema," 32(3), September 1, 2008, 603–611.

823. "Global Strategy for Infant and Young Child Feeding," World Health Organization, Geneva, 2003.

824. "A Time to Wean: The Hominid Blueprint for the Natural Age of Weaning in Modern Human Populations." Stuart-Macadam & Dettwyler 1995.

825. Kevin Y. Urayama, "A Meta-Analysis of the Association between Day-Care Attendance and Childhood Acute Lymphoblastic Leukaemia," *International Journal of Epidemiology* 39(3), June 2010, 718–732.

diseases. Every time humanity attempts to destroy a deadly disease, a deadlier one seems to appear. Smallpox remains the only major human disease that has been wiped out, after a global campaign that ended in 1977. Not a long ago, contracting AIDS was a death sentence, now people with HIV or AIDS can live relatively long lives with the appropriate care and drug treatment. However, this marked medical advancement has only fed a growing complacency about the disease: the number of heterosexual men with HIV has almost tripled in the past decade. In 2005, for the first time since the height of the AIDS epidemic in the 1980s, more than a million Americans were living with HIV.[826]

AIDS gets at least 23 cents of every health dollar going to poor countries, although globally, AIDS causes fewer than 4% of deaths.[827] Compared to global clean water shortage, AIDS is small potatoes. All the other crises the world is facing, be they famine, malaria, global warming, pollution, or civil war, pale in comparison with the problem regarding water. There are over 1.1 billion people in the world today who lack access to safe drinking water. Two million die each year from water-related diseases, which make up 80% of all maladies in developing nations.[828] Water and waste pipes in the United States are also rusty and leak about 23 gallons of precious fresh water per every American each day.[829] The irony is that unsafe water and inadequate sanitation are among the few global problems that are genuinely solvable over the short term and require no new technology. The greatest public health advance of mankind is not vaccines, or antibiotics, or disposable diapers, or refrigeration, or mosquito netting, but plumbing. But while AIDS and "climate change" engage major scientific minds, no-one is going to win a Nobel for putting in latrines. However, it is rather pointless to develop novel crops if the water they need is not there.

While fears for our health tend to focus on dramatic threats like Ebola or swine flu, about 70% of deaths and costs in developed countries are attributable to chronic diseases that can be prevented or controlled. However, fewer than half of adults in the U.S. receive preventive care.[830] Most health care providers put urgent care ahead of preventive services, and most health insurers invest little in prevention, knowing that other insurers will reap the benefits later. Should medical science develop an expensive but effective treatment for e.g. childhood diabetes or multiple sclerosis, it would undoubtedly be adopted, whatever the cost. And since the money will have to come from health care fees, it will ultimately be paid by those whose ailments are not life-threatening. The government will need to prioritize, i.e. decide who will receive treatment. The losers are the 80% of the population who expend 20% of the health care costs. The power of money will grow, while priority is going to be determined by

---

826. Joint United Nations Programme on HIV/AIDS 2006.

827. Ravishankar, et al. Op. cit.

828. Margaret Wertheim, "Drying the Tears of Thirsty Nations," *Los Angeles Times*, September 12, 2004.

829. "2009 Report Card for America's Infrastructure." Op. cit.

830. Jeanne M. Lambrew & John D. Podesta, "Health Prevention as a Priority: Creating a 'Wellness Trust,'" *Washington Post*, October 17, 2006.

the cost-effectiveness of the different treatments. Expensive treatment will be given if it is deemed effective, but less potent therapies will be discontinued.

Employer health benefits have been a middle-class mainstay in the United States since World War II, when federal wage controls prompted American companies to offer health insurance instead of pay rises. But as the cost of health insurance soars, the number of uninsured will grow. Health costs are going to depress wage gains, raise taxes, and cut down other government programs. Ironically, any health care system that satisfies most of the people as individuals will hurt society as whole. The problem is, people want a health care system that does three things: first, to provide the necessary care to everyone, regardless of income; second, to maintain our freedom to choose physicians and their freedom to recommend the best care for us; third, to control costs—and these goals are sadly incompatible. We can have any two of them, but not all three: if everyone receives care with complete choice, costs will explode; we can control costs, but that means denying care or limiting choices.

However, improving fairness and lowering costs, while maintaining quality, is theoretically possible given all the waste—unnecessary operations, the huge legal costs, paying for patented medicines when generics are available, etc.—even if the political way to solutions is barred by vested interests. President Obama's rhetoric quickly shifted from health care reform to health insurance reform, but getting more people access to a system that provides worse outcomes at higher costs is not an option for a sustainable health care system, let alone a sustainable economy. The Obama administration made health care neither a right, nor a privilege, but an obligation for individual Americans and a government-mandated profit centre for U.S. corporations. For the first time in American history, a bill uses the coercive power of the federal government to force every citizen to purchase the products of a private company. And if a citizen cannot afford that product, government will subsidize him, thereby directing public money to private profit.

For years, the paradigm of poverty dominated the discussion about why the sickness and death rates of the lower social classes are two or three times the norm. According to this paradigm, the disparity supposedly stems from differences in access to care, or in other words, differences in wealth. In the UK and other countries where universal health care was thought to sever the tie between health and social class, the resulting increase in health differences was greeted with astonishment. The less educated and lower income individuals tend to seek preventive—as opposed to curative—care less often than the more educated and higher income individuals even if that care is free.[831] According to a 2005 study conducted by the Helsinki University Department of Public Health in collaboration with the Danish Public Health Institute, highly educated and highly paid individuals are much less likely to be overweight than the less educated. The wealthier individuals have more money to spend on healthy pastimes and healthy foods.[832] The higher the social ladder the lower

831. Linda S. Gottfredson, "Intelligence: Is It the Epidemiologists' Elusive 'Fundamental Cause' of Social Class Inequalities in Health?" *Journal of Personality and Social Psychology* 86(1), January 2004, 174–199.

832. Sirpa Sarlio-Lähteenkorva, et al. "The Social Patterning of Relative Body Weight and Obesity in Denmark and Finland," *European Journal of Public Health* 16(1), February 2006, 36–40.

the sickness and death rates, except for cancers and tumours, which are twice as prevalent among the well educated, but rare in comparison to diabetes and high blood pressure.[833] Obviously, if everyone committed to healthy living, health care crises would disappear, insurance premiums would go down, and Big Pharma would be left out in the cold.

For years now, American medical professionals have had to deal with the threat of multi-million dollar negligence suits. Recent figures indicate that one in seven doctors in the United States refuse to deliver babies because they cannot afford the insurance cover needed to protect them.[834] The Hippocratic oath states: "May I always act so as to preserve the finest traditions of my calling and may I long experience the joy of healing those who seek my help." However, as far as I am concerned, organizations such as Médecins Sans Frontières rest on misplaced professional pride. It is easier to deal with children starving in Africa than the health care crisis at home. Every day, mass media brings suffering that is not in front of us to our living rooms and offices. Is it any wonder that physicians have the highest suicide rate of any profession?

In today's medicalized society, even mental health is seen as mechanical, and repairable through pharmaceutical means. The therapy culture, in which we currently live, tells us what the right feelings are, what the correct intensity of those feelings is, and should one's feelings be wrong, anger or frustration for instance, this is seen as causing mental problems. As the late psychotherapist and publisher Dr. Christopher S. Hyatt (1943–2008) put it: "Mental health is the ability to deny reality and repress feelings within the boundaries and parameters established by one's peer group(s)."[835] People these days no longer know how to live life with its joys and sorrows and getting through difficulties at an individual pace. In the modern quartal economy, man is a unit of production, who must be at his best 24/7 and in a constant manic state, in order to be normal according to the output measures of global finance. If one makes the mistake of crying or takes one's time weathering the tribulations of life, a prescription for antidepressants is soon to follow.

There was a marked and broad expansion in antidepressant treatment in the United States from 1996 to 2005. An astonishing 10% of the U.S. population was prescribed an antidepressant in 2005, in comparison to 6% in 1996. Over this period, Americans treated with antidepressants also became more likely to receive additional antipsychotic medications and less likely to undergo psychotherapy.[836] Educated people have actually come to view depression as a biochemical disorder that requires medical treatment. Yet, in truth, modern medicine has not advanced in the mapping of the neurological basis of mental illnesses since the days of Atreya, founder of ancient Indian medicine. He wrote his work around three centuries before the dawn of the common era. Only the terms have changed: where a modern neurologist talks

833. Gottfredson, op. cit.

834. "The 2005 Report to the Secretary: Rural Health and Human Service Issues," The National Advisory Committee on Rural Health and Human Services, Washington, D.C., April 2005.

835. "'Prescription for Rebellion'—Revisited." Hyatt, op. cit. 39.

836. Mark Olfson & Steven C. Marcus, "National Patterns in Antidepressant Medication Treatment," *Archives of General Psychiatry* 66(8), August 2009, 848–856.

about neural transmitters and neuron synapses, Atreya spoke of fluids and channels. No truly scientifically effective psychiatric drugs have been developed, degenerative brain diseases continue to wreak havoc on our brains, nor has there been much progress in the field of neural regeneration.

If you have seen a physician about emotional problems some time during the past twenty years, you will have been told that you may have a chemical imbalance and need pills to correct it. It is not just the medical profession that thinks this way either. Television, newspapers, magazines, and internet sites have all pushed the idea that conditions such as depression, anxiety, and schizophrenia can be treated by drugs that help rectify an underlying brain problem. People with mental conditions are told that they need to take psychiatric medication for the rest of their lives to stabilize their brain chemicals, just like a diabetic needs to take insulin. The trouble is, there is little or no justification for this view of psychiatric drugs. However, if doctors told their patients that they have no idea what is going on in their brain, but that they could take a pill that would make them feel different and might help suppress their thoughts and feelings, then many of them might choose to avoid taking drugs. And if placebos can make people better, then depression can be treated without medication that comes with serious side effects, not to mention costs.

Unlike other fields of medicine, psychiatry diagnoses behaviour that society does not like. Yesterday, it was homosexuality, tomorrow it will be homophobia. The "diagnosis" of such "pathological behaviour" is based on social, political, and even aesthetic values. If even psychiatrists acknowledge the boundary line between troublesome behaviour and mental illness to be blurry in adults, then in children, whose brains are still a work in progress, it is fuzzier still. The notion of Attention Deficit Hyperactivity Disorder, along with all the other frequently diagnosed learning or behavioural "syndromes" or "dysfunctions" is logically absurd. If a child who is unable to concentrate (the main diagnostic "symptom" of the "disorder") suffers from ADHD, then a child who cannot ride a bicycle must be suffering from Bicycle Riding Deficit Disorder. As psychiatric diagnosis and medication of children are becoming more widespread, overworked teachers, well-meaning neighbours and relatives, and parents themselves are less willing to accept youthful misfits for who they are and to help them adapt without prescribing drugs or attaching labels. If Einstein were born today, his parents would get a comprehensive evaluation and poor little Albert would undoubtedly end up on Ritalin. Deprived of his daydreams, he might focus more on his math homework, but would probably not discover relativity.

New guidance in the UK advises physicians that treatments such as Ritalin should be avoided wherever possible—as if *all* drugs should not be avoided wherever possible. Instead, Britain's National Institute for Health and Clinical Excellence recommends training for parents to help them tackle their child's difficult behaviour.[837] Funny how there were no diagnosed cases of ADHD until parents stopped disciplining their children. Children need boundaries and they also need chastising to keep them in line. Every species of mammal disciplines its young and

837. "Attention Deficit Hyperactivity Disorder: Diagnosis and Management of ADHD in Children, Young People and Adults—NICE Clinical Guideline 72," NICE, London, September 2008.

children who are not punished for breaking the rules go mad, just like undisciplined dogs. It has also been acknowledged for some time now that there is a lot of commonality between the symptoms of a tired child and the symptoms of a child with ADHD.[838] It has been suggested that some children who lack sleep do not appear tired, but instead behave badly.

A joint study by scientists from the University of Helsinki and Finland's National Institute of Health and Welfare found that a good night's sleep can reduce hyperactivity and bad behaviour among children. The study examined 280 healthy children aged seven or eight and found those who slept for fewer than eight hours to be the most hyperactive.[839] While it is recognized that chronic sleep deprivation is a problem for many adults in Western countries, with poor sleep being linked to depression, heart disease, strokes, lung disorders, traffic and industrial accidents, sleep has been largely ignored as an important aspect of health. It has been estimated that a third of American children do not get enough sleep; on average, teenagers are having seven hours and 53 minutes of sleep a night, much less than the nine hours recommended at that age.[840] Even an extra 30 minutes per night has been shown to lend a major improvement in objective cognitive tests, improving reaction times, impulsivity, and attention spans.[841]

The fact that so many people work so hard to keep the patently absurd idea of attention deficit disorders alive can only mean that it is a very profitable hoax. All these vaguely defined diseases satisfy medico-economic needs by generating additional income for the growing number of psychiatrists, psychologists, and related professions. This is an industry that invents chronic diseases, be it restless legs syndrome, dry eye syndrome, or unspecified sleep disorders that require taking nightly doses of habit-forming tranquilizers; this is an industry that makes up conditions like social phobia, generalized anxiety disorder, and oppositional defiant disorder to sell mind-altering drugs. We now have 3-year olds on antidepressants. Why? Because Big Pharma, just like Big Tobacco, knows that if you get them while they are young, you have a customer for life.

For-profit medicine and its business partners operate as a legalized drug trade, procuring thousands of young patients, many of whom eventually become clients of illegal drug dealers. Reports of adverse effects of ADHD medication have grown in recent years even as their use has increased. According to U.S. Food and Drug Administration estimates, 4 to 5 million Americans, mainly children but also an increasing number of adults, are now taking ADHD medication regularly. FDA records dating back to 1969 reveal that nearly three-quarters of all serious reported

---

838. R. E. Dahl, et al. "The Impact of Inadequate Sleep on Children's Daytime Cognitive Function," *Seminars in Pediatric Neurology* 3(1), March 1996, 44–50.

839. E. Juulia Paavonen, et al. "Short Sleep Duration and Behavioral Symptoms of Attention-Deficit/Hyperactivity Disorder in Healthy 7- to 8-Year-Old Children," *Pediatrics* 123(5), May 1, 2009, e857–e864.

840. James E. Gangwisch, et al. "Earlier Parental Set Bedtimes as a Protective Factor Against Depression and Suicidal Ideation," *Sleep* 33(1), January 1, 2010, 97–106.

841. Avi Sadeh, et al. "The Effects of Sleep Restriction and Extension on School-Age Children: What a Difference an Hour Makes," *Child Development* 74(2), March/April 2003, 444–455.

problems with amphetamines and half of all serious side effects—such as heart problems, hallucinations, elevated aggression, and suicidal tendencies—with drugs such as Ritalin occurred between 1999 and 2003.[842]

Of course, the mechanistic relationship with one's own body and health has spawned an entire industry of soft alternatives. When Daniel Yankelovich, a leading market researcher and social scientist, studied the seemingly non-conformist people of the 1960s and '70s, he realized that they were not anti-consumerist at all; they simply wanted products that expressed their individuality, self-direction, and self-actualization. A comprehensive study reported in the *Journal of the American Medical Association* put the number of patient visits to alternative-medicine practitioners at 629 million a year in 1997, far surpassing the 386 million visits to conventional physicians.[843] When people do no wish to sculpt their minds and bodies with the happy pills of conventional medicine and the knife of a plastic surgeon, they wear harmony-radiating coloured crystals or drink rejuvenating herbal teas. But in the end, they too are adopting an extremely simplified, medicalized conception of health.

In times past, disease was a condition one wished to get rid of, now it has become part of one's identity. Should I suffer from, for example, obsessive compulsive disorder, I can nonchalantly announce that my name is Antti Balk and I have OCD. In the olden days, the Church invented Hell, told us what it was like, and then offered us a solution. People today seek similar solutions to problems they assume they have. We are told that there are right kind of feelings and wrong kind of feelings and that we must be ready to get help—the right kind of help—from professionals. It is no use fighting it, like there was no use fighting hellfire in the past; if an expert tells you that you have a problem, then you have a problem even if you do not see it yourself. Indeed, the fact that you do not see it might be a symptom of the very problem—you are clearly in denial about it. You say that you don't have a problem, you don't feel that you're depressed, or addicted to this or that. No, no, you are wrong; you just cannot admit it to yourself.

This incessant and limitless psychologizing starts as early as day care and kindergarten. The small human embryos are brainwashed into believing that they have certain skills and certain shortcomings and weaknesses, which they need to make do with for the rest of their lives. In other words, we are taught from a very young age to interpret ourselves and our environment though psychologizing. Instead of focusing on our "problems," would it not be more sensible to further our talents, our skills, our desires, and our sensibilities in such a way that every single one of us could fulfill most of our opportunities in the course of this limited existence, regardless of how much these differ from current "norms"? All this comes to head in the "psychology of happiness," according to which happiness is the normal state.

All emotions are obviously valid—that is the only way they could have evolved;

842. Kate Gelperin, "Studying Cardiovascular Risk with Drug Treatments of ADHD: Feasibility of Available Study Methods in Children and Adults," FDA Drug Safety and Risk Management Advisory Committee, Silver Spring, MD, February 9, 2006.

843. David M. Eisenberg, et al. "Trends in Alternative Medicine Use in the United States, 1990–1997." *JAMA* 280(18), November 11, 1998, 1569–1575.

whether a feeling is perceived as negative or positive is always a value judgement. Even the more "spiritual" Westerners cannot be reminded too often that Buddhism emphasizes relating to our emotions as they are, versus trying to strike an idealized meditative pose. In the words of the late occult historian Gerald Suster (1951–2001), "New Age is merely softened down and tarted up Christianity; an outmoded religion once adhered to by primitive mammalian primates based upon ludicrous notions of sin and guilt. Under Christianity, perfectly natural desires were called 'sinful'. Under New Age, you still have to be guilty as sin for the same, for the words and phrases are 'unspiritual'—whatever that may mean—or 'not virtuous'. Whatever words are used, people still end up feeling guilty over perfectly natural and honourable feelings like love, hate, lust, anger *et al.*"[844] As Dr. Stanley Turecki, author of *The Difficult Child*, put it: "We are suffering . . . from a shrinking tolerance for the broad limits of normality."[845]

So just what *is* disease? There is a range. At one extreme, we find conditions that cause agony or premature death, at the other lay cosmetic correctness, like hair growing out of the ears. The ailments in between are the ones society debates about. Most deaf people consider themselves a minority, just like blacks or gays; some of them are against fitting the hearing impaired children of deaf couples with inner ear implants, because they feel the "right" to a sign language community is more important than the right to hearing. So is giving a child the ability to hear a cure or an act of genocide? What about hereditary albinism? If political correctness had been in the fashion when the polio vaccine was developed, perhaps the vaccinations would have been outlawed as unethical? Or what about height? Human growth hormone is recommended for the shortest 3% of the population; but even if the average height increases dramatically, there will always be a shortest 3%. It is easy to scare people with all sort of risk groups, since we all fall into one risk group or another—"On a long enough timeline the survival rate for everyone drops to zero."[846] Or as William L. Roper, director of the CDC from 1990 to 1993, saw it: "Death is the ultimate negative patient health outcome."[847]

Dr. Leon R. Kass, chairman of President Bush's now-dissolved Council on Bioethics, called for a "moratorium" on the research that gave birth to it until we sort out the moral issues involved. But we already know all we are ever going to know about the moral issues, and no crash research program can produce any dazzling new bioethical principle we never thought of before. All new medical technologies and treatments entail ethical dilemmas and risks. Interspecies organ transplantation contains the risk of a global epidemic, and for the umpteenth time, medicine is again posing the question about the essence of humanity. In the past, organ transplants always had a clear medical reason: one cannot make do without a heart, liver, or at

---

844. 1990, 88–89.

845. As quoted in Melissa Healy, "Are We Too Quick to Medicate Children?" *Los Angeles Times*, November 5, 2007.

846. *Fight Club*, op. cit.

847. Timothy Leary & Eric Gullichsen, "Twenty-Two Alternatives to Involuntary Death." Hyatt, op. cit. 293.

least one kidney, but one will survive without a womb or a face.

When you have more scientists working on a problem, you increase the chance of solving it; if you put more ethicists onto a problem, you only end up with more problems. For example, it never occured to anyone before that cloning embryos from stem-cells "exploits women as egg donors not for their benefit."[848] It is perfectly understandable that people demand safety from new medications and therapies. But sometimes the principle of caution can turn on itself, for if medicine did not take any risks, it would not advance either. The demands of some ethicists are bordering on the monomaniacal: medical science is immoral when the treatments fail, but even more immoral when they succeed. It was only a century and a half ago that Western religious leaders argued anaesthetics should not be used for women in childbirth, because labour pains were prescribed by God as punishment for Eve's transgression.

There are genuine problems in medicine which are obscured by the current ethics debate. Every med student hears this story at some point: Graduation day comes and the newly minted doctors assemble to pick up their diplomas; the dean gazes out and announces abashedly: "I am sorry to tell you that half of what we taught you is wrong; the problem is, we don't know which half." Whatever has been in vogue in medicine in one decade has been declared ineffective, dangerous, and sometimes even barbaric in the next. Some see the fact that only a handful of pharmaceutical substances have survived thirty years or more as strong testament to the capacity of the profession to acknowledge its mistakes; but because drug patents only last a few years, there is a substantial benefit to drugs having a limited lifespan—Big Pharma is able to charge big money for a certain period and then release a new, high-priced drug to replace the off-patent generic.

Many medical procedures that became common before their effectiveness was tested are so ingrained in tradition that they continue to be practised even though their usefulness has been disproven. An episiotomy, for example, is an incision many pregnant women receive ostensibly to reduce the risk of tissue tears during delivery. It has been one of the most common surgical procedures performed in the United States since the 1930s, and was not subject to careful evaluation until the '80s. Common sense dictates that making any incisions in the skin can only promote tearing, just like a piece of fabric will not tear well until you get it started. However, twenty-five years later, the procedure was still performed in about one-third of all vaginal births, making it more common than hysterectomies and Cæsarean sections.[849]

Chemotherapy, the use of poisonous substances to kill cancer cells, was invented more than six decades ago. The first such substances were nitrogen mustards, originally developed in the 1920s and '30s as chemical warfare agents. Modern chemotherapy treatments are in fact so potent that they can actually cause secondary tumours in patients. Like the other current cancer therapies, surgery and radiation, they only attack the equivalent of Hydra's head. In the '80s and '90s, oncologists were convinced that high-dose chemotherapy followed by a bone-marrow transplant was

848. Leon R. Kass, as quoted in Gina Kolata, "South Koreans Streamline Cloning of Human Embryos," *New York Times*, May 19, 2005.

849. Katherine Hartmann, et al. "Outcomes of Routine Episiotomy: A Systematic Review," *JAMA* 293(17), May 4, 2005, 2141–2148.

the best treatment for women with advanced breast cancer. Many cancer specialists refused to enroll their patients in randomized clinical trials that were designed to test transplants against the standard therapy. They asserted that the trials were unethical, because they knew transplants worked. However, when the studies were concluded in 2000, it turned out that bone-marrow transplants were actually killing patients.[850] The sole effective strategy for defeating cancer lay in treatments that will check cancer's ability to regenerate, just as Herakles finally slew the ancient beast by cauterizing each of its necks. And this requires action on the level of the DNA.

Similarly, the technology used to produce flu vaccine dates back to the 1930s, when scientists discovered that influenza virus can be grown by inserting it between the membranes of fertilized chicken eggs and then keeping the eggs warm. Afterwards, the egg matter and chicken embryo must be separated carefully and the virus purified—any slip-up can introduce bacteria. The original flu vaccine virus is over 70 years old, and has been passaged, cultured, and manhandled so that it will grow in mice, in eggs, in ferrets. Alone, this strain will not protect anyone from anything, but needs to be mixed with the particular strain scientists predict will be circulating eight months from production. Influenza viruses mutate with incredible speed and each flu season sees slightly different genetic versions of the viruses that infected people the year before. Every year, the World Health Organization and the CDC collect data from roughly a hundred nations on the flu viruses that circulated the previous year, and make an educated guess on which viruses are likely to circulate in the coming autumn. In 2003, they picked the wrong strain.[851]

People tend to think they have the flu anytime they fall ill with an ailment that brings on headache, fever, coughing, sneezing, and the feeling that you have been sleeping on a bed of rocks, but according to scientists, at most half, and perhaps as few as 7 or 8 percent, of such cases are actually caused by an influenza virus in any given year.[852] Rather than a symptom of a viral infection, a high fever is the body's natural defence mechanism that checks the growth of the virus. The high temperature keeps the viral RNA from making copies of itself—it is an immune response only warm-blooded mammals have developed to prevent the spread of viral infections. More than two hundred known viruses and other pathogens can cause "influenza-like symptoms," including bocavirus, coronavirus, enterovirus, rhinovirus, and respiratory syncytial virus.[853] You can even catch two separate strains of cold at the same time, and those strains can then swap their genetic material inside your body to make a whole new strain. But depending on the season, in up to two-thirds of the cases of flu-

---

850. Michelle M. Mello & Troyen A. Brennan, "The Controversy Over High-Dose Chemotherapy With Autologous Bone Marrow Transplant For Breast Cancer," *Health Affairs* 20(5), September 2001, 101–117.

851. Wendy Orent, "They're Sticking It to Us With Antique Vaccines," *Los Angeles Times*, December 19, 2004.

852. Shannon Brownlee & Jeanne Lenzer, "Does the Vaccine Matter?" *The Atlantic*, November 2009.

853. W. Garrett Nichols, et al. "Respiratory Viruses Other than Influenza Virus: Impact and Therapeutic Advances," *Clinical Microbiology Reviews* 21(2), April 2008, 274–290.

like illness, no cause whatsoever can be found.[854]

And even when the match between vaccine and virus is dead on, the vaccine is only partly effective, vaccinated people being 70% less likely to catch the virus.[855] However, recombinant DNA technology could produce appropriate vaccines very rapidly. Cell culture technology would give vaccine developers greater flexibility and allow them to grow vaccine strains in huge quantities. With molecular biology, you can make a recombinant vaccine using the old internal genes from the original virus and a sequence from a human carrier. This would be infinitely safer than taking a virus sample from a sick person's throat, since only the virus' genetic sequence is used and no other infectious agents can come along for the ride. But the money is in new drugs, not in new vaccines, so the latter are never put on a fast tract by the FDA.

Sometimes, an old-fashioned polio vaccine strain regains the ability to paralyze and kill: four polio outbreaks, most recently one in 2004, have been caused by vaccines. And while vaccines for polio and, say, whooping cough dramatically reduced death rates from those diseases, the impact of flu vaccine has been more difficult to determine. Flu comes and goes with the seasons, and usually does not kill people directly, but rather only contributes to deaths by making the body more susceptible to secondary infections like pneumonia or bronchitis. The people who get these complications from influenza are precisely the ones who do not develop immunity from the vaccine due to their weakened vital functions. In short, the flu vaccine is only effective on those who do not need it. Case in point: in 2004, vaccine production fell behind, causing a 40% drop in immunization rates, yet mortality did not rise.[856]

The global swine flu threat of 2009 awakened governments from Egypt to India to the need for flu vaccines. In the most ambitious vaccination program mounted since the anti-polio campaign in the 1950s, the U.S. government commissioned MedImmune and four other companies to produce enough vaccine to cover the entire population of the country. As headlines and news briefs warned of a possible pandemic, patients more worried than truly sick began clogging emergency rooms across the nation. The mere presence of this sneezing, coughing, infectious tide of humanity in the ER endangered the lives of the really ill. Random swabs taken by the UK Health Protection Agency show that, at the end of the first wave of the "pandemic" in Britain, just one in twenty people calling the National Pandemic Flu Service with symptoms of the disease had it.[857] Across Europe, governments are now trying to resell their stockpiles of swine flu vaccine.

Studies show that when there is ER crowding, mortality goes up, because patients who need immediate attention fail to receive it. When patients with even mild flu symptoms show up in the hospital, they vastly increase the spread of the virus, simply because they inevitably sneeze and cough in rooms that are jam-packed with other people. It is hardly an exaggeration to say that there is no worse place to go than the

---

854. Brownlee & Lenzer, op. cit.

855. Orent, op. cit.

856. Brownlee & Lenzer, op. cit.

857. Alex J. Elliot, et al. "Monitoring the Emergence of Community Transmission of Influenza A/H1N1 2009 in England: A Cross Sectional Opportunistic Survey of Self Sampled Telephone Callers to NHS Direct," *British Medical Journal* 339, August 27, 2009, b3403.

hospital during flu season. Conversely, social distancing can blunt the impact of an epidemic: avoiding public places, washing hands diligently, and having a supply of canned goods and water are highly effective steps in slowing the spread of the virus. Our reliance on vaccination may have the opposite effect: it breeds feelings of invulnerability and leads some people to ignore simple measures like more stringent hygiene, staying away from those who are sick, and staying home when they feel ill.[858]

Meanwhile, the health care industry is reaping the benefits of the global swine flu pandemic scare. Large pharmaceutical companies reported windfall sales from flu drugs and H1N1 vaccines. Small biotech firms won fresh attention from investors and governments looking for quicker and less expensive ways of making vaccines to protect their populations. And diagnostic companies grew their revenues as doctors ordered more flu tests. However, the WHO is facing charges from many European politicians that it exaggerated the dangers of swine flu. In early 2010, the Council of Europe launched a formal investigation into whether pharmaceutical companies influenced public health officials to spend billions of euros unnecessarily. The council's Social, Health and Family Affairs Committee praised Poland's Health Minister Ewa Kopacz for her decision not to order any H1N1 vaccines in spite of pressure from Big Pharma and health organizations.

Thanks to the anti-swine flu strategy adopted by Poland, fewer fatal cases of the virus were reported and the virus was less virulent than in member nations that spent millions of euros on vaccines.[859] Since the 1970s, the U.S. government has shielded vaccine-makers from lawsuits over the use of childhood vaccines; instead, a federal court handles claims and decides who will be paid from a special fund. During the previous swine flu epidemic in 1976, more people were crippled by and died from the vaccine than the virus itself.[860] Under a document signed in 2009 by the U.S. Secretary of Health and Human Services, Kathleen Sebelius, vaccine-makers and federal officials are granted total legal immunity from lawsuits that result from any new swine flu vaccine. In the end, it is all a matter of gross national product—governments are afraid that people will stay home sick instead of slaving away at work.

Today's debates about genetic manipulation enforce, for their part, the mechanistic view of the human body and the notion that man can be influenced on the physiological level. The new medicalization is represented by the potency drugs Viagra and Cialis, the antidepressants Prozac and Celexa, the cholesterol lowering Crestor and Zetia, pharmaceutical products that offer an instant solution to our problems. Humans are hard-wired for immediate gratification; across the developed world, prescription pills have become a societal force: adults and children alike rely on them for a growing list of maladies, one of the newest being shyness, for which few medical alternatives were available a generation ago. Now that we have effective remedies for nearly every disease and symptom, it would be "unethical" to leave them

858. Brownlee & Lenzer, op. cit.

859. Paul Flynn, "The Handling of the H1N1 Pandemic: More Transparency Needed," Council of Europe, Strasbourg, March 23, 2010.

860. Cyril H. Wecht, "The Swine Flu Immunization Program: Scientific Venture or Political Folly," *American Journal of Law & Medicine* 3(4), Winter 1977–1978, 425–445.

untreated. Yet the fact is that the U.S. pharmaceutical industry spends almost twice as much on product promotion as it does on research and development.[861]

Worse still is the growing trend to invert the whole process and promote diseases to fit existing drugs. The strategy is to convince as many people as possible that they have medical conditions that require long-term drug treatment. The internet has given patients more and more self-initiative; according to a recent Finnish study, more than half of all patients have a clear picture of what is wrong with them and how they should be treated even before they see a doctor.[862] One prominent disease-mongering tactic is to attach polysyllabic, clinical-sounding names to what used to be seen as trivial or passing conditions. These new, formidable names usually come with official acronyms that add even more gravitas. Occasional heartburn becomes "gastro-esophageal reflux disease" or GERD; fidgeting legs become "restless leg syndrome" or RLS; shyness becomes "social anxiety disorder" or SAD; impotence becomes "erectile dysfunction" or ED—Viagra® was originally designed as a heart medicine but failed.

The United States is probably the only country in the world that permits advertising of drugs which are available only through a doctor. Efficient direct-to-consumer drug marketing promises us happier, more fulfilled lives: according to a 2001 Kaiser Family Foundation survey, 30% of Americans had spoken to their physician about a medication they had seen advertised and 44% of those had been given the prescription they asked about.[863] I thought the whole point of prescription drugs was that it is not safe to let us simply buy them over the counter. They are either so strong or so habit-forming that it is up to a professional to decide whether we really need them. Advertising changes that relationship by sending us to the doctor's office filled with nameless dreads about the symptoms of diseases we might have, along with a detailed knowledge of the drugs that might help. "This is America I guess. The land of 8-minute abs, 6-minute facelifts and 10 plastic surgery procedures in one day. . . This is the land where Restless Leg Syndrome is cured by a drug that can cause an uncontrollable urge to gamble."[864] As the ads say: "The only thing more effective is diet and exercise."

The growing use of prescription drugs has led to new problems; one in six Americans take three or more different prescription pills daily, by and large in combinations never tested on animals.[865] The elderly are assuredly the best group of customers for the pharmaceutical industry: many of them take so many pills every day that they can no longer tell what they all are for. With over 15,000 prescription drugs in use and some 300,000 over-the-counter products, it is impossible to track all the

---

861. "Profiting from Pain: Where Prescription Drug Dollars Go," Families USA, Washington, D.C., July 2002.

862. Hanna K. Toiviainen, et al. "Physicians' Opinions on Patients' Requests for Specific Treatments and Examinations," *Health Expectations* 8(1), March 2005, 43–53.

863. Rideout, op. cit.

864. Denis Leary, "I Feel Good," *Huffington Post*, May 11, 2010.

865. Critser 2005.

interactions any more.[866] Consequently, each year more people die in the United States from prescription drugs than in traffic accidents. On top of that, each year sees 2.2 million serious adverse drug reactions—defined as "those that required hospitalization, were permanently disabling, or resulted in death."[867] On the other hand, statistics show that placebos sometimes work even better than many of the most popular pills on the market today. Research also shows that the worse the side effects a patient experiences, the more effective the drug; patients apparently think that if the drug is so strong it makes them vomit and hate sex, then it must be strong enough to lift their depression. And the more expensive the snake oil, the better it works, according to studies.[868] It would seem that medication is not always necessary for healing, whereas the belief in healing is.

But although experts know that antidepressants are scarcely better than placebos, few patients or physicians do. Many general practitioners see with their own eyes and feel with their own hearts how the drugs lift the black cloud from their depressed patients. And since doctors are not exactly in the habit of prescribing dummy pills, they have no experience on how patients do on them, and never realize that a placebo would be almost as effective as a $4 pill. Hence the moral dilemma. The placebo effect rests on the holy trinity of belief, expectation, and hope, so telling this to someone who is being treated with antidepressants threatens to topple the whole house of cards. Should the doctor explain that it is all in their heads, that the reason the pill works is the same reason why Dumbo could initially fly only with a feather clutched in his trunk, the magic would dissipate like fairy dust in the wind.

The strength of the placebo effect drives drug companies crazy, since it makes the superiority of a new drug much harder to show. Over the decades, governments have chosen to allow a strange system for developing medicines to be constructed. Most of the research carried out by scientists to bring a drug to your local pharmacist is done in government-funded university laboratories and paid for with our taxes. Drug companies only come in late in the process of development, and finance part of the expensive but largely uncreative final trials. In return, they will own the exclusive rights to manufacture and profit from the resulting medicine—no-one else is allowed to make or sell it. Only 14% of their budgets go to research and development, and much of that is squandered on "me-too" drugs, medicines that do exactly the same thing as a drug that already exists, but have one molecule different, so the companies can take out a new patent and generate fresh profits.[869] The pharmaceutical industry has increasingly come to rely on blockbuster drugs whose long-term risks and long-term benefits are often more or less identical.

Before the U.S. Food and Drug Administration approves a new drug, it must undergo clinical trials. But these trials are not performed by the FDA itself, they are

---

866. Philip Aspden, et al. "Preventing Medication Errors," Institute of Medicine of the National Academies, Washington, D.C., July 20, 2006.

867. Jason Lazarou, et al. "Incidence of Adverse Drug Reactions in Hospitalized Patients: A Meta-analysis of Prospective Studies," *JAMA* 279(15), April 15, 1998, 1200–1205.

868. Kirsch 2009.

869. Angell 2004.

done by the drug companies. These trials usually use relatively few test subjects and the drug companies tend to choose subjects most likely to react well to the drug being tested. The trials are also often concluded in a matter of weeks, even though real-world users might be on the drug for months or years at a time. The worst side effects of the drugs could easily be far too complex and unexpected to discover via laboratory tests. And even when adverse effects show up during clinical trials, the drugs are sometimes released anyway. They might ultimately end up taken off the market because of those same adverse effects, even though the generally accepted estimate is that less than 10% of individual instances of adverse effect are ever reported to the FDA. One-fifth of all drugs will be either withdrawn or have a black box warning within 25 years of entering the market.[870]

Drugs are not released when they have been proven safe—that would require analyzing huge amounts of data on huge numbers of people over several decades. Drugs are released when enough FDA bureaucrats, many of whom are former or future pharmaceutical executives, can be convinced that the drug is not immediately deadly. Nor is the information that is used to convince the regulators necessarily published for public and scientific scrutiny, thus impairing not only the ability of clinicians and patients to make informed medical decisions, but the ability of scientists to design safer and more efficient trials in the future. Many doctors get their information about new drugs either during visits from drug company representatives or from articles published in major medical journals. Merck recently went so far as to cook up a phony "peer-reviewed" journal and publish favourable data for its products in it, but many articles in the real journals are also written by drug company physicians involved in developing the new medicines.

Lilly actually ghostwrote scholarly articles about its drugs, and asked doctors to put their names on them—with the rising malpractice premiums and lower HMO reimbursements, many doctors cannot even afford to practise these days without pharmaceutical consulting grants. Either way, many doctors will prescribe a new drug right away and rely only on what they read in the manufacturer's own summaries of trial results. The information they are getting always favours the new drug, with the studies almost invariably funded and controlled by the company making the drug. It was not until 1962 that the FDA was ordered by Congress to review all new medications for effectiveness. Thousands of drugs already on the market were naturally also supposed to be evaluated, but some manufacturers claimed their medications were "grandfathered" under earlier laws. The FDA estimates that unapproved prescription drugs still account for 2% of all prescriptions filled by American pharmacies, or about 72 million scripts a year.[871]

Depression has long been treated with pharmaceuticals, but antidepressants have only recently become the most commonly prescribed class of medications in the United States. First came the barbiturates. They were otherwise fine mood-alterers, except that an overdose usually resulted in death, and alcoholics were dropping like

870. Karen E. Lasser, et al. "Timing of New Black Box Warnings and Withdrawals for Prescription Medications," *JAMA* 287(17), May 1, 2002, 2215–2220.

871. Ricardo Alonso-Zaldivar & Frank Bass, "U.S. Pays $200M for Unapproved Drugs," Associated Press, November 24, 2008.

flies because they liked mixing them with booze. Something else had to be developed to replace them and so we got benzodiazepines, which had a similar effect but were hard to overdose on. They were, of course, seriously addictive, so the next generation of anti-anxiety medicines, which merely altered serotonin levels, was greeted with joy. Known as SSRIs, or selective serotonin reuptake inhibitors, they too came with some unfortunate side effects. As Denis Leary put it, "how depressed do you have to be when in order to feel better, you're walking around like a naked grape with a head full of bells and a sudden desire to punch a stranger in the throat?"[872]

What is more, SSRI withdrawal, even if done gradually, can be excruciating. Some of the more serious withdrawal symptoms include twitches, tremors, blurred vision, and nausea—but also depression and anxiety. However, depression and serotonin do not necessarily have anything to do with each other, so it is possible that SSRIs are based wholly on the placebo effect. There is a strong placebo component in the response to drugs for pain, asthma, irritable-bowel syndrome, various skin conditions, and even Parkinson's disease; but according to the most extensive study ever conducted on SSRI drugs, they are so ineffective as not to be drugs at all. The 2008 study by a University of Hull team concluded that the previous, distorted findings were a result of the drug companies withholding 90% of the trial data and publishing only 10%, i.e. the portion that was favourable.[873] However, their very real side effects include insomnia, psychoses, and school shootings.

We are told over and over again that psychotherapy is more effective than either drugs or placebos, but the reality of the matter is that most patients with depression are treated by primary-care doctors, not psychiatrists. And despite antidepressant prescriptions becoming more and more common, they are not used in the treatment of depression much more than before. In other words, antidepressants are used more often than before to treat unrelated disorders.[874] While most patients do not experience truly serious side effects, there is a small group of people who will become violent or dangerous and self-destructive. In other words, for them, the effects of the drug are a reverse of what they are supposed to be. It was first discovered in the United States that school shooters have almost without an exception been on SSRIs either during the shooting or just before it.[875] The shooters were, of course, highly disturbed individuals with murderous fantasies, but you should be able to guess what happens when those tendencies are further boosted with pharmaceuticals.

It has recently come to light that Lilly always knew about this side of the story, but knowingly manipulated the results or omitted them altogether. Lilly's own studies list the suicides as overdoses and/or accidents, and leave the horrible massacres entirely out of the research. Incredibly, the pharmaceutical giant has enjoyed its share of the spoils of war in Iraq. It has made an immensely lucrative deal with Washington, stipulating that Prozac® should used as the primary shell-shock treatment. The

872. Op. cit.

873. Irving Kirsch, et al. "Initial Severity and Antidepressant Benefits: A Meta-Analysis of Data Submitted to the Food and Drug Administration," *PLoS Medicine* 5(2), February 2008, e45.

874. Olfson & Marcus, op. cit.

875. Levine 2001.

National Center for Posttraumatic Stress Disorder recommends "SSRIs as first-line medications for PTSD pharmacotherapy in men and women with military-related PTSD."[876] Their side effects can even prove useful in a war zone: slaughtering a room full of people might be a problem in peace time, but the ability to do so is essential in Baghdad house raids. Consider the recent WikiLeaks video of U.S. forces killing a dozen or so Iraqi civilians—the attack on a second group of unarmed civilians who drove up to aid a wounded countryman was particularly striking.

Of course, the down side is that these drugs often leave the user suicidal. Armed forces personnel traditionally have had a much lower suicide rate than the general population, but the Iraq war veterans appear to be taking their own lives at an epidemic pace. Suicide rates have been rising every year since the start of the Iraq war and 2008 marked the highest rate of military suicides in decades. In January of 2009, the U.S. Army for the first time ever exceeded the civilian ratio of 19 deaths per 100,000 due to suicide. By then, suicide took the lives of more American soldiers than al-Qaeda and the Iraqi insurgency combined. In fact, more U.S. military personnel have taken their own lives than have been killed in either the Iraq or Afghanistan wars.[877] There is even talk of an "Iraq War Syndrome," which British soldiers who served in Iraq curiously seem to show no signs of. The possible connection of Prozac to the American military suicides has not been examined and probably never will be.

Medical services that are held sacred such as medications, procedures, and surgery often do not work or work poorly to treat the diseases that account for the majority of illnesses and costs today, namely heart conditions, diabetes, obesity, breast and prostate cancer, and several other chronic diseases. Yet the State reimburses for these services because of clinical practice guidelines established through industry influence or custom, not science. Tax dollars pay for medical care even if it is not proven effective, which leads to higher costs and worsened clinical outcomes. What is not reimbursed is the treatment of obesity, except for gastric bypass, a $100,000 operation, even though obesity accounts for around 10% of health care costs.[878] In fact, many are demanding that the obese, the smokers, and the alcoholics should pay higher insurance premiums than the rest of us. And such demands will only grow in the future, because we have been taught to hate all losers.

Generally speaking, what we hear about bodily ailments is a bunch of nonsense. A person suffering from a "bad back" is told that his back muscles are weak and they need to be strengthened. Modern medicine is starting to resemble a religion: whatever the complaint, the patient is to blame. He is either too lazy or too stupid. If exercise does not bring about the desired result, the patient has simply not tried hard enough. In reality, the cause of back pain is not muscular weakness, but muscular tension. Otherwise the fact that even top-ranking athletes suffer from back pain would not make any sense. In fact, most people suffer from it at one point or another. The pain comes and goes. It cannot be caused by the intervertebral disc or wear, since the disc

---

876. J. I. Ruzek, et al. "Treatment of the Returning Iraq War Veteran." Lande 2004.

877. Chiarelli 2010.

878. Mark Hyman, "Why Health Care Reform Will Fail: Part I—The Business of Disease: We Pay for What Doesn't Work," *Huffington Post*, August 19, 2009.

does not move back and forth, and a wear does not come and go. The pain emanates from the supporting muscles around the vertebrae. Attempting to strengthen those muscles through exercise is completely useless, because they function wholly outside the voluntary nervous system.

We have a tendency to condemn people with values different from our own, and it is easy to denounce a person whom we think does not pay enough attention to their own health—such a person should pay for his own medical care. What about joggers? They always seem to have one knee shot, and skiers and alpinists, they should have huge premiums. If we wish to be consistent in our values, we must ask ourselves why a top athlete with a titanium knee and a plastic jaw who is forced to retire at thirty should not pay for his own medical bill and should not be held accountable for ruining his own health. If we are to be consistent, we must condemn also this method of endangering one's health. The expression "athletics" is no doubt simpler and more concise than the "struggle of overtrained and crippled drug addicts paid for by advertisers and followed by factionalists."

Yet it is clear that athletics are great and exercise is terrible. The greatest athletic achievements embody elegance, brilliance, and virtuosity. They form a part of high culture because they consist of the cultivation and refinement of a certain human ability. Usain Bolt is superior in every meaning of the word. He is a "champion" in a way that is prone to cause elation in his fellow-men. This dimension of glory is completely absent from run-of-the-mill exercise. The red-faced panting and puffing that comes with it is the diametric opposite. We are told that exercise is not only "great for our health" but that it is downright "addictive." However, a glance at the etiquette book reminds us that when you engage in a solitary and unritualized activity for the sake of pleasure, you should not do it in front of others. The aristocratic nature of athletics is what makes them great—exercise is only demeaning.

Each successive post-WWII generation has enjoyed an increasingly sedentary lifestyle, and those lifestyles appear to have been accompanied by an inexorable increase in obesity. But might we have confused cause and effect? Terry Wilkin, professor of endocrinology and metabolism at the Peninsula Medical School in Plymouth, argues that we have. For more than a decade, he has been monitoring the health, weight, and activity levels of 300 subjects since the age of five. When his team compared the more naturally active children with the less active ones, they were surprised to discover absolutely no difference in their body fat or mass.[879] It is much harder to exercise when you are overweight and "high energy density" foods are quick to get us there. Obesity figures are not going to improve through government-sponsored programs such as PE time in school, extracurricular activities, and playing fields, which focus primarily on exercise while ignoring the gigantic food industry that pushes high-calorie junk to children.

It would be absurd to disapprove of exercise in itself, but claiming that it is unequivocally a good thing is no more reasonable—that would make it an ideology. Exercise is important, but its significance has been overemphasized, because too much

879. Brad S. Metcalf, et al. "Fatness Leads to Inactivity, but Inactivity Does Not Lead to Fatness: A Longitudinal Study in Children," *Archives of Disease in Childhood* 96(10), October 2011, 942–947.

strain is bad for our health and wears out our bodies. We only have a limited number of heartbeats, so is it really wise to waste so many on needless physical exertion? From treadmills to dumbbells, Jane Fonda to *Buns of Steel*, we understand and expect that getting in shape is going to require serious effort on our part. However, more and more research is emerging to show that exercise has a negligible impact on weight loss. For example, the Mayo Clinic, a prestigious non-profit medical practice and research group based in the U.S., reports that studies "have demonstrated no or modest weight loss with exercise alone" and that "an exercise regimen . . . is unlikely to result in short-term weight loss beyond what is achieved with dietary change."[880]

In theory, it is, of course, possible to burn more calories than you eat, but you have to do a lot more exercise than most people realize. However, even mild anaerobic exercise has great many salutary effects. Neck pain, for example, seldom if at all originates in the neck itself, but is rather caused by tight muscles of the upper back or the shoulders, which can be easily targeted and loosened up by little weight training. What is more, the latest scientific findings suggest that an intense workout in the gym is actually less effective than gentle exercise in terms of weight loss. Researchers at the kinesiology department of UMass Amherst have found evidence that moderate exercise such as walking may help burn calories without triggering a "caloric compensation effect," i.e. without making you reach for a snack the moment you are done. In one experiment, they showed that simply standing up instead of sitting used up hundreds more calories a day without increasing appetite hormones in the blood.[881] From a purely practical perspective, exercise is never going to be an effective way of slimming, unless you have the training schedule and willpower of an Olympic athlete.

The notion of eternal youth, health, and beauty was first entertained by the urban middle classes, but it soon spread even to the rural areas; today, every small town boasts at the very least a gym. This symbolic ascendancy of youth denotes a corporate infiltration of our daily lives, the creation of a new family structure that is ruled by the young, or through our perception of a youthful ideal. It is bewildering how people can act so uniformly in their pursuit of individualism. We have all but forgotten that, "Ageing is not a curse, it is a privilege." The customary respect for elders was a respect due for having survived past the historic life expectancy of twenty-five. Survival and old age do not require wisdom any more, or indeed, tips from the previous generation. However, today, as before, "Respect is something you earn."

Of course, old people no longer show any respect to the young either. Senior citizens bump unapologetically into other commuters in the train, never ask politely for room in a crowd, and always jump the queue. The old can be wise, but they are not so *by default;* most are just dead-set in their ways in a fashion a young person could never be—as Einstein famously put it, "Common sense is just the sum total of all prejudice deposited in the human mind prior to the age of 18." Or, as the now-ageing hippies used to say: "Never trust anyone over thirty." Mental powers, reasoning, speed of thought, and spatial visualization begin to dwindle in our late

---

880. Warren G. Thompson, et al. "Treatment of Obesity," *Mayo Clinic Proceedings* 82(1), January 2007, 93–102.

881. Brooke R. Stephens, et al. "Effects of 1 Day of Inactivity on Insulin Action in Healthy Men and Women: Interaction with Energy Intake," *Metabolism* 60(7), July 2011, 941–949.

twenties, marking the start of old age. Once you reach middle age, it is easier to do nothing new than to do something new, because by then risk presents more possibility of loss than gain, whence the saying: "You cannot teach an old dog new tricks." The elderly complain about their ailments and see their doctor on a regular basis, but refuse to give up salt, tobacco, or the morning coffee. Story upon story is devoted to how the baby boomers are "redefining" retirement, bringing the same level of self-indulgence to it that they have brought to every other period in their lives. When taking advice from your parents, it always boils down to "honour thy mother and father" versus "consider the source."

10

Always Remember That You're Unique, Just Like Everyone Else

"I have never let my schooling interfere with my education," as Mark Twain reputedly asserted. First there was the old European aristocracy, whose gentle manners and refined breeding could be explained by their noble birth. The modern bourgeoisie, who inherited the power of the nobility, could not pretend to be "naturally" upper class, and therefore had to compensate for the lack of ancestry and tradition with schooling—only proper education could take the place of the missing gentility. The habitus of the cultured burgher implied that high social standing came with certain responsibilities or obligations, namely a thorough command of the cultural heritage and good manners. This is the main reason why literature is often associated in our culture with the deluded notion that a person can ennoble and refine himself by the simple act of reading or writing books.

In advanced placement high school classes, students are rushed through tomes and required to read year round. Curricula demand that the AP students read classics, but they are not taught to understand the theme, the syntax, or the vocabulary, leaving them disinterested about the literature because it does not connect with them. Instructed to wring symbolism out of every word, teachers are left with no time to help their students make meaning of the complex texts. Teaching is reduced to telling the students what the texts mean, denying the students any opportunity to bring their thoughts into the analysis of meaning. Required reading leaves adolescents with no time to pick up books they think would be fun. It is this—not television, cell phones, or the internet—that has produced a generation that does not read anymore.

I say this emphatically: universities are the last vestige of mediaevalism in Western civilization. The Latin word *universitas* signifies a guild, and all modern universities are still based on the mediaeval guild system, with its consecutive degrees of apprentice, fellow, and master, which require information, knowledge, and learning that has not changed. Surely the basics are the same, you ask? Maybe, but then exactly what do we have the 12 years of comprehensive education for? Basic reading skills, addition and multiplication, recognizing a squirrel as a squirrel, are taught in the first and second grades. With this education, the students should be able to do just okay in society, provided that they also learn a trade with which to support themselves. In the Middle Ages, students generally entered university at the age of fourteen, or even earlier. Today, as before, most learning takes place during practical training, be the student's major field medicine, computer science, or economics—and the place of training will usually be the graduate's future employer, based on his earlier performance there, not on his grades from any theory class.

At the same time, public support for university professors conducting research in addition to teaching has hit a new low. People seem to think that if faculty members only stopped doing research, and in particular, if they stopped asking for tax-supported funding for it, they could focus on what is important: the education of our children. However, the question becomes: what exactly would the professors be teaching them, and where would they get the material? People tend not to realize that the information in textbooks and lectures has to come from someone, somewhere, finding things out, doing experiments, and putting the results together with the works of others, eventually developing a body of knowledge. What is taught at university is constantly changing as new research reveals new discoveries each day, leading to new conclusions.[882]

But as Matt Damon told a snotty college student in *Good Will Hunting*, "You wasted $150,000 on an education you coulda got for a buck fifty in late charges at the public library."[883] When universities first got started, there were no printing presses or college libraries, so back then the books would have cost the mediaeval equivalent of the aforementioned amount. The strongest rationale for having universities today is research, i.e. self-education, not teaching others. Before universities were widespread, scientists—or natural philosophers as they were then known—had to fund their own research through their personal fortunes or by acquiring wealthy patrons. Darwin, for example, was able to pursue his interest in the origin of the species largely due to the fact that he married his cousin, Emma Wedgwood, heir of the Wedgwood china dynasty.

We have since then turned science into a big business, but at the same time, failed to notice that many of the rules of science do not really fit with that model. Science has changed considerably in terms of competitiveness, the level of funding, and the

882. Marlene Zuk, "We Need Professors in the Labs as Well as in Classes," *Los Angeles Times*, December 13, 2004.

883. Dir. Gus Van Sant. Miramax Films, 1997.

commercial pressure. There is no dividing line between academic laboratories and commerce in the United States any more, as scientists are juggling between the one and the other with the help of money and cultural approval. Much of today's scientific misconduct is a direct result of the frustrations and injustices built into the modern American system of scientific rewards. According to a large-scale survey of scientific misbehaviour undertaken by the University of Minnesota, alarming number of U.S. researchers engage in fact-bending or deceit. For instance, more than 15% of the scientists who answered a confidential questionnaire confessed to having thrown out data when it contradicted their "gut feeling," while an equal portion admitted they had changed the design or results of a study to satisfy a sponsor.[884]

The university is supposed to be an insular environment: universities exist to pose difficult questions, to promote critical thinking, and to generally challenge prejudice and complacency; those within their walls are meant to be protected from outside political pressure in order that learning can take place. The true researchers do not lust after extra money; to them, quantitative recognition is not the bottom line. The recognition all scientists crave for is from those who truly understand their achievements—their peers and colleagues. What researchers wish to do the most is to research; freely, in peace. The problem with universities is that the days of the tenured professors are consumed by administration, supervising dissertations, and faculty disputes prompted by shrinking resources. The rest of the teaching staff is formed by part-time researchers, who live from hand to mouth.

The societal changes that came with industrialization at the end of the 19th century created a new demand for schooling in the West, which in many countries led to compulsory education. It was important to be able to predict educability: how to tell the educable children from those who probably could not be schooled. The premise was that intelligence is an unchangeable and mostly inherited trait. The basis for the larger trait theory lay in a belief characteristic of Western everyday thought which regards personality as describable with fixed traits and attributes. The efforts to group individuals into various personality types found its expression as early as 400 BCE, when Hippocrates proposed a connection between temper and personality. The idea was that every person could be described through the same basic traits, which explain their behaviour: e.g. Johnny is lazy because he acts in a lazy manner, and Johnny acts in a lazy manner because he is lazy.

This rather obvious exercise in circular reasoning was not challenged until the late 1920s, and at that time, governments paid no heed to such critique, because there was no other method available to satisfy the growing need for psychological testing prompted by the two world wars. During the Second World War, there was a great upsurge in the development of such tests, the goal being the grading and classification of the new conscripts. Trait theories offered a temptingly straightforward answer to this challenge, enabling the creation of simple, easy-to-administer tests for large groups of people. The period following WWII saw a dramatic growth of clinical psychology, necessitated by all the mental health problems caused by war. At that time, clinical thinking was still dominated by the medical view of illness, and traits

884. Brian C. Martinson, et al. "Scientists Behaving Badly," *Nature* 435(7043), June 9, 2005, 737–738.

were thought of as useful in the classification of mental disorders, just as medical symptoms are useful in dividing patients into different disease categories.

Indeed, the principal contribution of trait theories to clinical work has been the development of methods to diagnose psychiatric illnesses. The *Diagnostic and Statistical Manual of Mental Disorders*, or the DSM, which defines the emotional problems for which physicians prescribe drugs and insurance companies pay the treatment bills, grew out of a guidebook used by the military during World War II. The creation of these testing tools has been based on preliminary studies that have sought to discern intrinsic differences between "normal" individuals and those with various classes of mental health problems. The trouble is, almost every piece of human behaviour can be classified as being in some way aberrant: since WWII, the number of disorders in the DSM has tripled to 300, an increase parallelled by the rise in sale of drugs that pharmaceutical companies tout as remedies for emotional suffering. Yet the rot really began with the Victorian obsession with social measurement and ever more refined division of people into sad, mad, or bad, all of which needed to be hidden away from ordered society in a total institution—asylum, workhouse, or prison—in order to preserve social order.

However, the limitations of trait description have become obvious in several extensive studies made during the last three decades. The still growing critique has been levelled mainly against the presumption that human behaviour is unchangeable and thus against the ability of trait theories to explain human actions in changing situations. For example, the same person can be totally confident in one situation and wholly unconfident in another. This tendency to overestimate the importance of traits and to underestimate the importance of circumstances is known as fundamental attribution error. It renders trait theories incapable of predicting a person's behaviour, yet they form the basis of all psychometric personality tests, including those used in vocational selection and job recruiting. The laws on privacy demand that workplace personality tests give a flawless picture of the applicant's personality—but how many people even have a flawless picture of themselves?

Research shows that we define a stranger's personality after just ten seconds. With this thin slice of information, we begin to think and act differently toward them. Should we label them as open-minded and curious, we might prefer to spend more time with them; should we label them as disagreeable and neurotic, we might prefer to keep our distance. So an entire pattern starts to form in a few seconds, yet at any given moment, you could be sociable, but you could also feel like being alone or uncomfortable around other people. We all laugh and tease friends at "happy hour," but we can be equally serious and assertive when trying to get a late fee waived by a credit card representative. Simply by recognizing the breadth of our personalities, we can gain access to a greater variety of strategies in any given situation. If we believe that traits such as intelligence, perseverance, and creativity are fixed, we are powerless to change and begin to view failures as personal flaws, instead of attributing them to difficult situations or a lack of effort.

Enlightenment science sought to reduce reality to distinct constituent units: time, space, matter, etc., using the Newtonian model as a template. In the aftermath of the Nazi experience, philosophers like Michel Foucault suggested that the mechanistic paradigm leads inevitably to fascistic and bureaucratic societies, where people are just cogs in the greater machinery. In science, the theories of relativity and quantum physics, developed between 1905 and the late 1920s, overturned all the principal concepts of Newtonian mechanics and the Cartesian world view: all the carefully distinguished categories of Newtonianism were once again understood as interconnected phenomena. Unfortunately, the philosophical implications of modern physics never filtered into the political arena; as Nobelist Richard Feynman once remarked, "I think I can safely say that nobody understands quantum mechanics."[885]

Whereas in classical physics the properties and behaviour of the parts determine those of the whole, the situation is actually reversed in quantum physics. Yet we continue to teach our children Newtonian theory, ostensibly because the easy-to-learn classical formulæ remain useable in everyday life. "Everything you've learned in school as 'obvious' becomes less and less obvious as you begin to study the universe. For example, there are no solids in the universe. There's not even a suggestion of a solid. There are no absolute continuums. There are no surfaces. There are no straight lines."[886] The schoolchildren who visit the publicly funded Smithsonian Institution in Washington D.C. are caught in a similar scientific time warp. According to the palaeontologists at the National Museum of Natural History, congressional funding for their subject dried up in the 1980s, when political hostility towards science, and in particular, evolution, began to increase.[887] In January of 2009, the broadcaster Sir David Attenborough revealed that he had received hate mail from viewers for not crediting God in his nature programs.[888]

One of the key evidences presented for Creation is the recurring appearance of the Divine Proportion, or Golden Section, as it was known to the ancient Greeks, throughout the design of the human body and other life forms. However, as Chapman Cohen observed: "Regularity in Nature is not proof of the control of Nature by Divine intelligence; it is rather the reverse. If something—call it matter, or ether, or x—exists, it must operate in accordance with its innate qualities; and so long as this x remains uncontrolled, its manifestations will continue unchallenged—in other words, there will be 'order'. The same causes, the same results."[889] Thus: "The intelligent beings in these regions should . . . not be surprised if they observe that their locality in the universe satisfies the conditions that are necessary for their existence," as Stephen Hawking wrote in *A Brief History of Time*. "It is a bit like a rich person living in a wealthy neighborhood not seeing any poverty."[890]

Everything organizes all by itself; we come from self-organizing cells of four billion years ago. The cells have grown more complex over time, and the most intricate creature on Earth confirms this. According to biologists and physicists, all

885. 1965, 129.

886. Fuller 1970, 120.

887. David Rains Wallace, "Believe It or Not, Science Evolves Too," *Los Angeles Times*, July 17, 2005.

888. *The Guardian*, January 27, 2009.

889. 1928, 43.

890. 1988, 124.

life is but a method of organizing matter and information through duplication. The ability of carbon atoms to form long chains with other atoms is basic to the chemistry of life as we know it. Carbon and hydrogen together can combine in a countless number of chemical compounds. There is no need for a mysterious life force or a button pusher, for this "autocatalysis" is a naturally occurring phenomenon. Evolution does not inherently rule out the possibility of God, but nor does the idea that life sprang forth from nothingness require belief in a deity.

Living organisms change only a little from generation to generation, not too much. An organism that was too open to change would be destroyed by mutations in a few generations; a structure that would not permit any alteration could not adapt to changes in environment, making the organism vulnerable to climate change or other species taking over its territory. In fact, evolution appears to be an absolute prerequisite for all things living. For sure, "evolution is both fact and theory," while "creationism is neither." There is no doubt whatsoever that evolution exists in the world. Even the majority of creationists regard evolution as a fact of nature. Darwin's Theory of Evolution is not a theory arguing that things evolve, but a theory as to why and how animals have evolved, changed, and developed.

The word "evolution" means literally "change occurring through a course of time," and Darwin proposed that the cause of this change is what he termed "natural selection." It is this factor which defines Darwinism as a particular kind of evolutionary science, one that relies on the vast evidence that living things adapted through random mutation. Some may conclude from this evidence that there is no God, while others may arrive at the conclusion that it must have taken an intelligent agent to come up with such a marvellous way for the world to change and rebalance itself. Either view is valid, but neither is provable; both belong to the realm of philosophy or religion, not science.

As Stephen Jay Gould wrote in *Science and Creationism:* "Facts are the world's data. Theories are structures of ideas that explain and interpret facts. Facts don't go away when scientists debate rival theories to explain them. Einstein's theory of gravitation replaced Newton's in this century, but apples didn't suspend themselves in midair, pending the outcome. And humans evolved from ape-like ancestors whether they did so by Darwin's proposed mechanism or by some other yet to be discovered."[891] The term "intelligent design" is just a linguistic filler for something as yet unexplained by science. In essence, it is saying that if there is no natural explanation for x, then the explanation must be a supernatural one. Proponents of intelligent design cannot see how e.g. the bacterial flagellum could have evolved, but saying "intelligent design did it" does not explain anything. And because supernatural power is by definition beyond the natural world, the study of such power is by definition outside science.

At the same time, two-fifths of all Americans reject the scientific consensus that life on Earth evolved from a common ancestor over millions of years; nearly as many believe evolution was guided by God, and fewer than one in six that it occurred by

891. "Evolution as Fact and Theory." Montagu 1984, 118.

itself.[892] However, to put this in perspective, according to a 1986 poll, about one-third of college students in the United States also believed that Big Foot actually exists, that the lost city of Atlantis was real, and that space aliens visited Earth in ancient times; even a larger portion believed in ghosts and thought it is possible to communicate with the dead.[893] Meanwhile, a 1998 survey of the National Academy of Sciences revealed that contrasted with 90% of all Americans, only 7% of the nation's leading scientists believe in God.[894]

Religious accounts of life's origins have usually been kept out of the science classrooms, at times by court order. However, loyal to the stories they have learned in church, students often take it upon themselves to wedge creationism into the classroom, sometimes becoming so disruptive that many teachers dread the annual unit on evolution, or skip it altogether. But where is the harm in believing in creationism, you ask? If you do, you are also prone to dismiss all evolution, not only the organic variety, and to try and turn back the clock on it. Ancient Babylonian scientists were quite convinced that the world was intelligently designed by Marduk, god of gods, after he smashed the skull of Tiamat, primordial mother of all things, so that her blood ran streaming to the ends of the earth. Different Christian groups disagree over whether the world was literally created in seven days, whether those seven days were a metaphorical reference to seven epochs, or whether there were large gaps of time between the days.

Mainstream media wrongly describe this as a debate between creationism and evolutionary theory. In reality, the debate is between creationism and the whole of science as we know it. If the universe is only 6,000 years old, then all of geology and biology are wrong. The speed of light has been wrongly calculated, so Einsteinian physics is also wrong. The distance and speed of other galaxies has been wrongly calculated, which means that all of astronomy and therefore even Newtonian physics are wrong. For informed individuals to challenge accepted scientific orthodoxy on the basis of new evidence is always healthy, whereas debunking the whole of science on the back of a story passed down by Iron Age goat-herders would be dangerously delusional.

The idea that supernatural claims are not disproven until they are tested, that they "might be true," only encourages people to give them far more credence than they actually deserve, breeding gullibility and wishful thinking, which pose a real danger for students of science. If testing these claims might work, then testing them should be unnecessary, because if there was any chance at all of some of these claims being true, then we would hardly be able to move without stepping on elves and gnomes all over the place. Plenty of studies have shown the inefficacy of prayer, for example, but that has not stopped people anywhere in the world from praying, including the ones

---

892. Gallup Poll, December 17, 2010.

893. Raymond A. Eve & Francis B. Harrold, "Creationism, Cult Archaeology, and Other Pseudoscientific Beliefs: A Study of College Students," *Youth and Society* 17(4), June 1986, 396–421.

894. Edward J. Larson & Larry Witham, "Leading Scientists Still Reject God," *Nature* 394(6691), July 23, 1998, 313.

who took part in those studies.[895] Nor has the vast mountains of evidence in support of evolution stopped people from believing in creationism.

"We must respect the other fellow's religion," exclaimed H. L. Mencken, "but only in the sense and to the extent that we respect his theory that his wife is beautiful and his children smart."[896] A believer who asks non-believers to respect his taboos in a public debate is not demanding respect, but submission. "There is, in fact, nothing about religious opinions that entitles them to any more respect than other opinions get. On the contrary, they tend to be noticeably silly."[897] What the Sage of Baltimore forgot is that even opinions are usually based on facts, or on our interpretation of facts, whereas beliefs, by their very nature, are not—tolerance does not equal respect. Adults should, of course, be free to believe whatever they like, but children should only be taught the facts, so they can grow up to be able to make their own informed decisions.

Since advocates of intelligent design have been wholly unable to convince scientists that their so-called theory has any scientific merit, they have relied on political methods to gain admittance to school curricula. They have marketed their ideas to politicians through web sites, news releases, and even free textbooks. Although such proponents of I.D. as the Discovery Institute in Seattle claim that their intent is not to promote a literal interpretation of the Bible, many of the politicians they lobby are themselves creationists, who deny that evolution took place. Early copies of I.D. literature have been demonstrated to be sloppy rewrites of creationist literature, with "creationism" search-and-replaced with "intelligent design," sometimes resulting in such typos as "designists." Teaching intelligent design can only deprive students of a proper education, which will ultimately cause harm to the U.S. economy.

Science in the United States has all but died out over the last quarter of a century, even as the importance of science has grown. As Carl Sagan put it, "We've arranged a global civilization in which most crucial elements—transportation, communications, and all other industries; agriculture, medicine, education, entertainment, protecting the environment; and even the key democratic institution of voting—profoundly depend on science and technology. We have also arranged things so that almost no one understands science and technology."[898] At a period when fewer and fewer American students are heading into science and baby-boomer scientists are retiring, can U.S. taxpayers really afford to debate the facts of evolution?

In the popular folklore of U.S. history, there is a sense in which the various scientific achievements of the Founding Fathers—the electrical experiments of Franklin, the botany of Jefferson, etc.—serve only as an extracurricular activity. That is, they are seen as statesmen and political visionaries, who just happened to also be hobbyists in natural philosophy, albeit incredibly talented ones. Well, popular history

---

895. Kevin S. Masters, et al. "Are There Demonstrable Effects of Distant Intercessory Prayer?: A Meta-Analytic Review," *Annals of Behavioral Medicine* 32(1), August 2006, 21–26.

896. 1956, 3.

897. 1949, 80.

898. 1995, 26.

has it is exactly backwards. The Founders might have been hobbyists and amateurs at science, but so were all the other great scientific minds of the Enlightenment. What they shared was a fundamental belief that the world could improve if the light of reason was allowed to shine upon it. Their political innovations were modelled after the advancements in natural philosophy which they had all experienced. Adopting a know-nothing attitude towards scientific thought and hiding behind the cloak of piety would have been the gravest offence to the Founders. When U.S. political leaders take anti-science positions, or when they happily plead ignorance about some of the most important issues of our time, they are not just being anti-intellectual, they are being downright un-American.

The United States has long had the largest—and since World War II also the most respected—university system in the world. Although the U.S. counts higher education as one of its top five service exports, and is still recognized as the global leader in science, that position is now being challenged by others. A fierce contest for talent is under way to win a share of the three million students from around the world now enrolled in colleges and universities—a number that is expected to more than double by 2025.[899] American universities may attract the brightest students in the world, but only to have most of them thrown out of the country after they graduate. The U.S. issues a minuscule number of work visas and green cards, turning away thousands of skilled graduates who want to stay and work there. Overall, the number of foreign students in the U.S. is inching back up after a decline following the 9/11 attacks, led by surging numbers from India and China. The latter in particular is investing a great deal to achieve its own technological strength, rapidly expanding and upgrading universities and research institutes, as well as investing in the rigorous education of the general population. All in all, China is educating ten times as many students as the U.S.[900]

A generation of Arab men who once attended university in the United States, and returned home to become leaders in the Middle East, is increasingly sending the next generation to schools elsewhere. The leaders of many of these countries understand quite well that their economic growth, military power, and national security all rely on technological advances. Indeed, government funding for science and education has grown sharply in recent years in many Middle Eastern countries, with several being in the process of overhauling and modernizing their national scientific infrastructures. The rulers of several of the Gulf States are building new universities with labour imported from the West for both construction and academics. In Dubai, the government pays for the education of its citizens up to Ph.D. level. Neither is Iran the evil theocracy that Western media portray it to be. It has successfully cloned animals, it has designed and built some of the most sophisticated instruments for the new particle collider at CERN, and it publishes more scientific papers per-capita than any

899. Lesleyanne Hawthorne, "The Growing Global Demand for Students as Skilled Migrants," Migration Policy Institute, Washington, D.C., 2008.

900. Keith B. Richburg, "U.S. Experts Bemoan Nation's Loss of Stature in the World of Science," *Washington Post*, May 29, 2008.

other nation.[901]

Popular accounts of the history of science often suggest that no major scientific advances took place between the ancient Greeks and the European Renaissance. Parts of Western Europe may have languished in the Dark Ages, but that does not mean there was stagnation elsewhere; indeed, the period between the 9th and 13th centuries marked the golden age of Islamic science. The greatest period of sustained scientific advances during the 1,500 years between the Greeks and the Renaissance took place in the great centres of learning across the mediaeval Islamic empire, from Baghdad and Cairo to Córdoba and Samarkand. Brilliant advances were made in every field from mathematics, astronomy, and chemistry to physics, engineering, and medicine. For a period spanning over half a millennium, the international language of science was Arabic—and the next generation of scientists outside the United States might not speak English.

It is as if we are going backwards—the United States was founded as a secular society by people fleeing religious extremists and the Founding Fathers insisted on the separation of Church and State. "What influence in fact have ecclesiastical establishments had on Civil Society?" asked President Madison in 1785. "In some instances they have been seen to erect spiritual tyranny on the ruins of Civil authority; in many instances they have seen the upholding of the thrones of political tyranny; in no instance have they been seen the guardians of the liberty of the people."[902] Prior to World War I, all the significant "free speech" cases were about blasphemy. The time-honoured method used by totalitarian systems to supress criticism is to define it as an "insult," which is of course something you are legally entitled to punish. In science, no power has monopoly over truth or its interpretation, everything is susceptible to ridicule and being challenged. In fact, this questioning is the only legitimate method of approach in all scientific teaching and research that hopes to produce new knowledge.

"If dissent is now also to be thought of as a form of 'dissing,' then we have indeed succumbed to the thought police," declared Salman Rushdie.[903] You should never get personal in any debate, yet neither should you have an iota of respect for the other person's opinion; you should never be rude to your opponents, but you must always be allowed to get viciously rude about what they think. People must have the right to take an argument to the point where someone is offended by what they say: it is no great feat to support the free speech of someone with whom you agree or to whose opinion or cause you are indifferent. The defence of free speech begins when people say something you cannot stand; if you cannot defend their right to speak out, then you simply do not believe in free speech. As Voltaire famously put it: "I disagree with everything you say, but I would die defending your right to say it."

"The community which does not protect its humblest and most hated member in

---

901. Kiarash Aramesha & Soroush Dabbagh, "An Islamic View to Stem Cell Research and Cloning: Iran's Experience," *The American Journal of Bioethics* 7(2), February 2007, 62–63; M. A. Gomshi Nobary & R. Sepahvand, "Fragmentation Production of Triply Heavy Baryons at the CERN LHC," *Physical Review D* 71(3), February 1, 2005, 034024.1–11.

902. *Memorial and Remonstrance Against Religious Assessments.* Gaustad 2003, 235.

903. Speech to the American Society of Newspaper Editors, April 17, 1996.

the free utterance of his opinions, no matter how false or hateful, is only a gang of slaves," asserted the American abolitionist Wendell Phillips in 1837. "If there is anything in the universe that can't stand discussion, let it crack."[904] As Thomas Jefferson pointed out, "It is error alone which needs the support of government. Truth can stand by itself."[905] When the Mohammed cartoon row hit the Islamic world, even the "moderate" leaders of the community only condemned the actions of the mob—the torching of Western embassies—not their goals—the imposition of Muslim taboos on the West. Leadership in a free society requires the willingness and ability to challenge public opinion when it is based on misinformation, no information, prejudice, or plain stupidity. "Defamation of religion" has no validity in international law, because only individuals, not concepts or beliefs, can be defamed.

I personally cannot think of a more faithless pursuit than trying to prove the veracity of Scripture. To quote John Shelby Spong, Episcopal Bishop of Newark, "Literalistic Christians will learn that a God or a faith system that has to be defended daily is finally no God or faith system at all. They will learn that any god who can be killed ought to be killed."[906] One is not required to have faith in something that can be touched, measured, or quantified, something that can be seen by building a large enough telescope or a sensitive enough electron microscope. In *Finding Darwin's God*, Prof. Kenneth R. Miller, a devout Catholic, observed that, "If a lack of scientific explanation is proof of God's existence, the counterlogic is unimpeachable: A successful scientific explanation is an argument against God. That's why this reasoning, ultimately, is much more dangerous to religion than it is to science."[907]

I have a great respect for anyone with a genuine religious conviction, but in the words of Franklin: "When religious people quarrel about religion, or hungry people about their victuals, it looks as if they had not much of either about them." It was Oscar Wilde who dubbed religion "the fashionable substitute for belief,"[908] and I certainly do not believe in "conversion," that is, that a person would suddenly believe in every single dogma of his newly-found Church. Americans are by every measure a deeply religious people, but as the Pew Forum on Religion & Public Life discovered, they are also deeply ignorant about religion.[909] And Mark Twain was hardly alone in his contention that "It ain't the parts of the Bible that I can't understand that bother me, it is the parts that I do understand." Religion is not the answer, but rather a hint, a suggestion, a possibility for exploration meant to be sifted through for clues to the ineffable mystery of the universe.

I am strongly against organized religion, any organized religion—depriving people of personal religious experiences. "Real religion should be something that liberates men," declared Federico Fellini in a *60 Minutes* interview. "But churches don't want free men who can think for themself [sic] and find their own divinity within. When

904. The Freedom Speech of Wendell Phillips at Faneuil Hall, December 8, 1837.

905. *Notes on the State of Virginia*, Query XVII: Religion. 2002, 193.

906. 1994, 22.

907. 2002, 266.

908. *The Picture of Dorian Gray.* Op. cit. 135.

909. "U.S. Religious Knowledge Survey," Washington, D.C., September 28, 2010.

a religion becomes organized it is no longer a religious experience but only superstition and estrangement."[910] Conventional religions want you to feel like you need them, so they can continue to sell you real estate in Heaven. But true religion is supposed to be so empowering that it could empower you out of the very belief system that is doing the empowering. It is supposed to reconnect you to your personal divinity so wholly that you do not even need religion anymore.

"Praying as a public function, particularly when led by a clergyman, is a vulgar display of an exclusively personal matter," wrote the American freethinker Joseph Lewis.[911] Putting God's name into a pledge is taking God's name in vain; putting God's name on money is idolatry. Coerced belief is no belief at all—it is tyranny. Freedom of religion means that you cannot be forced into participating in a religious ceremony that is not of your choosing simply because you are out-voted. The U.S. Supreme Court ruled in 1962 that: "Neither the fact that the prayer is denominationally neutral nor the fact that its observance on the part of the students is voluntary can serve to free it from the limitations of the Establishment Clause."[912] And it does not take a rocket scientist to realize that a mandated moment of silence is a moment when the believers can say to the rest of the world: "This is me praying to my God. Maybe you should be praying too."

But as Nietzsche wrote, "this is the way in which religions are wont to die out: under the stern, intelligent eyes of an orthodox dogmatism, the mythical premises of a religion are systemized as a sum total of historical events."[913] In equating God with the structure and function of the material world, Christians are playing a losing game. God is turned into just another part of the natural world, thereby losing His transcendent mystery and divinity. Rational inference can never substitute for personal experience of the divine, which is—and must remain—the foundation of faith. And as the evangelical geologist Davis A. Young asks: "Can we seriously expect non-Christian educational leaders to develop a respect for Christianity if we insist on teaching the brand of science that creationism brings with it? Will not the forcing of modern creationism on the public simply lend credence to the idea already entertained by so many intellectual leaders that Christianity, at least in its modern form, is sheer anti-intellectual obscurantism?"[914]

"If God is omnipotent and omniscient, why didn't he start the universe out in the first place so it would come out the way he wants? Why's he constantly repairing and complaining? No, there's one thing the Bible makes clear: The biblical God is a sloppy manufacturer. He's not good at design, he's not good at execution. He'd be out of business if there was any competition."[915] Unless one wishes to attribute sheer malevolence to such a designer—like some Gnostic sects of old did—the manifold design flaws of life point distinctly to a natural, rather than a divine, process, where

910. Interview by Harry Reasoner, c. 1981.

911. 1957, 34.

912. *Engle v. Vitale*, 370 U.S. 421 (1962).

913. *The Birth of Tragedy*. 1967, 75.

914. 1982, 163.

915. Sagan 1985, 287.

living things were not created, but evolved. "Why has Christianity refused, whenever possible, to allow its beliefs to compete in a free marketplace of ideas?" enquired George H. Smith. "The answer is obvious and revealing. Christianity is peddling an inferior product, one that cannot withstand critical investigation. Unable to compete favorably with other theories, it has sought to gain a monopoly through a state franchise, which means: through the use of force."[916]

And it is not just Christianity, but most of the dogmatic religions that "have exhibited a perverse talent for taking the wrong side on the most important concepts in the material universe, from the structure of the solar system to the origin of man."[917] Ancient sun-worship is downright scientific in comparison: solar energy is the only energy we have, be it in the form of food or fossil fuel; man receives his sustenance, his life, ultimately as a gift from the Sun. Of course, "Religions die when they are proved to be true. Science is the record of dead religions."[918] There is only one traditional task of religion that science cannot fulfill: it does not have the ability to consolidate the communal bond through a system of morality. It is precisely this hole which the religious fundamentalists and moralists attack.

There are facts, but there are no moral facts; and as the Talmud says, "If you add to the truth, you subtract from it." The trouble with keeping your mind open is that people will come along and attempt to throw a lot of rubbish into it. In *The Burden of Skepticism*, Carl Sagan put it thus: "I maintain there is much more wonder in science than in pseudoscience. And in addition, to whatever measure this term has any meaning, science has the additional virtue, and it is not an inconsiderable one, of being true."[919] The science that was supposed to free us from all supernatural incomprehensibility has evolved into something more amazing than anything any religion has ever been able to produce. It has paraded before us a universe where particles seem to anticipate the position of one another, where cause and effect are turned on their heads, where energy vibrates in eleven dimensions, and where time travel may be feasible.

The universe of science is truly supernatural in that we can no longer discern it with our senses or through our three-dimensional mindset. Yet at the same time, most of us are convinced that this is the "most truthful" of all the models. It is precisely science, the force that was supposed to remove everything akin to religion from the world, that today fills us with a lofty sense of wonder. The business of science is to observe the physical world, to develop theories about how it works and then to test them; science in itself is neither atheistic nor godly. Only the Christian religion and science are mutually exclusive: the first couple was allowed to stay in paradise on one condition, that they did not eat of the tree of knowledge; "Moral: science is the forbidden as such—it alone is forbidden. Science is the first sin, seed of all sin, the original sin. This alone is morality. 'Thou shalt not know'—the rest follows."[920]

---

916. 1979, 114.

917. Simpson 1966, 214.

918. *Phrases and Philosophies*. Op. cit. 306.

919. *Skeptical Inquirer* 12(1), Fall 1987.

920. *The Antichrist*. Op. cit. 629.

"Do not believe in anything (simply) because you have heard it," says the Buddha. "Do not believe in traditions because they have been handed down for many generations. Do not believe in anything because it is found written in your religious books. Do not believe in anything merely on the authority of your teachers and elders. But after observation and analysis, when you find that anything agrees with reason, and is conducive to the good and benefit of one and all, accept it and live up to it."[921] Tenzin Gyatso, the 14th Dalai Lama, bids us to "conduct research and then accept the results. If they don't stand up to experimentation, Buddha's own words must be rejected."[922] As Mohandas Gandhi pointed out: "Truth never damages a cause that is just."[923]

Anti-religious atheism is a product of the Christian culture. Of course, basic Eastern religious doctrines, such as everyone being seen as their own redeemer, there being more than one deity, the ultimate object of religious pursuit being "uncreation," are considered downright Satanic in the West. Then there is the whole prayer-meditation divide: one seeks to gratify the ego, while the other seeks to dissolve it. "On two hypotheses alone is there any sense in prayer, that not quite extinct custom of olden times. It would have to be possible either to fix or alter the will of the godhead, and the devotee would have to know best himself what he needs and should really desire. Both hypotheses, axiomatic and traditional in all other religions, are denied by Christianity. . . .Christianity nevertheless maintained prayer side by side with its belief in the all-wise and all-provident divine reason (a belief that makes prayer really senseless and even blasphemous). . ."[924]

The Zen Buddhists say, "Wash your mouth every time you say 'Buddha!'" There will be no progress in Christianity until someone can get up in church and say, "Wash your mouth every time you say 'Jesus!'"[925] When the object of worship is externalized completely, that object, be it money, knowledge, Buddha, or Christ, becomes an obstacle that stands not only between the worshipper and the worshipped, but between the worshipper and their true self. When seeking enlightenment, every achievement won must be sacrificed or else one becomes a fanatic for whatever one happens to have reached; one must constantly refine, ceaselessly seek new paths and scale fresh heights before one can experience the whole—"If you meet Buddha on your road to enlightenment, kill him." Che Guevara had his own unique take on that Oriental saying: "If Christ himself stood in my way, I, like Nietzsche, would not hesitate to squish him like a worm."[926] Jesus is a false god, and if he were here today, I am positive he would agree and be outraged to see that his message has been transformed into a tool of idolatry and oppression. We would, of course, be fools to hope for a society in which organized religion completely dies out, but we should stop

---

921. Kalama Sutta, Anguttara Nikaya III:65.

922. *TIME*, April 11, 1988.

923. 1942–1948, II, 162.

924. *The Wanderer and His Shadow*, Passage 74. Nietzsche 1909–11, VII, 235–36.

925. Watts 1964, 112.

926. Dolores Moyano Martin, "The Making of a Revolutionary," *New York Times*, August 18, 1968.

behaving as if it deserved our collective respect.

There are things that we do not know and will never know, but none of them oblige us to say God, any more than they oblige us to say Quetzalcoatl. In fact, saying God gives us absolutely no answers at all. The Big Bang, on the other hand, gives us some very workable theories and answers. For example, the temperature of the universe and the quantities of matter is consistent with those expected if the Big Bang occurred. "In the popular imagination," writes Prof. Taner Edis, "the Big Bang is a great explosion; at one time there was nothing, then matter erupted into previously empty space. However, the Big Bang is the beginning of spacetime itself, not an event in time."[927]

The universe should really not exist at all. Zeno's paradox states that if an object is travelling from point A to point B, it has to logically reach a half way point between the two points. To reach that halfway point, it must reach a quarter of that distance first, and before that, it must travel an eight, a sixteenth, through an infinite gulf of increasingly impossible distances. This means that any motion, movement, distance, time, or even thought is in effect a logical impossibility. The Objectivist philosopher Leonard Peikoff contends that, "Existence exists, and only existence exists. Existence is a primary; it is uncreated, indestructible, eternal,"[928] and as Einstein phrased it in his day, "the only reason for time is so that everything doesn't happen at once."

"A human being is part of the whole, called by us 'Universe'; a part limited in time and space. He experiences himself, his thoughts and feelings as something separated from the rest—a kind of optical delusion of his consciousness. This delusion is a kind of prison for us, restricting us to our personal desires and affection for a few persons nearest to us. Our task must be to free ourselves from this prison by widening our circle of compassion to embrace all living creatures and the whole nature in its beauty. Nobody is able to achieve this completely but striving for such achievement is, in itself, a part of the liberation and a foundation for inner security."[929]

"All Bibles or sacred codes, have been the causes of the following Errors.

"1. That Man has two real existing principles Viz: a Body & a Soul. 2. That Energy, call'd Evil, is alone from the Body, & that Reason, call'd Good, is alone from the Soul. 3. That God will torment Man in Eternity for following his Energies.

"But the following Contraries to these are True.

"1. Man has no Body distinct from his Soul; for that call'd Body is a portion of Soul discern'd by the five Senses, the chief inlets of Soul in this age. 2. Energy is the only life and is from the Body and Reason as the bound or outward circumference of Energy. 3. Energy is Eternal Delight."[930]

The now challenged body-mind duality that was once prevalent in Western medicine is of Christian origin. As the Jesuit Father John L. McKenzie points out in the *Dictionary of the Bible*, "The immortality of the soul . . . was really an element foreign to Hebrew belief and Hebrew psychology which was never assimilated into

927. 2002, 94.

928. *The Philosophy of Objectivism*, Lecture 2. Rand 1988, 42.

929. Albert Einstein, March 4, 1950. Herbert 1985b, 250.

930. *The Marriage of Heaven and Hell*, pl. 4.

the Old Testament."[931] The Jews still believe in bodily resurrection—that is why they are required to bury their dead with all organs and limbs intact. Most Christians, however, would identify the ego with the soul, and in the 17th century, the French philosopher René Descartes declared that the mind and the body occupied different dimensional spaces, thus putting into words the old Christian paradigm known today as Cartesian dualism. However, modern scientific evidence has shown body and mind to have a far more integrated and interesting relationship.

Muscular tension, breathing, and posture have an effect on your emotions. When your body is tense, it produces different chemicals than when it is relaxed, so you of course also feel different. Your mental interpretations and your physiology are tightly intertwined in a so-called cybernetic circle. Should you alter either one, it affects the other immediately. Have you tried smiling when you are angry? It is difficult because the mind says one thing and the body says another. But if and when you were successful, you were probably taken aback by how much better you felt after this small change. If you tell your heart to beat faster, nothing happens. But if you visualize yourself walking in a gloomy, darkened alley late at night, your heart rate will rise. And these are only a few illustrations of just how strong the bond between mind and body is.

But how is it that emotions can create physical phenomena? The physical reality is supposed to be causally closed: i.e. every physical phenomenon must have a physical cause. Research has not unveiled any such abnormal states where a phenomenon would happen without a physical impetus—neither in the brain nor anywhere else. The only reasonable conjecture is that emotions are simply physical states of the brain. The physical effect of e.g. a placebo painkiller is explained by the release of endorphins, the body's own morphines. Our mental lives do not disappear just because we know their true, physical nature. Nor did light vanish when we learned that it was only a form of electromagnetic radiation.

The whole spirit-matter distinction is a philosophical construct: $E=mc^2$. Science fiction often entertains the notion that some day humanity will evolve to the point of becoming pure energy, but the truth is, we are *already* pure energy; atoms, protons, neutrons, electrons. "It was the sick and decaying who despised body and earth and invented the heavenly realm and the redemptive drops of blood," wrote Nietzsche, a classical philologist, "but they took even these sweet and gloomy poisons from body and earth."[932] The ancient Greeks made no separation between philosophy, religion, and spirituality. They spoke of Earth, Air, Fire, and Water; but also of a quintessence, a "fifth essence," which they called *physis*, and which constituted the spiritual aspect of it all, and from which we derive the word "physics."

Most of the Yoga masters, Hindu gurus, Buddhist monks, and other Asian teachers who started coming to the West in the 19th century emphasized the experimental dimension of spirituality—the demonstrable influence it has on individual lives. They presented their teachings as a science of consciousness with a theoretical component and a set of practical applications for testing those theories. As early as the 1890s,

931. 1995, 184.

932. *Thus Spoke Zarathustra*. Op. cit. 144.

Swami Vivekananda spent time with such scientific luminaries as Lord Kelvin, Hermann von Helmholtz, and Nikola Tesla. "Mr. Tesla thinks he can demonstrate mathematically that force and matter are reducible to potential energy," the swami wrote in a letter to a friend. "I am working a good deal now upon the cosmology and eschatology of Vedanta. I clearly see their perfect unison with modern science."[933]

According to physics, energy is neither created nor destroyed, only transformed. The laws of physics state that energy never gets quashed or erased. Does this mean that we are immortal after all? Well, we do not necessarily come back as our former selves, but our energy is certainly going to be used to fill another space somewhere. All the atoms of Jesus are still circulating around, and in fact, water molecules in the communion wine and wafer are bound to hold a few of his, making transubstantiation something more than just a silly Catholic dogma. Christians generally make fun of the Eastern concept of circular time, yet they never consider the absurdity of the Saviour of Mankind appearing on Earth at a particular point in time. As Stanislaw J. Lec asked, "When myth becomes reality, who wins? The idealist or the materialist?"[934]

The earliest humans probably never believed in a divinity at all. Even today, there are still many tribes that have absolutely no belief system as such; they simply accept that the world "is" and leave it at that. "Man always deceives himself when he abandons experience to follow imaginary systems," declared Baron d'Holbach. "He is the work of Nature. He exists in Nature. He is submitted to her laws. He cannot deliver himself from them. He cannot step beyond them even in thought."[935] We are told that "all things are possible with God,"[936] yet even He cannot boil an egg in cold water. "The imagination imitates," observed Oscar Wilde. "It is the critical spirit that creates."[937] Therefore, I have to agree with Harriet Martineau (1802–1876), the first female sociologist and an avowed atheist, who opined that "the one essential requisite of human welfare in all ways is scientific knowledge of human nature."[938]

Western civilization's adversarial relationship to nature mirrors an adversarial relationship of Westerners to their own nature. The dream of techno-utopia, which has been the primary enabling ideology of industrialism since the Age of Coal, and which was articulated by Sir Francis Bacon two centuries before that, parallels exactly the individual dream of finally getting your act together, controlling yourself, and living happily ever after. Both involve a conquest of nature—in the latter case, a conquest of your own nature, your biological drives. In Western religion, this idea takes the form of Original Sin and the concept of the Total Depravity of Man, but Western science, secular ethics, and even much of New Age thought agrees in a subtle way.

Of all the animals that walk the earth, man is the one predisposed to neuroses. Take any animal away from its natural environment, educate it away from its natural

933. Letter to E. T. Sturdy, February 13, 1896. 1964, 334.

934. Op. cit. 125.

935. 1816, I, 9.

936. Mark 10:27.

937. As quoted in Gide 1971, 797.

938. 2007, 645.

instincts, and you run the risk of a neurosis: head swaying in caged lions, crib biting in stabled horses, etc. Man, however, being as he is educated almost completely away from his instincts, has the dubious distinction of being the only animal predisposed to neurotic behaviour. Unlike animals, man can choose to ignore his instincts, indulging in which would often be not only immoral, or socially unacceptable, but against the law as well. At bottom, humans are animals with the burden of self-awareness.

Another trait that separates man from animals is our ability to anticipate the future and to plan long-term, goal-oriented actions. Countless psychological experiments have established that man alone is characterized by a wide-range, protracted memory. We are often urged to "live in the now" as a solution to all our problems, which is a bit of an oxymoron, since any conscious action requires knowledge of the past and anticipation of the future. However, it is equally absurd to make long-term plans: we may have excellent memories, but we are still not psychic. Contrary to conventional wisdom, time is not a dimension; in fact, time in itself does not even exist. What we call "time" is simply one aspect of the ever-changing relationship between moving objects in space—if nothing moved, there would be no time.

In Western society, time is a scarce resource. We turn everything into a race to the finish, but we never reach the finish line. We exist in a world where instant gratification is not fast enough, a world of not only speed dating, but even speed yoga. Yet every moment is eternal; there is no such thing as "waste of time," time itself being an abstract concept, one that all little children lack. As George Matthew Adams put it, "We cannot waste time. We can only waste ourselves." And the same goes for what most people refer to as "waste of energy." But as Brooks wrote back to his prison buddies in *The Shawshank Redemption*, "I can't believe how fast things move on the outside. I saw an automobile once when I was a kid but now they're everywhere. The world went and got itself in a big damn hurry."[939] All other animals go by the Sun, while humans are slaves to the artificial 24-hour clock and the arbitrary Daylight Savings Time that badly screws up our internal clocks twice each year.

Even as technological advancements have dramatically improved material lives in the West, many Westerners only feel increasingly worse. By practically every measurable yardstick, Western life has been getting better for decades. Standards of living keep on rising, with the average house in the United States now more than twice as large as a generation ago; middle-class income is still climbing, if more slowly than income at the very top; and more Americans graduate from college every year. Longevity is in on the rise, diseases—including most cancers—in decline. Pollution, except for greenhouse gases, is on the decrease. All these positive indicators notwithstanding, the percentage of Americans who describe themselves as "happy" has not increased since the early 1950s, while the incidence of clinical depression has jumped ten-fold over the last half-century.[940]

Urbanized, sedentary lifestyles, nutrient-deficient processed foods, synthetic but unsatisfying entertainment, are just some of the trends driving up the rate of true depression. But about one in four people who appear depressed are in fact struggling

939. Op. cit.

940. Easterbrook 2003.

with the normal mental fallout from a recent emotional trauma, like a failed marriage, the loss of a job, or the collapse of an investment. A study based on survey data from more than 8,000 Americans between 1990 and 1992 suggests that we need to be careful not to overdiagnose a normal, homeostatic response to loss and call it a disorder. Depression, suicide attempts, and deliberate self-harm can be rational bargaining tactics used to manipulate others into providing support they might otherwise withhold.[941]

Addictions, too, may be outgrowths of the changing social environment, including modern distractions such as bars and casinos. It was useful for our ancestors to follow their impulses strongly and spontaneously, but today, with temptations to indulge at every turn, suddenly you have a disorder. If we block the depressive symptoms with medication, we could be hamstringing the body's natural defences. In many cases, mere rest and a few outbursts of emotion are sufficient to gradually lift the depression. Pills do nothing but provide a pharmaceutical illusion of problem-free existence. At the same time, the field of mental health perpetuates this myth with the very concept of "mental health," which implies a state without suffering. This belief can eventually cause people to think that with enough effort they can eliminate suffering.

Obstacles, troubles, and problems do not have to cause sorrow. When we see them as uniquely our own, and face them as personal challenges to overcome, we can actually experience a great deal of joy in confronting them. In this way, a significant obstacle becomes a vehicle of "proving" ourselves against a threat to our personal will. Challenges and difficulties are essential prerequisites to all "spiritual growth," and what could be more challenging than mental "illness," which forces us to see how our brain works, and how we might improve upon our awareness in order to get on with our lives? In a foreword to *The Loss of Sadness*, Dr. Robert L. Spitzer, a major architect of the modern classification of mental disorders, acknowledges the imprecision of the DSM and "especially the question of how to distinguish disorder from normal suffering."[942] One has got to ask: when did the human condition become a medical condition?

"Negative" emotions such as fear and anger are inborn and tremendously important. We tend to think of anger as a dangerous emotion and are encouraged to practise "positive thinking," but that approach is only self-defeating and ultimately a damaging denial of reality. Studies show that people base their feelings about themselves on real evidence from their lives. Researchers from the University of Waterloo and the University of New Brunswick found that those with low self-esteem actually felt worse after repeating positive statements about themselves. The Canadian researchers found that, paradoxically, people with low self-esteem were in a better mood when they were allowed to have negative thoughts than when they were asked to focus on positive thinking.[943] Indeed, negative emotions are often crucial for

---

941. Jerome C. Wakefield, et al. "Extending the Bereavement Exclusion for Major Depression to Other Losses: Evidence From the National Comorbidity Survey," *Archives of General Psychiatry* 64(4), April 2007, 433–440.

942. Horwitz & Wakefield 2007, viii.

943. Joanne V. Wood, et al. "Positive Self-Statements: Power for Some, Peril for Others," *Psychological Science* 20(7), July 2009, 860–866.

survival. Negative emotions narrow and focus attention by boosting our dopamine levels so we can concentrate on the trees instead of the forest.

If people are instructed to focus exclusively on positive thoughts, negative thoughts might be especially discouraging, leading to self-reproach and pathological attempts to suppress them. Sometimes positive thinking is even used to treat genuinely sick people. In her book, *Smile or Die* (2010), the American journalist Barbara Ehrenreich relates how she fell ill with breast cancer and how she was then pushed the doctrine of positivity. The role of positive thinking in healing cancer patients was thought to be self-evident. According to Ehrenreich, the dogmas of optimism and positivity have become part of established medicine and there are even universities that seriously study the science of happiness. The deepest impact of the doctrine has been felt in the business world, which refuses to accept the possibility of failure—and we all know the results. Everyone feels anger, but individuals who learn how to express their anger, while avoiding the destructive consequences of unbridled fury, have achieved something incredibly powerful in terms of overall emotional well-being.

The reason for us feeling sick usually lay in our own stress reactions. That is why many turn to alcohol, cigarettes, or drugs to change how they feel—to cope with stress. However, stress is hardly a new phenomenon, having originally evolved in mammals to decrease the odds of being caught and eaten by something. In reaction to loud noise, sudden movement, or perceived danger, the area of the brain called the amygdala secretes a hormone called cortisol. Also known as the "stress hormone," it heightens the awareness of surroundings, while slightly sharpening vision and hearing. When a person detects a threat, adrenaline is released into his bloodstream, his heart rate quickens, his pupils dilate, his muscles tense up, his blood pressure rises, his digestive process is stopped, and his immune system is repressed. This is the fight-or-flight response.

This stress response is no less important an evolutionary adaptation today than it was in the day of sabre-toothed tigers. We need a certain amount of stress to motivate ourselves into certain actions, such as dodging speeding automobiles. When you drive at 70 mph with other vehicles only a car-length away, you had better have heightened awareness of sudden small movements. This can be called positive stress; but a constant, unnecessary, mental and physical stimulation can lead to illness. In fact, nine out of ten physical symptoms are either directly caused by stress or made worse by it.[944] If you are threatened, you need energy in order to react to the situation —the problem is that we are constantly preparing ourselves for dangers that never arise. Frightened people over-personalize the news, thereby increasing their worries. Fear is a warning system intended to alert us to impending danger: a terrorist strike, though a potential large-scale danger, is not impending. This type of stress is clearly the negative kind.

At the same time, we are under-rehearsed for real disasters exactly because our lives are over-alarmed. Most people stopped listening about the same time they became simply annoyed with their neighbour's car alarm sounding in the middle of the night, rather than getting concerned that there might be a prowler about.

944. Coleman, op. cit.

Between the noise pollution from cell phones, pagers, watches, and personal organizers, the supposed red flags have turned into nothing more than white noise. Just like in the case of the boy who cried wolf, we all have heard the warnings, however valid, too many times. So whenever an air-raid warning is sounded, we tend to immediately conclude it is the alarm being tested and not our survival skills. The constant drama of disaster is anaesthetizing: in the daily media, every little raindrop is a "storm," every little brush fire a "firestorm."

Nevertheless, the human brain was not designed to stress about the kind of things it stresses about today. A regular "day in the life" entails demands and strain: on your way to work you are stuck in the traffic, you argue with your spouse, an unexpected bill arrives in the mail, the children have made a mess, you are criticized. These kind of things may not seem like threats to you, but your nervous system does not differentiate between physical threats and the threats against the ego. Every time we shop in any modern supermarket, we run into more people than cavemen did during their entire lives. It is like some overlit funhouse, a massive attack on all our senses and a ***bona fide*** assault on our optic nerves. We are simply surrounded by too many stimuli.

News today is 24/7 and the media only get better at delivering us more information to worry about. The 19th-century prairie farmer may have fussed about the weather and the arrival of the Wells Fargo wagon, but he would have known scarcely anything about crimes in distant cities or rioting mobs in other nations. Now everyone gets minute-by-minute details of murders, natural disasters, and social unrest around the globe. As they say in the business, "Good news is no news, bad news is big news." Even as most things are getting better and better for most people, there are new additions to our list of worries each day, activating ever more stress. Home TV shopping, online browsing, pharmacies, even grocery shopping, are all round-the-clock. We have succeeded in eliminating the hours of the day and the time of the year by building heated and lighted cities.

The optical noise generated by brightly illuminated cities and suburbs is interfering with our sleep. Pitch black would give us a better rest at night. For countless centuries, poets, philosophers, and scientists have debated why humans spend more than a third of their lives asleep, but most agree on one thing: if nature made people sleep away so much of their lives, it must be crucial to their well-being—which is why Amnesty International lists sleep deprivation as a form of torture. We now know that cortisol production stops during sleep, giving our bodies a break from stress hormones. Sleep is not a waste of time, it is a very active time and we need it for things like memory and learning. We may acquire information during the day, but at night, we sort that information. Researchers believe that for most of human history, the norm was 10 hours of sleep nightly. A generation ago, the U.S. average was no longer more than eight hours per night; now it is seven and still falling—even though with the 24/7 society and information overload we need our sleep more than ever.[945] The resultant sleepiness has an incalculable effect on work productivity, on personal relationships, and even highway safety.

945. Easterbrook, op. cit.

Six in 10 adult Americans reported driving drowsy in 2004, and a federal study released in 2006 found that drowsiness was involved in nearly eight in 10 car crashes, being far more common than either alcohol or speeding.[946] According to the most recent studies, sleep deprivation can trigger many illnesses, including heart disease, diabetes, depression, or serious weight problems. The National Sleep Foundation asserts lack of sleep to be the number one killer in the West. It poses a greater health hazard than cancer or coronary disease. Is this any surprise when the average American spends more time viewing media such as TV and the internet than sleeping? One-third of that time, nine hours a day on the average, is consumed juggling two or more media at once.[947] We have all these things we are in the middle of, whether it is tending to an emergency at work, or a family situation, or some thing has just come up that occupies our mind. However, willed concentration—as opposed to obsession such as workaholism—requires relaxation.

Relaxation allows for a natural response, rather than the kind of reactive tension and fear that can come to control our lives. Your mind and body are in constant interaction. The body has slower rhythms because it functions in here and now, but the mind works restlessly. You are not going to come up with the Grand Unified Theory while dealing with three PIN numbers, six passwords, 12 preset radio stations, and several remote controls. There are now 500 channels, all the time. Unless you are checking your DVR 24/7, you might miss something. How can you sleep with any conceivable question un-Googled? After a department at software firm Veritas declared Friday an e-mail free day, it found that that day had become its most productive.[948] The very technology that was supposed to make us more efficient was found by a recent report on "info-mania" to be such a distraction that it cut our IQ points by 10.

The study commissioned by Hewlett-Packard found that excessive day-to-day use of modern technology, whether it was sending e-mails or using cell phones, reduces workers' mental sharpness in a class equal to missing a whole night's sleep. In the study, an average worker's functioning IQ fell 10 points when distracted by ringing telephones and incoming e-mails, that is, more than double the four-point drop seen in studies on the impact of smoking marijuana.[949] This notwithstanding the fact that neurological research by the National Institute of Drug Abuse shows that cannabis

946. "2005 Adult Sleep Habits and Styles," National Sleep Foundation, Washington, D.C., March 2005; "The Impact of Driver Inattention On Near-Crash/Crash Risk: An Analysis Using the 100-Car Naturalistic Driving Study Data," National Highway Traffic Safety Administration, Washington, D.C., April 2006.

947. Robert A. Papper, et al. "The Media Day," Center for Media Design, Ball State University, Muncie, IN, Fall 2005.

948. Marlon A. Walker, "The Day the E-Mail Dies," *Wall Street Journal*, August 26, 2004.

949. "Abuse of Technology Can Reduce UK Workers' Intelligence," London, April 22, 2005; Peter Fried, et al. "Current and Former Marijuana Use: Preliminary Findings of a Longitudinal Study of Effects on IQ in Young Adults," *Canadian Medical Association Journal* 166(7), April 2, 2002, 887–891.

might actually cause changes in the molecular structure of the cerebral arteries.[950] And, unlike cannabis, technology has not been shown to stimulate the growth of new brain cells in rats.[951]

As it turns out, those who multitask the most are the ones who are worst at it. According to a Stanford University study, multitaskers are more easily distracted and less able to ignore irrelevant information than those who do less multitasking.[952] Most people think multitasking means having half a dozen things going on at once and trying to pay attention to all of them simultaneously—which I reckon goes by another, less flattering name. Anyone who understands information processing knows that what we call multitasking is actually attention shifting. When attention is divided, both performance and self-evaluation drop, so we end up with people who think they drive normally while talking on the phone. Multitasking affects memory, retention, and the sorting of information. If we wish to carry out our tasks quickly, efficiently, and completely, we should do them one at a time—"Thou must (1) Find out what is thy Will. (2) Do that Will with a) one-pointedness, (b) detachment, (c) peace."[953]

In a wired society accustomed to having well-nigh unlimited information and the boundless choices of online shopping, it seems downright heretical to suggest that the infinite possibilities of modern life leave us less satisfied rather than more. In his book, *The Paradox of Choice: Why More Is Less* (2004), Swarthmore psychologist Barry Schwartz challenges the orthodoxy that in order to maximize freedom and welfare we need to also maximize choice. While Dr. Schwartz considers choice in general a good thing, he points out that people in the West are confronted with so bewildering an array of choices that it leads to paralysis. His local supermarket alone boosts a choice of 175 salad dressings, 40 toothpastes, 75 ice teas, 230 soups, and 285 different varieties of cookies. With so many options available for almost any decision, the chance that we will regret our eventual decision is also much higher.

The abundance of choices only raises our expectations, causing us to expect perfection. A "wrong decision" can lead to regret, which can lead to self-blame, which can lead to depression, which can lead to suicide. Some choice is better than no choice, but more choice does not necessarily make things better still. "Only through hard work and perseverance can one truly suffer." What makes a worry a worry is worrying—things only have meaning when you attach it to them. All of us have problems that seem a lot bigger than the above, but the fact is, both the big hardships and big successes affect the quality of our lives a lot less than the everyday choices we make. "This is the object of the usual monastic vow of poverty, chastity, and obedience. If you have no property, you have no care, nothing to be anxious about;

---

950. Ronald I. Herning, et al. "Cerebrovascular Perfusion in Marijuana Users During a Month of Monitored Abstinence," *Neurology* 64(3), February 8, 2005, 488–493.

951. Wen Jiang, at al. "Cannabinoids Promote Embryonic and Adult Hippocampus Neurogenesis and Produce Anxiolytic- and Antidepressant-like Effects," *Journal of Clinical Investigation* 115(11), November 1, 2005, 3104–3116.

952. Eyal Ophir, et al. "Cognitive Control in Media Multitaskers," *Proceedings of the National Academy of Sciences* 106(37), September 15, 2009, 15583–15587.

953. *Liber II: The Message of the Master Therion.* Op. cit. 42.

with chastity no other person to be anxious about, and to distract your attention; while you are vowed to obedience the question of what you are to do no longer frets: you simply obey."[954]

The key is to stop thinking; to observe, and not to judge. You should not underestimate the effect of this form of simple escape and recalibration on your overall sense of well-being. Many diseases stem from stress symptoms that could be cured with simple relaxation—but medication is prescribed all too readily. There is a cultural conditioning that proclaims "what you see is what you get," even though we do not see electrons, we do not see a virus, we do not see the future. At the same time, perception is reality, reality but perception—"what you see you create." As Epictetus put it nearly two thousand years ago, "Men are not the least influenced by events, but only their interpretation of those events."[955] If you do not assume responsibility for your attitudes, someone else will do it for you: the advertisers, politicians, religious leaders, or self-help gurus.

Of course, most of us want nothing more than to give it up, to hand over control of our lives and our thinking and our deepest beliefs to the government, drug companies, churches, and TV shows, which we depend on to tell us what to think, how to behave, what to eat, how to exercise, and whom to respect. We wilfully shut down our intuition, the feelings deep inside, largely because such intense cognition would require actual effort on our part. We do not realize that happiness is a state of mind, an inner quality independent of circumstances. No other can "stand in the way of your happiness." Many people associate their fulfilment with some external thing or physical factor, such as money, sex, property, or work. But if you concentrate on your inner life, you can feel fulfilled every day the moment you wake up. You will then be able to direct your attention to the outer existence, and you no longer need to manipulate others into giving you what you need to feel good.

"Being happy" has become everyone's duty in Western society. If you are not happy, you are a pathetic loser with poor life management skills—and poverty is out of style. However, only lobotomy-patients are always *content*. For most of history, the word "happiness" had a broader meaning that was more equated with living a good or virtuous life. Focusing on happiness so much, by tackling it head on as it were, is kind of counterproductive, because happiness is a byproduct of a life lived well. Happiness is different from pleasure, which comes and goes. True happiness is a profound sense of well-being in the midst of pleasure and pain, gain and loss. You can have a good meal and it feels great, but then it is over. Pain and difficulties will also come and go. How would you behave if all your problems were suddenly and mysteriously solved? I am willing to wager that you would create more problems almost immediately. As the Puritan saying goes, "The devil finds some mischief still for idle hands to do."

Without suffering, we would not try to change things, to act. However, our own suffering desensitizes us to the suffering of others—we should always take care of our own, inner well-being first. Let us say that you stand in line at a soup kitchen and

954. Idem. 1969, 12.

955. *Enchiridion*, 5.

give out food to a couple of hundred disadvantaged people. Then you go about your middle-class life and wait until the next time to engage in some more charity and/or ego massage. Should you, on the other hand, sit silently in your asana at home, freeing your mind of anger and fear, you would also be doing something good in the world. Emotions are easily passed from person to person, often without either party realizing it. When somebody who is nervous boards the metro, everyone around him picks up on that immediately. When somebody who is serene and happy gets on, they feel that too. We all receive and broadcast states of mind the whole day long.

Melancholy is not apathy, but a dynamic state that pushes you forward, to growth. Only by visiting the deepest recesses of our being can we create new ways to see and experience our selves and the world around us. The compulsion of happiness destroys our humanity. When an individual gives up their right to feel melancholy, either though the psychology of happiness, the jargon of positivity, or little pink pills, they become vapid, and perilous in their vapidity. What good could possibly come from a culture that does everything it can so people would not need to grieve, grow old, or die? The end of the road for the American dream is an addiction to the vapid mall mentality with its non-stop muzak soundtrack. The happiness addict is a zombie whom the powers that be can steer whichever way they want.

Whereas a positive mood seems to promote flexibility, co-operation, and reliance on mental shortcuts, negative moods trigger more attentive, careful thinking, and greater attention to the external world. In other words, being unhappy makes us think more clearly. In contrast to the happy zombies, miserable people are better at decision-making and far less gullible, according to Prof. Joe Forgas from the University of New South Wales. The Australian research indicates that a grumpy person can cope with more demanding situations than a happy one because of the way the brain promotes information processing strategies. Sad people are also better at stating their case through written arguments, which to Forgas shows that a "mildly negative mood may actually promote a more concrete, accommodative and ultimately more successful communication style."[956]

"Artificial intelligence" does not and will never work because it is emotions that drive people. Not even human thought is rational. Most of the human brain is dominated by automatic processes, rather than deliberative thinking; and much of what happens in the brain is emotional, not cognitive. Oscar Wilde defined man "as a rational animal who always loses his temper when called upon to act in accordance with the dictates of reason."[957] Experiments have shown rational thinking to be absolutely dependent on the adequate functioning of the parts of the brain responsible for primaeval emotions. The traditional juxtaposition of "sentimental" and "coldly rational" acts is ostensible. The word apathy literally means the "absence of feeling." Lack of volition is one of the symptoms of depression, and will-less automatons without a sense of self have no rational interest in self-preservation.

No matter what the circumstances, our emotions are self-generated: e.g. no-one reaches inside your brain and flips the anger-switch. The more a child learns to get

956. *Australasian Science Magazine*, November/December 2009.

957. *The Critic as Artist.* Op. cit. 1001.

things easy and ready-made, the less his connection to his own volition will develop; the thinner the line to the outside world, and the more vague the feeling that one exists—a self. Prosperity produces an infinite number of diversions irresistible to the young, but all these amusements do nothing to prompt developing minds and imaginations to ponder life's big questions: Who am I? What am I doing here? How can I make my life matter? The ubiquity, vulgarity, and superficiality of the 24/7 commercial culture trains children to focus on surfaces, to give too much weight to fashion, appearance, fame, and wealth.

The economic recession only reinforces the belief that success is, at bottom, dependent on happiness. And happiness is up to you. What you give up will be given to you. If you give up your reason, you will be given easy answers. Or you might even experience a miraculous cure. At least one line of business is always thriving in a recession: pseudo-scientific psychobabble and self-help "literature." The internet and the shelves are brimming with humbug: happiness guides, healing stones, positive psychology, and angel trinkets. What you give up will be given to you. If you give up your doubts and your money, you will be given a ticket to a New Age universe, where whales sing, getting rich is up to you, and cosmic energy heals all wounds. It is cheap compared to what women are willing to pay for lotions, creams, serums, and diet plans.

It is customary in our culture to sweep the real problems under the rug, and tell ourselves that if we could only get a bigger car, more jewelry, admirers, money, lovers, or some such, our lives would somehow get better. At the workplace or at school, the stress response helps people to be on guard regarding problems, and to work harder. Studies show that "successful" or high-income individuals generally have more cortisol pumping thorough their systems. However, prolonged stress can disrupt the immune system, increase the risk of heart disease, and take its toll on the body in countless other ways. Research also reveals that those who enjoy career success and exhibit stress symptoms are twice as likely as the general population to describe themselves as "very unhappy."[958]

"Grass is always greener on the other side." There is no silver spoon: a rich man's worries may differ from a poor man's in quality, but not in quantity. E.g. even if I could afford a Ferrari, I would be far too stressed about dents and scratches to park on the street, any street, or to go to the local supermarket for a six-pack of micro-brew if I happen to run out in the middle of watching an award-winning foreign film on the brand new 60" plasma—the colours of which are to my great annoyance already starting to fade. Such purchases might make you feel better temporarily, but if you embark on that road you have to feed your habit constantly. Children and adults alike are ticking off gift lists in Christmas catalogues and trying to attain the happiness promised by advertising. The outside world is pushing in to the soul of even the smallest child with its ready-made images, leaving little or no space for one's own fancies and imagination.

"Be careful what you wish for—you might just get it." A preschooler screaming for the lures of the candy and toy shelves at the supermarket with his face red, drenched

958. Easterbrook, op. cit.

in sweat, is an everyday spectacle. Wow, there's a strong-willed child. Think not! It is perfectly natural for the child to want the toy or the candy. And if the adult only gives him the room to want, the child will probably switch his attention quickly to the next temptation. One does not need to get a thing, if one gets to want. In the mind of the adult, wanting has come to mean getting. Wanting in itself is denied as an expression of inner will. The adult feels it is her responsibility to either give or deny the object of a child's desire, resulting in a verbose argument as to why the child cannot have what he wants. This deepens the misconception in his mind that getting things is important, not wanting them. What is worse, it also deepens the misconception that he is not allowed to be who he is. And this applies to the inner child just the same and lay behind many an adult depression and anxiety.

When you're living it, you don't dream it. "When the gods wish to punish us, they answer our prayers."[959] By definition, you can never get what you want; and once you have got what you have wanted, you start to fear losing it. People play the lottery because everyone has dreams they cannot afford to realize: travelling, taking time off work, enjoying trivialities. Everyone, that is, except those who have won the lottery. The latter are characterized by the lack of dreams and the inability to remember whether they had them in the first place or why they ever played the lottery. In fact, the only moment of happiness for the lottery winner is when he first learns that he has won, but has not yet received the cheque, and everything is still possible. Every lottery winner has heard the cautionary tale about the winner who spent it all, partying like there was no tomorrow, buying whatever caught his fancy, and plain giving it away. The tale is a legend: there is no record of this ever actually having happened anywhere. The real tragedy of a lottery winner is not wasting money, but not being able to; rather than money, he has found money trouble.[960]

That does not mean that you cannot achieve success in the physical world; it just means that most of us prefer peace, love, and understanding over material possessions. Still, it would be wrong to argue that it is the poor people who are happy and the rich people who are miserable. It is statistically untrue, since the poorest countries in the world also tend to be the least happy. But once you get past a certain level of income, additional money no longer makes these countries any happier, and the same is true for individuals.[961] For example, Qatar is a place where it seems like the entire nation has won the lottery. And are they happy? No, basically not, even thought the reasons for their unhappiness are different from what they were fifty years ago, when they were eking out a meagre living in the desert sands.[962] Only the truly desperate are able to apply themselves with the focus and fortitude necessary for thinking themselves into better circumstances.

Ask yourself, which would you rather worry about: finding the money to fix the run-down old car (which affects your quality of life and is something you have control over) or if your latest investment will pay off (which does not really affect

959. *An Ideal Husband.* Op. cit. 617.

960. Lau & Kramer 2005.

961. Layard 2005.

962. Weiner 2008.

your quality of life, nor do you have any control over it)? “The solution of every problem is another problem,” as Goethe memorably put it. By concentrating on our actions rather than on some specific goal, we can free ourselves of our subconscious habits. As children, we were put in school soon after our selves had begun to develop, at the pivotal stage of our individuation, when we start to move from the instinctual world of the small child into the conscious stage of late childhood. We are put under great pressure straight away, and in our reading, writing, adding, and subtracting, we are judged by our progress, not how we apply ourselves. Instead of success, results are demanded of us, and thus we become very goal-oriented early on. Is it any wonder that the generally very well-adjusted 5-year olds end up tense and uncoordinated 7-year olds?

11

Man Is the Only Animal That Trips Twice on the Same Stone

People are, at bottom, the same, not different. As Oscar Wilde quipped, "It is only the superficial qualities that last. Man's deeper nature is soon found out."[963] Think about yourself for a second: what about you exactly is a fact—true in the sense that everyone would agree with you on that? Height, weight, age, sex, name; everything else is belief. This makes people predictable, a fact abused by all sorts of charlatans. On the other hand, since we are all neurologically the same, anything anyone else in the world can do, so can you, if only you use your nervous system in the same way as that someone else.

The human mind could be compared to an iceberg, the visible top of which would be the conscious part, with the unseen bulk being the subconscious. This is what Einstein meant when he stated that we only use 10% of our brain capacity. The noted futurologist Ray Kurzweil has estimated that supercomputers will reach the human brain in computing capacity in the first half of this decade; however, the brain is also energy efficient, running as it does on about 10 watts of power—a computer with the same processing power would consume about a billion watts. In a way, we function mostly with the support of the subconscious mind: we are generally not conscious of

963. *Phrases and Philosophies.* Op. cit. 308.

our autonomic functions or thoughts, although the subconscious receives two million messages from our senses each second. There is no way the conscious mind could process all those messages, which is why the subconscious sorts them out and presents the conscious mind with a summary.

Why is it then that we interpret reality for ourselves? It is precisely because the conscious mind can only handle a few tasks at the time, whereas the subconscious processes a couple of million different ones every second. It would simply be an insurmountable challenge to process reality consciously, to try and make sense of those millions of sensory messages that bombard us each second of each day. This is why we filter our reality; and since our filter is formed by the assessments, views, and concerns we have at the particular moment, we are constantly screening reality in order to find what we think is important and useful to us. And it is precisely this that explains the differences in people's beliefs, for every person has a filter unique from everyone else's.

Everything that happened to you during your first six years—the formative period —especially everything that evoked intense emotions, forms the basis of your thinking and acting for the rest of your life. There are millions of neural pathways in the human brain, and every thought and memory has its own path. Every time we have a powerful experience, our brain encodes the whole chain of actions into our memory. If the experience was unpleasant, we learn to avoid those particular actions. The system is extremely efficient: should a toddler for example stick his finger into something hot, he feels pain and knows not to do it again. Every time we experience something new, we create a new neural path through which we can revisit the particular experience. Each time we repeat an action, we reinforce the pathway. The common assertion that it takes three weeks to form a habit is largely true; but if the experience is emotionally very powerful, a habit can form in a day.

The way we apply ourselves defines how our minds and bodies function. We generally apply ourselves in accordance with our habits—we do what we are used to doing; it is, after all, less taxing than having to re-invent the wheel every single day. Our habits guide our thoughts and actions. Throughout our lives, we react to situations and demands in a totally predictable fashion. We adjust to circumstances and events without being at all conscious of what we are doing. We experience stress, pressure, nervous tension, and our health declines. Usually this results in bad posture and reduced mobility, respiratory and digestive problems. We slump our torsos, causing both physical and mental harm. In unfamiliar situations, we go off the rails, are lost, and don't know how to react. We struggle to achieve something, but often our efforts are misdirected and contrary to our goals. We must learn to control our responses consciously and sensibly.

Both the images from outside ourselves, such as perception and memory, and from within, like imagination, use the same neural network and have in principle the same effect on our behaviour. Our behaviour depends on who we think we are, and we constantly monitor ourselves and the feedback the world gives us to define who we are. In other words, the process is circular, and our sense of self requires ceaseless reinforcement. We interpret our behaviour and receive feedback through our sense of self. There is no way out of the circle. By about the age of ten, you formed your first permanent impression of yourself: attitudes towards and beliefs about yourself. Those attitudes and beliefs have influenced what you have ventured, wanted, done, or left undone. And they continue to influence you today, even though you might not be conscious of it.

Beliefs, true and false, direct people into such actions as affirm these same beliefs. Our beliefs and values govern what kinds of abilities and skills we will develop. If you think you cannot influence your own health in any way, you will not be interested in your diet or pay attention to the needs of your body. You will not seek the required knowledge or buy the hogwash about exercise and what not that your friends try to sell you. If, on the other hand, you do believe you can influence your health, you might be willing to try different things, find out about things, go to classes, and learn more every day, so that sooner or later, you will discover ways to keep yourself healthy.

Beliefs thus place restrictions on what abilities and skills we are able to acquire. Our abilities and skills again determine which responses we start to use and learn to apply. Some of our responses are eventually turned into automatic reactions, habits, and rituals. Through these reactions, we interact immediately and concretely with the limitations and possibilities of our environment. Thus our identity, through our beliefs and values, abilities and reactions, determines how we are able to utilize our physical and social environment. When you understand how the mechanisms of your mind work, you can better control your life; when you are conscious of your beliefs, you are in command of every situation.

Animals learn as a byproduct of other behaviour, instead of consciously seeking a particular skill. Humans, too, learn a lot unconsciously and unintentionally. Should a toddler be required to willfully acquire all the skills he does during his first years, the task would prove impossible. A small child does not learn on purpose, but as the child grows, he will more and more aim at learning; it becomes a goal in itself and a branch of activity. The unique feature of human learning is that it is often conscious: we consciously look for connections between things. Psychology may not be an exact science, but the concept of associative memory links all the varied theories of psychology, from (spiritual) Freud and Jung through (mental) behaviourism to (materialistic) neuroscience.

Association is the basis of both human thinking and science—"Once is a fluke, twice is a coincidence, three times is a similarity, four times is a trend." One definition of insanity is to keep doing the same thing in the same way and expect different results. Superstition is when you connect two or more unconnected things. Some people are amazed how others cannot see the absurdity of some of their mental associations, but "Humans can find a pattern in just about anything, and we must find such a pattern if we are to comprehend things," as Dr. J. J. Hahn famously contended. "Mightn't people be mistaking this order imposed by the human mind for order caused by God?" The paranoid mentality is even more inclined towards such superstitions than the rest of us, and will often be looking for proof of the existence of spirits, magic, and paranormal phenomena; the paranoid will forever be searching for new magical occurrences, and since they have no understanding of the things they are meddling with, they will take at face value what they observe.

Humans are hardwired to need answers: the caveman who heard a rustle in the bushes and checked to see what it was lived longer than the one who assumed it was just the wind; the trouble is, when we fail to find a logical answer, we tend to settle for a stupid one. It is, of course, entirely possible to derive true conclusions from false premises: we may, for example, say that pigs are birds, birds cannot fly, and therefore pigs cannot fly. People also often tend to confuse cause and effect: e.g. men do not want sex because they look at porn, they look at porn because they want sex—i.e. it also matters greatly *how* the two things are connected. One cannot deduce on the basis of a correlation that a certain thing causes a certain other thing. One can only surmise that there is a connection between the things. Then there is the Fallacy of the Undistributed Middle, or going from point A to point Z, jumping over all the important steps in between: "All pugs are dogs. All chihuahuas are dogs. Therefore, all pugs are chihuahuas." Or to use a more topical example: "Terrorists attacked America. Therefore, terrorists hate freedom and democracy."

Countless studies have shown that a person can consciously pay attention to only a limited number of units at the same time. However, these units can be multiform, equally and simultaneously e.g. letters, words, or sentences. This is why it is important to learn how to assemble things into meaningful, practicable units that contain useful information. The main thing is not the data in itself, but how a person sorts out and interprets it in his mind—remember the words of Epictetus. This all requires the gradual automatization of many functions during the learning process. For example, when we teach ourselves how to read, we start to gradually notice the individual letters automatically, without consciously observing every separate letter.

And once a person has learned to read, he tends to use the same circuitry regardless of his second language or its alphabet; which is why Chinese writing is so hard for Westerners to master. The automatization enables us to form larger perception units, to focus our attention on full words, phrases, and trains of thought. A similar transition of conscious focus and direction to larger wholes takes place in the acquisition of many other skills. The diversity of the forms of communication, languages based on gestures and sounds, and especially the abundance and subtlety of symbols separates humans from all other creatures. And what is mind-boggling is that statistical analysis shows over 80% of all existing information and technology available today to have been in use only for a single generation.

New scientific and technological breakthroughs are occurring in every field at a breath-taking pace. People are communicating with each other over ever-increasing distances, studying and shaping the world around us. Calculations which used to take years, journeys that used to take months, can now be made in a few hours. Advances advance, and wherever we are going, we are going there fast. Nowadays, most people put infinitely more effort into learning how to use the new digital camcorder than how their own brains work. We can quick-link, cross-text, and multi-chat while being wholly ignorant of how these very advances are stealthily destroying a crucial human skill—the slower, longer, harder, and subtler art of deeper understanding.

If you have been in a room full of teenagers lately, you will understand the above phenomenon perfectly. They are wired like a telephone pole, routinely using more computing power than was used to get Apollo 11 to the Moon. In fact, 15-year-old girls today are so obsessed with gizmos like cell phones, digital music players, digital cameras, and hand-held organizers, that they have become the world's top consumers of computer chips. They are fluent in the jargon and adept at ring-tone programming, and nothing in the hi-tech field seems to get by them, so you think these teens must be super-geniuses by now—but then you hear them speak. You hear them struggle to form a complete sentence, a single nuance and careful thought about an actual subject of interest that has nothing to do with what they TiVo'ed or watched on their PlayStation or which of their little friends just texted them on their new pink phone.

For the "instant-message generation," the internet has become a form of social interaction. Most of the content they access has been generated by their friends. And this does not apply just to the teens. Increasingly, it is the way of America.[964] It has been suggested that Google and other search engines satisfy us because they are less likely to take us into areas where our preconceptions are challenged; the collections of search engines, news feeds, and social media encourage us to link to, follow, and read only that which we can easily assimilate. People today are expert on allusion, on skimming over the surface of things, on referencing the world around them more proficiently, while comprehending it less. Yet as far back as 1913, Aleister Crowley had already observed that: "Very many people go about nowadays who are exceedingly 'well-informed,' but who have not the slightest idea of the meaning of the facts they know. They have not developed the necessary higher part of the brain. Induction is impossible to them. . . This is the great fault of modern education—a child is stuffed with facts, and no attempt is made to explain their connection and bearing. The result is that even the facts themselves are soon forgotten."[965]

Our educational establishment guides the pupils into surface learning, the teaching being largely focused on unconnected details. Standardized testing mostly measures only memory skills. You can get good grades by mere surface learning, even if you do not properly understand the lesson. Having to memorize too many facts means that there is no room left for critical thinking. People seldom try to learn or recall things that do not evoke any mental associations. And there needs to be an emotional response, such as a Eureka moment (though the response does not need to be positive), in order for an association to form; which is also why religious propaganda is always far more effective than its rational counter—and why SATs are counterproductive. "You've had nature explained to you and you're bored with it, you've had the living body explained to you and you're bored with it, you've had the universe explained to you and you're bored with it, so now you want cheap thrills and, like, plenty of them, and it doesn't matter how tawdry or vacuous they are as long as it's new and as long as it flashes and fuckin' bleeps in forty fuckin' different colours."[966]

Fingers are pointed at various aspects of the educational system—overcrowded classrooms, incompetent teachers, lack of funding, etc.—but these are all just

964. Amanda Lenhart, et al. "Social Media & Mobile Internet Use Among Teens and Young Adults," Pew Internet & American Life Project, Washington, D.C., February 3, 2010.

965. 1969, 84.

966. *Naked.* Dir. Mike Leigh. Channel Four Films, 1993.

secondary problems. One of the foremost behavioural scientists, B. F. Skinner (1904–1990), was always depressed by the fact that the American school system refuses to see what education is about. In his professional opinion, the schools themselves create the very problems they complain about. Children should be allowed to advance at their own pace and get to know immediately if they have done right or wrong—two things that he considered essential in education. Schools would be able to teach twice as much over the same period, but the school system, based as it is on a series of grade levels, cannot be amended. "People do not realise one simple fact . . . that what people call reward and I call reinforcement must occur precisely at the moment that the thing is done."[967]

Reward is more effective than punishment; it teaches one what to do, whereas punishment only teaches one what "thou shalt not" do. If you prohibit one thing, the "delinquents" will just do it another way—the only thing people learn from punishment is how to avoid being punished. And of course, the only thing worse than not doing something out of fear is doing something out of fear. Rewarding behaviour produces faster and much more precise learning results than punishment does. But even punishment should be applied immediately following the undesired behaviour in order for it to have any effect; and the violators still need to learn how they *should* behave—wherein lay the failure of the modern criminal justice and prison system; our entire legal system is still, at a very basic level, about retribution, not reform.

Our self-imposed regimen of self-control, threat and incentive, which begins in childhood, is scarcely any different. What is the greatest fear of a small child or, indeed, any young mammal? It is, of course, abandonment by the parent, a certain death sentence. Parental rejection and conditional approval tap into this very fear, and as we grow older, we internalize them as shame and guilt on the one hand, and conditional self-love on the other. As if our self-loathing and disgust, our guilt and shame, could motivate us to do better next time. This is the mentality of punishment and control. If you hurt yourself with enough self-abuse, surely you will not do it again? Wrong. Ask any addict, or spouse of an addict, how well this kind of control works.

Written tests and exams also represent fear-based learning, the very opposite of learning based on desire. Fretting with pre-test jitters, students stuff their minds with information which they then regurgitate on exam sheets, never to visit it again. It is pretty basic psychology that if you think you are not allowed to fail, sooner or later you will explode. Modern examination rituals border on institutional child-abuse, taking a heavy toll on our youth. Depression and anxiety are endemic among teenagers, and rising still. Pharmaceutical researchers routinely subject animals to a regimen of "chronic mild uncontrolled stress" to test putative new antidepressants and see if the condition can be experimentally reversed by patentable drugs. The "chronic uncontrolled stressors" which our school system routinely inflicts on adolescent humans have no less harmful effects on the mental health of the confined students, who often go on to self-medicate with alcohol, tobacco, and illegal narcotics. If our society treated any other group of people the way it treats children, it would be

967. "Interview with B F Skinner," *The Psychologist* 1(4), April 1988.

considered a human rights violation.

Man is naturally active; he is learning something all the time—or at least buttressing his old preconceptions. So the question is not does man learn, but what does he learn. Today, all over the world, education is moving towards more and more testing, more examinations and more qualifications. There is a great deal of teaching to the test, so that in trying to increase scores, schools develop an understandable focus on the test, resulting in a narrowing of the curriculum. Even the youngest students quickly realize that the parental pressure is for grades, not knowledge, and cheating is of course the simplest path. Worse yet, the original purpose of examinations, to assess students' progress, has become confused with school accountability and the performance management of teachers. Consequently, instructors cheat as well, inflating grades because that is easier and less frightening than confronting parents or the head master—"Falsehood is invariably the child of fear in one form or another."[968] Many of these behaviours start when grading first begins, and many of the kids who cheated their way through high school cheat their way through college. A 1999 study by Donald McCabe of the Center for Academic Integrity found that cheating is common at all universities. In the survey of 2,100 students on 21 campuses, half admitted to cheating on written assignments, and one-third to serious cheating on tests.[969] A further 16% of students in some American universities admit to using Ritalin—a stimulant designed to treat hyperactive children—to maximize their learning power.[970]

Time spent studying, doing homework, and practising the piano is time not spent doing other things—like chasing boys or girls, which is fairly instrumental in making us well-rounded people. As Barnaby C. Keeney, the twelfth president of Brown University and the first chairman of the National Endowment for the Humanities, once exclaimed: "At college age, you can tell who is best at taking tests and going to school, but you can't tell who the best people are. That worries the hell out of me."[971] American society has an abundance of people who were academic achievers in high school, but were so driven by a high grade-point average that their inner lives remained stunted. Or which parts of their lives do you think were sacrificed to conform to the societal assumption that doing well in tests means doing well in life? According to a recent survey by Hudson Highland Group, a quarter of Americans who work on a computer admit to searching for a new job on company time. The number remains the same even if the workers assume their employers are monitoring their internet use. Twenty-four percent of executives and 23% of employees admitted to using company time and company computer in job search.[972]

Einstein, for one, flunked geometry. In fact, until 1905, nobody had any idea

968. Crowley 1979, 401.

969. Donald L. McCabe, et al. "Academic Integrity in Honor Code and Non-Honor Code Environments: A Qualitative Investigation," *The Journal of Higher Education* 70(2), March–April 1999, 211–234.

970. Martha J. Farah, et al. "Neurocognitive Enhancement: What Can We Do and What Should We Do?" *Nature Reviews Neuroscience* 5(5), May 2004, 421–425.

971. "Close-Up," *LIFE* 61(12), September 16, 1966.

972. Rasmussen Poll, March 11–13, 2006.

Einstein was capable of anything like what he accomplished. He had been an average student at the University of Zürich, and had not been allowed into graduate school because he had constantly smarted off to his teachers. The only job he had been able to get was as a third-class patent clerk. Yet, as he later admitted, if he had landed a university job straight away, he probably would not have had the time for the quiet, unpressured reflection absolutely necessary for his breakthroughs. As Robert A. Heinlein wrote: "A human being should be able to change a diaper, plan an invasion, butcher a hog, conn a ship, design a building, write a sonnet, balance accounts, build a wall, set a bone, comfort the dying, take orders, giver orders, co-operate, act alone, solve equations, analyse a new problem, pitch manure, program a computer, cook a tasty meal, fight efficiently, [and] die gallantly. Specialisation is for insects."[973]

Of course, "They teach you anything in universities today. You can major in mud pies."[974] Man will adapt to anything—unfortunately. For instance, humans are the only actual omnivores in the animal kingdom, as evidenced by our astonishingly varied national cuisines. However, horses, for example, with their one toe, are, strictly speaking, further "evolved" than man with his five toes. Yet specialization has progressed to such a point that people are now expected to acquire more than one profession. A growing number of college students opt for double or even triple majors, as they seek extra credentials to help them compete in a tightening job market. The more and more specialists there are in an information economy, the more people there are whose skills are less portable than they used to be: e.g. jobs designing microchips may vanish due to fundamental advances or changes in the design or production of integrated circuits. And when there is an excess supply in the job market, employers can afford to hire people with actual experience, as opposed to nominally qualified applicants who have merely taken a couple of classes in the speciality.

Meanwhile, getting retrained is getting increasingly difficult. Burgeoning fields, such as nursing, often require years of study that many jobless cannot afford. In the field of science, a counter-reaction can already be detected in the form of growing interdisciplinary enterprises—an inevitable consequence of ever-narrowing disciplines. However, it was precisely the disdain for artificial boundaries between academic fields that fostered the discovery of the structure of DNA at the Cambridge Laboratory of Molecular Biology back in 1953. Science typically advances in the sort of situations where one particular phenomenon is discovered to go back, or be reducible, to another, more fundamental and common phenomenon. This is what happened for example when scientists learned that visible light is merely a subset of electromagnetic radiation.

The trouble is, "Expertise in one field does not carry over into other fields. But experts often think so. The narrower their field of knowledge, the more likely they are to think so."[975] Or to quote the noted psychologist Abraham Maslow, "I suppose it is tempting, if the only tool you have is a hammer, to treat everything as if it were a

973. Op. cit. 248.

974. Orson Welles, attributed.

975. Heinlein, op. cit. 349.

nail."[976] Our brains work fast. The moment you think about some past event, the emotion or meaning you associate with it reawakens and is intensified so quickly that it is often the only one you consciously recognize. And since on the level of your nervous system, everything has taken place automatically and instantly, you might even think that this particular emotion is the only possible way to feel. Thus, in the words of Gore Vidal, "To learn and not to think over what you have learned is perfectly useless. To think without having first learned is dangerous."[977]

Every academic degree is, by design, attainable by the average student and this is a fact that today's self-satisfied academics would do well to remember. The people who have said some of the most idiotic things I have ever heard have had letters after their names. President Obama is a perfect example of the autocratic professional technocrats who have increasingly gained power in the United States—a group long on education and short on wisdom and judgement. The 19th-century American educator Brander Matthews described people like this as having been "educated beyond their intellect." Their skills centre around matters like the law or economics, formerly considered professions supportive, not determinative, of things that others do.

One might be a good politician and a good lawyer, but not a good politician simply because one was a lawyer. Franklin Roosevelt and Abraham Lincoln were both lawyers, but that did not define their place in history. However, there has been a change in the role of law in society. Law has moved from being a necessary tool helping us organize our society and restrain its excesses to becoming an end in itself. The United States has passed more laws since 1976 than it did in its first two centuries and the key to this has been law schools that were churning out tens of thousands of new attorneys each year. And it is not just the law. In the 1950s, American business schools produced less than 5,000 MBAs a year; by 2005, this number had soared to 142,000. In seven years, the nation produced a million MBAs and still faced huge trade and budget deficits, a dying automobile industry, two costly and unwinnable wars, and a growing division between rich and poor.[978]

Since the 1980s, MBAs with no real-life experience have taken over business, lawyers and economists have taken over politics, and over-professionalized journalists have taken over the media. Spin has replaced reality and action at every level. As the post-Keynesian economist Joan Robinson pointed out, "The purpose of studying economics is not to acquire a set of ready-made answers to economic questions, but to learn how to avoid being deceived by economists."[979] The government has assigned a plethora of practical tasks to people who think in abstractions, speak in clichés, use paperwork as a pacifier, and convert policies into a bunch of numbers or legal restrictions. People who can and will think for themselves are a threat to those with formal and rigid ways of thinking. Pavlovesque, obedient human robots may be safer to the modern élites, but the results could also be catastrophic, since nothing new or

---

976. 1966, 15–16.

977. 1981, 434.

978. Sam Smith, "Flotsam & Jetsam: Moderate Extremism," *Progressive Review*, July 13, 2009.

979. 1955, 30.

revolutionary is created.

The modern educational system is geared too much towards producing resources for the needs of market fundamentalism, rather than serving the gifted, creative, and intelligent in society. No-one is served by an educational system that set us up for jobs that could be automated, for work that need not be done, for labour without meaningful reward. In short, students are only taught to be dumb but diligent workers, who believe blindly in the official truth and consider anyone who questions it a kook. They have been trained into repeating countless silly and sillier tasks one day after another, just as they will be expected to do when they graduate. This, combined with ultimate efficiency and maximal utilization of working hours, is Taylorism pure and simple.

Mental associations can and do work against you, most of the limitations in people's lives being the result of their own associations. We tend to think that should we face something unexpected and unfamiliar, we will rise to the occasion. But we do not—we default to our level of training. Some 95% of those who perish in cold water are not actually hypothermic. More often than not, their body temperatures turn out to be almost normal. It is not the cold that kills them, it is the terror, which leads to drowning and heart attacks.[980] Some people will immediately fall into a helpless state of mind should they be required to speak to an audience, others when confronted with an intimate situation. Phobias are an extreme example of how external stimuli can trigger a negative mental state; the body remembers the distressing events it has experienced. The memories of trauma—mental as well as physical—are stored in the body's muscular and tissue memory. We are not aware of them, however, because the body has insulated itself from the pain: when the trauma was inflicted, the muscles and other tissue of the pain area would be only as active as absolutely necessary. This inactivity began to change the natural structure of the body, so that the feeling of pain would gradually disappear and we could put it behind us. We did, but at a price: the resulting bodily armour prevents us from experiencing life with the sensitivity and spontaneity of a child.

People maintain this defence mechanism themselves and even think of it as a part of who they are. In reality, it is internalized oppression and our entire upbringing is based on it. The character armour is a way to prevent emotion—a cold world is an easier place to live in when we are cold ourselves. Wilhelm Reich noticed during his therapy sessions that even those memories, that had caused his patients to lock up on muscular level, returned when the muscular armour was crushed. Indeed, Reich proclaimed that all muscular tension had its genesis and its purpose. Thus man is always carrying his own prison with him. Reich is fond of using the image of a soldier who is being systematically alienated from the true feeling of life. A stiff-necked, stone-chested, and unnaturally straight-backed person makes for the best possible killing machine. One grows into a good soldier by getting detached from authenticity at an early age, as a result of which the person will long ever more passionately for the life he has lost, but also feel ever further away from it.

Repetition reinforces our mental associations and makes them more permanent.

---

980. Giesbrecht & Wilkerson 2006.

When the body encounters a new but similar situation, it accumulates more tension, unless the previous tensions have been relieved through exercise, massage, yoga, or other means. A small change in how we use our bodies and what we express through our gestures can effect a big mental change. By learning to know our bodies more deeply and by facing the pent-up tensions, fears, and pains, we can let go of those entirely. If we have accumulated tension for a long time and in traumatic circumstances, we may not be able to freely direct our bodily postures and movements. We will subconsciously avoid certain postures and movements, ones that would enable us to relax and unwind. Man was born both lively and relaxed, free and vigilant—achieving this state again is entirely possible.

Your beliefs or generalized and quasi-factual notions about yourself, others, and the cause, effect, or meaning of things shape the focus of your attention. For example, if you believe that you are not liked in certain company, you will one-sidedly notice and store in your mind signs that confirm your belief; or if there are not any, you might become a "mind reader": "There they are, all smiles and trying to appear nice on the outside—but I know what they are really thinking." Beliefs tend to have a self-reinforcing effect. As soon as a belief is formed, your perception is directed towards things that support the belief, or to interpret things in a way that supports the belief. A person who thinks he is blessed with good luck, only remembers his successes. A person who thinks people cannot be trusted, only notices the incidents that offer further proof of people's treachery.

The belief-reinforcing interpretation is often formed in a flash and almost by itself. Different incidents bolster your beliefs until they become an intrinsic part of your thinking, regardless of their veracity. All your new beliefs are tested through your old ones, planting your older beliefs even deeper into your mind. This eventually comes to mean that you will only accept such information as buttresses your established notions and automatically dismiss everything that undermines them. This is one of the greatest tragedies of humanity: every kind of intolerance, bigotry, racism, and almost all conceivable prejudice stems from notions that have been fed to you from the outside and which you have accepted as "truths."

When our minds record an incident, the information received by our senses is not stored one hundred percent. We pick and choose parts of the event, usually unconsciously and automatically. We filter some things out, whereas some things connected with the incident are transformed on the basis of our beliefs and interpretation, and we can generalize an event in such a manner that its whole emotional significance is determined by that generalization. Tyler Durden got it right when he thundered, "Fuck what you know. You need to forget about what you know, that's your problem. Forget what you think you know about life, about friendship, and especially about you and me."[981] By picking and choosing the information around us we alter—subconsciously—our mental states and emotions. But we can also do all this consciously.

Since our beliefs are generalizations, good warning words are "always," "never," "everyone," "no-one," "people," "others," "men," "women," etc. Our entire

981. *Fight Club*, op. cit.

understanding of the universe is based on our thoughts, which are generated by our emotions, which are generated by our reactions to things that happen to us. Not since we were tiny infants have any of us directly perceived the world we live in. We are all walking through life in a dream state that amounts even at best to a funhouse-mirror image of reality. "Zen mind, beginner's mind" is a phrase popularized by Zen master Shunryu Suzuki and it means exactly what it says: the Zen mind is a beginner's mind, open, questioning, and joyous, devoid of all preconceptions and fixed ideas. "There is no emotion which does not leave a mark on the mind, and all marks are bad marks."[982] Dissociate!

Our thoughts are mainly controlled by our subconscious minds, which were largely formed before the age of 6, and we cannot change our subconscious by just thinking about it. This is also why "positive thinking" does not work for most people: the subconscious is like a record player, and until you change the record, it will not change. There are several ways to do this, one being "mindfulness," a Buddhist exercise where you live consciously in the moment rather than falling back to previously programmed behaviour. To improve our sensory perceptions, we need to temporarily stop making snap judgements, and be ready to try something to which we are not accustomed. We should aim at objective and unprejudiced observation, through which we can experimentally study our own behaviour, perhaps forcing us to question our basic assumptions. If we are persistent, our lives and learning transform from collecting habits and routines to fundamental change and progress. Observe, don't judge!

The next time you walk down your street, notice the direction of your gaze: are you staring at the pavement or straight ahead? Stop and expand your field of vision. Quit focusing on one thing at a time and start to become aware of what is happening on the edges of your visual field. Assimilate consciously what you are seeing, take note of the richness of colours and shapes. Then feel the ground below you feet, how your feet touch the ground on each step. Start to notice the breath of air blowing against you. Listen attentively to every sound that you have never paid any attention to before; notice when you hear the sounds and when you do not. When you talk to someone, take note of as many things about the person as possible: do not limit yourself to the substance of the conversation, but notice the details of your surroundings, the smallest changes in the other person, like subtle facial movements. On what topic do his pupils dilate? When does a little smile appear on his lips? When does he twitch nervously or scratch himself? The alternative is being stuck in "Groundhog Day."

We often do not pay any real attention to our bodies until they protest and become ill. Do we concern ourselves with our bodies at all when they are functioning properly? Do we remember to thank them for taking us wherever we happen to be going? For making our wishes come true? Or do we only notice them when they are no longer capable of functioning in the fashion we take for granted? Do we not know how to listen to our bodies' messages, because there is no interaction, because the communication between our minds and bodies is strictly one-way? Your body is

982. Crowley 1969, 95.

receptive to the experiences of your mind. Your body carries the suppressed feelings, happy and sad, whether you like it or not. Should our bodies and minds conflict with each other, we are in danger of falling sick. Our bodily postures and movements reflect our mental attitudes and beliefs. The body communicates our inner feelings and experiences to the outside world.

There is always an abundance of information around us, just waiting to be discovered. After a while, you will start to automatically experience your environment in a new way, and you life will become more nuanced. When you begin to observe more, you begin to see and understand more. Soon you will become aware of each person's characteristic manners and signs, which comment on their actions and words. The more carefully you observe the way certain signs relate to certain emotions in each person, the better and more versatile your interaction with them can become. Studies show that anywhere from 55 to 95 percent of communication is nonverbal. You, too, might be sending one message with your mouth and quite another through your body language.

Although all people are supposedly wonderful, unique individuals, sometimes we seem more like zombies just reacting to stimuli. We all pass through a trance at least twice each day: once upon waking, and the second time upon retiring. The lethargic or "hypnagogic" state we experience on a Sunday morning, when, with our eyes still shut, we think to ourselves "Shall I wake up or not," knowing full well that we are already awake. On the way to work, we get stuck in traffic, causing a *time distortion:* the car in front of you appears to take forever to cross the intersection. And then a *time displacement* takes place—you picture yourself arriving late, getting reprimanded by your boss—which again causes a *time regression:* you recall a previous confrontation with an authority figure, such as a teacher or a parent.

You arrive at work, notice a member of the opposite sex, and experience a *positive hallucination:* you imagine yourself in an intimate relationship with the person. Someone calls you from the opposite end of the office, but you have a *negative hallucination* and do not hear him because you are daydreaming. Before leaving, you have an argument with someone and undergo an *age regression* to childish reactions, with both of you throwing tantrums and shouting *post-hypnotic suggestions* at each other, viz. "You always mess up everything" and "You are constantly on my case." As a way to free ourselves from this automation, Dr. Stephen Wolinsky recommends in his book *Trances People Live* (1991) actions which he calls "witnessing." Simply, by stepping outside your problem into the shoes of a witness, you will be able to put the problem into a larger context—the main thing is that you move towards observing and away from identifying with your day-to-day trances.

After a while, you will begin to realize that you are not your trances: you are the creator of your trances, and when you purposely create one trance after another, you learn how to control them. Ultimately, all that is left is you, the observer and creator of your experiences. Certain practices of some Eastern religions are based on this exact method, which, if taken to the extreme, can produce some quite fascinating results. The above-mentioned Buddhist practice of "mindfulness" aims at stopping "the suffering caused by lust and greed." When you raise your hand, know that you are doing it. When you bend your wrist, know it. Know when you are walking forward, when back, when turning left, when right. When you look down or up, when your eyelids move or when your mouth opens, when you breathe in and when you breathe out. Stay aware!

As you observe your movements, thoughts arise: you need to let them pass and focus only on watching them; man is trapped by his thoughts when he identifies with them. One should observe one's thoughts, not destroy them, but become a "silent watcher," a detached observer—anyone can do this. These few simple mental practices can help us free ourselves of the ready-made trances offered by our culture. We are constantly forming mental associations about the stimuli in our environment, most of them unconsciously. Some people only need to use a certain tone of voice and your emotional state changes instantly. Certain smells, listening to an old song, noticing a patrol car in your rear-view mirror, all trigger a different mental state.

Since every moment of your life has been stored in the memory of all your senses, an entire past mental state can be easily brought back by the appropriate visual, auditory, tactile, gustatory, or olfactory stimulus. A simple glance at an old school photo can inundate the mind with whole childhood experiences. Often one will hear a song on the radio and start daydreaming about the past. Millions of sensory messages bombard our minds every second of every minute of every hour of every day. Some of these messages come from our friends and relatives, some come from advertisers, politicians, media, and religious groups. Messages permeate our consciousness from all around us and shape us—most people fail to notice this everyday hypnosis at all.

Perhaps the biggest misunderstanding about advertising is that people think of it as background noise. People keep the television or radio on, thinking that because it is only in the background, they will not be influenced by it. But it is precisely from the background that advertising has its strongest effect, working as it does largely through the subconscious mind. We associate Pepsi with Britney Spears and we know what goes "snap, crackle, pop." Funny commercials make us laugh, and laughing produces mental associations that tie the advertised product to the feeling of happiness. Advertisers know that it is no use trying to influence us through reason: Martini-drinkers are portrayed as young, rich, and handsome jet-setters, who don't have a worry in the world; but if you stop and think about it, youth, wealth, and looks have nothing to do with the brand of alcohol you consume. The most important thing in advertising is to create an association; the association need not be logical, it just needs to be positive.

Similarly, many religious people who attend a Mass enter a trance state during the holy service, if unknowingly. In a church, the cross forms a focal point for the viewer, incense dulls the senses, chants are repeated, eyes are closed, and the preacher may have personal magnetism. "Close your eyes and let the Lord enter your heart" is an exhortation very similar to the stage hypnotist's "Close your eyes and let calm enter your body." The high priests of every organized religion know full well that all the chanting and ceremony are no idle choice of style. The members of a cult may receive hypnotic suggestions during a meditation session, which is in itself a mind-altering process. A bartender may put a few dollar bills in the tip jar, so it will appear that it is customary to tip with paper money, and the sexton does the same with the offertory plate.

Dr. Wolinsky made note of the fact that it is through a trance that a person creates and sustains his psychological symptoms. He noticed that all symptoms and problems are firmly related to one another through at least one classic deep trance event. Let us for example examine the blight of migraine, a condition that has been studied for over two millennia. It affects about 45 million people in the United States alone. It has broken up more marriages, ruined more chances of promotion, and upset more plans than any other medical condition. More than one in seven people suffer migraine attacks, the symptoms of which include a blinding headache, flashing light before the eyes or ringing in the ears, accompanied by nausea, vomiting, or dizziness. Migraines can be extremely debilitating; in fact, the World Health Organization rates the effect of a severe migraine attack at a par with being psychotic or quadriplegic.[983]

The unusual fact about migraines is that they seem to be prevalent all over the world, affecting every race, gender, and creed, with one notable exception: migraine is absolutely unknown in primitive African tribes. Had ancient Romans not suffered them 2,000 years ago, this would lend to the belief that migraine is an illness of modern civilization. So rather than it being something we are doing in our culture that produces migraine, perhaps it is something we are not doing. Diet has to be ruled out, since none of the tribals who had been Westernized after an African upbringing had succumbed to migraine. Climate and weather conditions were discounted for the same reason. Yet, a particular foodstuff—especially cheese, chocolate, ice cream, nuts, or citrus fruit—will often precipitate an attack.[984]

We know that the primitive African tribes attach a great importance to the transition from youth to maturity. The initiation ceremonies for boys and girls at puberty are made up of ritualistic procedures handed down from time immemorial. The ritual dancing, the symbolic smoking, and the monotonous chanting have all the necessary elements to produce a hypnotic trance in the participants. Could it be then that the African tribes are immune to migraines because they dispel their childhood repressions at the correct time, effectively banishing their symbolic demons, in reality the hang-ups of youth? If you think about migraines as being a blanking action of the mind, a shutting out of consciousness of unpleasant memories and emotions, it all makes sense. Can you imagine a more likely foodstuffs to trigger subconscious recall of childhood than cheese or chocolate?[985]

Every person is walking around full of repressions which could have been fairly easily released at the time of puberty, had Judaeo-Christianity not swept up and corrupted the age-old rites of passage. It takes hardly more than a second for a strong enough incident or emotion to arise to succumb to a repression, and our childhood to puberty is made up of around 400 million seconds. There should really be no need for psychoanalysts. There should be no such things as phobias, psychosomatic disorders, or people generally externalizing and identifying with their anxieties. Were there a system of transition rites in place today, it would reduce the costs of medical care enormously. I am not sure that the manufacturers of benzodiazepines, beta-blockers,

983. World Health Organization 2008, Table 8.

984. French 1984.

985. Ibid.

and selective serotonin reuptake inhibitors would be too pleased though.

Consciousness can be altered without resorting to psychopharmaceuticals for example by repeating some word or phrase, a practice that is popular in many Eastern religions. You can repeat any sound, movement, or image. When you say or do something for the first time, your conscious mind tests the veracity of the words or actions, but when the same thing is repeated, the veracity check is no longer necessary and the stimulus moves from conscious control to subconscious watch. We often run into this phenomenon in daily life. Let us for example consider the fact that a person living near a railroad does not notice the passing trains, but a person visiting him will. The conscious mind tends not to pay attention to repetitious sounds, letting the subconscious deal with them instead.

At first, a *mantra* is repeated consciously, but its subsequent repetition is monitored by the unconscious mind, where the *mantra* has been planted through constant repetition. However, empowerment gurus are doing their disciples a great disservice by making them "think positive" about situations in which the odds are overwhelmingly against them. The most dangerous people in government and business are the highly enthusiastic incompetents, who are running faster and faster in the wrong direction, doing catastrophically counterproductive things with winning enthusiasm.

"What you pay attention to grows." If you tell yourself: "I am not tense," you will focus on being tense. Instead, you should always phrase your goals in a positive fashion, viz. "I am getting more and more relaxed." This cannot be emphasized enough. Behavioural changes cannot be enforced through will, never mind the program of threat and incentive that we mistake for will. The fatal flaw of negative expressions such as "Thou shalt not kill" or "Thou shalt not steal" is that the negation only happens in the language, not in the mind. When you hear a prohibition, you are forced to image the prohibited thing in your mind before you can try to replace it with something else, if you are still capable of doing so. Do not think about a pink elephant! Do not in any circumstances thing about a pink elephant! . . . and what happened with the elephant?

Sensitivity training only makes people pay more attention to sex, ethnicity, and physical appearance. The more we talk about illnesses, the sicker people think they are. Can you guess what country has the highest level of sick leave per worker? The socialized health care paradise of Sweden![986] All the research suggests that the more anti-drug messages you show adolescents, the more likely they are to actually take drugs. At least nine out of ten dieters fail—a worse failure rate than that of heroin addicts trying to break their habit.[987] This is not because food is more addictive than heroin, but due to the fact that the would-be slimmers have to struggle to eat less in a world where they are constantly bombarded with advertisements that seek to get everyone to eat more.

The focus of your attention can be conscious or subconscious. What you hold to be important steers your perception so you will be especially sensitive to the presence

986. "OECD Economic Surveys: Sweden," Organization for Economic Co-operation and Development, Paris, August 2005.

987. Coleman, op. cit.

and even more the absence of this thing. At the same time, you may not even notice other things that are essential to a more favourable emotional experience. If, for example, you price perfection and absolute success above all things, even a small slip-up may receive a disproportionate attention in your mind and in how you subconsciously assess the situation. You may not even notice how much better some other thing has worked out or be aware of all the things you have learned.

Trying implies failing; if you want to relax, you should not concentrate on relaxation, but on something you associate with relaxation. Think back to a situation where your mind and body were suddenly calmed, even though you started out in a stooped and stiff posture; by not settling for just one case, but calling to mind many similar incidents, you should be able to find out what they all have in common. A person can alter his bodily sensations and actions by changing the state of his mind. But often the fastest way is to go the other direction: by changing, either consciously or subconsciously, through some impulse, the state of his body, a person can very strongly affect his mind. This often happens like a force of nature, all by a sudden, automatically, making it difficult to tell which changed first, the body or the mind.

Urging people to "drive safely" is more productive than urging them to "drive carefully," since care does not equal safety. Parents often try to instruct their children through forbiddance. Every child seems to climb a fence wherever they see one, prompting parents to yell: "Don't fall!" or "That is dangerous!" or "You'll hurt yourself!" Instead, parents could tell their children: "You have a great balance," or "You are so agile," or even "Hold on!" Then they could instruct their offspring to get off the fence, if necessary. Positive exhortations invariably work better than negative ones. Begging your children not to wet their pants because there are no restrooms nearby does not work half as well as assuring them that they will be able to hold it.

The realization that the subconscious will faithfully discharge bad ideas as well as good ones led Dr. Émile Coué to assert that where there is a conflict between the imagination and the conscious will, the imagination will always carry the day: "In the conflict between the will and the imagination, the force of imagination is in direct ratio to the square of the will."[988] This is termed the Law of Reversed Effort; when the conscious will attempts to oppose the imagination, the will's efforts are reversed into the exact opposite. If you fear an event happening, it inevitably will. Place a three-foot wide plank on the ground and most people could safely walk along it, but suspend the same plank 50 feet up, and the reaction will be very different. Struggle to remember a name; the more you struggle the less likely you are to remember—abandon your struggle and what happens?

It is impossible to always do your best, and doing your best is not always good enough—I always say "I'll do what I *can*." Scolding is seldom productive, praise never. Positive feedback is stronger than negative: success goes to the head, but losing goes to the heart. An earthworm learns only slowly, after dozens of random actions; humans form associations much faster. Even a single successful action can lead to change in behaviour, especially if the person has consciously aimed at what the action accomplished. The down side is, you can do everything right, and all can still go

988. 1922, 18.

wrong. It is no argument that, in hindsight, you should have acted differently—you simply did not have that knowledge then.

Humans are the only animals that have the ability to think about the future. That means people spend much of their time not so much enjoying life as thinking about future pleasure and taking steps to ensure its attainment. However, very little about real life can compete with imagined life. All disappointments require advance planning in the imagination: one has imagined things to go a certain way and when they do not, you feel bad. The process is reinforced as you discover more and more detailed sensory information. "Misanthropy comes when a man without knowledge or skill has placed great trust in someone and believes him to be altogether truthful, sound, and trustworthy; then, a short time afterwards he finds him to be wicked and unreliable."[989]

Trusting yourself is confidence, trusting others, arrogance. "You trust me to do what?" "You trust me to take your money, but not your picture?" "Those are two different kinds of trust."[990] "Oh, I trust you alright, I trust you to betray me." The paradox is, you cannot trust other people, but—in a society—you have to. Laws about swearing on the Bible and against "lying under oath" are some of the few remaining feudal relics. Trust is a notion that underlies everything from individuals making decisions together to huge policy questions between nations. "The greatest folly of human existence is the ease with which we can be made to believe, and even fight for, a lie—provided that lie is something we want to hear."[991]

"The sin which is unpardonable is knowingly and wilfully to reject truth, to fear knowledge lest that knowledge pander not to thy prejudices."[992] There is no "how things should be." That is the basic motivating premise behind any rejection of reality. "The truth is what it is, not what should be. What should be is a dirty lie."[993] We spend our lives expecting people to behave in a certain way, and when they do not behave according to our expectations, we become angry, sad, confused, and sometimes frightened. "I forgive you." "For what? I wasn't aware I was in your debt!" Yes, "If you want something done right, you have to do it yourself," but: "When things go wrong, it is almost always possible to trace the error to one's own self-willed and insolent presumption in insisting that events shall accommodate themselves to our egoism and vanity."[994]

Humans process information selectively and interpretively, which under normal circumstances is necessary and useful. However, when operating and monitoring complex instruments, this type of information processing can become a risk factor. The communication between pilots and the air traffic control is recorded. By listening to the tapes, it has been discovered that expectations and interpretations influence the processing of information. Should a pilot have the wrong expectation, he is going to

989. *Phædo*, 89d.

990. *8MM*. Dir. Joel Schumacher. Columbia Pictures, 1999.

991. Andrew Somers, "The Right to Be Ignorant," *Civil Liberties*, August 13, 2005.

992. *Liber Libræ*, 15. Crowley 1909–13, I, 19.

993. Bruce 1972, 236.

994. Crowley 1961, 173.

choose the information he processes so that it will conform to that expectation. As they say, "Assumption is the mother of all fuck-ups." When one is required to make quick decisions, assumptions can prove fatal.

Take for example a pilot approaching a familiar airfield by night. On basis of several previous experiences, he assumes he can lower the plane once he is past a certain ground point. Due to an unusually heavy head wind, the speed of the plane is lower than usual and it crashes into the hills in front of the runway. Many factors contribute to the fact that some assumptions are more persistent than others. One such factor is previous experience: an expectation that has been fulfilled several times is not going to change quickly. Another factor is connected with emotions: if an assumption has an emotional component, it is more difficult to change.

The automatic cooling system of the Chernobyl nuclear plant and the computer controlling it was turned off and the system was under manual control before the fateful accident. When the computer was on-line, it conveyed steady reports on the state of the plant. According to experts, the last report by the computer contained information on the basis of which the plant should have never been transferred to manual control. The operator who made the transfer had been preparing the experiment for a long time. The intention was to try out a new cooling mechanism, which would improve plant security by immediately activating itself in the event of a power failure. It is possible that the operators' enthusiasm for the experiment kept them from seeing the warning in the computer report. They were killed when the plant exploded.

The ability to tell lies is a vitally important ***human*** trait—requiring as it does self-awareness. Lying involves multiple brain processes, such as integrating sources of information and manipulating the data to one's advantage. It is linked to the development of brain regions that allow "executive functioning" and employ higher order thinking and reasoning. Researchers from the Institute of Child Study at the University of Toronto have found that the ability to fib at the age of two is a sign of a fast-developing brain and means the child is more likely to have a successful life. The more plausible the lie, the more quick-witted the children will be in later years and the better their ability to think on their feet. At the age of two, 20% of children will lie; by three, this rises to 50%, and by four, almost to 90%. The most deceitful age is twelve, when almost every child tells lies.[995]

As adulthood approaches, youngsters learn instead to use the less harmful "white lies" that everyone tells to avoid hurting other people's feelings. The Finnish people are often accused of being "honest to a fault," for "It is dangerous to be sincere unless you are also stupid."[996] The proverb says, "Ask no questions, hear no lies," and it is quite impossible to actually "tell the truth, the whole truth, and nothing but the truth." Unfortunately, man also has infinite capacity for self-deception; it is part of his defence mechanism, the ego: "Man is a Religious Animal. Man is the only Religious Animal. He is the only animal that has the True Religion—several of them. He is the only animal that loves his neighbor as himself, and cuts his throat if his theology isn't

995. Victoria Talwar & Kang Lee, "Social and Cognitive Correlates of Children's Lying Behavior," *Child Development* 79(4), July/August 2008, 866–881.

996. *Man and Superman.* Shaw 1903, 192.

straight."[997]

A recent analysis of data from dozens of studies, involving thousands of participants, sheds new light on how we choose what to hear and what not to hear. Led by researchers at the University of Illinois and the University of Florida, the study found that while people tend to avoid information that contradicts what they already think or believe, certain factors can prompt them to seek out, or at least consider, other points of view. Unsurprisingly, the researchers also found that people are more resistant to new points of view when their own ideas are associated with political, religious, or ethical values. As Nietzsche put it: "Convictions are more dangerous enemies of truth than lies."[998]

"The world is our picture," explained Carl Jung in his Tavistock lectures. "Only childish people imagine that the world is what we think it is. The image of the world is a projection of the world of the self, as the latter is an introjection of the world. But only the special mind of the philosopher will step beyond the ordinary picture of the world in which there are static and isolated things. If you stepped beyond that picture you would cause an earthquake in the ordinary mind, the whole cosmos would be shaken, the most sacred convictions and hopes would be upset, and I do not see why one would wish to disquiet things. It is not good for patients, or for doctors. It is perhaps good for philosophers."[999]

However, most of people's problems are philosophical, not psychological. If you cannot find a word for any one thing in your brain's vocabulary, it is very hard to fit that thing into your personal universe. Still, it is self-deception, the uniquely human ability to tell ourselves that everything is okay, that makes the world go round. Even Adam Smith knew that happiness, though largely illusory, is the best motivator, "the deception which rouses and keeps in continual motion the industry of mankind."[1000] Ultimately, all deception is self-deception; that is why we get so mad at the person who lies to us—it is not that *he* tricked us, but that he tricked *us*. "You can't con an honest man."

Self-awareness is the condition of observing one's self from the outside: thus, the idea of an ultimate deity with self-awareness, with an ego, is not only an insult to my intelligence, but an affront to all that I find good and holy. I whole-heartedly agree with the notion that God can become human to interact with the world: "To know itself, each such Star, or Soul, must eat the Fruit of the Tree of Knowledge of Good and Evil, by accepting labour and pain as its portion, and death as its doom. That is, it must reveal its nature to itself by formulating that nature as duality."[1001] But that moment God ceases to be God and can only become God again by dissolving the ego. Strip away everything of yourself that is conditional—your name, your language, your relationships, your acquired knowledge, your body parts—and what are you left with? Nothing except a point of awareness. And since your awareness is independent of all

---

997. *Man's Place in the Animal World.* Twain 2010, 121.

998. *Human, All-Too-Human*, Sec. 483. 1909–11, VI, 355.

999. 1968, 66.

1000. 1761, 272.

1001. Crowley 1974, 118.

that is conditionally you, it is identical to my awareness and that of everyone else. Not identical as in "separate but the same," but identical as in "one and the same." We are all the same being taking different points of view.

Over and over again, Jesus denied having any special status, affirming that we are all "children of God." It was Paul who formulated the black magic of "vicarious atonement," the corrupt, vile doctrine that only one man could unite transcendent and immanent spirit, a doctrine which Jesus himself rejects in the Gospels. Pauline Christianity allows only Christ to be "one with the Father," despite the fact that Jesus denied this very doctrine repeatedly. Can you imagine if Buddhism taught that only Siddharta could become a Buddha? Yet what mainline Christianity teaches is that no-one can completely attain the union with the transcendent and escape from the illusory (or fallen) immanent—only Christ can say "I and my Father are One." So, historically, any Christian mystic, who saw through this and experienced the highest of all communions, was usually burned for heresy, if he was brave or stupid enough to talk about it.

Western psychology, like Western religion and philosophy, is obsessed with the ego. If we agree with the Cartesian proclamation "I think, therefore I am," then what happens in those rare moments when we are not thinking? Do we cease to exist? Of course not, unless we never existed at all, unless our actual identity is a nothing that embraces everything; since an everything cannot look at itself, we create the illusion of separate selves, leading to the illusion of survival, and on to all our pain and suffering. It is the ego's fear of death that led to the notions of Heaven, and then of Hell. The Easterners actually view reincarnation as a bad thing—get rid of the ego and all that is left is ecstasy. "If we identify ourselves with our thoughts or our bodily instincts, we are evidently pledged to partake of their partiality. We make ourselves items of the interaction of our own illusions."[1002]

Your ego is created by other people; this is the single thing all modern theories of psychology agree on. We do not exist as individual selves, immutable, unchanging, and separate; ultimately, there is no self staring us back in the mirror—we are all mutually defined. Every aspect of a person's behaviour is explainable. The person himself may not be able to explain it, or can only explain it erroneously, but that does not alter the fact that every effect has a cause. As Dr. Richard Bandler puts it, "people are not broken." One's whole personality is made up of early, perfectly natural shocks to the system, to which it responds perfectly naturally—though not always "normally." The mentally "ill" are not diseased: behaviour cannot be "pathological," it can simply conform to, or not conform to, our non-medical expectations of how people should behave.

The therapeutic model asserts that there are no "bad people," only personal injuries that lead to bad behaviour. Unfortunately, this model is in complete harmony with the story an abuser tells himself. "In reality, abuse springs from a man's early cultural training, his key male role models, and his peer influences. In other words, abuse is a problem of values, not of psychology."[1003] In *Why Does He Do That?* (2002), Lundy

1002. Ibid. 206.

1003. Bancroft 2003, 75.

Bancroft attacks the idea that abusers should go into therapy and explains in detail how therapy can, in fact, make someone a more effective abuser. If an abuser sees the destructive behaviour that is the result of implementing their values as a legitimate expression of their feelings, or as a "mental illness," it is even more unlikely that they will ever change; in fact, it gives them a weapon to use against anyone who suggests that they should. Therapy, the secular humanists' version of the confessional, might be beneficial for people who have no other emotional outlet, but this is hardly the case for the abuser.

"Self-improvement is masturbation"[1004]—get rid of the ego and you get rid of the problem or "neurosis." "Why treat symptoms, when we can eradicate the disease, especially as in this case the symptoms are sheer hallucinations on the part of the patient."[1005] Zealous individualism has often formed a mass movement of self-deception. Its newest brain-child is the "man without qualities"—people who have all the likeable traits, but no anchor to the self. We are very judgemental of our emotions. If we think that they are too raw, too impolite, or too awkward, we try to dress them up with positive thoughts and make them appear more respectable. Between our massages, acupuncture, and yoga, who has a minute to himself? And we all partake in these comforting anaesthetics without really believing in any of them.

The irony is, you can be fully-realized and a total asshole at the same time; in fact, it's almost a requirement: just witness the plethora of swamis who sleep with their female devotees and lamas who boast a fleet of luxury vehicles. High morals have nothing to do with enlightenment; whether you "let go" at the face of death because you think it is the right thing to do or because you're plain exhausted, the result is the same. Just because someone can remain calm and composed in a situation that has you bouncing off the walls doesn't mean that he's a better person—he has simply mastered a particular talent. No-one can become a "spiritual person," if they are not already one; but even a paedophile can be an otherwise "good person," and even a "good father."

One has to make do with what one has got. We are not in perpetual need of repair; the true grunt work of self-improvement is simply being aware of what one thinks, feels, says, and does. "If it ain't broke, don't fix it." One can of course use one's powers for good or for evil: "The majority of people will find most trouble with the Emotions, and thoughts which excite them. But it is both possible and necessary not merely to suppress the emotions, but to turn them into faithful servants. Thus the emotion of anger is occasionally useful against that portion of the brain whose slackness vitiates the control"[1006]—"For though it be Illusion, it is by the true Analysis of Falsehoods that we are able to destroy them, just as the Physician must understand the Disease of his Patient if he is to choose the fitting Remedy."[1007]

Many people say that they cannot meditate because their minds are too active. What they fail to understand is that the "taming of the mind" is a result of sustained

1004. *Fight Club*, op. cit.

1005. Crowley 1986, 117.

1006. Idem. 1969, 79.

1007. Idem. 1991, 26.

meditation, not the practice itself. "Clearing your mind" is not how you meditate; the notion that you are supposed to turn your mind into a blank slate devoid of any thoughts as you sit down on a cushion is a popular, albeit mistaken one. As far as I know, the only spiritual movement that has ever taught it that way is Aum Shinrikyo, the small Japanese cult responsible for the 1995 nerve gas attack on the Tokyo subway —which alone should be ample evidence that they are doing it wrong. And even in their system, the "blank mind" is only viewed as the end goal of the process, not the starting point.

Like fire, ego is "a good servant but a bad master." We need creative and useful habits in order to survive in this complex world of ours. It is important that our intellect should monitor the effects of our habits and decide where to make changes. This is analogous to the industrialist overseeing and directing his employees without attempting to do their jobs. It is useless to merely know these things; you have to also remember them at the right moment—and be constantly reminded of them in order not to forget: "All truly wise thoughts have been thought already thousands of times; but to make them truly ours, we must think them over again honestly, till they take root in our personal experience."[1008] Spiritual growth—or whatever you want to call it—is actually a continuous circular process in which the journey is more important than the goal. Letting go is not a one time thing; it is something you do every day over and over again.

"The secret of living without frustration and worry is to avoid becoming personally involved in your own life."[1009] Anxiety and depression are normal, healthy human responses, but unfortunately our culture associates chronic depression with a heroic, artistic stance, one we think mankind would be worse without. Since the time of ancient Greece, our philosophy, arts, and letters have elevated this clinical condition to a height no other emotional state comes close to reaching: it is seen as evidence of a more refined cast of mind, of a deeper and more sensitively attuned intellect. We meet a person who is bashful, ambivalent, and troubled over things that do not trouble other people, and we think that these are moral qualities. That attitude, to put it simply if not clinically, is plain nuts.

We are all familiar with the stereotype of the tortured artist. Vincent van Gogh's ear-cutting, Salvador Dalí's various neuroses, and Sylvia Plath's depression come to mind. Scientists claim that they now know why: a genetic mutation that is linked to psychosis and schizophrenia also seems to influence creativity. The neuregulin 1 mutation apparently dampens the prefrontal cortex, a brain region that reins in mood and behaviour. This mutation could unleash creative potential in some people and psychotic delusions in others. This could also explain why mutations that increase a person's risk of developing mental disorders such as schizophrenia have been preserved, and even preferred, during human evolution.[1010]

In order to understand this "illness," we must examine primitive cultures. All of

---

1008. Goethe 1883, 171.

1009. Wilson 1988, 160.

1010. Szabolcs Kéri, "Genes for Psychosis and Creativity: A Promoter Polymorphism of the *Neuregulin 1* Gene Is Related to Creativity in People With High Intellectual Achievement," *Psychological Science* 20(9), September 2009, 1070–1073.

them have shamans or medicine men, who have the ability to travel to the "other world" and heal people. Becoming a shaman is not based on free choice, but the tribes are able to identify their future shamans at an early stage, and it takes many chaotic years before the shaman is able to control his abilities. Interestingly enough, the effects of turning into a shaman are very similar to the "symptoms" of schizophrenia. Indeed, Western psychiatrists have managed to dupe some primitive tribes into believing that their shaman-in-training is, in fact, schizophrenic and in need of medication. Unfortunately, it seems that antipsychotic substances prevent the process from completing, causing the person to be lost in the abyss between the two worlds.

"Joy and Beauty are the evidence that our functions are free and fit; when we take no pleasure, and find nothing to admire, in our work, we are doing it wrong."[1011] Ascetic religions try to convince us about the ennobling effects of suffering, but the truth is: "If you're not having fun, you're doing something wrong." Our culture teaches people what to think, but not *how* to think. Many people assume that when they hear a voice in their heads, they need to listen to it, even if doing so would not be advantageous. "Just have a good time all the time—nothing else makes sense."[1012] Suffering helps none. Since we cannot ultimately know what is really happening, and are only interpreting everything for ourselves, why not make our interpretations such that they increase our happiness? Even the Bible says: "Eat, drink and be merry, for tomorrow you might be dead."[1013]

Conversely, "To suffer heartaches and not to be a poet? Whatever for?"[1014] The opposite of self-denial is not the avoidance of pain: "Each new thing that we know about ourselves helps us to realize what we mean by our 'Star.' . . . One should plunge passionately into every possible experience; by doing so one is purged of those personal prejudices which we took so stupidly for ourselves."[1015] We should not try to block out the pain of living through what Tyler Durden termed "premature enlightenment." We have to suffer for our past evil deeds, even though we might not understand what we have done wrong, because our nervous system is wired that way. Not even a sadist or a psychopath can escape this, for small flaws do not alter our basic architecture.

We should therefore attempt to become enlightened, that is, to learn how to live without dreams of a life after death, where the burdens accumulated in this life no longer bother us. In fact, this might well be what that grinning lardass from Nepal was trying to explain to us all along. Buddhism, after all, started out not as a religion, but as a philosophy of life. Even the Buddhist word for religion, Dhamma, does not literally translate to faith. The Pali version of the Sanskrit concept of Dharma, it is a very complex word taking several meanings based on the context in which it is used. The word "Buddhism" itself is an invention of British scholars and Christian missionaries who were trying to make sense of Indian religion during the 19th

---

1011. Crowley 1974, 210.

1012. Mick Mondo. "Do It For the Show." *Mondo's House of Wax.* Unreleased, 1996.

1013. Isaiah 22:13.

1014. Lec, op. cit. 131.

1015. Crowley, op. cit. 186, 189.

century.

If we are going to understand ourselves, much less other people, we need to look beneath our patterns and face our emotions in their natural, unmasked state. Being stuck at the level of our habitual dramas is like going through the day half awake, barely conscious of the world's brilliance. A part of us may prefer this half-asleep state, where nothing is too bright or too strange, but there is another part that can hardly wait to be free, to take a chance, to see what is on the other side of the mountain. "Conquer every Repulsion in thy self, subdue every Aversion. Assimilate all Poison, for therein only is there Profit. Seek constantly therefore to know what is painful and to cleave thereunto, for by Pain cometh true Pleasure. Those who avoid Pain physical or mental remain little Men, and there is no Virtue in them. Yet be thou ware lest thou fall into the Heresy which maketh Pain, and Self-sacrifice as it were Bribes to corrupt God, to secure some future Pleasure in an imagined After-life."[1016]

Pride and dignity are not the same thing. "The noble soul has reverence for itself."[1017] The Buddhists teach self-compassion. "When a faculty is freely fulfilling its function, it will grow; the test is its willingness to 'strive ever to more'; it justifies itself by being 'ever joyous'."[1018] Happiness stimulates brain cell growth in the hippocampus, enhancing memory and cognitive skills; by contrast, reduced hippocampal volume is anatomically characteristic of depressives, correlating with the length of their depression. In other words, depression makes you dumber! A number of American studies have estimated the annual workplace cost of depression at $40 billion. The World Health Organization estimates that by 2020, clinical depression will be second only to heart disease in terms of disability; but it strikes people at a much younger age and has a more lasting impact on their lives.[1019]

Suicide is already the third leading cause of death among young people—that's two places higher than traffic accidents.[1020] WHO figures show a suicide takes place somewhere in the world every 40 seconds, making it a major public health problem.[1021] If you judge by the mainstream media and the public education programs, you might be inclined to think that it is teenagers and young adults that are the age group most likely to take their own lives. Indeed, according to the National Mental Health Association, the rate of suicide among young Americans between 15 and 24 years of age has nearly tripled since 1960, being now the second leading cause of death among college-age adolescents; yet they still have the second-lowest rate of suicide.[1022] The absolute lowest rate is among children aged between five and fourteen—children younger than that are deemed incapable of consciously choosing

1016. Idem. 1991, 24.

1017. *Beyond Good and Evil*, Verse 287. Op. cit. 256.

1018. Crowley, op. cit. 162.

1019. Murray & López 1996.

1020. Victor R. Wilburn & Delores E. Smith, "Stress, Self-Esteem, and Suicidal Ideation in Late Adolescents," *Adolescence* 40(157), Spring 2005, 33–46.

1021. Krug, et al. 2002.

1022. Wilburn & Smith, op. cit.

to end their lives.[1023]

Certainly more suicides among the old succeed, compared with the young, for whom it may sometimes be just a cry for help. The sky-high suicide rate among the elderly applies to the entire world, not just the United States. Plotted in a graph, suicide rates by age group around the globe gently curve upwards as age increases, until the line suddenly spikes when the graph reaches the final group. All in all, nearly a million people take their own lives every year, more than those murdered or killed in war.[1024] In the West, 65 to 90 percent of the people who commit suicide are estimated to be clinically depressed; in China, where there are a disproportional 300,000 suicides a year, these are committed by and large to preserve one's honour—shame also keeps Easterners from seeking financial or medical assistance.[1025]

1023. Krug, et al. Op. cit.

1024. Ibid.

1025. S. J. Blumenthal, "Suicide: A Guide to Risk Factors, Assessment, and Treatment of Suicidal Patients," *Medical Clinics of North America* 72(4), July 1998, 937–971; Yi-Ju Pan, et al. "Suicide by Charcoal Burning in Taiwan, 1995–2006," *Journal of Affective Disorders* 120(1–3), January 2010, 254–257.

12

Prediction Is Very Difficult, Especially If It's About the Future

"Intuition is merely not knowing what one knows." Which is why a "gut feeling" is usually right. Most of the stimuli we encounter do not register consciously; the blind do not develop heightened senses—they just pay more attention to the remaining ones. "Coincidence, noun: You weren't paying attention to the other half of what was going on."[1026] Or, as Prof. John Allen Paulos put it in *Innumeracy: Mathematical Illiteracy and Its Consequences*, "A tendency to drastically underestimate the frequency of coincidence is a prime characteristic of innumerates, who generally accord great significance to correspondences of all sorts while attributing too little significance to quite conclusive but less flashy statistical evidence."[1027]

Krishnamurti asserts that "your belief in God is merely an escape from your monotonous, stupid and cruel life,"[1028] the only reason the mad-at-god atheists believed in God in the first place. However, "The Universe is not fair, it's exact." Everyone deserves what they get. Verily, "Sins of the fathers are visited upon the

1026. Brunner 1968, 31.

1027. 1988, 26.

1028. 1968, 206.

children unto the third and fourth generation."[1029] That is to say, the challenges and opportunities faced by each generation are dependent on the fortunes of the previous one. As sure as night follows day, guilt follows sin, and punishment follows guilt. When guilt has no outlet, our mental reminder, i.e. punishment, enters the stage and begins to control us by setting different restrictions. As a rule, the guilt-ridden restrict their lives in some ways. They feel like they do not "deserve" certain things or are "not worth it." Restrictions of this type were created by the person himself, even though he is scarcely aware of them.

"You know, I used to think it was awful that life was so unfair. Then I thought, wouldn't it be much worse if life were fair, and all the terrible things that happen to us come because we actually deserve them? So now I take great comfort in the general hostility and unfairness of the universe."[1030] The creation is perfect, disease and all—but only if you suppose it was not created by an omnipotent benevolent being: "God's only excuse is that He does not exist."[1031] The universe is expanding at exactly the right speed to keep it from flying apart or collapsing back into itself. If an airplane should lose its wings at 30,000 feet and not fall to the ground, then we would be living in a world where people could stick rockets up their backsides and fly to Hawaii for a three-day weekend. If you do not find that to be an improvement on the laws of nature, then I think you will have to agree with me: things are perfect.

"In a universe of blind physical forces and genetic replication, some people are going to get hurt, other people are going to get lucky, and you won't find any rhyme or reason in it, nor any justice. The universe we observe has precisely the properties we should expect if there is, at bottom, no design, no purpose, no evil, and no good, nothing but blind, pitiless indifference."[1032] And, "When man comes to the realization that he is not the 'favorite' of God; that he was not specifically created, that the universe was not made for his benefit, and that he is subject to the same laws of nature as all other forms of life, then, and not until then, will he understand that he must rely upon himself, and himself alone, for whatever benefits he is to enjoy; and devote his time and energies to helping himself and his fellow men to meet the exigencies of life and to set about to solve the difficult and intricate problems of living."[1033]

Humans, alone on Earth, can rebel against the mechanistic indifference of nature. According to Oxford zoologist Richard Dawkins, understanding the pitiless ways of natural selection is precisely what can make humans moral. It is human agency, human rationality, and human law that can create a world more compassionate than nature, not a religious view that falsely sees the universe as fundamentally good and benevolent. "In that world, you'll be able to rise in the morning with the spirit you had known in your childhood: that spirit of eagerness, adventure and certainty which

1029. Exodus 34:7, Numbers 14:18.

1030. "A Late Delivery from Avalon." *Babylon 5*. PTEN. April 22, 1996.

1031. Stendhal, as quoted in Nietzsche 1909–11, XVII, 39.

1032. Dawkins 1995, 133.

1033. Joseph Lewis, "An Atheist Manifesto," Freethought Press Association, New York, 1954.

comes from dealing with a rational universe."[1034] We can choose to inhabit a world in which we are rewarded for "good" behaviour and punished for "bad," but this will almost certainly entail creatively re-interpreting reality to sustain that view.

To discover the cause of a series of effects is valuable knowledge, but to call that cause "good" or "evil" on account of its effects is simply ludicrous. Karma is not about retribution, vengeance, or reward. "By doing certain things certain results will follow."[1035] In nature, there are neither rewards nor punishments, there are only consequences. "Whatever a man prays for he prays for a miracle. Every prayer reduces to this: 'Great God, grant that twice two be not four.'"[1036] Destiny, by definition, cannot be changed. So are miracles possible? No. In fact, this is exactly what makes them miracles. In this sense, the erasure of miracles is perhaps the greatest achievement of the scientific age. And it is not that the field of unexplained would have been narrowed by science. It is that science disproves miracles in principle: whatever happens, it is, at all events, natural.

"Every action has an equal and opposite reaction," i.e. "If you piss into the wind, you get wet"—but not because you are being punished. "It'll get worse before it gets better." "What goes up must go down." "It's darkest before the dawn." "We have to pay for the pleasure with pain. We sat up all last night, and now we must go to bed early; we drank too much champagne, and now it is the turn of Vichy."[1037] Consequently, Taoists subscribe to *Wu-Wei*, the doctrine of doing everything by doing nothing. "Thus thy true Nature is a Will to Zero, or an Inertia, or Doing Nothing; and the Way of Doing Nothing is to oppose no Obstacle to the free Function of that true Nature."[1038]

"Grant me the serenity to accept the things I cannot change, the courage to change the things I can, and the wisdom to know the difference." Habits are a useful aid in getting through daily routines; we cannot afford to waste time and energy pondering our breakfast every morning, so we act on habit. We need not decide every day whether we will walk to work, take the bus, or drive. We even tend to fall in love and handle our relationships in a perfectly predictable fashion. Our bad habits tend to establish themselves in our minds and bodies, leaving us feeling impotent to change them. With feelings of self-pity and fatalism, we begin to accept the situation, notwithstanding the knowledge that we have the power to choose our actions—this is what separates man from animals. Otherwise we will live our lives as slaves of habit and prisoners of coincidence. Human dignity lay in our ability to respond, rather than merely react.

The centuries old controversy between free will and determinism was solved by the Edwardian magus Aleister Crowley, when he posited a True Will. In the words of the great American poet Walt Whitman: "While we are from birth to death the subjects of irresistible law, enclosing every movement and minute, we yet escape, by

1034. Rand 2005, 1068.

1035. *Liber O vel Manus et Saggittæ*. Crowley 1909–13, II, 13.

1036. *Prayer*. Turgenev 1904, 323.

1037. Crowley 1986, 115–116.

1038. Idem. 1991, 29.

a paradox, into true free will. Strange as it may seem, we only attain to freedom by a knowledge of, and implicit obedience, to Law. . . The shallow, as intimated, consider liberty a release from all law, from every constraint. The wise see in it, on the contrary, the potent Law of Laws, namely, the fusion and combination of the conscious will, or partial individual law, with those universal, eternal, unconscious ones, which run through all Time, pervade history, prove immortality, give moral purpose to the entire objective world, and the last dignity to human life."[1039]

"With the majority of people their actions cancel each other out; no sooner is effort made than it is counterbalanced by idleness. Eros gives place to Anteros. Not one man in a thousand makes even an apparent escape from the commonplace of animal life."[1040] Man is the only creature capable of sidestepping his biology. He can decide not to build the tower he has planned, not to use the weapon he has invented, and not to cheat on his wife. He can sit down next to himself, take a look at the strait-jacket of his nature and undress himself. He does not have to take vengeance on his enemies, he does not have to buy things that he does not need, he does not have to be a robot that reacts to stimuli from inner and outer space. If it is going to happen anyway, we should make it happen the way we want it to happen.

"Little prigs and three-quarter madmen may have the conceit that laws of nature are constantly broken for their sake."[1041] People still seem to think that adverse weather—in the form of hurricanes and tsunamis and so on—is a punishment from above for men's sins, such as polluting the environment. But nature has always been inhospitable; it is not "doing it on purpose." As Stanislaw J. Lec observed, "You can change your faith without changing gods. And vice versa."[1042] Modern neo-pagans differ from the ancient pagans precisely in their nature worship; man has not had any kind of mastery over nature until late—people of old approached nature with fear.

One of the great engineering achievements of the ancient world was draining the Pontine Marshes, which enabled the city of Rome to expand. But such a project could never be undertaken today, as the vast swamp would be protected as wetlands. The attitude of conservationists is patronizing in the extreme—nature does not need conserving. Should a freeway not be repaved, the forest will break through it. In time, the road will vanish from sight like the ruins of an ancient edifice. There is incredible power in one, small, innocent sprout. Nothing that man can build will last forever. Nature's counters rain down like hellfire: planes crash, ships sink. Nature triumphs over man every time, prompting Kurt Vonnegut to declare: "If people think nature is their friend, then they sure don't need an enemy."[1043] Christianity makes man the "crown of creation," but as James Randi remarked, "To recognize that nature has neither a preference for our species nor a bias against it takes only a little courage."[1044]

If we banned building on risky terrain altogether, the world would be empty. In

---

1039. *Freedom*. 1904, 336.

1040. Crowley 1969, 103.

1041. *The Antichrist*. Op. cit. 618.

1042. Op. cit. 85.

1043. 1991, 111.

1044. 1987, 303.

one way or another, every part of the globe is uninhabitable. Take California, for instance: it has the most advanced agriculture in the world, the most advanced machine tool sector in the world, and the most advanced infrastructure in the world —that is the only reason people can live in California, because otherwise the place is a scorching desert with earthquakes, mud-slides, and forest fires. Tornadoes have been observed on every continent except Antarctica; hurricanes roam the Atlantic, Pacific, and Indian Oceans; blizzards occur in the north and the south; overflowing rivers have washed away entire cities. "Religious ideas have sprung from the same need as all the other achievements of culture: from the necessity for defending itself against the crushing supremacy of nature... A great deal is already gained with the first step: the humanization of nature. Impersonal forces and destinies cannot be approached ... if everywhere in nature there are Beings around us of a kind that we know in our own society . . . we can apply the same methods against these violent supermen outside that we employ in our own society; we can try to adjure them, to appease them, to bribe them, and, by so influencing them, we may rob them of a part of their power."[1045]

But tree-hugging? Can you get more out of touch with nature? There are no tree-huggers among farmers. The human impact on the environment began much earlier than the industrial revolution. Trees are much more terrifying than bandits or animals: one can always make the thug think the police are on their way, one can even try to dissuade the wild beast, but if a tree feels like falling, it will fall. "The 'only way to live in harmony with Nature is by living at a subsistence level,' as the animals do."[1046] One cannot communicate with nature; it understands neither humour nor philosophy. Can anything be more alien or menacing? Aestheticizing nature as a landscape is the invention of urban intellectuals. The rural populace has a practical relationship with nature: to them, it is a backyard, the basis of livelihood, a world of danger and utility. Historically speaking at least, only the idle cityfolk can afford to admire the scenery.

What is unnatural is wilderness. The so-called wilderness of pre-colonial America was inhabited by Indians, who changed their environment, cutting down trees, burning forests, running buffaloes over cliffs—they were not dancing with wolves. Wilderness is the least natural part of the planet. However, man has traditionally understood himself as more a part of the culture he has created than as a part of nature. Through cultural heritage, he has carried from generation to generation the message of human uniqueness among the species. But what if our evolved culture is merely an expression of our biological imperative? Man is larger than an ant and has more folds in his brain. Correspondingly, our technical and social structures are larger and more complex. They just are not proof of any real difference between the two species.

Man is not apart from nature, but very much of nature, so whatever man does is natural. However, environmentalists tend to view human activity as a blemish and animal activity as noble and good. If Manhattan had been built by ants,

---

1045. Freud 1957, 34–35, 25.

1046. "The Environmentalist Threat." Rockwell 1990, 293–94.

environmentalists would undoubtedly make it a World Heritage Site; had the Grand Canyon been the result of coal mining, Al Gore would say, "This is dreadful." But nature has no master-plan; nature is not god. Quite the opposite, "Mother Nature's a mad scientist," as Cosmo Kramer put it.[1047] Evolution is random: people get alarmed about things getting out of control, but the production of life is out of control to begin with—it is simply not an orderly process. The reason runaway genetic effects are not observed in nature is that natural selection has spent countless aeons conditioning living things to resist runaway genetic effects.

There is a technological imperative which insists that everything that can theoretically be done, will be done: space weapons, supertoxins, human clones. Or can you point to a technological breakthrough that was actually prevented, wisely? Maybe biological warfare, for a few decades, in some parts of the world. Compared with all the episodes where blocking progress for fear of the unknown turned out to be either futile or misguided, it is surely rare. Science has no choice but to push relentlessly forward—it is society that always seems to be sliding backward. Should we allow our government to block valuable areas of research such as human cloning, our scientists will simply move to other countries. Even nanotechnology is a natural progression of science; solid state physics, chemistry, electrical engineering, chemical engineering, biochemistry, biophysics, and material science working together.

As Einstein pointed out, "The whole of science is nothing more than a refinement of everyday thinking."[1048] Scientific thought is merely an outgrowth of the same kind of careful observation that allows a Bushman to identify, by their tracks alone, the species, age, health, and time of passage of dozens of different animals. That skill is neither arrogant, inhuman, or heartless, and the knowledge thus gained is extremely useful to everyone in the tribe. As science has matured, it has realized that the whole world is made up of tracks that can be read, understood, and correctly interpreted. Yet, "Men have never fully used [their] powers to advance the good in life, because they have waited upon some power external to themselves and to nature to do the work they are responsible for doing."[1049]

"In the Middle East, the Bronze Age people of Canaan—the ancient region between the River Jordan and the Mediterranean that roughly corresponds to Israel—also failed to adapt to the drying out of their lands around 2200 BC[E]. In their case, says Arlene Rosen of Ben Gurion University of the Negev, it was their beliefs that were their undoing. 'In Canaan, people believed that environmental disasters were caused by a deity unhappy with the people,' she says. 'Like the Mayans, the Canaanites could have coped with the new conditions by introducing new irrigation systems for their crops. Instead, they attributed the shift in climate to the wrath of the gods, built more temples and prayed for better times. Within a short time, the cities and towns were abandoned and the people became nomadic herders.'"[1050]

1047. "The Yada Yada." *Seinfeld.* NBC. April 24, 1997.

1048. 1954, 290.

1049. Dewey 1934, 46.

1050. Stephanie Pain, "'Rigid' Cultures Caught Out by Climate Change," *New Scientist* 1915, March 5, 1994.

Genetically modified crops and livestock, in the form of cross-breeding, are the very basis of human civilization, without which *Homo sapiens* would probably no longer exist. Biotechnology has been around since the advent of farming and animal husbandry. For better or worse, genetic engineering is the ultimate taming of the wild. The ability to slice and dice DNA is perfectly natural, so the idea that we are violating some fundamental barrier in doing genetic engineering is spurious; whether it is safe or not, it is going on in nature all the time. Old-fashioned breeding has produced astonishing results: traditional farmers have created turkeys that are unable to mate, because their oversized breasts prevent them from getting close enough to copulate. It was standard breeding that produced the high-yield crops of the Green Revolution.

Never in the history of humanity has food been scrutinized so closely as the GM foods are today. The approved products are safe. Traditional crops and foodstuff would not pass the same requirements. In fact, only in this connection have we begun to accumulate knowledge on the food we have been eating until now. We consumed rape for four and a half millennia "as nature had intended" it. It contained harmful erucic acid and toxic glucosinolates. These hazardous substances were removed by traditional breeding thirty years ago. Rapeseed oil as man wanted it is already healthier than olive oil.[1051]

The new technologies allow us to analyze all the thousands of compounds that the plants produce in their cell tissue. The results confirm that genetic engineering enables a much more precise breeding than do the old techniques. In the future, biotechnology may offer the world a second green revolution, by producing drought- and flood-resistant plants or varieties that can withstand pest attacks. When conventional rape was compared with GM rape, no compound concentration was any different. When it was compared to the original toxic rape—which is still grown by the ton for industrial use—it was discovered that traditional plant breeding had altered the concentration of over a hundred different compounds.

Your run-of-the-mill vegetable foods cause allergies, peanuts, tree nuts, wheat, and soy being among the worst in that respect. Raw potatoes, like other starchy vegetables, are actually indigestible. When eaten peeled, the potato is completely nutrient free; unpeeled, it contains nature's own toxin, solanine, which causes gastrointestinal and neurological symptoms. It is an historical relic from an era when the poor of Europe, and particularly of Ireland, simply had nothing else to eat. All the GM varieties have been thoroughly tested, and none of them cause any new allergies. In fact, since food allergies kill about as many people as lightning strikes do each year, we probably do not need to put warnings on every product saying it was "made in a factory that also manufactures items containing peanuts, soy, wheat, eggs, milk, shellfish or other things that might be bad for your body." There has certainly never been a mythical "fish-laced strawberry" on the market. GM companies avoid using animal genes especially in food crops. The reasons are commercial, not technical. A polar salmon is very cold-resistant, but a much more cold-resistant gene is found in rye grass. However, not every fish gene is allergenic. It is less expensive and a lot safer

---

1051. Gunstone 2002.

to produce medical proteins in GM plants than to extract them from animals, donors, or dead people.

Ten years after GM crops were first planted commercially in the United States, 89% of soybeans, 83% of cotton, and 61% of corn is genetically engineered to resist herbicides or to produce their own pesticides.[1052] And since most processed foods contain at least small amounts of soy lecithin, corn syrup, or similar ingredients, nearly everyone in the country has consumed some amount of genetically modified food. GM-produced hormones, antibodies, and edible vaccines for the developing world are on their way. The enzymes in breast milk can be grown in rice grains for the treatment of AIDS orphans. But persistent misperceptions, particularly in Europe, about genetically modified foods have led to their underuse and even prohibition as food aid in needy countries. Environmental activists are saying much the same thing about "gene food" as religious leaders were saying about inoculation in 1796.

More and more people are eating more and better food than ever before. World cereal consumption has doubled in the last three decades, while meat consumption has tripled since 1960 and the global fish catch has grown six-fold in half a century.[1053] None of that happened by magic, but only by giving nature a massive helping hand. At the turn of the millennium, the U.S. Global Change Research Program (USGCRP) estimated that half of all the commercial fertilizer ever produced had been applied since 1984.[1054] While global population doubled to 6 billion people in the 40 years after 1960, global food production more than kept up. The proportion of undernourished people in developing countries fell in those four decades from 37% to 17%. That figure is still an outrage, but it is also the lowest such figure in human history.[1055]

Obesity is a consequence of *Homo sapiens* carrying into an era of abundance, leisure, and warmth the physiology that evolved in a world marked by barely enough food, constant physical activity, and dangerous cold. Until relatively recently, if you were not healthy enough to hunt, grow, or trade for your food, you starved to death—today is the only time in history when people can eat until they are literally unable to move and still survive. There are now more overweight people across the globe than hungry ones. Obesity is the global norm, and although undernutrition remains a problem in a few countries and in certain populations of some others, it is no longer the dominant ailment. Excess fat is already apparent all over Europe and the United States, but its disastrous consequences will be seen with a small delay.

According to statistics, studies, and research, obesity is soon going to be the number one cause of death in the West. Scientists say that the Western youth of today may be the first generation whose life expectancy is shorter than that of their

---

1052. Jorge Fernandez-Cornejo & Margriet Caswell, "The First Decade of Genetically Engineered Crops in the United States," U.S. Department of Agriculture, Washington, D.C., April 2006.

1053. "Diet, Nutrition and the Prevention of Chronic Diseases: Report of a Joint WHO/FAO Expert Consultation," World Health Organization, Geneva, 2003.

1054. Tony Socci, "Ecological Consequences of Human-Induced Changes in the Global Nitrogen Cycle," Washington, D.C., February 26, 1997.

1055. "The State of Food Insecurity in the World 2005," Food and Agriculture Organization of the United Nations, Rome, 2005.

parents. Meanwhile, the burden of obesity, with its related conditions, is shifting from the rich to the poor, not only in urban but in rural areas around the world. A recent survey on obesity has shown that the world's most overweight region is actually the South Pacific. The tiny republic of Nauru is apparently the fattest nation on Earth—an estimated 94% of its adult population is overweight. In fact, eight of the ten most overweight countries in the world are located in the South Pacific. The World Health Organization estimates that 90% of men and women in these isolated corners of the Pacific are obese or overweight.[1056]

The world produces enough to feed everyone, but the food is often in the wrong place, or unaffordable, or cannot be stored long enough. Making sure that everyone has enough to eat is more about politics than science. In the EU, up to a third of the food grown never makes it to the shelves of the retailers because it is a funny shape or colour.[1057] Despite reservations in some parts of the world, notably Western Europe, genetic modification is becoming one of the staple tools to enhance developing world agriculture. Global food economy is based on around 120 species of plants, nine of which produce three-quarters of world foodstuff. These nine are rice, maize, potato, soybean, sugarcane, wheat, barley, cassava, and sorghum. They are a tiny fraction of the over 300,000 species of green plants in the world, or even the 20,000 that are edible for humans. A large portion of the foodstuff is used to feed animals, rice being by far the most important human staple—half of the world population live on it.

When production is on such a narrow basis, the risks grow. Two million people died during the Irish Potato Famine and 700,000 emigrated. What happened in Ireland during the 19th century is not just a bleak chapter of history. Banana is presently in the same situation. The banana plantations are plagued by a serious fungal disease, reducing the harvest by half in many places. All the banana field is genetically identical, since the new seedling is grown from the old rootstock. We have already been forced to stop growing one dominant subspecies of banana, and we may soon have to abandon another one.

Not so long ago, the entire existence of mankind was spent jamming anything we could find down our throats and nobody gave a damn where it came from, as long as it had some calories in it. Then suddenly we started worrying about things like health and the environment, and everything got complicated. Just a few generations ago, people looked to science and technology as salvation; it was the age of Tupperware, Kool-Aid, and pasteurized processed cheese. Today, there is an increasing emphasis on "natural" and demonization of anything in our food that comes out of a laboratory. Enter the $25 billion a year culinary juggernaut known as the organics industry with its promise of food that is better for you and for the planet. Pesticide-free, hormone-free, antibiotics-free—the one thing it is not is free.[1058]

As people have become more interested in health and environmental issues, many companies have started to advertise their products as having been made of natural

---

1056. Lauren Streib, "World's Fattest Countries," *Forbes*, February 7, 2007.

1057. Jenny Gustavsson, et al. "Global Food Losses and Food Waste: Extent, Causes and Prevention," Food and Agriculture Organization of the United Nations, Rome, 2011.

1058. "2011 Organic Industry Survey," Organic Trade Association, Brattleboro, VT, April 2011.

ingredients. According to Dara O'Rourke, a professor in environmental policy at Berkeley, about a third of all new food products launched in 2008 claimed to be "natural."[1059] But if you stop and think about it, you will realize that these claims are absurd, since *everything* comes from nature—the atomic bomb uses nature's own nuclear energy, but it takes only one to ruin your day! And are we not imbibing a million different synthetic compounds every day, just by existing, walking, breathing? Are there not trace amounts of a hundred different pharmaceuticals in our water supply and hovering in the air that we breathe? There are 100,000 chemicals in the registry of substances tracked by the Environmental Protection Agency; if all classified compounds in the EPA database are toxic, then I would recommend paving the planet with clean cement—except cement also makes the list alongside bog peat and cat urine.

What about synthetic hormones in milk and how they lead to early puberty in little girls? Well, that theory falls apart when you take into consideration the fact that the same phenomenon is happening in Europe, where farmers are not allowed to use any exogenous hormones. By 8-years-old, more than one in ten girls have already begun to develop breasts, which technically marks the start of puberty for girls. Earlier breast development is now so typical that the Lawson Wilkins Pediatric Endocrine Society has urged changing the definition of "normal" development.[1060] The trend goes hand in hand with the obesity epidemic: the reason why girls are going to puberty earlier is because people are fatter. At the same time, however, there is less evidence to suggest that the average age of menarche has come down, even if earlier pubertal onset means that girls' lifetime risk of exposure to estrogen is increased.

Fatty tissue is a source of estrogen, so chubbier girls are exposed to more estrogen. Girls will not go into puberty until they have enough body fat to support growing a baby in the womb—which is why a lot of Olympic gymnasts do not hit puberty until after they have stopped competing professionally. The fact of the matter is that everybody gets estrogen from milk, even organic milk, and if the cow happens to be pregnant at the time it was milked, we get 35 times more of it and it is all completely natural. Every glass of milk we drink, every cut of beef, chicken, or pork we eat is chock full of natural hormones. They are in the organic products too and they are necessary for life. Neither "organic" nor "fair trade" is synonymous with "good." These labels only tell us that the foods have been produced in strict accordance with certain carefully laid out principles, but even organic foods are mass-produced and industrially processed. Organic means "healthy" to many people, but organic junk food is still junk food—just because these products are organic does not necessarily mean that they are the healthiest options.

For many consumers, the organic label conjures up an image of a place where safer food, better flavour, and a healthier environment all intersect. By buying from farms that have been certified organic, they imagine that they are getting the best-tasting produce while saving the environment, supporting small producers, and protecting

1059. Suzanne Goldenberg, "American Shoppers Misled by Greenwash, Congress Told," *The Guardian*, June 21, 2009.

1060. Sandra Steingraber, "The Falling Age of Puberty in U.S. Girls: What We Know, What We Need to Know," Breast Cancer Fund, San Francisco, August 2007.

their own health. However, the fact is that many of the farmers most respected by chefs for the quality of their produce eschew organic farming. Nor does every conscientious farmer agree that pesticides are a bad idea. Meanwhile, mainstream supermarkets are overflowing with organic fruits and vegetable from huge agribusiness conglomerates. Most food travels at least 1,200 miles to get to Americans' plates and this is also the case for most organic foods, which generally come from large producers in California. Consumers who think they are buying from a small local farm may actually be buying from a company moving up to half a million pounds of lettuce a day. About half of all organic milk and dairy products come from Horizon Organic, a company owned by Dean's Foods, one of the largest food corporations in existence.[1061]

Organic convenience foods and snacks might be manufactured by small American companies from local ingredients, but, increasingly, they are being made from ingredients bought cheaply from as far away as South America or China. In fact, 20% of the world's organic fruits and vegetables are grown in China.[1062] And under U.S. law, there is no way of knowing whether a product, organic or not, was grown in China or in Brazil. You can label a product "U.S. grown," but that is almost never done, and more often than not, it is not the case. The extra shipping and global delivery these "industrial organic" producers employ to obtain and deliver organic ingredients pumps so many chemicals back into the environment that it counteracts any saved in growing the stuff organically in the first place.[1063] Many people also think that organic produce has more vitamins and minerals than does conventional produce, but that is not true either.

Over 400 nutritional studies show no evidence that organic foods have any more nutrients than regular foods do. Researchers from the London School of Hygiene and Tropical Medicine recently looked at all the evidence on nutrition and health benefits from the past fifty years. Their report, which was commissioned by the UK Food Standards Agency and published in the *American Journal of Clinical Nutrition*, found no differences in most nutrients in organically or conventionally grown crops, including in vitamin C, calcium, and iron. The same was true for studies looking at meat, dairy, and eggs.[1064] In other words, you are not getting any benefits from buying organic even though you are typically paying 30% to 50% more than you otherwise would. Any standards invariably support big producers over smaller ones, and higher prices charged for certified organic produce are no guarantee that you will be getting better food.

Once seen as the domain of wild-eyed hippies, organic farming was domesticated in the United States in 2002, when the department of agriculture began setting the standards through the National Organic Program. Government rules and regulations

1061. Carol Ness, "Green Giants: Mega-Producers Tip Scales as Organic Goes Mainstream," *San Francisco Chronicle*, April 30, 2006.

1062. "Organic Foods." *Penn & Teller: Bullshit!* Showtime Networks. July 30, 2009.

1063. "The Organic Myth: Pastoral Ideals Are Getting Trampled as Organic Food Goes Mass Market," *BusinessWeek*, October 16, 2006.

1064. Alan D. Dangour, et al. "Nutritional Quality of Organic Foods: A Systematic Review," 90(3), September 2009, 680–685.

made organic farming safe for big business and stores like Safeway and Wal-Mart suddenly started packing their shelves with organic products. The largest food manufacturers scarfed up some of the best-known organic brands and started their own organic lines: Coca-Cola owns Odwalla, General Mills has Muir Glen and Cascadian Farm, Smuckers bought out Knudsen and Santa Cruz Organic, etc. The USDA pays lip service to the hippie ideals by defining organic farming as a system designed to "foster cycling of resources, promote ecological balance, and conserve biodiversity," but there is no enforcement mechanism for these abstractions.[1065] Fallowing and on-farm composting, key components of the theory of organic farming since J. I. Rodale launched *Organic Farming and Gardening* Magazine in 1942, are not required by the USDA. On the other hand, many of California's smaller conventional farms employ a variety of organic practices even if they do not seek government certification.

There is a reason a pound of organic carrots costs almost twice as much as a bag of standards carrots the same size—organic food is more expensive to farm. And that is because the yield per acre for organics is usually lower than for standard crops since organic fertilizers are not as effective. Nor does the relative degree of "naturalness" necessarily correspond to the effect on human and environmental health. The environmental effects of Chilean nitrate are similar to synthetic fertilizers, but it is considered organic because it is mined from a natural source. Nor is there such a thing as pesticide-free farming: all organic farmers use pesticides, some of them quite toxic, because they cannot use the synthetic varieties. What is more, residues from neighbouring non-organic fields are always possible; even though it was banned in the '70s, DDT is still routinely found in soil samples.[1066]

However, by most definitions, the synthetic insecticide DDT is not a toxin at all. Indeed, its growing popularity since the '40s was based on the fact that it is not toxic to humans. It is toxic to flies and other insects, because it enters their nerve cells directly through their skin, whereas you can only enter human nerve cells through what we ingest. DDT was very efficient at combatting insects that produce all kinds of diseases and the banning of DDT forty years ago has, in fact, cost millions of lives. Before the ban, the inventor of DDT—the only effective agent against the malaria mosquito—won the Nobel Prize, because he had saved more lives than anyone else in the history of the planet. He had all but eradicated one of the greatest killers of children in the Third World. There were still 50,000 deaths from malaria per year, but when DDT was banned, the number of deaths went up to a million per year—mostly children under the age of 5—and stayed there for the next four decades.[1067]

DDT was banned for no good scientific or environmental reason whatsoever, and much of the synthetic pesticides we use today are many times safer. But instead of some of the safest pesticides ever devised by humanity, the organic farmers are left using more harmful alternatives. Judicious use of synthetic pesticides also means that

---

1065. 7 C.F.R. § 205.2 et seq.

1066. Max Withers, "The Many Meanings of 'Organic,'" *Los Angeles Times*, May 4, 2005.

1067. Gerald Weissmann, "DDT Is Back: Let Us Spray!" *The FASEB Journal* 20(14), December 1, 2006, 2427–2429.

the conventional farmer can spray less than his organic cousins, who have to rely on a small list of approved substances. And even the American Cancer Society says there is no scientific evidence that pesticide or herbicide residues are a cause of cancer in the United States.[1068] In fact, the average cup of coffee contains a thousand times more carcinogens than a year's worth of synthetic pesticide residues. However, banning man-made pesticides and fungicides puts us at great risk, since fungi produce the most potent carcinogens in nature.[1069]

One problem of growing crops with "natural fertilizers," or cow manure, is that it is a hot spot for pathogens like *E. coli* and *Salmonella*, but the biggest problem for organics is that it takes so much more land to produce a given amount of food. If we tried to do a conversion to organic agriculture on a global basis, 2 billion people would starve to death, because we simply would not be able to produce enough food for them. Nobel Peace laureate Norman Borlaug (1914–2009), driver of the Green Revolution, calculated that organic farming could, at most, feed 4 billion people. Trouble is, there are almost 7 billion people in the world. Borlaug's high-yield, disease-resistant crops helped world food production more than double between 1960 and 1990, saving hundreds of millions of lives and averting a worldwide famine.[1070] Yet there is tremendous nostalgia right now for an imagined past in which everything we ate was pure and came straight out of magically clean earth. The pre-industrial age was not the garden of Eden: livestock got horrible plagues, crops would fail for no apparent reason, and millions of people starved—all thanks to organic farming.

The demand for food is growing year by year. Even by the most conservative estimates, food production needs to double over the next five decades to feed the world's growing population, even though we cannot acquire any more arable land and the water supply is shrinking. Many scientists believe that only genetic engineering can solve these problems. In Argentina, for example, the use of GM soybean has greatly expanded the crops, while significantly lowering both the production costs and carbon emissions. Not only that, but thanks to the new GM varieties, the use of pesticides has markedly decreased.[1071] One-third of agriculture's greenhouse emissions are caused by the production of nitrogen-based fertilizers, but some of the biggest names in GM are developing crops whose greater efficiency would mean higher yields for less fertilizer. In developing countries, especially in Africa, the Western debate on the ethics of GM food seems distant. There is no money for fertilizer, only a little water, and few thriving crops, so every innovation is welcome. At the turn of the millennium, Sir Robert May, chief scientific adviser to the UK government, said people who were anti-GM displayed "the attitude of a privileged élite who think there

---

1068. Lawrence H. Kushi, "American Cancer Society Guidelines on Nutrition and Physical Activity for Cancer Prevention: Reducing the Risk of Cancer With Healthy Food Choices and Physical Activity," *CA: A Cancer Journal for Clinicians* 56(5), September/October 2006, 254–281.

1069. Rockwell, op. cit. 298.

1070. Ronald Bailey, "Billions Served: Norman Borlaug Interviewed by Ronald Bailey," *Reason*, April 2000.

1071. Graham Brookes & Peter Barfoot, "Global Impact of Biotech Crops: Socio-Economic and Environmental Effects in the First Ten Years of Commercial Use," *AgBioForum* 9(3), 2006, 139–151.

will be no problem feeding tomorrow's growing population."[1072] Several African countries have banned GM crops, because they would otherwise lose what little export market they have in the anti-GM Europe.

As believers in "organic medicine," the Nazis urged the German people to eat raw fruits and vegetables, since the preservation, sterilization, and pasteurization of food meant "alienation from nature."[1073] The Nazis were also anti-pesticide and Hitler's personal physician, Theodore Morell, declared that DDT especially was "both useless and dangerous."[1074] They campaigned against artificial colourings and preservatives, and demanded more use of organic pharmaceuticals, cosmetics, fertilizers, and foods. Government medical journals blamed cancer on red meat and chemical preservatives —you did know that Hitler was a vegetarian? Drinking was actively discouraged, and there were stern penalties for anyone caught driving drunk, with the police, for the first time in history, empowered to give mandatory blood alcohol tests. The morphine-addict Himmler shared Hitler's hatred for alcohol, and had his SS promote fruit juices and mineral water as substitutes.

There is still a strong ideological component to choosing to be all organic: I am purer than thou, I am more committed to being green and eco-friendly than you are. Organics has been rightly called the dietary equivalent of the Toyota Prius. People are trying to convince themselves and others that they are nice people who want to save the planet and eat healthier, but there is no scientific evidence that they are actually achieving that. A recent study of nearly 4,000 American consumer products found "greenwashing" in nearly every product category. More than 98% of supposedly natural and environmentally friendly products in the United States are making potentially false or misleading claims.[1075] There is a proliferation not only of products claiming to be green, but of certification programs purporting to back up those claims. At the same time, the average consumer still has difficulty perceiving even the difference between Certified Organic and Fairtrade Certified™.

Fairtrade was a pioneering concept twenty years ago, offering farmers in poor countries a better price for their produce by having Western consumers pay a little more. But with several hundred competing certification programmes, consumers are bombarded by all sorts of labels touting the green, natural, eco-friendly, recyclable, and non-toxic properties of goods. All the various green, organic, and eco labels easily become generalized to denote everything good and decent. Supermarkets prefer not to say who makes their store brands; manufactures resist efforts to have labels that say where ingredients actually come from; and marketers create the illusion that all things organic come from picture-perfect small farms. Environmental, health, and fairness claims become mixed up in the minds of consumers—as soon as you have a label for something, people get stupid about it and stop educating themselves.

It is quite common to demand perfect ethical and ecological compliance from an

---

1072. As quoted in Robin McKie, "Why the West Must Swallow Gene Foods," *The Observer*, January 23, 2000.

1073. Proctor, op. cit. 231.

1074. Ibid. 238.

1075. Goldenberg, op. cit.

alternative product. But whether such thinking leads to a favourable outcome is another thing entirely. A key mechanism of the Fairtrade system is to guarantee a certain minimum price for co-operatives of small farmers in the developing world. So why are they not selling Fairtrade tobacco as well as Fairtrade coffee? Tobacco, exactly like coffee, is an important export for many developing countries, and only a tiny portion of the profits go to the impoverished farmers. However, a positive Fairtrade label would not sit well in the packaging of a hazardous product. "Fair" and "tobacco" do not go together, because they create a moral contradiction. The ethics that is sold to the consumer must be clear and simple—too bad that the world is actually pretty complicated.

Fairtrade does not pretend to offer an alternative to global capitalism; on the contrary, multinational companies like Starbucks have been crucial to its success. These days it is precisely the large corporations that go on and on about "civic responsibility" and the "protection of nature." Consumer boycotts are seen as a way to influence corporations, but do they really work? Black-listed companies like Unilever and Nestlé have not seen their sales or market shares drop. It is hard to even identify their products in the supermaket, because they have so many different brands. McDonald's is a lot easier to boycott. But staring just at numbers might not be a good criteria for a boycott. Boycotts seek to influence the consumer's image of the corporation. Maintaining positive image requires constant effort on the part of the companies and image can be an important competitive advantage when the products are similar.

For decades, scientists have sought to calculate how much fossil fuel goes into our food by measuring the amount of energy expended in growing, packaging, shipping, consuming, and ultimately disposing of it. A growing portion of the organic food sold in the United States comes from other countries, yet the food miles argument has to be one of the most criminally oversimplified in the whole green debate. Food does not need to travel from an exotic location in order to clock up food miles. Domestically produced food can also travel considerable distances between farm, processors, storage depot, and the supermarket. What is more, the food miles argument completely ignores the concept of scale. A small local farm might produce ten tonnes of lamb, but might have a truck that can carry only one tonne at a time. If the distance to the nearest market is 100 miles, you get lamb with 100 food miles, but the farmers have to make 10 trips to transport the meat. Meanwhile, lamb from a bigger farm 500 miles away would travel 500 miles, but would only need to do it once.

A study at New Zealand's Lincoln University showed that lamb shipped to Britain produced one-quarter of the carbon emissions of British lamb, when they accounted for the relative reliance on fertilizer and energy-hungry irrigations systems, as well as the mode of transport.[1076] Apples from New Zealand may also be "greener" than those grown locally, because the climate there allows for much greater yields, and farms rely mostly on electricity generated by renewable sources. Should the Brits grow greenhouse vegetables all the year round, that would take a horrendous amount of

1076. Caroline Saunders, et al. "Food Miles—Comparative Energy/Emissions Performance of New Zealand's Agriculture Industry," Agribusiness and Economics Research Unit, Lincoln University, Christchurch, July 2006.

electricity, requiring vast amounts of coal or other fossil fuels. So produce imported from a warmer climate is much more ecological than domestic produce in the winter, unless the produce is shipped via air freight—shipping emissions have been shown to be about one-60th of those produced by air travel. Still, as the UK Trade and Development Minister said at a recent seminar: "Driving 6.5 miles to buy your shopping emits more carbon than flying a pack of Kenyan green beans to the UK."[1077]

Storing and cooking food also consumes energy. In the case of UK grown cooked vegetables, over half of all energy used during the food's life cycle is expended in the kitchen, that is, more energy than went to sowing, growing, harvesting, packaging, storing, and transporting it. Boiling vegetables is incredibly energy intensive, and it alone dwarfs the energy consumed during their production and transport.[1078] Yet no-one doubts that agriculture is a major polluter. Soil itself produces greenhouse gases, including carbon dioxide, methane, and nitrous oxide. The gas emissions occur as the millions of bacteria living in the soil break down carbon-based molecules. According to a Cornell University study, 30% of fossil-fuel expenditure on farms growing conventional crops is found in chemical fertilizer. This 30% is not consumed on organic farms, but only if the manure used as fertilizer is produced very close to the farm—if farms have to truck bulk manure more than a few miles, the savings is eaten up in diesel consumption.[1079]

It could be argued that since livestock and poultry are not part of the natural ecosystem, they are actually more ecological to eat than fish and game. Yet some people who disdain the hunting and trapping of free, wild animals pay others to raise, kill, and butcher animals under unnatural and often inhumane conditions. It is also unnatural that we have become so insulated from violence and death that we think they are somehow unnatural. In times past, children got used to death early, they witnessed the butchering of chickens and pigs at the family farm, and the dead were not taken to funeral homes. The truth is that life is not possible without death—no matter what you eat, something has to die to feed you. Organically reared livestock provide less meat per acre than their conventional cousins, and their ecological impact is greater than that of vegetables. It takes 7 to 10 pounds of vegetable protein to produce a pound of meat protein.

However, the calculations on energy used, calories consumed, humans fed, are all based on the notion that animals eat grain. You can certainly feed grain to animals, but it is not the diet they were designed for. Grain did not even exist until humans domesticated annual grasses some 10,000 years ago, while the wild progenitors of the domestic cow grazed the prairies for two million years before that. For most of human history, grazers and browsers have not been in competition with us. They ate what we could not eat—cellulose—and turned it into what we could eat—protein and fat.

1077. As quoted in Simon Usborne, "Inconvenient Truths: Don't Believe the Greenwash," *The Independent*, March 3, 2009.

1078. Llorenç Milà i Canals, et al. "Life Cycle Assessment (LCA) of Domestic vs. Imported Vegetables: Case Studies on Broccoli, Salad Crops and Green Beans," Center for Environmental Strategy, University of Surrey, Guildford, May 2008.

1079. David Pimentel, et al. "Environmental, Energetic, and Economic Comparisons of Organic and Conventional Farming Systems," *BioScience* 55(7), July 2005, 573–582.

Grain, organic or not, will dramatically increase both the growth rate of beef cattle and the milk production of dairy cows; but it will also kill them. Ruminants have evolved to eat grass. They have a rumen, the first in a series of multiple stomachs that acts as a fermentative vat. What actually happens inside a cow or a sheep is that bacteria eat the grass, and the animals eat the bacteria. A grain diet will disturb this delicate bacterial balance and the rumen will turn septic. Even chickens get fatty liver disease if they are fed grain exclusively, but it is the ruminants that should really never touch the stuff.[1080]

The UN has calculated that a third of the increased demand for food over the next three decades will come from people shifting their dietary habits to meat and dairy as they become able to afford it. Yet some would have us believe that the worth of a human being is measured by his culinary preferences. Is a vegetarian teetotaller really more spiritual and evolved than the rest of us? Many small, intense subcultures have cult-like elements, and veganism is certainly no exception. The vegans preach their diet, nay, lifestyle with the proselytizing zeal of early Christian missionaries. In 2002, a Dutch animal-rights activist, Volkert van der Graaf, murdered the populist politician Pim Fortuyn. The noted vegetarian and teetotaller Adolf Hitler was also against animal testing—he preferred to experiment on humans. I say: "Never trust anyone who doesn't eat meat." Or, indeed, any other intellectually dishonest person.

We should not be cruel to animals and we should take care of our pets. This is a genuine moral issue. Both Judaism and Islam have ancient rules of sacrifice meant to lessen an animal's suffering and bring a quick and merciful death. But I leave the room when people turn the question into metaphysics and start talking about the morals of animals. The Nazis outlawed medical research on animals, with Hermann Göring threatening anyone who broke the law with being "deported to a concentration camp."[1081] He jailed a fisherman for six months for cutting off a bait frog's head while it was still alive, prompting a German humour magazine to run a cartoon with a platoon of frogs giving Göring the Nazi salute. Saying that you "can't hurt an animal" means that you put animals above your fellow-humans. Burglary, conspiracy to blackmail, and offences against animal research operations—animal rights extremists have long conducted a campaign of harassment and intimidation against the animal research industry, seeking to achieve their objectives by creating a climate of fear.

Morality is a human creation, a conceptual and normative system focused on human behaviour. Other animals are not "good," if not "evil" either. They have no rights, but nor do they have responsibilities. In order to speak of the "moral right" of an animal, one has to assume that the animal is able to make a moral demand, to conceptualize good and evil, right and wrong. One can say that an animal likes certain things and dislikes others, but these are just primitive valuations, not moral judgements. As Orson Scott Card put it, "If pigs could vote, the man with the slop bucket would be elected swineherd every time, no matter how much slaughtering he

---

1080. Keith 2009.

1081. Proctor, op. cit. 227.

did on the side."[1082] The argument that pigs are as intelligent as dogs only works for people who like to think that dogs are intelligent; they are, in fact, little smarter than slugs, if often a lot cuter. This is actually one reason why we love them so much—they do not hold grudges, act in petty ways, or seek revenge. In 2010, voters in Switzerland overwhelmingly rejected a proposal put forward by animal rights groups to introduce a nationwide system of publicly-funded lawyers to represent animals in court.

"Six million Jews died in concentration camps," says a PETA spokeswoman, "but six billion broiler chickens will die this year in slaughter houses."[1083] And the People for the Ethical Treatment of Animals are not alone in assuming that "cage-free" chickens are somehow superior to "caged" chickens—not from a gastronomical or nutritional standpoint, but from the standpoint of ethics. The thinking goes that it is more humane to let cooped-up chickens mill around freely. This, of course, means that layers of chicken excrement build up on the floor, which is what the eggs lay in until someone picks them up. But more to the point, when chickens are crowded together, rather than separated into cages, they peck each other incessantly. This is where the phrase "pecking order" comes from; it is animal instinct, an avian attempt to establish a social hierarchy. After months of going at each other, older birds have few feathers left on their scarred necks. Meanwhile, "free-range" hens run around loose, outside, being pursued by foxes and dogs; some get hit and killed by cars. All in all, cage-free chickens have twice the mortality rate of the caged variety.[1084]

Seeing our pets the way we see ourselves—as having human thoughts and needs—is just another kind of abuse. Crating a human child is cruel, whereas crating a dog is often helpful and soothing. No human being would care to spend five minutes in a kennel, yet a good kennel may be the safest and best place to leave our dogs when we leave home. When we see dogs as deprived, abused, and needy, we tend to treat them unwisely. Overfeeding and the resulting epidemic obesity is cited as a major killer of dogs and cats by American veterinarians. How many times have you heard a pet owner say, "I just can't resist when they beg for food"? Any vet or animal nutritionist will tell you that such a person is doing as much harm to their cute little beggars by overfeeding them as they would by kicking them.

For the last time, dogs are not "people" of another species—they are another species! In order to train and care for them property, we must understand this fact. Busy and guilt-ridden owners often think that their dogs have already suffered so much that they could not possibly inflict any more criticism. Yet it is exactly the firm, effective training that would make those dogs happier and more secure. Many Westerners today see their pets as family members, emotional support systems, metaphors for their own past issues, aids for growth and healing, children with fur. As dog and cat ownership has expanded to nearly two out of three U.S. households, Americans have taken to giving their animals more human-sounding names. By 2007,

---

1082. 2001, 315.

1083. *Washington Post*, November 13, 1983.

1084. Linda Valdez, "Cage-Free Egg Farms Peck Away at Consumer Reality," *Arizona Republic*, August 10, 2008.

17 out of the top 25 tags for cats and dogs in the San Francisco area were typical people names—such as Jennifer, Lucy, and Samantha, or Marcus, Kevin, and Charlie.[1085]

According to a survey by the American Pet Products Manufacturers Association, the number of U.S. households with pets jumped from 56% in 1988 to 63% in 2006; but spending on pets more than doubled just between 1994 and 2007, according to the same survey, to an excess of $40 billion a year.[1086] As the market for pet pampering products has exploded, the century-old pharmaceutical giant Eli Lilly has begun making a chewable, beef-flavoured version of Prozac "to treat separation anxiety in dogs." The growing anthropomorphizing of canines affects the decision when to euthanize a sick or elderly pet. Vets say their biggest recent problem is people who see their pets so human that they simply cannot end their lives or suffering, no matter the pain or cost. And who could forget Leona "Only the Little People Pay Taxes" Helmsley's decision to leave $12 million to her dog in her will.

Socrates said it 2,400 years ago: society is on the path to destruction when animals have human rights, teachers fear and flatter their students, and parents try to act like their children for fear of appearing disagreeable or authoritarian. In 2001, the Malawi environmental affairs minister Harry Thomson told reporters: "We know that crocodiles are a menace here—they are eating people. But since we are members of Cites our hands are tied."[1087] International treaties classify crocodiles as an endangered species. The natural order is superior to mankind, opined ecologist John Muir more than a century ago, because Nature is "unfallen and undepraved" and man is always and everywhere "a blighting touch." Therefore, according to Muir, alligators and other predators should be "blessed now and then with a mouthful of terror-stricken man by way of a dainty."[1088]

When rainforests fall to beef, environmentalists are outraged, aware, ready for a boycott; but when the culprit is wheat and the victim is a prairie, they are silent. Most of them have embraced as an article of faith that vegetarianism is the way to salvation for both mankind and the planet—how could it be destroying either? Many vegans think animals should be protected from being killed not only by humans, but by other animals. They would build a fence down the middle of the Serengeti, thereby dividing the predators from the prey. Killing is always wrong and no animal should ever have to die, so the big cats and wild canines would go on one side and the wildebeests and zebras would live on the other. Carnivores do not need to be carnivores—that is just a lie the meat industry tells. We have all seen dogs eat grass, so dogs can obviously live on grass. Except that dogs, lions, and humans do not have a ruminant's digestive system. They have no mechanism to digest cellulose and therefore cannot survive on it. They may occasionally eat grass, but only medicinally, as a purgative to clear their digestive tracts of parasites.

1085. Erin McCormick, "Man's Best Friends Getting Man's Best Names," *San Francisco Chronicle*, May 1, 2008.

1086. "APPMA National Pet Owners Survey 2007–2008," Greenwich, CT, June 2007.

1087. Raphael Tenthani, "Malawi: Chiefs Want Better Care From Government," Panafrican News Agency, February 2, 2001.

1088. Rockwell, op. cit. 291.

On the carnivore side of the fence, every animal would be killed by starvation. Some would last longer than others, for example, the ones that ended their days as cannibals. On the ruminant side of the fence, the naturally vegetarian species would reproduce as effectively as ever. But without predators to check their number, there would quickly be more grazers than grass. The poor animals would outstrip their food source, eat the plants down to the ground, and then they, too, would starve to death. Ultimately, without grazers to eat the grass, the whole land would turn into a desert. Without grazers, the perennial plants would mature and shade out the basal growth point at the plant's base. In a brittle environment like the Serengeti, decay is mostly physical—or weathering—and chemical—or oxidative—not bacterial and biological as in a moist environment. The ruminants take over most of the biological functions of soil by digesting cellulose and returning nutrients in the form of urine and feces. Without them, the plant matter will pile up, reducing growth, and start killing the plants. As the bare earth is exposed to wind, sun, and rain, the minerals leech away and the soil structure is destroyed.[1089] Congratulations, you have just killed everything.

And we should note that the site for this animal protection fence was Africa. No animal rights activists seem concerned about the North American prairie, where carnivores and ruminants alike have been extirpated for the annual grains that vegetarians push. Plants and animals need to be eaten as much they need to eat. The grazers need their daily cellulose, but the grass also needs the animals. It needs the manure, with its nitrogen, minerals, and bacteria. It needs the resources stored in animal bodies and freed up by degraders when they die. The number of wild animals killed per hectare in crop production is twice that killed in ruminant-pasture.[1090] The grass and the grazers need each other as much as do predators and prey. These are not one-way relationships, much less arrangements of dominance and subordination. We are not exploiting each other by eating; we are only taking turns.

As Sir Albert Howard noted in *An Agricultural Testament*, "Mother earth never attempts to farm without live stock."[1091] Animal agriculture can have an extremely negative impact on the ecosystem, or it can bring benefits to it. When animals are raised in large confinement systems and fed grain, their production generally uses more energy and causes more pollution than the production of field crops. But when animals are raised in small groups primarily on pasture, their production uses less energy and causes less pollution than do field crops. The modern meat industry uses 78 kJ of fossil energy to produce 1 kJ of beef energy and studies show that eating meat contributes more to greenhouse gas emissions than does driving a car. Similarly, contaminated runoff from slaughter houses is a major source of water pollution, and livestock itself releases more "global warming pollutants" than all the plains, trains,

1089. Keith, op. cit.

1090. Steven L. Davis, "The Least Harm Principle May Require That Humans Consume a Diet Containing Large Herbivores, Not a Vegan Diet," *Journal of Agricultural and Environmental Ethics* 16(4), 2003, 387–394.

1091. 1940, 4.

and automobiles put together.[1092] So vegetarianism might be good for the planet after all, but the question remains: is it good for *you?*

Spinach, tomatoes, lettuce. Fresh produce seems to be the culprit in one episode of food-borne illness after another. According to the CSPI, the number of produce-related outbreaks of food-borne illness in the United States has increased from about 40 in 1999 to 86 in 2004. Indeed, Americans are more likely to get sick from eating contaminated produce than from any other food item.[1093] The two main contributing factors to the rise in outbreaks are: 1) greater consumption of fresh produce, especially cut fruits and vegetables; and 2) an ageing population more susceptible to food-borne illness. The numerous federal and state regulations that are supposed to ensure food safety have become less effective as the American produce supply has grown increasingly industrial. Produce presents a great food safety challenge because, unlike meat, which can be cleansed of bacteria through proper cooking, it is often consumed raw.

Whether "meat is murder" or not, meat eating is more natural than vegetarianism. As hunter-gatherers, we are designed, from our teeth to our rectums, to eat meat; our teeth have crowns unlike greens-eaters', whose teeth never stop growing. Vegetarianism has no verifiable health benefits for humans, but several verifiable health hazards. Historically, the typical diet of poor people consisted of grains, vegetables, and very little meat. In contrast, wealthy classes have always eaten lots of meat and fat, and they also tend to live longer. Indeed, strict vegetarians seem to die earlier than people who eat a balanced diet. There is little research into the area that excludes all the other contributing factors, but one study that does concluded that the annual all-cause death rate of vegetarian men was slightly more than that of non-vegetarian men (.93% vs. .89%), while the annual death rate of vegetarian women was significantly more than that of non-vegetarian women (.86% vs. .54%).[1094] The most extensive research on the subject has probably been made in India, where the mortality and malnutrion rates of its different regions and populations have been compared with each other. Some Indian ethnic groups are strictly vegetarian, while others enjoy a mixed diet—the latter again fare better, despite their often lower socio-economic status.[1095]

Finding the right balance of nutrients is much harder when you take meat out of the equation. Somehow I doubt many vegetarians really understand what makes up a truly balanced diet. Vegetarian diets typically lack iron, omega-3 fatty acids, and several other nutrients from zinc to B-12. Creatine, a nutrient associated with muscle strength, is only found in meat and fish. Ask yourself, how many vegetarian athletes

---

1092. Henning Steinfeld, et al. "Lifestock's Long Shadow: Environmental Issues and Options," Food and Agriculture Organization of the United Nations, Rome, 2006.

1093. "Outbreak Alert! Closing the Gaps in Our Federal Food-Safety Net," Center for Science in the Public Interest, Washington, D.C., December 2007.

1094. Michael M. Burr & Peter M. Sweetnam, "Vegetarianism, Dietary Fiber, and Mortality," *American Journal of Clinical Nutrition* 36(5), November 1982, 873–877.

1095. T. A. B. Sanders & Sheela Reddy, "Vegetarian Diets and Children," *Ibid.* 59(5S), May 1995, 1176S–1181S; Sonia Bhalotra, et al. "The Puzzle of Muslim Advantage in Child Survival in India," *Journal of Health Economics* 29(2), March 2010, 191–204.

do you know? Most sports professionals scarf meatballs and skirt steaks to replenish the gaping caloric hole left by daily exercise. As for vegans, who abstain from all animals products, including milk and eggs, the consequences can be even more dire: a vegan couple from Atlanta was recently sentenced to life in prison over the death of their malnourished baby—the baby died six weeks after birth due to being fed a diet largely made up of soy milk and organic apple juice. In short, cutting animal products out of your diet does not necessarily mean that you are doing your body any favours.

One's diet can have a remarkable effect on one's behaviour, mood, satisfaction, and quality of life in general. Food impacts all of our emotions, memories, and even our sense of self-worth. Food can be more effective than medicine, because food molecules act like hormones, regulating and balancing the functions of our bodies. According to research, food can even alter the genes that influence the rise of depression and schizophrenia.[1096] Any time we choose to limit the options in our diet, there is potential for coming up short. Many vegetarians are depleted; their immune systems do not functions as well, and they get sick more often. Vitamin and mineral deficiencies result in a greater vulnerability to colds and other illnesses. Zinc, for instance, is a powerful antioxidant that is more easily gleaned from lean meats like chicken and turkey. There is no plant-based source at all for B-12, a vitamin found readily in meat, fish, and milk. B-12 deficiencies can, among other things, impair cognitive development, and they have been linked to depression and memory failure. Older people with lower than average B-12 levels are more than six times more likely to experience brain shrinkage, which is associated with a significantly higher risk of developing dementia.[1097] Vegetarians might not even be aware of their B-12 deficiency, because high levels of folate from green vegetables can mask the shortfall in blood test readings.

What is more, the type of iron found in plant foods can clash with a plant-based chemical called phytate, which blocks iron absorption and can lead to deficiency and anaemia. An iron deficiency is one of the greatest pitfalls of a vegetarian diet, especially for women, who lose iron during menstruation. While you might think you are eating plenty of tofu and broccoli, the iron offered by plant foods is more sensitive to substances that block absorption, including fiber and caffeine, so your body might actually be rejecting the iron in the foods you eat. Spinach, too, is a very good source of iron, but unlike the iron from meat, you need complementary foods such as wholegrains or tomatoes to absorb it property. Meat and fish, on the other hand, naturally provide useful nutrients, usually in the precise way you need them. For twelve years, Dr. Sara Holmberg followed the eating habits and health of nearly two thousand Swedish men living in the countryside. Her research uncovered an interesting connection between animal fat intake and fruit and vegetable consumption: those who ate fruits and vegetables daily had a very low cardiovascular

---

1096. Malcolm Peet, "International Variations in the Outcome of Schizophrenia and the Prevalence of Depression in Relation to National Dietary Practices: An Ecological Analysis," *British Journal of Psychiatry* 184(5), May 2004, 404–408.

1097. Anna Vogiatzoglou, et al. "Vitamin B12 Status and Rate of Brain Volume Loss in Community-Dwelling Elderly," *Neurology* 71(11), September 2008, 826–832.

risk, but only if they also ate a lot of fat.[1098]

The fact of the matter is, how you eat will affect your physiology. Meat tends to satiate, and give you ample time to do other things besides think of your next meal. Animals who are plant-eaters cannot stop eating, and it consumes much of their time and thought. In place of meat, many vegetarians end up eating a lot of bread, potatoes, refined-flour pasta, and white rice. You are bound to gain weight with a diet so heavy in carbohydrates if you do not also exercise regularly. The largest and longest-running comparison of diet plans funded by the National Institutes of Health and the Community Foundation for Southeast Michigan found that Atkins dieters saw sharper drops in triglycerides and blood pressure, and steeper increases in HDL, or "good" cholesterol, than people on the low-fat, high-carb diet, which has for decades been touted as the model of healthy eating.[1099] Since vegetarians often load up on snack foods to satisfy cravings, they can actually overload on empty calories. These high-glycaemic foods act like sugar in the bloodstream, which leads to energy swings and stimulates insulin production. The higher the insulin levels, the more likely a person is to be fat and have low levels of protective cholesterol, and to develop Type 2 diabetes and premature heart disease.[1100]

The human genome is still in the process of adapting to the relatively new starch- and sugar-based agricultural diet. By comparing the genetic profiles of diabetics with those of healthy controls, researchers have found some recently spreading genes that seem to protect against diabetes by affecting the body's ability to digest starches. This may explain why Native Americans, who came to farming relatively recently, have a higher risk of diabetes.[1101] A diet rich in bread, potatoes, and white rice may be contributing to a silent epidemic of a dangerous liver condition. All bread, white bread or whole wheat, has the same glycaemic index. High-glycaemic foods, rapidly digested by the body, can cause "fatty liver," increasing the risk of serious illness. At the population level, simultaneously with a large reduction in animal fat consumption, the number of people with weight problems and obesity has increased sharply—a meat-free diet is not the healthiest kind simply because it is low in fat.

Many benefit from the prevalent "fat theory" at the moment, including, of course, the food industry, specifically margarine industry. Vegetable fats such as soy, sunflower, and rapeseed oil make for excellent tractor fuel, but they are unfit for human consumption. It is very likely that humans have received their nutrition mostly from other animals, so animal fats have been an important factor in the evolution of human digestion and metabolism. But due to current governmental

---

1098. Sara Holmberg, et al. "Food Choices and Coronary Heart Disease: A Population Based Cohort Study of Rural Swedish Men with 12 Years of Follow-up," *International Journal of Environmental Research and Public Health* 6(10), October 2009, 2626–2638.

1099. Christopher D. Gardner, et al. "Comparison of the Atkins, Zone, Ornish, and LEARN Diets for Change in Weight and Related Risk Factors Among Overweight Premenopausal Women," *JAMA* 297(9), March 7, 2007, 969–977.

1100. Abraham Lustgarten, "Confessions of a Fallen Vegetarian," *Alternative Medicine*, November/December 2004.

1101. George H. Perry, et al. "Diet and the Evolution of Human Amylase Gene Copy Number Variation," *Nature Genetics* 39(10), October 2007, 1256–1260.

recommendations throughout the Western world, butter and lard have been replaced by polyunsaturated fats like vegetable oils and their hardened derivative, margarine, which elevate blood fat levels considerably more than does butter.[1102]

Animal and vegetable fats are mixtures that contain both saturated and unsaturated fatty acids, and in the typical meat fats, the portion of good, unsaturated fats is very high, between 60 and 80 percent. At the same time, the benefits of plant-derived polyunsaturated fats remain to be proven. When we talk about the dangers of red meat, we are talking about the meat from artificially fed animals. Modern forms of meat production reduce the amount of omega-3 in our foods, contributing to a global omega-3 deficiency in most people's diets. Animals that graze on grass have higher omega-3 content in their meat, and the longer they are out to pasture, the more omega-3s accumulate in their meat. Today, however, the great majority of animals dine on corn, which is completely devoid of omega-3s. What is more, only animal-derived omega-3 is proven to help with brain, heart, and joint function, plant-derived omega-3 does not appear to help at all.

Most of the typical animal fats have no trans-fats, which not only raise bad (or LDL) cholesterol in the blood, but also lower the levels of good (or HDL) cholesterol. Saturated fats, although they raise bad cholesterol, raise good cholesterol as well. Trans-fats also raise the levels of blood triglycerides and inflammatory proteins. Having too high a proportion of polyunsaturates reduces the body's ability to deal with inflammation and makes you more vulnerable to heart disease and arthritis.[1103] During the past decade, numerous studies from Scandinavia, Britain, and the United States have said the same thing: there is no evidence of the dangers of animal fats to blood vessels and the heart. Yet the opposite nutritional dogma has been repeated since the 1960s, when a physiologist named Ancel Keys first published his "Seven Countries" study that purported to show that animal fat consumption strongly predicts heart attack risk.[1104]

Keys' conclusions have influenced American and North European dietary guidelines for decades, even though other researchers pointed out that if 21 other countries had been included in his study, the associations that he observed would have been extremely weak. Moreover, there was actually no connection between heart attacks and cholesterol within the individual countries. Keys claimed that coronary artery disease was five times as prevalent in Finland as in Japan due to a different diet, but he did not bother to explain why the disease was five times as prevalent in eastern as in western Finland, although both the diet and cholesterol levels were similar.

Three large international meta-analyses have been published in recent years that assemble hundreds of individual studies on links between fats and heart disease. All three analyses, totalling 800,000 subjects, concluded that the link between saturated

---

1102. Lena Ohlsson, "Dairy Products and Plasma Cholesterol Levels," *Food & Nutrition Research* 54(0), 2010, 5124.

1103. Simon Hemelryk, "The Super-Food Diet," *Reader's Digest*, September 2009.

1104. "Epidemiological Studies Related to Coronary Heart Disease: Characteristics of Men Aged 40–59 in Seven Countries," *Acta Medica Scandinavica* 460 (Suppl.), 1966, 1–392.

animal fat consumption and cardiovascular mortality and disease was nonexistent.[1105] One reason for this disparity might be the fact that the older studies, among them the infamous North Karelia Project, did not make a distinction between the effects of animal fats and those of trans-fats, which the Finnish diet of the time was brimming with. Indeed, one of the meta-analyses found that polyunsaturated vegetable oils strongly increase cardiovascular deaths—this result applies to practically all oils with the exception of olive oil and rapeseed oil with certain reservations.[1106] Nor did the older studies figure in the health risks of a starchy diet.

It is really quite strange that industrially processed food has displaced natural food. We eat, often unknowingly, large quantities of highly processed vegetable oils like soybean oil, canola, sunflower, corn, and cottonseed oils. In the early 20th century, the average annual consumption of butter per person was 18 pounds; this was on top of all the lard, duck and goose fat, and other animals fats, as well as the unpasteurized whole fat dairy products that were used copiously back then—yet the percentage of deaths from heart disease in the early 1900s was only around 8%. The U.S. Food and Drug Administration estimates that, on average, Americans now eat almost 5 pounds of trans-fats each year, while butter consumption per person barely reaches 4 pounds; at the same time, the percentage of deaths from heart disease hovers around 40%.[1107]

Once upon a time, trans-fats were considered a wonderful and healthy addition to the human diet—and a boon for the agricultural industry as well. Back in the early 1900s, chemists figured out how to create them in a laboratory. They would mix liquid oils with hydrogen gas and atoms of hydrogen would attach to the oils, making them stiff at room temperature, just like butter and beef tallow. Hydrogenation, as the process is called, not only made vegetable oils usable in frying and baking, but extended their shelf-life as well. It was a handy and profitable way to dispose of the huge quantities of cottonseed oil produced as a byproduct of the cotton-growing industry. Hydrogenated oils could be put into processed foods and ready-made mixes for cakes and drinks. Of course, they have no nutritional value, but were used because they were cheap, added bulk to products, and had a neutral flavour. "Partially hydrogenated" oils could be fashioned into a cheap butter-like spread, margarine.

Today, the international scientific community has no doubts about the health risks of the long-chained, industrially hydrogenated fatty acids. There is ample experimental evidence from both clinical and epidemiologic studies conducted on three continents. Trans-fats have been shown to correlate more pronouncedly than saturated fats with cardiovascular diseases. Some studies estimate trans-fats are twice as bad for the heart, while others put the risk as much as ten times higher. A review

---

1105. Andrew Mente, et al. "A Systematic Review of the Evidence Supporting a Causal Link Between Dietary Factors and Coronary Heart Disease," *Archives of Internal Medicine* 169(7), April 13, 2009, 659–669; C. Murray Skeaff & Jody Miller, "Dietary Fat and Coronary Heart Disease: Summary of Evidence from Prospective Cohort and Randomised Controlled Trials," *Annals of Nutrition and Metabolism* 55(1–3), September 2009, 173–201; Patty W. Siri-Tarino, et al. "Meta-Analysis of Prospective Cohort Studies Evaluating the Association of Saturated Fat with Cardiovascular Disease," *American Journal of Clinical Nutrition* 91(3), March 2010, 535–546.

1106. Mente, et al. Op. cit.

1107. Fallon & Enig 2001.

by the *New England Journal of Medicine* in 2006 concluded that eliminating artificial trans-fats from the food supply could prevent between 6 and 19 percent of heart attacks and related deaths each year.[1108] The nation of Denmark was sufficiently convinced of the dangers to ban industrial trans-fats three years earlier in 2003, and New York became the first city in the United States to ban them in 2008. Several major cities have since followed suit, with the state of California banning hydrogenated frying oils in its restaurants in 2010. However, under FDA rules, "zero grams of trans fat" equals less than half a gram per serving—if someone ate several servings of those foods a day, they could still consume a significant amount of trans-fat. The FDA applies this same rounding principle to zero calories, fat, and carbohydrates.

Proteins should make up to 15–20% of your diet, but getting the right type is just as important as the amount. Tofu gets called the "perfect protein," but it is not quite.[1109] By and large, plant protein does not contain enough amino acids to be converted effectively into muscle. Animal-based proteins contain a more complete suite of amino acids that aid in everything from sleep to calcium absorption. If you are not getting enough protein in your diet, you are going to be tired. You will not have what you need to sustain energy, alertness, muscle repair, and muscle maintenance. In children, protein deficiencies can lead to stunted growth. Wheat-based protein, for instance, is only half as available to the body as animal protein, and leaves out many essential amino acids. Isolated soy—like the kind in vegetarian "steaks" and other fake meat—will provide most of these missing aminos, but not in the same highly usable form as those found in meat. All meat and fish are high in protein, so you should choose them based on other factors, like omega ratios and the amount of saturated fat.[1110] While saturated fat appears to have no effect on cardiac health, eating too much can crowd out vitamins, minerals, and fiber needed for optimal health.

Soy is 95% of the vegetable protein in the world. It no longer qualifies as an organic source for protein, since modified genes have transferred from one plant to another and the vast majority of the world's soy is tainted in this sense. However, soy products are a major alternative protein source to meat for many people in the developing world. Protein is more important than petrol—you can live without petrol, but you cannot live without protein. But soy consumption is also on the increase in the West, which buys a lot of cheap soy from such countries as Brazil and Argentina. In the early 1980s, U.S. farmers produced four-fifths of the world's soybeans, today they only produce a third. Meanwhile, the soy boom in South America is changing lifestyles, ecosystems, and economies. The production of soy is far less labour-intensive than the traditional cattle farming industry, and other plantations are torn down to cultivate soy. Exports to Europe and China, which need soy to feed their meat and poultry industries, are propelling record trade surpluses.

Animal feed consists mostly of genetically modified soy and vegetable oil, which

---

1108. Dariush Mozaffarian, et al. "Trans Fatty Acids and Cardiovascular Disease," 354(15), April 13, 2006, 1601–1613.

1109. "Energy and Protein Requirements: Report of Joint FAO/WHO Expert Consultation," Food and Agriculture Organization of the United Nations, Rome, 1991.

1110. Lustgarten, op. cit.

tip the fat profile of the animals in a pathological direction. Vegetable fats are mostly omega-6, which causes inflammation. The infections do not have time to manifest themselves, because the animals are butchered young and fed steady doses of antibiotics, but people digest these fats in their everyday diet. We have been led to believe that the best quality food is local food. But what constitutes local food when the feed is imported? In many countries, the whole food chain is controlled by one feed factory. Chickens, swine, and even cows are fed basically the same animal feed—the formula is only slightly altered to make it suitable for different animals. Cows are fed the same soy as chickens, although cows are grass-eating ruminants. Mad cow disease came about when cows were fed bovine offal; the long-term effects of feeding soy to ruminants are still unknown.

We have all been taught in school that everything that is good in human culture flowed from the invention of agriculture. Science, technology, and art were born, and the endless struggle against starvation, disease, and violence could be won, just because humans figured out how to grow their own food. The reality, of course, is that agriculture has been a net loss for both human rights and culture. It was agriculture that brought about slavery, militarism, nationalism, imperialism, class divisions, chronic hunger, epidemic disease, and organized religion. The question is not why some people were slow to adopt agriculture, but why anyone took it up at all. Agriculture has also been devastating to the other animals with whom we share this Earth, and ultimately to the life support systems of the planet itself. If we really want a sustainable world, we need to start examining the power relations behind the foundational myth of our civilization.

Brazil was the last country in the Americas to officially abolish slavery, in 1888, just before it became an independent republic. For more than three and a half centuries, African slaves had been shipped in the millions to work on Brazilian sugar plantations and other large agricultural estates or *fazendas*. And even today, Brazil is still plagued with similar practices. There are more people of African descent in Brazil than in any other country outside the African continent; but higher you go in Brazilian society, the less evident this reality appears. The modern slaves are mostly found in the vast Amazon region of the country, a frontier territory that the state cannot always control or police properly. They are taken by a *gato*, or gangmaster, usually to clear areas of the jungle. Human rights and labour organizations estimate that between 25,000 and 40,000 people are forced to work in this inhuman way. Yet violence in the Amazon was only brought to the world's attention when an American nun was killed in the city of Anapu in 2005.

There is great concern about the loss of the Amazon rainforest and the deforestation that been done to clear the land for soybean production in not only Brazil but Paraguay as well. Any plan to crack down on deforestation, however, depends on the government's ability to enforce its laws, which according to local farmers is practically nonexistent in the jungle. Brazil's government was named the worst illegal logger of Amazon forests by one of its own departments in 2008. Topping the Environmental Ministry's list of the 100 worst offenders was the Institute of Colonization and Agrarian Reform (Incra), a government department responsible for distributing land to the poor. According to Environmental Minister Carlos Minc, the six largest deforested areas since 2005 all belonged to Incra.[1111] His predecessor, Marina Silva, had resigned from her post because the pressure on her for taking the measures she took against deforestation became unbearable.

The dense and steamy habitat of the Amazon straddles eight countries and is home to up to 20% of the world's fresh water and 30% of its plant and animal species.[1112] The 1.5-million-square-mile Brazilian Amazon is larger than the entire nation of India and accounts for more than half of the ecosystem. It contains more than 40% of the world's rain forests, and according to the Brazilian government, about a fifth of it has already disappeared.[1113] However, recent studies suggest deforestation of the Brazilian Amazon has been underestimated by at least 60%. It is happening on such a massive scale that the only way of measuring it is by using satellites. While traditional aerial images can show areas that have been completely destroyed, they do not reveal selective logging, i.e. where loggers pick out trees of value while leaving the surrounding forest intact.[1114]

Ever since saving the Amazon became fashionable in the '80s, the jungle has consistently been likened to an enormous recycling plant, "lungs of the world" that sucks up carbon dioxide and pumps out oxygen for us all to breathe. But far from cleaning the atmosphere, the Amazon is now a major source for greenhouse gases. Globally, about three-quarters of man-made carbon dioxide come from power plants, transportation, and industrial activity, but more than 70% of Brazil's emissions come from deforestation.[1115] Rampart burning and clearing of forests release 250 million tons of carbon emission into the atmosphere each year, which translates into several times that amount in actual CO_2. Brazil has become the world's fourth-largest producer of greenhouse gases, ahead of industrialized nations such as Canada and Italy, but its consumption of fossil fuels creates less than half what the fires spew out.[1116]

Even without the massive burning, the popular notion of the Amazon as a giant oxygen factory is misguided. Left unmolested, the forest does generate enormous amounts of oxygen through photosynthesis, but it consumes most of that itself in the decomposition of organic matter. The Amazon also plays a role in keeping the region cool and relatively moist, which has a hugely beneficial effect on agriculture, the same interests that are trying to cut down the forest. About 40% of the precipitation in southern Brazil—where much of the country's agriculture, industry, and population is based—comes from moisture evaporated off the rain forest's thick tree

---

1111. Raymond Colitt, "Brazil Government Biggest Illegal Logger in Amazon," Reuters, September 30, 2008.

1112. Henry Chu, "Rain Forest Myth Goes Up in Smoke Over the Amazon," *Los Angeles Times*, June 8, 2005.

1113. Jack Chang, "As Brazil's Rain Forest Burns Down, Planet Heats Up," McClatchy Washington Bureau, September 7, 2007.

1114. Gregory P. Asner, et al. "Selective Logging in the Brazilian Amazon," *Science* 310(5747), October 21, 2005, 480–482.

1115. Chang, op. cit.

1116. Chu, op. cit.

cover.[1117] The jungle's humidity, as much as water from the ocean, is instrumental in creating rain over both the Amazon River basin and other parts of South America. The hydroclimatic cycle of the Amazon depends on having forest there; its destruction would take away half of the annual rainfall in Brazil, the ripple effect of which could disrupt weather patterns in Antarctica, the Eastern United States, and even as far as Western Europe.[1118]

In a campaign without peacetime precedent, U.S. mainstream media is warning about global warming. Never, other than during the two world wars, has there been such a concerted effort by opinion-forming institutions to indoctrinate Americans, 83% of whom now deem global warming a "serious problem."[1119] Much of the American public has come to believe that anyone who is skeptical about the dangers of global warming is an enemy of the environment, even though many of the skeptics are passionate environmentalists. They are horrified to see the obsession with global warming distract public attention from what they see as more serious and more immediate dangers to our planet, including problems of nuclear weaponry, environmental degradation, and social injustice. In 1992, the first UN environmental summit held in Rio de Janeiro made the political decision that scientific uncertainly should not stand in the way of launching preventive measures against global warming—and this is what the Kyoto Protocol of 1997 is based on.

The Kyoto Protocol, which came into force in 2005, is a comprehensive set of rules for reducing and restricting greenhouse gas emissions; however, the trouble with faith-based rules is that they might very well be wrong. The Intergovernmental Panel on Climate Change is presenting a consensus view that has been approved by a very large number of interests. Established in 1988, the IPCC does not carry out its own original research, nor does it monitor climate or related phenomena itself. It is merely tasked with providing policymakers with neutral summaries of the latest expertise on climate change. According to the IPCC, the climate is warming at such a rapid pace that preparing for it will be cheaper than forgetting about it. This might be so, but at the same time, we have created a milieu where even healthy criticism appears irresponsible and skepticism, a hallmark of science, is frowned upon—"Let's be clear: the work of science has nothing whatever to do with consensus. Consensus is the business of politics. . . What is relevant is reproducible results. The greatest scientists in history are great precisely because they broke with the consensus."[1120] Indeed, global warming is more about politics than about science.

The claim of consensus has historically been the first refuge of scoundrels. It is a way to avoid debate by claiming that the matter is already settled. "Whenever you hear that the consensus of scientists agrees on something or other, reach for your wallet, because you're being had."[1121] Of course, there is not even a consensus on

1117. Chang, op. cit.

1118. Chu, op. cit.

1119. George F. Will, "Fuzzy Climate Math," *Washington Post*, April 12, 2007.

1120. Michael Crichton, Lecture at the California Institute of Technology, Pasadena, January 17, 2003.

1121. Ibid.

climate change—far from it. Although the IPCC reports are described in the media as representing a "consensus" of "the world's top 2,500 climate scientists," only a few dozen of their contributors are strictly climate specialists and most are not really scientists at all. When the IPCC produced its first report in 1990, Richard Lindzen, professor of meteorology at the MIT Department of Earth, Atmospheric, and Planetary Sciences, pointed out that the computer models on which the IPCC based its projections were fundamentally skewed by several crucial factors they had missed, such as the negative feedback effect of the most potent greenhouse gas of all, water vapour. The IPCC's second report in 1996 provoked Dr. Frederick Seitz, the former president of the National Academy of Sciences, to exclaim that he had never known such a perversion of established scientific procedure in all his 60 years as a scientist.

Consensus is only ever invoked in situations where the science is not solid enough: nobody says the consensus among scientists is that $E=mc^2$; nobody says the consensus is that the Sun is 93 million miles away—a theory accepted by 99% of scientists may be wrong. Not long ago, every physiologist knew that stomach ulcers were due to excess acid caused by stress and could only be cured by diet; then Barry J. Marshall and J. Robin Warren showed that the actual cause was a microaerophilic bacterium called *Helicobacter pylori* and that antibiotics were the correct treatment. The existence of the greenhouse effect is an indisputable physical fact, without which there would be no life as we know it on this planet; there is, however, no hard evidence of any human contribution to climate change. The signature statement of the Nobel Prize winning 2007 IPCC report may be paraphrased as follows: "We are 90% confident that most of the warming in the past 50 years is due to humans."

The 2007 report upgrades the IPCC's previous assessment from 2001, which dubbed human behaviour as the "likely" culprit for the recent warming trend. The words were selected to correspond to precise numerical assessments of our guilt, with the 2001 report calculating a 66% chance of human culpability. These assertions are based on computer models, not direct observation: the science summary from the science section of the most recent IPCC report plainly states that we cannot detect a human influence in the climate, but the "Summary for Policymakers" completely ignores the science and unilaterally concludes that 95% of global warming is due to human activities.[1122] The simple fact is that thermometers do not come with markers saying "this much is human-caused" and "this much is natural." In general, we use numbers and percentages when talking about statistical probability, and phrases like "doubtful" or "almost certain" when talking about subjective judgements—by tagging subjective judgements with percent values, the IPCC blurs the long-standing distinction between chance and *raison de croire*.

The main basis of the claim that man's release of greenhouse gases is the cause of global warming is based almost entirely on computer models. The argument goes that the current models used by the IPCC could not reproduce the warming from about 1978 to 1998 without some forcing, and that the only forcing they could think of was man. There is no reason to demonize carbon or carbon dioxide. CO_2 is a naturally-occurring, transparent inert gas, the catalyst for photosynthesis, without which there

1122. Solomon, et al. 2007.

would be no vegetation to support terrestrial mammalian life. As Mr. White put it, "Carbon is at the centre of it all. There is no life without carbon. Nowhere—that we know of—in the universe. Everything that lives, lived, will live—carbon."[1123] All life on this planet is carbon-based, so to be "carbon neutral" is to be dead.

Carbon dioxide is an essential element in Earth's climate control system, and if we did not have any, it would be too cold for humanity to be here. Ninety-seven percent of all CO_2 emitted every year in the world is naturally caused, meaning only about 3% stems from human activity. All 7 billion of us, China, India, the United States, factories, cars, and coal plants are generating only 3% of Earth's CO_2. The biggest sources are decaying plants, volcanoes, and forest fires.[1124] CO_2 is nothing new, there have been periods on this planet when its atmospheric concentration was up to 7,000 ppm, or roughly 20 times what it is today. In fact, CO_2 now occupies only one-tenthousandth more of the atmosphere than it did in 1750; and if we try really hard, and refuse to cut any of our CO_2 emissions, we might be able to occupy another one-twothousandth part of the atmosphere in the next hundred years.[1125]

Yes, the global atmospheric concentration of CO_2 has risen over the last hundred years from about 0.028% to 0.038%, but its effect on Earth's temperature pales in significance to that of water vapour and cloud cover.[1126] Human contribution to the total volume of greenhouse gas in the planet's atmosphere is less than 0.3% and nothing in any climate model can show that a 0.3% input or lack of input creates a measurable difference in the trend of global temperatures. The biggest component of greenhouse gases in the atmosphere is water vapour and we have no control over that gas. What is more, the entire greenhouse effect of the entire atmosphere, once you net off the albedo effect of the clouds, is only 33°F. So the IPCC apparently thinks that if we alter one-twothousandth of the composition of the atmosphere over the next hundred years, this is somehow going to have the same effect as one-sixth of the existing atmosphere.[1127]

Climate change is normal and natural. There was a Mediaeval Warm Period, for example, long before BP existed. Over the last several million years, climate change has followed a pattern: ninety to a hundred thousand years of icing, followed by a ten to fifteen thousand year period of warming, called the interglacial, or "between icings." We are currently almost 15,000 years into the latest interglacial period, so global cooling could be expected at any time. For roughly the past 10,000 years, since the end of the last Ice Age, humans have enjoyed a relatively stable, comfortable period, during which they have invented everything from agriculture to moon rockets. Nomadic bands of hunter-gatherers have given way to nearly 7 billion people, most of them city dwellers. The effects of urban development play a major role in warming, as thousands of square miles of dry shrubland are transformed into highways, housing tracts, and strip malls—all of which retain heat.

1123. "Peekaboo." *Breaking Bad.* AMC. April 12, 2009.

1124. "Being Green." *Penn & Teller: Bullshit!* Showtime Networks. July 24, 2008.

1125. Lord Christopher Monckton, Speech at Bethel University, St. Paul, MN, October 14, 2009.

1126. Solomon, et al. Op. cit.

1127. Monckton, op. cit.

It is straightforward to get a temperature reading that is precise in space and time from an individual weather station. But some countries have several weather stations, while others have only a few, and there are sizeable areas of the globe with no surface measurements at all. Modelling 101 says that the most important phase in building a model is "validation." The role of carbon dioxide in the speculated climate change is a *cause célèbre* in scientific circles, because while its atmospheric concentration has risen steadily over the last hundred years, global temperatures have not followed suit, but have fallen between 1940 and 1970, and again from 2002 on, as all internationally accepted databases (NASA GISS, RSS MSU, UAH AMSU, and HADLEY) show. Correlation does not prove causation, but the lack of correlation disproves causation. In fact, the entire point of the scientific method is to rule out premises that are contradicted by observational evidence.

If the world really were on the verge of disaster, then why would the global warming activists support legislation that their own models show will do virtually nothing? If there was a way to reduce our CO_2 emissions substantially, that is, by at least half or two-thirds, it would be reckless not to do that. But there is a fundamental problem here that no-one really cares to mention: there is nothing humanity can do, from a practical standpoint, to greatly reduce CO_2 emissions, because everything we do depends on energy, and fossil fuels are the only affordable and abundant source of energy we have right now. They are the backbone of all national economies, making up about 80% of the world's energy. They sustain economic growth, which—in all modern societies—buttresses political and social stability.[1128] It is pointless for the West to criticize China for its energy consumption when so much of China's industry is concentrated on producing goods for Western markets.

Until we can replace fossil fuels, or find practical ways to capture their emissions, no government will sanction the deep energy cuts that would truly make a difference. To reduce emissions significantly, governments would have to suppress electricity use, which would depress economic growth, and fan popular discontent. Political leaders everywhere deplore global warming—and then do little about it. Except for Eastern European nations, where dirty factories have recently been shuttered, few countries have cut emissions. In 2008, a little-publicized report for the UK Department for Environment, Food and Rural Affairs showed that rather than going down 5% as British ministers claimed, CO_2 emissions had gone up 18% between 1992 and 2004, growing in line with the economy. But under the internationally-agreed system for carbon accounts, emissions from international aviation, shipping, and imports are not included in a country's greenhouse gas statistics, so the British government was able to calculate that its greenhouse gases had been falling since the 1990s.[1129]

WWF has called the Defra figures "breathtaking" and says they make a mockery of the United Kingdom's claims of global leadership.[1130] They are a massive blow to the claim that Britain has grasped the holy grail of climate policy, i.e. decoupling

1128. Robert J. Samuelson, "Global Warming and Hot Air," *Washington Post*, February 7, 2007.

1129. Thomas Wiedmann, et al. "Development of an Embedded Carbon Emission Indicator: A Research Report to the Department for Environment, Food and Rural Affairs by the Stockholm Environment Institute and the University of Sydney," Defra, London, July 2008.

1130. Roger Harrabin, "UK in 'Delusion' over Emissions," BBC News, July 31, 2008.

economic growth from emissions growth. But even if rich countries actually managed to curb their emissions, it would matter little, since poor countries would offset the reductions. In fact, as manufacturing in the UK has closed down, some of the production has shifted to countries where manufacturing is more carbon intensive than it would be in Britain. So it makes no difference whether Europe signs on to an updated Kyoto Protocol. It makes no difference whether the United States adopts Cap and Trade. Even if both areas could roll their emissions back to 1970 levels, it would not affect the present situation in the slightest. Reducing global CO_2 emissions to 60% of 1990 levels before 2050, while China, India, and possibly even Africa modernize, is inconceivable.

Poor countries are not going to sacrifice their economic gains and political stability to placate the rich nations' global warming fears. The practical consequence of the Stern policy would be to slow down the economic growth of China today in order to reduce damage from climate change a hundred years later. Several generations of Chinese citizens would be impoverished to make their descendants only slightly richer—the slowing-down of growth would be far more costly to China than the climatic damage. Besides, Chinese statistics show that the country has always done better economically when it has been warmer. Indeed, general knowledge of the period from about 900 CE through the early 14th century clearly shows that global warming was also a good thing for Western Europe a thousand years ago. That was a period when civilization advanced, trade expanded, agriculture thrived, and populations increased. Holding China and India responsible for emissions from the manufactured goods they sell us could prove very hard to negotiate.

On a per-person basis, the CO_2 emissions of China and India are only about one-fifth the level of Western countries. In Africa, less than 40% of the population even has electricity.[1131] A relatively low-exergy source of energy, such as sunlight, cannot be used to replace a relatively high-exergy source such as coal. The demand for energy in the world is growing so rapidly that there is no other way to satisfy it than with fossil fuels. Research on solar, wind, hydro, and geothermal energy have been in progress for decades, but their efficiency is not good enough to make them cost effective, even with the oil prices as high as they are. Renewable energy is in the same class of ideas as perpetual motion: the specific problem with wind energy is that you cannot always have the wind when you need the energy—this is why although more than 15% of German energy capacity is wind power, it produces only 3% of German energy. An average kilowatt from wind costs 10 cents, whereas the average cost of electricity is only about one-third as high.[1132]

Industrial wind power does not produce the claimed benefits of reduction in fossil fuel consumption and CO_2 emissions when back-up generation inefficiencies are taken into account. Even in the best case scenario, wind-natural gas combos result in only marginally lower CO_2 emissions than natural gas units alone. In some locales and circumstances, even the best pairings of wind and fossil-fired generators would

1131. Samuelson, op. cit.

1132. *One Planet.* BBC World Service. February 25, 2005.

produce more CO_2 than would be the case with no wind at all.[1133] Now, one could correctly state that burning hydrogen, as some advocate, would reduce CO_2, but the byproduct of burning hydrogen is water vapour, a much more powerful greenhouse gas. And when you figure in the electricity used in the production of hydrogen, its pressurization and gas conversion, its transport and distribution, the hydrogen car ends up using many times as much energy as a petrol car. There is little sense in converting water into hydrogen, when the same amount of energy could turn carbon dioxide into gasoline. And since most of our hydrogen comes from natural gas, its use would not reduce out dependence on greedy oil states.

George W. Bush famously stated that "America is addicted to oil," but he conveniently left out the fact that the U.S. is also addicted to corn. Maize is a main feed grain for poultry, cattle, and hogs in the country, but it is also the main raw material for ethanol, an alternative to gasoline. The production of maize for biofuel has recently overtaken the use of the plant as food. By 2009, the grain grown to produce fuel in the United States was enough to feed 330 million people—the entire national population—for one year at average consumption levels.[1134] When the price of a grain drops, the farmers usually plant more for next year; while they earn less, there is an over-supply of cheap corn, and that means having to find ever more ways to use it up. In Europe, too, more and more farmers are switching to biofuel crops, encouraged by rising prices and cuts in subsidies for food production.

Touted as an alternative fuel of the future, ethanol has long been a cornerstone of some U.S. lawmakers' efforts to curb dependence on foreign oil. But more recently, the growth in biofuel production has been driven by the desire to find less environmentally-damaging alternatives to oil. The trend has contributed to a sharp rise in food prices as farmers switch production from wheat and soy to corn, which is then turned into ethanol. As more farmers switch to corn to take advantage of the high prices, fewer fields of other grains and food crops are planted, causing prices to rise for those as well. The price of wheat doubled in less than a year, while other staples such as corn and soy were trading at well above their 1990s averages, sparking "the first real economic crisis of globalisation."[1135] Because the international community decided that global warming was a problem, one-quarter of the agricultural land in the United States has been taken out of growing food for people who need it, and devoted to growing biofuels for clunkers that do not.

In 2008, the British *Guardian* newspaper revealed a secret World Bank report that concluded the drive for biofuels by American and European governments had pushed food prices by 75%, in stark contrast to U.S. claims that prices had risen only 2–3% as a result.[1136] The higher prices mean that investment in agriculture has become more attractive, but the increased interest in agriculture also has a downside, as speculators

---

1133. Kent Hawkins, "Wind Integration: Incremental Emissions from Back-Up Generation Cycling," National Wind Watch, Rowe, MA, November 2009.

1134. John Vidal, "One Quarter of US Grain Crops Fed to Cars—Not People, New Figures Show," *The Guardian*, January 22, 2010.

1135. Aditya Chakrabortty, "Secret Report: Biofuel Caused Food Crisis," *Ibid.*, July 4, 2008.

1136. Donald Mitchell, "A Note on Rising Food Prices," April 8, 2008.

have come into the agricultural commodity market. Commodities have recently become especially enticing to investors as the credit crisis has roiled other investment opportunities such as stocks and debt-related securities. The recent flood of investment money has transformed the market for wheat, cotton, and other agricultural goods into a volatile realm that some insiders call the "Wild West of Wall Street." Apart from drought, speculation was the other factor named by the UN Food and Agriculture Organization as being responsible for the record highs and the recent volatility in markets.[1137]

For Westerners, paying two dollars instead of one for a hamburger is an inconvenience, but for the people in Haïti who are living on mud pies made with real mud, the doubling of world food prices means they cannot even afford the mud. The U.S. Agency for International Development has had to significantly scale back emergency food aid to some of the world's poorest countries because of soaring food prices, and needs to reduce the number of recipient nations, the amount of food provided to them, or both.[1138] The UN humanitarian relief program is confronting similar pressures, seriously complicating already strained efforts to combat global hunger, particularly in Africa, Central Asia, and Latin America—there are 800 million people in the world who did not have enough to eat on a daily basis even before the recent record rise in prices.[1139] Josette Sheeran, executive director for the UN World Food Program was quoted as saying that "This is really the first emergency we've faced without a drought, war, natural disaster."[1140]

The United Nations has described the rapid rise in food prices as a "silent tsunami" hitting poor countries.[1141] According to the head of the World Bank, it could push another 100 million people in poor countries below the poverty line. His warning followed that from the director of the International Monetary Fund, who said hundreds of thousands of people were at risk of starvation.[1142] There have been food riots in a dozen regions of the world in the last few years and the World Bank estimates 33 countries face potential social unrest.[1143] The rising food prices have led to protests in countries as far apart as Mexico, the Philippines, Indonesia, Ivory Coast, and Ethiopia. Many argue that it was skyrocketing food prices that ultimately caused the toppling of North African dictators from Ben Ali to Mubarak in 2011.

Protests have also begun in the United States—in Congress. Representatives of the dairy, poultry, and livestock industries, which rely on corn as a principal animal feed, demand an end to subsidies for corn ethanol in hope of stabilizing corn prices. In the

---

1137. "Food Outlook: Global Market Analysis," Food and Agriculture Organization of the United Nations, Rome, June 2008.

1138. Anthony Faiola, "Soaring Food Prices Putting U.S. Emergency Aid in Peril," *Washington Post*, March 1, 2008.

1139. United Nations Fund for Population Activities, op. cit.

1140. Faiola, op. cit.

1141. "The Silent Tsunami: Food Prices Are Causing Misery and Strife around the World," *The Economist*, April 17, 2008.

1142. "World Bank Echoes Food Cost Alarm," BBC News, April 13, 2008.

1143. Robert B. Zoellick, Speech to the Center for Global Development, Washington, D.C., April 2, 2008.

UK, pig farmers are protesting at Downing Street over the price of feed. Most of the corn today feeds livestock, not people, and high feed prices have discouraged meat producers from expanding, resulting in higher retail prices; in some countries, prices for milk and meat have more than doubled. For the first time in 40 years, there has actually been a decrease in U.S. poultry production. The government's subsidies for corn-based ethanol are thus worsening inflation, perhaps permanently.[1144]

Make no mistake about it, Americans are paying twice: once in taxes, and again at the supermarket cash register for more expensive food. Biodiesel production is entirely dependent on government subsidy, since its production cost remains higher than the cost of conventional diesel production. The UN Secretary General stressed that individual governments should look again at the subsidy and tariff protection policies they have adopted for growing biofuels.[1145] Continuing to divert more food for fuel, as is mandated by the U.S. government in its renewable fuel standard, will likely reinforce the rise in world hunger. In 2007, the OECD countries spent up to $15 billion on support to biofuels, including tax breaks—this is incidentally the same amount that Oxfam estimates is needed immediately to help the most vulnerable people affected by the food crisis.[1146]

In the past four decades, cultivation of vegetable oil crops has increased faster than any other major type of food or industrial crop. At the same time, per capita human consumption of vegetable oils has increased more rapidly than any other food. Palm oil is the fastest-growing and highest yielding source of vegetable oil in the world. It can be separated into a wide range of distinct oils with different properties that can be used in a variety of products. Its largest consumer is still the food industry, but its demand in biofuel production is rapidly growing. However, many analysts doubt that "sustainable" palm oil exists, because any palm oil used for fuel simply swells the demand for the product oil on the global market which is mainly governed by food firms. A recent WWF report shows that palm oil based biofuels are among the smallest in their carbon footprint, but this requires that the plantations are established on idle land.[1147]

Because oil palms do not absorb as much CO_2 as the rainforest or peatlands they replace, palm oil can generate as much as ten times more carbon than regular petroleum.[1148] The destruction of Indonesia's peat swamps has often been cited as an example of biodiesel folly. The swamps are one of the richest stores of carbon on the planet and they are being burned to produce palm oil—deforestation already accounts

1144. Robert J. Samuelson, "The Upside of Recession?" *Washington Post*, April 25, 2007.

1145. Ban Ki-Moon, Remarks to the General Assembly Meeting on the Global Food and Energy Crisis, UN Headquarters, New York, July 18, 2008.

1146. "Another Inconvenient Truth: How Biofuel Policies Are Deepening Poverty and Accelerating Climate Change," Oxfam International, Oxford, June 2008.

1147. Guido Reinhardt, et al. "Rain Forest for Biodiesel?: Ecological Effects of Using Palm Oil as a Source of Energy," WWF Germany, Frankfurt, 2007.

1148. Eric Holt-Gimenez & Isabella Kenfield, "When Renewable Isn't Sustainable: Agrofuels and the Inconvenient Truths Behind the 2007 U.S. Energy Independence and Security Act." Jonasse 2009.

for up to 25% of all greenhouse gas emissions.[1149] And once the forests are gone, they can no longer soak up the carbon from industry, transport, and power plants. The rapidly growing production of biofuels increases the number of oil palm plantations especially in Southeast Asia, but production is increasing in Oceania and South and Central America as well. The conversion of rainforests, peatlands, savannas, and grasslands to produce biofuels has dramatic consequences for biodiversity.

The natural forests that are cut down in Southeast Asia to make room for oil palm plantations are so-called mega-biodiversity centres that contain 10% of the world's biodiversity. These plantations pose a threat to many endangered species, including the orangutan, the tiger, and the rhino. The EU has adopted a mandatory 10% goal for biofuels in transportation by 2020. By 2020, the acreage of oil palm plantations is set to quadruple in Indonesia, and double in Malaysia; together the two countries already produce 80% of the world's palm oil. If the forests continue to be cleared at the present pace, the rainforests of Sumatra and Borneo will disappear by 2022.[1150] Thanks in large part to oil palm plantations, Indonesia already has the dubious honour of being the world's third-largest emitter of CO_2, trailing only China and the United States.

In just the four years between 2007 and 2010, rainforest destruction alone is estimated to have released more carbon into the atmosphere than every flight from the dawn of aviation until 2025.[1151] It would be politically and economically much easier to make massive reductions in deforestation than to achieve similar cuts in air travel, but ironically most people get far more exercised over the evils of aviation than they ever do over forest loss. Biofuel producers in developing countries are often eligible for millions of dollars in development money from the World Bank, but at the same time, the UN estimates that 60 million indigenous people, who depend on forests almost entirely for their survival, are at risk of being evicted from their lands to make way for these biofuels.[1152]

Brazil is the world's second-largest ethanol producer and the biggest exporter of sugar-based ethanol. The Brazilian ethanol is also the cheapest in the world, prompting the United States to impose an import tariff on it in order to protect the American corn farmers. Together with the United States, Brazil produces about 70% of the world's ethanol. The country's tropical climate allows it to efficiently grow sugarcane for ethanol production, which now provides half of Brazil's transport fuel. However, Brazilian sugar is still produced via the feudal latifundary system, a model of production that became obsolete in Europe four or five centuries ago. In fact, sugarcane is produced in Brazil exactly as it was produced back in the 1500s, using slave labour and devastating the environment—the only difference is that the cane

1149. Andrew W. Mitchell, et al. "Forests First in the Fight Against Climate Change," Global Canopy Programme, Oxford, May 2007.

1150. Reinhardt, et al. Op. cit.

1151. Mitchell, et al. Op. cit.

1152. Victoria Tauli-Corpuz & Parshuram Tamang, "Oil Palm and Other Commercial Tree Plantations, Monocropping: Impacts on Indigenous Peoples' Land Tenure and Resource Management Systems and Livelihoods," United Nations Permanent Forum on Indigenous Issues, New York, May 7, 2007.

hacked from the modern fields is part of an energy revolution.

The biofuel industry began in the 1970s and has turned Brazil into an agricultural superpower. The country was hit hard by the oil crisis and the then military government launched a subsidized drive to embrace the alternative energy source. If there was no ethanol, fuel would be a great deal more expensive in Brazil. Latifundios are huge landed estates based on the cultivation of just one crop—or monoculture; they belong to private landowners known as "sugar barons." This distorted landownership is probably Brazil's biggest problem, and the reason behind all its other deep social issues. Millions of landless workers struggle for survival in the Brazilian countryside, crowding the slums of the cities in desperation. Out of this poverty and anger rises the crime that cripples the whole Brazilian society. Almost everything is owned by the top 50,000 Brazilians (out of a population of 165 million), while 4 million peasants get to divide 3% of the land between themselves.[1153] Judging from the UN Human Development Index (HDI), Northeast Brazil, the traditional area of sugar production, is one of the worst places on the planet.

The Brazilian land reform got off to a promising start in the 1990s, but then hit a brick wall when the global ethanol boom began. Tens of thousands of rural families have had their houses torn down and their small farms destroyed, to make way for huge sugarcane estates. They have been expelled to the *favelas*, the shanty towns, of nearby cities, and consigned to a miserable existence; the girls have a future in prostitution, the boys have a future in small crime, narco-traffic, and death squads—creating an even more violent society. It is quite common for large Brazilian estates to comprise of tens of thousands of hectares of land, with the biggest ones being hundreds of thousands of hectares in size. Estates this large require their own troop of guards, a private army of sorts, despite the fact that both the police and the judiciary system give the large landowners their full support. Sugarcane estates require an extremely large work force, especially during harvest. Migrant workers are freighted in, illegally, from thousands of miles away. They are housed in heavily guarded barracks that bear an uncanny resemblance to prison camps. Armed guards also watch the sugarcane fields from sentry towers positioned at regular intervals. The more money we invest in sugarcane, the more people are enslaved and the more leaders of the landless movement are murdered.

Monoculture does not occur in nature. It does not leave any room for other plants, animals, birds, insects, or humans. An unbroken chain of sugarcane fields envelop over 5 million hectares of land in Brazil. The plan is to clear 4 million hectares more over a decade to meet the global demand for biofuels. Sugarcane is responsible for the devastation of the Atlantic Rainforest in Brazil: over the last thirty years, more forest has been destroyed by the sugar barons than in the previous five centuries since the Portuguese invasion.[1154] When tropical woodland is cleared to produce sugarcane for ethanol, about 50% more greenhouse gas is released than what occurs from the production and use of the same amount of gasoline—and that statistic holds for at

1153. Bales, op. cit.

1154. "Etanoliorjat." *MOT.* Yle TV1. December 4, 2006.

least two decades.[1155] Making ethanol requires up to six times more energy than the finished fuel actually contains, so the energy expended during production alone easily outweighs the consumable energy in the end product.[1156]

The IPCC's description of Brazilian ethanol production as "highly advanced" and "a model" is somewhat of an exaggeration. The Brazilian mode of farming happens to be incredibly energy inefficient. In order to speed up the harvest, the farmers first burn the foliage: during the harvest season, the air of the sugar region and the nearby cities is filled for weeks by acrid smoke and soot. A third of the energy contained in the biomass is scattered to the wind through this process. This corresponds to 5% of the annual oil production of the OPEC countries. 700,000 barrels of gasoline is used just to create the sugarcane fields.[1157] On the day after the burning, the fields swarm with cane cutters who suck the ash and soot of the burn-beaten land into their lungs. It is probably the hardest job in Brazil. Those who think using the "green" fuel will reduce fossil fuel consumption are deluding themselves. People tend to see ethanol as an endless cycle: grain is used to produce ethanol, ethanol is burned and gives off CO_2, and grain uses the CO_2 as it grows. But that is not the case—fossil fuel actually drives the whole cycle.

Taking grain apart, fermenting it, distilling it, and extruding it uses a lot of fossil energy. If we take into account little-considered inputs like the energy required to extrude alcohol from corn, produce fertilizers and pesticides, transport crops and dispose of wastewater, we discover that ethanol contains 65% less usable energy than is consumed in the process of making it.[1158] Every sugarcane harvest extracts 80 tonnes of organic matter per hectare, which means that the fields require especially heavy fertilization. Nitrous oxide, or N_2O, is a vastly more potent greenhouse gas than CO_2, and it is released when fertilizer breaks down. It alone undoes any benefit gained through the reduction in use of fossil fuels.[1159] Studies indicate that the global warming potential of the greenhouse gases released in growing biofuel crops is up to twice as high as the reduction gained from fossil-fuel savings. Measurements of emission from the burning of biofuels derived from corn and rapeseed have been found to produce up to 50% and 70% more greenhouse gases respectively than fossil fuels; biodiesel derived from palm trees planted on rainforest lands was determined to be more than twice as bad in this regard as petroleum diesel.[1160]

In tropical conditions, you also need to use an abundance of pesticides, including an herbicide by the name of Diuron that has a nasty tendency to pile up in the soil.

1155. Joseph Fargione, et al. "Land Clearing and the Biofuel Carbon Debt," *Science* 319(5867), February 29, 2008, 1235–1238.

1156. Tad W. Patzek, "Thermodynamics of the Corn-Ethanol Biofuel Cycle," *Critical Reviews in Plant Sciences* 23(6), 2004, 519–567.

1157. *MOT*, op. cit.

1158. Patzek, op. cit.

1159. P. J. Crutzen, et al. "N_2O Release from Agro-Biofuel Production Negates Global Warming Reduction by Replacing Fossil Fuels," *Atmospheric Chemistry and Physics* 8(2), 2008, 389–395.

1160. Ibid.

The worst problem, however, is water. Only 7% of the Atlantic Rainforest remains.[1161] The trees do not call the rain anymore. With the decrease in rainfall and the increase in heat, the Brazilian sugar barons are irrigating their green deserts with the waterways, the streams, and the rivers. As a result, not only are the rivers of the sugar region drying up, they are also flush with fertilizers, pesticides, and the distillation residue from the sugar and ethanol plants. In the United States, corn is the crop most likely to leach chemical contaminants into waterways. When you dump nitrogen fertilizer on corn fields, it runs away in surface water, into the Mississippi River and Gulf of Mexico. The excess nitrogen introduced into the water causes out-of-control algae growth, creating an oxygen-poor "dead zone" where other marine flora and fauna cannot survive.[1162]

The health effects from ethanol use are the same whether it was made from corn or other plant products. In addition to greenhouse gases, biofuel production creates phosphorous and fine particle emissions. Ethanol may produce fewer carbon monoxide emissions than regular gasoline, but it releases much higher levels of nitrogen oxides, one of the principal ingredients of smog, when burned.[1163] Should ethanol gain widespread use as a "clean" alternative to gasoline, people with respiratory illnesses would be in trouble. Pollution from ethanol could end up creating a far worse health hazard than gasoline, especially for people with asthma and other respiratory diseases. According to a Stanford University study, ethanol-burning cars could boost levels of toxic ozone gas in urban areas, and the Los Angeles Basin might be among the hardest hit because of the area's reliance on cars and topographic factors that tend to concentrate smog there.[1164]

Pollution from ethanol is more risky to humans than pollution from gasoline, because when ethanol breaks down in the atmosphere, it generates considerably more ground-level ozone. When inhaled even at low levels, ozone can harm lungs, aggravate respiratory problems, and impair immune systems. It is a highly corrosive gas that not only damages the delicate tissues of the lungs, but it can crack rubber and wear away statues. The use of ethanol as fuel also releases formaldehyde and acetaldehyde, not to mention benzene and butadiene—these are dangerous carcinogens and, as such, a threat to public health. Everything that produces soot and similar pollutants kills people and causes an irregular and uneven thermal load on the planet. Back in the '70s, we were all forced to install catalytic converters on our cars because they converted carbon monoxide to a safe gas, carbon dioxide. The impact of diesel fumes on air quality and human respiratory problems is far worse than that of petrol fumes, from 10 to 100 times worse for each particle of carbon emitted.[1165]

1161. *MOT*, op. cit.

1162. Patzek, op. cit.

1163. Ibid.

1164. Mark Z. Jacobson, "Effects of Ethanol (E85) versus Gasoline Vehicles on Cancer and Mortality in the United States," *Environmental Science & Technology* 41(11), June 1, 2007, 4150–4157.

1165. Chris A. Jakober, et al. "Oxygenated Organics in Fine Particle Emissions from Gasoline and Diesel Vehicles for Source Apportionment," Department of Environmental Toxicology, UC Davis, Davis, CA, February 2005.

Whenever there is a public transportation strike in my home town, the emissions are actually lowered and the air quality improves. Traffic also tends to flow much more smoothly, even though there are more cars on the road and they still cannot use the bus lanes. Never mind that public transport is subsidized and cannot pay for itself. Children and the elderly are particularly susceptible to smoke particles from diesel exhaust. The minute particles can cause asthma, bronchitis, lung disease, and heart problems. Want to know the best way to prevent colds? Stay away from airborne particle pollution. While tiny viruses are the actual cause of colds and flu, ultra-fine particles from combustion sources can aggravate, and even lay the foundation for, the virus to embed itself and for the infection to take hold. Breathing in diesel fumes can also raise the risk of potentially deadly blood clots and increase the chances of heart disease and stroke. Diesel emissions elevate the risk of premature death, cancer, and other chronic disease. According to the California Air Resources Board, diesel soot is responsible for 70% of the state's cancer risk from airborne poisons. Thousands of Americans die every year from diesel particles in California alone.[1166]

Saying that public transport is greener than using your car is an insult to the victims of diesel emissions. Public transport systems are designed to meet peak demand, but have to offer a frequent service all day long. People will not use buses or trains unless they know they can get to where they want when they want. In terms of CO_2, full buses and trains are significantly less polluting per passenger than cars, but unfortunately, buses and trains are far from full for most of the day. Cars appear very inefficient because often just one person travels in a car, but if you pack in extra passengers you quickly make the car a dramatically greener option. If you pack a family of five into a car, the average emissions per passenger falls from 180 g/km to just 45 g/km. According to the U.S. Department of Energy, a bus with average occupancy (9 people) is more polluting than a car with average occupancy (1.57 people).[1167] I have a 10-mile drive to my office, which takes about twenty minutes. The only way I could do it by bus would be to take a bus into the city centre then another bus out again to work. It would be over 20 miles and take an hour. Can you see the difference between the relative carbon footprints of the two journeys? It has been said that public transport is a means of getting from where you are not, to where you do not want to go, at a time you do not wish to travel, in the company of people you would normally cross the street to avoid.

Brazilian ethanol made from sugarcane produces about twice as much ethanol per acre as corn. However, the CO_2 emissions of a car running on sugarcane-based fuel are still only one-fourth lower than those of a petrol car. In order to significantly reduce the global traffic emissions, biofuels would need to completely replace regular petrol and diesel. This is not physically possible, since there is not enough raw material in existence. To fill up one SUV with pure ethanol would require 550 pounds of corn, or roughly the amount of calories to feed a person for a year—and that is just one tankful. Even if all the corn crop and all the soy crop in the United States were

1166. Don Anair & Patricia Monahan, "Sick of Soot: Reducing the Health Impacts of Diesel Pollution in California," Union of Concerned Scientists, Cambridge, MA, June 2004.

1167. Stacy C. Davis, et al. "Transportation Energy Data Book: Edition 28," Center for Transportation Analysis, Oak Ridge National Laboratory, Oak Ridge, TN, June 2009.

converted to ethanol, this would only be enough to replace 12% of the petrol demand and 6% of the diesel demand.[1168] In order to meet the global road transport demand for fuel, we would need 600 million hectares of sugarcane fields, or 200 times what Brazil has today. Most of the biofuels would have to come from less economical crops, and all the agricultural land in the world would not be enough, nor would all the existing forests. Some researchers place their hopes in biotechnologies, such as genetic engineering, to boost crop yields, but advances have been slow since the spectacular successes of the Green Revolution, which was incidentally almost entirely driven by fossil fuels.

All the oil, coal, and natural gas that people use today was itself plant residue millions of years ago. This residue got buried before it could fully decompose, and heat and pressure within the Earth cooked it into its present form. In essence, modern science is trying to develop a technology that skips the burial step, converting biomass directly into fuel. Unfortunately, the ethanol program fails to reduce emissions and hurts poor people all over the world by raising the price of food. Biotechnology could be a great equalizer, spreading wealth over the world wherever there is land, air, water, and sunlight, but this has nothing to do with the misguided effort to reduce carbon emissions by converting food crops into ethanol. After we have mastered biotechnology, the rules of the game will be radically changed, and it is likely that biotechnology will dominate our lives and our economic activities during the second half of the 21st century, just as information technology dominated our lives and our economy during the second half of the 20th.

"The car of the future runs completely on electricity," we are told. "No more dependance on gas; no more choking on toxic fumes." But electric cars are not futuristic—they are positively retro. Cars powered by electricity have been around since the 1800s and actually predate the gasoline-powered variety. Thomas Davenport, a Vermont blacksmith, built the first rotary electric motor in 1833 and it was used to power a model train the next year. In the late 1830s, Robert Davidson, a Scottish inventor, rigged a carriage with an electric motor powered by batteries. It was not until 1895 that gasoline-powered cars, or converted carriages with a two-cylinder engine, were sold commercially, and then only in minute numbers. Around the turn of the century, the average car buyer got to choose between gas, electric, and steam. When the automobile industry was taking form, no-one knew which type of vehicle was going to become the standard, and at that time, over a hundred companies placed their bets on electricity. Henry Ford and Thomas Edison teamed up to design an electric car, but the prototypes never went into production. By the 1920s, the market for electric vehicles was minuscule, and things never got better.

Many companies tried to combine the best of both worlds, with cars than ran on a mixture of electricity and gas. The Pope Manufacturing Company of Hartford, Connecticut, built a working prototype of a hybrid vehicle in 1898. Commercial models were brought out in Belgium and France the next year, beating the Toyota Prius to the market by almost a century. Even Ferdinand Porsche and the Daimler

---

1168. Jason Hill, et al. "Environmental, Economic, and Energetic Costs and Benefits of Biodiesel and Ethanol Biofuels," *Proceedings of the National Academy of Sciences* 103(30), July 25, 2006, 11206–11210.

Company had a go at it. Since its launch in 1997, the Prius has become a big seller, with its drivers including a clutch of celebrities led by Leonardo DiCaprio. It has become a symbol of everything a standard car is not: green, clean, and ethical. It is also the only reasonably-priced car a Hollywood A-lister can drive without everyone thinking his career has gone down the toilet. Hybrid cars, which combine a battery with a petrol engine, do have a lot of potential, but most existing or planned hybrids provide fairly small boosts in fuel economy. Even the Prius only delivers impressive results in city driving, when running on battery power. Drivers who spend most of their time on freeways might well get better mileage in a conventional Toyota Echo. Indeed, tune-ups and proper tire air pressure would probably save more energy.

There is no way hybrids can substitute for oil-burning vehicles, because manufacturing hybrid batteries requires rare elements that are even more scarce than oil. That hulk of a battery contains almost 14 kilograms of nickel, which is mined and smelted in Sudbury, Ontario, in a plant that has caused so much environmental damage and acid rain that NASA uses the dead zone around it to test its moon rovers. A thousand tonnes of zinc is mined and smelted in Canada and then shipped 10,000 miles to Europe for refining and again to China to be made into zinc foam, then to a battery factory in Japan, and finally all the way back to the United States. The Prius, therefore, requires more energy to build than a standard car of similar size. In fact, when you combine all the energy it takes to build and drive a hybrid, it adds up to almost 50% more than it does to build and drive an SUV. A report from CNW Marketing Research concludes that in "dollar per lifetime mile," a Prius costs $3.25, compared with $1.95 for a Hummer H3.[1169] In terms of money, you perhaps save on fuel, but because you do so, studies show that people are driving more, resulting in more fuel consumption.

There is even a study that says people contribute more to greenhouse gas emissions by walking than by driving, since the increased energy it takes to walk requires people to eat more, which causes the proliferation of slaughterhouses. Among the 51 exhortations in *TIME* Magazine's "Global Warming Survival Guide," No. 22 says a BMW is less responsible than a Big Mac for climate change. This is because the global meat industry produces over half of all man-made greenhouse gas emissions, i.e. much more than transportation.[1170] Nitrous oxide in manure has a 100-year average global warming potential (GWP) 296 times greater than that of carbon dioxide, while methane from animal flatulence is 23 times as potent as CO_2.[1171] Australia's Department of Climate Change and Energy Efficiency says over two-thirds of the country's agricultural emissions are released as methane from the gut of livestock.[1172] Even the IPCC estimates that atmospheric concentrations of methane are about two

1169. "Dust to Dust: The Energy Cost of New Vehicles from Concept to Disposal," Bandon, OR, March 2007.

1170. Bryan Walsh, "Skip the Steak," April 9, 2007; Steinfeld, et al. Op. cit.

1171. Crutzen, et al. Op. cit.; Walsh, op. cit.

1172. "Australia's Emission Projections 2010," DCCEE, Canberra, December 2010.

and a half times those seen in pre-industrial times, mostly due to farming.[1173]

The methane levels remained stable for about a decade, until they jumped sharply in the beginning of 2007, according to researchers from the MIT. The levels rose simultaneously all over the world, which further perplexes the researchers. They think it is too early to say whether it is just a short-term phenomenon and admit that they do not yet fully understand the atmospheric cycle of methane.[1174] Some 80% of anthropogenic CO_2 emissions originate outside the transportation sector, from power generation and from fuels for industrial, commercial, and residential use. Cars could be completely emission-free if their manufacture and freight, the production and transmission of "emission-free" energy for their engines, and the maintenance of road networks did not require any help from polluting industries. Black carbon or soot should be included in the climate agenda, since its warming effect is as great as that of carbon dioxide—at least on the Northern Hemisphere.[1175] If there really is a need for governments to lower planetary temperatures, other mechanisms would be a lot cheaper and much more effective than regulation of CO_2.

In its 2001 report, the IPCC famously declared the 20th century to be the warmest in the last millennium. However, it measures the 11th to the 19th centuries using tree ring samples and the 20th using thermometers. The resultant graph looks like a hockey stick, but only because the IPCC is using incompatible sets of data. According to their survey, most of the supposed warming occurred in the early 20th century, that is, when the United States was still a predominantly rural economy. So if the report proves anything, it is that as Americans switched their horses to automobiles, the rate of global warming slowed down. Indeed, what is to say that the rise of carbon dioxide is not just a symptom of the global warming, rather than its cause?

The IPCC's 2007 report warned that "glaciers in the Himalayas are receding faster than in any other part of the world."[1176] Given that this is the highest mountain range in the world and its meltdown implies a massive flooding of India, China, and the entire Asian region, it was a major selling point for the warmist agenda. Al Gore also says that Mawenzi has lost a lot of ice on its summit because of global warming, but satellite records of the temperature on the summit of Kilimanjaro over the last thirty years indicate that there has, in fact, been a regional cooling in the area. The cooling has dried the atmosphere, so the ice is ablating, not melting; it cannot melt, because the average temperature on the summit is -7°C, or about 13°F below freezing. Not only that, but the snows of Kilimanjaro have actually been in retreat since the 1880s; the climate there is not getting warmer, it is getting drier—it simply will not snow.[1177]

1173. Kenneth L. Denman, et al. "Couplings Between Changes in the Climate System and Biochemistry." Solomon, et al. Op. cit.

1174. M. Rigby, et al. "Renewed Growth of Atmospheric Methane," *Geophysical Research Letters* 35, 2008, L22805.

1175. Stacy C. Jackson, "Parallel Pursuit of Near-Term and Long-Term Climate Mitigation," *Science* 326(5952), October 23, 2009, 526–527.

1176. Rex Victor Cruz, et al. "Asia." Parry, et al. 2007.

1177. *An Inconvenient Truth*. Dir. Davis Guggenheim. Paramount Pictures, 2006; Lonnie G. Thompson, et al. "Kilimanjaro Ice Core Records: Evidence of Holocene Climate Change in Tropical Africa," *Science* 298(5593), October 18, 2002, 589–593.

The statement on the glacier melt in the 2007 IPCC report contains other serious errors, such as a claim that the "total area [of the Himalayas] will likely shrink from the present 500,000 to 100,000 km^2 by the year 2035."[1178] There are only 33,000 square kilometers of glaciers in the Himalayas. A table in the report states that between 1845 and 1965, the Pindari Glacier shrank by 2,840 meters, but then says that is a rate of 135.2 meters a year, when it is really only 23.5 meters a year—the authors have managed to divide the total loss measured over 121 years by 21, instead of 121. One passage estimates the world's glaciers are melting so fast that those in the Himalayas could vanish completely by 2035. This date is not just a little bit wrong, but far out of any order of magnitude. Most Himalayan glaciers are hundreds of feet thick and could not melt fast enough to vanish by 2035, unless there was an immense rise in global temperatures. The maximum rate of decline in thickness seen in glaciers at the moment is two to three feet per year, with most being far lower.[1179] According to a report published by the Indian government in 2009, Himalayan glaciers "have not in any way exhibited, especially in recent years, an abnormal retreat."[1180]

As it turns out, the basis of the stark glacier meltdown statement by the IPCC was not even a scientific study of melting data. Rather it was a reference to a newspaper article cited by the ecological advocacy group, World Wide Fund for Nature, in 2005. The original source of the IPCC statement appeared in a 1999 issue of the British popular science magazine, *New Scientist*, and was cited in passing by the WWF. This magazine article was itself based on a short telephone interview with Syed Hasnain, a little-known Indian glaciologist then based at Jawaharlal Nehru University in Delhi. He has since admitted that the claim was pure "speculation" on his part and was not supported by any actual research.[1181] Despite the lack of scientific validation, the decade-old claim ended up in the IPCC's fourth assessment report published in 2007. *The Sunday Telegraph* has documented at least 15 other non-peer-reviewed reports from the WWF that were used in the UN's climate-change bible, which calls for capping man-made CO_2.[1182]

Earth's temperature is dependent to a large extent on the Earth's axis in relation to the Sun, and sunspot activity on the surface of our parent star. The Sun is the *only* thing that provides heat and energy to our *entire* solar system. The Milankovitch orbital cycle is closely associated with the onset of ice ages. This is based on the fact than when the Earth's orbital parameters (eccentricity, obliquity, precession, and position of perihelion) change and certain conditions are met, the amount of solar

1178. Cruz, et al. Op. cit.

1179. Jonathan Leake & Chris Hastings, "World Misled over Himalayan Glacier Meltdown," *The Sunday Times*, January 17, 2010.

1180. Vijay Kumar Raina, "Himalayan Glaciers: A State-of-Art Review of Glacial Studies, Glacial Retreat and Climate Change," Ministry of Environment & Forests, New Delhi, November 2009.

1181. Leake & Hastings, op. cit.

1182. Richard Gray & Rebecca Lefort, "UN Climate Change Panel Based Claims on Student Dissertation and Magazine Article," *The Sunday Telegraph*, January 31, 2010.

radiation wanes to the point where glaciation can begin.[1183] The Earth's oceans function as both efficient temperature equalizers and the greatest carbon sink in the world—the top three and a half meters of the ocean have a thermal capacity greater than the entire atmosphere.[1184] Yet figuring these factors into climate models is still in its infancy. The Sun is not some stable "lightbulb" in the sky, but a battlefield of violent eruptions, the repercussions of which can be quite unexpected.

According to recent studies, polar temperatures can vary by 2 or 3 degrees Celsius due to solar wind.[1185] When the Sun is in its active phase, the solar wind becomes stronger and polar temperatures rise. The polar ice caps of Mars have shrunk at the same pace as those of Earth, even though Martians, to my knowledge, have not accumulated "climate debt toward developing countries."[1186] Small changes in the Sun can result in large changes on Earth and the other planets. The changes in the amount of solar radiation are very small, under 0.1 percent—but that is enough to bring on ice ages.[1187] The so-called Little Ice Age lasted in Europe from circa 490 CE to 1400 CE. At its coldest phase, the River Thames was used for ice skating while the European ports were frozen solid. And as solar activity wanes, cosmic radiation increases. Earth is thus a playground to many different celestial forces and mechanisms.

There are so many different natural causes for warming and cooling that even if man is warming the planet, it is negligible compared to nature. We do not have a clear picture of what is happening in the climate now, never mind what will happen in the future. We live on a dynamic Earth, with so many constantly changing variables, that it is impossible to list everything, let alone measure them all. Chemistry, physics, and some medicine is truly "reproducible" experimentally, but a published work on earth sciences is not so easily reproduced. It is nearly impossible for an oceanographer, meteorologist, or climatologist to publish data and have others go out and reproduce it exactly. Which is precisely the problem. Because of the difficulty in measuring a lot of the stuff out there, a degree of mathematical speculation has crept into science. And as Bertrand Russell pointed out, "Physics is mathematical not because we know so much about the physical world, but because we know so little."[1188]

Climate-change forecasts are like financial forecasts, but involve an immensely more complex array of variables. They require the interpretation of innumerable feedback loops, all the convective forces, the evaporation, the winds, the ocean currents, the changing albedo of Earth's surface, etc. etc. The models do not

---

1183. Ji-Feng Ju, et al. "Recognition of Milankovitch Cycles in the Stratigraphic Record: Application of the CWT and the FFT to Well-Log Data," *Journal of China University of Mining and Technology* 18(4), December 2008, 594–598.

1184. "Annual Report on the Ocean Observing System for Climate," National Oceanic and Atmospheric Administration Office of Climate Observation, Silver Spring, MD, September 2007.

1185. Annika Seppälä, et al. "Geomagnetic Activity and Polar Surface Air Temperature Variability," *Journal of Geophysical Research* 114, 2009, A10312.

1186. Shane Byrne, "The Polar Deposits of Mars," *Annual Review of Earth and Planetary Sciences* 37, May 2009, 535–560.

1187. J. Beer, et al. "The Role of the Sun in Climate Forcing," *Quaternary Science Reviews* 19(1–5), January 2000, 403–415.

1188. 1995, 125.

realistically include ice sheets or the biosphere—all the flora and fauna on this planet. We do not even know all the things that we do not know. To think we humans are so clever that we can create computer code that accurately reproduces the millions of processes that determine climate is pure hubris. Even if every atom in the universe were co-opted into a mind-bogglingly vast computational matrix, it still would not be able to calculate every possible permutation on a chess board, let alone anything truly complex. As Nikola Tesla once complained, "scientists have substituted mathematics for experiments, and they wander off through equation after equation, and eventually build a structure which has no relation to reality."[1189]

There are many warnings from history about placing too much reliance on mathematics. The Ptolemaic model of the universe is one of the most famous examples of the dangers of the mathematical approach. It used a series of epicycles to explain the motions of the planets in a geocentric universe, which, with a few tweaks, would still work today. However, despite being mathematically correct, the Ptolemaic model failed to reflect the underlying reality. Today's computer models, on the other hand, cannot even predict the weather in two weeks, much less a hundred years. The CO_2 saturation model used by the IPCC resulted in projections according to which global temperatures rise by 0.2°C per decade in tandem with the CO_2, but none of these projections worked for even one decade—nature proved them wrong. Climate models can at best be useful in explaining climate changes after the fact.

The climatologists at the University of East Anglia refuse to publish the computer code they use to model global climate, yet they claim a scientific consensus exists based on other scientists believing their conclusions without ever having seen the raw data, testing it, or reproducing their results. Scientists should always be willing to expose their ideas to independent verification by others, and evidence should always trump theoretical expectations, no matter how highly the theory might be regarded. The mistake Pons and Fleischmann made when they announced their discovery of cold fusion was to publish their data and allow other scientists the opportunity to try to reproduce their results; if they had kept their data secret and just asked other scientists to sign a petition, they, too, might have walked away with a Nobel Prize. In any case, it should be wholly inappropriate for the verification of the integrity of the scientific process to depend on appeals to Freedom of Information legislation.

Climate forecasts, based on computer models that analyze the past, tell us that we do not know how much warming is occurring, whether it is temporary or permanent, nor how much warming is dangerous, or perhaps beneficial: e.g. modest temperature increases may actually benefit crops in rich temperature countries, making growing seasons longer. However, one of the most widely quoted and most alarmist passages in the IPCC's 2007 report was a warning that, by 2020, global warming could reduce crop yields in some African countries by 50%. Unlike the glacier claim, which was confined to a section of the technical *Working Group II* report, this claim forms part of the key *Synthesis Report*, the production of which was the personal responsibility of the chair of the IPCC, Dr. Rajendra Pachauri. The origin of this claim turns out to be a 2003 paper written for a Canadian environmental think tank—not a peer-

1189. "Radio Power Will Revolutionize the World," *Modern Mechanics and Inventions*, July 1934.

reviewed scientific journal—by Ali Agoumi, a Moroccan activist who draws part of his income from advising on how to make applications for "carbon credit." As his primary sources, he cited reports from three North African governments, but none of these even remotely support anything he wrote.[1190] The report from the Algerian government, for example, predicted that, on current projections, *la production agricole devra plus que doubler à l'horizon 2020*, "agricultural production will more than double by 2020."[1191] This demonized molecule, CO_2, is not some kind of a toxin or contaminant or pollutant—it is a fertilizer.

Uncertainty is intrinsic to the scientific process, and sometimes one needs to have the courage to stand up and say "maybe." In the effort to understand climate, certainty comes only with the hindsight of centuries. Forty years ago, pretty much everyone thought that we had messed up the Earth with careless and selfish fossil fuel emissions—and were headed into an ice age. Today, the same fossil fuel emissions are blamed for global warming. On the first "Earth Day" in 1970, environmentalists warned that we faced global cooling unless the government took immediate and massive action. After four decades of falling temperatures, the *Christian Science Monitor* reported on August 27, 1974, that Nebraska's armadillos were retreating south from all the cooling. On August 14, 1975, the *New York Times* reported "many signs" that "Earth may be heading for another ice age," and on December 10, 1976, *Science* Magazine warned about "extensive Northern Hemisphere glaciation."[1192] In the '80s, the greatly respected astrophysicist Carl Sagan still made a warning of catastrophic global cooling, and many of the television programs he produced making that claim were shown in schools across the United States and Europe. Even the most prominent scientific figure supporting man-made global warming today, Prof. James Hansen of NASA, once predicted that the Earth was about to enter a global ice age.

More recently, researchers from the UK's National Oceanography Centre said changes to ocean currents in the Atlantic may cool European weather within a few decades. Their conclusions, reported in a 2005 issue of the scientific journal *Nature*, are based on 50 years of Atlantic observations.[1193] However, computer models have regularly predicted that the North Atlantic Conveyor may reduce in intensity or even turn off altogether, a concept that was pushed beyond credibility in the Hollywood blockbuster *The Day After Tomorrow*.[1194] If it turned off completely, even computer models predict Europe would cool by only 4 to 6 degrees Celsius. The North Atlantic Conveyor forms a part of a larger movement of water, the Atlantic Meridional Overturning Circulation, which is itself but one component of the global thermohaline system of currents. Should the Gulf Stream run down from the glaciers melting, would they not freeze again and all soon return to normal? I doubt the

1190. Christopher Booker, "African Crops Yield Another Catastrophe for the IPCC," *The Sunday Telegraph*, February 14, 2010.

1191. "Elaboration de la stratégie et du plan d'action national des changements climatiques," Direction Générale de l'Environnement, Alger, March 2001.

1192. As quoted in Contoski 1997, 441.

1193. Harry L. Bryden, et al. "Slowing of the Atlantic Meridional Overturning Circulation at 25° N," 438(7068), December 1, 2005, 655–657.

1194. Dir. Roland Emmerich. Twentieth Century Fox, 2004.

theory only works one way, if it works at all. The oceanic currents depend on the Earth's rotation and the location of the continents—man could not change those even if he tried. Indeed, the North Atlantic Conveyor undergoes a natural 70-year cycle of strengthening and weakening, with a northern cooling until the mid-1970s and a warming afterwards.[1195] But the alarmists are a hardy bunch; they just will not give up. As nature switched from global cooling to global warming, so did they.

Until now, the climate, like all cyclic systems, has behaved dynamically. It cools. It warms up again. It has been like this for a few billion years. There is a popular misconception that global change is a spatially uniform and chronologically regular process, even though every climate scientist readily accepts that there is all kinds of natural variability in the system. When you are looking for a signal in a very noisy record, you have to do as much averaging as possible; the quality of the data is poor and the changes are small, so it is easy to nudge such data a few tenths of a degree in any direction. It is therefore quite surprising that research in an area that depends so heavily on statistical methods has not been carried out in close collaboration with professional statisticians. When Terry Mills, professor of applied statistics and econometrics at Loughborough University, looked at the same data as the IPCC, he found that the warming trend reported over the past 30 years or so was just as likely to be caused by random fluctuations as by the impact of greenhouse gases.[1196]

For some reason, the warmists always pick as the starting point for their time series a suitably cold year from the bleak '50s through '70s. Should they choose a point from the '30s or '40s, they would draw a completely different picture: ice caps and glacier thickness have either remained the same or even grown since industrial CO_2 emissions began to rise. Nor can greenhouse gases alone melt the Arctic at the alarming rate that has been reported recently. In July 2008, numerous voices in the scientific community expressed fears of a mass melting of the polar ice caps, including Dr. David Barber, Canada's Research Chair in Arctic System Science, who told the *National Geographic*, "We're actually projecting this year that the North Pole may be free of ice for the first time [in history]."[1197] However, according to collated data from the NASA Marshal Space Flight Center and the University of Illinois, Arctic ice extent was actually 30% greater in August 2008 than it was in the previous August.[1198]

There is, in fact, a strong growth trend in the sea ice at the planet's other polar region, the Antarctic. Due to oceanic currents, the Antarctic is thermally insulated from the rest of the Earth. The whole Antarctic region south of the 60th latitude is covered with ice sheets several kilometers thick. This is more ice than covered the whole Northern Hemisphere during the last Ice Age. In the last couple of decades, the area of sea ice in the Antarctic has grown by about 13,000 sq. km per year.[1199] The East

1195. Michael E. Schlesinger & Navin Ramankutty, "An Oscillation in the Global Climate System of Period 65–70 Years," *Nature* 367(6465), February 24, 1994, 723–726.

1196. Terence C. Mills, "'Skinning a Cat': Alternative Models of Representing Temperature Trends," *Climatic Change* 101(3–4), August 2010, 415–426.

1197. Aalok Mehta, "North Pole May Be Ice-Free for First Time This Summer," June 20, 2008.

1198. Steven Goddard, "Arctic Ice Refuses to Melt as Ordered," *The Register*, August 15, 2008.

1199. Jiping Liu, et al. "Interpretation of Recent Antarctic Sea Ice Variability," *Geophysical Research Letters* 31, 2004, L02205.

Antarctic Ice Sheet, which covers 75% of the Antarctic's total land area, thickened at an average of 1.8 cm per year between 1992 and 2003.[1200] This bulge is probably due to the couple of degrees Celsius cooling experienced in the region. It was downplayed by the IPCC in preference to highlighting the small, seasonal decline in sea ice in the Arctic, probably because sea ice was projected to shrink in both the Arctic and Antarctic under all its Special Report on Emissions Scenarios.

Since the Antarctic contains the bulk of our planet's ice, understanding its growth or shrinkage is critical to predicting future sea-level changes. Some fear that if the Earth's oceans swell significantly, it will cause devastation on populated low-level islands and coastal regions. The flood deaths of Bangladesh and other low-lying regions are used as examples of climate change, although countless people have died in these annual floods for longer than I can remember. The IPCC also infamously claimed that rising sea levels endanger the 55% of the Netherlands it says is below sea level; the actual portion of the Netherlands below sea level is 20%, prompting the Dutch environmental minister to exclaim that she will no longer tolerate the climate body's errors.[1201] The IPCC further claims that the Maldives are in imminent danger of sinking below the sea, although Prof. Nils-Axel Mörner, who in 2004 to 2007 did the most thorough investigation of sea levels ever done in the Maldives, concluded that there had been no sea-level rise there for over a thousand years.[1202]

Obviously, the IPCC cannot be considered a reliable purveyor of the true state of climate science. Flaws in its seminal 2007 report range from typos in key figures to sloppy sourcing. A key role in this report was played by the Climate Research Unit at the University of East Anglia. One of three international agencies compiling global temperature data, the CRU has been long suspected of manipulating the data, something that was conclusively proved when 160 megabytes of its e-mails were leaked on the internet in 2009. We now know that the researchers wrote programming notes in the source code of their own climate models admitting that results were being manually adjusted to conform to their wishes. We now know that the CRU took out most of the Siberian weather station data when Siberia is supposed to have experienced significant warming, and that it progressively removed Japanese weather stations over 300 meters, so that older measurements included data taken at high altitudes, while recent ones did not.

We now know that the "climate researchers" supplemented the original elevation readings at the Maldives (which show that the sea levels have not risen) with readings taken in Hong Kong (2,000 miles away), which show a 2.3 mm rise per year. This figure is not due to the sea levels rising, but due to Hong Kong sinking. The e-mails suggest criminal conspiracy, collusion in exaggerating warming data, illegal destruction of embarrassing information, organized resistance to FOI requests, private admissions of flaws in their public claims, and much, much more. One of the most

---

1200. Curt C. Davis, et al. "Snowfall-Driven Growth in East Antarctic Ice Sheet Mitigates Recent Sea-Level Rise," *Science* 308(5730), June 24, 2005, 1898–1901.

1201. "Sea Level Blunder Enrages Dutch Minister," Radio Netherlands Worldwide, February 4, 2010.

1202. "Sea Level Changes and Tsunamis, Environmental Stress and Migration Overseas: The Case of the Maldives and Sri Lanka," *Internationales Asienforum* 38(3–4), 2007, 353–374.

damaging e-mails was sent by the head of the CRU himself, Dr. Phil Jones, who wrote: "I can't see either of these papers being in the next IPCC report. Kevin and I will keep them out somehow—even if we have to redefine what the peer-review literature is!"[1203] While the mainstream media seems to be determined to keep this scandal under the rug, it may well turn out to be the biggest scientific hoax in history because of the global policy implications.

Even before this so-called "Climategate," a British High Court judge issued an opinion that Al Gore's movie about global warming should come with a warning that it features "partisan political views" and numerous serious errors. The case was brought by a Kent school governor who felt the UK government was "brainwashing" children by mandating that the movie be shown in schools. For example, Gore asserted that melting of ice in either West Antarctica and Greenland would cause a sea-level rise of up to 20 feet "in the near future." The judge found this "distinctly alarmist" and it was common ground that if Greenland's ice did melt, it would release this amount of water, "but only after, and over, millennia."[1204] But then, Gore knew this all along. In 2005, the year he predicted imminent catastrophic sea-level rise, he bought a $4 million St. Regis Tower condo in San Francisco—just feet from the ocean at Fisherman's Wharf.

By 2007, Gore's film had made more than $50 million worldwide. Fifty thousand DVDs had been given away to schools and non-profit organizations. His book had sold nearly one million copies—with a separate edition for children.[1205] In 2009, the former Vice President said he would donate 100% of the proceeds from his latest propaganda piece, *Our Choice: A Plan to Solve the Climate Crisis*, to the Alliance for Climate Protection, a "non-partisan advocacy group" of which he just happens to be the chairman.[1206] It has since been revealed that some of the footage in *An Inconvenient Truth* was CGI; the ice shelf collapse was taken from the previously mentioned disaster movie *The Day After Tomorrow*. Even Gore's favourite picture of those two polar bears on a melting iceberg about to drown turns out to have been shot only a short distance from land, because the wind-sculpted ice looked so pretty. The bears were not drowning, they were waving![1207]

The population of polar bears has actually increased dramatically since the '50s, from about 5,000 to about 25,000.[1208] This is hardly the profile of a species in imminent threat of extinction, but even if their habitat was in danger from environmental conditions, they would probably adapt like the brown bear has. After all, we lose infinitely more people to death by cold each year than we lose to death by

---

1203. To Michael Mann, July 8, 2004.

1204. *Dimmock v Secretary of State for Education & Skills* [2007] EWHC 2288 (Admin).

1205. Ellen McGirt, "Al Gore's $100 Million Makeover," *Fast Company*, July/August 2007.

1206. John M. Broder, "Gore's Dual Role: Advocate and Investor," *New York Times*, November 3, 2009.

1207. Christopher Booker, "The Mother of All Scares: Presentation to the 2009 International Conference on Climate Change," The Heartland Institute, Chicago, March 16, 2009.

1208. J. Aars, et al. "Estimating the Barents Sea Polar Bear Subpopulation Size," *Marine Mammal Science* 25(1), January 2009, 35–52.

heat. However, it is doubtful that the shrinkage of some of Greenland's glaciers can be attributed to supposed global warming, since the mean temperatures in the region have fallen markedly over the last few decades. In fact, the ablation began in 1880, as did many of the other glacial recessions observed around the world, some of them as early as 1820. Most of the melting has happened long before humans could have had any influence on the glaciers whatsoever.[1209]

Greenland was melting faster in the 1920s than it is melting today.[1210] It was during the Viking Age about 1,000 years ago that the island got its name, from its greenness. The Norse were relocating there in droves at the time because the living conditions were favourable, but then the climate changed and it got cold there. Some of the possible explanations include changes in precipitation, cyclic changes in the North Atlantic Oscillation (NAO), and the still continuing recovery from the Little Ice Age. Technically speaking, we are still living in an ice age today, if not in the glaciation phase. The fact that the poles are covered with ice is the very definition of an ice age. Temperatures have not risen globally since 1998, when El Niño warmed the world, although CO_2 levels in the atmosphere have continued rising.

Yet, somewhere along the line, global warming became the explanation for everything. No-one can discuss any meteorological and geophysical event in the media without immediately pulling the climate-change card. It is now common practice to lay the blame for every hurricane, tornado, wildfire, drought, and flood on global warming. Unfortunately, there is absolutely no scientific basis for this. Climate experts at the Jet Propulsion Laboratory and Scripps Institution of Oceanography recently issued a joint statement saying that no single event—no matter how unusual—could be directly attributed to global warming.[1211] Every textbook on meteorology will tell you the main source of weather disturbances is the temperature difference between the tropics and the pole, and in a warmer world, this difference is smaller. This means that we would have less variability and fewer storms, but since that cannot be considered catastrophic, the warmists would have us believe the opposite.

The argument that Hurricane Katrina was an offspring of global warming ignores meteorological records showing that the number of hurricanes has been cycling up and down for decades—the Atlantic has a natural 25-year cycle of hurricane intensity.[1212] A few hundred years ago, a Katrina-scale calamity would have been attributed to God's wrath. But in the modern Western view, nature must be tamed, and therefore all disasters are unnatural. We blame, often quite rightly, anything that goes wrong not on the deities in the sky, but on the gentlemen in Washington. The catastrophe that Katrina caused in New Orleans can easily be attributed to civil engineers who erected inadequate levees, city planning that allowed neighbourhoods

---

1209. Monckton, op. cit.

1210. Ibid.

1211. Robert Lee Hotz & Erin Cline, "Hot? Yes. Global Warming? Maybe." *Los Angeles Times*, July 26, 2006.

1212. Stanley B. Goldenberg, et al. "The Recent Increase in Atlantic Hurricane Activity: Causes and Implications," *Science* 293(5529), July 20, 2001, 474–479.

to be built below sea level, and Bush administration officials who failed to do their jobs.[1213]

And what about the Iowa floods? Farmland in the Midwest has been plumbed with drainage pipes, streams have been straightened, most of the wetlands have been engineered out of existence, and land set aside for conservation is being put back into corn production to meet the demands of the ethanol boom—tell me that this is not a landscape begging to have 500-year floods every decade! The wettest year on record was way back in 1993. The second wettest: 1881. Third wettest: 1902. What makes Iowa an awkward place to talk about global warming is that the state has been a bit cooler in the summers than it was in the first half of the 20th century. Some think the widespread shift to annual plants, such as corn and soybeans, and away from perennial grasses may have altered the climate. The ten hottest summers in Iowa have been, in order, 1936, 1934, 1901, 1988, 1983, 1931, 1921, 1955, 1933, and 1913. When Iowa set a state record with a high temperature of 117°F in 1936, no-one blamed it on global warming.[1214]

On to the wildfires and mudslides in California, then. Building homes in wildfire-susceptible forests, overgrown with vegetation due to decades of fire suppression, is like putting a match to gasoline. And if you want to have a house on a mountain slope, you should not complain if you get mudslides in the basement. The 2005 Atlantic hurricane season had been the busiest in record, and at the start of the 2006 season, forecasters issued alarmingly specific predictions of more danger to come. Countless families in the vast swath of the U.S. Southeast were turned into survivalists as households stockpiled ready-to-eat meals and scarfed up emergency radios, propane stoves, home generators, shutters, and candles. In May 2006, the National Oceanic and Atmospheric Administration came out with the announcement that the year might be "hyperactive." That prediction, along with all the others, turned out to be wrong; the storm totals did not even reach the averages of the previous ten years.[1215] When everything gets reduced to a global-warming narrative, the real danger is that we will be unable to see the trees for the forest.

As soon as Governor Schwarzenegger announced that "the science is settled," two-thirds of California's citrus crop was destroyed. I suppose all those oranges and lemons must have been wiped out by drought? No, they were wiped out by an exceptionally bitter frost.[1216] The past few years across the world have seen some of the heaviest snowfalls and coldest temperatures ever recorded. A severe ice storm in December 2007 was blamed for the deaths of at least 22 people in the central United States. In December 2008, the southern U.S. was hit by rare snowfall that blanketed parts of Louisiana and Mississippi, blocking roads and forcing offices to close. Meanwhile in the northeast, one of the worst ice storms in a decade knocked out power to more

1213. Davis, et al. 2006.

1214. Joel Achenbach, "Global Warming Did It! Well, Maybe Not." ***Washington Post***, August 3, 2008.

1215. Peter Whoriskey, "South Spent Millions on a Hurricane Season That Wasn't," ***Ibid.***, October 19, 2006.

1216. Lord Christopher Monckton, Closing Keynote Address to the 2009 International Conference on Climate Change, New York Marriott Marquis, New York City, March 10, 2009.

than half a million homes and businesses in New England and upstate New York. For the first time in 37 years, Canada received a coast-to-coast white Christmas.

As Arctic air made its way south from Canada, the northeast and midwest U.S. experienced some of their coldest weather in years. Schools were closed because of the cold in January 2009 in Michigan, Iowa, Ohio, Illinois, and New York state, but frosty weather also hit Alabama, Georgia, and South Carolina. Heavy snow fell across large parts of the United Kingdom in February 2009, while the icy winds made temperatures feel "sub zero," as the coldest winter in 13 years continued. All London buses were pulled from service and Heathrow's runways were closed because of the worst snow Southeast England had seen for 18 years. The UK Highways Agency said there were too many minor accidents on the roads "to put a number on."[1217] The same snowfront battered France and Spain, disrupting travel and closing hundreds of schools. Switzerland, which usually has 2 weeks of winter, and hardly any snow, had a winter that lasted for 4 months and came complete with snow and frost. The same was repeated the next year.

In October 2009, it snowed more in the Austrian Alps than it had snowed in October in 25 years.[1218] In December, blizzards in the Midwest of the U.S. also brought record snowfalls again, bringing chaos to road and air transport from Texas to Minnesota. Meteorologists in Iowa recorded the highest snowfall since 1988, while the University of Wisconsin was forced to cancel classes for the first time since 1990.[1219] Scores of churches even cancelled Christmas services and drivers were encouraged to pack emergency kits before setting out during what is normally one of the busiest travel periods of the year. According to the National Weather Service, the storm spanned two-thirds of the country, but record low temperatures chilled even Florida in January 2010, endangering fruit and vegetable crops and taxing the power grid of a state unaccustomed to the cold. The 36°F recorded at the Miami airport beat an 82-year-old record.[1220]

While the IPCC alleges that there is a link between global warming and coral reef degradation, the coral reefs in Florida were dying because of the exceptionally cold winter. Coral dies when it has to cope with temperatures under 60°F for prolonged periods. In Miami, the mercury has regularly dipped below 35°F at night during the last few winters. Due to the cold, the corals, which are often hundreds of years old, lose their pigmentation and ultimately die. Their death gravely affects the delicate tropical ecosystem in the area, because the micro-organisms that feed on them need to find their food elsewhere. Cold-blooded lizards are also suffering from the recent chill in Florida. Their mobility declines when the temperatures fall below 60°F and Floridians have lately witnessed iguanas falling from trees.[1221] However, Florida was

1217. "Heavy Snow Hits Much of Britain," BBC News, February 2, 2009.

1218. Barbara Sladkowska & Kuba Jaworowski, "Central Europe Hit by Heavy Snow, High Winds," Reuters, October 14, 2009.

1219. "Heavy Snowfall Buries US Towns," BBC News, December 10, 2009.

1220. Tamara Lush, "Cold Imperils Florida's Fish, Fruit and Veggies," Associated Press, January 11, 2010.

1221. Juan Castro Olivera, "Florida's Cold Snap Disaster for Tropical Wildlife," AFP, January 8, 2010.

still the only state in the union that did get any snow in the brutal winter of 2010–2011.

I have met numerous Americans who are seriously embittered over how their children are going to die because a 2-degree temperature rise will cause them to starve, the sea levels to rise, or Mexicans to move north because their farmlands have been ruined. One would expect even people who do not understand the science to recognize the illogic of arguing that colder temperatures are due to warming. But as George Orwell famously pointed out, "There are some ideas so absurd that only an intellectual could believe them." When a Rasmussen poll showed decline in public concern about global warming in 2008, alarmists were forced to take increasingly ridiculous positions to defend the indefensible.[1222] The information can sometimes be so contradictory and confusing that it is easy to feel overwhelmed with a sense of futility, especially when people are running around screaming that the end is nigh.

The truth is that hurricanes, ice storms, and tornadoes, brutal cold fronts and heat waves, cycles of flood and drought, are not unforeseeable interruptions of normalcy, but simply the way the planet we live on does its business. There is a widespread perception that the risk of dying in earthquakes and volcanic eruptions is higher than that from everyday hazards. In actual fact, earthquakes, wildfires, and hurricanes combined account for less than 5% of deaths from natural hazards in the U.S.[1223] In some parts of the world, hurricanes provide a third of the annual rainfall. What we call "climate" is really an average of the extremes of heat and cold, precipitation and drought.[1224] "Sustainability" is an attempt to define a condition that does not exist in nature. Nature is not in balance like a scale, so much as it is a stream of energy and matter, a continuum that fluctuates according to internal and external forces and yet is flexible enough to maintain its core character.

In a recent poll by the marketing agency BBMG, nearly 9 in 10 Americans identified themselves as "conscious consumers." About the same number said that if products were equal in price and quality, they were more likely to buy from companies that manufacture energy-efficient products and commit to environmentally friendly practices.[1225] The notion that the choices of an individual make a big difference crystallizes in the oxymoronic concept of a "green consumer." We tend to think that good and green choices protect the environment and promote sustainable development. "It is up to you" and "vote with your wallet" are slogans that emphasize individual responsibility. The premise is that people are free to act and that it is their rational choices that decide whether the environmental problems are solved or not. Unfortunately, this is wholly unrealistic. We are only deluding ourselves if we think that the small efforts and little good deeds of individual consumers will add up

---

1222. "Fewer Americans Worried About Climate Change," Angus Reid Global Monitor, December 22, 2008.

1223. Kevin A. Borden & Susan L. Cutter, "Spatial Patterns of Natural Hazards Mortality in the United States," *International Journal of Health Geographics* 7(1), 2008, 64.

1224. William H. Hooke, "Avoiding a Catastrophe of Human Error," *Washington Post*, January 5, 2005.

1225. Raphael Bemporad & Mitch Baranowski, "Highlights from the BBMG Conscious Consumer Report," BBMG, New York, November 2007.

to sustainable development.

If we look at the environmental issues the world faces today, climate change is one of the poorest investments you can make in terms of cost and benefit. Because there is so much CO_2 involved, we can only make a tiny fraction of a difference in its amount, meaning that there will be virtually no change in whatever the climate is going to do. In order to forestall just one Celsius or two Fahrenheit degrees of global warming—assuming the UN is right about the effect of CO_2 on global warming—we would have to forgo two trillion tonnes of carbon emissions, the equivalent of 67 years of the world's entire annual output, meaning that we would have to close down the global economy entirely, go back to the stone age without even being allowed to light a fire in our caves—and that is what we would have to do just to knock off 1°C of global warming.[1226] However, if we attacked things like water pollution, where we know how to clean up water, then we would be talking about saving millions of lives today.

Even if we cured ourselves of our addiction to fossil fuels and stabilized Earth's climate, we would still have an environmental crisis on our hands. When CO_2 became the focus of the environmental movement, it was taken up as a political cause and soon became the only cause for many. The worry about global warming has since obscured ozone depletion, environmental toxins, and all the waste dumped at sea. The constant pumping of poisons and chemicals into our environment causes untold horrors that directly affect us in the form of cancer and disease. This is indisputably man's doing and something needs to be done about it. You do not need a climate model to detect a huge oil spill in the Gulf of Mexico. The reason BP was drilling there in the first place is that production off the California, North and South Carolina, and Florida coasts is banned, although there is an estimated 30 billion barrels of oil there. Rich people in places like Santa Barbara do not want their views ruined by a distant drilling platform.

Now, I do not mean to infer that the environmental movement has not accomplished anything, but there is so much more still to do. All this is in peril, if it keeps telling the world that humanity can only be saved if everyone believes that the climate is warming because of CO_2 emissions. The emphasis on man-made CO_2 always appealed to a certain strain of environmentalists, who thought the best thing to do was to go back to the way things were in mediaeval times and get rid of all the dreadful cars and factories. To them, CO_2 was a perfect emblem of industrialization. It could be used to legitimize a whole sweep of pre-existent myths that were anti-car, anti-growth, anti-development, and above all, anti-capitalism. Lord Monckton, former science adviser to British Prime Minister Margaret Thatcher, dubbed it "the traffic light tendency: they call themselves green, because they're too yellow to admit that they're really red."[1227]

People today want to continue to aspire to middle-class consumption patterns, but they also want to feel like they are responsible citizens who care about social and environmental issues. The only way to reconcile that is to go shopping for something

1226. Lord Christopher Monckton, Speech at Bethel University, St. Paul, MN, October 14, 2009.
1227. Ibid.

that declares itself to be ecologically friendly. In terms of emissions, we are constantly battling against increases of wealth. Every year, we fail to improve our energy efficiency to keep up with wealth increases, let alone to cut emissions. The notion that you can go green by spending money is more artificial than a plastic Christmas tree. And even if you reduce your consumption, it only lowers the price for the rest of us, so we can consume more. Corporate social responsibility is a nice idea, but in order for corporations to be socially responsible, they would have to sacrifice consumer deals and investor returns—which they will not do.

The responsibility for building sustainable development lay with the politicians, not the consumers. The federal government is America's single largest polluter; of 1,255 "Superfund" sites, the Pentagon is responsible for 129—the most of any entity.[1228] It is nice that a person makes the right choices, but it is simply not enough. We cannot solve environmental issues without global treaties. Al Gore says that we can fix the problem of global warming if we switch to compact fluorescent light bulbs, buy hybrid cars, and turn the lights off when we leave the room. But even if everyone in the whole world does this, CO_2 emissions are going to continue to rise, because these are very minor components of all the energy we use. Until we find a new energy source of the kind we cannot currently envision, we are stuck with fossil fuels. Considering this reality, one can only view all the pious exhortations to "do something" as naïve, self-interested, misinformed, stupid, or dishonest. Politicians wish to be seen as reducing global warming; companies want to polish their image and exploit markets created by new environmental regulations.

Electricity companies have noticed that when they justify their price hikes with carbon trading, this makes it an ecological necessity and those who are against it must want the world to be destroyed. Oil companies have also followed the situation and begun to support the notion of global warming, because the same trick can be used to hike up their prices as well. In fact, BP was a founding member of the U.S. Climate Action Partnership (USCAP), a lobby dedicated to passing a cap-and-trade bill. As the largest producer of natural gas in the country, BP saw many ways to profit from climate legislation, notably by persuading Congress to provide subsidies to coal-fired power plants that switch to gas. The reality is that the oil-and-gas industry decided to hedge its bets a long time ago and rebrand themselves as "energy suppliers," not oil-and-gas players. They know that their main product will stay in demand until it runs out sometime within the next hundred years; because of this natural expiry date, they have nothing to gain by opposing a reduction of fossil-fuel use, and can use the global warming bandwagon to get grants from taxpayers to fund the research needed to find their next energy "product."

BP, for instance, has lobbied for and profited from subsidies for biofuels and solar energy, two products that cannot break even without government support. Their industry is not just about extraction, but also distribution, and within a couple of decades, they will begin to need a new product to distribute. Similarly, the banks that made money on oil futures have recently realized that they are futures traders, not oil traders, and have opened new carbon exchanges. The governments that tax oil will

---

1228. Lyndsey Layton, "States Accuse Pentagon of Threats, Retaliation: Allegations Arise in Base Cleanup Hearing," *Washington Post*, September 19, 2008.

soon need a replacement revenue stream, and although they have not worked out quite what it is yet, they know they must back the green horse. You are delusional if you think that all the extra taxes on flying, gasoline, electricity, etc. actually go to green issues and initiatives. It is just one more way governments can get money out of the taxpayer and say look at us, we raised funds in green taxes for the environment. As for journalists and pundits, I can come up with no explanation except shallowness or herd mentality.

Various factions have monetary, political, and even emotional interests in cultivating fears. Climate scientists need there to be a problem in order to get funding. They have a vested interest in creating panic, because that way the research money will flow to climate science. Tens of thousands of jobs depend on global warming. Prior to the 1990s, the level of funding for climate and climate-related sciences was somewhere around the order of $170 million a year—reasonable for the size of the field. But then it jumped to $2 billion a year, by a factor of more than 10. This brought a lot of new people, who otherwise were not interested, into the field. There was now a whole cadre of people whose only interest in climate science was man-made global warming. Research relating to this topic is one of the best funded areas of science today, with the U.S. government alone spending more than $4 billion a year.[1229]

The difficulty in publishing scientific papers that question the global-warming orthodoxy has been long recognized. If university departments cannot get their papers published in reputable journals, they will not receive money for research. Any researchers interested in debating the issues are silenced, because they risk becoming financial liabilities to their departments. Yet the common prejudice is that scientists who do not agree with the theory of man-made global warming must be paid by the oil-and-gas industry to tell lies. Why is money from a private source considered more controlling and directing than money from government? Is funding from an environmental group less directing than money from anywhere else? We live in a world where political correctness demands that we admire non-profit organizations and do not question their expertise or methods of operation. But since no-one can claim to be a purely impartial expert, no-one should be elevated above all criticism.

"Where are your sources and your references?" This is what a person gets asked when the facts he presents do not conform with the dominant paradigm. It lets you know that information can only exist in one set of circumstances, within specific information-producing institutions known as universities, outside of which everything must be plain misinformation. Yet peer review is only as good as the peers; if alchemists had been asked to write peer reviews, they might have come up with all sorts of justifications for the work of their colleagues, and the lay reader would not have been any wiser. As Richard Lindzen, Alfred P. Sloan Professor of Atmospheric Science at MIT, recently lamented in the *Wall Street Journal:* "Scientists who dissent from the alarmism have seen their grant funds disappear, their work derided and themselves libeled as industry stooges, scientific hacks or worse. Consequently, lies

1229. *The Great Global Warming Swindle.* Channel 4. March 8, 2007.

about climate change gain credence even when they fly in the face of the science."[1230]

Until recently, "being green" was not especially attractive to large corporations. The image of a green consumer was gray, puritanical, and sombre: the green consumer denied himself everything beautiful, pleasurable, and joyful. Until recently, Al Gore was seen as the flawed man, uncomfortable in his own skin, and incapable of uniting the nation. He was caricatured by some American political commentators as a serial exaggerator, the guy who invented the internet, who was the model for *Love Story*, who applied a little too much passion to that kiss he delivered to his now ex-wife, Tipper, at the Democratic National Convention in 2000. After the election, everyone expected Gore to quietly withdraw from public life, write a memoir here, hold a visiting professorship there, and maybe deliver the occasional keynote speech. Instead, in what may be the greatest brand makeover in history, Gore is now being hailed as a visionary who was right about everything while even the super-rich are driving hybrids.

The son of a senator, Albert Arnold Gore, Jr. was raised for the presidency; his movie and his speeches are, to paraphrase Clausewitz, a continuation of politics by other means. Yet as Gore himself put it, global warming is not even a political issue, but a moral issue. After all, ethics is not a branch of science, but a branch of philosophy. Should a scientist challenge the "received truth," he will be branded not only a hack, but downright evil. For centuries, people took natural disasters to be a form of divine retribution, God or Mother Nature punishing man for his transgressions. In a way, many still do. The main point Gore and his followers make is religious, rather than scientific. There is a worldwide secular religion, which we may call radical environmentalism, which holds that humans are "stewards of the Earth" and that despoiling the planet with waste products of our luxurious living is a sin. The ethics of this environmental faith are taught to children in schools and kindergartens all over the world.

Our ecological concerns often manifest themselves as worries that there is a revenge of nature taking place. Man has attempted to rise above nature, to "play God," if you will, and now Mother Nature is striking back. If we do not repent, doomsday will surely follow. What the concerned citizen usually fails to realize is that the ecological concerns were brought to public attention by the scapegoat itself, modern natural science. Every day, television, newspapers, and the internet bombard us with the message that we are destroying our planet, the ice caps are melting, and polar bears are drowning. We have messed up the environment beyond all repair and we must now pay the piper. Is it any wonder so many people are suffering from green guilt? Well, no need to worry, you may be a carbon sinner, but you can buy yourself a clean, green conscience for cash. Happy Earth Day everyone!

Dreamed up by politicians and businessmen rather than scientists, carbon offsetting has been described by Friends of the Earth as "a smokescreen to avoid real measures to tackle climate change."[1231] A carbon credit is something you buy to offset your emissions that contribute to global warming. In the same way as the mediaeval

1230. "Climate of Fear," April 12, 2006.

1231. Press Release, January 18, 2007.

Church allowed the rich to buy their way out of sin, so offsetting allows the wealthy to salve their consciences for all those shopping trips abroad. Of course, it would be far greener not to spend the carbon in the first place; in fact, offsetting has been found to create perverse incentives, encouraging firms only to grow their carbon footprints in order to earn money by implementing a carbon reduction program. And that is before going into the impossibility of accurately calculating how much carbon is emitted in the first place and ensuring the "offset" does not involve planting a tree that will end up emitting even more carbon.

Besides flights, you can offset car journeys, home energy usage, and food consumption. You can even buy offsets as a Christening present, according to JP Morgan's Climate Care website. Businesses, governments, and individuals buy carbon offsets every day. This can be done by investing in renewable energy, including wind and solar power and the use of biomass, while other kinds of project include tree planting or "reforestation." There are no standards, there is no oversight. Basically, carbon credit companies can make up their own formula for charging their clients whatever they want. Not only that, but they can spend the money on whatever project they want as well. According to the findings of a six-month investigation by reporters from *The Christian Science Monitor* and the New England Center for Investigative Reporting, many carbon offsets are empty promises and some are outright scams.[1232]

Carbon offsets are the environmental equivalent of financial derivatives: complex, unregulated, and in many cases, not worth their price. What you are buying may help you feel good, but there is absolutely no evidence that it compensates for global warming. Even UN certified projects have been criticized for failing to prove they provide emissions reductions which would not have happened without them.[1233] That is what all this hoopla is about: not saving the planet, just feeling less guilty. The average citizen, a mom or dad, wants to tell their children that they are carbon neutral. Companies buy offsets in bulk to help project a green image. In the United States alone, offset sales have tripled in five years.[1234] The real Inconvenient Truth is that Al Gore owns the company he supposedly buys his carbon credits from; he is carrying on the time-honored American tradition of snake oil salesmen.

In 2004, two years before his Oscar-winning movie, Gore founded a private equity firm called Generation Investment Management (GIM), which now has nearly $1 billion under its management. Governments worldwide are contemplating mandatory offset programs, like that established in Europe under the Kyoto Protocol. These funds are traded on the European Climate Exchange, half of which is owned by CCX, itself a creature of Gore's firm, GIM. As a private citizen, Gore is not required to disclose his income or assets, but financial disclosure documents released before the 2000 election put the Gore family's net worth at $1 to $2 million. Gore does not reveal his present net worth, but the fact that he was able to single-handedly make a $35 million

1232. Doug Struck, "Buying Carbon Offsets May Ease Eco-Guilt but Not Global Warming," *Christian Science Monitor*, April 20, 2010.

1233. Damian Kahya, "Who Pays and Who Gains from Carbon Offsetting?" BBC News, November 26, 2009.

1234. Struck, op. cit.

investment in Capricorn Investment Group should give us a clue. He is poised to reap hundreds of millions of dollars from investments in the companies that will benefit from the increased emphasis of the U.S. government on green technology, and according to the *New York Times*, he could become the world's first "carbon billionaire."[1235]

The head of the UN's climate change panel, Dr. Rajendra Pachauri, is also accused of making a fortune from his links with carbon-trading companies. Although Dr. Pachauri, co-awardee of the Nobel Prize with Mr. Gore, is often portrayed as a scientist, with the BBC even describing him as "the world's top climate scientist," his Ph.D. is actually in economics and he has no qualifications in climate science whatsoever. He has, however, established an astonishing worldwide portfolio of business interests with bodies that have billions of dollars invested in organizations dependent on the IPCC's policy recommendations. These include banks, oil-and-gas companies, and investment funds involved in carbon trading and "sustainable technologies," which together constitute the fastest-growing commodity market in the world, estimated to soon be worth trillions of dollars a year.[1236]

No-one in the world exercised more influence on the events leading to the disastrous Copenhagen climate conference in 2009 than Dr. Pachauri. Under the UN Clean Development Mechanism (CDM), corporations and consumers in the developed world pay for the right to exceed their "carbon limits" by buying certificates from companies in countries such as India and China, which in turn rack up "carbon credits" by showing that they have in some way reduced their carbon emissions. The Adaptation Fund, established by the Kyoto Protocol signatories in 2001 to transfer cash to countries vulnerable to the changing climate, gets its money from a 2% levy on the sale of carbon credits issued by the CDM. However, it apparently took years to set up the structure and appoint the required staff, so the fund was not actually established until late 2007. To date, no projects in developing countries have received any money from the fund, although several million dollars have been spent establishing the program and paying for administration.[1237]

Negotiations at the UN climate summit in Copenhagen were suspended after developing countries withdrew their co-operation, because they saw the money meant to help them cope with climate change as just a relabelling of existing aid commitments.[1238] In the end, delegates passed a motion simply taking note of the U.S.-backed climate deal, without formally adopting it. The price of carbon futures fell sharply in the European markets following the summit. EU allowances for December 2010 delivery were trading nearly 10% lower the day after the disappointing conclusion.[1239] In practice, no plausible "cap-and-trade" program can significantly

---

1235. Broder, op. cit.

1236. Christopher Booker & Richard North, "Questions over Business Deals of UN Climate Change Guru Dr Rajendra Pachauri," *The Sunday Telegraph*, December 20, 2009.

1237. Rob Young, "Poor Nations Await UN Kyoto Cash," BBC News, December 9, 2009.

1238. Felix Fallasch & Laetitia De Marez, "New and Additional?: An Assessment of Fast-Start Finance Commitments of the Copenhagen Accord," Climate Analytics, Potsdam, October 7, 2010.

1239. Fiona Harvey & Chris Flood, "Carbon Prices Drop in Wake of Climate Talks," *Financial Times*, December 21, 2009.

curb global warming; to do that, quotas would need to be set so low as to shut down the economy, or the cost of scarce quotas would skyrocket and be passed along to consumers in much higher energy prices—not that such a program would not be a bonanza for lobbyists, lawyers, and consultants vying for exceptions and special treatment.

Climate change and carbon trade are big business and you should not stick your nose too far into them. Rent-seeking, or the "wolf," has been disguised as environmentalism, or the "sheep." One can tell this just from the fact that the world's biggest proponents of global warming are people like Al Gore. We knew something was wrong when Ken Lay proposed a cap-and-trade scheme and Goldman Sachs positioned itself to ride the carbon trading bubble. Rent-seeking and totalitarian measures always need to be disguised as something that appeals to people's conscience and morality. Among those labels are children, welfare, nature, health, etc. These terms are used in politics when there is a need to prohibit or make money on something. When you appeal to conscience, you loosen people's purses and get them to pay the extra costs for energy caused by carbon trade. Besides, the media loves the preacher con man combination, which has been known to create enormous fortunes.

Since outright tax increases are bad politics during a recession, they cannot be implemented. However, the Obama administration's health care and cap-and-trade agendas have been described as "taxation Trojan Horses festooned in righteousness and sanctimony."[1240] During fiscal years 2012 through 2019, the U.S. government expects to collect $646 billion in "climate revenues," a completely new tax category.[1241] The promotion of green jobs with stimulus money, a bastard child of Obama's environmental and economic agendas, has been a top priory for the White House since day one. His administration claims to have created nearly 200,000 green jobs, but in lieu of settling on a straightforward definition of a green job, it has adopted an extraordinarily broad description of such jobs. They include not only financial advisers, wholesale buyers, and reporters, but also marketing managers, public relations specialists, and several more occupations that, as far as I can tell, have nothing to do with protecting the environment.[1242]

The global recycling movement was born in Germany a quarter of a century ago with Greenpeace and Friends of the Earth serving as midwives. The German environment minister, Klaus Töpfer, managed to pass a law that obliged the trade and industry to take back all the waste they had produced. This was the starting point for the producer responsibility based EU-wide recycling program. The multi-billion euro recycling industry tells us that this is the right thing to do, but many others think that it would be a much better idea to convert the waste directly into energy as near as possibly to the place of its origin. At the moment, the waste has to be collected, transported, washed, sorted, warehoused, transported again, cleaned up, crushed, melted, and fashioned into new products. All these operations consume a lot of energy

1240. Dougherty, op. cit.

1241. Ibid.

1242. Byron York, "Obama Team Uses Flimflammery to Inflate Job Numbers," ***Washington Examiner***, September 23, 2010.

and only strain the environment further.

We should be glad that plastic does not biodegrade: being inert, it does not introduce toxic chemicals into the environment. Rocks do not biodegrade either—why should we mind having styrofoam buried under our feet as opposed to rocks? Styrofoam, being man-made, is apparently evil, whereas rocks are natural, and therefore good. Even though PDF is a paperless and an "archival quality" format, it represents consumption, the destruction of the environment, and the maximization of profits, because every time you read a file, you need not only electricity, but a computer that has to replaced every couple of years. A paper book does not consume anything after it has been printed and it stays readable from father to son, even after the world where electricity is cheap and abundant has come to an end.

We tend to cry "This can't go on!" only when things are going well. Most of humanity has had their life expectancies extended, their health, food, and water quality improved, and their daily lives made easier. The recycling movement warns us that the United States is in danger of becoming covered in garbage, because the average American generates 8 lbs. a day. In fact, Americans create less than 3 lbs. of garbage each, which is much less than people in Mexico today or Americans a hundred years ago. Gone, for example, are the 1,200 lbs. of coal ash each U.S. household used to generate. The modern packaged foods actually mean less rubbish, not more.[1243] If we only practised forestry in the regions where forests grow the fastest, i.e. the subtropical zones, all the wood and paper used today could be produced in an area about the size of New England, and we could leave the rest of the world's forests alone.

What will we do when all the world's problems have been solved? Saving the planet cannot be the ultimate goal of our existence. However, were it not for the obvious ramifications for ratings and circulation, the news media would love to cover the end of the world. There has been a long succession of overhyped "scares" in the last few decades. We have repeatedly seen supposed experts hitting the headlines by raising some new fear, some terrifying new threat to human health or well-being: the "mad cow disease" was supposed to kill half a million people, the avian flu was supposed to kill 150 million, and the "millennium bug" was supposed to bring civilized life to a halt by knocking out all the computers. Our worries today are disproportionately about the world's dwindling water supply, air pollution, and carcinogenic chemicals.

According to H. L. Mencken, "The whole aim of practical politics is to keep the populace alarmed (and hence clamoring to be led to safety) by menacing it with an endless series of hobgoblins, all of them imaginary."[1244] While some people respond well to scare tactics, others melt into little puddles of jelly. The former variety will get pumped, put on a hard hat, and become a block leader, while the puddle of jelly will go home, cower in a corner, and have nightmares that he is one of the polar bears in Al Gore's movie. It would be far more helpful if all the Chicken Littles would just stop yelling doom, calm down, and maybe promote a little common sense. We are not

1243. Rockwell, op. cit. 296.

1244. 1949, 29.

going to stop driving cars, nor are we going to give up meat. If you spend a gallon less of gas, do you honestly think that no-one else is going to spend it? If you eat one less porterhouse, do you honestly think that juicy steak is not going to get eaten? The group, people, nation that refuses to consume anything only makes itself suffer while others use up the saved resources.

There is no sense in seeking zero risks—due to the minimal health risks of pesticides, for instance. We should always put the benefits and harms into perspective. Perhaps the biggest problem is that we prioritize the wrong things or pay too much attention to factors that have little effect on anything. We tend to spend a lot of resources on trivial issues while ignoring things that really matter and have a big impact on our health. A team of American researchers recently proposed severe limits on the consumption of salmon due to the toxic chemicals they contain. The researchers estimated that a couple of hundred cases of cancer were caused by the fish each year. Their suggested restrictions would cut cancers by 50 cases, leaving 150 cases. However, fish consumption prevents 30,000 heart deaths each year, so if people eat less fish only 23,000 deaths get prevented, meaning that 7,000 die while only 50 are saved.[1245]

As Lynn White, Jr. (1907–1987), a professor of mediaeval history at Princeton, Stanford, and UCLA, put it, "we shall continue to have a worsening ecologic crisis until we reject the Christian axiom that nature has no reason for existence save to serve man."[1246] As a species, we have been hellbent on wrecking our environment pretty much since the day we figured out how to make fire. Must I quote Agent Smith from *The Matrix?* "Every mammal on this planet instinctively develops a natural equilibrium with the surrounding environment, but you humans do not. You move to an area, and you multiply, until every natural resource is consumed. The only way you can survive is to spread to another area. There is another organism on this planet that follows the same pattern. A virus. Human beings are a disease, a cancer on this planet, you are a plague, and we are the cure."[1247]

The Bible tells us to "be fruitful and multiply," and it is this global swarming that is driving global warming. Why are we expected to cut back on our car emissions and plane emissions, but not our baby emissions? Are we really supposed to celebrate the pitter-patter of tiny carbon footprints? The government of China brags that its greatest contribution to the fight against global warming has been its policy of punishing, imprisoning, or sterilizing women who have more than one child. Of course, there are two-child families all over China, as parents earn enough money to pay fines or find loopholes in the policy, which is more porous than most outsiders imagine. For example, parents who were both only children are allowed a second child, as are rural parents whose first-born was a girl. Growing populations have strained the planet's ecosystems over the past half a century, threatening international efforts to combat poverty and disease, a UN-sponsored study warns.

1245. Eiliv Lund, et al. "Cancer Risk and Salmon Intake," *Science* 305(5683), July 23, 2004, 477–478.

1246. "The Historical Roots of Our Ecologic Crisis," *Ibid.* 155(3767), March 10, 1967, 1203–1207.

1247. Dir. Andy and Lana Wachowski. Warner Bros. Pictures, 1999.

Over the past five decades, humans have changed ecosystems more rapidly and extensively than any comparable period in history, according to the four-year, $24-million Millennium Ecosystem Assessment (MA) released in 2005. Increased human demands for food, clean water, and fuels could speed up the disappearance of forests, fish, and fresh water reserves and lead to more frequent disease outbreaks over the next 50 years.[1248] But the horrors of population growth have also been greatly exaggerated. A century ago, just one in seven of the world's people lived in cities; within the next 20 years, that number will rise to 95% of humans.[1249] The fact that global population is concentrated in cities means that it does not spread out to destroy large areas of land. Every month, about 6 million people move from the countryside to the cities. Only about 36% of the population of Africa currently lives in urban areas, but the continent is experiencing urbanization rates twice as high as those seen in the West during the industrial revolution.

UN-HABITAT predicts that Africa will be an urban continent by 2030, as rural inhabitants flee droughts and land left infertile by overfarming.[1250] But which is more ecological from the standpoint of global warming, city living or rural life? There is clear evidence that the greenhouse gas emissions of most rural dwellers are three or four times as high as those of a typical urbanite, simply because the distances travelled are usually much longer, the trips are done by car, and there tend to be more square feet to heat and light up in a country house. People think burning wood is fine and healthy because it is a natural substance, and we associate the smell of wood smoke with good things, like camping and cooking over the fire. In reality, breathing the particles that emanate from wood-burning fireplaces is no different from breathing tobacco smoke. A more ecological solution would be to live in downtown New York, in a small apartment with central air conditioning, and move around short distances on the subway, rail, and bus.

We are not in danger of running out of food either, although Lester Brown from the Worldwatch Institute has predicted this since the 1970s. Current food production per unit of land is dreadfully inefficient, with the United States, for instance, producing less than half of the wheat the EU does, hectare for hectare.[1251] According to a recent study, the number of obese people is growing fast in African cities; the urban poor can only afford cheap, high-fat and high-sugar foods.[1252] The noted economist and Nobel laureate Amartya Sen observed in the '80s that famine is seldom caused by a shortage of food. In most cases, it has to do with poverty and availability. We cannot get food to where it is needed, and those who need it cannot afford to buy it. The UN food and agriculture organization FAO recently pointed out that much of the famine in Africa is due to armed conflicts and the mass migration they cause.

1248. Millennium Ecosystem Assessment 2005.

1249. "World Urbanization Prospects: The 2005 Revision," Department of Economic and Social Affairs of the United Nations Secretariat, New York, 2006.

1250. United Nations Human Settlements Programme, op. cit.

1251. Lomborg 2001.

1252. Abdhalah K. Ziraba, et al. "Overweight and Obesity in Urban Africa: A Problem of the Rich or the Poor?" *BMC Public Health* 9, December 2009, 465.

When people are forced to leave their homes, they also lose their fields and their livestock.[1253]

Countries that are at war or preparing for war sink what little money they have into building their armies. It was recently discovered that millions raised by Band Aid and Live Aid for famine relief in Ethiopia were diverted to pay for weapons by a hard left-wing rebel group. Known as the Tigrayan People's Liberation Front, they were fighting the Ethiopian army, then the largest in Africa.[1254] When conflicts end, all the money goes to rebuilding. People die in Kenya, because they have no food, yet the crops of the Kenyan farmers rot, because there is no market for their produce. "The world has more than enough resources to accelerate progress in human development for all and to eradicate the worst forms of poverty from the planet. . . For example, it has been estimated that the total additional yearly investment required to achieve universal access to basic social services would be roughly $40 billion, 0.1% of world income, barely more than a rounding error. That covers the bill for basic education, health, nutrition, reproductive health, family planning, and safe water and sanitation for all."[1255]

Yet most of the entreaties of the UN's millennium assessment are the exact same type of banalities found in earlier warnings about the dangers of technology, such as the famous observation by the 18th-century demographer Thomas Malthus that unchecked procreation would lead to population growth that would exceed the food supply over time. He thought mass starvation was inevitable because population increases geometrically while food production grows arithmetically, but he failed to anticipate the advent of the Industrial Revolution. Malthus' prediction was thwarted by advances in agricultural science that vastly increased our ability to produce food. Similarly, his successors in the 1960s, like Paul Ehrich and the Club of Rome, did not see the Green Revolution that was just around the corner.

The highly urbanized North America and Europe do not have problems of deforestation. In fact, North American tree cover has been increasing over the last two centuries. Ancient forests must be axed; it might not be picturesque, but it is practical. Wheezy old trees simply cannot suck up the carbon like they used to. A tree absorbs roughly 1,500 tonnes of CO_2 until it reaches 55 years of age, after which absorption slows; and when that tree decomposes, it belches all the CO_2 back out again.[1256] The wood can be better used to make furniture, houses, and many of the products we currently manufacture from less suitable materials. According to Worldwatch, the forest and tree cover of the world has shrunk; according to the Danish professor of statistics Bjørn Lomborg, this cover has grown—both use the same statistics published by the UN.[1257] To quote economist Jeff Faux, "if you torture a statistic long enough, it will confess to anything."

1253. "Linking Conflict and Development: A Challenge for the MDG Progress," Committee on World Food Security, Rome, May 23, 2005.

1254. "Aid for Arms in Ethiopia." *Assignment.* BBC World Service. March 11, 2010.

1255. United Nations Development Programme 1998, 37.

1256. Usborne, op. cit.

1257. Lomborg, op. cit.

Due to the chequered forest reporting of local authorities, it is difficult to calculate a global trend. The images taken by NASA's satellites, on the other hand, are incredibly detailed, clear, and impartial. They can be used to assess the amount of biomass on every continent with great certainty. The Vegetation Index (VI) thus derived gives the total amount of the green biomass contained in forests and other vegetation. According to NASA, the VI values have grown especially steeply in the Northern Hemisphere since the 1980s. The reason for this might well lay in the direct fertilizing effect of man-made carbon emissions and the thus improved climate. Maybe we are living in a CO_2-starved world; we do not know. If we had not pumped the atmosphere full of CO_2, we might be fast heading to a new ice age; we do not know.

There may be evidence that the planet is getting warming, but we cannot be sure we are causing it, and even if we did cause it, we do not know that we can fix it, and even if we could fix it, we do not know how. "We do not know" terrifies some people, but many critical numbers are beset by bigger doubts than is generally admitted. Cutting back our quality of life is not the right way to fix things. Hell, we are not even sure of that. The one thing we do know is that it will not do us any good to buy forgiveness from a former politician who is building his new career on our guilt. Gregg Easterbrook has a "Law of Doomsaying": predict catastrophe no later than 10 years hence, but no sooner than 5 years away—soon enough to terrify, but far enough off that people will forget if you are wrong.

Malthus was the first in a long string of eco-pessimists who assumed that nations would invariably wreak environmental havoc by mechanizing the world and mining its natural resources. In every last one of these false alarms, nature and technology spiked their prophecies. According to the eco-alarmists of the 1970s, there was not supposed to be any oil industry to be a stooge of by now. It is not entirely accurate to say that there is a diminishing amount of resources, because human genius always finds new ways to use what is there. Two centuries ago, no-one could have conceived that the Sun's rays or the oceans' waves are a resource to be used, yet solar and tidal power make it so. The pace of scientific development is faster than ever and all the new technologies are going to emerge "out of the blue."

In the '70s, the world shook off the illusion that cheap oil would be available in perpetuity, even if the governments' own foolish price controls were the ultimate cause of the massive shortages. However, such organizations as the Club of Rome got many people into believing that all the Earth's resources were about to run out. This made economic growth the number one enemy of the environmental movement and government controls on consumption were required. But if we really were running out of oil, for instance, its price would skyrocket, prompting consumers to use less and entrepreneurs to seek substitutes. In fact, when the U.S. oil supply was threatened by the Iraq War, that is exactly what happened. The Club of Rome's claim that global economic collapse was imminent due to the rapid depletion of critical resources is a direct precursor to the current warnings. It, too, based its alarms not on any scientific analysis of specific issues, but on a computer model, which was predestined to give the results they wanted.

Eleven crucial minerals, including oil, natural gas, copper, gold, silver, tin, and zinc were supposed to run out by the beginning of 2000.[1258] Being in the pocket of the oil-and-gas companies should be about as lucrative as being in the pocket of the buggy-whip industry. Yet Exxon boasted a net profit of $11.68 billion in the second quarter of 2008, which just happens to be the largest quarterly profit ever earned by an American company—and Exxon Mobil only has 2% of the world's oil production.[1259] Despite the Iraq War and the resulting production disruptions, despite the moratorium on drilling in the Gulf of Mexico, despite turmoil in Nigeria and quarrels in Central Asia, the United States has more petroleum on hand today than it has had since at least the beginning of the first Gulf War.[1260] The world is so awash with oil that it is running out of storage places. Banks have rented supertankers and are parking the oil, driving up the price to make money.

Oil should be $10 a barrel by now and gas 99 cents a gallon, prompting U.S. regulators to look for evidence of market manipulation, while the IMF is examining the role of traders in the price spike. Meanwhile, hedge funds and big banks are taking advantage of loopholes in federal trading limits to buy massive amounts of oil contracts, helping push oil prices to record highs. Goldman Sachs persuaded pension funds and other large institutional investors to invest in oil futures, i.e. agreeing to buy oil at a certain price on a fixed date. This push transformed oil from a physical commodity, rigidly subject to supply and demand, into something to gamble with, like a stock. As speculators in oil futures are allowed to buy more contracts, more contracts are sold than there are barrels of oil in existence. Between 2003 and 2008, the amount of speculative money in commodities grew from $13 billion to $317 billion, an increase of 2,300%. By 2008, a barrel of oil was traded 27 times, on the average, before it was actually delivered and consumed.[1261] Over the same period, investors have become such a force on commodity markets that their appetite for oil contracts has been equal to China's increase in demand. The era of *cheap* oil may be over, but there is still plenty of energy and resources left.

Even if conventional oil production should peak in the coming decades, there is still 15 times as much "unconventional oil" left.[1262] Bitumen from oil sand can be separated and processed into raw oil suitable for refineries. Turning coal into diesel fuel is an old idea. The Nazis did this during World War II, after they no longer had access to the Romanian oil fields—Germany has plenty of coal, but precious little oil. South Africa used the same technique when international sanctions were imposed on its Apartheid régime in the 1980s—half of the cars in the country now run on coal-based fuels. There will be cheap coal and uranium for centuries to come. "We're running out of atmosphere faster than we're running out of oil," as Dr. Daniel

1258. Meadows, et al. 1972.

1259. Tom Petruno, "If Only Exxon Could Earn Money Like Disney," *Los Angeles Times*, July 31, 2008.

1260. Richard Martin, "What Peak Oil?: Why an Oil Glut Is Ahead," *Fortune*, September 8, 2010.

1261. Matt Taibbi, "The Great American Bubble Machine," *Rolling Stone*, July 9, 2009.

1262. International Energy Agency, op. cit.

Kammen, professor of energy at UC Berkeley put it.[1263]

One cannot help feeling that the depletion of natural resources is used as an objective-sounding argument in the cultural critique against the Western way of life, consumer society, and economic growth, to which each and all can in some degree subscribe. But let us try and put numbers to the price of energy a thousand years ago, when horses and donkeys did the job of internal combustion engines and electric motors. As a benchmark, we will assume that electricity costs at present about 8 cents per kilowatt-hour. This puts the costs of power in the Middle Ages at approximately $90 per kWh. To be even more concrete about this and how this translates into the modern world, a gallon of gasoline contains 40 kWh of energy, so for the energy costs to rise to the mediaeval levels would require gasoline prices at $3,600.00 per gallon.

It is precisely industrial societies that have become progressively cleaner by developing new technologies to reduce air pollution and remove toxins from drinking water. China overtook the United States as the world's biggest energy user in 2009, and it uses more oil incrementally than the U.S. because its growth is less energy efficient.[1264] China's emissions can be lowered by a startling amount merely by raising the energy efficiency requirements of its buildings and equipment to European levels. For years, the Kyoto Protocol has worsened China's carbon intensity, because the country is seen as a developing nation with low per capita emissions; instead of tackling pollution, the environmental movement has lobbied for carbon caps. Due to the premature politicization of the global warming research, Westerners have all but forgotten about the real, old-fashioned pollutants.

Even as we are being pressured into expensive eco-production, the so-called developing countries get to use cheap and dirty production methods with the help of our money. The most tragicomic part of this whole global warming hysteria is that it increases pollution in the Third World, as the "climate commitment" of the West drives industrial production from clean and energy-efficient plants to China and other developing nations, where the exit gas clean-up and wastewater treatment technologies are at a level they were in the West 50 years ago. As production moves to countries where environmental responsibility is a fairly unknown concept, this leads to an absolute increase in the total amount of pollution in the world and a more wasteful exploitation of natural resources.

Of course poor countries have not signed Kyoto—they are not going to sacrifice poverty reduction, bigger middle classes, and all the other economic gains just to combat global warming. Carbon reduction is often justified on basis of the need to protect the Third World poor, who are believed to suffer the most from the consequences of climate change. But any process that makes energy more expensive and less accessible is only going to degrade the quality of life, especially for those who are already poor and have difficulty acquiring energy. All advancements in equality throughout the history of mankind ultimately boil down to reducing the cost of energy and creating new inventions to use that energy. Al Gore and his followers are trying to pass new regulations and taxes that would end up raising the global price of

1263. Keynote Address to the 11th Annual Meeting of the National Collegiate Inventors and Innovators Alliance, The Quorum Tampa, Tampa, FL, March 22, 2007.

1264. International Energy Agency, op. cit.

fuel—fuel that the poor in Africa need to cook or pump water, to get their crops to market and their children to school or to a doctor. The enormous cost of reducing carbon emissions compelled Pulitzer-winning columnist George Will to write that global warming legislation "could cause in this century more preventable death and suffering than was caused in the last century by Hitler, Stalin, Mao, and Pol Pot combined."[1265] It is buffoons like Al Gore who are destroying this planet, believe me before it's too late!

Without energy, life is short and brutal. When you talk about raising the price of energy, you are talking about killing people. There is a better way to control population than to withdraw the one effective agent against one of the world's greatest killers, and that is to raise the standard of living of the poorest. As every demographer knows, if we make the poor wealthy, the population will stabilize. Conversely, if we make the wealthy poor, it will start to increase again. If the environmental movement was really serious about saving the planet from a huge carbon footprint, they would not pursue policies that will make you poor, but would try to make everyone rich. Yet the American Clean Energy and Security Act of 2009 proposed that the United States shut down five-sixths of its economy.[1266] Never before in history, with the exception of Japan's self-imposed isolation in the 17th century, did a government actively force its people away from economic activity and industry. Never before have politicians come up with proposals so astronomically costly or potentially damaging to their own national economies. Global warming legislation also poses a very real threat to our civil liberties, leading another Pulitzer-winner, Charles Krauthammer, to warn that "other than rationing food, there is no greater instrument of social control than rationing energy."[1267]

The recession threw the world economy into turmoil, but the environment is grateful. Carbon emissions were globally lowered by as much as 3% in 2009, according to the International Energy Agency (IEA). The reduction was historic, since emissions have not fallen so steeply since the end of the Second World War.[1268] Yet the announcement should have not come as a surprise: emissions have always followed business cycles—booms and busts. The greatest fall in emissions was recorded after the depression of 1930, when they fell by a fourth. Despite that, the 1930s were warm, in many places warmer than the temperature peaks 70 years later. Emissions also fell in the '40s and the '70s, but more importantly, rose sharply during the '50s and '60s.[1269] That was the period when the growing industrial production in the West was fuelled by cheap oil. In spite of growing emissions, the climate cooled down in the '50s and the '60s, and began to warm up a little again following the oil crisis of 1973. Even Al Gore no longer refers to carbon emissions, but to "global

---

1265. "An Inconvenient Price," *Newsweek*, October 13, 2007.

1266. Monckton, op. cit.

1267. "Carbon Chastity: The First Commandment of the Church of the Environment," *Washington Post*, May 30, 2008.

1268. International Energy Agency, op. cit.

1269. Elina Kervinen, "Taantuma laskee päästöjä eniten sitten toisen maailmansodan," *Helsingin Sanomat*, November 7, 2009.

warming pollution."

There is a widespread perception that if the U.S. and the EU could only get their greenhouse gas emissions under control, the problem of climate change would be solved—but nothing could be further from the truth. The IEA predicts that by 2035, world energy demand and greenhouse gases will increase by over a third, with developing countries accounting for about two-thirds of the growth.[1270] In fact, the whole global warming scare can be seen as a war against China and India. From a developmental point of view, these countries are at the stage the West passed some time ago. As a result, their very real industrial needs can be portrayed as evil by Western politicians, who care not that their own nations had exactly the same failings during their early stages of industrialization. Donald Trump has got it right, Al Gore should return his Nobel Prize: eco-alarmism does not deliver world peace, it threatens it.

Measures to curb climate change cannot succeed, but they can do much harm. Reports say that electricity prices could double in Europe if power companies are to meet emissions reductions targets under the Kyoto Protocol.[1271] Yet governments, led by the European Union, have proposed even more ambitious measures to change the world's climate, intended not just to meet the original Kyoto targets, but to go far beyond them. But then, vilifying and taxing success is exactly what government is for—otherwise the rest of the citizenry might develop self-esteem issues. This was marvellously addressed by Robert Heinlein, who wrote: "Throughout history, poverty is the normal condition of man. Advances which permit this norm to be exceeded—here and there, now and then—are the work of an extremely small minority, frequently despised, often condemned, and almost always opposed by all right-thinking people. Whenever this tiny minority is kept from creating, or (as sometimes happens) is driven out of a society, the people then slip back into abject poverty."[1272]

Before the Japanese tsunami of 2011, there was a growing consensus that nuclear power was the best way for China and India to modernize without adding disastrously to global warming. Nuclear power emits only 2–6% of carbon per kWh of that emitted by the cleanest fossil fuel, natural gas—and that is after factoring in everything from the uranium mining to plant decommissioning.[1273] John Ritch, head of the World Nuclear Association, argues that the world will need 10,000 civilian nuclear reactors by the end of the century, compared with just 440 today.[1274] The trouble is, no nuclear plant has ever been built anywhere in the world without public money. In theory, there is nothing to stop a private firm from proposing to build a nuclear power station, but given the amount of investment needed, explicit

---

1270. Op. cit.

1271. "Countdown to Kyoto 2008–2012: The Carbon Challenge for Europe's Electric Power Sector," Global Energy Decisions, Boulder, CO, November 2006.

1272. Op. cit. 244.

1273. "Meeting the Energy Challenge: A White Paper on Nuclear Power," Department for Business, Enterprise & Regulatory Reform, London, January 2008.

1274. David Ignatius, "Good Nukes, Bad Nukes," *Washington Post*, March 1, 2006.

government support is necessary to persuade firms to do so.

Poverty matters because it leaves many people no choice but to exploit the environment. China's influence in developing nations is growing, because it has had to move some of its own polluting industry abroad as its middle classes have grown. We have a tendency to think that if rural culture disappears, all that is left is chaos. We conclude that as the culture of greeting, visiting, and chatting fades away, manners in general will vanish—as if the urban world would not offer anything in its place. City is a natural unit of economy. Cities were the source of progress and enlightenment. People have a need to gather together, invent new things, and find a mate—cities make this possible. But many Westerners see the flight from the countryside as a problem. They think that country living is somehow superior, that country folk are somehow closer to nature, which is not true: everything good and decent in the world has its origin in cities, including civilization, culture, and freedom. Idolizing nature as something original, untouched, beautiful, and noble is called romanticism. The term is usually used in a derogatory sense, because it is easy to show that the romantics are wrong: the idyllic rural community in the middle of unspoiled nature is a figment of their own imagination. Returning to the past is impossible, not due to the irreversibility of modernization, but because that past never existed.

Small islands, fringed with picture-postcard beaches and far from madding crowds, are often on the top of the wish list for eco-travellers. Living as they do six days off the coast of Africa, Tristanians tend to be romanticized by the island's few visitors, who are usually dissatisfied with their contemporary Western life. Though Tristan may lack most of the distractions of modern civilization, its inhabitants still have all the natural human vices. There are single women with children by married islanders, there are tragic love affairs with South African sailors who dock only once a year.[1275] Homicide rates among traditional cultures lacking written laws and police forces are far higher than those in modern Western cultures. Among the Gebusi of Africa and the Yanomamo of Venezuela, for example, almost a third of men die by being murdered.[1276] There is no jail, but there is whispering and plenty of secrets. Gossip and fear of the outside are the primary forms of social control in every isolated community. Their self-sustaining economies offer little room for individuality and there are few man-made avenues though which to invest one's energy and express one's creativity. Lacking immunity to the germs of the mainland, old people of Tristan scurry indoors at the sight of foreigners.[1277]

It is not a bad thing that tourists travel to artificial oases designed expressly for them. All the main destinations in the Caribbean are adult sandboxes built just for tourists. They have everything a holidaymaker might need. Mass tourism is the most ecological form of tourism. When people fly alone to the jungles of Borneo to see the aboriginal people, their environmental impact is much greater. The thought that there

1275. Gregory Rodriguez, "Sin Gets Around. . . Even in Paradise," *Los Angeles Times*, November 5, 2004.

1276. Buss 2005.

1277. Rodriguez, op. cit.

was anything truly original, something that had only ever existed in one specific place, is a complete myth. All the cultures of the world are hybrids, formed through the intermingling of various different elements, through the constant migration of people. In its volume and pace, modern mass tourism may be something never seen before, but that does not mean that people did not travel before. It was only 10,000 years ago that people first began to settle down in one place, instead of moving around all the time.

Extinction is completely natural, just as new species are discovered every day. What is more, evolution is faster when it is warmer. According to a recent study reported in the *Proceedings of the Royal Society*, climate has a direct effect on the speed of "molecular evolution" in mammals. Researchers found that, among pairs of mammals of the same species, the DNA of those living in warmer climates changes at a faster rate.[1278] These mutations, where one letter of the DNA is substituted for another, are the first step in evolution. This could explain why the tropics are so species-rich—more than 50% of life on Earth is in tropical forests, which cover less than 7% of the planet's surface.[1279] In warmer climates, the germ cells that eventually develop into sperm and eggs divide more frequently, providing more opportunities for mutations in the population over a given time; this increases the probability of advantageous mutations that are selected for within the species.

In 2003–2004, two teams of scientists working independently in Africa many miles apart discovered a new species of monkey—the first new primate known to science in more than 20 years. Approximately 1,100 of the animals, now named the "highland mangabey," or *Lophocebus kipunji*, live in the highland Ndundulu Forest Reserve in Tanzania.[1280] They were quickly classified as "critically endangered species" by the International Union for Conservation of Nature, meaning that their numbers have decreased, or will decrease, by 80% within three generations. In fact, a global review of the world's primates says 48% of species face extinction.[1281] Similarly, when a team of Australian scientists identified a new dolphin species in 2005—the first for 56 years—these "snubfin dolphins," or *Orcaella heinsohni*, immediately became a high conservation priority, even if they are only considered "near threatened" by the IUCN.[1282] Dolphins, whales, porpoises, and sirenians are so difficult to survey that declines that should result in a "vulnerable" listing go undetected at least 70% of the time.[1283]

1278. Len N. Gillman, et al. "Latitude, Elevation and the Tempo of Molecular Evolution in Mammals," *Proceedings of the Royal Society B* 276(1671), September 22, 2009, 3353–3359.

1279. Mitchell, et al. Op. cit.

1280. Trevor Jones, et al. "The Highland Mangabey *Lophocebus kipunji:* A New Species of African Monkey," *Science* 308(5725), May 20, 2005, 1161–1164.

1281. "The IUCN Red List of Threatened Species™," International Union for Conservation of Nature, Cambridge, October 2008.

1282. Isabel Beasley, et al. "Description of a New Dolphin, the Australian Snubfin Dolphin *Orcaella heinsohni* sp. n. (Cetacea, Delphinidae)," *Marine Mammal Science* 21(3), July 2005, 365–400.

1283. Jan Schipper, et al. "The Status of the World's Land and Marine Mammals: Diversity, Threat, and Knowledge," *Science* 322(5899), October 10, 2008, 225–230.

"The purpose of life is to be defeated by greater and greater things," as Rainer Maria Rilke famously declared. Life was not always as complex as it is today. We have come a long way from bacteriological lichens and amoebas to the more sophisticated range of bird, mammal, and reptile we are today. Most species in the fossil record last a few million years and then become extinct. Why not allow this to continue? A typical species becomes extinct within 10 million years of its first appearance, although some species survive virtually unchanged for hundreds of millions of years. In lieu of God, they were created by blind nature, and there have been many failings and poor designs along the way, now scrapped by the natural process of extinction. Frogs have been called "living fossils," because these small creatures have survived for 200 million years. However, amphibians are also one of the most threatened groups of organisms in the world. Their skins easily absorb pollutants, their habitats are being squeezed by human expansion, and some species are even hunted, but the single biggest threat is actually a disease caused by *Batrachochytrium dendrobatidis*—this rapidly spreading deadly fungus was discovered and named as a new genus in 1998.

But how exactly do scientists ascertain that a species is extinct? It is not like they can ever know for sure. We still often hear the claim first made by biologist Norman Myers in 1979 that we lose 40,000 species a year, but there is no evidence for these figures. Back in 1995, the inaugural UN biodiversity report noted that the estimated and the substantiated extinction figures did not coincide with each other.[1284] It is difficult to make reliable estimates of impending extinction. It is hard to put a number on extinctions when we do not even know how many species there are. In 2005, *Science* Magazine reported that the spectacular ivory-billed woodpecker, declared extinct in 1920, had been found alive in North America; among the world's largest woodpeckers, the red, white, and black ivory-bill is one of only six North American bird species suspected to have gone extinct since 1880—the report was suppressed for over a year.[1285] The truth is, we cannot tell for certain which species are truly endangered. The butterfly catching methods, for example, have changed several times during recent history and are not comparable. Nor is it possible to deduce from the data on birds and mammals what will happen to smaller species, of which only a fraction are known.

Like the modern environmentalists, who place every bug and weed above humans, the Nazis, too, were ardent conservationists. They passed a host of laws to protect "nature and nature's animals," especially "endangered" plants and animals.[1286] If some people wish to preserve this or that dying species for scientific or entertainment purposes, on their own land and at their own expense, I am all for it. Zoos and universities do this all the time. But the rest of us should not be taxed and regulated, and have our property rights taken away, to save every bug and weed. Some people only want to protect species that they like, such as whales and parakeets; unfortunately, most of the life on this planet is made up of insects, fungi, and what

---

1284. United Nations Environment Programme 1995.

1285. John W. Fitzpatrick, et al. "Ivory-billed Woodpecker (*Campephilus principalis*) Persists in Continental North America," *Science* 308(5727), June 3, 2005, 1460–1462.

1286. Proctor, op. cit. 227.

not. An estimated 5 to 50 billion species have lived here, but only about 50 million are alive today, meaning that 99.9% of all species that have ever lived are now extinct. Even colossal extinction events, such as the Permo-Triassic extinction, which wiped out 95% of all marine species and 70% of land species 251 million years ago, make way for other species to thrive.[1287] Some scientists even theorize that without these natural catastrophic events, Earth would be a dead planet.

As far as Nietzsche could see, the struggle for survival is not the rule of nature, but the exception in life. By far, it is the richness of resources that prevails in the world, not the want of them. And most importantly, where there is a struggle for life, it is the strong, not the weak, who always seem to come up short. Obviously, the strong should not look after the weak, the weak—like everyone else—should look after their own. The term is not the "survival of the strongest," but the survival of the fittest. It is usually the smartest who survive—not the best, but the best adapted. Human fatness, slowness, and clumsiness poses a constant dilemma for inventors. Even if they could make every appliance much smaller than it is today, our fat sausage fingers simply could not operate the controls. Albert Einstein always resisted the quantum theory's spooky behaviour, "God does not play dice" being among his most famous objections. But experiments eventually proved that He apparently does, and laid the technical foundations for today's quantum information revolution—cryptography, computation, and teleportation.

Science no longer paves the way for engineering, it is the other way around. A chip manufacturer figures out a way to make wire only a few molecules thick, but why the circuits function is not important, as long as they do. Science can take years, if not decades, to catch up with an adequate explanation of the quantum mechanics involved. This is the final triumph of Edison over Einstein, God chastising Albert for telling Him what to do. The biggest problem for people who design computers, smartphones, and other gadgets is not that it is difficult to create a device that fulfils the existing needs of people. The real problem is that the gadgets must always be ahead of the users, and it is not easy to market a new device or function. Of course, they are always accepted in the end—not because they meet existing needs, but because consumers are creative, inventive, curious, and endlessly gullible. People are constantly adapting their everyday behaviour to fit new technological demands.

There are no equal signs between evolution, progress, and change. The idea of progress itself contains many concepts that are difficult to reconcile. Firstly, it claims that progress, according to the prevalent standards (living standards, technology, liberty, equality, etc.) has actually taken place. Maybe it has, but were things not measured by different standards before the Age of Enlightenment and the advent of capitalism? Yes, they were, so we have to conclude that there has been progress also in the measuring system itself. If the value of progress is the product of progress, by what standard is the progress of standards supposed to be measured? The inevitability of progress is entirely dependent on our point of view: if we did not consider our present standards better than the old ones, we would not have them. Progress does not make things better, it only changes our standards. "Reactionaries" view the

1287. "Dinosaurs: Ancient Fossils, New Discoveries," American Museum of Natural History, New York City, May 14, 2005.

present through the standards of the past, whereas "progressives" measure the past with the standards of today.

Homo sapiens was weaker than *Homo erectus*, yet the former triumphed. In fact, humans are weaker than any other large primate: gorilla, orangutan, even the chimp. As Voltaire famously observed, "God is not on the side of the big battalions, but on the side of those who shoot best." The dinosaurs grew very big very fast. This probably resulted in them not being able to survive the Chicxulub meteor disaster. Small animals always fare better in catastrophic circumstances, because they need less food. However, the cockroach would actually be one of the first insects to die in a nuclear blast, according to research published in 1959.[1288] And in any case, "the quickest and most economical way of winning a military decision is to defeat an enemy not at his weakest but at his strongest point."[1289]

True strength lay not in giving blows, but in taking blows—professional athletes constitute perhaps the most patched-up segment of the population. A "math genius" does not use more but less brain power than the average man to figure out what 123 times 456 is; similarly, the more you try to remember something, the less likely you are to do so—the trick is knowing which specific parts of the brain to activate for any given task. As it says in *The Devil's Dictionary*, "Certain old men prefer to rise at [dawn], taking a cold bath and a long walk with an empty stomach and otherwise mortifying the flesh. They then point with pride to these practices as the cause of their sturdy health and ripe years; the truth being that they are hearty and old, not because of their habits, but in spite of them. The reason we find only robust persons doing this thing is that it has killed all the others who have tried it."[1290]

1288. D. R. A. Wharton & Martha L. Wharton, "The Effect of Radiation on the Longevity of the Cockroach, *Periplaneta americana*, as Affected by Dose, Age, Sex and Food Intake," *Radiation Research* 11(4), October 1959, 600–615.

1289. Epaminondas, as quoted in Green 1970, 24.

1290. Bierce, op. cit. 63.

13

Men Are from Mars, Women Are from Venus, Self-Help Books Are from Uranus

Since at least the French Revolution, politicians and activists have preached ideological *fraternité*, but in 1913, the "Great Beast" Aleister Crowley declared "the brotherhood of all things created" a fact of nature.[1291] According to his younger countryman and fellow atheist, Richard Dawkins, being pro-life "in debates on abortion or stem cell research, always means pro *human* life, for no sensibly articulated reason."[1292] In Dawkins' view, the fact that humans think of themselves as distinct from—and superior to—other animals, is a sort of racism. Evolution shows that bullfighters and fox hunters are tormenting their own distant cousins, prompting Dawkins to send money to anti-bullfighting groups in Spain and to ban fox hunting on his family farm. In his essay *Gaps in the Mind*, he wrote: "the melancholy fact is that, at present, society's moral attitudes rest almost entirely on the . . . speciesist imperative."[1293] The fact that over 90% of the existing species' genetic material is the

---

1291. "Mysteria Mystica Maxima: Constitution of British Section," Ancient Order of Oriental Templars, London, February 15, 1913.

1292. *Son of Moore's Law.* 2004, 114.

1293. Ibid. 25.

same should form an ample basis for morality.

Ultimately, to quote Carl Sagan, "We are made of star-stuff,"[1294] or, to put it less eloquently, of thermonuclear waste—none of us would exist without three generations of stars dying and being born. "There is not a single atom in our bodies that hasn't been forged in the furnace of the Sun."[1295] We are 18% carbon and exist on the basis of carbon chains. This carbon was formed inside stars and became a part of our planet billions of years ago. Of the 92 natural elements, it is carbon that seeks companions and gathers other elements around itself. Carbon atoms link together in chains the foundations of life, amino acids. It is within the carbon chains that those amino acids and bases form DNA, the basic blueprint of all known life. It is highly probable that life on other planets is also based on carbon, because it is so common and bonds with other elements so easily. All space programs basically search for . . . us. That is, understanding of how we came to be. As Robert Heinlein pointed out, "A generation which ignores history has no past and no future."[1296] Knowing the past, building everything on what has gone before, is necessary for appreciating the present and in contemplating the future.

The importance of Copernicus was not simply that he figured out the truth, but that his revelation finally allowed scientists to make accurate calculations about Earth's orbit and the movement of other planets. Realizing that Earth was not the centre of the universe did not make earthlings any less important—it just allowed them to do their sums right. As late as the 17th century, common people were not allowed to look through either telescopes or microscopes, because they altered people's perceptions of the universe. The microscope can be considered a spiritual doorway, because it shows how we are all connected; on a molecular level, we are all the same. We are all stardust, made from molecules that have partaken of the life of stars; in our protomolecular form, we have all lived for billions of years. We might have more of one thing than another, but we are all still related at the atomic level; at the level of DNA, every living thing on the planet has the same code. "We are machines for propagating DNA," as Dawkins puts it. "It is every living object's sole reason for living."[1297] Every living organism is just a husk, discarded as soon as DNA no longer needs it; individual animals die, and whole species may go extinct, but an unbroken genetic line connects every living thing on Earth. As for the molecules of your body, they are returned to the universe and reappear as other life forms or celestial objects—here is immortality you can count on.

It is a given in physics that matter or energy can be neither created nor destroyed. In recent years, scientists have extended this notion also to information. As simple molecules grew into more complex ones, they kept moving into ever greater complexity. You would think that once an organic chemical reached thousands of individual atoms, it would break apart, instead of building itself into an even more

---

1294. 2000, 190.

1295. *I Heart Huckabees.* Dir. David O. Russell. Fox Searchlight Pictures, 2004.

1296. Op. cit. 241.

1297. "Growing Up in the Universe: Waking Up in the Universe." *The Royal Institution Christmas Lectures.* BBC. December 30, 1991.

complex molecule. Yet life has evolved inexorably; evolution has kept adding on without wiping out the lower forms of life. The blue-green alga, a very primitive life form, is still with us, even if it no longer rules the scene. Nature constantly reminds itself of earlier forms of life: a human foetus develops from a single fertilized ovum, passing through stages that repeat the biology of fish, reptiles, lower mammals, and so on, before becoming fully human. Nothing of value is ever forgotten.

Human dignity, should it be understood in any meaningful way, cannot be diminished by the fact that a fruit fly has almost as many genes as we do. If you compare humans and animals from a purely biological perspective, there are no fundamental differences. Many genes are interchangeable among species and vastly different organisms use similar genetic building blocks. The Cambrian explosion happened primarily through the reshuffling of existing genes into new and more complex arrangements that created all the basic animal forms. The human brain has between 1 and 10 trillion neurons, whereas the worm ***Cænorhabditis elegans*** has only 302; but the genes in those 302 neurons make many of the same chemicals that the human brain does. Like musical notes, genes can produce incredible diversity depending on how they are orchestrated. Everything has to do with what genes are turned on and off—that is the whole secret of life. "But let your communication be, Yea, yea; Nay, nay: for whatsoever is more than these cometh of evil."[1298]

Genes are drugs and DNA is the largest and most powerful pharmacy imaginable. Its products—proteins and enzymes—repair wounds, attack infectious invaders, and destroy diseased or cancerous cells every day. As Voltaire famously quipped, "The art of medicine consists in amusing the patient while nature cures the disease." Sealed in the double helix is the ability to create every cell in the body and scientists today are trying to figure out how to tap this potential. In theory, embryonic stem cells can be grown into any type of cell in the body, so they are seen as holding the key to a new era of regenerative medicine—to developing cells with the ability not just to arrest illness, but to reverse it. Therapeutic cloning has been legal in the UK since 2002, but opponents say it is wrong to create human embryos solely for the purpose of destroying them. Some also fear that such research could hasten the arrival of the first cloned baby—something that virtually all parties to the debate expressly oppose.

Foetal cells are cloned all the time; even Mother Nature does it, every time she makes identical twins. Asexually produced offspring are also clones. The fact is, underlying cultural beliefs have a much stronger influence on people's opinions about cloning than science-based information about its potential and pitfalls. But after reading countless papers and watching endless news reports on the matter, I have yet to hear a genuinely ethical objection to cloning, be it of humans or of sheep. The objections given are not ethical, but religious in nature, and essentially boil down to the tired old accusation of "playing God." If you clone a human being, will the two clones share the same soul, or will God have to create a new one? Since God is perfect, and man imperfect, surely if we attempt to create a clone, it must necessarily be imperfect. Will it be soulless? Mechanical? Dangerous? Able to destroy its creators?

Even identical twins—and clones—are identical only on the level of DNA, i.e. only

1298. Matthew 5:37.

the "blueprint" is the same. Identical twins do not look as alike as people think they do, but there are also deeper differences. If one twin is gay, for example, the other is usually straight. If one twin gets diabetes, there is only a 30% chance that the other will get it too. The same goes for schizophrenia. The odds that both will get these two diseases are much higher than for regular siblings, but nowhere near 100%.[1299] Does the shared DNA of identical twins prevent us from respecting them as individuals? Why is the question of dignity raised specifically in connection with cloning? Are we not dealing with primitive doppelganger fears, viz. "Am I the real me?" Everyone can see from their own fingerprints that those on the right and the left hand fingers are not totally identical, even though the genes and the environment are absolutely the same. There is an elusive third factor in the development of an organism, known as developmental noise.

It is a common misconception that DNA creates life on its own. Actually, DNA interacts with its molecular environment through an unimaginably complex web of chemical reactions, responding to chemicals in the womb, in the body, in the food that we eat and the air that we breathe. Even after a child is grown, DNA keeps interacting with the environment, and new generations of cells bear the imprint of that interaction. Every living substance in the body, from bone to blood, along with every action of the body, from mobilizing antibodies in the immune system to firing synapses in the brain, is created by an interaction with DNA. The developmental noise is completely random, and it stems from e.g. the fact that the concentration of certain rare molecules varies randomly between the right and left sides of the body. Thus even identical twins, and even clones, will have somewhat different fingerprints, even though their genes are absolutely identical. The string of biochemicals that cause the billions of neurons in each person's brain to develop in distinct ways makes it possible for even twins to develop minds of their own. It might be a paradox, but our genes predetermine that we are not predetermined.

There is not nearly enough information in the human genome to account for all the different brain cells and synapses. The brain cannot be hardwired for the simple reason that it must learn. Experiences and memories shape and reshape its circuitry, strengthening those synaptic connections that fire frequently and letting others weaken. When an infant comes into the world, its genes have created an immense amount of neurons and synapses; by the age of three, a child's brain has, on the average, twice as many neurons and neural connections as an adult's. As the baby matures, that number dwindles, as the synapses that do not get used are eliminated—at a rate of thousands per second. Even middle-aged brains generate thousands of new neurons every day in areas crucial to learning and memory. Each brain changes throughout a lifetime, altered by experience and ageing, as neurons and synapses vie for sensory stimulation. Studies show that even the simplest mental activities can involve slightly different areas in different people's brains.[1300] A "criminal gene" will never be found, because crime encompasses too wide a range of behaviour and because the very concept is socially defined.

1299. Bouchard & Propping 1993.

1300. Gazzaniga 2004.

We also need to get rid of the idea that mammals, and humans in particular, are somehow the pinnacle of evolution. If your high school biology teacher told you that humans sit at the top of the food chain, he was dead wrong: literally millions and millions of microscopic organisms—viruses, bacteria, protozoa, and fungi—feed on us and reproduce within us. What confuses people is their assumption that parasites are only damaging things, when in fact, the overwhelming majority of viruses are not harmful to their hosts. Each one of us is infected with a huge array of viruses; the human genome itself contains more retrovirus sequences than actual genes. That is true of nearly all eukaryotes, and the more complicated the organism, the more of those sequences it has.[1301] We also need to understand that evolution is not linear, but an intricate branching process. We cannot expect, for example, to trace a structure in the human brain back to other current vertebrate species. The crow shows far more advanced cognitive behaviour than the chimp, the closest genetic relative of humans. New Caledonian crows design and make intricate tools, whereas no chimpanzee has ever been known to make even a simple tool without being carefully coached by humans.[1302]

The term "birdbrain" is an arrogant, anthropocentric insult to an avian race that evolved more than 50 million years after the first mammals crept, crawled, and stood on the world's stage. And those bird brains have been evolving even more rapidly than mammalian brains ever since. Because the cognitive ability to think and learn was formerly assumed to lay in specific layers of brain cells within the cerebral cortex, birds—having no similar cortex—were believed to act only through instinct. However, modern brain researchers have discovered that bird brains have large clusters of nerve cells occupying the pallium, and that these cell clusters are equally responsible for reasoning, learning, and concentration.[1303] Magpies are the first non-mammals scientists found could recognize themselves in a mirror. Japanese psychologists found that they could teach pigeons to discriminate between the impressionistic paintings of Monet and the abstract works of Picasso.[1304] Some birds are known to play games in which they intentionally tell lies. However, the ancient symbol of wisdom, the owl (spotted or otherwise) ranks among the dumbest of our feathered friends.

The human brain is designed to look for differences as a way of discerning the features of the world—this is necessary for our survival. However, it also makes stereotyping a consistent and universal human trait. Noticing certain differences is unavoidable: your subconscious mind will automatically fix on the one feature or characteristic of the person or group that is different from what you are used to. Just as Caucasians find Asian eyes too slanted and narrow, Asians find Caucasian eyes too round. As soon as we notice some recognizably different feature about someone and

---

1301. Villarreal 2005.

1302. Susan Gaidos, "Humans Wonder, Anybody Home?: Brain Structure and Circuitry Offer Clues to Consciousness in Nonmammals," *Science News* 176(13), December 19, 2009, 22–25.

1303. Erich D. Jarvis, et al. "Avian Brains and a New Understanding of Vertebrate Brain Evolution," *Nature Reviews Neuroscience* 6(2), February 1, 2005, 151–159.

1304. Ann B. Butler, "Evolution of Brains, Cognition, and Consciousness," *Brain Research Bulletin* 75(2–4), March 18, 2008, 442–449.

see that the same trait appears in a group of people, we have the beginnings of a stereotype. All it takes is an emotional response—either negative or positive—and the stereotype is born. The "Muslim" racial category, for example, can be defined by a woman with a head scarf or a brown-skinned man with a beard. In reality, of course, Muslims include Chinese and African people, as well as women who do not wear head scarves.

Similarly, the Jewish people never existed as a "nation-race" with a common origin, but are a colourful mix of groups that at various stages in history adopted the Judaic faith. We have been taught that the Jews do not convert people, and this may be how it is today, but it was not always so. In fact, Judaism was the first proselytizing religion—this is why there are Jews everywhere in the world. The people did not spread, the Jewish religion did. Not only are the North African Jews mostly descendants of pagans who converted to Judaism, but so are the Jews of Yemen and the Ashkenazi of Eastern Europe. The common Jewish history as we know it was not written until the 19th century. The exile of the Jewish people was originally a Christian myth that depicted the event as divine punishment imposed on the Jews for having rejected Jesus. The Romans did not exile peoples and could not have done so even if they wanted to. They had no trains or trucks to deport entire populations—that kind of logistics did not exist until the 20th century.[1305] Apart from those who were taken as slaves to Rome, the Palestinian Jews actually converted gradually to Christianity or Islam. A malicious person might claim that the Palestinian Christians and Muslims are more closely related to the original Israeli Jews than the modern Jewish immigrants.

Yet, compared to other mammals, humans are a quite homogenous species. I am not saying that there are no differences between populations, skin colour being the most conspicuous. As we all know, the Nazis justified the death camps on the grounds that Jews and Gypsies were genetically inferior; what is less known is that the German National Socialist Party took their cue from eugenics legislation passed in the United States.[1306] Americans define race primarily by skin colour, but skin pigmentation is just one trait and it is no guarantee of genetic variation. The physical stereotypes of race—including eye shape, hair type, and skin pigment—reflect superficial differences. In earlier times, Irish, Italian, and Eastern European Jewish immigrants were not considered as whites. On the other hand, Hispanics were not counted separately by the census until the 1960s and Asian Indians used to be classified as whites.[1307] Second World War internment camps were erected for Asian Americans, not German Americans, although the latter constituted the largest immigrant group in the U.S. at the time. The patriotism of relatively few German or Italian Americans was ever questioned, whereas 120,000 Japanese Americans were rounded up and shipped off to camps.[1308]

1305. Sand 2009.

1306. Proctor, op. cit.

1307. Sam Roberts, "In a Generation, Minorities May Be the U.S. Majority," *New York Times*, August 13, 2008.

1308. Hixson 2008.

With the number of African immigrants in the U.S. tripling since the 1990s, the use of the term "African-American" is becoming increasingly strained.[1309] Modern America is home to millions of immigrants who were actually born in Africa. They have last names like Mbeki and Agbaje, and speak languages like Yoruba and Swahili. Meanwhile, American descendants of African slaves neither knew their African ancestors nor even have elder relatives who knew them. If they did, they would know that it was other Africans who sold them into slavery in the first place. The North African states also sent slave ships to Europe for three centuries to kidnap European Christians for their slave pens, because they were not allowed to enslave their fellow-Muslims. Between one and 1.25 million Europeans were taken into slavery over that period.[1310] Male captives were worked to death building palaces for the Sultans while women were sent to the rape pens known as "harems." This is why there are so many people with green eyes living in Morocco today. In fact, the French first invaded Algeria to put a stop to the Algerian-sponsored slave raids against Europe.

On a global scale, it is the white people who are the minority. What is more, most people of the world do not even see each other in terms of colour or race, but in term of family or tribe. South Africans growing up during Apartheid were basically born into a caste system. South Africa has several different tribes and just because you were black, another black person might not be considered equal to you. One black tribe thought themselves above another black tribe, the whites thought themselves above the black tribes, the blacks thought they were above the Indians, and the Indians thought themselves above the blacks—Apartheid was about far more than the colour of one's skin. The barriers that individuals use to separate themselves from the members of other ethnic groups are cultural, linguistic, religious, economic, and political. The issues of economic disparity have not changed since Apartheid ended: many white South Africans are leaving the country because they are targeted by black criminals and the post-Apartheid government does nothing to protect them. In 2009, one white man from South Africa was given refugee status in Canada after claiming persecution from black South Africans.[1311] And if the history of the country is studied, the appalling violence and hatred was not just white versus black, but largely black versus black. The greatest genocide of the 21st century, that of Rwanda, involved black people killing other black people. "African-American" cuisine is more southern U.S. than Senegalese and a working-class black man in Ohio has more in common with a working-class white man in Connecticut than with a Nigerian.

Even after the horrible lessons learned during the Holocaust, Germany still defines Germanness based on bloodlines. Russians of German descent, who speak no German but have the right genes, are thus able to acquire German citizenship far more easily than people of Turkish descent born in Germany, who speak fluent German and identify with German cultural practices. The whole concept of race could be dismissed on the simple basis that there is more genetic variation within populations

---

1309. McWhorter 2003.

1310. Davis 2003.

1311. Immigration and Refugee Board, Refugee Protection Division, #MA8-04910, August 27, 2009.

than between them.[1312] Ethnic groups are marked more by cultural than blood differences. Every person's DNA is a mosaic of segments that originated at various different times and places. Even if we should examine just a small village of Pygmies, they would show almost all the genetic variation catalogued in the world. "White people" do not share a common genetic heritage, but come from different lineages that migrated from Africa and Asia. Light skin colour is required in northern climes for the sun's ultraviolet rays to penetrate into the body. The mutation responsible for this may have arisen at different times, in different ancestral groups, and on different points along the DNA. I might be closer in my DNA to an African than to another European in the street and this is true for every race. Ultimately, all hominids came from Africa, so everyone in the U.S. should check the box next to "African-American" in their census forms.

Mitochondrial DNA shows that all humans living today descend from one maternal source—dubbed "Mitochondrial Eve"—who lived in East Africa between 100,000 and 200,000 years ago. Similarly, the Y chromosome reveals that all men have a common ancestor, "Y-chromosome Adam," who lived at approximately the same time. Both analyses indicate that modern humans descend from a small founding population of about 10,000 men and women. Since the mutation clocks of mitochondrial DNA and the Y chromosome tick at different speeds, the fact that they both indicate humans emerged at the same historical moment makes this evidence all the more convincing. Recent studies of ancient climate data further suggest that East Africa went through a series of massive droughts between 135,000 and 90,000 years ago; it is possible that the harsh environment and changing climate forced populations to migrate north in order to survive.

Inbreeding and the small original population of our ancestors might be the reason why we have so many hereditary diseases today. Man and chimp began to diverge from a common ancestor about 6 million years ago. Humans show much less genetic variation than do chimpanzees and gorillas. This is thought to stem from the fact that humanity has gone through several "population bottlenecks" in the course of its evolution. The fact that there will soon be 7 billion of us is not matter of course. There used to be fewer people in the world than there are nonhuman apes at present. A population of 10,000 individuals would not be considered viable today. There are, for example, about 21,000 chimps and 26,000 gorillas in the world at the moment and both species are deemed critically endangered. The number of early humans may have shrunk as low as 2,000 before numbers began to expand again in the Late Stone Age. In any case, ***Homo sapiens*** was probably on the verge of extinction before it started its migration from Africa to the other continents over 100,000 years ago. Each of us has at least 100 new mutations in our DNA, but due to our diminutive founding population, the elimination of the harmful varieties has been slow and difficult.

Research into mutations of DNA has revealed something quite surprising. Women seem to have always moved from tribe to tribe and clan to clan more often than men. In men, the changes in the Y chromosome are mostly regional.[1313] To make the

1312. Cavalli-Sforza 2000.

1313. Jobling, et al. 2003.

comparison, the geneticists studied the molecular clock. Almost all human cells contain tiny bacteria-like entities called mitochondria, which provide energy to the cells. They have their own DNA, separate from the DNA that actually makes a person. Since there are no mitochondria in sperm cells, they are inherited only from the mother. This means that each person actually inherits more genetic material from the mother's than the father's side, so surnames should really also come from the maternal side. In Europe, the genetic variation of women is greater than that of men, meaning that they have either voluntarily married into another village or been abducted by men from other villages. Men in Europe have a higher likelihood of having lived near the place in which they were born, prompting some geneticians to suggest that we should refer to "father tongue" rather than mother tongue.

Our looks mostly come from the father's side, since this is the only way to tell who our father is in lieu of DNA testing; our intelligence, on the other hand, comes largely from the mother's side, because intelligence is more important to the survival of the fairer sex. In fact, since an unusually large number of brain-related genes are situated on the X chromosome, Nobelist sperm banks are a brazen scam. There are other ways to propagate a species besides sex, but all the higher species reproduce sexually. Asexual reproduction reduces genetic diversity and this makes it harder for the organism to adapt—to changed environmental conditions or the emergence of a new disease, for example. Typically, when a species reproduces asexually, harmful changes creep into its genes over several generations. The species will eventually have problems reproducing at all and can often fall victim to extinction. With sexual reproduction, the mixing of maternal and paternal DNA introduces genetic novelty which can give the species new traits that might be advantageous in their new circumstances.

Like "START treaty" or "stupid idiot," the phrase "reproductive organ" is redundant —all organs are reproductive organs. Where do the wings of a bird come from? A bearded man in the sky who thinks that flying is really neat? No, the bird's wings are there because they contributed to the reproduction of its ancestors. So too the bird's heart, lungs, and genitals. At most, it might be practical to distinguish between directly reproductive organs and indirectly reproductive organs, and this observation holds true also of the human brain, the most complex organ system known to biology. Some of our brain functions are directly reproductive, like lust, while others are indirectly reproductive, like anger. Where does anger come from? The neural circuitry of anger is a reproductive organ as surely as a penis or a vagina. Anger exists in *Homo sapiens* simply because angry ancestors had more children—there is no other way it could be there.

Testosterone is what makes the sex drive in both men and women more aggressive. It is *the* sex hormone. It makes us want to have sex, pursue sex, initiate sex, and perhaps dominate the sex act. Women's sex drive is linked to testosterone levels just as men's. Testosterone is what motivates both sexes to strongly desire specific genital intercourse and release by orgasm.[1314] Without sexual reproduction, without death, there would be no need for aggression. Sex and violence are intrinsically linked. *This*

1314. Crenshaw 1997.

is the Fall of Man; only, Adam was created from Eve's "rib," not the other way around! Orson Welles explained it best: "If there hadn't been women we'd still be squatting in a cave eating raw meat, because we made civilization in order to impress our girl friends. And they tolerated it and let us go ahead and play with our toys."[1315] It is an old joke that all new technology is driven by porn: a big attraction for digital cameras was the ability to take bedroom photos without having to take film to the corner photo shop; similarly, the rapid spread of VHS and, later, DVD and Blu-ray sales is partly explained by the ability to watch adult movies without going to the local theatre.

Man is a sexual being—that is why there are two genders. (Well, actually more than two, but we will get to that later.) There are some advantages to asexual reproduction, because it avoids the energetic cost of producing males, and doubles the number of reproductive females produced each generation from 50% to 100%. Parthenogenesis is a type of reproduction that occurs when an egg cell is triggered to develop as an embryo without the addition of any genetic material from a male sperm cell. Literally Greek for "virgin birth," it occurs in a number of lower animals; insects such as ants and bees use it to produce drones, for example. However, while asexual reproduction of males from unfertilized eggs is a normal part of some insect reproduction, similar reproduction of females is exceedingly rare. Vertebrates in general have evolved away from parthenogenesis to boost genetic diversity and enhance evolutionary potential.

Yet it is often the case that males have to work very hard to convince females to mate with them. In most animal species, males have to put on elaborate courtship displays to impress females, and that includes even the tiny fruit fly: male fruit flies vibrate one of their wings to produce a barely audible song. Orson Welles hits the nail on the head again: "I think we're a kind of desperation. We're sort of a maddening luxury. The basic and essential human is the woman, and all that we're doing is trying to brighten up the place. That's why all the birds who belong to our sex have prettier feathers—because males have got to try and justify their existence."[1316] Nothing says "men need not apply" like a phial of mail-order sperm and a turkey-baster. In the absence of the shame historically attached to unwed motherhood, babies can now be custom-ordered without the muss and fuss of human intimacy.

What is happening today is important in the context of our continuing evolution as a species. Men's ability to read maps, lift heavy objects, and set the clock on the VCR makes them useful, and the female of the species tends to respond to the male who displays the most utility. The sole function of sperm is to fertilize the egg, as a reward for which it gets to contribute half of its genome to the resulting embryo. However, a group of scientists in Britain recently announced their intention to fertilize an egg without the use of sperm cells, using the genetic material from another egg instead. As Campbell Scott ranted in *Roger Dodger:* "The species is not static. We're in a constant state of flux. Two genders has been the default setting for one reason only: So far it's been the only way to propagate the race. . . .10 or 15

1315. McBride 1977, 52.

1316. Frost 1970, 32.

generations from now, men will be reduced to servitude. Technology and evolution will have combined to exclude sperm from procreation, and our final destiny will be to lift couches and wait for that day when telepathy overcomes gravity and our gender's last remaining utility is lost forever. Forever."[1317]

A female inherits one X chromosome from each parent, a male inherits an X chromosome from his mother and a Y chromosome from his father. But while scientists once believed that one of the X chromosomes in women was relatively passive in relation to the other, new research shows that there is enormous variation in the interactions between the two. It turns out that as many as 25% of the genes in the second X chromosome are active, meaning that as many as 300 genes may be activated differently among women than among men.[1318] In the light of modern science, the Y chromosome appears to have come about as a byproduct of the X, diverging from it hundreds of millions of years ago. The Y and the X still retain some completely identical genes. It was the divergence of the Y that gave birth to sex—and sex has proven to be an efficient way to survive and adapt. Almost all living animals, including sea anemones, worms, insects, fish, and humans, share the exact same gene involved in the production of sperm. This suggests the ability to produce sperm arose just once, about 600 million years ago, to be conserved through all subsequent animal evolution.

The Y chromosome has thrown out most of the genes it once had, and that the X still has, concentrating on what it does best, providing the recipe for making sperm. However, if the Y was destined to shrink further, some of the non-sperm genes that humans and chimps share on their Y chromosomes would have disappeared in the 6 million years since the two species diverged. Instead, all 16 of the non-sperm genes on the human Y have counterparts on the chimp chromosome.[1319] In all, man has at least 30,000 genes. The X-Y chromosome pair is unique in that its two halves are not even remotely similar in appearance or content, unlike the other 22 pairs. The X chromosome contains as many as 1,500 genes, whereas the Y only has 78. All embryos start out as female, and the body of a developing foetus only becomes male if the male-determining gene known as SRY is present. The Y chromosome's proudest and almost only possession, this dominant gene turns the reproductive tissue from its ovarian course and switches it into becoming testes. It is the testes and their Leydig cells that take care of the rest with hormones: puberty, sperm, and body hair.

It is the Y chromosome that is ultimately responsible for the angry male hormone, testosterone, whereas a woman is much more deeply affected by hormonal surges that fluctuate throughout her life. However, as men age, the testosterone-estrogen balance does start to shift, with testosterone decreasing and estrogen increasing, which partly explains why so many men seem to mellow out as they get older.[1320] The brains of all

1317. Dir. Dylan Kidd. Artisan Entertainment, 2002.

1318. Laura Carrel & Huntington F. Willard, "X-Inactivation Profile Reveals Extensive Variability in X-Linked Gene Expression in Females," *Nature* 434(7031), March 17, 2005, 400–404.

1319. Jennifer F. Hughes, et al. "Conservation of Y-Linked Genes During Human Evolution Revealed by Comparative Sequencing in Chimpanzee," *Nature* 437(7055), September 1, 2005, 100–103.

1320. Crenshaw, op. cit.

foetuses appear "feminine" prior to the testosterone surges that cause the masculine features of the male embryos.[1321] A wealth of research in the last ten or fifteen years have underlined the fact that the human brain is a full-fledged sex organ in the sense that the two sexes have profoundly different versions of it.[1322] However, the differences in adult brains do not seem to affect IQ test results and even the differences between mathematical skills only appear with puberty, again probably because of testosterone. This hormone is also the reason why men are so prone to start fights for little or no reason at the hot-dog stand and in the hockey rink—the male equivalent of "three irrational days a month."

Whereas women often find it difficult to counter aggression, when men push back, it earns them the respect of other men. This also applies to verbal duelling: many men find that their adrenaline gets going when someone challenges them; it sharpens their minds, making them think more clearly and get better ideas. The male of the species thrives under competition and is driven to improve his rank in whatever hierarchy he is in. His bravado is fed in his teenage years when a massive increase in testosterone makes him perceive other people's faces as more hostile than friendly.[1323] But the reaction is different for those who are not biologically inclined to this mode of exchanging ideas, including most women: feeling attacked, they back off, and simply do not do their best thinking under those circumstances. "Manliness seeks and welcomes drama and prefers times of war, conflict, and risk."[1324] It entails assertiveness, even stubbornness, and explains why men, who are naturally inclined to assert that "our policy and our party is better than yours," continue to dominate in the political sphere.

This is also one of the main reasons why many women who are talented and passionate about science drop out of the profession. It is not that they are not fascinated by the discipline, or that they would lack the talent to come up with new ideas, but that they are put off by the competitive, cut-throat culture of science. The assumption that arguing is the only way to explore ideas is deeply rooted in Western civilization. It is to be found in the patriarchal roots of the Christian Church and an educational system that traces back to the all-male universities of the Middle Ages where students learned by oral disputation. To even things out, girls get better grades than boys and are much more likely to graduate from high school, go to college, and get a degree. Boys, on the other hand, are much more likely to get in trouble or be labelled as learning disabled. In fact, boys are five times as likely as girls to receive a diagnosis of attention-deficit hyperactivity disorder. Boys are far more likely than girls to be disciplined, suspended, held back, or expelled. Girls are much better

---

1321. John A. Morris, et al. "Sexual Differentiation of the Vertebrate Nervous System," *Nature Neuroscience* 7(10), October 2004, 1034–1039.

1322. Larry Cahill, "Why Sex Matters in Neuroscience," *Nature Reviews Neuroscience* 7(6), June 2006, 477–484.

1323. Brizendine 2010.

1324. Mansfield 2006, ix.

disposed to sit still and follow instructions.[1325]

From the first day of school, an average boy is already developmentally two years behind the girls in reading and writing, yet he is usually expected to learn the same things in the same way and in the same amount of time. Boys have less of the "calming chemical" serotonin and more testosterone, making them more fidgety and impulsive. While every nerve in their bodies tell them to run, they have to keep quiet and listen for almost eight hours a day. Boys' brains also go more frequently into a "rest state," leading to "zoning out" or moving around to try and stay focused. Biologically, a boy needs about four recesses a day, but he is lucky if he gets one, since many lawsuit-wary schools have banned them altogether. Should he hug a girl, he could be labelled a "toucher" and be suspended—a result of what some believe is an increasingly anti-boy culture that pathologizes their natural behaviour.[1326] According to U.S. education statistics, boys are 2.5 times more likely to be suspended from school and 3.4 times more likely to be expelled.[1327] If a boy falls behind, he is apt to be moved to special ed, where he will find that more than 70% of his classmates are also boys.[1328] It is out of manliness that even grown men do not like to ask for directions when lost. Women look after themselves from the age of eleven, because they start to bleed, while men, short of serious accidents or health crises, are traditionally no-shows at the doctor's office. Women early on establish a lifelong pattern of paying attention to their bodies, including regular check-ups, preventive screenings, and actually listening to medical advice.[1329]

Since 1970, American women's undergraduate enrollment in college has risen three times as fast as men's, and women now make up 57% of U.S. college students.[1330] By 2009, women also earned a majority of doctoral degrees in the United States. By field of study, women receiving doctorates outnumbered men in six of the eleven graduate fields: Arts and Humanities, Biology, Education, Health Sciences, Public Administration, and Social Studies. Men still outnumbered women in fields like Engineering (78.4%), Math and Computer Science (73.2%), and Physical Sciences (66.6%).[1331] Back in the 1990s, the Clinton administration began to enforce Title IX of the Civil Rights Act in a new way. Colleges were required to have an equal male-to-female ratio in their sports programs as in their student bodies. Athletic directors tried to get more women to go out for sports, but most colleges failed to scare up enough

1325. Sarah O. Meadows, et al. "Assessing Gilligan vs. Sommers: Gender-Specific Trends in Child and Youth Well-Being in the United States, 1985–2001," *Social Indicators Research* 70(1), January 2005, 1–52.

1326. Michelle Conlin, "The New Gender Gap: From Kindergarten to Grad School, Boys Are Becoming the Second Sex," *Business Week*, May 23, 2003.

1327. Gurian & Stevens 2005.

1328. Conlin, op. cit.

1329. Sebastian Kraemer, "The Fragile Male," *British Medical Journal* 321(7276), December 23, 2000, 1609–1612.

1330. Gurian & Stevens, op. cit.

1331. Nathan E. Bell, "Graduate Enrollment and Degrees: 1999 to 2009," Council of Graduate Schools, Washington, D.C., 2010.

female athletes and were forced to terminate men's teams instead.[1332] At the same time, of course, Title IX refuses to acknowledge cheerleading as a sport, although it produces twice as many athletic injuries as the next ten most dangerous college sports combined.[1333] Female co-eds have higher GPAs than male co-eds, and one would think that lagging at schoolwork was more serious than lagging at playground participation. Unfortunately, male students are not accustomed to viewing themselves as a gender; to realizing that they are subject to certain societal pressures just because they are men. There will be no calls for government studies on the gender gap in graduate school enrollment, or increased government funding to address the problem, and nobody will refer to it as a "crisis."

Men and women are equal, but they are also very different both physically and emotionally. All in all, men and women may differ by as much as 2% of their entire genetic inheritance—to put this figure in perspective, the hereditary gap between *Homo sapiens* and its closest relative, the chimpanzee, is only 1%. Small differences in the genotype can result in big differences in the phenotype: humans have 99% of active genes in common with the chimpanzee and no-one is claiming that humans and chimps are even the same species. Because of that 1% difference, humans now dominate every ecosystem on the planet, while chimps and other great apes are on the verge of extinction.[1334] The human female's care in selecting mates, combined with the quick selection made possible by men's lack of a back-up X chromosome, may have driven the divergence between male and female brains. Women are not just small men with different plumbing and hormone problems; there are differences pretty much everywhere scientists have looked, in all the physiological systems of the body.[1335] The "sex" of donor tissue actually influences how it is received by the patient's immune system, so men who get cells from a female donor are at an increased risk of dangerous "graft-versus-host" disease, while women who get "male" cells are more likely to reject them.[1336] From hearts to brains, from livers to intestines, from skin to blood, and from chromosomes to cells, the vast and fascinating differences between the two sexes are only slowly being understood.

It is not surprising that the rebellion against the sexual stereotypes of patriarchal society has sometimes fallen into the trap of denying that there is *any* difference between man and woman, besides the "purely anatomical" ones. This is a completely forgivable reaction to being told that you are "unsuitable" for some or other profession —usually an influential or well-paid one—just because you are a woman. It is also forgivable in cases where a woman actually *is* a sound professional in some male-dominated field, but has difficulty in being taken seriously, because she happens to be

1332. David Gelernter, "Inequality, by the Numbers: Don't Fight Bigotry with Stats and Ratios," *Los Angeles Times*, June 10, 2005.

1333. "Catastrophic Sports Injury Research: Twenty-Sixth Annual Report," National Center for Catastrophic Injury Research, University of North Carolina, Chapel Hill, NC, Spring 2008.

1334. Tarjei S. Mikkelsen, et al. "Initial Sequence of the Chimpanzee Genome and Comparison with the Human Genome," *Nature* 437(7055), September 2005, 69–87.

1335. Wizemann & Pardue 2001.

1336. Alois Gratwohl, et al. "H-Y as a Minor Histocompatibility Antigen in Kidney Transplantation: A Retrospective Cohort Study," *The Lancet* 372(9632), July 5–11, 2008, 49–53.

sexually attractive. But understandable or not, the unisex stereotypes are just as dangerous and distorting as the patriarchal ones, because there *are* basic differences between the male and female natures—the most obvious difference being that every woman is potentially or actually a child-bearer. In fact, this is basically the only difference which patriarchy regards as important. It says a great deal about the power of hormones that, in spite of these stereotypes, so many millions of men and women have managed to achieve happy sexual partnerships.

If you are a woman and have ever complained that your man does not "get" you, it may surprise you to discover that you do not get him either. The male brain is a lean, mean, problem-solving machine, which is why the man in your life tries to solve your problems rather than listening attentively while you vent. Techniques for imaging the brain show that men and women use their brains in different ways even when they are doing the same thing. When faced with a personal problem, a man uses his analytical brain structures, instead of his emotional ones, to find a solution—and it is frustrating to him when his partner does not let him try to help in this way. The male brain area for sexual pursuit is 2.5 times larger than the one in the female brain, so a man cannot stop his desire any more than a woman can stop wanting to talk or cuddle. A woman feels like a man loves her when he listens to her and wants to spend time with her, but a man feels like a woman loves him when she has sex with him and enjoys it.[1337]

Double standards for genders are perfectly valid, if only because men cannot bear children. However, since the early 1990s, the public discourse on gender, youth, and education has been largely set by feminist academics and activists. Well, I am not a feminist, mostly because I support equality. You can say that society puts pressure on women to take care of the family and raise the children, and that is not fair. But society also puts pressure on men to be the provider and to make good money and be successful, and that is not fair either. Yet the feminists argue that a woman should be able to have a successful career *and* a good family life, that the State should provide some social service for the children to be taken care of while she dedicates herself to work. Over 90% of the people who die at work are men—does this mean that men are socially oppressed? No, this is because men are physically stronger and take more risks, and they become construction workers and firemen.[1338]

Women's rights activists have already made it possible for women to train themselves as plumbers and for men to become nurses—is this not equality? Universal male suffrage resulted in compulsory military service, but universal suffrage seems to only have resulted in free daycare. It is a woman's instinct to raise children and take care of the sick and elderly; that has been their role for nearly all of human history, pre-history, and even before we evolved into *Homo sapiens*. When women were given the right to vote, they naturally used their vote to demand that the government help them in their main historic role—and they got their demands since politicians wanted their vote. One prominent Finnish feminist recently argued that daycare is not even a right, but the basis for women to participate equally in life and society. Of

1337. Brizendine, op. cit.

1338. Al-Tuwaijri, et al. Op cit.

course, "most propaganda is not designed to fool the critical thinker, but only to give moral cowards an excuse not to think at all."[1339]

As women have entered the work force, both unemployment and prices have risen considerable. Americans used to be able to buy new cars, vacation homes, and raise a family on one salary. Today, more than 70% of U.S. mothers work outside the home, compared to less than 40% in the 1970s, and that is often still not enough to pay the mortgage.[1340] As the famous social critic and "dissident feminist" Camille Paglia attests, by "getting women out of the kitchen and into the office, we have simply put them in another bourgeois prison."[1341] A recent report from the Bureau of Labor Statistics has some dire information of what went on between 2000 and 2005 in the U.S. economy. American women are apparently not only taking more than half of the new jobs created, but their jobs are absolutely necessary to the survival of the family.[1342] Four out of five U.S. couples are dual-earner couples today, and women in dual-earner households contribute about 44% of the family income, up from 39% in 1977. Their jobs still tend to be lower-paid jobs, but the biggest growth in the economy is exactly among these lower-paid jobs.[1343]

There has been "a massive change in our way of life."[1344] The generations working today work anywhere from 10 to 15 hours more per week than any prior generation, yet it now takes two people to make one living. There are still a few stay-at-home mothers, but they tend to be either on maternity leave, childcare leave, unemployed, or even retired, because one salary is no longer enough to support a family. Women's employment itself has meant new costs, from daycare through extra cars to more meals out. At the same time, young women's sexual behaviour and alcohol consumption are getting closer and closer to those of young men.[1345] The work pressures of today's 25- to 40-year-old women seem to lead to the same type of behaviour that was once thought to be characteristic of men. In his 1970s bestseller, *A Nation of Strangers*, Vance Packard depicted the United States as "a society that is coming apart at the seams."[1346] He was only one in a long line of futurists who predicted an America of ever-increasing "spatial mobility" that would give rise to weaker families, childlessness, and anonymous communities.

In earlier generations, extended networks helped American families withstand the

---

1339. Michael Rivero, *WhatReallyHappened.com.*

1340. Peter G. Gosselin, "If America Is Richer, Why Are Its Families So Much Less Secure?" *Los Angeles Times*, October 10, 2004.

1341. 1994, ix.

1342. Marlene A. Lee & Mark Mather, "U.S. Labor Force Trends," Population Reference Bureau, Washington, D.C., June 2008.

1343. Ellen Galinsky, et al. "Times Are Changing: Gender and Generation at Work and at Home," Families and Work Institute, New York, August 2011.

1344. "A Good Childhood: Searching for Values in a Competitive Age," The Children's Society, London, February 2009.

1345. Mark A. Bellis, et al. "Sexual Uses of Alcohol and Drugs and the Associated Health Risks: A Cross Sectional Study of Young People in Nine European Cities," *BMC Public Health* 8, May 2008, 155.

1346. 1972, 2.

dislocations of the westward expansion or of immigration. The ever expanding chain of relocations in the endless attempt to get a bigger apartment, the insecurity of short-term jobs, and the growing length of generations have led to the parents of small children not having any help from their family or neighbours. Mothers in particular have reached the limit in balancing between housework, childcare, and their jobs. On the other hand, all problems with children's growth and development are far too easily blamed on the lack of maternal care. Many with children work because they have to; others stay home because they have to. Many work and wish they did not have to; others do not work and wish they could. Many work part time or do one thing and then another. What ever happened to parenting support and societal responsibility? Never before in history has society demanded that a healthy, working-age adult withdraw from the community to raise her children by herself until they go to school.

It might not take a village to raise a child, but for the longest time, the village did raise the children. There were no more single parents than there were nuclear families. In the past, the knowledge and experience required to raise and educate children were passed on down through generations within families and communities, resulting in there being a recognizable tradition of child rearing almost everywhere in history. These traditions were based on the experience of millions of parents over many centuries, but the last few decades have seen an interruption of these traditions. I am not one to romanticize the 1950s, but back in those days, women still had sewing circles. Every door was open and people actually felt responsible for other people's children. Today, no-one would think of going next door for a cup of tea or to discuss a personal problem. You have to coordinate your schedules and meet at a park or a restaurant. There is none of the fluid interchange of aid and support that previous generations of mothers had.

The women of Western Europe have long ago surpassed men in their level of formal education. Women make up the majority in universities and are also better students than men. So should the length of one's education show in one's pay? It is easy to think that "in the name of fairness" it should, but no employer hires people as a reward for education, and different fields of education simply yield different results. Women's recent academic achievements have not greatly increased their number in leading positions in business or society. Men in the West continue to earn more than women—approximately $1 for every 75 cents that women make in the United States. But after accounting for different job choices, hours worked, and time taken off to raise children, economists such as June O'Neill and Claudia Goldin have concluded that it is these factors, not discrimination, that account for most of the difference.[1347]

The fact is that men have traditionally shouldered the more onerous and dangerous jobs, including entrepreneurship and national defence, which is also why men have risen to powerful positions in society. I am sure that many women would be perfectly suitable for these positions, but how many of them would really even want these kind of jobs? Yet the pay gap between men and women is used to justify so-called "positive discrimination" in favour of women, for example by demanding that public companies

1347. June O'Neill, "The Gender Gap in Wages, circa 2000," *The American Economic Review* 93(2), May 2003, 309–314; Goldin 1990.

institute female quotas in their boards of directors. Almost half of the corporations listed on the Helsinki Stock Exchange have no female board members at all. They do not have a single female president between them. The state-owned entities, on the other hand, are required by the Finnish government to have at least 40% of women on their boards.[1348]

It is easy to hire secretaries—sorry, administrative assistants—who do not intend to make the job their life's work, but it not as easy to promote people up the corporate ladder who do not. It is not ability or discrimination that hold women back, but the impossibility of making a full-time commitment to both work and family in a culture that not only demands 80-hour weeks, but is unusually obsessed with children as well. Girls continue to be given the impression that getting married and having children is more important for women than for men, and that these things are something to aim for in lieu of a career. Of course, women also have some practical problems due to pregnancy, but the greatest problem is in their own heads—they have a guilty conscience for wanting to work when they have a toddler at home.

Indeed, there are only two sorts of working mothers: ones that feel guilty at work for neglecting their children and ones that feel guilty at home for neglecting their work. Each path has both benefits and costs for the children, but it is impossible to answer whether one path is "better" in the abstract. However, a recent study of a thousand 3rd to 12th graders asked: "If you were granted one wish that would change the way that your mother's work affects your life, what would that wish be?" At the same time, another study asked mothers to guess what their children would wish for. This is what they found: "Most mothers (56%) guessed that their children would wish for more time with them. In fact, only 10% of children made that wish. Their most frequent wish: 'I want my mom to be less stressed and tired' (34%)."[1349]

According to a recent analysis of U.S. census data, women in their twenties actually out-earn coeval men in NYC, Boston, Chicago, Dallas, and several other big cities. These women have more education than their male peers and are less likely to be married and raising a family than their suburban female counterparts.[1350] Can we thus assume that everyone who wants and is qualified to hold a leading position will achieve that position? For both men and women, this takes a lot of work and even then, that goal is not always reached. However, entrepreneurship and managership are more often the goals of men than of women. The overwhelming majority of women work a few years and then take a large portion of their productive years to raise children, after which they may or may not return to the labour force. As a result, they tend to seek the type of work that does not require a long-term commitment to a career.

Surveys show that for every woman who wants to be a politician, there are 8 to 10 men who want that job. Obviously, there will always be more male than female politicians, since so few women want to be in politics. Often female politicians are

---

1348. "Government Report on Gender Equality," Ministry of Social Affairs and Health, Helsinki, 2010.

1349. Galinsky 1999.

1350. Sam Roberts, "For Young Earners in Big City, a Gap in Women's Favor," *New York Times*, August 3, 2007.

promoted for being women, because the system needs them since half of the voters are female. A British sociologist, Catherine Hakim, recently found that out of 3,700 working-age women she surveyed, about a third were fully focused on their jobs, about a third were fully focused on their families, and about a third wanted a mix of the two—meaning that they took the sort of jobs that do not lead to fast-track promotion.[1351] If these numbers stay the same, there will never be a 50/50 split between men and women at the highest professional or managerial levels in any field. The ratio will always remain around two to one.

Men are more vocal at demanding raises, more interested in promotions, and have more experience than women, if the latter have spent two years taking care of their children. Never-married women, who do not have children, tend to earn more than married women or women who have children, and in fact, never-married women earn on average more than never-married men.[1352] These roles explain the alleged disparities between male and female salaries. We live in a market economy and this is a free country—everyone has the right to choose their own profession and place of employment. Managerial positions are not conducive to married life, or more precisely, to parental life, and many women who could have these jobs opt not to pursue them. Pair-bonding mechanisms also influence what kind of jobs people take, and they are monstrously unequal. Leadership, or power, is an important quality in men, but even the best male models make only a fraction of what female supermodels do.

The potential for upward mobility for attractive lower-class girls is enormous, infinitely more so than for lower-class men. A good salary does not mean just a livelihood for men: a man's salary and status are of fundamental importance to his ability to find a mate. The men with the lowest income are left without a spouse more often than the others. A respected position and high pay are consequently sought after even by the men who do not much care about these things. At the same time, women usually try to find a job that they like doing, rather than one that pays well. In a man's list of happiness priorities, work comes both first—his pay—and second—his career; for a woman, work comes a distant third and even then in the form of job satisfaction. Whether by reason of biological wiring or social conditioning, most women are simply not willing to give up as much of family life as leadership positions inevitably demand. Highly educated women come third in a Finnish happiness survey. Their happiness stems from a successful partnership, good health, and a satisfying job.[1353]

Do women want to see the pay in female-dominated fields raised just because so many women work in them? That would not be equality. We are often told that nurses are not valued enough, but neither are firemen or paramedics. The idea that one's wage could be determined on basis of how "important" the work is sounds a lot

---

1351. "Lifestyle Preferences as Determinants of Women's Differentiated Labor Market Careers," *Work and Occupations* 29(4), November 2002, 428–459.

1352. "Women Making Significant Financial Gains," Employment Policy Foundation, Washington, D.C., April 2, 2002.

1353. Liisa Martikainen, "Suomalaisten nuorten aikuisten elämään tyytyväisyyden monet kasvot," *Jyväskylä Studies in Education, Psychology and Social Research* 287, 2006.

like incomes policy to me. In the age of global free markets, no salary can be too far from supply and demand, apart from certain exceptions that stem from a particularly strong bargaining position—as in the case of commercial pilots who can bring air traffic to a halt just like that—or a particularly weak bargaining position—as in the case of nurses who simply cannot strike very efficiently. Nations that provide universal health care from the public purse cannot afford to have nurses earn astronomical wages. In a market economy, wage levels are not and cannot be determined on the basis that some feminists think the job in question is equally "demanding" as a better paid profession. If everyone rushed to become engineers, supply and demand would lower the engineers' pay and the interest to become an engineer. In the real world, however, not everyone has the talent or motivation for the job.

What if the die-hard feminists are right, and men and women are really born exactly alike? In that case, there is no sense in advocating pay hikes in female-dominated professions in the name of equality. If there truly are no male or female professions, the issue is solved when women take jobs in better paid fields, that is, after having been liberated from the ideological notion of "female jobs." For some reason, the pay-gap debate is dominated by the idea that one's salary somehow measures one's "value to society." It does not, because society does not determine our wages. What people earn is determined by the supply and demand of labour and the added value that the employee provides to the employer. When a field has "value to society," it only lowers the wages in that field, because it makes more people seek jobs in the field, thereby raising the supply and lowering the demand. When the status and rewards of a job are such that people are only willing to do it for money, the employer will have to pay a little extra in order to recruit enough workers.

Men are, in general, paid a little more even for the same jobs, but should we immediately assume that this is because of discrimination? If you look at some other statistics, you will see that this is not necessarily the case. Firstly, men work more hours per week than women in the same jobs; depending on the industry and also on the country, male workers put in 3 to 8 hours a week more than female workers. Secondly, women take more days off than men; they have to choose between caring for a family at home or maximizing their career opportunities in a workplace that measures performance by the number of hours put in. Thirdly, and largely for the same reasons, men tend to take more risks and work in more hazardous situations than women in the same line of work.[1354] Should the average wages of women rise to the same level as men's, women would actually become wealthier than men. Women get money not only from their employer, but from men. As a result, women's standard of living and level of education are higher than one would deduce from just a pay comparison.

Women also live longer, and thus collect Social Security and pensions longer. Widows also tend to inherit valuable property and even while the husband is alive, his income invariably benefits his wife. As far as I can tell, women are very much in charge of household spending. Men may earn more, but women spend more.

1354. Elaine L. Chao & Philip L. Rones, "Women in the Labor Force: A Databook," U.S. Department of Labor, Washington, D.C., September 2007.

Advertisers certainly know this, and the people who lay out the shopping malls clearly know this as well. Admitting the differences between men and women is not chauvinism, just like admitting the differences between ethnicities is not racism; what constitutes chauvinism or racism is treating a person differently just because of their sex or race—this happens when we institute positive discrimination. During both the First and the Second World War, Jews were overrepresented in the U.S. military relative to their number in the population. So did the military discriminate against Gentiles? No, prejudice obviously ran exactly the other way. Numbers tell us absolutely nothing unless we understand the underlying social context.[1355]

The number of homosexuals discharged from the U.S. military under the "Don't Ask, Don't Tell" (DADT) policy dropped significantly every year since the Afghanistan and Iraq conflicts began, until President Obama was finally forced to repeal the whole policy in 2011. It was the Second World War that brought women into the industrial workforce for the first time. Before the War, industrial work was a man's job, but in some wartime shipyards, 40% of the workers were women.[1356] Since then, the average hours worked per week in all jobs has increased for women, but not for men. American women worked significantly more hours in 2008 than in 1977—40 hours and 43 hours, respectively—while the average work hours per week remained steady at 48 hours for men.[1357] If women were just as productive as men in the same jobs and are paid significantly less for the same work, why would anyone hire men? Why would any business-owner whose goal is to make a profit be willing to pay more money to get the same results? Employers who keep paying below a person's marginal product will only hurt themselves by losing their best workers and thereby lowering profits. If women continue to have lower pay and poorer jobs even after correcting for maternal leaves, then the reason for this must be that their marginal productivity is, on the average, lower than men's. I have no argument with the principle of equal pay for equal work. However, I find it intellectually dishonest to claim that wage equality is the key to equality in general.

There are fundamental differences between men and women that have been shaped over millennia of evolution. For one, men and women think differently—brain scans prove this, as does plenty of other research. On average, women gather more data, consider the context, sympathize with others, and think more long-term. Men, on the other hand, are more focused, think linearly, focus on rules and the short term. You can blame the difference on testosterone. In the ages past, men tended to be the hunters and needed to focus; women, in contrast, had a much broader field of responsibilities, which included bringing up children and picking the plants. Double-income families are not a modern invention: in prehistoric times, double incomes were the norm, with women putting 60–80% of the food on the table; in Africa and Asia, women still grow 80% of the crops. However, following the invention of the plough and the resulting need for hard manual labour, the balance of power shifted. Only since the World Wars have women re-entered the Western workforce and

---

1355. Gelernter, op. cit.

1356. Honey 1984.

1357. Galinsky, et al. Op. cit.

begun to regain their status in our society.[1358]

Women have constituted a growing share of the once heavily male workforce for nearly a century, with big bumps in their favour during epochal events like the Great Depression and the Second World War. In fact, women are now on the verge of outnumbering men in the American workforce for the first time in history. This historic reversal is caused not only by long-term changes in women's roles, but also by the massive job losses men suffered during the latest recession. The only parts of the U.S. economy that are still growing—health care, education, and government—have traditionally had a female majority. And that dominance has only increased because federal stimulus funding has directed money to precisely these fields.[1359] American men are doing worse than American women in several walks of life: men make up, for example, the majority of prisoners, homeless, long-term unemployed, victims of violent crime, and disenfranchised youth.[1360] The U.S. Postal Service is cutting tens of thousands of blue-collar jobs dominated by men, while new hires are expanding in teaching and other fields dominated by college-educated women. According to the Bureau of Labor Statistics, state and local governments have cut 86,000 men from payrolls during the recession, while adding 167,000 women.[1361]

The problem is not in the biological differences of men and women any more than in wage discrimination, but rather in the upbringing of girls and the role given to women by society. Dress, grooming, dating, courtship, contraception, and abortion patterns were fanatically conventionalized in tribal and feudal societies. Our core identities are based on gender; however, gender roles—viz. the "Whore" and the "Madonna"—are Christian and Western. In Thailand, home to a petite, from-a-Western-point-of-view feminine-looking people, an estimated 10–15% of children identify as transgendered; this small East Asian country carries out more sex-change operations than any other nation in the world.[1362] The number of gay people is probably the same there as in other countries, but because Thai society and culture tend to be very soft and very sweet, the male homosexuals tend to be transgender. Personally, I blame it on all the tofu in their diet.

The first question asked about a newborn baby is its sex. From day one, boys are dressed in blue and girls in pink; children are taught at kindergarten what boys and girls are supposed to be like. If a four-year-old boy knows any truths to be self-evident, it is that pink is for girls. He is not born with this notion, but after a lifetime of seeing girls swaddled in pink, dressed in pink, dragging around pink dolls, riding pink tricycles, and sleeping in little pink bedrooms, the connection is hard to miss. Gender identity provides us with the most basic guide as to how we relate to others, while it also affects the way in which we experience ourselves and our own gender

---

1358. Helen Fisher, "Female/Male Mind: Capitalizing on the Male and Female Minds to Grow the Bottom Line," World Economic Forum, Davos, January 25, 2008.

1359. Dennis Cauchon, "Women Taking Over Job Marker," *USA Today*, September 2, 2009.

1360. Farrell 1993.

1361. Cauchon, op. cit.

1362. Sam Winter, "Thai Transgenders in Focus: Demographics, Transitions and Identities," *International Journal of Transgenderism* 9(1), 2006, 15–27.

identity. When we can clearly tell who is a man and who is a woman, we know how to relate to each other; when gender identity is ambiguous in someone else, it challenges our conception of who we are ourselves. Even homosexuals, transvestites, and transsexuals usually have a clear sense of their own gender identity, even if it does not correspond to what they look like—what is intolerable to our minds is gender ambiguity.

However, our society is still clinging to the Victorian dress code. No ancient civilization anywhere dressed its men in trousers and shirts. And what is with the notion that men should not have long hair? This is a relatively new phenomenon. Free men have worn their hair long for most of recorded history. During the 17th and 18th centuries, it was also fashionable for men to decorate their hair. Conversely, slaves, soldiers, sailors, and other "workers" have traditionally had closely cropped haircuts in contradistinction to free men. Egyptian and Aztec men even wore make-up, and not just war-paint like the Celts. There is only one era in world history besides our own when short hair on men was in vogue: in the Roman Empire, free men had short hair to distinguish them from the long-haired barbarians—that is, everyone else. However, for the last thousand years of the Empire, even the Romans wore their hair long. The hairstyles of European men only changed with the Industrial Revolution over the course of the 19th century. It was thought that long hair would get in the way of working in factories, offices, and other industrial settings. When men's military service became compulsory in the West during the 20th century, long hair was considered unsoldierlike. Women, on the other hand, were not allowed to wear knickers for the longest time, since any kinds of pants were considered strictly male attire; in fact, wearing men's clothing was one of the crimes that got Joan of Arc burned at the stake.

Although the terms "sex" and "gender" are often used interchangeably, there are crucial distinctions. Strictly speaking, sex is the classification of living things generally as male or female according to their reproductive organs and the way that the X and Y chromosomes are organized. While the majority of people conform to what is thought of as male (male genitalia with XY chromosomes) or female (female genitalia with XX chromosomes) there is actually a sizeable portion of the populations that does not.[1363] There are women with XY chromosomes, and people with genitalia that is not easily classified as either male or female. However, a "true" hermaphrodite, i.e. an organism born with a complete set of male and female reproductive organs, only exists among other species such as the earthworm. The lines of gender, on the other hand, get blurry around the edges, and involve a person's self-image and how that person is responded to by society based on the way the person presents him or herself.

Gender is not as binary as people are brought up to think, and the assignment of gender identity is something that is conferred and constructed, rather than simply a biological given. It is, of course, rooted in biology, but also shaped by environment and experience. Cosmetic surgery cannot change sex—men still will not be able to bear children and women still will not be able to ejaculate. Yet the relative simplicity of the three-and-a-half-hour procedure illustrates the physical similarities between

---

1363. M. Blackless, et al. "How Sexually Dimorphic Are We?: Review and Synthesis," *American Journal of Human Biology* 12(2), March 2000, 151–166.

the two sexes. The biggest complaint of the Thai "ladyboys" is that they cannot change their legal status.[1364] Spain allows transsexuals who have not had a gender-realignment operation to nevertheless alter their gender on birth certificates and other documents. In fact, only a third of Spanish transsexuals opt for this kind of surgery, but if they do not otherwise look like the sex on their identification, they face ridicule, discrimination, and unemployment.[1365] However, unlike Western and East Asian transsexual women, *hijras* of South Asia generally do not attempt to pass as females. Research shows that other animals engage, for example, in bondage, polygamy, group sex, homosexuality, and sex with inanimate objects, but no study has yet found another animal that engages in cross-dressing.

Feminism is predicated on patriarchalism. The patriarchy and chauvinistic views permeate absolutely everything in our culture and society, including the feminist movement. One glaring example is the fact that Christian Churches call their female clergy "women priests" rather than priestesses, like all the ancient pagan religions did. I continue to be perplexed by women fighting for the right to be Catholic priests. The entire faith and its textbooks are so sexist that it seems as crazy as Jews fighting for the right to join a Nazi party. Of course, it is amazing how many Jewish neo-Nazis there are! Is it not gender discrimination to not treat a woman as a woman, but to try and make her more like a man in order for her to be appreciated? Gender roles can, at best, be liberating. Everyone should be free to choose their own role, whether that involves being the complete opposite of their traditional gender role or its full manifestation.

Since times immemorial, it has been customary for male divinities to be served mainly by male clerics and celebrants, and for female deities to be served by priestesses. Even the divinities invoked in ancient oaths were divided by sex, with men calling on gods and women calling on goddesses. Verily, God is not a "She," but then again, feminists are not interested in returning to matriarchy, but having a patriarchy with women in the male roles. Male devotees of the Great Goddess Cybele were required to actually castrate themselves, and in the figurative sense, the modern feminists are doing the same thing to themselves. Just like a male chauvinist uses the terms that most degrade femininity, the female chauvinists use similar terms about men. There is no fundamental difference between being called a wanker on a public forum such as the internet or being called a whore on Hollywood Boulevard—both are predicated on Christian, or patriarchal, sexual morality.

In mainline Christian tradition, Eve is the counterpart of the Devil. Her crime, like the Devil's, is disobedience to God. She dared to exercise her own will, embrace her sexual power, and initiate her boyfriend, Adam. The eating of the fruit and acknowledgement of sexuality was the ultimate act of rebellion against the *status quo* and its allegedly divine upholder, Yahweh. Most modern-day feminists sacrifice their feminine natures, and thereby their true power, in a quest for "equal rights." Professional women in particular are quickly becoming "equal," that is, alienated from their own bodies and souls. Women's basic nature is stifled at the workplace, but men

---

1364. Winter, op. cit.

1365. "Spain Eases Law for Transsexuals," BBC News, March 1, 2007.

suffer as well, because they must close their eyes at the sight of a sexy woman, repressing their natural instincts for fear of sexual harassments suits. We are told that boys today no longer have male role models, when in fact, it seems to me that girls are the ones who lack female role models. The modern woman, who kicks men in the groin while spewing out obscenities, does not exactly qualify as one. Have you not noticed that feminists are always trying to prove that they are just as good as men in gender-specific tasks, never gender-neutral ones? The amount of female chauvinists may be just a fraction of male chauvinists, but it is among the chauvinists that we find both the woman-beaters and the few violent women.

Glorifying violence has always been a part of American television entertainment. However, apart from a couple of isolated formats, this "entertainment" invariably portrays violence against women negatively, so it not a huge issue. The bigger issue lay in how violence against men is portrayed. Television shows tend to be unmoved by violence against men, except when the assailant is female, in which case the violence is considered funny or even justified. When the victim is female and the assailant male, the reaction is shock, even if the violence was instigated by the female party. Many women simply do not understand that they are not allowed to hit men just because female entertainers constantly batter male actors in a "positive" fashion. For some reason, this phenomenon has hardly generated any debate among the various "councils" and such. Female violence has been legitimized and become an integral part of today's illusion of equality. It is precisely women who are the most avid readers of violent suspense and crime novels. Yay for girlpower!

Since the influence of Oriental martial arts films on the U.S. market began, Western audiences have been treated to countless film and television scenes of petite women and girls duking it out with big bruisers. Unfortunately, since even a woman with the same muscle mass as a man the same size is still weaker physically, this has given many girls a false sense of security. According to violence statistics, two or three men are beaten up per every woman—by other men, of course, but presumably the same ones that beat up on the women.[1366] Israeli field experience shows that male soldiers cannot handle seeing dead female comrades, which, of course, should be an argument against men in the military. Let's face it, men are squeamish, they faint at the sight of blood, whereas women bleed three days straight every month; and it is not like women soldiers are going to go around raping enemy civilians. Women may be inferior in hand-to-hand combat, but we are not fighting with swords and axes anymore. "Every damn fool can pull the trigger"—which is how conscription got started in the first place—but how many feminists do you hear arguing for involuntary draft of women? What could be a more basic gender equality issue than the fact that one sex is categorically coerced into forced labour?

However, brain scan research shows that men and women respond differently to danger. A team of Polish radiologists found more activity in the emotional centres of women's brains.[1367] When viewing negative images, women show stronger and more extensive activity in the left thalamus, an area which relays sensory information to

---

1366. Farrell, op. cit.

1367. L. Podsiadlo, et al. "Functional Magnetic Resonance Imaging of Different Genders in the Activation of Brain Emotional Centers," *Iranian Journal of Radiology* 8(S1), 2011, 82–83.

the pain and pleasure centres of the brain. Men, on the other hand, show more activity in an area of the brain called the left insula, which plays a key role in controlling involuntary functions such as respiration, heart rate, and digestion. In essence, activity in this area primes the body to either run from danger or confront it head on—the so-called "fight or flight response." This means that when faced with dangerous situations, men are more likely than women to take action, whether that is to avoid or confront the situation.

It is a common fallacy to suggest that there would be no wars if women were in power. Women do not get along with each other; it is men who naturally form associations—besides, you cannot have a war if no-one is taking care of things back home. Before the Iraq War, it was suggested that the anti-war women should start a campaign of celibacy. The idea came from the ancient Greek play and protagonist by the name of *Lysistrata*, "army-disbander." Unfortunately, there was no wide enthusiasm to withhold sexual privileges, one supposes, because female solidarity is not something to be counted on. Do you really think that all women—wives, lovers, and other man-eaters—would ever strike together? And even if they did, there would immediately be a stream of female reserves flowing in from third countries.

Watch children of any age play. Little boys set up wars and play-fights; little girls fight, but not for fun. Starting a fight is, in fact, a common way for boys to make friends: one boy shoves another, who shoves back, and pretty soon they are playing together. However, when a boy tries to make friends with a girl by shoving her, she is more likely to try and run away from him. A cartoon published recently in *The New Yorker* captured this well. It showed a little girl and a little boy eyeing each other. She is thinking: "I wonder if I should ask him to play." He is thinking: "I wonder if I should kick her."[1368] Older boys and grown men have their own version of "agonism," using fighting as a model for doing things that have nothing to do with actual, physical combat. They show affection to each other by mock-punching, getting a friend's head in an armlock, or playfully trading insults.

War is not violence, but a highly-organized, intellectual exercise. Sun Tzu, Julius Cæsar, Napoleon, Clausewitz, Schwarzkopf—not exactly a pack of savages. There is no such thing as "inhuman violence." Cruelty is practised only by the most intelligent creatures, humans, dolphins, etc. The past century was among the cruellest in the history of mankind. Because dolphins are intelligent, sociable, and have jaw structures that make them appear as if they are smiling, we tend to think of them as playful and peace-loving. However, dolphins are known to engage in much the same type of bullying as schoolchildren do, ganging up on a weaker member of the species. In fact, the bottlenose dolphin has a sex life which rather resembles that of an LA gang member. Male bottlenose dolphins form alliances of two or three in order to isolate and have sex with a single female they like. They will keep other males away while repeatedly copulating with her for weeks at a time.[1369] In the human world, this is known as rape.

Men think in terms of status and rank, while women prefer flat hierarchies. Men

1368. Bruce Eric Kaplan, October 18, 2004.

1369. R. C. Connor, et al. "Two Levels of Alliance Formation among Male Bottlenose Dolphins," *Proceedings of the National Academy of Sciences* 89(3), February 1, 1992, 987–990.

can have tunnel vision, while women may fail to get to the point. Men are more analytical, while women are better at long-term planning. "Emotional intelligence" is an insult to both intelligence and emotions (or empathy). Successful businessmen and women are not known for their introspection—they are very externally focused and have to have real, rational intelligence. And that is the one thing that is not included in the increasingly broad definition of EI. Which does not subtract from the fact that, by some criteria, modern IQ tests are better measures of low-grade autism than mature intelligence. We have been taught that getting along with people is more important than personal success. The ugly truth is that a successful person cannot be friends with everyone. A successful person needs the ability to be aggressive, self-centered, and even slightly narcissistic, and has to be willing to ignore other people's feelings, when they are in the way of his or her own gain. But who wants to raise a girl with the above attributes? It is, however, what we must do, if we want women to be successful.

Evolution has made sure, as far as possible, that the species will survive, by building in a mechanism which ensures that, when confronted with a situation where a species could be decimated, the losses are likely to be repleted by "appropriate action"—an upsurge of sexuality. The aftermath of danger—once the danger has been met and overcome—is a return to normal, followed by an arousal of the sexual factor. Just consult the birth statistics of a nation at time of war—sky high! After Saddam Hussein was ousted, the number of nuptials in Iraq soared; party planners, judges, and clergy members estimate that the number of weddings doubled since the uneasy months before the U.S.-led invasion in 2003.[1370] Ask any veteran who has been "over the top" with machine-gun blazing what he felt when he reached the safety of a dug-out—amazed at his arousal! Ask a fighter pilot what he felt like when he landed safely after aerial combat—the same thing!

Ask a teenage girl whether she said "yes" before or after a high-speed dash on her boyfriend's motorcycle, when she felt so afraid and exhilarated. People are simply more likely to feel aroused in scary settings. It is pretty simple psychology: you are feeling physiologically aroused, and it is ambiguous why; then you see an attractive person, and you think, "Oh, that's why!" Women in the military often face more danger from their male counterparts than from their enemies. As U.S. Congresswoman Jane Harman put it, "a female soldier in Iraq is more likely to be raped by a fellow soldier than killed by enemy fire."[1371] Recently, in the rather inaptly named Democratic Republic of the Congo, the main distinction between the UN blue helmets and the roving militias seems to be that the peacekeepers pay local girls for sex with scraps of food, while the militias simply rape.[1372]

"All things that exist," wrote Marquis de Sade, "including especially every impulse,

---

1370. Louise Roug, "The Time Seems Ripe to Tie the Knot in Iraq," *Los Angeles Times*, June 12, 2005.

1371. As quoted in Nancy Gibbs, "Sexual Assaults on Female Soldiers: Don't Ask, Don't Tell," *TIME*, March 8, 2010.

1372. Susan A. Notar, "Peacekeepers as Perpetrators: Sexual Exploitation and Abuse of Women and Children in the Democratic Republic of the Congo," *Journal of Gender, Social Policy & the Law* 14(2), 2006, 413–429.

however bizarre, violent or anti-social, is natural and has its place in nature."[1373] Eros and Thanatos are eternally linked, death being a result of sexual reproduction. "Sex and death go together like bacon and eggs," says the legendary horror filmmaker David Cronenberg. "I wish I could take credit for being the first one to think of that, but human art began with that perception 50,000 years ago. Sex is a way to conquer death. It's also an affirmation of the body. . . There's a reason people who have just escaped death tend to be very sexy: if death is everywhere then we'd better reproduce right away. It's an encoded, genetic thing."[1374] Any kind of physiological arousal will probably do the trick: couples, who ride a roller coaster, laugh at a really funny comedy, or flee a restaurant together without paying the bill, get an emotional jolt and are liable to attribute the feeling to the attractiveness of the other. People in the throes of passionate love are willing to take exceptional risks for their loved one. Successful men have been the ones who took risks that paid off; the losers are found among the unsuccessful bachelors, who, by definition, failed to contribute to succeeding generations of men—or to their inclinations.

Roughnecks say that they feel more alive when they brawl, more at one with life and death and the beauty of blood—"Killing with gloves on is like fucking with a condom." Throughout the centuries, we find examples of beatings that would today be called "senseless violence." But they are not senseless, because the acts have a clear motive: the pleasure brought on by violence. Our minds are designed to kill—it is part of human nature. Over the grand sweep of time, killing has conferred such powerful advantages in the ruthless game of reproductive competition that natural selection has made every last one of us "capable of murder." Genes of murderers prevailed over those of their victims, and we are their descendants. Whether you like it or not, killing has proved to be a disturbingly effective way to solve an array of adaptive problems in the unforgiving game of survival. It can be used to prevent injury, rape, or death; to protect one's children; to eliminate a rival or an enemy; to acquire their resources; to secure access to their mates; to prevent them from appropriating one's own mate; and so on and so on. The evolutionary struggle is all about reproductive competition and the strategies that lead to greater reproductive success are the ones that, over aeons, come to characterize any given species.

Evolutionary theory also explains why 87% of killers worldwide are men.[1375] Men kill so much more than women because women are the more valuable reproductive resource; women, not men, bear the burden of the nine-month investment to produce a child—competition is always fiercest among the sex that invests less. Road rage, neighbours feuding over intrusive flora or fauna, and other personal space disputes stem from responses selected through evolution to protect resources and ensure survival of the species. When someone cuts us off on the road, it triggers an ancient evolved adaptation to protect our social reputation. We can either become known as the kind who refuse to take any, or the kind others can exploit with impunity. Should we fail to respond to a trespass, we would signal exploitability. It is not just about a

---

1373. Hyatt, op. cit. 34.

1374. Jamie Graham, "The Total Film Interview: David Cronenberg," *Total Film*, October 2005.

1375. Buss, op. cit.

bruised ego: people who are exploitable are also less likely to attract a mate and propagate—the precise mandate behind most territorial behaviour. We need to face the fact that "violence is a part of sexuality, and vice versa," as Mr. Cronenberg puts it.[1376]

Mating is inextricably intertwined with murder. Watch a herd of buffalo, wildebeest, or rhino, and you will see the males competing for the females—often extremely aggressively. Rhino sex is always violent; it looks like two Jeeps going at it. Once copulation begins, they are locked together for well over an hour. It makes sound biological sense that the species—which wishes to survive—should be propagated by a process of natural selection, by the fittest, healthiest, and most virile and aggressive of their numbers. Sexual coercion is extremely common among animals: males of many species harass, coerce, or force females of their own kind to mate, and occasionally even harass sexually a member of closely related species. Male grey seals, for example, are known to harass and mate with female harbour seals, producing hybrids. One of the most common sexual fantasies for women is being taken by force; mind you, this does *not* mean that any of them would like to get raped for real—the instinct of self-preservation simply tends to be followed by the instinct of procreation. Why do you think men are so turned on by catfights?

"There is a fine line between pleasure and pain," they say. In the American world of sado-masochism, one man recently begged to be tied on a spit and roasted over sizzling coals; his dominatrix counterpart reached an orgasm merely watching his pain. In Japan, some women are turning to electrically charged squid for sexual satisfaction, and couples everywhere are looking for more intensity in their sex lives. After the pain threshold is crossed, they describe a type of ecstasy called "flying," which is no longer painful, but creates an entirely sexual, transcendent place. In 2003, a German computer technician advertised on the internet for a well-built male prepared to be slaughtered and then consumed. His willing victim agreed to have his penis cut off, flambéed, and served up to eat together before he died. There was debate in the courts whether his death constituted murder, after all, the victim had solicited the act.[1377]

Domestic violence has been a subject of discussion for so long that no-one dares to say that it is okay to beat up a nagging wife any more. A violent man is able to remain a gentleman by saying that he has "never hit a woman." After repeating this line a few times, he is allowed to put as many men in the hospital as he likes. Almost every single man has been beaten up one time or another. Yet these men do not have the good sense to feel like the victims of male violence or experience justified feelings of iniquity. This may be because most men who get beaten up also get blamed for getting beaten up. Since humans kill to prevent being killed, attempting murder is a dangerous evolutionary strategy. A UN study of 21 mainly developed countries found that boys, especially in the 15-to-17 age group, are up to four times more likely to be

1376. Op. cit.

1377. "German Cannibal Tells of Fantasy," BBC News, December 3, 2003.

murdered than girls of the same age.[1378] Even the boys who never get battered by other boys are forced to dodge and evade their fists. The fear of getting beaten up is so everyday for men that no-one thinks to even mention it.

Till the end of his days, a man must elude hoodlums who are always looking for a fight. It is enough to look in the wrong direction, to take the wrong seat on the bus, or to give a wrong answer to a question that has no right answer. The typical verbal situation is such where the woman in the party keeps arguing, when the man knows that they need to leave and quick. Arguing is really not in either one's interest, but it is the man, who will get beaten up, not the woman. It all boils down to centuries-old moral standards: a man of honour takes care of his own business, and it is practically one's duty to strike a slanderer. When both parties are men, even aggravated assault gets spoken of like it was just a squabble between kindergartners: "Who started it? Did he provoke it?" The fact is, the act of fighting should have resolved the issue in and of itself. Often times men in a bar agree to "take it outside." Afterwards, they might shake hands and have a beer together. Women are not privy to this world. According to statistics, they are more likely than men to fear unknown assailants, although they have a considerably smaller risk to encounter anonymous violence.[1379]

Domestic violence is common in all patriarchal societies, be the abusive party male or female; in fact, it is the most common form of violence. In three-fourths of rapes, the victim knows the rapist; wherever you live in the world, if you are a woman and you are attacked, the most likely perpetrator is your partner.[1380] However, sexual assault and domestic abuse are among the crimes that have historically suffered from underreporting by the public. Until the 20th century, the law said that a man was allowed to physically discipline his wife, children, and servants "to a reasonable measure." In England, for example, this meant that a husband had the legal right to beat his wife, provided he used a stick no thicker than his thumb. It is important to realize that men who "resort to" violence have not lost their self-control, but are in fact asserting control over their spouses. From their skewed perspective, they are creating a highly functional home life through bullying and intimidation that, far from being problematic for them, actually provides them with numerous benefits and advantages.

Home is, in fact, the most dangerous place for a woman to be. But men are not safe there either. Female domestic violence is a subject that is not widely discussed. There are many women who beat their husbands or boyfriends, and this subject has been a taboo for a long time. Men tend not to report an abusive spouse, because people would laugh at them if they did. It is embarrassing for a man to admit that he has been brutalized by a woman—people will just tell him to man up. Similarly, women who try to seek help for their violent tendencies are often turned down by the social

---

1378. Paulo Sérgio Pinheiro, "World Report on Violence against Children," United Nations Secretary-General's Study on Violence against Children, Geneva, 2006.

1379. Hannah Scott, "Stranger Danger: Explaining Women's Fear of Crime," *Western Criminology Review* 4(3), July 2003, 203–214.

1380. Shannan M. Catalano, "National Crime Victimization Survey: Criminal Victimization, 2003," Bureau of Justice Statistics, Washington D.C., September 2004.

authorities.[1381] In 99% of the cases, it is the man who gets dragged away from his home by the police, even if the woman had started the dispute. The same people who say rapes are not sexual acts claim that men cannot be raped; but you cannot have it both ways—arousal does not equal consent. Feminists tend to bring up domestic violence as an issue of equality, seeking to make the male party in the debate feel guilty. Did you know, for instance, that accredited universities teach it as a fact that men dominate women through violence and threat of violence? As far as I know, violence has nothing to do with equality, and assault is a crime regardless of sex.

Mothers discipline their children as much as the fathers do, and women have uncontrollable fits of jealousy as well. The vast majority of female acts of violence are never reported to the police, although the perpetrators of infanticide, for example, are mostly women.[1382] Not long ago it was believed that mothers were incapable of killing their children—now they are the first suspects. When we hear that a mother has hurt her baby, our first reaction is: how in the world could a mother do such a thing to her own child? We think of a mother who beats her children as a freak of nature, who has somehow lost her marbles. If a man hits another man in the taxi queue, no-one asks how he could do such a thing, but when a mother assaults or sometimes even murders her child, the first question on everyone's lips is exactly that. We have the patently false impression that motherhood somehow trumps everything else, erases every wicked thought and thwarts every evil deed. A crying baby and a depressed mother make a really bad combination, and children under a year old are mostly abused by their mothers. Only a small portion of battered babies are ever admitted to the emergency room and most cases never end up in the official statistics.[1383] Rather than there being one type of woman who is violent, women of all types, regardless of age or education, can resort to violence. One's gender does not protect a person from mental instability, physical exhaustion, or even postpartum depression.

Even though gender equality has improved, equality in terms of physical strength will probably never happen. A Detroit study shows that three-quarters of wives who killed their husbands were not even charged, since prosecutors found their acts to have been necessary to protect their lives or the lives of their children.[1384] When a woman gets angry, she may attack her spouse, but in the absence of edged weapons, no real damage is usually done. However, she may vent her frustration and pain by punching, kicking, scratching, and biting. She might not feel like she was doing anything wrong, presumably because as the weaker person, she thinks that her fists do not hurt. There are actually plenty of men who are abused by their wives or their partners. Some women throw things at them, scream and spit at them, and the men do not fight back. As the saying goes, "Never hit a woman."

Our culture seems to have accepted the notion that women have the right to beat on a member of the "stronger" sex. But what can a man do in this situation? If a man

---

1381. Cook 1997.

1382. Hrdy 1999.

1383. Tanja Henttonen, "Vauvojen kaltoinkohtelu: Tunnistaminen ja puuttuminen ensikodeissa," Federation of Mother and Child Homes and Shelters, Helsinki, 2009.

1384. Kates 1990, 24–25.

gets angry, frustrated, and uses his fists, we call it domestic violence. One might ask whether women as the physically weaker party have the same accountability as do men. In half of all spousal abuse cases today, the victim is male.[1385] If it comes as a surprise to you that teenage girls are much more violent than teenage boys, you might be the victim of feminist propaganda or gender studies.[1386] A man who hits a woman gets swarmed by a veritable army of social workers, but if a man gets beaten, it is always his fault or proof of his wimpiness and unmanliness. Should a woman begin to insinuate that she cannot handle it anymore, her violence is glossed over with comments like "We all get mad sometimes" or "You look exhausted, why don't you take a rest?" All the women surveyed by the Federation of Mother and Child Homes and Shelters in Finland between 2004 and 2008 were terrified by their own violent behaviour.[1387]

Female acts of violence are often not just of the physical variety, but usually entail quite a bit of psychological violence as well. Physically abusive women taking part in a Norwegian study told the researchers that psychological violence, and insults in particular, was still their most frequently used form of abuse. All the women taking part in the study said that they used insults and personal attacks before resorting to physical or material violence. They would call their spouses dumb, hit them verbally where it hurts, and say things that they knew would make them absolutely furious.[1388] Domestic abuse can also entail intimidation, threats, pressure, defamation, and malicious innuendo. Many angry women will underline how much they hate and despise their spouses, and reckon that their anger gives them the right to call the father of their children a monster and a pig in front of them. Some even think it is perfectly okay to make statements such as "I'll cut your balls off with these scissors while you sleep." It is easy to put a man down both physically and mentally: a man who is abused by a woman gets scorned and ridiculed by others—he cannot discuss these issues with anyone if he wishes to remain a man.

The sole justification for endless criticism, picking, and nagging is often the particular emotional state the woman happens to be in. Violence, both physical and psychological, is a behaviour, and it should not be confused with a feeling. Being angry is not the same as acting out the anger. Women discuss sensitive and personal issues with other women more than men do with other men. Even as babies, females send out stronger signals than males that they are open for communication. Little girls raise their eyebrows, open their eyes wide, and give people the impression that they really want to talk. Wanting to talk and learning to speak about intimate feelings serves women well for a lifetime. Men, women, and children all seek their comfort from women.[1389] Every guy I know is completely dependent on some woman for a

---

1385. Cook, op. cit..

1386. Margaret A. Zahn, et al. "Violence by Teenage Girls: Trends and Context," Office of Justice Programs, Washington, D.C., May 2008.

1387. Hannele Törrönen (ed.), "Vaiettu naiseus: Ajatuksia naisen väkivallan tunnistamisesta, nimeämisestä ja hoitamisesta," Federation of Mother and Child Homes and Shelters, Helsinki, 2009.

1388. Isdal 2000.

1389. Kraemer, op. cit.

major part of how his life functions, whether it is emotional or housekeeping, childcare, what have you. Men confide their secrets, worries, and fears only to their own female friends or spouses. This means that a man is completely helpless when a woman insults him in a way only a woman can. Opening up to her turns out to have been nothing but surrendering one's weapons. From this vantage point, the constant advice from wives, mothers, and social workers to talk more appears in a somewhat different light.

There is plenty of dating advice out there, and most of it is for women trying to deconstruct men's hearts. The usual premise is that men are complicated, emotionally stunted creatures who are incapable of direct action. Many delightful, attractive women are in relationships with men who do not call, do not bother, and do not care. When a man is truly interested in a woman, he pursues her. That is the way it has always been and equality has not changed this fact. If a man is into you, he will call, no matter how busy he is, because you are the bright spot in his day. He will want to have sex with you, and will stop having sex with other women. He will want to be with you when he is sober, not just to party. And if he is really truly head over heals in love with you, he will want to marry you. He is not, however, into you, if he keeps disappearing with no explanation, or is married to someone else. But why do men lie? And not just lie, but kiss and compliment and generally mess with women's heads rather than saying "I'm just not that into you"?

The truth is, honesty can make a woman defensive and confrontational. She may ask the man countless questions about what she did wrong, a situation no man wants to be stuck in. Men are, for good reason, afraid of women being upset or yelling. In a fight with other men, they know what is what: it gets verbal and then it gets physical. With women, they have no idea where it is going to go, but they know it cannot and should not get physical. Men are quicker to anger than women, because the female brain has an extra "stomach" for chewing anger that theirs does not have. They go from zero to fist fight in a second. A Swedish study shows that holding back one's anger elevates the risk of cardiac episodes in men. Those men who held back their fury and did not deal with conflicts had a much greater risk of getting a heart attack than those who tackled the problems head on. Scientists from the Stress Research Institute at the University of Stockholm believe that suppressed anger can lead to a rise in blood pressure and, if recurrent, could gradually cause heart disease.[1390]

Men and women are physically equal only as toddlers, and although there is no doubt nature has given men a stronger physique, women cope better. Mentally, girls develop faster and earlier than boys. Girls' death rate in the 15-to-19 age group is half that of boys, and boys have higher death rates at all ages than girls. Boys age 12 to 19 are 40% more likely to be the victims of violent crime than girls, and are significantly more likely to suffer from alcohol or drug addiction.[1391] In truth, boys and girls are not equal even at birth: infant mortality rates in developed countries are considerably

---

1390. C. Leineweber, et al. "Covert Coping with Unfair Treatment at Work and Risk of Incident Myocardial Infarction and Cardiac Death among Men: Prospective Cohort Study," *Journal of Epidemiology & Community Health* 65(5), May 2011, 420–425.

1391. Meadows, et al. Op. cit.

higher for boys.[1392] But the girls' biological advantage begins in the womb. The fertilized egg that becomes a girl gets a double dose of the X chromosome. Since females cannot have twice as much gene product, they turn off one chromosome: in half their cells, it is the mother's X, in the other half, it is the father's. A number of genetic diseases originate in the X chromosome, and with only one X, boys might get just the defective cells, while girls get a mixture of normal and defective cells.[1393]

Male embryos are also less robust than their female counterparts, and require a greater degree of nurturing throughout the pregnancy in order to survive to full term. Girl babies even survive adverse birth traumas more readily, while grown women fare better in life-threatening circumstances and are less affected by cold and disease. The female was given this edge to ensure the survival of the species: to repopulate a decimated community only one or two healthy males are needed, as long as they are outnumbered by healthy, fertile females. A male lion can have sex 50 times within 24 hours, in 30-second bouts—that is why it is called the "king of the jungle."[1394] In short, the females of the species must survive in reasonable numbers, but there need only be a few males. Yet roughly 106 boys are born for every 100 girls, which is thought to be nature's way of compensating for the fact that boys are more likely to die in their infancy.

Evolution implanted in the male a basic urge to protect the female and her young at the cost of his own life if necessary. However, deep down in his subconscious mind, man knows and resents this. He feels expendable, and quite frankly, he all but is. He might also resent the fact that a woman can go on receiving pleasure in the sex act time and time again, whereas a man, even in his sexual prime, cannot maintain continuous erections. There is thus no equality between the genders even in sexual intercourse. A 30-year-old man going out with a 20-year-old woman is dating someone of his own maturity, but a 30-year-old woman dating a 20-year-old man might just as well be dating a 12-year old. Now, a woman might reach her sexual peak in her 30s and a man in his 20s, but that is just more proof that there is no god; also, the sexual peak only measures lust, not skill.

A former U.S. schoolteacher recently made national headlines by marrying an ex-pupil a decade after she "raped" him when he was just twelve. Another American teacher apparently had a sexual affair with her 13-year-old pupil, got pregnant, was sent to prison, had the baby, met the pupil after getting out, got pregnant again and was put back into prison. What a horrific crime it was to force sex on these young, innocent boys, who must have been too traumatized to come forth and accuse their rapists of such dastardly deeds. Face it America, the only "trouble" these boys are going to have is taking care of all the girls who would like to find out what their teachers taught them. According to the international Population Council and the United Nations Children's Fund (UNICEF), one in every seven girls in developing countries will get married before they turn 15 and one in three before they turn

1392. World Health Organization 2008.

1393. Barbara R. Migeon, "The Role of X Inactivation and Cellular Mosaicism in Women's Health and Sex-Specific Diseases," *JAMA* 295(12), March 22/29, 2006, 1428–1433.

1394. Patricia Yollin, "Not Your Mama's 'Birds and Bees': The Zoo's X-Rated Animal Sex Tour Is Graphic, Kinky," *San Francisco Chronicle*, February 15, 2006.

18.[1395] Boys are married off young as well, but almost everywhere in the world, men marry later then women—the fact is, boys simply hit puberty later.

The patriarchal notion of the monogamous female and the promiscuous male is supposed to be a typical pattern for both human and nonhuman primates. The argument goes that since males have an unlimited supply of spermatozoa, they are predisposed to make use of any and every opportunity to mate. Since there is little if any parental follow-through required, males of most species are supposed to be aggressive sexual adventurers, inclined to engage in sex with multiple partners whenever they can, because males who succeed in so doing leave more descendants. The female germ is more unique than the male one and requires maturation, so females are supposedly much more careful when choosing a mate. While the male cheerfully squirts his sperm around all over the place, the smart female makes the best males compete for her—eggs are costly to produce, so one should not waste them. However, field studies of nonhuman primates suggest that natural selection actually drives female primates to seek multiple partners as well. Chimpanzees, for example, are notoriously promiscuous, with half of the offspring in one group of female chimps studied in West Africa turning out not to have been sired by the males in residence.[1396] And the same appears to be true for early human communities.

Females of most species only have sex when they have the ability to get pregnant. The majority of mammals have an oestrous cycle: they come "into heat" periodically, and at other times have no interest in mating. Female porcupines, for example, are in season only four hours a year. Ovulation is their only peak and having sex means begetting young, nothing else. Males know the right moment from various visible and chemical signs, and when the time is not right, males look at other choices. But things are different for monogamous birds and humans. With Old World monkeys, apes, and *Homo sapiens*, an immense evolutionary change took place. The mating-signal of genital blood was wrested from its former place at ovulation to a new position at menstruation—when it is very unlikely that conception can occur. At the same time, sexual libido was spread over most of the cycle, which means that primate females have sex even when they know they cannot get pregnant.

Is a male required to move from female to female, siring as many children as possible, in order to ensure that his genes will survive? Many scientists now suggest that sticking around might be a better strategy for human males. Since the human female does not go into heat, the roving male is liable to miss the two or three days a month that she is fertile. And even when she is ovulating, there is only about a 20% chance of him impregnating her. This makes it more probable that males will stay in a relationship. In fact, marriage was invented by human males as a form of "mate-guarding." Having regular sex with one particular woman was much easier than roaming from one random female to another, not to mention much more effective in terms of reproductive success. Magnus Enquist from Stockholm University has come to the conclusion that male monogamy is the first choice in species where one cannot

---

1395. "Supporting Married Girls: Calling Attention to a Neglected Group," Population Council, New York, December 2007; "Progress for Children: A Report Card on Child Protection," United Nations Children's Fund, New York, 2009.

1396. Hrdy, op. cit.

tell from the outside whether the female is ovulating.[1397]

Most primate females signal their fertile period by swollen labia—on human females, the labia swell when they are aroused. These kinds of sexual messages are often typical of just one sex. Their purpose is to either attract partners or to flaunt at the competition. Women give a wide variety of subtle signals to advertise the fact that they are ready to conceive. The human breasts also have signal value, although females of other primate species only develop sexual characteristics when they are in constant competition over males of the species. Gibbon couples and single orangutan females have not evolved any particular bodily signals, unlike chimps living in a group. An appropriate layer of fat might act as an honest signal of when a woman is able to take care of children. Before our species domesticated dairy animals, insufficient milk secretion would have proved fatal for a child.

On the other hand, breasts are hardly an honest signal of the ability to lactate, because the milk does not issue from the fatty tissue, but from the mammary glands. The evolution of fatty breasts has resulted in males having a random preference for large mammaries. Often times our preferences are "merely" aesthetic, without any greater purpose. However, large glands happened to be beneficial for females due to the better ability to take care of their young; therefore the males who preferred larger glands would have more viable offspring. They thus inherited two useful features: big glands in the females and a fondness for big glands in the males. This could have easily led to a self-perpetuating and growing pressure for ever larger breasts. After all, breast budding—the first visible sign of puberty—seems to be arriving ever earlier.

Producing mammary glands, however, requires resources. It would be far easier to resort to "cheating" and make use of nature's silicone, the fatty tissue around the glands. With this innovation, the size of the female breasts has exploded and no longer has any real advantage in survival—rather the reverse. Plastic surgery saw great advances after World War I, when it was used to rehabilitate badly disfigured soldiers, but it was later embraced by healthy people who wanted larger breasts and fewer wrinkles. In 1992, the year silicone implants were banned for general use in the United States, an estimated 32,607 American women underwent augmentation—elective surgery to enhance breast size. Since then, augmentations have soared to more than a quarter of a million a year, according to the American Society of Plastic Surgeons.[1398] The typical augmentation patients are either women who never developed breasts during puberty or women whose breasts have sagged due to ageing, pregnancy, or breastfeeding. The median age of augmentation patients is 34, and 75% of them are married.[1399]

What is unusual about human breasts is the fact they develop so early, long before the female is able to conceive or needs them in order to nurse. The gap between the first appearance of breast buds and menstruation is close to three years on the

1397. Joanna Marchant, "Sex, Lies and Monogamy," *New Scientist* 2288, April 28, 2001.

1398. "ASAPS 2003 Statistics on Cosmetic Surgery," Arlington Heights, IL, August 12, 2004.

1399. V. Leroy Young, et al. "Initial Report From an Online Breast Augmentation Follow-Up Survey," *Aesthetic Surgery Journal* 24(3), May 2004, 229–243.

average.[1400] Now, other primates do have protruding breasts, but they only show up just before nursing and disappear soon afterwards. Why would young women have inconveniently protruding and large breasts, if they served no evolutionary purpose? The obvious down-side is this: while sexual harassment was first recognized as a legal claim for discrimination in the U.S. 35 years ago, sexual harassment in American workplaces is as prevalent now as it was before it was made illegal.[1401] The cultural narrative about the roles of men and women has changed very rapidly in the West over the last four decades, but human behaviour has not. As Dr. Gregory House once observed about a female patient, "either she cracked under the whip or she started to realize that her evolutionary purpose is to arouse men, not to castrate them."[1402]

Both men and women want intimacy, but for men, intimacy is a physical matter. As far as men are concerned, more sex means more intimacy and a stronger relationship. To women, however, intimacy is something quite different, a product of the feelings and heart. It is the male biological urge to "hunt" and "conquer," but women could never invent weapons that kill, only ones that make you feel really bad and guilty until you surrender. The male genitalia is on the outside and a man's interest in a woman is made obvious by his erection. While a man is a sexual extrovert, a woman is usually a sexual introvert; her sexual organs are within her and she has trouble speaking of her deepest sexual longings and feelings. However, females use signals of male genetic quality, such as the size and shape of a peacock's tail, to select a mate. Men like to have all their stuff—their books, their CDs, and their DVDs—on display to impress their friends and potential love interests, while women like to hide things in cupboards.

Studies suggest that women want to conceal their ovulation from males other than their chosen partner. It is in a woman's best interest to form a closer attachment to one man to help raise children, rather than to advertise her fertile time and possibly be approached by a large number of competing males. The system for sexual orientation and arousal make men go out and find people to have sex with, whereas women are more focused on accepting or rejecting those who seek intimate relations with them. A woman must feel loved by and comfortable with a partner before she will open up, either figuratively or literally; for her, sexual passion is a result of intimacy, rather than the other way around. And this, my friends, is why men who openly sleep with multiple partners will always be seen by others as "studs," while women who do the same will always be branded as "strumpets."

1400. Kaplowitz, op. cit.

1401. McKinnon 2005.

1402. "Dying Changes Everything." *House M.D.* FOX. September 16, 2008.

14

As Knowledge Is the Outcome of Ignorance, So Is Also Virtue the Outcome of Vice

One of the common mistakes of youth is to assume that once you know all about sex, you know all about life, that you have uncovered the *primus motor* of all human affairs. Or is it? The mere fact that there are two sexes means that we are sexual beings. It is received opinion in zoological circles that the development of the menstrual cycle—or non-stop libido—was responsible for the evolution of primate and eventually human societies. But how could this possibly be a survival factor? The answer has to be that sexuality in primates must have become of benefit and importance to the individual as well as to the species by breeding. Many apes and especially our nearest primate relation, the bonobo or "pygmy chimpanzee," as well as toothed whales, and dolphins in particular, have sex not only to propagate the species, but to experience the pleasure it brings. Oral sex, for example, might be much more common in the animal kingdom than we think: according to the primate researcher Frans de Waal, oral sex is probably underreported, because scientists tend to be too bashful to mention it.

Many scientists, for instance, use euphemisms like "reproductive instinct." In addition to sexual morality and needless modesty, there is a purely religious aspect to this: people have wanted to see some sort of a divine plan at work, a "creative force," if you will. They have not dared to state or even admit the plain truth: the purpose of sex is not procreation, but sexual pleasure; reproduction is just a—often unwanted—side-effect. Sex between higher animals, as between humans, is frequently simply a matter of enjoyment, and that applies to animals of the same sex as well as opposite sexes. Male dogs will lick each other and hump on each other, females in heat will hump on other females, and males will lick females even out of season; in fact, even neutered males will have sex with females in heat. In the blockbuster movie, ***March of the Penguins***, these flightless birds were loving and caring parents that stayed in a monogamous relationship throughout their lives.[1403] In truth, 15% of emperor penguins change partners each year and some of them are homosexual.[1404]

According to the Oslo Natural History Museum, homosexuality has been observed among 1,500 species, and that in 500 of those it is well documented.[1405] This includes not only short-lived sexual relationships, but even partnerships that may last a lifetime. While homosexuality would appear to contradict evolutionary imperatives, scientists say it appears to do no harm and may actually help in some circumstances. Sometimes a pair of male birds may rear eggs "donated" by a female: in the case of flamingos, for instance, two males can maintain a much larger territory than a heterosexual flamingo pair, meaning that more chicks can grow up. In some penguin colonies, as many as one in ten pairs may be same sex, while female penguins sometimes "prostitute" themselves to get stones for nest-building. It is completely justified to say that the higher the animal is in the scale of evolution, the more complex its sexual behaviour. Non-stop libido was an evolutionary adaptation favouring the development of social and economic co-operation. Patriarchal religions may have tried to narrow sex down to copulation for breeding, but evolution knows better.

Many people are under the impression that the Old Testament specifically forbids masturbation, when in reality, the Bible does not even mention masturbation. The story of Onan in Genesis 38 is often cited as an example of how God will punish masturbators—it is, after all, where we get the term "Onanism." After his brother died, Onan was commanded by God to impregnate his brother's widow, but Onan defied God by pulling out before he ejaculated, so she would not get pregnant. This was why his seed spilled on the ground, but the detail came to be equated with masturbation by people who had their own agenda. Circumcision was developed, and is still used, to control a child's sexuality—this is the core motive behind circumcision and any other explanation is secondary or a pretext. Although the Judaic faith holds that the reason circumcision was commanded was to seal in one's flesh a symbol of the covenant between Yahweh and His people, even noted Jewish philosophers such as Moses Maimonides and Philo Judæus believed that the real reason was to control the male's sexual impulses.[1406]

Circumcision diminishes sexual sensation. Not only that, but the movement of the

---

1403. Dir. Luc Jacquet. Buena Vista International, 2005.

1404. Matt Walker, "Penguins Are Not People," *New Scientist* 2519, October 1, 2005.

1405. "Against Nature?: An Exhibition on Animal Homosexuality," October 12, 2006.

1406. *Guide of the Perplexed*, III.49; *De Specialibus Legibus*, I.9.

skin layers of the foreskin provides a natural lubrication, usually making it easy to masturbate without additional lubricants when a foreskin is present. Until the late 19th century, circumcision was never practised among Christians in Europe, who instead regarded it with repulsion. According to the Christian point of view, children were innocent and had no sexual nature. Europeans considered children as amusing pets, whom they tickled and excited for their own entertainment. They did not pay any attention to children pleasuring themselves until the 18th century, when the battle against the corruption of children was aimed at the children themselves. The adults began a cruel and futile war against children's genitalia, and over the next century, the violent suppression of childhood autoeroticism turned into a full-blown obsession. No child could escape its horrors: every little person was made to believe that touching their privates would wither their bodies and paralyze their brains, lead to madness and impotence and countless other terrifying and shameful ailments.

By the 1830s and '40s, the masturbation panic had spread to the United States, with Christian evangelical and medical quacks warning that those who fell victim to the practice would be reduced to a state of utter degradation. American parents were cautioned to be on the lookout for early signs of self-abuse in their children, and by the 1890s, infant circumcision had become a popular technique to prevent, or cure, masturbatory insanity. According to the Royal College of Surgeons in Great Britain, the foreskin could cause "nocturnal incontinence," hysteria, epilepsy, and irritation that might "give rise to erotic stimulation and, consequently, masturbation."[1407] At the same time as circumcisions were advocated on men, clitoridectomies were also performed to treat female masturbators. The "Orificial Surgery Society" for female "circumcision" operated in the U.S. until 1925, and the procedure continued to have its advocates through the 1930s.

The war on children's sexuality did not relent until the beginning of the 20th century, when the view on sexual matters in general underwent a fundamental change. Approximately one-sixth of males worldwide are still circumcised today, but the vast majority of them for religious reasons. The United States is the only country in the world that continues to routinely circumcise a majority of male infants for non-religious reasons, but the medical rationale for the procedure developed long after it was in wide practice. Even though all major medical organizations in America now judge the benefits of neonatal circumcision to be too small to justify the risks associated with performing it routinely, it nonetheless remains the single most common surgical procedure carried out in the country.[1408] The practice never spread beyond English-speaking countries, however, if only because the persistently anti-Semitic Christian denominations on the Continent always considered the arguments for it to be theologically suspect.

No more than 50 years ago, masturbation was thought to cause everything from softening of the brain to the eating of clay. Today things are different, and masturbation is considered a healthy and normal form of sexual behaviour. It has been

1407. As quoted in Karen Ericksen Paige, "The Ritual of Circumcision," *Human Nature* 1(5), May 1978, 40–48.

1408. Caleb B. Nelson, et al. "The Increasing Incidence of Newborn Circumcision: Data from the Nationwide Inpatient Sample," *Journal of Urology* 173(3), March 2005, 978–981.

dubbed the "only safe sex," but it is also a great way to learn how to climax. An orgasm, like urination, is a reflex, but both functions can be controlled in large part by will. Every woman is responsible for her own orgasm, and masturbation is the only proven form of sex therapy. Some children start masturbating when they are only a few years old, others a little later. A boy child will experience his first ejaculation somewhere between 13 and 15 years of age. As men age, however, they may not have as many ejaculations as they did when they were younger, and this might actually be adding to the problem of infertility. The longer sperm hang around in the testes, the more likely they are to accumulate DNA damage, and the warm environment could also make them more sluggish after a while.

Research shows daily ejaculations to reduce the amount of DNA damage seen in sperm samples.[1409] Apparently, the saying "Use it or lose it" applies just as much to sexuality as it does to muscles and brains. A report by Finnish researchers says older men who have sex more often experience fewer erection problems. The five-year study of 989 male Finns aged 55 to 75 showed that having sexual intercourse less than once a week doubled the risk of erectile dysfunction compared to having sex once a week.[1410] The prostate sits near the nerves that govern erection as well as the ability to control urine flow. The prostate is a muscle, and like all muscles, it must be used if it is to remain strong. Not only that, but regular use also helps to cleanse the gland—it is no accident that the highest incident of prostate cancer occurs in celibate men.[1411] Viagra® is snake oil.

Scientifically speaking, masturbation is good for you. In one of the first major attempts to measure the cancer risk of male sexual activity, researchers at the National Cancer Institute discovered that men having the most orgasms reduced their prostate cancer risk by a full third.[1412] Prostate cancer is one of the leading causes of death in older men, and frequent ejaculations will help to keep the gland healthy. Like early childbirth in women, a lot of orgasms early in a man's life may be like running an engine, prompting youthful cells in the critical region to develop into a whole lot of robust prostate cells. Penile tissue is like other tissue: oxygen is good for it. However, unlike the muscles in your forearm, for example, the corpora cavernosa spend no more than three hours a day—if you are lucky—fully oxygenated.

When a man is sexually aroused, whether by stimulation of the penis or by his favourite porn movie, more blood flows into his member. In the two flexible tubes of spongy tissue that extend the length of the shaft, muscle tissue slackens. Their caverns swell with blood, straining against the surrounding membranes and trapping the blood in the organ. The result is a longer, stiffer penis, but also, because of all the oxygen brought along by the blood, a thoroughly oxygenated one. Some scientists

---

1409. "Daily Sex Helps to Reduce Sperm DNA Damage and Improve Fertility," European Society of Human Reproduction and Embryology, Amsterdam, June 30, 2009.

1410. Juha Koskimäki, et al. "Regular Intercourse Protects Against Erectile Dysfunction: Tampere Aging Male Urologic Study," *The American Journal of Medicine* 121(7), July 2008, 592–596.

1411. G. G. Giles, et al. "Sexual Factors and Prostate Cancer," *BJU International* 92(3), August 2003, 211–216.

1412. Michael F. Leitzmann, et al. "Ejaculation Frequency and Subsequent Risk of Prostate Cancer," *JAMA* 291(13), April 7, 2004, 1578–1586.

even wonder if the real reason for unconscious nocturnal erections might be to make sure oxygen levels in the corpora cavernosa stay high. Since it is apparently between that and succubi, my money is on the former. In any case, the fact that even twelve-week old foetuses can have erections in the womb is probably because periodic oxygenation is so important. Oxygen-deprivation might also explain why some men lose erectile function after prostatectomies and never recover it.[1413]

The Bible does not condemn, and indeed cannot condemn, homosexuality. The concept was not invented until the Renaissance. The Bible does not condemn homosexual practices either—what it condemns is sodomy, be it with a man or a woman. It condemns sodomy for the same reason it condemns *coitus interruptus:* both acts waste semen. In the 13th century, St. Thomas Aquinas rated masturbation as a graver sin than rape, because it was "unnatural," since the seed was spilled. In a rape, the semen at least went to the right place, even if this happened by force. The original purpose of marriage was to produce legitimate offspring or heirs; it had nothing to do with love, heterosexual or otherwise. Times were bad, and sex was for procreation only, to ensure the survival of the tribe. "Be fruitful and multiply!" Jesus is the only unmarried prophet in the Bible, and it was St. Paul who finally made celibacy the ideal.

During the Italian Renaissance, however, the Neoplatonic philosopher Marsilio Ficino developed a concept now known as "Platonic love," which had far-reaching consequences in the European social tradition. While Ficino believed that the human soul pursued contemplation more or less in isolation, he acknowledged the fact that human beings are fundamentally social. When the spiritual relationship between God and the individual was reproduced in a friendship or love with another person, that constituted what he called "spiritual love." In other words, when the love and spiritual bond between friends mirrors their love for God, then the two individuals have attained the highest type of friendship they can. While Renaissance thinkers, artists, and other cultural leaders only adopted Neoplatonism in part, the doctrine of Platonic love diffused quickly throughout the culture. It completely changed the Western experience of sexual love, which, since antiquity, had always been closely related to eroticism and physical attraction.

Sex has been around since the dawn of time, since the first single-celled critter got a pseudopod over on a nearby proto-hottie and delivered his precious load of DNA. Sex meant that the offspring of that original sex machine were able to adapt to changing environments and, thus, survive. The headaches and hang-ups did not start until much later, after "love," or more precisely, "romantic love," came into existence. All of a sudden, you had writers, poets, and philosophers discussing sexual love in terms of spiritual bonds, as reflecting the relationship between the individuals and God; you had people swooning and mooning and duelling and falling on swords and taking poison—none of which are particularly good survival traits. The act of sex became disentangled from the deep-seated feelings of affection that people had grown to associate with it. The highest form of love was no longer passion that led to sex, but

---

1413. Alexander Müller, et al. "The Effect of Hyperbaric Oxygen Therapy on Erectile Function Recovery in a Rat Cavernous Nerve Injury Model," *The Journal of Sexual Medicine* 5(3), March 2008, 562–570.

passion that chastely steered clear of sex altogether, ultimately resulting in misery, violence, and death. Rather than being considered pathological, all this tragic perturbation was viewed as "romantic."

Platonic love also gave homosexual eroticism a new language. While homosexuality was quite common in the Middle Ages, it was not regarded as an identity trait, as it is today. When a man had sex with another man, he was a "sodomite" for the duration of the act; after that, he was someone who had committed the sin of "sodomy"—but homosexuality as a steady state did not yet exist. Self-described "sodomites" did not generally eschew marriage or heterosexual intercourse the way that modern "gays" are usually assumed to do. The mediaeval sodomite categorized himself mainly in ethical terms, and the word "sodomy" implied moral degradation and damnation. The language of Platonic love, however, gave the Europeans a language with which to define non-sexual male-male relationships. Once understood in spiritual terms, male-male sexual relationships could also be discussed in the same terms, and this Renaissance-era language is still a key element in the modern day debates of homosexuality.

Since gay men have about one-fifth as many children as straight men, any gene favouring homosexuality should quickly disappear from the population. So it is true that no-one is born gay, but nor is anyone born straight either—it is a question of identity. And an identity takes a long time to develop. According to the American Psychiatric Association, "The potential risks of 'reparative therapy' are great, including depression, anxiety and self-destructive behavior, since therapist alignment with societal prejudices against homosexuality may reinforce self-hatred already experienced by the patient."[1414] However, a recent U.S. study of anonymized credit card receipts from a major online adult entertainment provider found little variation in consumption between states. In fact, those states that consumed the most porn tended to be more conservative and religious than the states with lower levels of consumption. Residents of the 27 states that have laws banning gay marriage, for example, boasted 11% more porn subscribers than states that do not explicitly restrict same-sex unions.[1415] Thus the people who are most outraged by porn turn out to be the largest consumers of the very thing they claim to be outraged by.

Broadly speaking, homosexuality is of far more concern to both the individual and society when it is "latent" rather than "blatant." When a person's homosexual urges are latent and concealed from his intellectual awareness, the effect upon their psyche is far more detrimental. "I couldn't stand another woman to touch me and I find it difficult to even shake hands with women," says the latent lesbian. Listen to the bravado of a youth about to go out and "bash some queers" because he "hates all puffs," and you can be confident the very same youth would really like to "bash" the homosexual feelings out of himself. Show me a vociferous anti-sex fundamentalist of any religious or political bent, and will I show you secret fantasies so kinky and twisted that it would make even Max Hardcore shudder. Life in Lubbock, Texas,

1414. "Psychiatric Treatment and Sexual Orientation: Position Statement," Arlington, VA, December 1998.

1415. Benjamin Edelman, "Red Light States: Who Buys Online Adult Entertainment?" *Journal of Economic Perspectives* 23(1), Winter 2009, 209–220.

taught Butch Hancock two things: "One is that God loves you and you're going to burn in hell. The other is that sex is the most awful, filthy thing on earth and you should save it for someone you love."[1416]

Whether women describe themselves as straight or lesbian, studies show that their sexual arousal seems to be relatively indiscriminate, i.e. they are aroused by both male and female images. Researchers from the University of Georgia have now also investigated the role of homosexual arousal in exclusively heterosexual men who admitted negative feelings toward homosexual individuals. Participants in the study consisted of a group of homophobic men and of a nonhomophobic control group. All the men were exposed to sexually explicit erotic stimuli consisting of heterosexual, male homosexual, and lesbian film material, while changes in their penile circumference were monitored. Both groups exhibited arousal in response to the heterosexual and female homosexual stimuli, but only the homophobic men showed an increase in erection when viewing male homosexual material.[1417] The study thus confirms that homophobia is indeed associated with homosexual arousal that the homophobic individual is either unaware of or denies—"The lady *doth* protest too much, methinks."

Here is what makes Republican Senator Larry Craig and people like him rife with potential for some of the most dishonest and dangerous abuses humans are capable of: the ability to ignore the incredible hypocrisy of your own life, the unbelievable amount of self-loathing and the pathetic insincerity; the ability to join a political party that not only openly loathes, but violently condemns, your choice in sexual partners. If you are capable of toeing the party line and swallowing such an ignorant doctrine in the middle of who knows how many secret gay affairs, I would not put anything past you. To my mind, you are capable of anything, no matter how sinister or disgusting. In the black community, men on the "down low" have sex with other men while keeping a heterosexual public identity. When STDs are seen as results of forbidden acts, infections tend to stay untreated and spread. Consequently, the U.S. capital Washington D.C. has a higher rate of HIV/AIDS than either Port Au-Prince, Haïti or Dakar, Senegal.[1418] In 2002, African-Americans accounted for more than half of new HIV cases reported in the United States, though they make up only 13% of the population.[1419]

Many black men who practise bisexuality do not accept that they are gay, and therefore are hard to reach via safe sex gay education programs. The nature of down-low partners means that girlfriends and wives may not know about them until they test positive for HIV. In fact, black women are currently being diagnosed with HIV at

1416. Regnerus 2007, 83.

1417. Henry E. Adams, et al. "Is Homophobia Associated with Homosexual Arousal?" *Journal of Abnormal Psychology* 105(3), August 1996, 440–445.

1418. *The Other City*. Dir. Susan Koch. Cabin Films, 2010.

1419. "Cases of HIV Infection and AIDS in the United States, by Race/Ethnicity, 1998–2002," *HIV/AIDS Surveillance Supplemental Report*, Centers for Disease Control and Prevention, Atlanta, 2004.

a rate twenty times that of white women.[1420] According to the UN, AIDS is the leading cause of death among black women aged 25 to 34, because they are half as likely to receive the latest drug therapy compared with other population groups.[1421] Most black women with HIV say they were infected through heterosexual contact, but are unclear as to how their male partners were infected. Many men on the down low find it difficult to view themselves as gay because of the intense negative stigma attached to homosexuality in the black community. Black churches and mosques are not exactly known for being tolerant of homosexuals, and being gay risks rejection by friends and family. Neither do blacks identify with gay culture, because they see it as white and effeminate. In the rare cases when they do venture into the predominantly Caucasian gay communities like San Francisco's, they feel unwelcome.[1422]

Sexuality for people, unlike some lower species, is an important form of social interaction, not just blind reproduction. To discuss a person, to discuss his or her problems, is surely to discuss their sexuality as well. Sexuality intrudes into many, many aspects of our lives—if not *all* aspects of our lives. To deny one's own or anyone else's sexuality is to deny the person's humanity, and that, to me, constitutes the only true perversion. In Christianity, sexuality is seen as a weakness of sinful flesh and considered an animal instinct. Much of this can be traced back to Saint Augustine, who reasoned in the 5th century that sexual pleasure was integral to the Fall of Man. Adam's sin, he argued, was not one of pride or disobedience, but of sex. All sexual pleasure is thus born out of evil, and our best hope for salvation lay in repudiating the sexual impulse and the burden of guilt inherited from the first man. This interpretation of the story of the Garden, along with the castrated manhood of Jesus, underlines our culture's perverted relationship to the power that flows from between our legs.

Gilgamesh is different: "for six days and seven nights Enkidu stayed aroused, and had intercourse with the harlot until he was sated with her charms."[1423] And thus did he become wise like a god and could no longer eat grass with the gazelles. Sexuality was rightly understood as the great moving power of civilization and culture, one that curtails our animal qualities and ennobles our souls. Sexual professionals were also properly esteemed in ancient Mesopotamia. Shamhat the harlot was a good and talented woman, who used not only her body but her words to transform the wild Enkindu from a beast into a human being. Tying sexuality to marriage and procreation is not only against nature, but in the long run, mentally damaging, both to one's self and to others—it is, therefore, in actual fact, morally reprehensible. If God made our bodies, but we think of them as dirty and shameful, are we not shunning His divine creation?

The United States is a country that is inundated with sex, yet Americans have an

---

1420. Gregorio Millett, et al. "Focusing 'down low': Bisexual Black Men, HIV Risk and Heterosexual Transmission," *Journal of the National Medical Association* 97(7), July 2005, 52S–59S.

1421. Joint United Nations Programme on HIV/AIDS 2006.

1422. Jason B. Johnson, "Secret Encounters of Bisexual Black Men Could Be Creating Wave of Infected Women," *San Francisco Chronicle*, May 1, 2005.

1423. Verses 175–177.

incredibly hard time talking about it like grown-ups. Will there ever be, in our lifetime, a U.S. President, a Senate subcommittee, or a government program that will dare come up with a new sex-positive guideline suggesting that we should all get naked as often as possible, so long as we enjoy ourselves responsibly and respectfully, because it will make the country and the world a better place? A 2007 study published in the *New England Journal of Medicine* found that about half of men and women ages 57 to 85 had at least one bothersome sexual problem, yet only 38% of men and just 22% of women over 50 discussed sex with their physician.[1424] Remember Joycelyn Elders? This feisty and outspoken Surgeon General, appointed by President Clinton back in 1993, had the audacity to suggest that masturbation was fine and healthy and should be taught to teens as a safer alternative to riskier forms of sex. Needless to say, Clinton was forced to ask Elders for her resignation. She later famously stated that, "As long as I was in Washington, I never met anybody that I thought was good enough, who knew enough, or who loved enough to make sexual decisions for anybody else."[1425]

For the last two millennia, we have been told that sex is filthy and the body is a disgusting, shameful vehicle. Life is merely a miserable purgatory where we scratch and claw for money and power while we eagerly await the Second Coming of Christ. This mentality is responsible for a great portion of violent sexual crimes, child abuse, sexual dysfunction, neurosis, etc. Any psychologist will tell you that sex, when repressed, will come out in other ways. It is, after all, the most powerful of all human urges, linked to the most powerful of all, the urge to survive, offering as it does a way for the species to survive as opposed to personal survival. A person who is sexually inhibited has an unconscious anxiety, and a person who has an unconscious anxiety is sexually inhibited—the two things are forever joined together. Pauline Christianity has turned the beauty and selflessness of surrendering one's self to another into a hideous crime against God. Every day, sexual therapists come face to face with the countless psychological knots that plague people who have been shamed and bullied into denying their own sexuality.

A quickly suppressed report by a group of psychotherapists in conservative New Zealand revealed that, of 1,000 subjects investigated, all 1,000 had been subjected to a sexual assault in their forming years, and that in over a third of the cases it had been carried out by a close relative.[1426] After sexual trauma, people commonly continue to experience negative and upsetting reactions to sex, closeness, intimacy, and even to their own desire, leaving them feeling ashamed, protective, or angry. Many people understand intellectually what happened to them, but when put in a stressful situation like having sex, their bodies continue to respond as they did during the abuse. A person might be making love with someone she cares about deeply, and suddenly become agitated and start reacting to the lover as if he were the perpetrator of the abuse that took place a long time ago. Because of our automatic survival

---

1424. Stacy Tessler Lindau, et al. "A Study of Sexuality and Health among Older Adults in the United States," 357(8), August 23, 2007, 762–774.

1425. "Abstinence." *Penn & Teller: Bullshit!* Showtime Networks. June 5, 2006.

1426. French, op. cit.

reactions to trauma, people seldom realize the extent to which they have been harmed until later in life. With sexual abuse, this realization might happen in a loving relationship, when the victim feels safe enough to start feeling the hurt, or with the birth of a child, when the body has to open.

Unfortunately, instead of engaging with the misuse of sex and sexual violence or coercion, the sex-positive movement likes to concentrate on pleasure, desire, education, and sexual empowerment. This is because larger cultural influences such as mainstream media and the Department of Justice seek to continually and erroneously connect things like committing rape and viewing porn, or experiencing sexual trauma and becoming a sex worker. At the same time, the sexual abuse survival movement has tended to ignore sexual pleasure and even adult sexuality altogether and focused exclusively on the abuses. It has proven exceedingly difficult to acknowledge both sexual trauma and a fulfilling sex life without triggering accusations or hysteria, even though we know that sex-positivity and healing from abuse are not mutually exclusive. In fact, pleasurable sex and intimacy is an essential part of the healing process.

Sex is a normal and healthy part of being human, and having good sex is one of the most powerful experiences anyone can have. Not having that can be as detrimental as having it can be powerful. People who have been abused often avoid sex altogether, in order to avoid bringing up feelings about the abuse. However, to heal they must go toward and eventually through whatever triggers memories of the abuse. The French-Jewish filmmaker Pierre Rehov's politically incorrect documentary, ***Suicide Killers***, minimizes the role that Israel's territorial occupation has on Palestinian anger and emphasizes the sexual repression he thinks contributes to the bombers' actions. Several of the young men whom he interviews behind bars say they are eager to reach Paradise and the 72 virgins promised by Islamic theology. "Those who blow themselves up get a good bonus from God—they marry 72 virgins," one tells Rehov. One jailed woman even talks about wanting to be the "prettiest" among the heavenly virgins.[1427]

Yet, Islamic sexual morés are not only about veiling women, segregating the sexes, and abstinence. Quite the contrary, sex is there to be enjoyed to the fullest by married Muslims, and there are numerous religious exhortations on the importance of foreplay, mutual titillation, and sexual satisfaction for both spouses. Should a husband fail to satisfy his wife sexually, or vice versa, that is considered grounds for divorce under Islamic law.[1428] It is the Judaeo-Christian cultures where women's sexuality has been repressed—if it was even acknowledged—for almost 2,000 years. In Victorian society, an "androcentric model" of sexuality was the accepted norm, meaning that "sex" consisted only of the act of penetration to male orgasm. Anything else just plain was not considered sex. Intercourse, as practised by most of society, was robotic and pleasureless, especially for women. It is almost impossible for a woman to reach orgasm in the "missionary position," where the penis never makes contact with the G-spot.

1427. City Lights Pictures, 2006.

1428. Diwan & Diwan 1997.

Based on the ancient Greek idea of a "wandering womb seeking its proper place," female hysteria was a very common catch-all diagnosis in the Victorian era. The symptoms of hysteria could range from excessive masturbation to excessive novel reading and a tendency to wander. Common treatments for hysterical women included opium, the removal of the clitoris, and incarceration. Nineteenth-century physicians even used vibrators to massage women to "hysterical paroxysm," that is, orgasm. Originally, however, the good doctor just reached down there and manually massaged the clitoris until he brought the patient to climax. Now, since this did not involve penetration, the Victorians did not consider it sex; in fact, the introduction of the speculum and the tampon created more controversy. It is reported that with some medical professionals, "pelvic massage treatments" comprised more than half of their business.[1429] With this sort of demand, it was inevitable that the burgeoning Machine Age would invent a device to decrease the work and increase the profits.

By 1900 A.D., a wide selection of electro-mechanical vibrating devices was available for the licensed physician. They ranged from hand- or foot-powered models to those powered by batteries, air pressure, water turbines, gas engines, and street current through lamp socket plugs. Eventually, companies like the Sears-Roebuck Co. and General Electric began mass-producing a variety of home massagers that retailed for $5 to $15. The vibrator was actually the fifth household device to be electrified, after the sewing machine, cooling fan, tea kettle, and toaster, preceding the vacuum cleaner and flat-iron by about a decade.[1430] However, once they showed up in 1920s porn, electric vibrators went underground until they were rediscovered by feminists giving workshops on women's sexuality in the 1970s. In the decades in between, the devices were marketed as "face massagers" in the ubiquitous and respectable mail order catalogs that were a staple in every American middle-class neighbourhood.

Although hysteria—the most frequently diagnosed female disorder in history—was not officially removed as a disease by the American Psychiatric Association until 1952, the widespread availability and popularity of vibrators has helped normalize discussions concerning the female libido. It should be noted, however, that sex aids have been commonplace throughout human history. Ancient Greek literature, for example, often describes women playfully masturbating with the assistance of a contraption known as *olisbos*. In *The Two Friends* of Herodas, two young women converse excitedly about these *olisboi*, and the conversation ends with the girl without one hurrying off to acquire such a "treasure" for herself. In the previously mentioned *Lysistrata* of Aristophanes, the female characters grieve the loss of the special leather dildos that used to be made to perfection by the women of Miletus. Classical Greek pottery unashamedly depicts their use in every conceivable manner, position, and combination.

In the 20th century, Western culture moved toward the belief that women were incapable of intense orgasm, except by clitoral manipulation. This misguided notion was reinforced by Masters and Johnson, whose pioneering research claimed that the clitoris was the only source of female pleasure. The belief persisted until 1950, when

1429. Maines 1999.

1430. Ibid.

an article by a German gynaecologist Ernst Grafenberg discussed the G-spot area. His research showed that women had a spot on the inside of the front wall of the vagina, which, when stimulated, produced intense orgasms and, in some women, even ejaculation of some unknown substance thicker and slicker than urine. We now know that the female prostate acts just like the male prostate: it swells up when rhythmically prodded and discharges fluid through the urethra. To reach the prostate gland in a male, you have to reach in through his anus; in the female, you must reach in, at a similar angle, through her vagina.

Of course, ancient cultures accepted what we have only recently "discovered." As early as the 4th century BCE, writings speak about the distinction between a woman's "red and white fluid."[1431] Even Native American folklore mentions the "mixing of male and female sex fluids."[1432] It might be time to take on the traditions of pre-colonial, pre-missionary Hawaii. There, older women taught young people the art of sexuality over the course of several years, beginning at puberty. In some African cultures, "revered" older women still guide younger boys into their manhood. There is no such thing as "frigidity"—a term coined by Freud—only lousy lovers. The most sexually satisfied women are the ones that take the initiative and/or control, while the least satisfied are the women who expect their partners to know how to satisfy them.

According to consistent reports, two out of three women never or hardly ever reach orgasm during intercourse and one-fifth hardly, if ever, achieve climax even during masturbation. If we continue to be shocked by women using vibrators or attending sex parties, then we are doing the female population a great disservice. Ours is supposed to be a progressive, liberated society, yet sexually empowered women are often seen as threats, bitches, dykes, and ball-busters by both women and men alike. Sexually independent women are stigmatized as evil temptresses, obstacles between man and a heaven filled with sexless wusses. Women have been led to believe that they are simply not allowed to enjoy life in such a way. Neither are men meant to dig too deep into what it means to be human, flesh and blood. Young women are taught to not flaunt themselves in front of men, lest they become sexual objects. Yet it is biology that has made them into sexual objects and they should be damn proud of it while it lasts.

"If you got it, flaunt it!"—"The exposure of innocence is a lie."[1433] The secret is out: women watch porn. A recent poll by *Glamour* Magazine found that 87% of women ages 25 to 39 enjoy pornography as part of their sexual lifestyles—more than use sex toys.[1434] Because disabled people can experience difficulty in forming intimate relationships, accessing adult entertainment can provide an alternative outlet. But saying that erotica can only be enjoyed by people who cannot have a "real relationship" must be one of the most hurtful myths around. Erotic films and magazines are an excellent way to make yourself feel sexually self-reliant and satisfied between partners, and they are routinely enjoyed by couples—together or separately

---

1431. Mishnah, Zabim 2:3.

1432. Keeler 1960, Figure 40.

1433. AL II:22.

1434. Blue 2006.

—as well. In fact, there is no question that sexually explicit material enhances some relationships, and sex therapists frequently recommend explicit materials as a means of fostering sexual arousal in normal, healthy monogamous relationships and marriages.

Sometimes people just go to porn for things they wish they could do in real life. It can fill a gap in their own relationship, if they have a partner who does not like oral sex, for instance, and they love it themselves. Because they are in a relationship and they want to stay in it, they go and look at images of oral sex. There is absolutely no evidence to suggest that exposure to pornography leads to a higher percentage of break-ups or marital problems. As Oscar Wilde pointed out, "A man who moralises is usually a hypocrite, and a woman who moralises is invariably plain."[1435] But in our culture, admitting that our bodies matter is almost an admission of failure. Women will never really experience freedom until they own their sexuality. Beauty is decidedly *not* in the eye of the beholder. Men might argue over whether they prefer Angelina Jolie or Gwyneth Paltrow, but you will never hear anyone say Susan Boyle. "Sex sells," and as Penn Jillette argues, "It is not the sex that's gratuitous. It's all the stuff around the sex that's not needed."[1436]

Despite all the incredible gains made for middle-class white women by reformist feminism, the younger generations seem to, quite frankly, be turning into sluts. Just look around: the streets are littered with half-naked young hussies vomiting their LSATs into spillovers with their skirts hoisted round their waists. At the first sight of a web-cam, young ladies from good homes will flash their tits for the *Girls Gone Wild* team. Feminism means they can do anything they want, but all the little tarts seem to want is boob-jobs, bikini waxes, and attention of the opposite sex. Every generation of teenagers has been criticized for its fashions. The trends of the 1960s, '70s, and '80s were no less shocking than the fashions of the noughties. Today's penchant for the skin-tight, the low-cut, and the high-rise makes this era of dress one of the most sexualized, but as one teenage girl explained to Children's Express: "Teenage girls are not nuns and it doesn't affect what they think about world hunger when they wear a short skirt. It's not as if what people wear is connected to their brains."[1437]

Why should teenage girls not be proud of their burgeoning womanhood? The sexual phobias of the adults should not have any place in this conversation—you could not call a grown woman "whore" in the newspaper and get away with it. Those who judge only by appearance are too shallow to get close enough to someone to find out what they are really like. There are those who mutter that the flamboyant, underwear-exposing fashions of today are further evidence of an overall decline in public morals and decency. The close similarity to fashions worn by noble Englishwomen in the Tudor period suggests otherwise: the ladies who wore the smock- and undershirt-revealing styles of the late 16th century were seen as paragons of virtue by all society. No high-born woman could risk being construed as provocative on account of what she wore.

1435. *Lady Windemere's Fan.* Wilde 1997, 518.

1436. "Sex, Sex, Sex." *Penn & Teller: Bullshit!* Showtime Networks. February 28, 2003.

1437. "Debate: Short Skirts in School," *Independent on Sunday*, March 21, 1999.

If adults think students' dress styles are too revealing, they should look beyond clothes for the source of the problem. It is quite a different thing if a 15-year old dresses in high heels and a push-up bra than if a grown woman of thirty does the same. The former may just be reacting to parents who are trying to shelter her from some of the less innocent, but perfectly natural aspects of adolescence. The over-the-top sex-bomb "rebellion" that adolescent girls engage in is a direct response to a culture that is suffering from sexual repression. If people did not get so freaked out over the idea of young people as sexual beings, there would be no need for young people to be so comically "hypersexualized." No-one does scary costumes on Halloween anymore. In the last few years, the Halloween costume industry has figured out a way to sexualize almost every conceivable option. Witch costumes now come complete with fishnet stockings and velvet miniskirts—warts and stringy hair have been long discontinued. Blame it on the movie ***Mean Girls:*** "Halloween is the one night a year when girls can dress like a total slut and no other girls can say anything about it."[1438]

Adults do not give young people enough credit these days. Children are maturing much faster, but that does not mean that they are all sex-crazed maniacs. Teachers are not used to seeing girls as young as twelve wear make-up and have "boyfriends," but they do not appear to have much confidence in older pupils who wear short skirts either. Of course, it might be more the fear of mature women that their husbands or male co-workers will want to jump these girls, or perhaps rather just being annoyed at their wandering eyes—men are only human, you know. There are some dangerous people out there, but is regulating skirt lengths really the best way to protect teenagers? When they leave campus, they are free to do what they like. Young people need lessons on personal safety—something that will stay in their minds forever, not just until they are out of uniform. Boys do not get branded as aspiring serial killers for smothering themselves in blood, which, as it happens, many American schools have banned on Halloween in recent years.

Humans enjoy watching beautiful people, whether they be of the same or opposite sex, of age or not, whether they admit it or not. "There are no ugly people on TV." The ancient Greeks considered it normal for any man to be drawn to the beauty of a boy, just as much as to that of a woman; but in Christianity, you have sinned merely by thinking of sinning. Recommendations to censor or age-restrict sexual images in advertising and music videos, along with the associated notion that all sexual messages are inherently "damaging" to women, assume that our current, restricted, plasticized, heteronormative social view of female sexuality is in some way or form "normal." The present Western sexual culture is not the logical conclusion of social libertinism; it is rather specific, quite peculiar, and not all that permissive.

Bisexuality was originally a physiological term: as a physical organism, we are all inherently bisexual, and have been so since time immemorial. Examine either sex and you will find attributes of the other sex within the blood, the cells, and even the genitals. No reasonable person could have any cause to deny this. Part of the mammary glands is evident on the male, just as a vestigial penis is evident on the

---

1438. Dir. Mark Waters. Paramount Pictures, 2004.

female. However, the rate at which our species is proliferating across the planet is ample evidence of the fact that our physical bisexuality is carried forward into physical reality in only a minority of cases. The word "bisexual" first appeared in its modern sense in a 1914 issue of *American Medicine:* "By nature all human beings are psychically bisexual—capable of loving a person of either sex."[1439] There is tremendous societal pressure to be either "gay" or "straight," even though the Kinsey Scale puts most of us somewhere nearer the middle than very far on one side or the other.[1440]

No sexually liberated person cares what sex his or her partner or object of affection is. Besides, sex is better by yourself anyway. I am not convinced that females even have a sexual orientation—what they do have is strong sexual preferences. Women tend to be very picky, and most choose to have sex with men. So are homosexuality and heterosexuality fictions? Of course they are, but as Gore Vidal quipped, "it makes a lot of girls happy."[1441] The gay identity constructed by West Europeans is irrelevant to the lives of, for example, the Latin American men who can sleep with other men without considering themselves homosexual. The clinical definition of a fetishist is a person unable to experience sexual pleasure from any other form of sexual release, which may make homosexuality a fetish, but no more than heterosexuality. Everyone trying to analyze everybody else's sex lives to make sure that they are not the bat-shit craziest one in town is a colossal waste of time.

What is abnormal may not necessarily be unnatural; to paraphrase Kinsey, "the only unnatural sex act is the one you cannot perform." Sex is sex—do not try to analyze it and always ask nicely the first time! Paraphilias, or socially unacceptable sexual practices, are much more common than most ordinary teleiophiles would imagine. Homosexuality, for instance, is nothing unusual among animals, but as far as I know, there is only one species that engages in homophobia. As the pioneering American rocket scientist Jack Parsons wrote: "The ruthless examination and destruction of taboos, complexes, frustrations, dislikes, fears, and disgusts hostile to the will is essential to progress. Even in the case of pet preferences and prejudices, it must be realized that those things are only significant to the individual—meaningless and often silly to the larger world. On a hot day, Galahad probably stank under his armor. And that sensibility which is nauseated by the sex odor of its own kind, and titillated by the sex odor of plants, might be profitably studied under the heading of a perversion."[1442]

As any biologist will attest, the genitals and the anus were deliberately placed close together in all mammals simply because the smell of the one points the way to the other. Thus, if you like assholes, or feel attracted to them, there is nothing wrong with you—and I am not talking figuratively. Humans are not naturally repulsed by feces; this no small feat is usually accomplished through potty training. Anal intercourse used to be the only method of contraception in various ancient cultures,

---

1439. Wilhelm Stekel, "Masked Homosexuality," *American Medicine* XX, August 1914.

1440. Kinsey, et al. Op. cit.

1441. Hari, op. cit.

1442. "Living Thelema." Hyatt 2000, 91.

which is not surprising, since the anus is an erogenous zone by itself. Whether you like it or not, the anal and vaginal region and the penis share the same nerve roots. Anal play is nothing to be ashamed of, although many people today are. It started in our earliest childhood: touching the anus is generally accepted as the first sexually related exploration every baby does and even some yet unborn foetuses do.

Stimulating the anus on a woman causes sexual arousal and the amazing sensation that somebody is touching your vagina from the outside. The buttock muscles are the strongest in the human body and they come into play during almost any form of sexual activity, including masturbation. Some women have been known to masturbate just by contracting and relaxing their muscles and this includes the "back door." And if you though butt sex was just for the select few, Kinsey found that half of both men and women had had some experience with anal stimulation or penetration.[1443] A little more recent research shows that over 10% of heterosexual married couples in the United States have regular anal intercourse.[1444] For the man, the main advantage of penetrating the anus with his penis is that the opening is not only very narrow, but the circular muscle around it is also much stronger. As a result, he is going to feel much more sensation compared to penetrating the relatively soft and receptive vagina. The vaginal contractions he feels only during the female orgasm is what he feels constantly while penetrating the anus. However, as Carol Queen stated some 20 years ago, when she sold her millionth strap-on harness to a heterosexual couple, "Straight couples are re-inventing anal sex."

Alexander the Great was not gay, the controversy over the Oliver Stone film notwithstanding; he did it with men and women—just like every other person back then. Hellenic paederasty, as idealized by the Greeks from archaic times onward, entailed a formal bond between an adult male and an adolescent boy outside his immediate family, consisting of intimate and often sexual relations. The custom was initially employed by the upper class as a means of teaching the young and conveying to them the essential male attitudes, such as *arete* (excellence) and *sophrosune* (restraint). It was also integral to Greek military training, and even a factor in troop deployment, with lovers often fighting side by side. As such, it was seen as a fundamental part of the Hellenistic culture from the time of Homer, and: "In the centuries of Rome's great military and political success, there was no differentiation between same-sexers and other-sexers; there was also a lot of crossing back and forth. Of the first twelve Roman emperors, only one was exclusively heterosexual."[1445]

As William Amstrong Percy III wrote in *Pederasty and Pedagogy in Archaic Greece*, "the Greeks we most admire almost always practiced pederasty, at least before marriage."[1446] Homer's works only hint obliquely at homoerotic relationships, as in the myth of Zeus and Ganymede in the *Iliad* and in the Homeric Hymn to Aphrodite. There are more than four dozen examples of young men who were lovers of male divinities in the Greek myths. Tradition ascribes Zeus, Apollo, Pan, Hermes,

1443. Op. cit.

1444. James R. Petersen, et al. "Playboy Readers' Sex Survey, Part I," *Playboy*, January 1983.

1445. Hari, op. cit.

1446. 1996, 9.

Dionysos, Orpheus, and Herakles to such love; in fact, all the chief gods of the Hellenic pantheon except Ares had these sorts of relationships. Alcæus, Pindar, and Sappho sang poems about paederastic love, and Æscylus, Sophocles, and Euripides wrote plays on the subject. Of the Athenian political leaders, Solon, Peisistratus, Hippias, Hipparchus, Themistocles, Aristides, Critias, Demosthenes, and Æschines all were recorded to have had same-sex relationships; same goes for Pausanius, Lysander, and Agesilaus of Sparta, and of course, Philip II and Alexander of Macedon.

In ancient times, the institution of paederasty was inseparable from organized sports. The gymnasium was the main venue for men to educate boys in the arts of athletics, warfare, and philosophy; it was also one of the principal venues for paederastic relationships. Socrates, Plato, and Xenophon all describe the inspirational power of love between men, and upon the death of Plato, the presidency of the Academy passed between lovers; of the great Stoic philosophers, Chrysippus, Cleanthes, and Zeno fell in love with young men. With the coming of democracy, whose heroes were the lovers and tyrannicides Harmodius and Aristogeiton, access to gymnastic and sympotic culture widened, and the relationships associated with it became more widely admired and imitated. According to public sentiment, as expressed in Pausanias' speech in Plato's *Symposium*, paederastic couples were seen as fundamental to democracy and feared by tyrants, because the bond between friends was stronger than the bond of obedience to a despotic ruler.

In general, once the young man came of age, the sexual relationship ended, but he would remain on close terms with his mentor throughout their lives. However, the Greeks also had a saying for those male lovers who continued their affair after the usual period: "You can lift up a bull, if you carried the calf." This was long before Judaeo-Christianity had shackled our sexuality, and ironically, Alexander is partly to blame: if he had not freed the Jews and founded Alexandria, Judaism might have remained an obscure Levantine sect and much of the world might still retain a healthy outlook on sexuality. All of this is closely related to the great cultural battle of the Hellenistic era, during which the Greeks sought to extend their culture and religion with its homoerotic ideals across the entire Mediterranean region, causing widespread rebellion. Jews, in particular, were aghast at all the nude athletics and overt homosexuality. It was a Christian emperor, Justinian, who finally put an end to the institutions that sustained Hellenic culture, including Plato's Academy and the Olympic Games.

Make no mistake about it, there is quite a bit of sex going on even in today's Olympics. When you have a lot of young people who are in great physical shape, you have a lot of testosterone to go around and everyone is attracted to everyone else. At the Albertville Winter Olympics, condom machines in the Athletes' Village had to be refilled every two hours. In Sydney, the organizers' original order of 70,000 condoms was depleted so fast that they ordered 20,000 more, but the supply was still exhausted three days before the competition schedule was over. Salt Lake City went even bigger, handing out 250,000 condoms in 2002, over the objections of the host town's Mormon leadership.[1447] When you pack thousands of fit people in the tightest clothes possible

1447. Paul Hochman, "Let the Games Begin," *Scotland on Sunday*, July 18, 2004.

into a gladiator-style arena for weeks on end, make them compete, sell tickets, and broadcast it around the world, it is the ultimate form of sex selling. No wonder sex workers in Vancouver wanted to open a legal co-op brothel just in time for the 2010 Winter Olympics.

A culture that integrated and even valorized some aspects of same sex love endured for a thousand years. Scholars such as William Percy hold that paederasty was formalized in ancient Crete around 630 BCE as a means of population control, together with delaying the age of marriage for men to thirty years. Pubescent boys were considered substitute women because they had no power, and their still developing bodies were more similar to a woman's than an adult male's. Paederasty was fully institutionalized and comparable to marriage—every Greek aristocrat did it. There was, however, a difference between it and marriage: boys usually had to be courted and were free to choose their male companion; girls, on the other hand, were used for economic and political advantage, and their unions were contracted at the discretion of their father and the suitor. Boys entered into a paederastic relationship from age of 12 to about 18 or 19, which was around the same age that girls were given in marriage, also to adult men several years their senior. At the end of the relationship, the older man would be ready for marriage and fatherhood, while the younger man would be ready to select his own protégée. To be sure, marriage has always been between a man and a woman, since its purpose is not sex, or even love, but the production of legal heirs.

Like homosexuality, infidelity is prevalent in animals. Female opossums even have double wombs: they can get pregnant even when they are pregnant—it is every woman's worst nightmare. Jealousy, a powerful human emotion, would make no sense if man was naturally monogamous, or indeed, if he was naturally polygamous. However, most people are only ever in love with one person ***at a time***. Marriage was not originally instituted in recognition of the naturalness of monogamy, but rather in recognition of its unnaturalness. It is clear that social monogamy (i.e. physical association and child rearing between a male and a female) and sexual monogamy are two different things. The former is common, while the latter is exceedingly rare. For the longest time, men and women married for money, power, etc., and had a string of lovers on the side. If your partner should cheat on you with a member of his or her own sex, it might hurt less, because there is no chance of progeny. On the other hand, if he or she actually leaves you for a member of the same sex, you could feel worse, neutered, like you could not procreate either.

Not long ago, all women without children were known as "childless," implicating a state of loss; throughout most of history, a man could divorce his wife, if she failed to bear children. Nowadays, however, an increasing number of women insist on using the term "childfree," which emphasizes liberation. According to the Guttmacher Institute, the average American woman wants two children, and spends approximately five years conceiving and having them—she spends another thirty years of her life trying to prevent getting pregnant.[1448] A recent study shows that women in the United States are having children at an all-time low rate. One in five

---

1448. "Fulfilling the Promise: Public Policy and U.S. Family Planning Clinics," New York, 2000.

women of reproductive age will not have any children at all. The more educated women are, the higher the childfree rate is.[1449] In Germany, a full 30% of women are childfree—the highest proportion of any country in the world. It is notable that child-wariness is not only characteristic of highly developed Germany and northern Europe as a whole, but that it rises from 30% to more than 40% among college graduates.[1450]

However, single people and homosexuals will always be second-class citizens in a society founded on procreation. In feudal times, unmarried men were not even considered adults, but at least singlehood was no longer a stonable offence. No society wants people to be mateless; it needs to perpetuate itself. For a culture to survive, the average birth rate has to be at least 2.1 per capita—any less and civilization will crumble.[1451] The societal pressure is always towards relationships, and if you resist, you will be considered antisocial or deranged. There is no open debate about the subject. People flat out refuse to believe that not everyone wants to have children. They always think it is simply because you have not met the "right person" yet. Singles routinely face tax and insurance penalties, housing discrimination, and inequities in Social Security benefits solely on basis of their marital status. No political candidate will ever utter the "S" word. They will refer to "marriage," "family," and "seniors," but nobody acknowledges singles. Not even Ralph Nader—and he is one of them.

This is why the gay community wants marriage and adoption rights. Historically, marriage has always been used a method of oppressing a despised group. For 150 years, the penal laws in Ireland provided that no Protestant could marry a Catholic. In the early part of the 20th century, 38 American states used the marriage license as a mechanism to prohibit white people from marrying blacks, Asians, and Native Americans. The rules against marriage between a "colored" person and a white person were struck down by the California Supreme Court in the 1940s and the U.S. Supreme Court in the 1960s, but using the marriage ceremony as a method of expressing societal disdain towards a particular group is as old as civilization itself. Of course, the problem with using this argument in relation to gay marriage is that, historically, the object of marriage was not the official recognition of an intimate relationship between two (or more) people, but the transfer of property to legitimate offspring.

Then again, the counter-arguments are just as silly: we have lately heard a lot about the "sanctity of marriage," as if that were something that has been around forever, when in reality the phrase was not even invented until 2004. There is not a single reference to it anywhere before the Massachusetts Supreme Court legalized same-sex unions in that state. Opponents of gay marriage needed a logical reason to overturn a legal precedent, and the only thing that trumps the Constitution is God Himself. People who are worried about gay marriage and its effect on the "sanctity" of the institution are often on their own third marriage and cheating on that spouse just

---

1449. Gretchen Livingston & D'Vera Cohn, "Childlessness Up Among All Women; Down Among Women with Advanced Degrees," Pew Research Center, Washington, D.C., June 25, 2010.

1450. David P. Barash, "Sex Is Essential, Kids Aren't," *Los Angeles Times*, May 10, 2006.

1451. Ferriss 2010.

like they cheated on the first two. Adultery, spousal abuse, etc. have no bearing on the "sanctity of marriage," just homosexuality. Yet it was heterosexuals who revolutionized marriage to the point where gays and lesbians began to say, "Hey, this applies to us now."

What, then, is the real "gay agenda," what is it that 99% of all gay couples wish for every single day? Above all else, they seem to want a simply inexcusable level of normalcy. For some inexplicable reason, they think that they should be allowed to live their lives in peace like everyone else, with full support and assistance of the government. Which is, perish the thought, remarkably similar to what straight people want. Guilt is a wonderful tool of oppression: you are not likely to assert your rights if you are feeling guilty, for example, about your sexuality. The recognition of gay marriages does not actually increase the number of homosexuals, even though it tends to bring the subject more into the public limelight. Gay marriage is just the next logical step of "gay pride." Same-sex weddings have recently been drawn into the national spotlight in America precisely by attempts to make the unions illegal; the increased attention to the marriage issue has encouraged more gay couples to formalize their relationships, even if in most states, the ceremonies remain purely sentimental.

The number of gay unions has remained relatively low where their registration has been made possible. A right does not equal an obligation. More gay couples were married in California in the first three months that same-sex unions were legal than were married in the first four years they were legal in Massachusetts. Even so, the number of marriages only represents about 10% of the same-sex couples in California.[1452] Here is something for you to try: call a married woman's spouse her boyfriend—if she protests, saying "He's my husband," just tell her you no longer recognize marriage. Suddenly, the majority gets to feel what the minority feels, to know what it is like to have their relationship downgraded, and to have a right they take for granted called into question because of someone else's beliefs. Mature gay couples who marry after 20 years of being together do it in order for society not to treat them as complete strangers, but allow them to register each other as next of kin and beneficiaries of their insurance plans. Now how devious is that? The nerve of these people to desire the same sort of lives as everyone else.

Banning same-sex unions would not undo the existence of alternatives to traditional marriage. Estimated 6 to 14 million children are being raised by gay and lesbian couples in the United States already.[1453] For decades, it was the done thing for family court judges to lean toward a maternal preference in custody disputes. But what if both parents should be women or neither one is? Judges in Massachusetts have been struggling with that question since gay and lesbian couples began filing for divorce in 2004—seven months after the state supreme court legalized same-sex marriage. In every U.S. state, judges are already forced to apply the principles of marriage law to same-sex couples, if only to regulate child custody should the couple

---

1452. Gary J. Gates & Christopher Ramos, "Census Snapshot: California Lesbian, Gay, and Bisexual Population," The Williams Institute, UCLA School of Law, Los Angeles, October 2008.

1453. Jenn Shreve, "The Gay-by Boom: Gay Couples No Longer Immune from Feeling the Pressure to Procreate," *San Francisco Chronicle*, September 29, 2004.

part their ways.

California courts have had to recognize Canadian marriages and Vermont civil unions in order to dissolve them. Courts in other states have granted visitation rights to same-sex partners who have bonded with the other's biological child, even if those rulings did not include such rights as inheritance or Social Security and health insurance coverage for the children. Divorce can be financially ruinous for same-sex couples. Heterosexual couples may claim a tax deduction from alimony payments, but that benefit is not available for gay and lesbian spouses because the IRS does not recognize their marriages. Retirement savings and pensions plans, painlessly split for heterosexual divorcées, would have to be cashed out and would be heavily taxed.

As absurd as it sounds, what we are seeing is an LGBT version of the nuclear family. Though some gays and lesbians who choose not to raise children are embracing their roles as doting uncles and aunties, many in the LGBT community wonder whether this trend could spell the end to the homosexual lifestyle as we know it. For gays and lesbians who are ambivalent about having children, and for those who have never wanted them at all, it can be a little unnerving to watch all your friends modelling the latest Baby Bjorns. After all, it was not that long ago when being gay meant having your parents lament never getting to have any grandchildren. Having a child has much greater implications when you belong to a socially disadvantaged group, whether that group be the homosexuals, the blacks, the immigrants, or the unemployed. However, gays and lesbians who decide *not* to have children often find themselves in the same unpleasant position as straight married couples who remain childless: having to constantly fend off inquiries into their "plans" and to listen in horror as formerly hip friends set up playdates for their rugrats.

Governments are wooing parents with longer maternity pay, paternity leave, flexible hours, and family tax breaks—this is clearly a redistribution of money from people without children to those with them. In fact, the only reason singles, childless couples, and gays are tolerated in society is that they are good for market economy. The gay community has by far the highest average income of any minority, and in most gay couples, both spouses work. They do not waste money on the basic expenses of heterosexual couples, such as the children's hobbies and education, so they tend to have more disposable income than other households. Homosexuals are commonly estimated to make up about 6% of the population, which means over 18 million people in the United States alone. More and more American companies are launching advertising campaigns with specific gay and lesbian themes in a bid to capture a piece of the $743 billion market.[1454] Big corporations are also waking up to the growing and largely untapped pool of singles who already account for a quarter of all travel and a third of home purchases. In 2004, De Beers Jewellery actually began marketing diamond rings for the right hand with the slogan, "Your left hand says we; your right hand says me."

In his enormously influential book, *The Rise of the Creative Class* (2002), Richard Florida, a professor of regional economic development, sought to identify the tools for

1454. "The Gay and Lesbian Market in the U.S.: Trends and Opportunities in the LGBT Community," Witeck-Combs Communications & Packaged Facts, Washington, D.C., July 2010.

success in an information age. His conclusion was simple: the locations that do the best are the ones that succeed in attracting creative people. Florida laid the sociological foundation for an idea many Silicon Valley residents already understood intuitively: that it is creative people, not multinational corporations, government offices, or public infrastructure, that fuel economic development. The "creative class" will find its way to places that have a tolerant atmosphere, a rich cultural scene, colourful street culture, and a happening nightlife. By comparing American cities, Florida found that the more gays and freelance artists live there, the better the cities do. Tomorrow's winners will include cities like San Francisco, Seattle, and Boston, whereas among the losers are Miami, Pittsburgh, and Detroit. Many gays and lesbians are creative, hard-working, and thus also economically productive people, but according to Florida, this is not enough to explain why the cities favoured by the LGBT community fare better than others.

Florida contends that gay people have a keen sense of the prevailing atmosphere, fleeing the narrow-minded localities in favour of the more tolerant areas. They are the "canaries of the creative economy," telling us where there is not enough oxygen. According to Florida, the key people of modern economy, the creative talent, are looking for exactly the same atmosphere. Many of them feel different, dress funny, sport strange body art, perhaps want to work at night. They are on the lookout for a town and a job that accepts them as they are. Florida includes almost a third of the labour force in the creative class: artists, researchers, teachers, lawyers, physicians, programmers, craftsmen—people who use creativity in their jobs, instead of repeating ready-made formulas. Information technology has changed a lot about our society and economy, but most creative people still want to live and work together in a real community of other interesting people. The science and technology of China and India are advancing rapidly, but Beijing still only produces as few patents as Phoenix and Shanghai about the same amount as Salt Lake City.[1455]

For the first time in U.S. history, there are more women living without husbands than with them. Thanks to high divorce rates, increased longevity, and the rising age for first marriage, American women now spend more of their adult lives single than married. Not only are women marrying later, they are also less likely to remarry right away if divorced or widowed.[1456] The assumption is that women want more than sex, and that men are more than happy to give it to them. But the fear of commitment does not fit the definition of fear, prompting the smarter psychologists to claim that it is really fear of abandonment. The truth is, many people do not really wish to share their lives with anyone—which is where "fuck buddies" and "friends with benefits" come in. Most of us are simply too busy, too lazy, or too unattractive to find a new person to have sex with every night. Now, jealousy is definitely fear, and many married people are terrified of their single friends stealing their spouses.

In Britain, half of single women are perfectly happy to stay unattached, according to a survey for market research group Mintel. The 2005 poll found that 56% of single women in the UK were "very happy" with their lives as they were and had absolutely

---

1455. Florida 2008.

1456. Sam Roberts, "51% of Women Are Now Living Without Spouse," *New York Times*, January 16, 2007.

no desire to be married. Forty-six percent of single men felt the same, and almost half of them said the biggest downside of living alone was "not having enough sex." For women, however, the biggest gripe was that everyone always assumed they wanted to be in a relationship.[1457] Decades ago, unmarried women of a certain age were considered sad old maids, while the men were seen as dirty old bachelors. Singlehood continues to be demonized by romantic love, which, incidentally, has never been more valued than it is today. In popular mythology, promoted in everything from movies and music to books and greeting cards, a partner is supposed to fulfill all of one's needs for emotional intimacy, financial security, and romantic passion. To me, this is just another example of the modern quest for happiness outside one's self.

We have come to the point in our culture where we think the only route to happiness and a meaningful life is coupling. Single people, like atheists, are defined by what they do not have. But as Tyler Durden pointed out, "We're a generation of men raised by women. I'm wondering if another woman is really the answer we need."[1458] It was not until the last century that the perfect couple assumed a central place in the Western imagination; around the turn of the 20th century, it was far more common for adults to maintain rich relationships with their same-sex peers. Something that is difficult for many women to admit or understand is that after about the age of seven, boys prefer the company of men. A woman is perceived as just another mother, and boys basically want to hear variations on only two phrases from their mothers: "I love you" and "Do you want your eggs fried or scrambled?" At the end of a long school day, boys really do not want to sit quietly and listen to yet more women speak soothingly about important subjects. Over the past twenty years or so, we have managed to create a new generation of child-men, perpetual adolescents who see no point in growing up. "I can't get married—I'm a thirty-year-old boy."[1459]

People can be quite protective of their life choices, and expressing your desire to either remain single or get married will leave people who have not made the same choice feeling that you are in some way looking down on what they have chosen. Far from being lonely, singles comfortable with their status report having dynamic social lives with time for frequent engagements with friends and family. Instead of being overwhelmed by loneliness and longing, they find that their lifestyle choice gives them an independence and spontaneity unknown to most couples. Studies have found that happier singles usually have a strong passion for some or other recreational or intellectual pursuit, and much of their joy derives from nurturing and maintaining a strong network of same-sex friends. Dinner parties and impromptu outings enrich their lives and fulfill their needs for human companionship, while higher-paying jobs allow them to live by themselves.[1460]

I have never understood the phrase "more than friends." Has everyone not seen

---

1457. "Marketing to Singles," Mintel International Group Ltd., London, February 2005.

1458. *Fight Club*, op. cit.

1459. Ibid.

1460. Martin Miller, "Unattached, Thank You, and Loving It: As More People Live the Single Life, Society Slowly Catches on to 'a Different Kind of Happiness,'" *Los Angeles Times*, September 2, 2004.

When Harry Met Sally? ". . . no man can be friends with a woman that he finds attractive. He always want to have sex with her. – So, you're saying that a man can be friends with a woman he finds unattractive? – No. You pretty much want to nail 'em too. – What if they don't want to have sex with you? – Doesn't matter because the sex thing is already out there so the friendship is ultimately doomed and that is the end of the story."[1461] This is, of course, also one cause of male homophobia, thinking that every gay man wants to shag you. "Remember when you were a kid and the boys didn't like the girls? Only sissies liked girls? What I'm trying to tell you is that nothing's changed. You think boys grow out of not liking girls, but we don't grow out of it. We just grow horny. That's the problem. We mix up liking pussy for liking girls. Believe me, one couldn't have less to do with the other."[1462]

Despite their protestations to the contrary, women do no really want a "nice guy"—not the kind of women men are attracted to, anyway. Sex is not romantic; at best, it is erotic. People only ever "make love" in bad Hollywood movies, prompting Marla Singer to exclaim: "I haven't been fucked like that since grade school."[1463] In fact, according to a study conducted at Heriot-Watt University in Edinburgh, watching romantic comedies can spoil your love life. Psychologists at the family and personal relations laboratory at the Scottish university say rom-coms promote unrealistic expectations when it comes to love. They studied 40 top box office hits from 1995 to 2005, and identified common themes which they believed to be unrealistic. They found fans of films such as *Notting Hill* and *Runaway Bride* often fail to communicate with their partner, because they think that if someone is "meant" to be with you then they will know what you want without you needing to tell them. While these films do capture the excitement of new relationships, they also suggest that trust and committed love exist from the moment people meet, when in fact these are qualities that usually take years to develop. Most people know that the idea of a perfect relationship is unrealistic, but some are more influenced by media portrayals than they realize.[1464]

"Romantic love is 80% sex." Attracting a heterosexual partner is all about the dance of polarity. Energy flows between positive and negative electrodes, anode and cathode, magnetic north and south. If you fail to convey masculinity as a man or femininity as a woman, you are not going to attract a suitable companion of the opposite sex. Yet the metrosexual revolution would have us believe that women are yearning for nothing more in a man than another girlfriend. We need to face the fact that we are not going to find our "soul mate" among the opposite sex; otherwise, there would be no need for hormones—men and women are just wired too damn differently. Now, there are millions of reasons why straight people get married, being soul mates just is not one of them: very smart and successful women always have a

---

1461. Dir. Rob Reiner. Columbia Pictures, 1989.

1462. Jules Feiffer, dialogue later cut out of the film *Carnal Knowledge* (1971). As quoted in Schuth 1978, 103.

1463. *Fight Club*, op. cit.

1464. Kimberly Johnson & Bjarne Holmes, "Contradictory Messages: A Content Analysis of Hollywood-Produced Romantic Comedy Feature Films," *Communication Quarterly* 57(3), January 2009, 352–373.

harder time finding partners, because men want somebody intelligent enough to recognize the man's brilliance, but not enough to challenge them; nor, indeed, so smart that they find someone else more interesting.

Women are paid less than men for several of reasons, but primarily because money is not the same kind of fetish for women as it is to men. Everyone knows perfectly well that women want men who have money, even if women constantly deny this. A scientific study of 37 different nationalities, including Eskimos, Taiwanese, Pygmies, and Germans, confirms this cross-cultural universal.[1465] Around the world, high-ranking men have always enjoyed access to comparatively large numbers of women. Young and attractive women have, by and large, found such men appealing beyond what may be predicted from their immediate physical appearance. "Power," as Henry Kissinger famously remarked, "is the ultimate aphrodisiac." In fact, power is pretty much the default pheromone among mammals. Female baboons, chimpanzees, elephants, elks, seals, etc. eagerly mate with dominant males while disdaining subordinates—and they do so more or less in what humans would call harems. Before the homogenization of cultures as a result of Western colonialism, more than 85% of human societies likewise favoured polygamy.[1466] Throughout history, men who accumulate power, status, and wealth have gained additional wives and consorts, and even in avowedly monogamous cultures, successful males have commonly had additional lovers. For men at the top, such opportunities continue to be exceedingly frequent, not because they have higher sex drives than anyone else, but because they are dominant males in a two-sex species.

"Lust is honest." Arranged marriages were not barbaric, they were highly civilized—"In the real world women fall in love with men who beat them, men fall in love with their mothers; love is the most inexplicable, unscientific, irrational of all phenomenon. The only thing we know for sure is that it can happen to anyone, and usually does."[1467] People say that men trade love for sex and women trade sex for love, and that is exactly what is wrong with today's relationships. If either party approaches a relationship in this manner, it will eventually fail. Everyone wants sex, but many women do not admit that to themselves, much less anyone else, and look down on men because they do. Both parties may thus start straying from who they are, to become what they believe the other is looking for, just to get to the sex part. Yet there is obviously some truth to the assertion that, "Women can use sex to get what they want. Men cannot, as sex is what they want."

According to a 2009 book called *Why Women Have Sex* by psychologists Cindy Meston and David Buss, there are 237 reasons why women have sex—and most of them have little to do with romance or pleasure. Alfred Kinsey, the father of sexology, asked 7,985 Americans about their sexual histories in the 1940s and '50s, while Masters and Johnson observed people having orgasms for most of the '60s; but they never bothered to ask why. As it turns out, women can use sex for all sorts of resources: promotion, money, drugs, for revenge, to get back at a partner who has

---

1465. Buss 1994.

1466. Barash & Lipton 2001.

1467. "Green Christmas." *Boston Legal.* ABC. December 18, 2007.

cheated on them; to make themselves feel good, or to make their partners feel bad. Women can use sex at every stage of the relationship, from luring a man into it, to try and keep him content, so he will not stray. Some women use sex to tell their partner they do not want them any more—by sleeping with someone else. Some use it to feel desirable; some to get a new car. There are very few things women will not use sex for. To sum up: "All men are dogs; all women are evil."

Research shows that, in casual relationships, physical attractiveness is a priority for women, just as it is for men. For long-term mates, men keep preferring attractiveness, but women opt for social status, as well as empathy and trustworthiness. A man naturally seeks a young, fertile woman, because this is a prerequisite for the propagation of the species. Should the woman be young and beautiful, the man is willing to accept all sorts of flaws and vices. A man is better off accentuating his wealth—if he has money, he also has reliability and can thus be committed to. A man looks the better to a woman the more power, status, and dominance he has. His physical appearance is not nearly as important as men tend to think. The better socio-economic status a man has, the sexier he appears to women. The feeling is absolutely genuine, because women are instinctually seeking a dependable provider for their offspring. "Clooneyish" men tend to be unfaithful, because men have a different genetic agenda—they wish to impregnate lots of healthy women. A woman might use sex to land a less handsome but more loyal mate: he will have fewer genetic benefits but more resource benefits, because he will stick around. After their minimum requirements are met, both sexes choose well-rounded partners over those with the very best looks or the highest status.[1468]

These neolithic ideals continue to influence our mate selection even if we are not consciously looking to procreate. Until very recently, however, children and parents were rarely in conflict about whom to marry: both agreed that marriage was not about love, but about social and economic ties. As recently as four decades ago, most American men said they wanted wives who would be good housekeepers, while most American women said they wanted husbands who were "industrious." Today, men and women in the U.S. invariably say they want partners who are intelligent and attractive.[1469] Nearly everyone in the West—and a growing number of young people elsewhere in the world—now believes that marriage is about love, that you should marry the person you love, something that would have been ludicrous and dangerous a century ago. For thousands of years, marriage was all about family unions and property, and for most of the world, it still is. Arranged marriages and marriages of convenience are globally much more common than so-called marriages of love. In Africa, most of Asia, India, China, even highly industrialized Japan, arranged marriages are the rule. This is, after all, how marriage was designed in the first place. At the same time, all sorts of matchmakers are becoming more and more common among the busy Western singles—the only difference being that matchmaking is a big business in the West, while marriages in other cultures are usually arranged according

---

1468. Norman P. Li & Douglas T. Kendrick, "Sex Similarities and Differences in Preferences for Short-Term Mates: What, Whether, and Why," *Journal of Personality and Social Psychology* 90(3), March 2006, 468–489.

1469. Coontz 2005.

to family interests.

Historically, married couples have seldom voluntarily slept in the same bed as each other. Sleep is vital for both our physical and mental health, and it is not sensible to share the bed space with someone who is making noises and who you have to fight with for the covers. The modern tradition of the marital bed only began with the Industrial Revolution, when people moving to overcrowded cities found themselves short of living space. In ancient Rome, the marital bed was a place for sexual congress, but not for sleeping. According to a recent Austrian study, sharing a bed with someone can temporarily reduce your bain power, especially if you are a man. Women who share a bed fare better because they sleep more deeply and are pre-programmed to cope better with broken sleep. A lot of events in women's lives disturb sleep, including bringing up children, the menopause, and even the menstrual cycle. Men tend to "sleep with one eye open" and when they spend the night with a bed mate, their sleep is disturbed whether they have sex or not, and this impairs their mental ability the next day.[1470]

That one small word, "love," stands for a hotchpotch of feelings and drives: romance, lust, passion, attachment, commitment, and caring—"There is the love of a child for its parents, a disciple for his master, a man for his mistress, the human for the divine and vice-versa—there are other forms as well."[1471] The danger lay in taking one aspect of love for the whole. Love can be a verb—to love someone—but in recent times, love seems to have become more and more a feeling—to be in love. Unfortunately, feelings are fickle and fleeting, and tend to lead to irrational and often even self-defeating choices. Love does not justify anything—love is temporary insanity. Even Freud called it a "lovely state of psychosis." The French give reduced sentences for crimes of passion. People who are in love beg and pray for mercy, swear oaths and sleep in doorways. They submit voluntarily to more humiliating slavery than real slaves ever do. If it were an attempt to gain wealth or power, such activities would be banned; but "all is fair in love and war."

As Ethan Hawke observed in ***Before Sunrise***, "If you think about it, love is the most selfish thing there is."[1472] Socrates had it right in the 4th century BCE: "These things, dear boy, you must bear in mind, and you must know the fondness of the lover is not a matter of goodwill, but of appetite which he wishes to satisfy: 'Just as the wolf loves the lamb, so the lover adores his beloved.'"[1473] Friendship does not aim at immediate pleasure, but also looks into the future. You would do well to avoid marriage, or you too might suffer the emotional pain, humiliation, expense, and logistical difficulty of breaking up a long-term union at midlife for something so demonstrably fleeting as love. Getting married thirty years ago was part of a tradition. People got married because their parents were married and could not imagine their children not getting married, or having children outside of marriage. Nowadays, couples who do not wish

1470. John Dittami, et al. "Sex Differences in the Reactions to Sleeping in Pairs versus Sleeping Alone in Humans," ***Sleep and Biological Rhythms*** 5(4), October 2007, 271–276.

1471. G. J. Yorke, "Tantric Theory," ***The Scribe***, Spring Equinox 1996.

1472. Dir. Richard Linklater. Columbia Pictures, 1995.

1473. ***Phædrus***, 241c–d.

to tie the knot are not rebelling against religion, but merely want to keep the State from contractually dictating the parameters of their relationship. For them, loving someone does not have anything to do with society—it is personal.

"Consider Love. Here is a Force destructive and corrupting where by many Men have been lost. Yet without Love Man were not Man."[1474] Love is forever, only the partners change: "Each time one loves is the only time one has ever loved. Difference of object does not alter singleness of passion. It merely intensifies it."[1475] Your brain is playing a trick by associating something that just happened with pleasure and attributing the feeling to the magnificent specimen right before your eyes. And already we suspect that this is not going to end well. These things have short shelf lives—they are hard-wired not to last. "The passion you fulfill is the passion you kill." According to science, the most wonderful, elating feeling known to man amounts to no more than a narcotic high: the bodily chemistry which makes people sexually attractive to new partners lasts, at most, two years.[1476] Being in love is fantastic, but our bodies cannot be in that state all the time—they would fizzle out; as a species, we would die. Passion is destined to end, whether it mellows into long-term love or blows up on the freeway at 4 a.m. Our society does itself a disservice by glorifying passionate love so much. The search for eternal passion is a search for the perfect high that keeps people discarding relationships left and right. Once the initial euphoria fades, people want to break up, instead of recognizing it as normal.

When we fall desperately in love with someone, there is a chemical reaction in our brain. For most people, this is a relatively good thing: you can go on for days without sleep, you text with your crush constantly, when you are not actually on the phone with them—you simply cannot get enough of them. The problem arises when the object of your affection is someone who is unavailable. Everyone who has felt the pangs of jealousy knows how we can resent the other person. We might harbour violent, murderous fantasies about that person. Dopamine is rushing into the nucleus accumbens, the insular cortex, and the lateral orbitofrontal cortex. The brain of a jilted lover lights up in the areas associated with risk taking, addiction formation, physical pain, and obsessive-compulsive behaviour. According to a 1999 study published in *Psychological Medicine*, people newly in love have serotonin levels 40% lower than normal—exactly like people with obsessive-compulsive disorders.[1477] A neurotransmitter associated with obsession, depression, and racing thoughts, serotonin is affected right down to the molecular level by romance and surging dopamine. This, according to modern medical science, is why people become obsessed with lost love, and are sometimes driven to stalking, homicide, madness, and suicide.

However, even Elizabethan physicians recognized "love sickness" as a medical condition. People visited hospitals with symptoms such as depression, inflamed bodies, excessive erotic desire, irrational thoughts, and a loss of self-control. Feelings

1474. Crowley 1991, 44.

1475. *Dorian Gray*. Op. cit. 136.

1476. Donatella Marazziti & Domenico Canal, "Hormonal Changes When Falling in Love," *Psychoneuroendocrinology* 29(7), August 2004, 931–936.

1477. Donatella Marazziti, et al. "Alteration of the Platelet Serotonin Transporter in Romantic Love," 29(3), May 1999, 741–745.

of love sickness were particularly prevalent when people were not allowed to express love, which caused anger and frustration, and then turned into a mental illness. Love sickness was often the result of a class-crossed love, a rich person falling in love with a servant or a poor girl who they were not allowed to be with. "Love" was seen as an infectious malady caught through the eyes, and the prescribed remedies included potions, diets, mental exercises, and listening to music; in extreme cases, bloodletting was performed to release "blood and seed" from the body. However, the medical profession of the day believed that the most effective cure was simply having sex. According to early modern writers, sexual congress expelled the excess blood and semen, which had accumulated in the body and putrefied, releasing harmful vapours that could cause melancholy.

"The one that loves the least controls the relationship." Man wants to love more than to be loved. When someone loves you, do you really feel their love? In order for you to feel their love, we would have to assume that there are love particles or love waves that radiate from person to person. Yet when we look at our beloved and feel that special feeling, that person seldom looks up from their morning coffee, having become aware of being the lucky recipient of our love. And if they did look up, the only thing they would realize is that they had just spilled their drink on their pajamas. Their only inkling that you love them is when you smile and say, "Honey, would you like me to make some more coffee for you?" Which would not actually be feeling love as much as inferring love. I would go as far as to say that, when you are feeling loved, what you are actually feeling is the love you have for the other person. But would that not mean that if all we ever wanted was to feel loved, we would simply need to give love? No, I am willing to bet our partner would soon feel smothered and leave us.

When love becomes real, it loses its taste, or turns into its own opposite. Anna Karenina becomes a jealous harpy, an unbearable hysteric, a madwoman. Her love fills her with hate. Innocence is lost in the first moments of love: a person in love only knows the logic of victory or defeat, a constant dialectic movement, with no outside, and no reason. A person in love is so wrapped up in their own world that they can only identify one feeling: my beloved does not love me. As Jim Profit instructed his viewers, "If you want someone to love you, open your heart; if you want them to obsess over you, close it."[1478] It is better to show favour to someone who does not love you, than to one who does. For when your lover has ceased lusting after you, they will feel sorry for the kindness they have shown. The person who was never in love will not regret their kindness. "Friendship often leads to love, love never to friendship." Hate is akin to love, or to put it another way, "You cannot hate, till first you have felt love."

The people we should fear the most are the people we love the most—spouses, parents, siblings. If you become victimized, chances are it is going to be by someone in your family. Both love and anger release dopamine, which causes emotional tunnel vision. As with any addiction, love has its withdrawal symptoms; and hate is a good substitute. Studies show that anger lowers our IQ—which is why "revenge is a dish best served cold"—and there is ample evidence to suggest that the same is true for

---

1478. "Pilot." *Profit.* FOX. April 8, 1996.

love. The fact that "love is blind, and stupid too" is exploited by womanizers and man-eaters everywhere. When is the last time you heard an intelligent love song? (No, Lily Allen's "Fuck You" does not count.) Love is an ***emotion***. "There is no such thing as an amicable divorce"—not for marriages of love at least. Prenups should not be optional. For some reason, different, commonsensical rules apply for unwed couples: apparently, if it is easy to enter into and easy to exit, it is no longer a marriage.

Once we have bound ourselves to someone on paper, we are held to a higher standard. We would never say a single person is an adulterer. Society looks more closely at married couples because they have made this public stake: "We are willing to fulfill the obligations of this institution." Early on, we learn to use nouns instead of verbs. When we say, for instance, that your relationship is doomed, we are talking about that fluid concept as if it was something solid and unchangeable like a teapot, instead of discussing the act of relating which entails dynamic interaction. When we use nouns, we see our relationships as immutable and fail to take responsibility for the active and continuous process of relating to someone. Those who systematically speak with nouns limit their choices, because they see the world as stagnant and unalterable. "What is it that they say? 'Change or die.' Well, you know, that's the same for relationships too. You know, if we don't allow them to change, we run the risk of destroying them."[1479]

It is romantic love that has led to 50% divorce rates and depreciation of the institute of marriage in the West. The highest rates of divorce in the United States are in Bible Belt states such as Alabama, Tennessee, and Arkansas; the lowest rate—2.4 divorces a year per 1,000 inhabitants—is found in gay marriage-friendly Massachusetts.[1480] The national divorce rate hovers between 40 and 50 percent, while same-sex couples in officially sanctioned relationships appear to be separating at a much lower rate. In Vermont, the first state to enact civil unions, only about 1.4% of couples have terminated them.[1481] The traditional marriage vows can also serve as an instrument of guilt. The words "till death do us part" have defined how our society looks at marriage for generations. How can two people who once loved each other, shared so much with each other, saw each other naked both emotionally and physically, disintegrate into appalling behaviour in break-up battles? More often than not, the answer lay in those five small words.

Sigmund Freud compared the hypnotic state to falling in love: both the hypnotized patient and the person in love become accommodating, lose their critical ability, and focus on only one thing. The amorous person is in psychosis and in a symbiotic state. The decisions one makes while in the throes of romantic love are irresponsible, because the person lacks the ability to make decisions freely—contracts made while inebriated are not legally binding. The pretty words one has uttered can turn against oneself: when you have promised so much before so many people and then do something stupid, the feeling of shame is so overwhelming it starts eating at the

---

1479. "Papa Can You Hear Me?" ***Being Erica***. CBC. November 24, 2009.

1480. Ellen Barry, "It Must Be Love, but Let's Be Sure," ***Los Angeles Times***, May 21, 2005.

1481. Wyatt Buchanan, "The Battle over Same-Sex Marriage," ***San Francisco Chronicle***, November 13, 2006.

relationship. A common myth about marriage is that the solemn nature of the commitment makes you work harder at a problem, rather than just pack your bags and leave when things go wrong. Studies show that those people who have the strongest sense that marriage is sanctified and should last forever are most likely to see it as a failure and a betrayal and be more angry and disappointed.[1482]

Do you not think that it is unrealistic to expect that love flourish for a lifetime that now runs into our 80s and 90s? When a marriage lasts decades, it is a gift, but it is no longer the norm. The origins of modern marital instability lay largely in the triumph of what many people believe to be marriage's traditional role: providing love, intimacy, devotion, and all-round mutual fulfilment. For centuries, marriage was stable precisely because it was not expected to provide such Utopian benefits. When people break up because they have the expectation of forever, deep inside they feel like they have failed. In times past, too much affection in a marriage was seen as a distraction from God, and in the Middle Ages, people went so far as to argue that love in marriage was impossible—the only path to true romance was adultery. Should a couple have enough will to keep the marriage going, they can succeed in forming a good relationship even after a rocky start. The couple will thus have learned early on how to deal with difficulty. Couples who have experienced no hardships can often be completely helpless when the first crisis presents itself. And as soon as love became the driving force behind marriage, people began demanding the right to divorce if they fell out of love.

When these demands were first raised in the late 18th century, conservatives predicted that love would be the death of marriage. For the next 150 years, the destabilizing effects of the "love revolution" were held in check by women's economic dependence on men, the unreliable methods of birth control used, and the harsh legal treatment of illegitimate children, as well as the social ostracism of unwed mothers. As late as the 1960s, two-thirds of college-educated women in the United States said they would marry a man they did not love, if he met all their other, usually financial, criteria—marriage was still the best way a woman could invest in her economic future. Men also felt compelled to marry, if they wished to be promoted at work or to have political credibility.[1483] By the 1970s, however, American and Western European women could support themselves if they needed to and their growing economic self-reliance has made them less likely to marry for money. College education, financial independence, and abating societal pressure have changed the rules for women in the West. They no longer need to depend on their husbands for a living and know that if their marriage does not work out, they can just leave.

One in four American women now earn at least 10% more than their husbands, up from one in seven in 1997.[1484] Unfortunately, divorces are more common in couples where the wife earns more.[1485] A recent study conducted at Newcastle University

---

1482. Coontz, op. cit.

1483. Ibid.

1484. Galinsky, et al. Op. cit.

1485. Matthijs Kalmijn, et al. "Income Dynamics in Couples and the Dissolution of Marriage and Cohabitation," *Demography* 44(1), February 2007, 159–179.

suggests that rich men give their partners more orgasms, which surely also implies that monetarily challenged men deliver fewer climaxes.[1486] In other words, a woman who marries someone who is an economic and social drain might be better off single in today's world, because she can now earn her own living. But a consuming career is not exactly conducive to romance, and that is truer for woman than for men. Power as an aphrodisiac has its gender-based limits. Men compete with each other, and they also compete with the women. Women do not want someone to be rude and insult them going up a hill; they want encouragement. Indeed, a study by Betsey Stevenson and Justin Wolfers indicates that women's subjective happiness is lessening as men's happiness is increasing—women are less happy now than they were 40 years ago.[1487]

The very anxiety that can fuel the initial desire to bond sexually could also sap the ability to experience pleasure. Falling in love has a hormonal basis that evens out the differences between the couple and makes them willing to compromise. Scientifically speaking, love is a form of "long-term commitment insurance" that ensures your mate is less likely to leave you, should your arms or legs fall off. Some people even think that they will be able to change the other person's annoying traits later on, or that marriage will have a curative effect on that person's violent tendencies or drinking problem. Over time, the parties may realize that they are two very different people. Romantic love lasts on the average 3 to 7 years—the time it takes to bring up a baby. Child rearing is so much work that if love had not evolved, our rational species would never reproduce and would die out. Surely the propagation of the species is worth taking risks for, and alterations in the brain help ensure that the lovelorn will do just that.

When we are in love, we do insane things partly because certain brain regions associated with fear get deactivated. However, if you fell for a person's reckless devil-may-care attitude, that might not be so appealing after you have had your first baby; on the other hand, if he should lose those attributes and become a caring and responsible father, you might discover that he is "not the person you fell in love with." Children may rank as the highest source of personal fulfilment for their parents, but are one of the least-cited factors in a successful marriage, according to an American survey released in 2007. On a list of nine contributors to success in marriage, children were trumped by faithfulness, a happy sexual relationship, household chore-sharing, adequate income, good housing, common religious beliefs, and shared tastes and interests.[1488] In fact, whenever and wherever the research is done on this subject, the results are always the same: women with no children are generally happier than women with children. Babies, as it turns out, are a bundle of stress—they may give our lives purpose, trajectory, and meaning, but they do not give us happiness.

1486. Thomas V. Pollett & Daniel Nettle, "Partner Wealth Predicts Self-Reported Orgasm Frequency in a Sample of Chinese Women," *Evolution and Human Behavior* 30(2), March 2009, 146–151.

1487. "The Paradox of Declining Female Happiness," *American Economic Journal: Economic Policy* 1(2), August 2009, 190–225.

1488. "Generation Gap in Values, Behavior: As Marriage and Parenthood Drifts Apart, Public Is Concerned about Social Impact," Pew Research Center, Washington, D.C., July 1, 2007.

If before World War II, the typical American marriage ended with the death of one partner within a few years after the last child had left home, today couples can look forward to spending more than two decades together in an empty nest. Al and Tipper Gore's split after four decades is highly unusual. About half of marriages end in divorce, but most of them blow up in the first nine years. After forty years together, you settle: you have joint friends, you have assets in common, you have children in common, you have formed your interests around each other's interests. The growing length of time partners spend with only each other for company has made some individuals less willing to put up with an unhappy marriage, while women's economic independence means it is no longer essential for them to do so. Marriage today, like the rest of our lives, is about personal satisfaction. Today's relationships are so fragile precisely because we think we should leave them if they become unsatisfying.

Overall, about half of cohabiting relationships end within five years, and those that last longer often lead to marriage. According to the Tavistock Marital Studies Institute, more than three in five women marrying for the first time already live with their husband-to-be.[1489] Statistically, the risk of divorce is highest in marriages that have lasted 4 to 6 years. The younger the generation, the more often 2 to 3 year unions lead to divorce. Almost a third of female divorcées are under 35.[1490] The birth of the first child is an especially big risk factor: the weaker the common ground, the harder it is to handle the arrival of a third party. For most of history, it has literally taken "a village to raise a child"—far from being the "traditional family," the modern nuclear family stems from the emerging middle classes of the Enlightenment. Marriage counselling has been around for ages, but couples these days are undergoing counselling to see whether they should even get engaged. In the American South, the most religious and divorce-prone part of the United States, many churches recommend it. However, when researchers followed up on the PREPARE premarital inventory three years later, they found that while 27% of the couples had decided against getting married, 20% of those who did marry had either divorced or separated, and a further 23% described themselves as dissatisfied in the marriage.[1491]

More and more couples favour marrying at register offices, hotels, and stately homes, rather than having a church ceremony. Catholic marriage ceremonies have been in decline in the United States for four decades—from 426,000 marriages nationwide in 1970 to 168,400 in 2010—even as the number of Catholics continues to grow.[1492] College-aged girls may be indifferent about the institution of marriage, but they are zealous about being brides and having weddings. The once-divorced do not wish to make a big deal about their second marriage, and the second or third weddings are seldom church ceremonies. Show me a scientific experiment where 66% of the results turn out negative and induce emotional breakdown and therapy and

1489. Sarah Harris, "Marriage 'Will Be Extinct in 30 Years,'" *Daily Mail*, April 20, 2002.

1490. Ben Wilson & Steve Smallwood, "The Proportion of Marriages Ending in Divorce," *Population Trends* 131, Spring 2008, 28–35.

1491. Blaine J. Fowers, et al. "Predicting Marital Success for Premarital Couple Types Based on PREPARE," *Journal of Marital & Family Therapy* 22(1), January 1996, 103–119.

1492. "The Official Catholic Directory," P. J. Kennedy & Sons, Berkeley Heights, NJ, 1971 & 2011.

alcoholism, and I will show you a scientist who will quickly scrap the whole thing and start all over. If—like statistics show—50 to 60 percent of all men and women are unfaithful, then marriages where neither partner cheats are rare indeed; the fact is, we all want to sleep with multiple partners, but to have our partners sleep only with us.

The notion of finding, or there even existing, "the one" ultimately derives from the Christian concept of an eternal union—there are fruit flies that live for a week and even they do not mate for life. The end of a sexual relationship is not only an end, but a beginning of a new phase in life. Which is why some German pastors have suggested that there ought to be an ecclesiastical divorce ritual. True to its tradition of cashing in on the rites of passage, the Church would have couples walk down the aisle to withdraw their sacred vows. According to the Rev. Gerson Rabe of Munich, admitting one's failure before God could be therapeutic. The divorcing couple would utter these words: "I have been wronged and I have done wrong. I admit my guilt before God and ask for His forgiveness."[1493] Which does not really take into account the couples who have plain fallen out of love. But is it really any surprise that couples cheat in a culture where all sex is considered dirty or clandestine? Rule number one in all matters reproductive: "Never trust musty dogmatic mythology written by angry old men who never had sex."[1494]

The object of marriage or coupling, or even love, is not happiness, but reproduction —the only reason for a long-term monogamous relationship. We now live in a society that has successfully disentangled the sexual instinct from the production of children, but in a society where all sexual activity was confined to marriage the decisive factor in population control was the length of marriages. Step another rung down the evolutionary ladder, and look at man demonstrating the herding gregariousness of the species as wandering bands of nomads. Ask yourself, who would have mated with whom? Would the tribe have waited for a chance encounter with another wandering tribe, or is it more likely that mating would have taken place between members of the tribe? What I am trying to say, as tactfully as possible, is that man's sexual instinct is, at bottom, incestuous, and that particular bit of naughtiness has to be educated out of his playtime at a very early age.

This particular bit of education is usually complete by around age seven. Ask any mother at what age her son became capable of an erection and she will confirm that it was literally from the earliest hours of his life. At bath time and diaper changing times in particular, he often demonstrated that he was feeling a sensual arousal. I am using a male baby as an example, because he shows his feelings more obviously than the female, but do not think that since little girls do not show it, that it did not happen to them. When the baby boy, as Freud put it, "no longer mistakes the aims of his sensuality,"[1495] he will start to become rather coy with his mother and insist on putting his pajamas on behind the sofa. In a split second, he has torn apart two

---

1493. Heikki Aittokoski, "Saksassa hankkeilla kirkollinen avioerorituaali," *Helsingin Sanomat*, March 3, 2001.

1494. Mark Morford, "My Baby Has Rainbow Hair," *San Francisco Chronicle*, April 12, 2006.

1495. *Contribution to the Psychology of Love, II.* 1975, 181.

developing stream of his life—the two feelings of affection and eroticism have been parted and are unlikely to ever rejoin again. The fact that we do not recall having made this immense decision fully justifies giving it the title of a repression.

A repression always produces a symptom. The symptom here produced is our inability to experience affection and eroticism at one and the same time. Look back through history and you will see kings taking low-born girls to their bedchamber; look through popular fiction and you will see Lady Chatterley sleeping with the gamekeeper; look through modern Sunday papers and you will see the Governor of California taking his Guatemalan housekeeper as a mistress. Man feels affection for his well-brought-up wife, who is the mother of his children, and whom he has to face at the breakfast table the next morning. This affection acts as a brake on eroticism, whereas should he go with a random prostitute, he will be able to indulge himself freely. However, this is also why a loving husband will never leave his wife to marry his mistress. So the problem is not that we cannot separate love from lust, but that we *are* separating love from lust. A modern man is expected to turn from a devoted husband into a sexy beast at the flick of his wife's finger, and many men simply cannot pull that off. As Oscar Wilde pointed out, "A man can be happy with a woman as long as he does not love her."[1496]

Many women who have gone through divorce cite the husband's excessive sweetness and endless adaptability as one reason for the separation. Divorced women often say their former spouse just was not enough of a man for them. No-one is surprised if a woman wants to free herself from years of domestic abuse, alcoholism, and humiliation, but that is much less common. Growing apart spiritually and physically can turn a marriage into a sibling union. A woman might fall in love with a nice, decent, proper gentleman, and discover it is impossible to start a fight with him. She will soon know that she has him around her little finger, and he will do and believe anything that she says. Many women feel that it is the man who should wear the pants in the relationship and bear the responsibility for the important decisions. This can result in the unfortunate situation where the wife says she is leaving him for someone else, while secretly wishing that her husband would man up and stop her.[1497]

Conservative columnist Kathleen Parker caused a furore with her recent book, *Save the Males* (2008), in which she argues that feminism has neutered men and deprived them of their noble, protective role in society. The reality is that, for at least the past 30 years, men in the West have been under siege by a culture that embraces the notion that the male of the species is to blame for all life's ills. Males as a group are deemed wicked by virtue of their DNA. While women have been cast as victims and martyrs, men have quietly retreated back into their caves, to better fade out emotions that fluctuate between mild amusement—"Are all women crazy?"—and uncontrollable rage—"Yes, they are and they have our kids." In the process of building a more female-friendly world, modern Western society has managed to create a culture that is hostile towards males, contemptuous of masculinity, and cynical about the very differences that make men sexually attractive to women.

1496. *Dorian Gray.* Op. cit. 124.

1497. Lipponen & Wesaniemi 2003.

Western men have been domesticated to within an inch of their lives, attending birth training, counting contractions, even "breastfeeding" with the help of supplemental nursing devices.

None of this means that marriage is dead. On the contrary, most Westerners have a higher regard for the marital relationship today than when marriage was, in effect, mandatory. The great thing about the institution of marriage, and the reason it has remained relevant for thousands of years and through ever-changing times, is its ability to change with those times. Marriage as a private relationship between two individuals is taken more seriously and comes with higher emotional expectations than ever before in history. But: "As long as men feel marginalized by the women whose favors and approval they seek, as long as they are alienated from their children and treated as criminals by family courts, as long as they are disrespected by a culture that no longer values masculinity tied to honor, as long as boys are bereft of strong fathers and our young men and women wage sexual war, then we risk cultural suicide."[1498]

The greatest irony of the "traditional marriage" argument is that it seeks to preserve a peculiar tradition that has never existed at any point in history. For thousands of years, marriage was essentially a business transaction between the parents of the bride and groom. As late as the 17th century, it was the parents who arranged the marriages of even their grown sons, sold the little heiresses like cattle, and became suspicious if the parties of the marriage contract showed unexpected fondness towards each other. Over the last century, however, the West has finally seen the triumph of this new-fangled notion that marriage should be about a loving relationship between two consenting adults. Almost everything we associate with marriage and weddings—the white dress, the sacred vows, the Bridal Chorus, the layer cake, and the rice—dates back only 50 to 100 years at most. When Queen Victoria of England married Prince Albert in 1840, she defied tradition by wearing a beautiful white lace dress in order to promote the sale of English lace. As accounts of her wedding spread throughout Europe and across the Atlantic, élites followed her lead. However, middle-class British and American brides did not adopt the trend until after World War II. At some point, the white dress also inexplicably came to symbolize chastity, even though blue was traditionally the colour of virginity (as in "something borrowed, something blue").

However, giving away the bride is downright patriarchal, as is the fact that the bride's family is still supposed to pay for the wedding. Marriage, in olden days, was a barbaric custom little different from a crude exchange of livestock at its more civilized, and no more than ritualized abduction at its worst. It entailed the transfer of ownership of a woman from her father to a husband. That is why you will find no references to white weddings in the Bible, or the union of one man and one woman—because, until fairly recently, marriage had nothing to do with religion. It was an economic and juridical matter, plain and simple. It almost invariably involved a significant transfer of real or movable property from the bride's family to the groom's family, or a dowry, but also from the groom to the bride as insurance in case she

---

1498. Parker 2010, 197.

survives him, a dower. The wedding ring served as proof that the groom had means to marry—once placed on the bride's finger it denoted ownership.

Thanks to dowries, daughters were a considerable financial strain on a family, even if they could be used to cement social and political alliances. The size of dowries also narrowed down the circle within which one could get married. Only families of equal status could afford the kind of dowries that their social class demanded. In societies where women play a subservient role to women, men also find themselves playing subservient roles to other men. People today complain how family values have disappeared as careers have become so important, as if fathers have never previously put themselves before their families. Marriage is a most fundamentally patriarchal institution: "The Bible teaches that woman brought sin and death into the world, that she precipitated the fall of the race, that she was arraigned before the judgment seat of Heaven, tried, condemned and sentenced. Marriage for her was to be a condition of bondage, maternity a condition of suffering and anguish, and in silence and subjection, she was to play the role of a dependant on man's bounty for all her material wants, and for all the information she might desire."[1499] If the Bible is true, then Jesus is the bastard son of a rapist god.

We think of marriage today as an equal partnership, but it is the woman—we would like to think—who decides whether to open her legs or not. It was not always so; for most of recorded history, the institution of marriage deprived her of this very right. In fact, marriage was expressly created to reverse this marked disadvantage to men. There was a great outcry from women's groups and the United Nations in 2009, when Afghanistan's President, Hamid Karzai, signed a law which "legalized" rape in a bid to appease the Taliban ahead of elections. This new Shia Family Law negates the need for sexual consent between married couples, but we tend to forget that, even in the West, rape was not a crime within marriage until the 1970s. In fact, according to a report ordered by the UN High Commissioner for Human Rights Louise Arbour, rape within marriage has still not been made a crime in 53 nations around the world.[1500]

There has never been a society that did not control the reproduction of its members in some way or another. In European society, this control used to be exercised through marriage. Most children were sired within marriage. Societal attitudes and practices sought to prevent extramarital childbearing any way they could. Sexual intercourse outside marriage would have freed women from the control of men. Primitive or non-existent social services could not have handled a large amount of single women and their illegitimate children. Unrestricted childbearing outside marriage would have resulted in a population explosion which the economy of early modern Europe simply could not have withstood. It is no longer fashionable to question women's decisions, especially when it comes to having children, but the shame attached to unwed motherhood did serve a useful purpose at one time.

The norms and laws that once penalized unwed mothers and their children have weakened or been overturned in most of Europe, ending centuries of injustice, but

---

1499. Elizabeth Cady Stanton. *Academy.* Gaustad, op. cit. 44.

1500. Fareda Banda, "Laws that Discriminate Against Women," Geneva, April 4, 2008.

also further diminishing the role of marriage in determining the course of people's lives. In the early modern era, from about 1500 to 1750 CE, only 1–5% of children were born out of wedlock.[1501] While we may have retired the word "bastard" and the attendant emotional pain for mother and child, acceptance of childbearing outside marriage represents not just an immense shift in societal attitudes, but a potential restructuring of the entire human family. By elevating single motherhood from an unfortunate consequence of poor planning to a sophisticated act of self-fulfilment, Western society has helped usher in a world in which fathers are not just scarce, but in which men are superfluous. The fact is that marriage is declining across much of Western Europe, a pattern which some sociologists describe as a "soft revolution" in European society, a generational shift away from Old World traditions towards a greater emphasis on personal independence. And when domestic partners do tie the knot, it is only to make a social statement or to gain a tax break.

As more and more unwed couples prefer to live together, such countries as Finland have attempted to improve the legal protection of cohabiting partners. In 2009, a Finnish Ministry of Justice committee proposed that the country should enact a law to regulate the dissolution of informal unions.[1502] The law would apply to all who live together, but are not married or in a registered partnership. For example, a 2-year-old child could, in the future, forfeit her inheritance to her mother's new boyfriend. The proposed law would also make it theoretically possible for a "widowed" roommate to demand a portion of the dead roommate's property on the grounds that the two people have "cohabited" for some time. Who would risk bringing home a nice girl one had met in a bar when the result might be a lifelong obligation to provide alimony after a couple of nights of cohabitation? Many couples have chosen to remain unmarried for a reason. If the government starts enacting laws to "improve" the "rights" of cohabiting couples, they would then have to get married and sign a prenup in order to keep their assets separate. The law was passed in 2010 and came into effect in 2011.[1503]

Traditional marriage has ceased to be the preferred living arrangement also in the majority of American households. For the first time in history, less than half of U.S. households are headed by married couples.[1504] In 2006, the Centers for Disease Control and Prevention released data showing that almost 36% of all births in the United States are extramarital, the highest percentage ever recorded.[1505] Births are up among unmarried mothers, not because of teenage girls giving birth, but because more unmarried women in their twenties are having children. According to the 2000 Census, 40% of cohabiting couples had children in their household, almost as high a proportion as the 45% of married couples who had children. The incidence of

1501. Philip S. Gorski, "Calvinism and Revolution: The Walzer Thesis Reconsidered." Madsen, et al. 2001.

1502. "Yhteistalouden purkaminen avoliiton päättyessä: OMTR 2008:10," Oikeusministeriö, Helsinki, 2008.

1503. Laki avopuolisoiden yhteistalouden purkamisesta (26/2011).

1504. "2005 American Community Survey," U.S. Census Bureau, Washington, D.C., November 14, 2006.

1505. "Births: Final Data for 2004," *National Vital Statistics Reports* 55(1), September 29, 2006.

cohabitation and unmarried child-raising only continues to rise, as does the percentage of singles in the population. Marriage is no longer the main way in which societies regulate birth rates or organize the division of labour between men and women. Women's greater participation in education has raised the marriage age and the incidence of non-marriage everywhere, while fertility rates have been cut in half even in places where women's lives are still largely organized through marriage.[1506]

For the last three or four decades, rising rates of youth violence, substance abuse, and suicide have all been blamed on two social pathologies: divorce and unwed motherhood. We have been told that unless we reverse these trends, they will lead to social decay. Tying such dire predictions to divorce and single motherhood seemed credible back in the 1970s and '80s, but a funny thing happened in the '90s: almost every negative social trend tracked by the U.S. Census Bureau, the CDC, and the Department of Justice declined. Both violent and property crime rates are at the lowest levels in the history of the Bureau of Justice Statistics' survey, which started in 1973. The United States has seen the sharpest decline in teen crime in modern history. The numbers of violent crimes in schools halved between 1992 and 2002, while teen homicide rates have dropped to their lowest levels since 1966. Teen drug abuse, binge drinking, and smoking have all fallen, while teen suicide rates have decreased by 25%. Yet the number of couples living together unmarried increased by more than 70% in ten years, while the population at large increased only by 13% over the same period. The number of families headed by single mothers rose five times faster than the number of married-couple families, and gay and lesbian parenting has also become more common.[1507]

There is no question that single parenthood increases the risk of teens getting into trouble. But so do poverty, parental conflict, parental substance abuse, and even an emotionally distant relationship with married parents. Research shows that the majority of teens who exhibit serious behavioural problems have five or more separate risk factors in their lives.[1508] In fact, there are ways in which children from single-parent households do better than children of married parents. A study about single-parenting and reading performance published in the *Journal of Marriage and Family* compared the reading scores of 15-year olds in single-parent versus two-biological-parent household in five Asian countries. In only one of them, Japan, did the children in two-parent families read significantly better than children in single-parent families. In two of the countries, Thailand and Indonesia, the children from single-parent households were actually better at reading than the children from two-parents households.[1509] I am not arguing that we should create single-parent households for the good of our children, but we should stop pretending that the children of single parents are doomed.

It is possible to value two-parent families without denigrating other family forms.

1506. Coontz, op. cit.

1507. Ibid.

1508. Ibid.

1509. Hyunjoon Park, "Single Parenthood and Children's Reading Performance in Asia," 69(3), August 2007, 863–877.

It is even possible to acknowledge the positive aspects of growing up in a single-parent home without denying the good that can come with having two adults at home. "Traditional" nuclear families have been so sentimentalized in U.S. society that when most Americans think of them, they immediately jump to a fantasy of two fully-engaged and available adults lavishing their love and attention on one another and the children in a home free of anger and conflict. Sociologists, such as Rosanna Hertz and Faith Ferguson, who have studied single mothers, have found that single parents are rarely raising their children single-handedly. On the contrary, they have a whole ensemble of friends, relatives, and neighbours, who are invested in their lives and the lives of their children.[1510] In fact, it is precisely this, and not a nuclear family, that has been the preferred method of child rearing through most of history. In hunter-gatherer communities, men and women stayed together only for a few years before moving on to new partners.

The truth is that there is no ideal family structure, so quit pointing to the Bible before you hurt yourself. The patriarchal family model is essentially grounded in hypocrisy, because the father is not God, and does not actually have the power that he appears to have to the child. Realizing the truth can come as quite a shock to children reared in this type of environment, and they might feel the need for something to replace the comfortable illusion they had been under. And this is precisely what makes the patriarchal family model invaluable to totalitarianism: "More than the economic dependency of the wife and children on the husband and father is needed to preserve the institution of the authoritarian family. For the suppressed classes, this dependency is only endurable on the condition that the consciousness of being a sexual being is suspended as completely as possible in the women and the children. The wife must not function as a sexual being, but solely as a child-bearer."[1511]

The 1980s were an exceptionally traumatic time in America. The massive entry of women into the workforce during the '70s, followed by a surge in divorce, overthrew old family norms and gender roles before new social values had time to develop. By the '90s, Americans began to handle divorce better: more divorced fathers paid child support and more couples worked out joint custody agreements; more unwed fathers remained involved with their children and more couples settled their divorces amicably.[1512] There is a persistent belief that women get custody more easily than men. In reality, the cases that make it to court go pretty much fifty-fifty. However, when the parents settle the matter amongst themselves, the mother usually gets the custody. This may be a problem, but solving it is not that simple: it is about culture, gender roles, and the myth of motherhood.

Today, no man in his right mind would ever want to get married; of course, the decision to marry is seldom made in the right mind. Legally, women now hold all the cards. If a woman gets pregnant, she can abort, with or without her husband's consent. Should she choose to have the child, she gets a son or a daughter and the

1510. "Kinship Strategies and Self-Sufficiency Among Single Mothers by Choice: Post Modern Family Ties," *Qualitative Sociology* 20(2), June 1997, 187–209.

1511. Reich 1980, 105.

1512. John F. Sandberg & Sandra L. Hofferth, "Changes in Children's Time with Parents: United States, 1981–1997," *Demography* 38(3), August 2001, 423–436.

man gets an invoice. No-one is arguing that a man should not support his offspring, but by that same logic, should he not also have a say in whether or not he has children? I am not suggesting that the man should get to decide whether the woman has an abortion; but if he is not forcing her to have the baby, should he be forced to pay child support? At the moment, a man's rights end at ejaculation. Marriage was certainly never designed to be an equal partnership, but the pendulum of power has only recently shifted from the man to the woman.

Before 1919, no woman was tried by a jury of her peers, because there were no women on juries, and there were certainly no female judges or lawyers to defend them. Feminists today complain that the sacred vows do not refer to "husband and wife," but man and wife, yet the word ***husband*** itself literally means the "master of the house," while the word ***woman*** denotes a womb-man. A wife's official title in the eyes of the law is unchanged since the beginnings of marriage: "Mrs. John Smith." However, it is more than thirty years since the neutral prefix "Ms" began to gain ground among an American feminist movement keen to find a title which did not denote a woman's marital status. Decades later, French feminists petitioned their government to remove the title ***Mademoiselle*** from official administrative documents, citing the unfairness of forcing women to divulge their marital status whereas men only have to reveal their gender, and in 2009, the European Parliament banned the use of both "Miss" and "Mrs."

In the West, marriage has always been more of a secular tradition than a religious one, a private contract between two families. Up until the Renaissance, wedding ceremonies were considered too vulgar to be performed inside a church, and European couples were traditionally married on its front doorstep. There was, after all, implied sex in the vows, not to mention shameless displays of public affection. The most romantic—yet no less patriarchal—bit, "You may now kiss the bride," has never actually been part of the liturgy; it is a remnant from the pagan tradition where the couple consummated their marriage then and there in front of the guests. Similarly, the tossing of the garter evolved from a 14th-century tradition of ripping the clothes off of the bride's body as she was leaving, in order to loosen her up for the wedding night. Wedding guests fought over the choicest pieces of undergarment, with the garter being considered the greatest prize. Even today, Catholic marriages are not considered valid before the couple has consummated the relationship—hence also the Church's opposition to premarital intercourse. However, until the 17th century, Christian Churches accepted the validity of a marriage on the basis of a couple's declarations: if two people claimed they had exchanged vows they were considered validly married.

There is an upmarket clinic in Paris, France, where young Arab women are waiting for an operation that could save their lives. It costs about 2,000 euros and carries very little risk. Yet the operation is not medically necessary. The surgery they are waiting for is to restore their virginity. Re-connecting the tissue of the hymen takes about half an hour under local anaesthetic. An unknown number of women around the world face an agonizing problem: they have had sex outside marriage and if found out, risk being ostracized by their communities, or even murdered—the social pressure is so great that some women have even taken their own lives. More and more of them, however, are undergoing surgery to hide any signs of past sexual activity. Mind you, this has nothing to do with Shariah law: Christian communities in the Middle East tend to be equally firm in their belief that women should be virgins when they marry.

The Mosaic code was conceived in the barren desert and does not recognize romance, courtship, or dating; sex is purely a matter of ownership. Marriage was a way of passing property, land, and wealth to a male heir when one had only biological daughters: marry them off and their bodies, rights, and property all became possessions of their husband. Virginity only has value when women are property. In biblical times, a woman was always either someone's virgin daughter or someone's betrothed or wife. And you cannot lay a hand on someone else's property. If the sex act took place in the town, both parties were stoned, because the woman should have cried out for help. If the crime took place outside of a town, only the man was killed. If one suspected one's betrothed was not a virgin, the girl was taken to her father's door where she was then stoned to death.[1513]

The seller needed to prove that the merchandise was untouched at the time of the exchange. This was harder than it seems, since the hymen is often already broken at birth. Women suppressed their powerful natural instinct, sexuality, in order to preserve the honour and property of their family. This is still the only logical reason for a woman to stay a virgin before she marries. One's sexual awakening marks the beginning of one's independence from one's parents and—by extension—from God and country. At the coming of age, every boy of the Maasai tribe is sent into the jungle alone to kill a wild beast. The success lay not in the kill, but in the boy returning home after he has proven to be able to fend for himself. He can now survive without his tribe, but he would remain mateless without it. For better or for worse, marriage has been displaced from its vital position in personal and social life in the West, and will not regain it barring a Taliban-like counter-revolution.

However, young girls are still taught that their first time should be "special." This raises unrealistic expectations—your first time is going to be lousy no matter what. It takes time to get to know your partner sexually, and every person is different. Best case scenario: virgin girl who has zero experience with the joys of her own body, with men, or with sex toys, marries a man who has not the slightest clue as to what to do with a woman's body, and neither will be able to tell an erogenous zone from an elbow. The notion that abstinence before marriage will somehow lead to maximum wedded bliss is a microcosm of the idea that if we show restraint in this world we will have boundless joy in the next. In fact, there are many who, based on how they found the former notion to be untrue, worry that the latter might be a little overhyped as well. Many devout Christians end up getting married before they are ready, because they want the sex now, and marriage is the only way they can get it without going to Hell. Six of the seven U.S. states with the highest divorce rates in 2007, and five of the seven with the highest teen birthrates in 2006, voted red in the elections; in other words, "family values" are the bane of family values.[1514]

Of course, the Christian West has traditionally considered sexual pleasure a sin

1513. Deuteronomy 22.

1514. Cahn & Carbone 2010.

even between a married couple. In ancient Indian culture, sexual pleasure was a given —it was seen as something that held the spouses together. The entire concept of female sexual satisfaction is a fairly recent one in the West and it remains a taboo in the more conservative and religious areas of the United States. There is a special place for worshipping the feminine in Vedic culture. It holds that the male does not exist without the female and vice versa; they are not divided and they are worshipped equally. The female orgasm has been known to Indian culture for a very long time. If a woman was frigid, it was thought to be the man's fault. Unsurprisingly, this sort of thinking shocked and disturbed the Brits who conquered India in the 18th century. Even today, two-thirds of the sex ed text books in Britain neglect to mention both the clitoris and the female orgasm; apparently, our culture still has trouble coming to terms with the fact that women—regular women—have sexual needs too. Voilà., the standard recipe for roughly 17 years of vague marital misery capped off by divorce and 2.3 unhappy children.

The British rulers made Indians ashamed of their own culture's approach to eroticism. Like other Easterners, the Indians covered up their sacred sexual art after being colonized by the West. At the root of this was the patriarchal desire to control women and thus society itself. The state-sanctioned institution of marriage became the primary means of this control, and soon religion itself came to be ruled by social conservatives, like it was in the West. *Religion qua religion* is necessarily hostile to individuality, necessarily hypocritical, and necessarily unable to withstand the natural expression of the human sexual instinct. According to Reich, this last necessity manifests itself in the patriarchal family unit, which is the primary instrument of sexual repression. This totalitarian tool imprints on the populace the characteristics of obedience and servility that are essential for fascism to triumph. Sexual practices which were once considered healthy and even spiritual in the East suddenly became barbaric and immoral.

In the West, the chastity and asexuality of women were seen as the moral pillars of society. Yet, as Hugh Hefner famously pointed out, "*Playboy* degrades women like *Sports Illustrated* degrades sports." Physical and mental subjugation, creepy old men hovering around you, taking your money, that is what sports are all about. Weeks of hardbodies, no camera angle left unexplored—no wonder the original Olympians competed in the nude. It is a strange paradox that sex workers are considered the victims of horrible objectification, when sports if anything constitute sophisticated, institutionalized objectification. The one motif permeating the entire feminist movement is a strident opposition to men treating women as objects. This supposedly demeaning, debasing, and exploitative treatment extends from pornography to beauty contests, from advertisements with pretty models all the way to wolf whistles at girls in miniskirts. Meanwhile, the athlete running on a track is treated like a race horse or a machine, and the whole point of competitive sports is that nothing matters except how well you do in the ring or the rink.

Is the attack on women as "sex objects" not simply an attack on sex, period? Is female sexuality not something that actually empowers women? It this not precisely why patriarchal society shuns it? The fact remains that sex drive is a primal instinct. You are not going to get it up if you focus on respecting your partner as a person. If you are not able to see your partner as a sexual object, you might as well forget about the whole thing. There simply is not enough blood in the male body for both the brain and the penis. The feminists are out to destroy the age-old and world-wide custom of women dressing to attract men and succeeding. If we lived in a society where women's sexuality was celebrated and seen as proactive rather than passive, I doubt people would jump so quickly to the concepts of exploitation and dehumanization when they think of exotic dancers and glamour models. Honestly, which does a strip tease demean more, the confident performer or the slobbering punter? But pubescent girls are not taught to be proud of their genitalia, which figure so prominently in Eastern sacred art.

In fact, menstruating women are under ban in patriarchal societies. There are actually two peaks to the menstrual cycle—ovulation and menstruation—and these two peaks have quite different implications. Women make different sexual choices at different points in their menstrual cycle, opting for better-looking, more masculine-appearing men when they are at their most fertile.[1515] In a sense, the woman's body belongs to the race at ovulation: she is a mere carrier and potential passer-on of DNA. At menstruation, however, she belong to herself. She goes through a process of physical renewal as her womb sheds its wall and renews itself. At ovulation, she is typically receptive, passive, desiring penetration; at menstruation, she is more likely to be active, taking the erotic initiative, desirous of sex for its own sake, independently of its reproductive function. The more a woman accepts and understands this and ceases to regard it as a "curse," the more fulfilled she will be; and the more a man accepts and understands this, the better he will complement her.[1516]

Reproductive rights have been called the greatest civil rights battle for women to date. The pill and the coil were a major step in the road to female sexual equality. One really cannot overstate the revolutionary impact of having a birth-control method that allowed women to plan their families. The thing women were most afraid of until the 1960s was getting pregnant, because it would have destroyed the life of a young student. The pill was the first modern contraceptive available to millions of women in the United States and around the world. Before it, women relied on just about anything to delay or prevent pregnancy, from eating pomegranate seeds and drinking mercury to knocking back a potion of beaver testicles brewed in a strong alcohol solution. Over 90% of women of reproductive age use the pill at some point in their lives.[1517] Thanks to it, a fertile woman can plan her life better, knowing that it will not be over just because of a once-a-month possibility of becoming pregnant. Western women under 40 have no conception of a world where they do not have complete control over their bodies and their sexuality. For most of them, reproductive choice is simply a fundamental and indisputable human right.

"Because this is not about babies, again. It's about subjugation of women by male-

---

1515. Steven W. Gangestad, et al. "Women's Preferences for Male Behavioral Displays Change Across the Menstrual Cycle," *Psychological Science* 15(3), March 2004, 203–207.

1516. Shuttle & Redgrove 1978.

1517. David J. Hooper, "Attitudes, Awareness, Compliance and Preferences among Hormonal Contraception Users: A Global, Cross-Sectional, Self-Administered, Online Survey," *Clinical Drug Investigation* 30(11), November 2010, 749–763.

dominated societies. It's no more; it's no less." Thus the late great George Tiller, M.D., who was murdered by anti-abortionists in 2009.[1518] Before the advent of the pill, people were forced to get married if their premarital relations yielded fruit. As late as the 1960s, the fear and especially the consequences of a pregnancy were palpable and often dire. Young women died as a result of illegal abortions all around the world. It was not uncommon for parents to abandon their pregnant daughters or for high schools to expel them. Maternal and infant health have improved dramatically and the infant death rate has plummeted due to the widespread availability of reliable birth control. Women today are able to fulfill increasingly diverse educational, professional, and political aspirations. The number of women in undergraduate schools and getting advanced degrees in the United States now exceeds the number of men. All this because American women finally have an effective method of limiting and planning their families.[1519]

The pill definitely liberated women—from the fear of pregnancy, from forced marriage. One's first love could remain one's first love. Yet it was married women who accrued the greatest benefit. They and their husbands were freed from the abstinence that had been eating at both parties. The very factors that have made marriage more optional in modern times have also made it more satisfying. It is high time to stop predicting social disaster from the transformation of family life and start helping every family build on its particular strengths and minimize its weaknesses. Refusing to recognize the genuine progress that has been made serves no-one. As opposed to what most people think, using the pill actually increases the likelihood of getting pregnant. According to recent studies conducted by the Universities of Bristol and Brunel, women who have used the pill for years conceive more easily than women who have never been on it. The results are the same regardless of how many times they have been pregnant before. Having used the pill in the past increased the chances of getting pregnant for both first-time mothers and mothers who already had other children.[1520]

At first, only married women could obtain the pill, and few young wives had the courage to go ask for it. The pill was introduced in Europe in 1961, but was initially quite hard to get, and there was often a waiting period of over six months. For a long time, many physicians refused to write prescriptions for the young and the unmarried, and when they did, they prefaced them with moral sermons. The 1960s were still a very narrow-minded era, even if they have the very opposite reputation. You see, in order to rebel, you need something to rebel against. Picture Saint-Tropez on the French Riviera in 1964: going topless on a public beach was against the law, but it caught on quickly and spread throughout France in under a decade. Like the pill, toplessness was seen as a way for women to assert and control their own sexuality. So why is it that one hardly sees any Frenchwomen going topless any more? And when

1518. *A Voice for Choice.* Dir. Andrea Buchanan. Alligator Cowgirl Productions, 2004.

1519. Cecile Richards, "For Women, the Ultimate in Preventive Health Care: Birth Control," *Huffington Post,* June 4, 2010.

1520. Alexandra Farrow, et al. "Prolonged Use of Oral Contraception before a Planned Pregnancy Is Associated with a Decreased Risk of Delayed Conception," *Human Reproduction* 17(10), October 2002, 2754–2761.

one does, they tend to be mature veterans of feminist battles who refuse to give up any of the rights they fought for. As the right to go topless gradually evolved into an obligation to do so, many women started feeling self-conscious and the prevailing feminist perspective changed from revelling in a new-found freedom to refusing to participate in a trend that put half-naked women on billboards everywhere.

The Western way of thinking reached a turning point in regards to erotic literature already in the late 18th century. That is when Marquis de Sade penned his works and had to answer for them. The sadomasochistic undertones of Western pornography do not necessarily relate only to societal views on sexuality and eroticism. They are a part of the greater liberation from the moral and cultural shackles imposed on our society by Christianity, the punk rock of their era, if you will. Drastic prohibitions could only be broken with drastic measures. I may be an atheist, but some of the kinkiest sex I have had has been with Mormons and born-again Christians—all that repressed sexuality clearly needs an outlet. You are calling me a "pervert"? Nothing more natural than sexuality. Now celibacy, that is perversion! But from the point of view of Christianity, nature is the domain of the flesh and of sin. "God created sex. Priests created marriage."[1521]

Alarmingly, almost 60% of Ireland's clergy would happily give up celibacy, according to a recent survey carried out by Wilton Research and Marketing on behalf of *The Irish Catholic* newspaper.[1522] Why, you say? Well, if you were told that you only needed 4 hours of sleep a night instead of the traditional 8, thus meaning that you had wasted 4 hours of your life every day until now, would you be willing to accept this assertion? Yes? And why is that? Because you already sleep closer to four hours than eight? Exactly. In fact, the Conference of Bishops in Brazil, the world's most populous Catholic country, found that over 40% of its priests had had affairs with women—a smaller percentage had had them with men.[1523] Even in Poland, more than half of all priests would like to do away with celibacy to have a wife and family, according to the findings of Prof. Józef Baniak. In the land that produced the late John Paul II, where most churches are still full on Sundays, more than 12% of the clergy admitted they were already living in stable relationships with a woman.[1524]

We know paedophilia is more common among priests than in most professions, but it is also more common among teachers and coaches; and generally among people who work with children. Opportunity may not make the criminal, but the paedophile will select a profession where his opportunities are greater. The Church also has less oversight, which is the real problem, and stems largely from the shortage of clergy: there was one priest for every 2,677 Catholics in 2003, whereas the figure was one in

---

1521. Voltaire, attributed.

1522. Patsy McGarry, "Survey: 57% of Priests Say Celibacy Should Not Be Compulsory," *The Irish Times*, October 28, 2004.

1523. Centro de Estatística Religiosa e Investigações Sociais, "O Perfil do Presbítero Brasileiro," Conferência Nacional dos Bispos do Brasil, Itaici, 2004.

1524. "Priests Unhappy with Celibacy," *Krakow Post*, March 2009.

1,797 in 1978—that is a drop of one-third in 25 years.[1525] Believe it or not, the Vatican's official position is that it is not a sin to be gay. However, it is a sin to engage in any sexual activity outside of marriage, so all homosexual acts are basically grounds for eternal damnation. The ultimate irony is that there are few organizations with such a high portion of gay people in their employ: according to some studies, anywhere between 20–50% of all priests may be gay.[1526] Normal, healthy homosexuals do not go around raping little boys, but if you are willing to join an organization that actively condemns your sexuality, I would not put paederasty past you.

As Susan Sontag once observed, "Religion is probably, after sex, the second oldest resource which human beings have available to them for blowing their minds."[1527] Pornography is a sign of social decay. Moral decay was also the watchword in the Berlin of the 1920s, where people were experimenting with all kinds of sex and doing what they damn well pleased. All Utopias, religions, fascisms, and democracies wish to erase this evil decadence. According to Reich, "a clear sexual consciousness and a natural regulation of sexual life must foredoom every form of mysticism; that, in other words, natural sexuality is the arch enemy of mystical religion. By carrying on an anti-sexual fight wherever it can, making it the core of its dogmas and putting it in the foreground of its mass propaganda, the church only attests to the correctness of this interpretation."[1528] The French dub the orgasm *le petit mort*, the little death. Studies indicate parts of the brain that govern fear and anxiety are switched off when a woman is having an orgasm, but remain active when she is faking it.[1529] The fact that there is no deactivation in faked orgasms would seem to imply that letting go is a basic part of a real orgasm. The profound relaxation that typically follows sex may be one of the few times we allow themselves to completely let go, surrender, and relax. When you have an orgasm, the prefrontal cortex, the seat of reason and impulse control, shuts down, and you lose yourself.

Sex is basic to our humanity; and sexuality, like dreaming, is an arena that connects us to a part of ourselves we do not always fully understand or have words for. It is clear that Reich used the term "sexual process" to describe the same basic energy that primitive cultures called Mana, Orenda, Wakan, or at a somewhat higher stage, Tao, Brahman, Yahweh, Allah. Reich thought that he had found what classical physicists called "ether" and what the otherworldly mystics called God. To Reich, the orgasm was *unio mystica* without the mysticism. An orgasmic existence in relation to all life was the stated goal of his form of psychoanalysis. He called a healthy person a "genital character," one that had attained their "orgasmic potency." This orgasmic potency was

---

1525. General Secretariat of the Synod of Bishops & Libreria Editrice Vaticana, "Instrumentum Laboris: The Eucharist—Source and Summit of the Life and Mission of the Church," Liturgy Office of the Bishops' Conference of England and Wales, London, 2005.

1526. Gerard J. McGlone, "Prevalence and Incidence of Roman Catholic Clerical Sex Offenders," *Sexual Addiction & Compulsivity* 10(2–3), 2003, 111–121.

1527. 1969, 57–58.

1528. Op. cit. 178–79.

1529. Janniko R. Georgiadis, et al. "Regional Cerebral Blood Flow Changes Associated with Clitorally Induced Orgasm in Healthy Women," *European Journal of Neuroscience* 24(11), December 2006, 3305–3316.

the ability to surrender to life in the fullest, just like a healthy person can completely give one's self to another at the moment of sexual climax. Such a person is no longer bound by sexuality, but has reached a level that Reich calls "self-regulation."

"It is one of the superstitions of the human mind to have imagined that virginity could be a virtue."[1530] The early Christians were morbidly fixed on chastity and celibacy. Young girls allowed themselves to be put to death, in the most painful and debauched ways possible, because they had been brainwashed into believing that their virginity, if preserved, assured them a place in Heaven. Books about such martyrs, whose breasts were torn off with hot irons and who had red-hot swords thrust into their vaginas, were considered educational reading for Victorian children. Before reliable birth control, the only sex that anyone considered actual sex was the reproductive kind. Just as it is canonically impossible for a same-sex couple to consummate a marriage, a priest molesting an altar boy is technically keeping his vow of celibacy. Ironically, what enabled the sexual revolution also expanded sexuality to mean anything that results in an orgasm, instead of anything that results in a pregnancy.

"Essentially, the idealization and deification of motherhood, which are so flagrantly at variance with the brutality with which the mothers of the toiling masses are actually treated, serve as means of preventing women from gaining sexual consciousness, or preventing the imposed sexual repression from breaking through, and of preventing sexual anxiety and sexual guilt feelings from losing their hold. Sexually awakened women, confirmed and recognized as such, would mean the complete collapse of authoritarian ideology."[1531] The message women still receive is that sexual aggression is unfeminine, that a woman's primary sexual role is as regulator of male desire—to say yes or no, but not to pursue desires of her own. In conservative societies around the world, girls are not supposed to be actively seeking anything, a girl simply exists for someone to marry or divorce. The regulations governing prostitution refer to female body parts only; all of the Nevada Administrative Code is built around the female anatomy.

Even a generation after the sexual revolution, the female orgasm is still seen as a threat, and in extreme cases, something to subjugate. The term "sacred prostitute" seems oxymoronic, but in a sense, it is actually redundant. The Hebrew word *zonah* means both prostitute and prophetess. Sacred whores were once also known as the "holy virgins," priestesses of the goddesses Ishtar, Asherah, or Aphrodite. The Vestal Virgins, too, performed magical sex rituals in honour of the Roman matriarch Vesta. In case you wonder how a professed virgin could practise sex magic, the word "virgin" was not taken to mean that the hymen was intact or that these priestesses were kin to the immaculate mother of Christ. In ancient times, a virgin was simply an unmarried woman, a woman who claimed ownership of herself. More recently, Betty Dodson, the godmother of the masturbation movement, proclaimed that "Independent orgasms will lead to independent thoughts. Once a woman has given herself her own best

---

1530. Voltaire 1952, II, 313.

1531. Reich, op. cit. 105.

orgasm, she's on a roll."[1532]

A whole set of traditions that come out of the East continue to insist that the transcendent and the immanent are inseparable, that the body and mind, sex and spirit, the divine and the human, are really the same things on a deeper level. "The demonstration of anthropologists that all religious rites are celebrations of the reproductive energy of nature is irrefutable; but I, accepting this, can still maintain that these rites are wholly spiritual. Their form is only sexual because the phenomena of reproduction are the most universally understood and pungently appreciated of all. I believe that when this position is generally accepted, mankind will be able to go back with a good conscience to ceremonial worship. I have myself constructed numerous ceremonies where it is frankly admitted that religious enthusiasm is primarily sexual in character."[1533] And: "When you have proved that God is merely a name for the sex instinct, it appears to me not far to the perception that the sex instinct is God."[1534]

Powerful social taboos have always surrounded menstruating women. The word "menstruation" comes from the Greek *menos*, which means both "moon" and "power." In pre-patriarchal times, and in many "primitive" cultures to this day, menstrual taboos were for the purpose of safeguarding the woman at a receptive time, during which she might go inwards and produce prophetic information or a dream which could be useful to the community. In particular, the menarche, or first menstruation, was regarded as a point of both mental and physical opening, during which a girl would have dreams or other experiences that would guide her later in life, and if she were to become a shamaness or a witch doctor, this was the time when she came into a special relationship with the potent spirits of the menses.

With the patriarchal takeover, however, menstrual taboos became a protection *against* women and against their powerful magic. Awe of women's blood-magic may have well given rise to the patriarchal cruelties of blood sacrifice. Men obviously cannot menstruate, but there are other ways of producing blood for magical purposes. The menstruating shamaness was dangerous, so the patriarchate needed to neutralize her with taboos, and kill something—or someone—instead. Even St. Paul contends that, "without shedding of blood is no remission."[1535] *Hoc est corpus.* It is noteworthy that cultures with strong male-imposed menstrual taboos—including our own—seem to be the most prone to aggressiveness and anxiety. As Michael Rooker's character advises in *Keys to Tulsa*, "Never trust anything that bleeds for five days and doesn't die."[1536]

Many smart, accomplished females still feel self-conscious buying "femcare" products, especially from a male cashier. Many of them wryly refer to a visit from "Aunt Flo" or "paying the monthly bill." They would simply die of total mortification

---

1532. *Passion & Power: The Technology of Orgasm.* Dir. Emiko Omori & Wendy Slick. First Run Features, 2007.

1533. Crowley 1979, 554.

1534. Idem. 1909–13, III, 281.

1535. Hebrews 9:22.

1536. Dir. Leslie Greif. Gramercy Pictures, 1996.

if they leaked or bulged or accidentally dropped a tampon out of their bag. None of them even question terms they take for granted, like "sanitary" pads and feminine "hygiene"—words that imply an inherently disgusting function. No, most of them still cling to patriarchal superstitions and old wives' tales about the subject, thinking that menstrual blood is poisonous, that a tampon can get lost inside you, and that you cannot get pregnant if you have sex during your period. Toilet paper, tissue, towels, and soap are generally free in public restrooms, but not pads or tampons; quite the contrary, femcare is considered a "non-essential good" and is therefore subject to sales tax in many U.S. states.[1537]

In 2007, the U.S. Food and Drug Administration approved the first birth-control pill that was expressly designed to eliminate women's monthly period. Taken daily, the contraceptive continuously administers slightly lower doses of the same hormones that are found in many standard birth-control pills to suppress menstruation. Called Lybrel®, it is marketed for women who find their periods too painful, unpleasant, or inconvenient, and thus perpetuates a lot of negative myths and taboos about menstruation. Standard oral contraceptives consist of 21 pills that contain estrogen and progestin, which prevent ovulation, followed by seven dummy pills that allow menstruation. However, they were originally developed to mimic a normal cycle in the belief that women would find it more acceptable, not because it would be safer or more effective at preventing pregnancy. For most of history, women had fewer periods than they do today because they were either pregnant or breast-feeding for most of their reproductive years—they certainly did not have 13 natural periods year after year for decades on end.

Suppressing the menstrual cycle could have benefits for women who experience cramps, bloating, or mood swings, but there are more pleasurable ways of addressing these problems. The uterine contractions brought on by orgasm are just as powerful as those of child labour.[1538] The orgasmic contraction and relaxation of the uterine muscle can be used to relieve cramps during PMS and menstruation. Prostaglandin E, an ingredient of semen, stimulates uterine contraction and having sex late in pregnancy is a natural way to set off labour. Obstetricians now use artificial means to stimulate the onset of labour, usually to protect the foetus from the negative effects of more than 42 weeks of gestation. These methods include amniotomy, or artificial rupture of membranes, and medications that stimulate contractions. But these come with certain disadvantages, such as a higher rate of Cæsarean sections, forceps-assisted delivery, postpartum bleeding, and prolonged labour.[1539]

The smell of lactating women has been found to increase fellow females' sex drives, perhaps because it would have made sense for women in early communities to have their children at the same time.[1540] "The Christian view that all intercourse outside marriage is immoral was . . . based upon the view that all sexual intercourse, even

1537. Stein & Kim 2009.

1538. Crenshaw, op. cit.

1539. Carole Ann Moleti, "Trends and Controversies in Labor Induction," *American Journal of Maternal/Child Nursing* 34(1), January/February 2009, 40–47.

1540. Natasha A. Spencer, et al. "Social Chemosignals from Breastfeeding Women Increase Sexual Motivation," *Hormones and Behavior* 46(3), September 2004, 362–370.

within marriage, is regrettable. A view of this sort, which goes against biological facts, can only be regarded by sane people as a morbid aberration. The fact that it is embedded in Christian ethics has made Christianity throughout its whole history a force tending towards mental disorders and unwholesome views of life."[1541] Both sexes lose: men must choose between a nurturing mother or a titillating sexpot, while women learn to either use their sexuality as a tool of manipulation or to repress their sexuality altogether. Without the embodiment of the "sacred whore" in every woman, society remains dysfunctional and self-help books continue to be the biggest sellers in the publishing industry.

No-one wants to talk about Freud any more, but the one thing he knew that no modern scientist or psychologist can refute is how central, essential, and powerful our sex drive is. The fact that we are living with that kind of powerful drive within us is inherently threatening. Freud believed that the conflicting tendencies inherent in the libido would be destructive without the control of reason. The libido needed to be constrained in order for the creation of human culture and society to be possible. In his final work, *Civilization and Its Discontents* (1930), he was led to the conclusion that culture and society inevitably needs to use the superego and the ego to suppress the id, in order for culture and society to exist at all. This strange exercise in circular reasoning was not recognized in psychoanalytical circles for what it was except by Freud's former disciple, Reich, who went so far as to consider the work a personal attack upon himself.

The deepest layer of the subconscious mind is formed by the disavowed and constricted stream of vital and powerful genital impulses, the possibility of love. This is the feared "libido," the buttress of everything that lives, the suppression of which all "worldliness" is about. Freud and his daughter Anna led corporate psychologists to think they could tame the irrational "secret self" by giving people symbols of power in the form of private houses, personal territory, and consumer goods. Reich, on the contrary, believed that the irrational inner self was not dangerous unless it was repressed, and that is exactly what Freud's techniques did. Such people will start to hate both themselves and life itself. Life begins to, at least subconsciously, revolt them, because they see how other people are still able to enjoy it. Their efforts to return to life manifest in an exaggerated, nearly hysterical sexual urge. But rather than being liberating, their sexual activities lead to ever worsening bottling up of energy. Anna Freud, herself a virgin analyzed by her father for her excessive masturbation, was committed to her father's legacy, and determined to take Reich down. She discredited his work and got him kicked out of the International Psychoanalytical Association. Reich was ultimately thrown in prison and the FDA ordered all his books and records to be burned.[1542]

Denying a pleasure turns it into an obsession—"The only way to get rid of a temptation is to yield to it."[1543] When you enter a Buddhist order, you are required to take ten vows, one of which is not to abuse sexuality, but there is no specific

1541. Russell 2009, 29–30.

1542. Sharaf 1994.

1543. *Dorian Gray*. Op. cit. 16.

definition of what that means. In the earliest sanghas, they decided it meant you had to be celibate, and some orders still interpret it that way, but there is no concept of sexual sin in Buddhism. Aleister Crowley, whom Bruce Dickinson (tongue firmly in cheek) dubbed the "greatest spiritual leader of our time,"[1544] found the long periods of abstinence prescribed by mediaeval grimoires to be counterproductive. Otherwise known as "Britain's most intimidating asthmatic bisexual," Crowley discovered that while abstaining, sexual urges did not dissipate, but rather consumed him. Instead of slowly starving the impulse to death, he concluded a better strategy was simply to appease it and get on with the magical operation. He would later remark, "The stupidity of having had to waste uncounted priceless hours in chasing what ought to have been brought to the back door every evening with the milk!"[1545] Sex is a basic need, so tying sexuality to marriage or procreation constitutes a human rights violation—anyone who thinks otherwise needs to get laid.

"Sex is the main expression of the Nature of a person; great Natures are sexually strong; and the health of any person will depend upon the freedom of that function."[1546] Crowley considered sex to be an impulse like hunger or thirst, best divorced from the emotional baggage which society attaches to it. The flesh must be dealt with, but not through any of the silly techniques provided by ascetic religions. It must be mastered not on moral grounds, but on the functional grounds of wanting to be more than human. And for it to be mastered, it must first be fulfilled and respected—no repression, no denial, no chastisement, no nonsense. As William Blake put it, "Those who restrain desire, do so because theirs is weak enough to be restrained."[1547] The rejected elements will always remain latent and when given enough provocation and stimulus, they will invariably rise up to haunt the individual when he least expects it. They will therefore have to be faced, dealt with, and incorporated into the very heart of one's being—"Sooner murder an infant in its cradle than nurse unacted desires."[1548]

Eating, shitting, fucking; oral, anal, genital. Man is, by nature, hedonistic, actuated by pleasure, not by needs. Anorexia and obesity, extreme sports and suicidal tendencies, these are unique attributes of humanity. It is precisely this pleasure instinct that separates humans from animals. What do you think would happen if we were given access to limitless food and sex? Would we perchance become unrestrained in both areas, succumbing to both gluttony and promiscuity with equal glee? For the first time in history, we have an immense society in exactly this situation and the answer is not what everyone expected: "The great anxiety in Middle America was that we were under siege—my parents would see kids walking down the street who were Boy Scouts three years earlier suddenly looking like hippies, and they were scared. Culturally, it was October 2001 for a decade. For a decade. And once our parents realized we weren't going to disappear into dope and radicalism, the pressure

1544. *Chemical Wedding.* Dir. Julian Doyle. Warner Bros. Entertainment, 2008.

1545. 1979, 113.

1546. 1974, 134.

1547. *The Marriage of Heaven and Hell,* pl. 5.

1548. Ibid. pl. 10.

came off. That's the world we're in now—parents of boomers who would not drink a glass of wine 30 years ago are now kicking back with vodka. In a way, they've been liberated."[1549]

As Voltaire observed, "nothing would be more tiresome than eating and drinking if God had not made them a pleasure as well as a necessity."[1550] The human endocrine system automatically rewards desirable actions/thoughts and punishes the undesirables. We are pushed to wanting to do, and get pleasure out of doing, things that turn out to be good. We have to take care of our young on a one-to-one basis, which is a lot of work, but also a pleasure. We get pleasure out of doing these things because we have a hunger for them. Just like we get pleasure out of eating because we have a hunger for food. This satisfaction is largely neurological: the brain produces its own natural opiates—endorphins and oxytocins—and it even has a version of THC called anandimide. Forget about jogging or doing sit-ups, sex uses every muscle group in the body, gets the heart and lungs going, and burns about 300 calories per hour. Endorphins released during orgasm stimulate the immune system, helping keep mild illnesses like colds at bay. These endogenous narcotics act as a powerful analgesic, elevating the pain threshold and helping relieve the aches of conditions like arthritis, whiplash, and migraine.[1551] Yes, having sex is actually a *cure* for headaches.

Orgasms elicit strong activity in the nucleus accumbens, the reward centre, which also lights up in response to cocaine, nicotine, and chocolate. Every human culture and every class of animal makes use of certain plants for their psychoactive properties. According to UCLA psychopharmacologist Ron Siegel, the desire for intoxication is actually a fourth drive, as unstoppable as hunger, thirst, and sex. Our DNA seems to be programmed to grow brains that crave intoxicating plants and potions: the molecular components of the intoxicants we use fit so neatly and precisely into our neural receptors that it appears as if our brains were specifically wired to receive them. This symbiotic relationships between animal brains and plant intoxicants is as ancient as the birds and the bees, and also the reason why the War on Drugs is really a war against human nature.

We crave it because our brains tell us to: dopamine, God's little neurotransmitter; better known by its street name, "romantic love." Norepinephrine; street name, "infatuation." These brain chemicals are natural stimulants. When we fall in love, these chemicals and their cousins throw a party in the neurons of our brains, dancing the night away in the limbic system, setting off obsessive thoughts, focused attention, and the desire to commit immoral acts with your heart's chosen every minute of every day. Studies show that the brain in the first throes of love is very much like a brain on drugs. The ventral tegmental area makes dopamine and sends it out to other brain regions when we are in love. It is the same region affected when we feel the rush of cocaine. Love is not a craving, it is a high.

Despite it being a time of unprecedented sexual freedom in America, the practice

---

1549. Joe Scarborough, as quoted in Jon Meacham, "The End of Christian America," *Newsweek*, April 13, 2009.

1550. *Dialogues et entretiens philosophiques*, XXV.

1551. Crenshaw, op. cit.

of policing sexuality has continued unabated since the Puritans landed at Plymouth Rock and a profound discomfort with sexuality still plagues the nation. The Bush administration poured more than $1 billion in federal aid into state-run abstinence education programs because it decided there was an imbalance that favoured comprehensive sex education. Abstinence-only programs, which focus on pre-teens and teens, teach that abstaining from sex is the only effective and acceptable method to prevent pregnancy and STDs; they give no instruction on birth control or safe sex. The fact is that "education" does not work; this was proven ages ago by psychologists, yet it is retried time and again. The "true love waits" attitude is not the problem, the problem is the parents who are narrow-minded, stubborn, or naïve enough to believe that, if they teach their child to wait with sex, everything will turn out just fine and nothing bad will ever happen. Anyone teaching teenagers to "just say no" to sex instead of telling them the practical information is being criminally negligent. Thanks to all the new hormones surging through their bodies, teenagers are actually chemically insane. Teaching them that "Once you do it you're spoiled" and "There's no getting back virginity" only amps up the pressure to unbearable.

Public interest messages that seek to induce fear, guilt, or regret are worse than ineffective. Danger only inspires curiosity among young people, who have a poorly developed sense of their mortality. Motorcycles, bungee-jumping, and unprotected sex are popular with the young because of the danger, not despite it. At puberty begins a shift of loyalty from one's family to one's friends. Authoritarian advertisements are not going to convince drug users, who are notoriously unreliable and anti-authoritarian. The risks, the danger, and the illegality are all part of the attraction of narcotics. There was a time within living memory when heroin was legal. Heroin was not criminalized in Britain until 1968, and there were not many addicts at that point. It was only after the drug was banned that it became more popular. The gangsters got in on the act, and now you not only have thousands of adults shooting up with needles, you have children shooting each other with guns.

Getting high is a puberty rite and teenagers use drugs to boost their fragile self-confidence. Taking drugs also helps defy authority, enabling young people to show that they are brave and can take care of themselves. When the police raid drug parties, they only encourage more parties by giving the use of drugs a purpose. In other words, drug raids encourage drug use. Research suggests that young adults in Europe deliberately binge on alcohol and drugs to improve their sex lives. It is well known that use of alcohol and drugs is linked to risky sexual behaviour, but a recent British study shows that many young Europeans "strategically" binge drink or abuse drugs in order to have more sex.[1552] Meanwhile, an American study reveals that sexual precociousness and the age at which we lose our virginity might be determined by genetics rather than social factors.[1553] Whether the human body developed gradually over millions of years or appeared suddenly about six millennia ago, God or Mother Nature installed sexual plumbing that kicks into high gear around age 13; yet there is

1552. Bellis, et al. Op. cit.

1553. Nancy L. Segal & Joanne Hoven Stohs, "Age at First Intercourse in Twins Reared Apart: Genetic Influence and Life History Events," *Personality and Individual Differences* 47(2), July 2009, 127–132.

a huge gap between puberty and marriage due to relatively recent social changes that extend adolescence further than ever before.

The age of majority is not 18 in the West today because people under 18 are considered children; people under 18 are considered children in the West today because the age of majority is 18. The distinction is legal, not biological—it is both illogical and immoral to treat a person who can have children of his or her own as a child. If you had all the adult parts but were forbidden by your elders to play with them, you would be rebelling too! "You must understand the rules of the culture," writes San Francisco columnist Mark Morford. "You must understand that your happy teenage hormones must be held in check, beaten down, thwarted, stomped on and made deeply shameful until you become older and fearful and pathetic and sad. You know, just like us."[1554]

Could it be that the porn industry needs its detractors? Of course it does, for without censorship and regulation, porn would not have the allure of forbidden fruit. Remember, porn is legal in America; and no other field of entertainment is as heavily policed and scrutinized by the government. Pornography generates $12 billion a year in revenue in the United States alone, making it one of the biggest economic sectors in the country.[1555] The good news is that most porn films shows happy people doing things that happy people do when they are in bed with someone they want to have sex with. The bad news is that most porn films are not very good. They might give you a few minutes of pleasure, make you giggle, maybe wince at poor plastic surgery choices, or even turn you off completely. Is it any wonder teenagers are having sex, when they have been taught that masturbation is wrong?

Abstinence should, of course, remain a choice. Lives would be saved if people postponed their first intercourse by a year. And if people were to remain abstinent until marriage, unintended pregnancy, sexually transmitted disease, and poverty would be dramatically reduced. On the other hand, you cannot claim that abstinence is the value of the United States when it is not held by 95% of the population: according to a recent survey by the Guttmacher Institute, 95% of Americans say they have had premarital sex.[1556] Young people are both emotionally and physically less mature than adults; and if adults cannot control their urges, how could teenagers? After a 2008 hearing on abstinence-only education, Republican representative Mark Souder said the only fully reliable way young people can protect themselves is by "abstaining from sex until a committed, faithful relationship."[1557] An evangelical Christian known for his outspoken views on religion, he resigned from Congress in 2010 over an extramarital affair with a staffer.

Jonathan Swift's dictum was that "you do not reason a man out of something he was not reasoned into." Every time scientists have done research on the subject, they

1554. "You Dirty Kids!" *San Francisco Chronicle*, May 15, 2009.

1555. Jonathan Curiel, "Newspapers Turn to Sex and Celebs: Publications Employ Titillation in Their Pages and on Their Web Sites to Lure Back Readers," *Ibid.*, March 4, 2009.

1556. Lawrence B. Finer, "Trends in Premarital Sex in the United States, 1954–2003," *Public Health Reports* 122(1), January/February 2007, 73–78.

1557. As quoted in "Congressman Resigns over Affair with Staff Member," *The Telegraph*, May 18, 2010.

have found that education does not educate; the health heathens consistently refuse to accept what is best for them. The U.S. government's long-term evaluation of the abstinence-only initiatives, required by Congress in 1997, showed that these programs accomplish essentially nothing. A congressionally-funded study released in 2007 examined the impact of the no-sex-until-marriage programs funded under the federal welfare reform law of 1996. More than 2,000 students were randomly assigned to groups that received abstinence-only counselling and those who received no counselling, and numerous surveys were conducted over the next 4 to 6 years to determine the impact. No evidence was found that these programs increased rates of sexual abstinence; in fact, those who had received the abstinence-only education—some as often as every school day for up to 4 years—did not behave any differently than their peers.[1558] For better or for worse, teenagers are perfectly capable of making up their own mind about sex and everything else.

The study showed that the students participating in abstinence-only programs had a similar number of sexual partners as their peers not in the programs, and that the age of first intercourse was also similar for both groups. Ironically, this is hardly surprising considering the moral of this study, and countless similar studies before it: everyone is just going to keep doing what they have always been doing no matter what you tell them. All preaching is essentially preaching to the choir. No-one—least of all a teenager—is going to change their opinion on account of a little thing like the facts. As Henry Waxman, chairman of the House Government Oversight Committee, remarked, "American taxpayers appear to have paid over one billion federal dollars for programs that have no impact."[1559] On a positive note, the abstinence-taught students knew as much as the others about the risks of unprotected sex and the consequences of sexually transmitted diseases and were just as likely to use a condom. These finding were confirmed by an Oxford University team that reviewed 13 U.S. trials involving 15,000 people aged 10 to 21.[1560]

Everybody knows that there is nothing "better than sex." Adults gauge the success of their relationships by how much sex they have, but adolescents are not supposed to have any? Could there be a more insulting, demeaning program than one whose sole intention appears to be to deceive humanity and undermine every human impulse and induce 10 million teens to resent and mistrust adults even more than they already do? I do not care what age you are, if you are not having sex, you are not girlfriend and boyfriend, but just plain old friends. If you are old enough to reproduce, you are by definition old enough to have sex—having responsible sex is another thing entirely. Ectopic pregnancy, infertility, and cervical cancer are admittedly not the problems of a pre-teen; rather, they are the problems of an ill-educated person who had unprotected sex and did not suffer the consequences until twenty years down the line.

1558. Christopher Trenholm, et al. "Impacts of Four Title V, Section 510 Abstinence Education Programs: Final Report," Mathematica Policy Research, Princeton, NJ, April 2007.

1559. As quoted in Maggie Fox, "Abstinence Education Does Not Work: Report," Reuters, April 14, 2007.

1560. Kristen Underhill, et al. "Sexual Abstinence Only Programmes to Prevent HIV Infection in High Income Countries: Systematic Review," *British Medical Journal* 335(7613), August 4, 2007, 248–252.

Women and *men* in their forties are now discovering that HPV contracted through oral sex back in college has led to a throat or head and neck cancer diagnosis. When you have sex with a person, you are exposed to all the diseases of that person's past sexual partners and the past partners of those people; many of these diseases have no external symptoms, so most people do not even know that they are infected.

Virginity pledges were introduced in the early 1990s as part of the Christian Sex Education Project aimed at reducing teen pregnancy and raising moral values. However, morality and value-based decision-making demand that we use the most current science available to protect our young people. A study released by Representative Waxman in 2004 found that of the 13 most frequently used federally funded abstinence-only curricula, 11 contained "errors and distortions." The teaching materials consistently exaggerated the failure rate of condoms and minimized their ability to prevent STDs. One guide is quoted as saying that, "The actual ability of condoms to prevent the transmission of HIV/AIDS even if the product is intact, is not definitely known." This while the Centers for Disease Control and Prevention insists that "latex condoms provide an essentially impermeable barrier to particles the size of STD pathogens." Another guide apparently goes as far as to claim that touching another person's genitals "can result in pregnancy." Contradicting the teaching of leading obstetrics textbooks, other guides warn that abortions can result in increased fertility and premature births.[1561]

A non-partisan study commissioned by the Texas Department of State Health Services, surveying teens in 29 Texas schools, showed about 23% of 9th-grade girls, typically 13 to 14 years old, had sex before receiving abstinence-only education. After taking the course, 29% of the girls in the same groups said they had had sex. Boys in the 10th grade, about 14 to 15 years old, showed an even more marked increase, from 24% to 39%, after attending abstinence-only classes.[1562] Instead of using the world's most famous unwed teenage mother, Bristol Palin, to promote abstinence, why are they not using the success stories? Oh, right, there are none. Abstinent teenagers end up bitter adults who resent having waited so long after they found out how good sex is. In fact, Randall Tobias, President Bush's abstinence-promoting "AIDS Czar" resigned after admitting he was a customer of the infamous "D.C. Madam" when the escort service was about to surrender its records.

The U.S. teenage pregnancy rate continues its two-decade decline as American adolescents increasingly get into the habit of using condoms during intercourse. Despite the continuous decline, the country's teen pregnancy rate is still the highest among industrial nations, with about one-third of girls in the United States getting pregnant before they turn 20.[1563] According to a recent study published in the online medical journal ***Reproductive Health***, teenage mothers are more common in the U.S.

1561. "The Content of Federally Funded Abstinence-Only Education Programs," United States House of Representatives Committee on Government Reform, Washington, D.C., December 2004.

1562. Patricia Goodson, et al. "Abstinence Education Evaluation Phase 5: Technical Report," Department of Health and Kinesiology, Texas A&M University, College Station, TX, September 2004.

1563. Brady E. Hamilton, et al. "Births: Preliminary Data for 2006," *National Vital Statistics Reports* 56(7), December 5, 2007.

states that have a high concentration of religious conservatives. The connection remains even after taking incomes and abortions into account.[1564] In fact, Harvard researchers found that more than half the adolescents who had made virginity pledges give up on these signed, public promises within a year.[1565] Drs. Hanna Brückner and Peter Bearman, from Yale and Columbia respectively, also published a paper in the *Journal of Adolescent Health* showing that teenagers who pledge to be abstinent until marriage are less likely to protect themselves with condoms if and when they do have sex.[1566]

The opponents of early sex education argue that it will only induce children to engage in premature sexual experimentation. The fact is, 99% of teenagers have sex. Anyone can engage in sexual intercourse without any education at all. But nature does not teach about birth control. *That* requires instruction. Using birth control is always a victory of reason over biology. Instincts and desires tell us to reproduce, and nature has always taken care of this part without any education. If we can learn to control the most basic of all drives—the sex drive—then we can control drugs, alcohol, and abusive anger. Experimentation is part of growing up, and the challenge for the parent is how to frame that experimentation, because there comes a time in adolescence when saying "No" will not work. Learning to use birth control, to put up with its inconvenience, conceiving risk and bearing responsibility is hard and requires motivation. Telling teenagers to repress their blossoming natural urges that have only recently been delivered to them is like telling a music lover that Beethoven is a hack.

According to Brückner and Bearman, young people who sign a virginity pledge are more likely to experiment with oral and anal sex. Their eight-year study found that just 2% of youth who never took a pledge said they had had oral or anal sex but not intercourse, compared with 13% of "consistent pledgers."[1567] Teenagers who are engaging in oral or anal sex will tell you that they are practising abstinence, because they have not had "real sex" yet. While oral sex is not necessarily more prevalent today than it was in the past, it is certainly more accepted. There are stories about many a well-to-do Georgia peach who can honestly say she is a virgin on her wedding day after having gone down on half her high-school football team. But why should non-procreative sex acts even be discouraged among teenagers? They function as relatively innocent ways to relieve sexual tensions without resulting in unwanted pregnancy, and with a greatly reduced risk of sexually transmitted disease. As long she does not give her husband Chlamydia, Gonorrhea, or HPV on their wedding night, why should it even be an issue?

For a teenager whose sexuality is blossoming, peer validation is the social glue that binds their identity together. Children as young as twelve, who are *not* sexually active, are sending explicit and provocative pictures of themselves to their peers. "We

1564. Joseph M. Strayhorn & Jillian C. Strayhorn, "Religiosity and Teen Birth Rate in the United States," 6(14), September 17, 2009.

1565. Janet E. Rosenbaum, "Reborn a Virgin: Adolescents' Retracting of Virginity Pledges and Sexual Histories," *American Journal of Public Health* 96(6), June 2006, 1098–1103.

1566. "After the Promise: The STD Consequences of Adolescent Virginity Pledges," 36(4), April 2005, 271–278.

1567. Ibid.

ask again: Where are your boundaries? It's simply not fair, you being all young and smooth and fearless, just discovering the joys of your bodies and of modern technology and flirting and flaunting it all like you don't have a care in the world."[1568] In 2004, a 15-year-old Pennsylvania girl was arrested for taking nude photographs of herself and posting them on the internet. She was charged not only with possession and dissemination of child pornography, but with sexual abuse of children as well. In 2008, a 15-year-old Ohio girl was charged with felony child pornography for sending nude photos of herself to a 13-year-old male classmate in a text message, and will in all likelihood have to register as a "sex offender" for the rest of her life. In 2009, three teenage girls from Greensburg, Pennsylvania, sent nude cell phone camera self-portraits to three high-school classmates, resulting in everyone involved being charged with trafficking in child porn.

But it is not just an American problem; similar cases have also been reported in the UK, Australia, and New Zealand. These children are not being sexually exploited—their sexuality is being criminalized. A recent survey of more than 1,000 teenagers in the United States found that around one in five 13- to 19-year olds had shared nude or semi-nude pictures of themselves either by text or online.[1569] The people enforcing and deciding how to apply adult sexual laws to children across the nation seem not to realize that children are simply doing what they have always done. How will making the consequences of a dumb decision even harsher prevent the impulsiveness that is characteristic to adolescents and, by definition, involves failing to consider consequences? How about a good spanking or sending them to their rooms without dinner? It turns my stomach that prosecutors should use a law intended to protect minors to punish them for being stupid. "Incarcerating kids will solve the 'sexting' problem like incarcerating drug users has created a drug-free America."[1570]

In times past, the power of instincts and desires was fought against in other ways: encounters between young people always involved chaperones, and they were never left alone—to no avail. And this was back when people got married in their early teens; in fact, this was *why* people got married in their early teens. Another commonly used deterrent was the threat of sinning, and young people were also regaled with horror stories about rotting spines and genitals falling off—to no avail. According to the 1st-century historian Strabo, "The great mass of women and common people cannot be induced by mere force of reason to devote themselves to piety, virtue, and honesty. Superstition must therefore be employed, and even this is insufficient without the aid of the marvelous and the horrible."[1571] But as G. B. Shaw quipped, "we learn from history that men never learn anything from history."[1572]

Countless studies have shown that public health messages that playfully encourage people to protect themselves against disease are much more effective at changing

1568. Morford, op. cit.

1569. "Sex and Tech," National Campaign to Prevent Teen and Unplanned Pregnancies, Washington, D.C., December 2008.

1570. Maia Szalavitz, *Huffington Post*, March 20, 2009.

1571. *Geography*, I, ii, § 8.

1572. *Preface to Heartbreak House*. 1919, lii.

behaviour than stern, moralistic ones. Casual sex only causes emotional problems if the participants have been raised to believe that casual sex is shameful. Public health programs and sex education curricula should focus on real threats such as interpersonal violence, pregnancy risk, and STDs, not on the theory that casual sex is emotionally harmful. According to studies, teenagers postpone their first intercourse if they are told about other forms of intimacy, such as oral sex—it is ignorance and curiosity that lead to experimentation.[1573] However, even in Europe, sex ed is still very much about pregnancy and disease prevention, not pleasure; in fact, when the UK National Health Service launched an "Orgasm a Day" campaign aimed at British schoolchildren, it sparked quite a controversy.

For generations, parents have been complaining how their children are "growing up so fast," while, according to many modern pundits, the smallest among us are being exposed to more and more adult themes at ever younger ages. According to a global survey conducted in 2006, the age at which virginity is lost in developed nations varies between 15 and 19. In the United States, it is 16.[1574] This is the age at which people first have sex, not the first time they think about sex or are exposed to it. In fact, it is normal for children to experiment with their sexuality. Yet the automatic conflation by the media of all sexual images and ideas with misogyny is evidence of a dangerous trend in contemporary thought: the idea that young women and girls need to be protected from any and all sexual imagery for the good of our moral health. Religious conservatives and high-profile feminists are unanimous in their allegation that contemporary culture has turned all women under thirty into sexual victims.

There are countries that are not "hypersexualized" like our culture. In these countries, women are made to wear veils and stoned to death for adultery. Many men, who live in societies divided among gender lines, start viewing women—all women—as nothing but sexual objects. Religious customs mean that there is no sex before marriage, and when men become obsessed with sexual desires, and have no outlet for these urges, they may begin to view all women in a derogatory fashion. Sexual harassment of women is on the increase in the Arab world, and according to a 2008 survey by the Egyptian Centre for Women's Rights, observing Islamic dress code is no deterrent. Some men said they harassed women simply because they were bored, and one who abused a woman wearing the niqab said she must be beautiful, or hiding something.[1575]

In the United States, on the other hand, rape and attempted rape declined 85% just between 1980 and 2004, according to the U.S. Department of Justice figures. According to a distinguished American legal scholar, Prof. Anthony D'Amato, this decline is due to the fact that the female body is no longer mystified and no longer tied with the instinct of undressing women. The four states with the highest per capita access to the internet saw a 27% decrease in rape, while the four states with the

1573. Sarah Blenkinsop, et al. "Evaluation of the APAUSE SRE Programme," Teenage Pregnancy Unit at the Department of Education and Skills, London, April 2004.

1574. "The Face of Global Sex 2007: First Sex—An Opportunity of a Lifetime," SSL International, Cambridge, 2007.

1575. "Clouds in Egypt's Sky: Sexual Harassment—From Verbal Harassment to Rape," ECWR, Cairo, July 2008.

lowest per capita access actually saw a 53% increase in rape over the same period.[1576] Due to the explicit sexual content in the media, comprehensive sex education is more important than ever before. Marketers have long understood that sex sells, even to children who have never even been kissed. Easy access to sexual messages and images has shifted the bounds of what is considered socially acceptable. Being a porn star used to be a career, but today's biggest adult starlets, not to mention the occasional models, have entirely separate day jobs.

Pamela Anderson and Paris Hilton are famous equally for their legitimate TV work and their online sex tapes. Meanwhile, adult film actress Jenna Jameson has moved from X-rated movies to a bestselling sex manual and a VH1 documentary. Dance moves once exclusively associated with strippers are as common on MTV as tight leather pants on rock stars. Women who act in porn have fewer casual relationships than their "sexually liberated" co-ed sisters. Children are not stupid, they just know less than adults. The new media environment relays the same information to everyone at the same time. Knowledge is no longer controlled by the home or the school, and the uncontrollability of information creates a sphere where anyone can end up regardless of their age. A few years ago a country was so alarmed about these issues that they banned television and advertising altogether; the only trouble is, that country was Afghanistan under the Taliban—not, by any account, fun times for women and children.

KGOY, or Kids Growing Older Younger, is a buzzword among advertisers who target the pre-teen market. Most 8- to 10-year olds have no desire to look "sexy," they associate bare midriffs and thigh highs with being fashionable. Paedophiles have a sick fixation with children looking like children—not like adults. And the awful fact is that the vast majority of childhood sexual abuse takes place inside families, with nearly two-thirds of abuse by a female involving the child's own mother.[1577] In the entire United States, approximately 115 children are abducted by strangers every year.[1578] In 2010, the annual survey by the Center for Applied Research in the Apostolate at Georgetown University reported 345 credible episodes of abuse by Catholic priests and deacons—*down* from 898 in 2004, the first year of the survey.[1579] In fact, every study of childhood sexual abuse tells us that about 95% of all cases involve a person who knew the child and stood in a position of trust—parent, uncle, scoutmaster. However, the rates of child abuse have not risen during the last hundred years, the chances of getting caught have merely gone up; half a century ago, children played in the same room where the parents had sex; today, this would be grounds for state custody.

Another common misconception about childhood sexual abuse is that it is

---

1576. "Porn Up, Rape Down," Northwestern University School of Law, Chicago, June 23, 2006.

1577. Lorraine Radford, et al. "Child Abuse and Neglect in the UK Today," NSPCC, London, September 2011.

1578. Heather Hammer, et al. "National Estimates of Missing Children: Selected Trends, 1988–1999," Office of Juvenile Justice and Delinquency Prevention, Washington, D.C., December 2004.

1579. "2010 Survey of Allegations and Costs: A Summary Report for the Office of Child and Youth Protection, United States Conference of Catholic Bishops," U.S. Bishop's Office for Child and Youth Protection, Washington, D.C., April 11, 2011.

perpetrated by adults. Unfortunately, "you don't just wake up one day at 50 and become a pervert."[1580] A British Broadcasting Company investigation recently discovered that, on the average, a hundred young people under the age of 18 are charged with rape each year just in Scotland—the figure excludes cases of consensual underage sex.[1581] Directly comparable figures for the rest of the United Kingdom were not available, but a UK Ministry of Justice report paints a similar picture in England and Wales.[1582] The 2009 BBC investigation looked at the case of Scottish teenager Colyn Evans, who murdered 16-year-old Karen Dewar in 2005. He was accused of six sexual offences between the ages of 10 and 16, but was never registered as a sex offender.

A Britain-wide survey suggests that a third of girls aged 13 to 17 suffer sexual abuse in a relationship and a quarter experience violence at the hands of their boyfriends. Nearly 90% of the 1,400 English, Welsh, and Scottish girls surveyed had been in intimate relationships, and one in three said their boyfriends had tried to pressure them into unwanted sexual activity by either physical force or bullying; one in 16 said they had been raped.[1583] All in all, various studies show that between a quarter and a third of children who have been abused report that the perpetrators have been other children. Many survivors of childhood sexual abuse learn about sex through that abuse, which is not exactly a source of empowering information. A 2000 study commissioned by the Girl Scouts of America concluded that "Physically, girls' bodies are maturing earlier than ever before. Cognitively, they are acquiring information about the world at an accelerated pace. . . The dilemma is that these same girls do not have the emotional maturity, nor do they have the information, to match their accelerated aspirations and expectations."[1584]

Most young people learn about sex through their peers, who are often equally uninformed. "If he pulls it out, you can't catch anything." "If you take it in the back door, you're still a virgin." "If you shower after you do it, you have nothing to worry about." "If you rinse your vag with Coke, you're in the clear." When hormones are raging and the only answer you hear is "Just say no," you have only your friends to turn to for, um, cola douches. And if and when teenagers get the message about safe sex from their parents, it often comes after they have already become curious or nervous about the subject or received conflicting information from their just as clueless friends. By the time a blushing school teacher begins a sex ed class, the pupils have already run a thousand web searches on the subject. These questions and answers should really be addressed in earnest as early as kindergarten.

Many young people are having sex precisely because they want to find out what it is. Accurate information in itself does not result in sexual activity, it only prevents

---

1580. "Pilot." *Blue Bloods.* CBS. September 24, 2010.

1581. *The Dark Side of Teenage Sex.* BBC One. July 21, 2009.

1582. "Youth Justice Statistics 2009/10: England and Wales," Youth Justice Board, London, January 20, 2011.

1583. Christine Barter, et al. "Partner Exploitation and Violence in Teenage Intimate Relationships," NSPCC, London, October 2009.

1584. Whitney Roban & Michael Conn, "Girls Speak Out: Teens Before Their Time," Girl Scout Research Institute, New York, 2000.

risks that are otherwise far too easily taken. Just because you wear a seat belt does not mean that you are looking for an accident. In the end, sex is a big deal only if there is a chance that someone will get pregnant or infected. More than 200 million women around the world lack access to contraceptives. Estimated 175,000 women die in childbirth and botched illegal abortions each year.[1585] As the laws on abortion have been loosened, the rate of abortions has come down. Since 1997, 19 countries have loosened their abortion laws considerably and three countries have tightened them. Many Nicaraguan women and teenage girls in particular have been driven to suicide, because they can no longer obtain an abortion. Abortions are now illegal in Nicaragua even when the pregnancy is the result of rape or incest and imperils the mother's health. According to a report by Amnesty International, suicides by poison have become the main cause of maternal deaths for young Nicaraguan women.[1586]

Meanwhile, the number of abortions have fallen dramatically in the United States over the last two decades, and will continue to do so with the increasing availability of better contraception and technologies to terminate unwanted pregnancies earlier. Early medication abortions, notably through the use of the RU-486 regimen, accounted for 13% of all abortions in 2005, more than double the level in 2001. In fact, the rates of surgical abortion are so low that fewer and fewer American physicians know how to perform the procedure.[1587] Studies show that high-risk behaviour is reduced most effectively by sufficiently comprehensive and accurate education programs: "Obviously, a man's judgment cannot be better than the information on which he has based it. Give him the truth and he may still go wrong when he has the chance to be right, but give him no news or present him only with distorted and incomplete data, with ignorant, sloppy or biased reporting, with propaganda and deliberate falsehood, and you destroy his whole reasoning process, and make him something less than a man."[1588]

Ultimately, it all comes down to these two choices: the John Waters way is to "thank God I was raised Catholic, so sex will always be dirty,"[1589] while the Lorra Moore thinking goes, "If you can't giggle, scream, laugh, run around the room naked, pour liqueur on each other and lick it off, tie each other down, have whipped cream fights, dance and sing with each other then you are having sex with the person too soon."[1590] If you are unable to discuss these matters without anxiety when you are young, bringing them up after you are in a relationship can be very difficult. If you think you have something to hide, if you feel the need to live some sort of secret and

---

1585. "Family Planning and Poverty Reduction: Benefits for Families and Nations," UNFPA, New York, July 11, 2008.

1586. "Not Even When Her Life Is at Stake: How the Total Abortion Ban in Nicaragua Criminalizes Doctors and Endangers Women and Girls," Amnesty International, London, July 2009.

1587. Rachel K. Jones, et al. "Abortion in the United States: Incidence and Access to Services, 2005," *Perspectives on Sexual and Reproductive Health* 40(1), March 2008, 6–16.

1588. Arthur Hays Sulzberger, Address to the New York State Publishers Association, August 30, 1948.

1589. *Out*, May 2004.

1590. Attributed.

embarrassing double life, if you are constantly hiding pictures and data on your computer, if you cannot let someone browse through your sex-toy collection without blushing or fainting, perhaps you have made the wrong choice. Sex educators refer to discovering one's own sexuality—everyone should be able to answer the question of desire for themselves.

As Diane di Mauro, program director of the Sexuality Research Fellowship Program at New York's Social Science Research Council, puts it: "There's this unspoken assumption that the truth about sex will set you free, but that's not the point. It's not going to set you free. It's going to provide an awareness and understanding of where one has come from and where one might be headed. That's all, and that's the point."[1591] We live in an individualistic era, yet we need someone to constantly tell us what we are supposed to do. We are no longer able to sort out our own thoughts without the help of a professional therapist or engage in any physical activity without a personal trainer. Maintaining the right state of mind today requires an expert who tells you when your feelings are correct. We cannot resolve our relationship issues without professional help and head to couples' therapy immediately after exchanging the vows. Our personal finances are the worst they have ever been, even though we are richer and wealthier than ever before in human history. So what should we do? Well, you definitely should not take advice from a silly little book like this one.

1591. As quoted in Steven Winn, "Kinsey Let Us Talk About Sex: But We're Still Divided Over It," *San Francisco Chronicle*, November 22, 2004.

"Then anyone who leaves behind him a written manual,
and likewise anyone who receives it, in the belief
that such writing will be clear and certain,
must be exceedingly simple-minded."
— Plato

"Ah! Don't say you agree with me.
When people agree with me
I always feel that I must be wrong."
— Oscar Wilde

"A witty saying proves nothing."
— Voltaire

Select References[*]

Abbott, E. (ed.) (1969). *Historical Aspects of the Immigration Problem: Select Documents.* New York: Arno Press.

Adams, D. (1979). *The Hitchhiker's Guide to the Galaxy.* London: Pan Books.

Adas, M. (1989). *Machines as the Measure of Men: Science, Technology, and Ideologies of Western Dominance.* Ithaca, NY: Cornell University Press.

Aksyonov, V. P. (1987). *In Search of Melancholy Baby.* New York: Random House.

Al-Khalili, J. (2011). *The House of Wisdom: How Arabic Science Saved Ancient Knowledge and Gave Us the Renaissance.* New York: Penguin Press.

Alperovitz, G. (1995). *The Decision to Use the Atomic Bomb: And the Architecture of an American Myth.* New York: Alfred A. Knopf.

American Psychiatric Association. (1994). *Diagnostic and Statistical Manuals of Mental Disorders.* 4th ed. Washington, DC: American Psychiatric Publishing.

Amstrong, K. (1993). *A History of God: The 4000-Year Quest of Judaism, Christianity, and Islam.* New York: Alfred A. Knopf.

Angell, M. (2004). *The Truth About the Drug Companies: How They Deceive Us and What to Do About It.* New York: Random House.

Angelou, M. (1969). *I Know Why the Caged Bird Sings.* New York: Random House.

Angoff, C. (1934). *Arsenal for Skeptics.* (ed. R. W. Hinton). New York: Alfred A. Knopf.

Aquinas, T. (1948). *Summa Theologica.* 3 vols. New York: Benziger Brothers.

Ard, B. N. (ed.) (1975). *Counseling & Psychotherapy: Classics on Theories & Issues.* Palo Alto: Science and Behavior Books.

Arendt, H. (1963). *Eichmann in Jerusalem: A Report on the Banality of Evil.* New York: Viking Press.

Aristophanes. (1998). *Birds and Other Plays.* (trans. S. Halliwell). Oxford: Oxford University Press.

---

*Only book-length and/or frequently referenced works are listed here; all other sources, including short reports and magazine, journal, and newspaper articles, are cited in full in the footnotes.

Aristotle. (1966). *Ethica Nicomachea.* (trans. W. D. Ross). Oxford: Oxford University Press.

_____. (1972). *Politics.* (trans. H. Rackham). Cambridge, MA: Harvard University Press.

Ashcroft, J. (2006). *Making a Killing: The Explosive Story of a Hired Gun in Iraq.* London: Virgin Books.

Asimov, I. (1978). *Quasar, Quasar, Burning Bright.* Garden City, NY: Doubleday & Co.

Bacevich, A. J. (2008). *The Limits of Power: The End of American Exceptionalism.* New York: Metropolitan Books.

_____. (2010). *Washington Rules: America's Path to Permanent War.* New York: Metropolitan Books.

Bacon, F. (1824). *The Works of Francis Bacon, Baron of Verulam, Viscount St. Albans, and Lord High Chancellor of England.* 10 vols. London: W. Baynes & Son.

Bakunin, M. A. (1973). *Selected Writings.* (ed. A. Lehning, trans. S. Cox & O. Stevens). London: Jonathan Cape.

Bales, K. (1999). *Disposable People: New Slavery in the Global Economy.* Berkeley: University of California Press.

Balk, A. P. (2008). *Saints & Sinners: An Account of Western Civilization.* Helsinki: Thelema Publications.

Bancroft, L. (2003). *Why Does He Do That?: Inside the Minds of Angry and Controlling Men.* New York: Berkley Books.

Bandler, R. (1985). *Using Your Brain—For a Change.* (ed. C. & S. Andreas). Moab, UT: Real People Press.

_____ & J. Grinder. (1975). *The Structure of Magic I: A Book about Language and Therapy.* Palo Alto: Science & Behavior Books.

Barash, D. P. & J. E. Lipton. (2001). *The Myth of Monogamy: Fidelity and Infidelity in Animals and People.* New York: W. H. Freeman.

Barnett, T. P. M. (2004). *The Pentagon's New Map: War and Peace in the Twenty-First Century.* New York: G. P. Putnam's Sons.

Barrett, G. (1921). *Objections to Anarchism.* London: Freedom Press.

Bastiat, F. (1968). *Selected Essays on Political Economy.* (trans. S. Cain, ed. G. B. de Huszar). Irvington-on-Hudson, NY: The Foundation for Economic Education.

Baudoin, C. (1924). *The Inner Discipline.* London: Allen & Unwin.

_____. (1920). *Suggestion and Autosuggestion.* London: Allen & Unwin.

Bauer, P. T. (1976). *Dissent on Development.* 2nd ed. Cambridge, MA: Harvard University Press.

_____. (1981). *Equality, the Third World, and Economic Delusions.* Cambridge, MA: Harvard University Press.

_____. (2000). *From Subsistence to Exchange and Other Essays.* Princeton, NJ: Princeton University Press.

Baumeister, R. F. (ed.) (1993). *Self-Esteem: The Puzzle of Low Self-Regard.* New York: Plenum Press.

_____. (ed.) (2001). *Social Psychology and Human Sexuality: Essential Readings.* Philadelphia, PA: Psychology Press.

Beccaria, C. (2008). *On Crimes and Punishment: And Other Writings.* (trans. A. Thomas & J. Parzen). Toronto: University of Toronto Press.

Beck, H. (1997). *The Origins of the Authoritarian Welfare State in Prussia: Conservatives, Bureaucracy, and the Social Question, 1815–70.* Ann Arbor: University of Michigan Press.

Behrendt, G. & L. Tuccillo. (2004). *He's Just Not That Into You: The No-Excuses Truth to Understanding Guys.* New York: Simon & Schuster.

Benoist, A. de. (2004). *On Being a Pagan.* (trans. J. Graham, ed. G. Johnson). Atlanta, GA: Ultra Press.

Bentham, J. (1988). *A Fragment on Government.* (ed. J. H. Burns & H. L. A. Hart). Cambridge: Cambridge University Press.

_____. (1988). *The Principles of Morals and Legislation.* Buffalo, NY: Prometheus Books.

Berkman, A. (1929). *Now and After: The ABC of Anarchism.* New York: Vanguard Press.

Berne, E. (1964). *The Games People Play: The Psychology of Human Relationships.* New York: Grove Press.

Bhagwati, J. N. (2002). *Free Trade Today.* Princeton, NJ: Princeton University Press.

_____. (2004). *In Defense of Globalization.* New York: Oxford University Press.

Bierce, A. (1925). *The Devil's Dictionary.* New York: Albert & Charles Boni.

Bissinger, H. G. (1990). *Friday Night Lights: A Town, a Team, and a Dream.* Reading, MA: Addison-Wesley Publishing Co.

Black, B. (1986). *The Abolition of Work and Other Essays.* Port Townsend, WA: Loompanics Unlimited.

Black, D. J. (1980). *The Manners and Customs of the Police.* New York: Academic Press.

Black, W. K. (2005). *The Best Way to Rob a Bank Is to Own One: How Corporate Executives and Politicians Looted the S&L Industry.* Austin, TX: University of Texas Press.

Blake, W. (1975). *The Marriage of Heaven and Hell.* Oxford: Oxford University Press.

Bloch, A. (2003). *Murphy's Law: The 26th Anniversary Edition.* New York: Perigee.

Block, W. (2008). *Defending the Undefendable: The Pimp, Prostitute, Scab, Slumlord, Libeler, Moneylender, and Other Scapegoats in the Rogue's Gallery of American Society.* Auburn, AL: Ludwig von Mises Institute.

Blue, V. (2006). *The Smart Girl's Guide to Porn.* San Francisco: Cleis Press.

Booker, C. (2009). *The Real Global Warming Disaster: Is the Obsession with 'Climate Change' Turning Out to Be the Most Costly Scientific Blunder in History?* London: Continuum Publishing.

_____ & R. North. (2007). *Scared to Death: From BSE to Global Warming—Why Scares Are Costing Us the Earth.* London: Continuum Publishing.

Bouchard, T. J. & P. Propping. (eds.) (1993). *Twins as a Tool of Behavioral Genetics: Report of the Dahlem Workshop on What Are the Mechanisms Mediating the Genetic and Environmental Determinants of Behavior?* Hoboken, NJ: John Wiley & Sons.

Bourne, R. S. (1964). *War and the Intellectuals: Collected Essays, 1915–1919.* (ed. C. Resek). New York: Harper Torchbooks.

Bovard, J. (2006). *Attention Deficit Democracy.* New York: Palgrave Macmillan.

_____. (2000). *Freedom in Chains: The Rise of the State and the Demise of the Citizen.* New York: Palgrave Macmillan.

_____. (1995). *Lost Rights: The Destruction of American Liberty.* New York: Palgrave Macmillan.

Bowen, S. W. (2009). *Hard Lessons: The Iraq Reconstruction Experience.* Darby, PA: Diane Publishing.

Braben, D. W. (2008). *Scientific Freedom: The Elixir of Civilization.* Hoboken, NJ: Wiley-Interscience.

Bradlaugh, C. (1882). *Theological Essays.* London: Freethought Publishing Co.

Branden, N. (1973). *The Disowned Self.* New York: Bantam Books.

_____. (1996). *Taking Responsibility: Self-Reliance and the Accountable Life.* New York: Simon & Schuster.

Brandt, A. M. (2007). *The Cigarette Century: The Rise, Fall, and Deadly Persistence of the Product That Defined America.* New York: Basic Books.

Bremmer, I. (2010). *The End of the Free Market: Who Wins the War Between States and Corporations?* New York: Portfolio.

Briggs, A. (1968). *Victorian Cities.* 2nd ed. Harmondsworth: Penguin Books.

Brizendine, L. (2006). *The Female Brain.* New York: Morgan Road Books.

_____. (2010). *The Male Brain.* New York: Broadway Books.

Bronowski, J. (1973). *The Ascent of Man.* Boston: Little, Brown & Co.

Bruce, L. (1972). *How to Talk Dirty and Influence People: An Autobiography.* Chicago: Playboy Press.

Brunner, J. (1968). *Stand on Zanzibar.* Garden City, NY: Doubleday.

Bryce, R. (2008). *Gusher of Lies: The Dangerous Delusions of "Energy Independence".* New York: Public Affairs.

Buchholz, E. S. (1997). *The Call of Solitude: Alonetime in a World of Attachment.* New York: Simon & Schuster.

Buehrens, J. A. & F. F. Church. (1989). *Our Chosen Faith: An Introduction to Unitarian Universalism.* Boston: Beacon Press.

Bufe, C. (ed.) (1992). *The Heretic's Handbook of Quotations: Cutting Comments on Burning Issues.* Tucson: See Sharp Press.

Bullough, V. L. & B. Bullough. (1995). *Sexual Attitudes: Myths & Realities.* Amherst, NY: Prometheus Books.

Bunge, M. A. (2003). *Emergence and Convergence: Qualitative Novelty and the Unity of Knowledge.* Toronto: University of Toronto Press.

_____. (1980). *The Mind-Body Problem: A Psychobiological Approach.* Oxford: Pergamon Press.

Burke, E. (1790). *Reflections on the Revolution in France: And on the Proceedings in Certain Societies in London Relative to that Event.* 2nd ed. London: J. Dodsley.

Burroughs, W. S. (1985). *The Adding Machine: Collected Essays.* London: John Calder.

Burton, R. F. (1924). *The Kasîdah of Hâjî Abdû El-Yezdî.* New York: Alfred A. Knopf.

Buss, D. M. (2000). *The Dangerous Passion: Why Jealousy Is as Necessary as Love and Sex.* New York: Simon & Schuster.

_____. (1994). *The Evolution of Desire: Strategies of Human Mating.* New York: Basic Books.

_____. (2005). *The Murderer Next Door: Why the Mind Is Designed to Kill.* New York: Penguin Press.

Byron, G. G. (1943). *Don Juan: A Satiric Epic of Modern Life.* New York: Heritage Press.

Cahn, N. & J. Carbone. (2010). *Red Families v. Blue Families: Legal Polarization and the Creation of Culture.* New York: Oxford University Press.

Calhoun, J. C. (1953). *A Disquisition on Government: And, a Discourse on the Constitution and Government of the United States.* (ed. R. E. Crallé). New York: Liberal Arts Press.

Camerer, C. F. et al. (eds.) (2004). *Advances in Behavioral Economics.* Princeton, NJ: Princeton University Press.

Camus, A. (1991). *The Myth of Sisyphus: & Other Essays.* (trans. J. O'Brien). New York: Vintage Books.

Capra, F. (1975). *The Tao of Physics: An Exploration of the Parallels Between Modern Physics and Eastern Mysticism.* Boulder, CO: Shambhala.

_____. (1982). *The Turning Point: Science, Society, and the Rising Culture.* New York: Simon & Schuster.

Card, O. S. (2001). *Saints.* New York: Forge Books.

Carlson, S. & G. A. Larne. (1989). *Satanism in America: How the Devil Got Much More Than His Due.* San Francisco: Gaia Press.

Carson, L. (1998). *Caring for the Dead: Your Final Act of Love.* Hinesburg, VT: Upper Access Books.

Carvalho, S. et al. (2002). *Social Funds: Assessing Effectiveness.* Washington, DC: World Bank.

Cavalli-Sforza, L. L. (2000). *Genes, Peoples, and Languages.* (trans. M. Seielstad). New York: North Point Press.

Chafets, Z. (2009). *Cooperstown Confidential: Heroes, Rogues, and the Inside Story of the Baseball Hall of Fame.* New York: Bloomsbury USA.

Chambliss, W. J. (1988). *On the Take: From Petty Crooks to Presidents.* 2nd ed. Bloomington: Indiana University Press.

Chesterton, G. K. (1909). *Tremendous Trifles.* New York: Dodd, Mead & Co.

Chiarelli, P. W. (2010). *Army Health Promotion Risk Reduction Suicide Prevention Report 2010.* Washington, DC: U.S. Department of the Army.

Churchland, P. S. (2002). *Brain-Wise: Studies in Neurophilosophy.* Cambridge, MA: MIT Press.

Cialdini, R. B. (1988). *Influence: Science and Practice.* 2nd ed. Glenview, IL: Scott, Foresman & Co.

Clausewitz, K. von. (1932–34). *Vom Krieg.* 3 vols. Berlin: Ferdinand Dümmler.

Cochran, G. & H. Harpending. (2009). *The 10,000 Year Explosion: How Civilization Accelerated Human Evolution.* New York: Basic Books.

Cohen, C. (1928). *Essays in Freethinking.* London: Secular Society.

Cohen, M. R. & E. Nagel. (1993). *An Introduction to Logic.* 2nd ed. (ed. J. Corcoran). Indianapolis, IN: Hackett Publishing Co.

Cole, J. R. (2009). *Engaging the Muslim World.* New York: Palgrave Macmillan.

Coleman, V. (1992). *The Drugs Myth: Why the Drug Wars Must Stop.* London: Green Print.

_____. (1985). *Life without Tranquillisers.* London: Piatkus Books.

_____. (1975). *The Medicine Men.* London: Temple Smith.

Collier, P. (2010). *Wars, Guns, and Votes: Democracy in Dangerous Places.* New York: Harper Perennial.

Comfort, A. (1967). *The Anxiety Makers: Some Curious Preoccupations of the Medical Profession.* Camden, NJ: Nelson, 1967.

Conrad, J. (1905). *Lord Jim: A Romance.* New York: McClure, Phillips & Co.

Contoski, E. (1997). *Makers and Takers: How Wealth and Progress Are Made and How They Are Taken Away or Prevented.* Minneapolis, MN: American Liberty Publishers.

Cook, P. W. (1997). *Abused Men: The Hidden Side of Domestic Violence.* Westport, CT: Praeger.

Coontz, S. (2005). *Marriage, a History: From Obedience to Intimacy, or How Love Conquered Marriage.* New York: Viking Press.

Cooper, J. (1989). *Principles of Personal Defense.* 2nd ed. Boulder, CO: Paladin Press.

Coué, E. (1922). *Self Mastery Through Conscious Autosuggestion.* (trans. A. S. Van Orden) New York: Malkan Publishing Co.

Crenshaw, T. L. (1997). *The Alchemy of Love and Lust: How Our Sex Hormones Influence Our Relationships.* New York: Pocket Books.

Critser, G. (2005). *Generation Rx: How Prescription Drugs Are Altering American Lives, Minds, and Bodies.* Boston: Houghton Mifflin Company.

Crowley, A. (1969). *Book 4.* Dallas, TX: Sangreal Foundation.

_____. (1962). *The Book of Lies: Falsely So Called.* 2nd ed. Ilfracombe, Devon: Haydn Press.

_____. (1979). *The Confessions of Aleister Crowley: An Autohagiography.* London: Routledge & Kegan Paul.

_____. (ed.) (1909–13). *The Equinox.* Vol. I. 10 nos. London: Simpkin, Marshall, Hamilton, Kent & Co.

_____. (ed.) (1919). *The Equinox.* Vol. III. No I. Detroit: Universal.

_____. (1986). *The Gospel According to Saint Bernard Shaw.* San Francisco: Stellar Visions.

_____. (1991). *Liber Aleph vel CXI: The Book of Wisdom or Folly.* 2nd ed. (ed. Hymanæus Beta). York Beach, ME: Samuel Weiser.

_____. (1974). *Magical and Philosophical Commentaries on the Book of the Law.* (ed. J. Symonds & K. Grant). Montréal: 93 Publishing.

_____. (1961). *Magick in Theory and Practice.* New York: Castle Books.

_____. (1954). *Magick Without Tears.* (ed. K. J. Germer). Hampton, NJ: Thelema Publishing.

_____. (1998). *The Revival of Magick and Other Essays.* (ed. Hymanæus Beta & R. Kaczynski). Tempe, AZ: New Falcon Publications.

Cubberley, E. P. (1934). *Public Education in the United States.* Boston: Houghton Mifflin.

Dafoe, D. (1885). *The Life and Adventures of Robinson Crusoe.* (ed. E. O. Chapman). New York: Worthington Co.

Dampier, W. C. (1929). *A History of Science and Its Relation with Philosophy and Religion.* Cambridge: Cambridge University Press.

Davis, H. (2009). *Caveman Logic: The Persistence of Primitive Thinking in a Modern World.* Amherst, NY: Prometheus Books.

Davis, R. C. (2003). *Christian Slaves, Muslim Masters: White Slavery in the Mediterranean, the Barbary Coast, and Italy, 1500–1800.* New York: Palgrave Macmillan.

Davis, T. et al. (2006). *A Failure of Initiative: Final Report of the Select Bipartisan Committee to Investigate the Preparations for and Response to Hurricane Katrina.* Washington, DC: U.S. Government Printing Office.

Dawkins, R. (2004). *A Devil's Chaplain: Reflections on Hope, Lies, Science, and Love.* Boston: Mariner Books.

_____. (1995). *River Out of Eden: A Darwinian View of Life.* New York: Basic Books.

_____. (1976). *The Selfish Gene.* Oxford: Oxford University Press.

Deloire, C. & C. Dubois. (2004). *Les islamistes sont déjà là: Enquête sur une guerre secrète.* Paris: Albin Michel.

Denson, J. V. (ed.) (1999). *The Costs of War: America's Pyrrhic Victories.* 2nd ed. New Brunswick, NJ: Transaction Publishers.

_____. (ed.) (2001). *Reassessing the Presidency: The Rise of the Executive State and the Decline of Freedom.* Auburn, AL: Ludwig von Mises Institute.

DePaulo, B. M. (2006). *Singled Out: How Singles Are Stereotyped, Stigmatized, and Ignored, and Still Live Happily Ever After.* New York: St. Martin's Press.

Descartes, R. (1988). *Selected Philosophical Writings.* (trans. J. Cottingham, R. Stoothoff & D. Murdoch). Cambridge: Cambridge University Press.

Deutscher, G. (2010). *Through the Language Glass: Why the World Looks Different in Other Languages.* New York: Metropolitan Books.

Devan, J. et al. (2011). *Doing Business 2012: Doing Business in a More Transparent World.* Washington, DC: World Bank.

Dewey, J. (1934). *A Common Faith.* New Haven, CT: Yale University Press.

_____. (1920). *Reconstruction in Philosophy.* New York: Henry Holt & Co.

DiLorenzo, T. J. (2004). *How Capitalism Saved America: The Untold History of Our Country, from the Pilgrims to the Present.* New York: Crown Forum.

Dilts, R. et al. (1998). *Beliefs: Pathways to Health & Well-Being.* Portland, OR: Metamorphous Press.

Diwan, P. & P. Diwan. (1997). *Law of Marriage and Divorce.* 3rd ed. New Delhi: Universal Law Publishing Co.

Djankov, S. et al. (2005). *Doing Business in 2005: Removing Obstacles to Growth.* Washington, DC: World Bank.

Doctorow, C. (2008). *Little Brother.* New York: Tom Doherty Associates.

Doren, A. et al. (2009). *Transparency International Annual Report 2008.* Berlin: Transparency International.

_____. (2010). *Transparency International Annual Report 2009.* Berlin: Transparency International.

Dychtwald, K. (1986). *Bodymind.* Los Angeles: Jeremy P. Tarcher.

Easterbrook, G. (1995). *A Moment on Earth: The Coming Age of Environmental Optimism.* New York: Viking.

_____. (2003). *The Progress Paradox: How Life Gets Better While People Feel Worse.* New York: Random House.

Easterly, W. (2006). *The White Man's Burden: Why the West's Efforts to Aid the Rest Have Done So Much Ill and So Little Good.* New York: Penguin Press.

Edis, T. (2002). *The Ghost in the Universe: God in Light of Modern Science.* Amherst, NY: Prometheus Books.

Edwards, M. (2010). *Small Change: Why Business Won't Save the World.* San Francisco: Berrett-Koehler Publishers.

Ehrenreich, B. (2010). *Smile or Die: How Positive Thinking Fooled America & the World.* London: Granta Books.

Einstein, A. (1979). *Albert Einstein, the Human Side: New Glimpses From His Archives.* (ed. H. Dukas & B. Hoffmann). Princeton, NJ: Princeton University Press.

_____. (1954). *Ideas and Opinions.* New York: Crown Publishers.

Ellis, R. J. (2005). *To the Flag: The Unlikely History of the Pledge of Alliance.* Lawrence, KS: University Press of Kansas.

Emerson, R. W. (1982). *Emerson in His Journals.* (ed. J. Porte). Cambridge, MA: Harvard University Press.

Engelhardt, T. (2007). *The End of Victory Culture: Cold War in America and the Disillusioning of a Generation*. 2nd ed. Amherst, MA: University of Massachusetts Press.

Enig, M. G. (2000). *Know Your Fats : The Complete Primer for Understanding the Nutrition of Fats, Oils, and Cholesterol*. Silver Spring, MD: Bethesda Press.

Epictetus. (1890). *The Works of Epictetus: His Discourses, in Four Books, the Enchiridion, and Fragments*. (trans. T. W. Higginson). New York: Thomas Nelson & Sons.

Epicurus. (1993). *The Essential Epicurus: Letters, Principal Doctrines, Vatican Sayings, and Fragments*. (ed. & trans. E. M. O'Connor). Buffalo, NY: Prometheus Books.

Erikson, E. H. (1980). *Identity and the Life Cycle*. New York: W. W. Norton.

Erlandson, G. et al. (eds.) (2004). *Our Sunday Visitor's Catholic Almanac: 2005 Edition*. Huntington, IN: Our Sunday Visitor.

Erlich, H. J. (ed.) (1996). *Reinventing Anarchy, Again*. San Francisco: AK Press.

Esposito, J. L. (1998). *Islam and Politics*. 4th ed. Syracuse, NY: Syracuse University Press.

_____ & D. Mogahed. (2007). *Who Speaks for Islam?: What a Billion Muslims Really Think*. New York: Gallup Press.

Ewen, S. (1976). *Captains of Consciousness: Advertising and the Social Roots of the Consumer Culture*. New York: McGraw-Hill.

Fallon, S. & M. G. Enig. (2001). *Nourishing Traditions: The Cookbook that Challenges Politically Correct Nutrition and the Diet Dictocrats*. 2nd ed. Washington, DC: NewTrends Publishing.

Fallows, J. M. (2009). *Postcards from Tomorrow Square: Reports from China*. New York: Vintage Books.

Farrell, W. (1993). *The Myth of Male Power: Why Men Are the Disposable Sex*. New York: Simon & Schuster.

Federal Bureau of Investigation. (2006). *Crime in the United States 2005*. Washington, DC: U.S. Department of Justice.

_____. (2011). *Crime in the United States 2010*. Lanham, MD: Bernan Press.

Ferriss, A. L. (2010). *Approaches to Improving the Quality of Life: How to Enhance the Quality of Life*. Dordrecht: Springer Verlag.

Feynman, R. P. (1965). *The Character of Physical Law*. Cambridge, MA: MIT Press.

Fisher, H. E. (2004). *Why We Love: The Nature and Chemistry of Romantic Love*. New York: Henry Holt & Co.

Flora, P. et al. (eds.) (1983). *State, Economy and Society in Western Europe, 1815–1975: A Data Handbook in Two Volumes*. 2 vols. Frankfurt: Campus Verlag.

Florida, R. L. (2002). *The Rise of the Creative Class: And How It's Transforming Work, Leisure, Community and Everyday Life*. New York: Basic Books.

_____. (2008). *Who's Your City?: How the Creative Economy Is Making Where to Live the Most Important Decision of Your Life*. New York: Basic Books.

Flynn, T. (ed.) (2007). *The New Encyclopedia of Unbelief*. Amherst, NY: Prometheus Books.

_____. (1993). *The Trouble with Christmas*. Buffalo, NY: Prometheus Books.

Foote, G. W. (1893–94). *Flowers of Freethought*. 2 vols. London: Pioneer Press.

Forbes, S. (2005). *A Natural History of Families*. Princeton, NJ: Princeton University Press.

Foucault, M. (1977). *Discipline and Punish: The Birth of the Prison*. (trans. A. Sheridan). New York: Pantheon Books.

_____. (1978–86). *The History of Sexuality.* 3 vols. (trans. R. Hurley). New York: Pantheon Books.

_____. (1965). *Madness and Civilization: A History of Insanity in the Age of Reason.* (trans. R. Howard). New York: Pantheon Books.

_____. (1978–86). *The History of Sexuality.* 3 vols. (trans. R. Hurley). New York: Pantheon Books.

Fox, J. (2009). *The Myth of the Rational Market: Wall Street's Impossible Quest for Predictable Markets.* New York: Harper Business.

Frank, T. (2004). *What's the Matter with Kansas?: How Conservatives Won the Heart of America.* New York: Metropolitan Books.

Franklin, B. (1972). *An Historical Review of the Constitution and Government of Pennsylvania.* New York: Arno Press.

Fraser, M. (2003). *Weapons of Mass Distraction: Soft Power and American Empire.* Toronto: Key Porter Books.

Frazer, J. G. (1911–15). *The Golden Bough.* 3rd ed. 12 vols. London: Macmillan & Co.

Freeman, K. (ed.) (1948). *Ancilla to the Pre-Socratic Philosophers: A Complete Translation of the Fragments in Diels.* Cambridge, MA: Harvard University Press.

French, N. (1984). *Successful Hypnotherapy.* London: Thorsons Publications.

Freud, S. (2005). *Civilization and Its Discontents.* (trans. J. Strachey). New York: W. W. Norton.

_____. (1957). *The Future of an Illusion.* (trans. W. D. Robson-Scott, rev. J. Strachey). Garden City, NY: Doubleday Anchor Books.

_____. (1933). *The Interpretation of Dreams.* (trans. A. A. Brill). London: Allen & Unwin.

_____. (1960). *Jokes and Their Relation to the Unconscious.* (trans. J. Strachey). New York: W. W. Norton.

_____. (1975). *The Standard Edition of the Complete Psychological Works of Sigmund Freud.* Vol. XI. (ed. A. Freud, trans. J. Strachey). London: Hogarth Press.

Friedman, M. (1962). *Capitalism and Freedom.* Chicago: University of Chicago Press.

_____. (1993). *Why Government Is the Problem: Essays in Public Policy.* Stanford, CA: Hoover Institution Press.

_____ & R. D. Friedman. (1980). *Free to Choose: A Personal Statement.* New York: Harcourt Brace Jovanovich.

Fromm, E. (1942). *The Fear of Freedom.* London: Routledge & Kegan Paul.

_____. (1947). *Man for Himself: An Inquiry into the Psychology of Ethics.* New York: Rinehart & Co.

_____. (1976). *To Have or To Be?* New York: Harper & Row.

Frost, D. (1970). *The Americans.* New York: Stein and Day.

Frost, R. (1914). *North of Boston.* New York: Henry Holt & Co.

Fuller, J. F. C. (1907). *The Star in the West: A Critical Essay upon the Works of Aleister Crowley.* London: Walter Scott Publishing Co.

Fuller, R. B. (1982). *Critical Path.* New York: St. Martin's Press.

_____ et al. (1970). *I Seem to Be a Verb.* New York: Bantam Books.

Gagnon, J. H. & W. Simon. (2005). *Sexual Conduct: The Social Sources of Human Sexuality.* 2nd ed. New Brunswick, NJ: Transaction Publishers.

Galinsky, E. (1999). *Ask the Children: What America's Children Really Think About Working Parents.* New York: William Morrow.

Gallant, T. W. (1991). *Risk and Survival in Ancient Greece: Reconstructing the Rural Domestic Economy.* Stanford, CA: Stanford University Press.

Gandhi, M. K. (1948). *Gandhi's Autobiography: The Story of My Experiments with Truth.* (trans. M. Desai). Washington, DC: Public Affairs Press.

_____. (1942–1948). *Non-Violence in Peace & War.* 2 vols. Ahmedebad: Navajivan.

_____. (1935). *Young India, 1927–1928.* Triplicane, Madras: S. Ganesan.

Gatto, L. T. (2000). *The Underground History of American Education: An Intimate Investigation into the Problem of Modern Schooling.* New York: Oxford Village Press.

_____. (2009). *Weapons of Mass Instruction: A Schoolteacher's Journey through the Dark World of Compulsory Schooling.* Gabriola Island, BC: New Society Publishers.

Gaustad, E. S. (ed.) (2003) *A Documentary History of Religion in America: To 1877.* 3rd ed. (rev. M. A. Noll). Grand Rapids, MI: Wm. B. Eerdsmans Publishing.

Gaylor, A. L. (ed.) (1997). *Women Without Superstition: No Gods—No Masters.* Madison, WI: Freedom From Religion Foundation.

Gazzaniga, M. S. (ed.) (2004). *The Cognitive Neurosciences.* 3rd ed. Cambridge, MA: MIT Press.

Gelb, M. J. (1995). *Body Learning: An Introduction to the Alexander Technique.* 2nd ed. New York: Henry Holt & Co.

George, D. L. (ed.) (1918). *The Great Crusade: Extracts from Speeches Delivered During the War.* New York: George H. Doran Co.

Gibbon, E. (1840). *The Decline and Fall of the Roman Empire.* 4 vols. (rev. H. H. Milman). New York: Harper & Brothers.

Gibbs, D. N. (2009). *First Do No Harm: Humanitarian Intervention and the Destruction of Yugoslavia.* Nashville, TN: Vanderbilt University Press.

Gibran, K. (1923). *The Prophet.* New York: Alfred A. Knopf.

Gibson, R. & J. P. Singh. (2003). *Wall of Silence: The Untold Story of the Medical Mistakes That Kill and Injure Millions of Americans.* Washington, DC: Regnery Publishing.

Gide, A. (1971). *The André Gide Reader.* (ed. D. Littlejohn). New York: Alfred A. Knopf.

Giesbrecht, G. G. & J. A. Wilkerson. (2006). *Hypothermia, Frostbite and Other Cold Injuries: Prevention, Survival, Rescue, and Treatment.* 2nd ed. Seattle: Mountaineer Books.

Gilbert, D. (2006). *Stumbling on Happiness.* New York: Alfred A. Knopf.

Gill, I. S. et al. (2009). *World Development Report 2009: Reshaping Economic Geography.* Washington, DC: World Bank.

Gillis, J. R. (1996). *A World of Their Own Making: Myth, Ritual, and the Quest for Family Values.* New York: Basic Books.

Glassner, B. (2009). *The Culture of Fear: Why Americans Are Afraid of the Wrong Things.* 2nd ed. New York: Basic Books.

Glimcher, P. W. (2003). *Decisions, Uncertainty, and the Brain: The Science of Neuroeconomics.* Cambridge, MA: MIT Press.

Gödel, K. (1962). *On Formally Undecidable Propositions of Principia Mathematica and Related Systems.* (trans. B. Meltzer). New York: Basic Books.

Goethe, J. W. von. (1883). *The Wisdom of Goethe.* (ed. & trans. J. S. Blackie). Edinburgh: Blackwood & Sons.

Goldin, C. D. (1990). *Understanding the Gender Gap: An Economic History of American Women.* New York: Oxford University Press.

Goldman, P. (1960). *Growing Up Absurd: Problems of Youth in the Organized System.* New York: Vintage Books.

Goldman, R. (1997). *Circumcision, The Hidden Trauma: How an American Cultural Practice Affects Infants and Ultimately Us All.* Boston: Vanguard Publications.

Gould, S. J. (1996). *The Mismeasure of Man.* 2nd ed. New York: W. W. Norton & Co.

Green, P. (1970). *Alexander the Great.* London: Weidenfeld & Nicolson.

Greenwald, G. (2009). *Drug Decriminalization in Portugal: Lessons for Creating Fair and Successful Drug Policies.* Washington, DC: Cato Institute.

_____. (2007). *A Tragic Legacy: How a Good vs. Evil Mentality Destroyed the Bush Presidency.* New York: Crown Publishers.

Griffin, G. E. (1964). *The Fearful Master: A Second Look at the United Nations.* Boston: Western Islands Publishers.

Grinder, J. & R. Bandler. (1981). *TRANCE-formations: Neuro-Linguistic Programming and the Structure of Hypnosis.* Moab, UT: Real People Press.

Gunstone, F. D. (ed.) (2002). *Vegetable Oils in Food Technology: Composition, Properties and Uses.* Oxford: Blackwell Publishing.

Gurian, M. & K. Stevens. (2005). *The Minds of Boys: Saving Our Sons from Falling Behind in School and Life.* San Francisco: Jossey-Bass.

Guthman, J. (2004). *Agrarian Dream: The Paradox of Organic Farming in California.* Berkeley: University of California Press.

Haeckel, E. H. (1900). *The Riddle of the Universe at the Close of the Nineteenth Century.* (trans. J. McCabe). New York: Harper & Brothers.

Haines, S. (2007). *Healing Sex: A Mind-Body Approach to Healing Sexual Trauma.* 2nd ed. (ed. F. Newman). San Francisco: Cleis Press.

Haldane, J. B. S. (1934). *Fact and Faith.* London: Watts & Co.

Haldeman-Julius, E. (1931). *The Meaning of Atheism.* Girard, KS: Haldeman-Julius Publications.

_____. (1929). *The Outline of Bunk: Including the Admirations of a Debunker.* Boston: The Stratford Company.

Hale, E. E. (ed.) (1870). *Old and New.* Vol. II. New York: Hurd & Houghton.

Hall, R. E. & A. Rabushka. (1995). *The Flat Tax.* 2nd ed. Stanford, CA: Hoover Institution Press.

Hames, P. (ed.) (1995). *Dark Alchemy: The Films of Jan Švankmajer.* Trowbridge: Flicks Books.

Hand, B. L. (1952). *The Spirit of Liberty: Papers and Addresses of Learned Hand.* (ed. I. Billiard). New York: Alfred A. Knopf.

Hasegawa, T. (2004). *Racing the Enemy: Stalin, Truman, and the Surrender of Japan.* Cambridge, MA: Harvard University Press.

Hatfield, E. et al. (1994). *Emotional Contagion.* Cambridge: Cambridge University Press.

_____ & G. W. Walster. (1978). *A New Look at Love: A Revealing Report on the Most Elusive of All Emotions.* Reading, MA: Addison-Wesley Publishing.

Hawking, S. W. (1988). *A Brief History of Time: From the Big Bang to Black Holes.* New York: Bantam Books.

Hayek, F. A. (2011). *The Constitution of Liberty: The Definitive Edition.* (ed. R. Hamowy). Chicago: University of Chicago Press.

_____. (2008). *Prices & Production and Other Works: On Money, the Business Cycle, and the Gold Standard.* (ed. J. T. Salerno). Auburn, AL: Ludwig von Mises Institute.

_____. (1944). *The Road to Serfdom.* London: George Routledge & Sons.

Hazlitt, H. (1979). *Economics in One Lesson.* 2nd ed. New York: Crown Publishers.

_____. (1959). *The Failure of the "New Economics": An Analysis of the Keynesian Fallacies.* Princeton, NJ: D. Van Nostrand Co.

_____. (1964). *The Foundations of Morality.* Princeton, NJ: D. Van Nostrand Co.

Heagerty, J. J. et al. (1943). *Report of the Advisory Committee on Health Insurance.* Ottawa: King's Printer.

Hedges, C. (2003). *What Every Person Should Know About War.* New York: Free Press.

Heinlein, R. A. (1988). *Time Enough for Love: The Lives of Lazarus Long.* New York: Ace Books.

Helgerson, R. (1992). *Forms of Nationhood: The Elizabethan Writing of England.* Chicago: University of Chicago Press.

Heller, J. (1961). *Catch-22.* New York: Simon & Schuster.

Herbert, F. (1985a). *Chapterhouse: Dune.* New York: Putnam.

Herbert, N. (1985b). *Quantum Reality: Beyond the New Physics.* Garden City, NY: Anchor Press.

Herdt, G. H. (ed.) (2009). *Moral Panics, Sex Panics: Fear and the Fight over Sexual Rights.* New York: New York University Press.

Herman, E. S. & N. Chomsky. (1988). *Manufacturing Consent: The Political Economy of the Mass Media.* New York: Pantheon Books.

Herodas. (1922). *The Mimes and Fragments.* (ed. A. D. Knox). Cambridge: Cambridge University Press.

Hertz, R. (2006). *Single by Chance, Mothers by Choice: How Women Are Choosing Parenthood without Marriage and Creating the New American Family.* New York: Oxford University Press.

Higgs, R. (1987). *Crisis and Leviathan: Critical Episodes in the Growth of American Government.* New York: Oxford University Press.

_____. (ed.) (1995). *Hazardous to Our Health?: FDA Regulation of Health Care Products.* Oakland, CA: Independent Institute.

_____ & C. P. Close. (eds.) (2005). *Re-Thinking Green: Alternatives to Environmental Bureaucracy.* Oakland, CA: Independent Institute.

Hine, T. (1999). *The Rise and Fall of the American Teenager.* New York: Bard.

Hitler, A. (1943). *Mein Kampf.* (trans. R. Manheim). Boston: Houghton Mifflin.

Hixson, W. L. (2008). *The Myth of American Diplomacy: National Identity and U.S. Foreign Policy.* New Haven, CT: Yale University Press.

Hjelle, L. A. & D. J. Ziegler. (1992). *Personality Theories: Basic Assumptions, Research, and Applications.* 3rd ed. New York: McGraw-Hill.

Hobbes, T. (1994). *Leviathan: With Selected Variants from the Latin Edition of 1668.* (ed. E. Curley). Indianapolis, IN: Hackett Publishing Co.

Hochschild, A. R. (1997). *The Time Bind: When Work Becomes Home and Home Becomes Work.* New York: Metropolitan Books.

Hodgkinson, T. (2004). *How to Be Idle.* London: Hamish Hamilton.

_____. (2009). *The Idle Parent: Why Less Means More When Raising Kids.* London: Hamish Hamilton.

Hoffer, E. (1951). *The True Believer: Thoughts on the Nature of Mass Movements.* New York: Harper & Row.

Hoffman, B. (2006). *Inside Terrorism.* 2nd ed. New York: Columbia University Press.

Holbach, P. H. T. (1816). *Nature and Her Laws: As Applicable to the Happiness of Man, Living in Society; Contrasted with Superstition and Imaginary Systems.* 2 vols. (trans. M. de Mirabaud). London: W. Hodgson.

Honey, M. (1984). *Creating Rosie the Riveter: Class, Gender, and Propaganda during World War II.* Amherst, MA: University of Massachusetts Press.

Hoppe, H. H. (2001). *Democracy: The God that Failed.* New Brunswick, NJ: Transaction Publishers.

_____. (2006). *The Economics and Ethics of Private Property: Studies in Political Economy and Philosophy.* 2nd ed. Auburn, AL: Ludwig von Mises Institute.

Horwitz, A. V. & J. C. Wakefield. (2007). *The Loss of Sadness: How Psychiatry Transformed Normal Sorrow into Depressive Disorder.* Oxford: Oxford University Press.

Howard, A. (1940). *An Agricultural Testament.* Oxford: Oxford University Press.

Howard, M. (2002). *The Invention of Peace and the Reinvention of War.* 2nd ed. London: Profile Books.

Howard, V. (2006). *Brides, Inc.: American Weddings and the Business of Tradition.* Philadelphia, PA: University of Pennsylvania Press.

Hoy, M. (ed.) (1990). *Loompanics' Greatest Hits: Articles and Features from the Best Book Catalog in the World.* Port Townsend, WA: Loompanics Unlimited.

Hrdy, S. B. (1999). *Mother Nature: A History of Mothers, Infants, and Natural Selection.* New York: Pantheon Books.

Hubbart, R. & E. Wald. (1993). *Exploding the Gene Myth: How Genetic Information Is Produced and Manipulated by Scientists.* Boston: Beacon Press.

Hudson, M. (1977). *Global Fracture: The New International Economic Order.* New York: Harper & Row.

_____. (1972). *Super Imperialism: The Economic Strategy of American Empire.* New York: Holt, Rinehart & Winston.

Human Security Centre. (2006). *Human Security Report 2005: War and Peace in the 21st Century.* Oxford: Oxford University Press.

Hume, D. (1970). *Dialogues Concerning Natural Religion.* (ed. N. Pike). Indianapolis, IN: The Bobbs-Merrill Company.

_____. (1987). *Essays: Moral, Political and Literary.* (ed. E. F. Miller). Indianapolis, IN: Liberty Fund.

_____. (1978). *A Treatise of Human Nature.* 2nd ed. (ed. L. A. Shelby-Bigge, rev. P. H. Nidditch). Oxford: Oxford University Press.

Huxley, A. (2004). *Brave New World: And Brave New World Revisited.* New York: HarperCollins.

_____. (1965). *The Devils of Loudun.* New York: Harper & Row.

Huxley, T. H. (1893). *Darwiniana: Essays.* New York: D. Appleton & Co.

_____. (1896). *Methods and Results: Essays.* New York. D. Appleton & Co.

Hyatt, C. S. (ed.) (2000). *Rebels & Devils: The Psychology of Liberation.* 2nd ed. Tempe, AZ: New Falcon Publications.

Ingersoll, R. G. (1901). *The Works of Robert G. Ingersoll.* 12 vols. New York: The Dresden Publishing Co.

Inglis, A. (1918). *Principles of Secondary Education.* Boston: Houghton Mifflin.

International Energy Agency. (2010). *World Energy Outlook 2010.* Paris: IEA.

International Narcotics Control Board. (2009). *Report of the International Narcotics Control Board for 2008.* New York: United Nations Publications.

Isdal, P. (2000). *Meningen med volden.* Oslo: Kommuneforlaget.

Iyengar, S. (2010). *The Art of Choosing.* New York: Twelve.

Jacob, H. (1984). *The Frustration of Policy: Responses to Crime by American Cities.* Boston: Little, Brown & Co.

James, J. (1986). *Windows.* Seattle, WA: Bronwen Press.

James, W. (1902). *The Varieties of Religious Experience: A Study in Human Nature.* London: Longmans, Green & Co.

Jardine, L. (1996). *Worldly Goods: A New History of the Renaissance.* London: Macmillan.

Jefferson, T. (2002). *Notes on the State of Virginia: With Related Documents.* (ed. D. Waldstreicher). New York: Palgrave.

Jellison, K. (2008). *It's Our Day: America's Love Affair with the White Wedding, 1945–2005.* Lawrence, KS: University Press of Kansas.

Jobling, M. A. et al. (2003). *Human Evolutionary Genetics: Origins, Peoples & Disease.* New York: Garland Science.

Johnson, S. (2008). *The Invention of Air: A Story of Science, Faith, Revolution, and the Birth of America.* New York: Riverhead Books.

Johnston, D. C. (2008). *Free Lunch: How the Wealthiest Americans Enrich Themselves at Government Expense (and Stick You with the Bill).* New York: Portfolio.

_____. (2003). *Perfectly Legal: The Covert Campaign to Rig Our Tax System to Benefit the Super Rich—and Cheat Everybody Else.* New York: Portfolio.

Joint United Nations Programme on HIV/AIDS. (2006). *2006 Report on the Global AIDS Epidemic: A UNAIDS 10th Anniversary Special Edition.* Geneva: UNAIDS.

_____. (2010). *UNAIDS Report on the Global AIDS Epidemic 2010.* Geneva: UNAIDS.

Jolly, A. (1999). *Lucy's Legacy: Sex and Intelligence in Human Evolution.* Cambridge, MA: Harvard University Press.

Jonasse, R. (ed.) (2009). *Agrofuels in the Americas.* Oakland, CA: Food First Books.

Jong, E. (1977). *How to Save Your Own Life.* New York: Holt, Rinehart and Winston.

Jouvenel, B. de. (1949). *On Power: Its Nature and the History of Its Growth.* (trans. J. F. Huntington). New York: Viking Press.

_____. (1957). *Sovereignty: An Inquiry into the Political Good.* (trans. J. F. Huntington). Cambridge: Cambridge University Press.

Jung, C. G. (1968). *Analytical Psychology: Its Theory & Practice.* New York: Pantheon Books.

_____. (1928). *Two Essays on Analytical Psychology.* (trans. H. G. & C. F. Baynes). New York: Dodd, Mead & Co.

Kaczynski, T. J. (2010). *Technological Slavery: The Collected Writings of Theodore J. Kaczynski, a.k.a. The Unabomber.* Port Townsend, WA: Feral House.

Kampfner, J. (2009). *Freedom for Sale: How We Made Money and Lost Our Liberty.* New York: Simon & Schuster.

Kates, D. B. (1990). *Guns, Murders, and the Constitution: A Realistic Assessment of Gun Control.* San Francisco: Pacific Research Institute for Public Policy.

Katz, D. L. (2008). *Nutrition in Clinical Practice: A Comprehensive, Evidence-Based Manual for the Practitioner.* 2nd ed. Philadelphia, PA: Lippincott Williams & Wilkins.

Kauffman, S. A. (1995). *At Home in the Universe: The Search for Laws of Self-Organization and Complexity.* Oxford: Oxford University Press.

_____. (1993). *The Origins of Order: Self Organization and Selection in Evolution.* Oxford: Oxford University Press.

Kean, T. H. et al. (2004). *The 9/11 Commission Report: Final Report of the National Commission on Terrorist Attacks Upon the United States.* Washington, DC: U.S. Government Printing Office.

Keeler, C. E. (1960). *Secrets of the Cuna Earthmother: A Comparative Study of Ancient Religions.* New York: Exposition Press.

Keith, L. (2009). *The Vegetarian Myth: Food, Justice, and Sustainability.* Crescent City, CA: Flashpoint Press.

Kendrick, M. (2007). *The Great Cholesterol Con: The Truth About What Really Causes Heart Disease and How to Avoid It.* London: John Blake Publishing.

Kennedy, P. M. (1987). *The Rise and Fall of the Great Powers: Economic Change and Military Conflict from 1500 to 2000.* New York: Random House.

Kern, F. (1939). *Kingship and Law in the Middle Ages.* (trans. S. B. Chrimes). Oxford: Basil Blackwell.

Kerry, J. F. et al. (2009a). *Afghanistan's Narco War: Breaking the Link Between Drug Traffickers and Insurgents.* Washington, DC: U.S. Government Printing Office.

_____. (2009b). *Tora Bora Revisited: How We Failed to Get Bin Laden and Why It Matters Today.* Washington, DC: U.S. Government Printing Office.

Kick, R. (2003). *50 Things You're Not Supposed to Know.* New York: The Disinformation Company.

Kierkegaard, S. (1952). *The Living Thoughts of Kierkegaard.* New York: David McKay Co.

Kimball, R. (2008). *Tenured Radicals: How Politics Has Corrupted Our Higher Education.* 3rd ed. Chicago: Ivan R. Dee.

Kinsella, N. S. (2008). *Against Intellectual Property.* Auburn, AL: Ludwig von Mises Institute.

Kinsey, A. C. et al. (1953). *Sexual Behavior in the Human Female.* Philadelphia, PA: W. B. Saunders.

_____. (1948). *Sexual Behavior in the Human Male.* Philadelphia, PA: W. B. Saunders.

Kirsch, I. (2009). *The Emperor's New Drugs: Exploding the Antidepressant Myth.* London: Bodley Head.

Kitcher, P. (1982). *Abusing Science: The Case Against Creationism.* Cambridge, MA: MIT Press.

Klare, M. T. (2009). *Rising Powers, Shrinking Planet: The New Geopolitics of Energy.* New York: Henry Holt & Co.

Kleck, G. (1991). *Point Blank: Guns and Violence in America.* New York: Aldine de Gruyter.

_____ & D. B. Kates. (2001). *Armed: New Perspectives on Gun Control.* Amherst, NY: Prometheus Books.

Koestler, A. (1967). *The Ghost in the Machine.* London: Hutchinson.

_____. (1959). *The Sleepwalkers: A History of Man's Changing Vision of the Universe.* London: Hutchinson.

Kolana, G. B. (2007). *Rethinking Thin: The New Science of Weight Loss—and the Myths and Realities of Dieting.* New York: Farrar, Straus & Giroux.

Komisaruk, B. R. et al. (2006). *The Science of Orgasm.* Baltimore, MD: Johns Hopkins University Press.

Kopel, D. B. (ed.) (1995). *Guns: Who Should Have Them?* Amherst, NY: Prometheus Books.

Kopp, S. B. (1980). *If You Meet the Buddha on the Road, Kill Him!: The Pilgrimage of Psychotherapy Patients.* London: Sheldon Press.

Korzybski, A. (1950). *Manhood of Humanity: The Science and Art of Human Engineering.* 2nd ed. Lakeville, CT: Institute of General Semantics.

_____. (2000). *Science and Sanity: An Introduction to Non-Aristotelian Systems and General Semantics.* 5th ed. Brooklyn, NY: Institute of General Semantics.

Kovacs, M. G. (trans.) (1989). *The Epic of Gilgamesh.* Stanford, CA: Stanford University Press.

Kramer, P. D. (2005). *Against Depression.* New York: Viking Press.

Krishnamurti, J. (1968). *The First and Last Freedom.* Wheaton, IL: Theosophical Publishing House.

Kropotkin, P. A. (1988). *Act for Yourself: Articles from "Freedom" 1886–1907.* (ed. N. Walter & H. Becker). London: Freedom Press.

Krug, E. G. et al. (eds.) (2002). *World Report on Violence and Health.* Geneva: World Health Organization.

Krug, W. C. (1969). *What's Happening to Our Money?* Windsor, ON: Herald Press.

Kuhn, T. S. (1970). *The Structure of Scientific Revolution.* 2nd ed. Chicago: University of Chicago Press.

Kurzweil, R. (1999). *The Age of Spiritual Intelligent Machines: When Computers Exceed Human Intelligence.* New York: Viking Press.

La Boétie, É. de. (1975). *The Politics of Obedience: The Discourse of Voluntary Servitude.* (trans. H. Kurz). New York: Free Life Editions.

Ladas, A. K. et al. (1982). *The G Spot: And Other Recent Discoveries about Human Sexuality.* New York: Holt, Rinehart & Winston.

La Follette, S. (1926). *Concerning Women.* New York: Albert & Charles Boni.

Laing, S. (1850). *The Social and Political State of the European People in 1848 and 1849.* London: Longman, Brown, Green, and Longmans.

Lakoff, G. (1987). *Women, Fire, and Dangerous Things: What Categories Reveal about the Mind.* Chicago: University of Chicago Press.

Lande, R. G. et al. (eds.) (2004). *The Iraq War Clinician Guide.* 2nd ed. Washington, DC: U. S. Department of Veteran Affairs.

Landes, D. S. (1999). *The Wealth and Poverty of Nations: Why Some Are So Rich and Some So Poor.* New York: W. W. Norton.

Landor, W. S. (1920). *Selections from the Writings of Walter Savage Landor.* (ed. S. Colvin). London: Macmillan & Co.

Lane, C. (2007). *Shyness: How Normal Behavior Became a Sickness.* New Haven, CT: Yale University Press.

LaPierre, W. R. (2003). *Guns, Freedom, and Terrorism.* Nashville, TN: WND Books.

Laslett, P. (1977). *Family Life and Illicit Love in Earlier Generations: Essays in Historical Sociology.* Cambridge: Cambridge University Press.

Lau, C. & L. Kramer. (2005). ***Die Relativitätstheorie des Glücks: Über des Leben von Lottomillionären.*** Herbolzheim: Centaurus.

Layard, P. R. G. (2005). ***Happiness: Lessons from a New Science.*** New York: Penguin Press.

Leary, D. (2008). ***Why We Suck: A Feel Good Guide to Staying Fat, Loud, Lazy and Stupid.*** New York: Viking Penguin.

Leary, T. (1998). ***The Politics of Ecstasy.*** Berkeley: Ronin Publishing.

Lec, S. J. (1962). ***Unkempt Thoughts.*** (trans. J. Galazka). New York: St. Martin's Press.

LeDoux, J. E. (1996). ***The Emotional Brain: The Mysterious Underpinnings of Emotional Life.*** New York: Simon & Schuster.

_____. (2002). ***Synaptic Self: How Our Brains Become Who We Are.*** New York: Viking Penguin.

Lehrer, K. (1974). ***Knowledge.*** London: Clarendon Press.

Leigh, C. (2004). ***Unrepentant Whore: The Collected Works of Scarlot Harlot.*** San Francisco: Last Gasp.

Leoni, B. (1991). ***Freedom and the Law.*** 3rd ed. Indianapolis, IN: Liberty Fund.

Leopold, L. (2009). ***The Looting of America: How Wall Street's Game of Fantasy Finance Destroyed Our Jobs, Pensions, and Prosperity.*** White River Junction, VT: Chelsea Green Publishing.

Lévi, É. (1922). ***The Paradoxes of the Highest Science: With Footnotes by a Master of the Wisdom.*** 2nd ed. Adyar, Madras: Theosophical Publishing House.

Levine, B. A. (2001). ***Commonsense Rebellion: Debunking Psychiatry, Confronting Society—An A to Z Guide to Rehumanizing Our Lives.*** London: Continuum Publishing.

Lewin, K. (1936). ***Principles of Topological Psychology.*** (trans. F. & G. H. Heider). New York: McGraw-Hill.

Lewis, C. S. (1970). ***God in the Dock: Essays on Theology and Ethics.*** Grand Rapids, MI: Eerdmans.

Lewis, J. L. (1957). ***Ingersoll the Magnificent: To Which Has Been Added a Special Arrangement of Some Gems from Ingersoll for Inspiration, Wisdom, and Courage.*** New York: Freethought Press Association.

Lewis, S. (1935). ***It Can't Happen Here: A Novel.*** Garden City, NY: Doubleday, Doran & Co.

Lincoln, A. (1905). ***Letters and Addresses of Abraham Lincoln, 1832–1865.*** (ed. M. Maclean). New York: Unit Book Publishing Co.

Lindner, R. M. (1962). ***Prescription for Rebellion: An Attack on Some Modern Methods of Psychoanalysis.*** New York: Grove Press.

_____. (1944). ***Rebel Without a Cause: The Hypnoanalysis of a Criminal Psychopath.*** New York: Grune & Stratton.

Lingeman, R. R. (1980). ***Small Town America: A Narrative History 1620–The Present.*** New York: G. P. Putnam's Sons.

Lipponen, P. & P. Wesaniemi. (eds.) (2003). ***Nainen & ero: Kertomuksia parisuhteen päättymisestä.*** Helsinki: Kirjapaja.

Little Hoover Commission. (2004). ***Breaking the Barriers for Women on Parole.*** Sacramento: Little Hoover Commission.

Lloyd, E. A. (2005). ***The Case of the Female Orgasm: Bias in the Science of Evolution.*** Cambridge, MA: Harvard University Press.

Locke, J. (1960). ***Two Treatises of Government: A Critical Edition with an Introduction and Apparatus Criticus.*** (ed. P. Laslett). Cambridge: Cambridge University Press.

Lofmark, C. (1992). *What Is the Bible?* Buffalo, NY: Prometheus Books.

Loisy, A. F. (1924). *My Duel with the Vatican: The Autobiography of a Catholic Modernist.* (trans. R. W. Boynton). New York: E. P. Dutton.

Lomborg, B. (2001). *The Skeptical Environmentalist: Measuring the Real State of the World.* (trans. H. Matthews). Cambridge: Cambridge University Press.

Lott, J. R. (2010). *More Guns, Less Crime: Understanding Crime and Gun-control Laws.* 3rd ed. Chicago: University of Chicago Press.

Lovejoy, A. O. (1961). *The Great Chain of Being: A Study of the History of an Idea.* Cambridge: Harvard University Press.

Lucretius. (1969). *On the Nature of Things.* (trans. M. F. Smith). London: Sphere Books.

Lukacs, J. (2002). *At the End of an Age.* New Haven, CT: Yale University Press.

_____. (1994). *Historical Consciousness: The Remembered Past.* New Brunswick, NJ: Transaction Publishers.

Lustick, I. S. (2006). *Trapped in the War on Terror.* Philadelphia, PA: University of Pennsylvania Press.

Luther, M. (1857). *The Table Talk of Martin Luther.* (ed. & trans. W. Hazlitt). London: H. G. Bohn.

Lynn, B. C. (2005). *End of the Line: The Rise and Coming Fall of the Global Corporation.* New York: Doubleday.

Lyons, D. (1997). *Gender and Immortality: Heroines in Ancient Greek Myth and Cult.* Princeton, NJ: Princeton University Press.

Macaulay, T. B. (1849). *The History of England from the Accession of James the Second.* 5 vols. Leipzig: Bernh. Tauchnitz.

Machiavelli, N. (2003). *The Prince and Other Writings.* (trans. W. A. Rebhorn). New York: Barnes & Noble Classics.

MacKay, C. (1841). *Extraordinary Popular Delusions and the Madness of Crowds.* 3 vols. London: Richard Bentley.

MacKinnon, C. A. (2005). *Women's Lives, Men's Laws.* Cambridge, MA: Harvard University Press.

Madsen, R. et al. (eds.) (2001). *Meaning and Modernity: Religion, Polity, and Self.* Berkeley: University of California Press.

Magnusson, D. (ed.) (1981). *Towards a Psychology of Situations: An Interactional Perspective.* Hillsdale, NJ: Lawrence Erlbaum Associates.

Maimbo, S. M. & D. Ratha. (2005). *Remittances: Development Impact and Future Prospects.* Washington, DC: World Bank Publications.

Maimonides, M. (1963). *The Guide of the Perplexed.* 2 vols. (trans. S. Pines). Chicago: University of Chicago Press.

Maines, R. P. (1999). *The Technology of Orgasm: "Hysteria," the Vibrator, and Women's Sexual Satisfaction.* Baltimore, MD: Johns Hopkins University Press.

Malcolm, J. L. (2002). *Guns and Violence: The English Experience.* Cambridge, MA: Harvard University Press.

Maldelbrot, B. B. (1982). *The Fractal Geometry of Nature.* San Francisco: W. H. Freeman & Co.

_____ & R. L. Hudson. (2004). *The (Mis)behavior of Markets: A Fractal View of Risk, Ruin, and Reward.* New York: Basic Books.

Males, M. A. (1999). *Framing Youth: 10 Myths about the Next Generation.* Monroe, ME: Common Courage Press.

Malone, M. S. (1995). *The Microprocessor: A Biography.* Santa Clara, CA: TELOS.

Mansfield, H. C. (2006). *Manliness.* New Haven, CT: Yale University Press.

Manwaring, D. R. (1962). *Render unto Caesar: The Flag-Salute Controversy.* Chicago: University of Chicago Press.

Martineau, H. (2007). *Autobiography.* (ed. L. H. Peterson). Peterborough, ON: Broadview Press.

Marx, K. (1996). *Das Kapital: A Critique of Political Economy.* (ed. F. Engels). Washington, DC: Regnery Publishing.

_____. (1973). *Karl Marx on Society and Social Change: With Selections by Friedrich Engels.* (ed. N. J. Smelser). Chicago: University of Chicago Press.

_____ & F. Engels. (1998). *The Communist Manifesto: A Modern Edition.* London: Verso.

Maslow, A. H. (1966). *The Psychology of Science: A Reconnaissance.* New York: Harper & Row.

Masters, W. H. et al. (1985). *Human Sexuality.* 2nd ed. Boston: Little, Brown & Co.

Matthews, A. (1988). *Being Happy!: A Handbook to Greater Confidence & Security.* Los Angeles: Price Stern Sloan.

Matthews, G. et al. (2002). *Emotional Intelligence: Science & Myth.* Cambridge, MA: MIT Press.

Maugham, W. S. (1938). *The Summing Up.* Garden City, NY: Doubleday, Doran & Co.

Mayer, D. N. (1994). *The Constitutional Thought of Thomas Jefferson.* Charlottesville: University Press of Virginia.

McBride, J. (1977). *Orson Welles: Actor and Director.* New York: Harvest/HBJ Books.

McCabe, J. (1950). *A Rationalist Encyclopædia: A Book of Reference on Religion, Philosophy, Ethics, and Science.* London: Watts & Co.

_____. (1914). *Sources of the Morality of the Gospels.* London: Watts & Co.

_____. (1929). *The Story of Religious Controversy.* (ed. E. Haldeman-Julius). Boston: The Stratford Co.

McCoy, A. W. (2009). *Policing America's Empire: The United States, the Philippines, and the Rise of the Surveillance State.* Madison, WI: University of Wisconsin Press.

McEwen, B. S. (2002). *The End of Stress as We Know It.* Washington, DC: Joseph Henry Press.

McGrath, R. D. (1984). *Gunfighters, Highwaymen & Vigilantes: Violence on the Frontier.* Berkeley: University of California Press.

McKenzie, J. L. (1995). *Dictionary of the Bible.* New York: Touchstone.

McKinsey, C. D. (1995). *The Encyclopedia of Biblical Errancy.* Amherst, NY: Prometheus Books.

McNeal, J. U. (1999). *The Kids Market: Myths and Realities.* Ithaca, NY: Paramount Market Publishing.

McWhorter, J. H. (2003). *Authentically Black: Essays for the Black Silent Majority.* New York: Gotham Books.

_____. (2001). *Word on the Street: Debunking the Myth of "Pure" Standard English.* New York: Basic Books.

Meadows, D. H. et al. (1972). *The Limits to Growth: A Report for the Club of Rome's Project on the Predicament of Mankind.* New York: Universe Books.

Mencken, H. L. (1916). *A Book of Burlesques.* New York: Alfred A. Knopf.

_____. (1949). *A Mencken Chrestomathy: His Own Selection of His Choicest Writings.* New York: Alfred A. Knopf.

_____. (1956). *Minority Report: H. L. Mencken's Notebooks.* New York: Alfred A. Knopf.

_____. (1926). *Notes on Democracy.* New York: Alfred A. Knopf.

Merton, T. (1966). *Conjectures of a Guilty Bystander.* Garden City, NY: Doubleday & Co.

Meston, C. M. & D. M. Buss. (2009). *Why Women Have Sex: Understanding Sexual Motivations, from Adventure to Revenge (and Everything in Between).* New York: Henry Holt & Co.

Milgram, S. (1974). *Obedience to Authority: An Experimental View.* New York: Harper & Row.

Mill, J. S. (1956). *On Liberty.* Indianapolis, IN: The Bobbs-Merrill Company.

_____. (1862). *The Principles of Political Economy: With Some of Their Applications to Social Philosophy.* 5th ed. 2 vols. London: Parker, Son, and Bourn.

Millennium Ecosystem Assessment. (2005). *Ecosystems and Human Well-Being: Our Human Planet—Summary for Decision Makers.* Washington, DC: Island Press.

Miller, K. R. (2002). *Finding Darwin's God: A Scientist's Search for Common Ground Between God and Evolution.* San Francisco: Perennial.

Miller, T. et al. (2011). *2011 Index of Economic Freedom.* Washington, DC: The Heritage Foundation.

Milton, J. (1806). *The Prose Works of John Milton: With a Life of the Author.* 7 vols. London: J. Johnson.

Miron, J. A. & K. Waldock. (2010). *The Budgetary Impact of Ending Drug Prohibition.* Washington, DC: Cato Institute.

Mischel, W. (2008). *Introduction to Personality: Towards an Integrative Science of the Person.* 8th ed. (rev. Y. Shoda & O. Ayduk). New York: John Wiley & Sons.

Mises, L. von. (2009). *Human Action: A Treatise on Economics.* Auburn, AL: Ludwig von Mises Institute.

_____. (2006). *Nation, State, and Economy: Contributions to the Politics and History of Our Time.* (trans. L. B. Yeager, ed. B. B. Greaves). Indianapolis, IN: Liberty Fund.

_____. (1952). *Planning for Freedom: And Other Essays and Addresses.* South Holland, IL: Libertarian Press.

_____. (1953). *The Theory of Money and Credit.* (trans. J. E. Batson). New Haven, CT: Yale University Press.

Mitford, J. (1998). *The American Way of Death Revisited.* 3rd ed. New York: Alfred A. Knopf.

Moisander, J. (2008). *Representation of Green Consumerism: A Constructionist Critique.* Saarbrucken: VDM Verlag.

Molinari, G. de. (1977). *The Production of Security.* (trans. J. H. McCulloch, ed. R. M. Ebeling). New York: The Center for Libertarian Studies.

Molinos, M. de. (1911). *The Spiritual Guide.* 2nd ed. (ed. K. Lyttelton). London: Methuen & Co.

Moncrieff, J. (2008). *The Myth of the Chemical Cure: A Critique of Psychiatric Drug Treatment.* New York: Palgrave Macmillan.

Montagu, A. (1967). *The Anatomy of Swearing.* New York: The Macmillan Company.

_____. (ed.) (1964). *The Concept of Race.* London: Collier Books.

_____. (1999). *The Natural Superiority of Women.* 5th ed. Walnut Creek, CA: Altamira Press.

_____. (ed.) (1984). *Science and Creationism.* Oxford: Oxford University Press.

_____. (1969). *Sex, Man, and Society.* New York: G. P. Putnam's Sons.

Montaigne, M. de (1959). *Essays.* (trans. J. M. Cohen). Harmondsworth: Penguin Books.

Moreland, J. P. & K. Nielsen. (eds.) (1993). *Does God Exist?: The Debate between Theists & Atheists.* Buffalo, NY: Prometheus Books.

Morford, M. (2010). *The Daring Spectacle: Adventures in Deviant Journalism.* San Francisco: Rapture Machine.

Morin, J. (1998). *Anal Pleasure & Health: A Guide for Men and Women.* San Francisco: Down There Press.

Morris, D. (1977). *Manwatching: A Field Guide to Human Behaviour.* London: Jonathan Cape.

_____. (1967). *The Naked Ape: A Zoologist's Study of the Human Animal.* London: Jonathan Cape.

Moscovici, S. (1985). *The Age of the Crowd: A Historical Treatise on Mass Psychology.* Cambridge: Cambridge University Press.

Mothner, I. & A. Weitz. (1984). *How to Get Off Drugs.* New York: Simon & Schuster.

Murphy, P. L. (1971). *The Constitution in Crisis Times, 1918–1969.* New York: Harper & Row.

Murray, C. J. L. & A. D. López. (1996). *The Global Burden of Disease: A Comprehensive Assessment of Mortality and Disability from Diseases, Injuries, and Risk Factors in 1990 and Projected to 2020.* Cambridge, MA: Harvard School of Public Health.

National Research Council. (2008). *Protecting Individual Privacy in the Struggle Against Terrorists: A Framework for Program Assessment.* Washington, DC: National Academies Press.

Nehru, J. (2004). *The Discovery of India.* New Delhi: Penguin Books.

Nestle, M. (2007). *Food Politics: How the Food Industry Influences Nutrition and Health.* 2nd ed. Berkeley: University of California Press.

Nietzsche, F. W. (1967). *The Birth of Tragedy and The Case of Wagner.* (trans. W. Kaufmann). New York: Vintage Books.

_____. (1909–11). *The Complete Works of Friedrich Nietzsche.* 18 vols. (ed. O. Levy). Edinburgh: T. N. Foulis.

_____. (1974). *The Gay Science: With a Prelude in Rhymes and an Appendix of Songs.* (trans. W. Kaufmann). New York: Vintage Books.

_____. (1954). *The Portable Nietzsche.* (ed. & trans. W. Kaufmann). New York: Viking Press.

Noble, T. F. X. et al. (2011). *Western Civilization: Beyond Boundaries.* 6th ed. Boston: Wadsworth.

Nooten, B. A. van & G. B. Holland. (eds.) (1994). *Rig Veda: A Metrically Restored Text with an Introduction and Notes.* Cambridge, MA: Harvard University Press.

Norberg, J. (2009). *Financial Fiasco: How America's Infatuation with Homeownership and Easy Money Created the Economic Crisis.* Washington, DC: Cato Institute.

_____. (2003). *In Defense of Global Capitalism.* (trans. R. Tanner & J. Sanchez). Washington, DC: Cato Institute.

Office of Management and Budget. (2010). *Fiscal Year 2012 Budget of the U.S. Goverment.* Washington, DC: U.S. Government Printing Office.

_____. (2004). *Information Collection Budget of the United States Government.* Washington, DC: Office of Information and Regulatory Affairs.

O'Hair, M. M. (1974). *Freedom Under Siege: The Impact of Organized Religion on Your Liberty and Your Pocketbook.* Los Angeles: Jeremy P. Tarcher.

Omelaniuk, I. et al. (eds.) (2005). *World Migration Report 2005: Costs and Benefits of International Migration.* Geneva: International Organization for Migration.

O'Rourke, P. J. (1995). *All the Trouble in the World: The Lighter Side of Overpopulation, Famine, Ecological Disaster, Ethnic Hatred, Plague, and Poverty.* New York: Atlantic Monthly Press.

_____. (1988). *Holidays in Hell.* New York: Grove Press.

_____. (1991). *Parliament of Whores: A Lone Humorist Attempts to Explain the Entire U.S. Government.* New York: Atlantic Monthly Press.

Orwell, G. (2003). *Nineteen Eighty-Four: Centennial Edition.* New York: Plume Books.

_____. (2001). *Orwell and Politics: Animal Farm in the Context of Essays, Reviews and Letters Selected from The Complete Works of George Orwell.* (ed. P. Davison). London: Penguin Books.

Osiander, A. (2007). *Before the State: Systemic Political Change in the West from the Greeks to the French Revolution.* Oxford: Oxford University Press.

Pachauri, R. K. & A. Reisinger. (eds.) (2007). *Climate Change 2007: Synthesis Report.* Geneva: Intergovernmental Panel on Climate Change.

Packard, V. (1972). *A Nation of Strangers.* New York: David McKay Co.

Page, K. E. & J. M. Page. (1981). *The Politics of Reproductive Ritual.* Berkeley: University of California Press.

Paglia, C. (1994). *Vamps & Tramps: New Essays.* New York: Vintage Books.

Paine, T. (2009). *The Age of Reason: The Complete Edition.* Escondido, CA: Truth Seeker Co.

Pape, R. A. (2006). *Dying to Win: The Strategic Logic of Suicide Terrorism.* New York: Random House.

Parker, I. (2007). *Revolution in Psychology: Alienation to Emancipation.* London: Pluto Press.

Parker, K. (2010). *Save the Males: Why Men Matter, Why Women Should Care.* New York: Random House.

Parry, M. L. et al. (eds.) (2007). *Climate Change 2007: Impacts, Adaptation and Vulnerability.* Cambridge: Cambridge University Press.

Parsons, J. W. (2008). *Three Essays on Freedom.* (ed. Hymanæus Beta). York Beach, ME: Teitan Press.

Parsons, K. (ed.) (2003). *The Science Wars: Debating Scientific Knowledge and Technology.* Amherst, NY: Prometheus Books.

Partnership for a Drug Free America. (2005). *Partnership Attitude Tracking Study: Teens, 2004.* Washington, DC: Office of National Drug Control Policy.

Pascal, B. (2008). *Pascal's Pensées.* Fairford: The Echo Library.

Paulos, J. A. (1988). *Innumeracy: Mathematical Illiteracy and Its Consequences.* New York: Hill and Wang.

Peck, M. S. (1978). *The Road Less Traveled: A New Psychology of Love, Traditional Values and Spiritual Growth.* New York: Simon & Schuster.

Pendell, D. (1995). *Pharmako/Poeia: Plant Powers, Poisons, and Herbcraft.* San Fracisco: Mercury House.

Percy, W. A. (1996). *Pederasty and Pedagogy in Archaic Greece.* Urbana, IL: University of Illinois Press.

Pervin, L. A. (1980). *Personality: Theory, Assessment, and Research.* 3rd ed. New York: John Wiley & Sons.

Petraeus, D. H. & J. F. Amos. (2006). *FM-3-24 Counterinsurgency: The Army and Marine Corps Field Manual on Counterinsurgency.* Washington, DC: U.S. Department of the Army.

Petronius. (1987). *Petronius.* (trans. W. H. D. Rouse, rev. E. H. Warmington). Cambridge, MA: Harvard University Press.

Phillips, K. (2006). *American Theocracy: The Peril and Politics of Radical Religion, Oil, and Borrowed Money in the 21st Century.* New York: Viking.

_____. (2008). *Bad Money: Reckless Finance, Failed Politics, and the Global Crisis of American Capitalism.* New York: Viking.

Philo. (1993). *The Works of Philo: Complete and Unabridged.* (trans. C. D. Yonge). Peabody, MA: Hendrickson Publishers.

Pillsbury, P. (1883). *Acts of the Anti-Slavery Apostles.* Concord, NH: Clague, Wegman, Schlicht, & Co.

Pilzer, P. Z. (2007). *The New Wellness Revolution: How to Make a Fortune in the Next Trillion Dollar Industry.* 2nd ed. Hoboken, NJ: John Wiley & Sons.

_____. (1990). *Unlimited Wealth: The Theory and Practice of Economic Alchemy.* New York: Crown Publishers.

_____ & R. Deitz. (1989). *Other People's Money: The Inside Story of the S&L Mess.* New York: Simon & Schuster.

Pisani, E. (2008). *The Wisdom of Whores: Bureaucrats, Brothels, and the Business of AIDS.* London: Granta Books.

Plato. (1975–1984). *Plato.* 12 vols. (trans. H. N. Fowler, W. R. M. Lamb, P. Shorey & R. G. Bury). Cambridge, MA: Harvard University Press.

Plutarch. (1932). *The Lives of the Noble Grecians and Romans.* (trans. J. Dryden, rev. A. H. Clough). New York: Modern Library.

Pohl, R. F. (ed.) (2004). *Cognitive Illusions: A Handbook on Fallacies and Biases in Thinking, Judgement and Memory.* New York: Psychology Press.

Pollan, M. (2006). *The Omnivore's Dilemma: A Natural History of Four Meals.* New York: The Penguin Press.

Polybius. (1823). *The General History of Polybius.* 5th ed. 2 vols. (trans. J. Hampton). Oxford: W. Baxter.

Ponton, L. E. (2000). *The Sex Lives of Teenagers: Revealing the Secret World of Adolescent Boys and Girls.* New York: Dutton.

Pope, D. C. (2001). *Doing School: How We Are Creating a Generation of Stressed Out, Materialistic, and Miseducated Students.* New Haven, CT: Yale University Press.

Popper, K. (1972). *Objective Knowledge: An Evolutionary Approach.* London: Clarendon Press.

_____. (1945). *The Open Society and Its Enemies.* 2 vols. London: Routledge & Kegan Paul.

P-Orridge, G. B. (2010). *Thee Psychick Bible.* (ed. J. Louv). Port Townsend, WA: Feral House.

Prahalad, C. K. (2005). *The Fortune at the Bottom of the Pyramid: Eradicating Poverty Through Profits.* New Delhi: Pearson Education.

Pratchett, T. (1990). *Diggers.* London: Corgi Books.

Price, W. A. (2000). *Nutrition and Physical Degeneration.* 6th ed. La Mesa, CA: Price-Pottenger Nutrition Foundation.

Prins, N. (2004). *Other People's Money: The Corporate Mugging of America.* New York: The New Press.

Proctor, R. N. (1988). *Racial Hygiene: Medicine under the Nazis.* Cambridge, MA: Harvard University Press.

Proudhon, P. J. (1923). *General Idea of the Revolution in the Nineteenth Century.* (trans. J. B. Robinson). London: Freedom Press.

_____. (1994). *What Is Property?* (ed. & trans. D. R. Kelley & B. G. Smith). Cambridge: Cambridge University Press.

Raff, R. A. (1996). *The Shape of Life: Genes, Development, and the Evolution of Animal Form.* Chicago: University of Chicago Press.

Rand, A. (1946). *Anthem.* New York: Signet Books.

_____. (2005). *Atlas Shrugged: Centennial Edition.* New York: Dutton.

_____. (1988). *The Ayn Rand Lexicon: Objectivism from A to Z.* (ed. H. Binswanger). New York: Meridian.

_____. (1943). *The Fountainhead.* New York: The Bobbs-Merrill Company.

_____. (1964). *The Virtue of Selfishness: A New Concept of Egoism.* New York: Signet Books.

_____ et al. (1966). *Capitalism: The Unknown Ideal.* (ed. L. Peikoff). New York: New American Library.

Randi, J. (1987). *The Faith Healers.* Buffalo, NY: Prometheus Books.

Ravnskov, U. (2000). *The Cholesterol Myths: Exposing the Fallacy that Saturated Fat and Cholesterol Cause Heart Disease.* Washington, DC: NewTrends Publishing.

_____. (2009). *Fat and Cholesterol Are Good for You!: What Really Causes Heart Disease.* Sweden: GP Publishing.

Reagan, P. C. (2003). *Mind Games: A Primer on Love, Sex and Marriage.* Thousand Oaks, CA: SAGE Publications.

Regnerus, M. D. (2007). *Forbidden Fruit: Sex & Religion in the Lives of American Teenagers.* New York: Oxford University Press.

Reich, R. B. (2007). *Supercapitalism: The Transformation of Business, Democracy and Everyday Life.* New York: Alfred A. Knopf.

Reich, W. (1949). *Character-Analysis: Principles and Technique for Psychoanalysts in Practice and in Training.* 2nd ed. (trans. T. P. Wolfe). New York: Orgone Institute Press.

_____. (1972). *Ether, God and Devil & Cosmic Superimposition.* (trans. T. Pol). New York: Farrar, Straus & Giroux.

_____. (1948). *The Function of the Orgasm: Sex-Economic Problems of Biological Energy.* 2nd ed. (trans. T. P. Wolfe). New York: Orgone Institute Press.

_____. (1980). *The Mass Psychology of Fascism.* 3rd ed. (trans. V. R. Carfagno). New York: Farrar, Straus & Giroux.

_____. (1945). *The Sexual Revolution: Toward a Self-Governing Character Structure.* (trans. T. P. Wolfe). New York: Orgone Institute Press.

Reinhart, C. M. & K. S. Rogoff (2009). *This Time Is Different: Eight Centuries of Financial Folly.* Princeton, NJ: Princeton University Press.

Resnick, L. B. (ed.) (1976). *The Nature of Intelligence.* Hillsdale, NJ: Lawrence Erlbaum Associates.

Richardson, R. D. (1995). *Emerson: The Mind on Fire.* Berkeley: University of California Press.

Richman, S. L. (1994). *Separating School and State: How to Liberate America's Families.* Fairfax, VA: Future of Freedom Foundation.

Richmond, Y. (2003). *Cultural Exchange & the Cold War: Raising the Iron Curtain.* University Park, PA: Penn State Press.

Robbins, T. (1984). *Jitterbug Perfume.* New York: Bantam Books.

_____. (1980). *Still Life with Woodpecker.* New York: Bantam Books.

Robertson, I. (1987). *Sociology.* 3rd ed. New York: Worth Publishers.

Robinson, J. (1955). *Marx, Marshall and Keynes.* Delhi: Delhi School of Economics.

Rockwell, L. H. (ed.) (1990). *The Economics of Liberty.* Auburn, AL: Ludwig von Mises Institute.

Rogers, C. R. (1989). *The Carl Rogers Reader: Selections from the Lifetime Work of America's Preeminent Psychologist.* (ed. H. Kirschenbaum & V. L. Henderson). Boston: Houghton Mifflin Co.

_____. (1969). *Freedom to Learn: A View of What Education Might Become.* Columbus, OH: Charles E. Merrill Pub. Co.

Rosen, J. (2004). *The Naked Crowd: Reclaiming Security and Freedom in an Anxious Age.* New York: Random House.

Rosenfeld, A. & N. Wise. (2000). *Hyper-Parenting: Are You Hurting Your Child by Trying Too Hard.* New York: St. Martin's Press.

Rothbard, M. N. (2000). *Egalitarianism as a Revolt against Nature and Other Essays.* 2nd ed. Auburn, AL: Ludwig von Mises Institute.

_____. (1998). *The Ethics of Liberty.* New York: New York University Press.

_____. (1985). *For a New Liberty: The Libertarian Manifesto.* 3rd ed. New York: Libertarian Review Foundation.

_____. (1977). *Power and Market: Government and the Economy.* Kansas City, MO: Sheed, Andrews and McMeel.

Rousseau, J. J. (1999). *Discourse on Political Economy; and The Social Contract.* (trans. C. Betts). Oxford: Oxford University Press.

Rowling, J. K. (2005). *Harry Potter and the Half-Blood Prince.* New York: Arthur A. Levine.

Roy, O. (2004). *Globalized Islam: The Search for a New Ummah.* New York: Columbia University Press.

Rubin, P. H. (2002). *Darwinian Politics: The Evolutionary Origin of Freedom.* New Brunswick, NJ: Rutgers University Press.

Rummel, R. J. (1994). *Death by Government.* New Brunswick, NJ: Transaction Publishers.

Rushdie, S. (1991). *Imaginary Homelands: Essays and Criticism 1981–1991.* London: Granta Books.

Rushkoff, D. (2009). *Life Inc.: How the World Became a Corporation and How to Take It Back.* New York: Random House.

Russell, B. (1925). *The ABC of Relativity.* London: Kegan Paul, Trench, Trubner & Co.

_____. (1945). *A History of Western Philosophy: And Its Connection with Political and Social Circumstances from the Earliest Times to the Present Day.* New York: Simon & Schuster.

_____. (1954). *Human Society in Ethics and Politics.* London: Allen & Unwin.

_____. (2009). *Marriage and Morals.* Abingdon, Oxon: Routledge Classics.

_____. (1998). *Mortals and Others, Volume II: American Essays, 1931–1935.* (ed. H. Ruja). London: Routledge.

_____. (1995). *An Outline of Philosophy.* 2nd rev. ed. London: Routledge.

_____. (1957). *Why I Am Not a Christian: And Other Essays on Religion and Related Subjects.* (ed. P. Edwards). London: Allen & Unwin.

Sacks, O. W. (1985). *The Man Who Mistook His Wife for a Hat: And Other Clinical Tales.* New York: Summit Books.

Safer, J. (2000). *Forgiving & Not Forgiving: Why Sometimes It's Better Not to Forgive.* New York: Harper Perennial.

Sagan, C. (2000). *Carl Sagan's Cosmic Connection: An Extraterrestrial Perspective.* 2nd ed. Cambridge: Cambridge University Press.

_____. (1985). *Contact: A Novel.* New York: Simon & Schuster.

_____. (1995). *The Demon-Haunted World: Science as a Candle in the Dark.* New York: Random House.

_____. (1977). *The Dragons of Eden: Speculations on the Evolution of Human Intelligence.* New York: Random House.

Sahlins, M. (1972). *Stone Age Economics.* Hawthorne, NY: Aldine de Gruyter.

Said, E. W. (1978). *Orientalism: Western Conceptions of the Orient.* London: Routledge & Kegan Paul.

Salerno, S. (2005). *SHAM: How the Self-Help Movement Made America Helpless.* New York: Crown Publishers.

Samuelson, R. J. (2008). *The Great Inflation and Its Aftermath: The Transformation of America's Economy, Politics, and Society.* New York: Random House.

_____. (2001). *Untruth : Why the Conventional Wisdom Is (Almost Always) Wrong.* New York: Random House.

Sand, S. (2009). *The Invention of the Jewish People.* (trans. Y. Lotan). London: Verso.

Sapolsky, R. M. (1997). *The Trouble with Testosterone: And Other Essays on the Biology of the Human Predicament.* New York: Scribner.

_____. (1998). *Why Zebras Don't Get Ulcers: An Updated Guide to Stress, Stress Related Diseases, and Coping.* New York: W. H. Freeman & Co.

Sartre, J. M. (1992). *Notebooks for an Ethics.* (trans. D. Pellauer). Chicago: University of Chicago Press.

Schaff, P. (1877–84). *The Creeds of Christendom: With a History and Critical Notes.* 4th ed. 3 vols. New York: Harper & Brothers.

_____. (ed.) (1887). *Nicene and Post-Nicene Fathers.* Series I, Vol. II. Edinburgh: The Christian Literature Company.

Scheer, R. (2008). *The Pornography of Power: How Defense Hawks Hijacked 9/11 and Weakened America.* New York: Twelve.

Schieber, S. J. & J. B. Shoven. (1999). *The Real Deal: The History and Future of Social Security.* New Haven, CT: Yale University Press.

Schiff, I. A. (1977). *The Biggest Con: How the Government Is Fleecing You.* Hamden, CT: Freedom Books.

Schulz, K. (2010). *Being Wrong: Adventures in the Margin of Error.* New York: Ecco.

Schumaker, J. F. (1995). *The Corruption of Reality: A Unified Theory of Religion, Hypnosis, and Psychology.* Amherst, NY: Prometheus Books.

Schuth, H. W. (1978). *Mike Nichols.* Boston: Twayne Publishers.

Schwartz, B. (2004). *The Paradox of Choice: Why More Is Less.* New York: Ecco.

Scott, J. C. (2009). *The Art of Not Being Governed: An Anarchist History of Upland Southeast Asia.* New Haven, CT: Yale University Press.

Scull, A. T. (1993). *The Most Solitary of Afflictions. Madness and Society in Britain, 1700–1900.* New Haven: Yale University Press.

Seligman, M. E. P. (1975). *Helplessness: On Depression, Development, and Death.* San Francisco: W. H. Freeman.

Sen, A. (1981). *Poverty and Famines: An Essay on Entitlement and Deprivation.* Oxford: Oxford University Press.

Shakespeare, W. (1835). *The Dramatic Works of William Shakespeare.* 6 vols. (ed. S. Johnson & G. Steevens, rev. I. Reed). New York: George Dearborn.

Sharaf, M. (1994). *Fury on Earth: A Biography of Wilhelm Reich.* New York: De Capo Press.

Shaw, G. B. (1916). *Androcles and the Lion, Overruled, Pygmalion.* New York: Brentano.

_____. (1913). *The Devil's Discipline: A Melodrama in Three Acts.* Westminster: Archibald Constable & Co.

_____. (1919). *Heartbreak House, Great Catherine, and Playlets of the War.* New York: Brentano.

_____. (1903). *Man and Superman: A Comedy and a Philosophy.* Westminster: Archibald Constable & Co.

Shelley, P. B. (2002). *The Selected Poetry and Prose of Shelley.* Ware: Wordsworth Editions.

Shorter, E. (1975). *The Making of the Modern Family.* New York: Basic Books.

Shuttle, P. & P. Redgrove. (1978). *The Wise Wound: Menstruation and Everywoman.* London: Victor Gollancz.

Siegel, R. K. (2005). *Intoxication: The Universal Drive for Mind-Altering Substances.* Rochester, VT: Park Street Press.

Simpson, G. G. (1966). *This View of Life: The World of an Evolutionist.* New York: Harcourt, Brace & World.

Skinner, B. F. (1971). *Beyond Freedom and Dignity.* New York: Alfred A. Knopf.

Smith, A. (1804). *An Inquiry into the Nature and Causes of the Wealth of Nations.* 2 vols. Hartford, CT: Oliver D. Cooke.

_____. (1761). *The Theory of Moral Sentiments.* 2nd ed. London: A. Millar.

Smith, G. H. (1979). *Atheism: The Case Against God.* Buffalo, NY: Prometheus Books.

Smith, H. (1958). *The Religions of Man.* New York: Harper & Row.

Smith, J. S. (1990). *Patenting the Sun: Polio and the Salk Vaccine.* New York: William Morrow.

Solomon, N. (2005). *War Made Easy: How Presidents and Pundits Keep Spinning Us to Death.* Hoboken, NJ: John Wiley & Sons.

Solomon, S. et al. (eds.) (2007). *Climate Change 2007: The Physical Science Basis.* Cambridge: Cambridge University Press.

Sommers, C. H. (2000). *The War Against Boys.* New York: Simon & Schuster.

_____. (1994). *Who Stole Feminism?: How Women Have Betrayed Women.* New York: Simon & Schuster.

_____ & S. Satel. (2005). *One Nation under Therapy: How the Helping Culture Is Eroding Self-Reliance.* New York: St. Martin's Press.

Sontag, S. (1969). *Styles of Radical Will.* New York: Farrar, Straus & Giroux.

Soto, H. de. (2000). *The Mystery of Capital: Why Capitalism Triumphs in the West and Fails Everywhere Else.* New York: Basic Books.

Sowell, T. (2010). *Basic Economics: A Common Sense Guide to the Economy.* 4th ed. New York: Basic Books.

_____. (1998). *Conquests and Culture: An International History.* New York: Basic Books.

_____. (2011). *Economic Facts and Fallacies.* 2nd ed. New York: Basic Books.

_____. (1996). *Migrations and Culture: A World View.* New York: Basic Books.

_____. (1994). *Race and Culture: A World View.* New York: Basic Books.

Spencer, H. (1868). *Essays: Scientific, Political, and Æsthetic.* New York: D. Appleton & Co.

Spinoza, B. (1957). *The Ethics of Spinoza: The Road to Inner Freedom.* (trans. R. H. M. Elwes, ed. D. D. Runes). New York: Philosophical Library.

Spong, J. S. (1994). *Resurrection: Myth or Reality?* San Francisco: HarperCollins.

Spooner, L. (1972). *Let's Abolish Government: An Original Arno Press Compilation.* New York: Arno Press.

Sprading, C. T. (ed.) (1913). *Liberty and the Great Libertarians: An Anthology on Liberty—A Hand-book of Freedom.* Los Angeles: The Golden Press.

Stang, I. (ed.) (1990). *Three-fisted Tales of "Bob": Short Stories in the Subgenius Mythos.* New York: Simon & Schuster.

Statius. (2003). *Thebaid.* (ed. & trans. D. R. Shackleton Bailey). 2 vols. Cambridge, MA: Harvard University Press.

Stavrianos, L. S. (1981). *Global Rift: The Third World Comes of Age.* New York: William Morrow & Co.

Stearns, P. N. (1975). *European Society in Upheaval: Social History Since 1750.* 2nd ed. New York: Macmillan.

Stein, E. & S. Kim. (2009). *Flow: The Cultural Story of Menstruation.* New York: St. Martin's Press.

Stenger, V. J. (2007). *God, the Failed Hypothesis: How Science Shows That God Does Not Exist.* Amherst, NY: Prometheus Books.

Stirner, M. (1971). *The Ego and His Own.* (trans. J. Carroll). London: Jonathan Cape.

Stockholm International Peace Research Institute. (2010). *SIPRI Yearbook 2010: Armaments, Disarmament and International Security.* Oxford: Oxford University Press.

Stokes, A. P. (1950). *Church and State in the United States.* 3 vols. New York: Harper & Brothers.

Storr, A. (1991). *Human Destructiveness: The Roots of Genocide and Human Cruelty.* 2nd ed. London: Routledge.

Strabo. (1889–93). *The Geography of Strabo: Literary Translated, with Notes.* 3 vols. (trans. H. C. Hamilton & W. Falconer). London: George Bell & Sons.

Stuart-Macadam, P. & K. A. Dettwyler. (eds.) (1995). *Breastfeeding: Biocultural Perspectives.* New York: Aldine de Gruyter.

Substance Abuse and Mental Health Services Administration. (2005). *National Survey on Drug Use and Health (NSDUH): 2004.* Washington, DC: U.S. Department of Health and Human Services.

Suster, G. (1990). *The Truth About the Tarot: A Manual of Practice and Theory.* London: Skoob Books.

Suzuki, S. (1970). *Zen Mind, Beginner's Mind.* (ed. T. Dixon). New York: Weatherhill.

Szalavitz, M. & B. D. Perry. (2010). *Born for Love: Why Empathy Is Essential—And Endangered.* New York: HarperCollins.

Szasz, A. (2007). *Shopping Our Way to Safety: How We Changed from Protecting the Environment to Protecting Ourselves.* Minneapolis, MN: University of Minnesota Press.

Szasz, T. S. (2003). *Ceremonial Chemistry: The Ritual Persecution of Drugs, Addicts, and Pushers.* Syracuse, NY: Syracuse University Press.

_____. (1997). *The Manufacture of Madness: A Comparative Study of the Inquisition and the Mental Health Movement.* Syracuse, NY: Syracuse University Press.

_____. (1961). *The Myth of Mental Illness: Foundations of a Theory of Personal Conduct.* New York: Hoeber-Harper.

_____. (2001). *Pharmacracy: Medicine and Politics in America.* Westport, CT: Praeger.

_____. (1976). *Schizophrenia: The Sacred Symbol of Psychiatry.* New York: Basic Books.

Tannen, D. (1990). *You Just Don't Understand: Women and Men in Conversation.* New York: William Morrow & Co.

Tanzi, R. E. & A. B. Parson. (2000). *Decoding Darkness: The Search for the Genetic Causes of Alzheimer's Disease.* Cambridge, MA: Perseus Publishing.

Taubes, G. (2007). *Good Calories, Bad Calories: Challenging the Conventional Wisdom on Diet, Weight Control, and Disease.* New York: Alfred A. Knopf.

Tennyson, A. (1898). *The Poetic and Dramatic Works of Alfred Lord Tennyson.* (ed. W. J. Rolfe). Boston: Houghton Mifflin Company.

Thompson, H. S. (2003). *The Kingdom of Fear: Loathsome Secrets of a Star-Crossed Child in the Final Days of the American Century.* New York: Simon & Schuster.

Thompson, T. L. (1999). *The Bible in History: How Writers Create a Past.* London: Jonathan Cape.

Thornhill, R. & S. W. Gangestad. (2008). *The Evolutionary Biology of Human Female Sexuality.* New York: Oxford University Press.

_____ & C. T. Parker. (2000). *A Natural History of Rape: Biological Bases of Sexual Coercion.* Cambridge, MA: MIT Press.

Thornton, M. (1991). *The Economics of Prohibition.* Salt Lake City: University of Utah Press.

Tilly, C. (1992). *Coercion, Capital, and European States, AD 990–1992.* 2nd ed. Malden, MA: Blackwell Publishing.

Tocqueville, A. de. (2003). *Democracy in America: And Two Essays on America.* (trans. G. E. Bevan). London: Penguin Books.

Todd, E. (2002). *Après l'empire: Essai sur la décomposition du système américain.* Paris: Gallimard.

_____. (1976). *La chute finale: Essai sur la décomposition de la sphère soviétique.* Paris: Robert Laffont.

Toffler, A. (1990). *Future Shock.* New York: Bantam Books.

Toland, J. (1976). *Adolf Hitler.* 2 vols. Garden City, NY: Doubleday & Co.

Tolstoy, L. (2003). *Anna Karenina.* (trans. R. Pevear & L. Volokhonsky). London: Penguin Books.

Tucker, J. A. (2010). *Bourbon for Breakfast: Living Outside the Statist Quo.* Auburn, AL: Ludwig von Mises Institute.

Turecki, S. & L. Tonner (2000). *The Difficult Child.* 2nd ed. New York: Bantam Books.

Turgenev, I. S. (1904). *Dream Tales and Prose Poems.* (trans. C. Garnett). London: W. Heinemann.

Twain, M. (1990). *The Autobiography of Mark Twain.* (ed. C. Neider). New York: Perennial Classics.

_____. (2010). *Mark Twain's Book of Animals.* (ed. S. F. Fishkin). Berkeley: University of California Press.

_____. (1983). *Mark Twain: Selected Writings of an American Skeptic.* (ed. V. Doyno). Buffalo, NY: Prometheus Books.

_____. (1935). *Mark Twain's Notebook.* (ed. A. B. Paine). New York: Harper & Brothers.

United Nations Development Programme. (2005). *Democracy in Latin America: Towards a Citizens' Democracy.* (trans. M. Stevenson, et al.). Buenos Aires: Aguilar, Altea, Taurus, Alfaguara.

_____. (1998). *Human Development Report.* 9th ed. Oxford: Oxford University Press.

_____. (2010). *Human Development Report.* 20th ed. Oxford: Oxford University Press.

United Nations Environment Programme. (1995). *Global Biodiversity Assessment.* Cambridge: Cambridge University Press.

United Nations Fund for Population Activities. (2004). *State of World Population 2004: The Cairo Consensus at Ten—Population, Reproductive Health and the Global Effort to End Poverty.* New York: United Nations Population Fund.

United Nations Human Settlements Programme. (2010). *The State of African Cities 2010: Governance, Inequality and Urban Land Markets.* Nairobi: UN-HABITAT.

United Nations Office on Drugs and Crime. (2005). *World Drug Report 2005.* Vienna: United Nations Publications.

_____. (2009). *World Drug Report 2009.* Vienna: United Nations Publications.

Untermeyer, L. (1955). *Makers of the Modern World: The Lives of Ninety-Two Writers, Artists, Scientists, Statesmen, Inventors, Philosophers, Composers, and Other Creators Who Formed the Pattern of Our Century.* New York: Simon & Schuster.

Valenstein, E. S. (1998). *Blaming the Brain: The Truth about Drugs and Mental Health.* New York: Free Press.

Vidal, G. (1981). *Creation: A Novel.* New York: Random House.

_____. (1992). *The Decline and Fall of the American Empire.* Berkeley, CA: Odonian Press.

_____. (2002). *Perpetual War for Perpetual Peace: How We Got To Be So Hated.* New York: Nation Books.

_____. (2001). *United States: Essays 1952–1992.* New York: Broadway Books.

_____. (1991). *A View from the Diners Club: Essays 1987–1991.* London: Andre Deutsch.

Villarreal, L. P. (2005). *Viruses and the Evolution of Life.* Washington, DC: ASM Press.

Vivekananda. (1964). *Letters of Swami Vivekananda.* 2nd ed. Calcutta: Advaita Ashrama.

_____. (1896). *Raja-Yoga.* London: Longman, Green & Co.

Volokh, E. (ed.) (2011). *The First Amendment and Related Statutes: Problems, Cases and Policy Arguments.* 4th ed. New York: Foundation Press.

Voltaire, F. M. A. de. (1785). *Œuvres complètes de Voltaire.* Vol. 46. Kehl: La Société Littéraire-Typographique.

_____. (1856). *A Philosophical Dictionary.* 2 vols. Boston: J. P. Mendum.

_____. (1919). *Voltaire in His Letters: Being a Selection from His Correspondence.* (trans. S. G. Tallentyre). New York: G. P. Putnam's Sons.

_____. (1952). *Voltaire's Notebooks.* 2 vols. (ed. T. Besterman). Genève: Institut et Musée Voltaire.

Vonnegut, K. (1987). *Bluebeard: A Novel.* New York: Delacorte Press.

_____. (1991). *Fates Worse Than Death: An Autobiographical Collage of the 1980s.* New York: G. P. Putnam's Sons.

Waal, F. B. M. de. (1997). *Bonobo: The Forgotten Ape.* Berkeley: University of California Press.

_____. (1982). *Chimpanzee Politics: Power and Sex among Apes.* New York: Harper & Row.

Wann, T. (ed.) (1964). ***Behaviorism and Phenomenology: Contrasting Bases for Modern Psychology.*** Chicago: University of Chicago Press.

Warah, R. (ed.) (2008). ***Missionaries, Mercenaries and Misfits: An Anthology.*** Milton Keynes: AuthorHouse.

Washburn, L. K. (1911). ***Is the Bible Worth Reading: And Other Essays.*** New York: Truth Seeker Co.

Wasserman, J. (2004). ***The Slaves Shall Serve: Meditations on Liberty.*** New York: Sekmet Books.

Watson, R. T. & D. L. Albritton. (eds.) (2001). ***Climate Change 2001: Synthesis Report.*** Cambridge: Cambridge University Press.

Watts, A. W. (1964). ***Beyond Theology: The Art of Godmanship.*** New York: Pantheon Books.

_____. (1961). ***Psychotherapy East and West.*** New York: Pantheon Books.

Weber, M. (1930). ***The Protestant Ethic and the Spirit of Capitalism.*** (trans. T. Parsons). New York: Charles Scribner's Sons.

Weinberg, S. (2001). ***Facing Up: Science and Its Cultural Adversaries.*** Cambridge, MA: Harvard University Press.

_____. (1977). ***The First Three Minutes: A Modern View of the Origin of the Universe.*** New York: Basic Books.

Weiner, E. (2008). ***The Geography of Bliss: One Grump's Search for the Happiest Places in the World.*** New York: Twelve.

Welbon, G. R. (1968). ***The Buddhist Nirvana and Its Western Interpreters.*** Chicago: University of Chicago Press.

Welles, O. & P. Bogdanovich. (1998). ***This Is Orson Welles.*** New York: De Capo Press.

Wells, H. G. (1943). ***Crux Ansata: An Indictment of the Roman Catholic Church.*** Harmondsworth: Penguin Books.

_____. (1920). ***The Outline of History.*** 2 vols. London: Macmillan & Co.

_____. (1914). ***The Wife of Sir Isaac Harman.*** London: Macmillan & Co.

Wesson, R. & P. A. Williams. (eds.) (1995). ***Evolution and Human Values.*** Atlanta, GA: Rodopi.

Whitaker, R. (2010). ***Anatomy of an Epidemic: Magic Bullets, Psychiatric Drugs, and the Astonishing Rise of Mental Illness in America.*** New York: Crown Publishers.

White, A. D. (1896). ***A History of the Warfare of Science with Theology in Christendom.*** 2 vols. New York: D. Appleton & Co.

White, A. R. (1970). ***Truth.*** Garden City, NY: Doubleday & Co.

Whitehead, A. N. (1954). ***Dialogues of Alfred North Whitehead.*** (ed. L. Price). Boston: Little, Brown & Co.

Whitman, W. (1904). ***Prose Works.*** Philadelphia: David McKay.

Wiesenthal, S. (1973). ***Sails of Hope: The Secret Mission of Christopher Columbus.*** (trans. R. & C. Winston). New York: MacMillan Publishing Co.

Wilde, O. (1997). ***Collected Works of Oscar Wilde: The Plays, the Poems, the Stories and the Essays including De Profundis.*** Ware: Wordsworth Editions.

_____. (1916). ***The Prose of Oscar Wilde.*** New York: H. S. Nichols.

Willett, W. C. & P. J. Skerrett. (2002). ***Eat, Drink, and Be Healthy: The Harvard Medical School Guide to Healthy Eating.*** New York: Simon & Schuster.

Williams, W. E. (1999). ***More Liberty Means Less Government: Our Founders Knew This Well.*** Stanford, CA: Hoover Institution Press.

Wilson, A. N. (1991). *Against Religion.* London: Chatto & Windus.

Wilson, E. G. (2008). *Against Happiness: In Praise of Melancholy.* New York: Farrar, Straus & Giroux.

Wilson, R. A. (1990a). *Masks of the Illuminati.* New York: Dell Books.

_____. (1997). *Prometheus Rising.* 2nd ed. Tempe, AZ: New Falcon Publications.

_____. (1990b). *Quantum Psychology: How Brain Software Programs You & Your World.* Tempe, AZ: New Falcon Publications.

_____ & R. J. Shea. (1983). *The Illuminatus! Trilogy: The Eye in the Pyramid, the Golden Apple, Leviathan.* New York: Dell Books.

Wilson, T. (1988). *The Great Big Giant Book of Ziggy.* New York: Galahad Books.

Wilson, W. (1974). *The Papers of Woodrow Wilson: 1908–1909.* Princeton, NJ: Princeton University Press.

Wittgenstein, L. (2009). *Philosophical Investigations.* 4th ed. (trans. G. E. M. Anscombe, P. M. S. Hacker & J. Schulte). Oxford: Wiley-Blackwell.

_____. (1922). *Tractatus Logico-Philosophicus.* (trans. C. K. Ogden). London: Routledge & Kegan Paul.

Wizemann, T. M. & M. L. Pardue. (eds.) (2001) *Exploring the Biological Contributions to Human Health: Does Sex Matter?* Washington, DC: National Academy Press.

Wolf, F. A. (1989). *Taking the Quantum Leap: The New Physics for Nonscientists.* New York: Perennial Library.

Wolf, M. (2007). *Proust and the Squid: The Story and Science of the Reading Brain.* New York: Harper.

Wolfe, C. (1999). *101 Things to Do 'Til the Revolution.* Port Townsend, WA: Breakout Productions.

Wolinsky, S. H. (1991). *Trances People Live: Healing Approaches in Quantum Psychology.* Falls Village, CT: The Bramble Company.

Woods, T. E. (2004). *The Politically Incorrect Guide to American History.* Washington, DC: Regnery Publishing.

Wootton, D. (ed.) (2003). *The Essential Federalist and Anti-Federalist Papers.* Indianapolis, IN: Hackett Publishing.

World Health Organization. (2008). *The Global Burden of Disease: 2004 Update.* Geneva: WHO.

_____. (2004). *The World Health Report 2004: Changing History.* Geneva: WHO.

_____. (2005). *The World Health Report 2005: Make Every Mother and Child Count.* Geneva: WHO.

_____. (2011). *World Health Statistics 2011.* Geneva: WHO.

Wright, G. H. von. (1963). *The Varieties of Goodness.* London: Routledge & Kegan Paul.

Wright, L. (2006). *The Looming Tower: Al-Qaeda and the Road to 9/11.* New York: Alfred A. Knopf.

Yankelovich, D. (1974). *The New Morality: A Profile of American Youth in the 70's.* New York: McGraw Hill.

Yeats, W. B. (2000). *The Collected Poems of W. B. Yeats.* Ware: Wordsworth Editions.

Young, D. A. (1982). *Christianity and the Age of the Earth.* Grand Rapids, MI: Zondervan.

Zakaria, F. (2003). *The Future of Freedom: Illiberal Democracy at Home and Abroad.* New York: W. W. Norton.

Zelman, A. S. (ed.) (1993). *"Gun Control": Gateway to Tyranny—Proof that U.S. Gun Law Has Nazi Roots.* 3rd ed. Hartfort, WI: Jews for Preservation of Firearm Ownership.

_____ & R. W. Stevens. (2001). *Death by "Gun Control": The Human Cost of Victim Disarmament.* Hartfort, WI: Mazel Freedom Press.

Zemtsov, I. (1991). *Encyclopedia of Soviet Life.* New Brunswick, NJ: Transaction Publishers.

Zimmer, C. (2001). *Evolution: The Triumph of an Idea.* New York: HarperCollins.

Zinsser, H. (1935). *Rats, Lice and History.* Boston: Little, Brown & Co.

www.ingramcontent.com/pod-product-compliance
Lightning Source LLC
Chambersburg PA
CBHW020630230426
43665CB00008B/109
9789525700404